FOR REFERENCE

Do Not Take From This Room

Ethnic American Literature

Ethnic American Literature

An Encyclopedia for Students

EMMANUEL S. NELSON, EDITOR

 GREENWOOD

AN IMPRINT OF ABC-CLIO, LLC
Santa Barbara, California • Denver, Colorado • Oxford, England

Library of Congress Cataloging-in-Publication Data

Ethnic American literature : an encyclopedia for students / Emmanuel S. Nelson, editor.

    pages cm

  Includes bibliographical references and index.

  ISBN 978-1-61069-880-1 (hardcopy : alk. paper) — ISBN 978-1-61069-881-8 (ebook)

    1. American literature—Minority authors—Encyclopedias.   2. Minorities—United States—Intellectual life—Encyclopedias.   3. Minority authors—United States—Biography—Encyclopedias.   4. United States—Literatures—Encyclopedias.   5. Minorities in literature—Encyclopedias.   6. Ethnic groups in literature—Encyclopedias.   7. Ethnicity in literature—Encyclopedias.   I. Nelson, Emmanuel S. (Emmanuel Sampath), 1954– editor.

  PS153.M56E825   2015

  810.9'920693—dc23   2014031621

ISBN: 978-1-61069-880-1

EISBN: 978-1-61069-881-8

19 18 17 16 15   1 2 3 4 5

This book is also available on the World Wide Web as an eBook.
Visit www.abc-clio.com for details.

Greenwood
An Imprint of ABC-CLIO, LLC

ABC-CLIO, LLC
130 Cremona Drive, P.O. Box 1911
Santa Barbara, California 93116-1911

This book is printed on acid-free paper ∞

Manufactured in the United States of America

For Trevor again, with love

Contents

Preface

Certain foundational texts, such as encyclopedias, sourcebooks, and dictionaries, are indispensable for legitimizing as well as institutionalizing any distinct and emergent field of knowledge. Such books collect, organize, and present primary data about the subject. By doing so, they help define the new discipline, create a necessary knowledge base, and provide an epistemological framework that can be shared by students and scholars in the field. They serve as instruments of basic research and as foundations for advanced inquiry; they facilitate dialogue within and across disciplines. While this encyclopedia is such a reference work, it also gestures toward a singular goal: it has been designed specifically with high school and community college students and their teachers in mind.

This reference work seeks to offer a comprehensive yet concise introduction to a spectacularly diverse range of ethnic American writing. The focus is on these four major ethnic groups: Native American, Asian American, African American, and Latina/o. The more than 150 entries in this single-volume encyclopedia, that range in length from about 750 words to 5,000 words, address topics as diverse as African American young adult literature, Asian American autobiography, Mexican American drama, Iranian American writing, and Vietnamese American literature. These lengthy entries offer panoramic overviews that help the reader gain a historical perspective on the individual traditions. A large majority of the entries, however, are on individual authors. Many of those authors are major literary figures with international name recognition, such as Toni Morrison, Maxine Hong Kingston, and James Baldwin. Some of the entries are specifically on significant individual texts, such as Sandra Cisneros's *The House on Mango Street* and Gene Yang's *American Born Chinese*, which are frequently taught in high schools and community colleges. In addition, there are several substantial entries on general topics that have compelling relevance to our deeper understanding of American ethnic experiences (e.g., assimilation, bilingualism, Civil Rights Movement, ethnicity, whiteness).

Yet the central objective of this encyclopedia is not to define or redefine an ethnic literary canon; its primary goal is to provide reliable, thorough, and up-to-date information on dozens of ethnic authors, texts, topics, and traditions. Teachers will find this reference work a useful pedagogical tool. Its user-friendly style, format, and level of complexity make it accessible to high school students as well as community college students. For example, if you are a teacher interested in introducing a Mexican American autobiography to your students, you will find here a succinct entry that will give you a lively introduction to the autobiographical tradition in Mexican American literature. If, on the other hand, you are a student researching the works of individual authors, such as Alice Walker or N. Scott Momaday, you will be able to locate in this encyclopedia concisely crafted entries on their lives and works; those entries will also direct you to others in this encyclopedia that you will find useful.

Accessibility, in fact, is a salient feature of this reference work: I have made every effort to make it as user-friendly as possible. The entries, for example, are arranged in alphabetical order. If you have a particular author or topic in mind, you may go directly to that entry. You may also consult the elaborate Table of Contents that lists all the entries alphabetically. You will also find useful the index located at the end of the encyclopedia. Look under Leslie Marmon Silko, for instance, to find the main entry for that author, and to locate any other substantive discussion of her in the book.

Furthermore, the entries themselves are designed to facilitate cross-referencing. For example, whenever an author who is also the subject of an entry is first mentioned within another entry, his or her name appears in bold. Similarly, whenever a topic or concept (e.g., racism, immigration, pedagogy and U.S. ethnic literatures) on which there is a separate entry is first mentioned within another entry, the words appear in bold. Many entries also conclude with the "*see also*" feature: the entry on James Baldwin, for example, invites the reader to see also the longer-entry African American Novel to gain an understanding of Baldwin's significance in a wider context.

Over 100 scholars have contributed to this encyclopedia, so the entries reflect a wide spectrum of styles, perspectives, and approaches. However, the entries themselves generally follow a standard format. An entry on an individual author, for example, begins with the author's name (last name first), followed parenthetically by the year of birth and, when applicable, the year of death. The opening line is always a phrase that identifies the author's ethnic background and the genre(s) in which he or she has published. The rest of the entry offers a judicious discussion of the author's major works and themes. When the title of a text by the author is first mentioned, its year of publication is indicated parenthetically. If brief quotations from primary sources are introduced, page numbers are not included, largely because multiple editions of works are often available and page numbers would therefore be misleading. However, direct quotations from secondary sources are parenthetically documented and the sources listed in the Further Reading section that follows all entries. Entries on general topics (e.g., Civil Rights Movement, Hawaiian literature) also follow a standard pattern; they allude to major events, figures, and texts and relevant historical and cultural background information. Those entries, too, conclude with a Further Reading section.

All Further Reading sections direct interested readers to the most useful secondary materials available on the topics. Given the constraints of space, the contributors were specifically instructed to list only the most seminal and accessible secondary sources. Entries on topics that have received substantial critical attention (e.g., African American novel) have several entries listed in the Further Reading section. However, entries on authors (e.g., Anne Moody, Khaled Hosseini) list only two or three entries but they have been carefully chosen for their scholarly value and their accessibility to students in mind. A detailed and up-to-date Selected Bibliography placed toward the end of the book guides the readers to a large body of scholarship; students interested in conducting more advanced research will find it useful.

I would like to take this opportunity to thank all the contributors to this project. They have been immensely generous in sharing their knowledge and expertise; it is their participation—their enthusiastic and professional handling of the assignments—that has allowed me to gather and edit this substantial reference work in a timely manner. I want to express my special gratitude to Paul Lauter, whose lively and provocative introduction follows this preface. Finally, I would like to thank George Butler, who commissioned this project; and Erin Ryan, Senior Coordinator of Editorial Operations at ABC-CLIO, for her valuable technical guidance.

Introduction

Paul Lauter

When in 1782 some of the founders of the United States selected *E pluribus unum* as the motto on the new nation's Great Seal, they may have chosen even more wisely than they knew. They were very likely thinking of 13 disputatious colonies being bound up into a single nation, or at most of an America constituted, as J. Hector St. John de Crèvecoeur wrote, also in 1782, of a "mixture of English, Scotch, Irish, French, Dutch, Germans, and Swedes." "From this promiscuous breed," Crèvecoeur had continued, "that race now called Americans have arisen." But in fact, long before Europeans arrived in what they thought of as the "new world," this hemisphere was already inhabited by enormously diverse groups of Native Americans, speaking a huge range of distinctive and mutually unintelligible languages, and with a multitude of cultures, religions, forms of organization, food, and folkways. Some were hunters and gatherers, moving from place to place through forest or across plains; others constructed careful dwellings within forbidding cliffs or on protected mesas, maintaining control over fertile oases of green amid an austere landscape; still others built large, complex, and often very rich cities, complete with elaborate temples and playing fields; yet others lived where nature was extraordinarily fruitful, providing salmon, furs, and fruit in sufficient abundance to sustain a large class of artisans and artists. The artistic productions of Native Americans were as varied as the terrain they inhabited. Thus "America," well before the arrival of Europeans, was, as we would now call it, a "multicultural" world.

When the Europeans did come—first probably from Scandinavia, then from Italy, Spain, Portugal, France, Holland, and finally England and elsewhere in Western Europe—they, too, were a more diverse cast than Crèvecoeur's phrasing indicates. Differing in language, religion, and attitudes toward the native populations, toward the land, and toward the future, they were often at war, and even in peaceful times engaged in struggles over power, property, and cultural authority. By the time the United States was constituted as a nation in 1776, moreover, something like 10 percent of its population came not from Europe or from among native peoples, but from Africa. These people, too, came from differing nations or tribes in west and central Africa, and carried with them to the new world differing languages, customs, and memories.

Thus, when the constitution of the new United States was established in 1791, the country that would come to be called "America" was by any account a "multicultural" nation. To be sure, certain elements of culture were more dominant than others. While German was the common language in many parts of Pennsylvania and Dutch in New York—just as, later, French would be in some of Louisiana, Swedish in parts of the Midwest, and Spanish in the Southwest—English became the language of public discourse and of schooling everywhere throughout the United States. English jurisprudence—including the presumption of innocence and trial by a jury of one's peers—provided a basis for much of the legal structure of the United States, though such peculiar American legal institutions as the Southern "slave codes," the Chinese Exclusion Acts, the colonial statutes governing Puerto Rico and the Philippines, and the executive decisions that brought about the internment of Japanese Americans during World War II would have profound effects on culture and society. Likewise, throughout the 19th century and much of the 20th, American literature was seen solely as a branch of English stock. Only within the last 40 years or so have we come to appreciate the fact that writers in America were composing texts throughout that period in many languages other than English and, perhaps more important, even when writing in English were working out of artistic imperatives arising from a wide range of cultures and historical experiences.

The variety of subjects, artistic styles, and distinctive qualities that, we now see, have characterized American culture from its beginnings was seldom widely appreciated, and certainly not within the academic world, before the 1960s. Certainly there were some critics and anthologists, particularly those on the political left, who had earlier promoted a more diverse idea of American writing. Still, had you studied American literature in the 1950s—as I did at New York University, Indiana University, and Yale University—or at other predominantly white colleges and universities, you would seldom have encountered a writer of color. I knew only of three—Richard Wright, James Baldwin, and Ralph Ellison—but nary a Native American or Latino or Asian American author, and hardly any white women apart from Emily Dickinson and Marianne Moore. Autobiographies of Benjamin Franklin and Henry Adams graced most American literature curricula, but not such works as Frederick Douglass's *Narrative* (1845), Harriet Jacobs's *Incidents in the Life of a Slave Girl* (1861), or other slave narratives, most of which were not even in print in 1960. Many writers who today are familiar to any student of American literature, such as Langston Hughes, Zora Neale Hurston, Kate Chopin, and Mary Wilkins Freeman, existed on the far margins of cultural knowledge, if they existed at all. Indeed, the titles of widely used anthologies of the time, such as *12 American Authors* (1962), reflected the narrow conceptions of American literature then dominant. Similarly, had you studied music, you would have learned about Bach cantatas, Beethoven symphonies, and Verdi operas, but not about African American spirituals or the extraordinarily creative work then being produced by such jazz musicians as Charlie Parker and Dizzy Gillespie, much less the blues or Chicano *corridos*.

It has become a truism to assert—either with something of a sigh of regret or with delight—that the social movements of the 1960s changed forever how American culture can be thought about. It is an often-told tale, and one I will not repeat at length here. It is, however, worth underlining that a central political demand of the civil rights and feminist movements of the time readily translated itself into cultural and educational terms. The demand was for access: to the voting booth, to the front of the bus, to public accommodations, to jobs from which one had been largely excluded by virtue of race, ethnicity, or gender. "Where are the blacks?" and "Where are the women"? were among the questions of the moment. And those questions might be, and were, quickly focused on curricula, reading lists, critical texts, and anthologies, as well as upon the student bodies and faculties of educational institutions. Once asked, such questions and similar ones about other ethnic and minority groups, including gay people, could steadily if not readily be answered. There was something of a model for entry into the canon provided by the phenomenal explosion of highly regarded writing by and study of Jewish American authors in the 1950s: Bernard Malamud, Norman Mailer, Grace Paley, Saul Bellow, among many others. And there was the work of scholars who had, for example, long been investigating the texts of African Americans, especially at the traditionally black colleges; others slowly but surely picked up their knowledge and their distinctive insights about what fully constituted American literature and culture. Moreover, the increasing study of ethnic and minority writing helped foster the publication and wide dissemination of important new works by new authors, such as *The Way to Rainy Mountain* (1969) by N. Scott Momaday (Kiowa) and *The Bluest Eye* (1970) by Toni Morrison. Dialectically, the success of such works encouraged the study of earlier texts that had emerged from particular ethnic or minority cultures. Thus, even when the movements for social change began to falter during the 1970s, the processes of reconstructing American literature continued apace. By about 1980, it had become possible to think of producing an anthology that significantly represented the many cultures that, together, constituted the newly emerging multicultural conception of American literature. Anthologies, like encyclopedias, are in their nature consolidations of particular cultural moments. The anthology that a group of us initially at the Feminist Press planned to produce as part of a project modestly called "Reconstructing American Literature" would, we hoped, make more fully visible the literatures and histories of the full spectrum of the people of America by making their works better known, accessible, and teachable. Out of mind, out of sight, we argued, and the supporters of the project—the federal Fund for the Improvement of Post-Secondary Education, the Rockefeller Foundation, and the Eli Lilly Endowment—apparently agreed. The *Heath Anthology of American Literature*, which emerged from that project, took nearly another decade to produce, and it became part of a general shift in the study of American literature from its earlier narrow focus on a very limited number of authors, literary forms, styles, and texts to the much more diverse and pluralistic conceptions characteristic of American literary study today.

Multiculturalism is the name we give to the study of that *pluribus* that has so distinctively constituted the United States. It is not that America is altogether exceptional in being made up by a variety of cultures. To the contrary, in recent times nations across the world that once saw themselves as monocultural have discovered the true multiplicity of cultures, languages, and histories shaping their character; indeed, a major problem of 21st-century politics from Chechnya to Sri Lanka to Central Africa has to do with violent struggles of minority peoples to throw off what they regard as the oppressive yoke of dominant groups. In the United States, the reality of a relatively peaceful multiculturalism today needs to be seen in the context of the sometimes violent clashes between groups: the displacement and, often, extermination of native peoples by Europeans; the capture, transportation, and enslavement of Africans; the struggles over title to land between Spanish- and English-speaking peoples in the Southwest and in California; the discrimination embodied in the phrase "No Irish need apply"; and the attacks on Chinese laborers on the West Coast. These and other such events have deeply seared the historical experience not only of minority communities in America, but also, less observably perhaps, of the nation as a whole. As Toni Morrison has pointed out, for example, the very absence of African Americans from many American literary texts, which suggests a certain need to bury or displace elements of our history, is a central feature of much canonical literature in this country.

But multiculturalism is by no means constituted by the study of conflict and oppression. In part it has to do with the celebration of what is or was distinctive in the cultures and histories of groups of people now resident in America. The ethnic parades and festivals, the display and consumption of foodways and fabrics, the study and transmission of a group's original language illustrate the processes of often colorful celebration that many ethnic Americans have maintained. These are of value in and of themselves. But more fundamentally, they express what Randolph Bourne pointed to in his important 1916 essay "Trans-National America." "Each national colony in this country," he wrote, "seems to retain in its foreign press, its vernacular literature, its schools, its intellectual and patriotic leaders, a central cultural nucleus. . . . The influences at the centre of the nuclei are centripetal. They make for the intelligence and the social values which mean an enhancement of life. And just because the foreign-born retains this expressiveness he is likely to be a better citizen of the American community" (*Heath* 1720).

Still, the concerns of multiculturalism as an area of academic study go deeper. We ask: What, if anything, in the social and historical experience of a group of people persists and significantly shapes the cultural productions of artists from among them? What, if anything, in the forms of works of art marks them as distinctive to a particular ethnic group? Are there characteristic tropes, master narratives, sets of events and characters, evident functions that distinguish the cultural works of any particular group? How do region, ideas about gender and sexuality, religious practices, persistent class barriers inflect ethnic artistic and intellectual practices? How, if at all, do relationships with a "home" country affect how people think and act and create, and how does that change from one generation to the next? How do ideas, images, characters from one ethnic background, indeed from majority backgrounds, get incorporated into and transformed in other ethnic writings; indeed, to what extent are "ethnic" texts necessarily hybrid in practice? What, to paraphrase Maxine Hong Kingston, is ethnic: the time period, the region—or the movies? (6). Above all, perhaps, what are the roles of writers and performers in the struggles of ethnic communities for survival, visibility, progress? Such questions, and others, constitute a vast academic field, within which this encyclopedia is designed to play an important role for a number of reasons.

First, answering any of these questions demands a considerable range of knowledge, often of languages and of cultures to which one was not raised. No one could be at home in each of the multiple cultures that now constitute America. Thus multiculturalism is a collective enterprise, for which an encyclopedia, like an archive or library, is an essential tool.

Second, though most of the works with which this encyclopedia is concerned are written primarily in English, there remains a problem of "translation." In part that has to do with the fact that significant authors—for example, Jimmy Santiago Baca, Víctor Hernández Cruz, and Gloria Anzaldúa—write both in Spanish and in English and mix into predominantly English texts many Spanish words and phrases. That produces a sometimes difficult, occasionally irritating, but generally productive experience of disorientation for non-Spanish speakers. The use of Spanish or Yiddish or Italian words and phrases, and even of dialects, may serve as a proxy for identity, a counter toward verisimilitude, or even a challenge to the "outside"—that is, nonethnic—reader. But "translation" has more generally to do with the fact that common cultural knowledge in one group is often the stuff of mystery or at least of puzzlement to people from another. I have often been surprised, for example, by how often students need "translation" not only of such Yiddish terms as *mohyl* or *schnurrer* but also of concepts about the status of men and women, the nature of daily rituals, the roles of the rabbinate in the orthodox Jewry sometimes portrayed by Henry Roth or Rebecca Goldstein, among many others. Similarly, teaching James Baldwin's story "Sonny's Blues" confronts many students with altogether unfamiliar but crucial musical idioms that need "translation," such as the playing of "Bird," the theatrics of a Harlem street-corner preacher, or the jukebox of a 1950s black bar.

In many ways this process of what I have been calling "translation" is continuous with the need for understanding distinctive historical contexts upon which works of ethnic literature may in some measure depend. Most literary texts come more richly alive when they are understood within as well as beyond the historical moments of their creation, whether we speak of *Macbeth* or of *MacBird*. But Louise Erdrich's novel *Tracks* (1988) will be peculiarly puzzling for one unfamiliar with the impact of the Dawes Severalty Act of 1887 upon Indian land tenure. The events unfolding in Sui-Sin Far's (Edith Eaton's) 1909 story "In the Land of the Free" seem simply arbitrary and incomprehensible if one is ignorant of the Chinese Exclusion Act and its daily implementation. Even the title of John Okada's novel *No-No Boy* will make no sense to anyone unfamiliar with the range of responses within the Japanese American community to their internment during World War II. The compelling texture of Bernard Malamud's story "The Lady of the Lake" (1958) dissolves before ignorance of the debates among Jews in the 1940s and 1950s about authenticity and the denial of Jewish identity.

Identity is, of course, a significant element in ethnic writing and criticism; indeed, forming one's identity as a hyphenated American, or in opposition to that very classification of "hyphenated American," probably constitutes the single largest category of ethnic fiction. Ethnic identity, it is now generally understood, is not a fact of nature but a social construction—as is expressed in the title of George Sanchez's important study, *Becoming Mexican American* (1993). As Sanchez demonstrates, the content of the name "Mexican American" changes over time, as relationships with the country of residence, the country of origin, and second- or third-generation community, as well as within the immigrant, change. There is, then, a certain contingency to ethnic identity: it must always be historically grounded, often regionally inflected. The meanings of "Italian" or "Italian American" have changed radically from the moment of Sacco and Vanzetti, to the moment of *Christ in Concrete*, to the moment of Tony Soprano. Yet there are cultural continuities; what are these? The very name preferred by inhabitants of an ethnic or racial category change: Negro, black, African American.

Are there cultural continuities, and if so are they the products of material conditions, of ideology, or of stereotypes imposed by the majority society?

To be sure, we resist stereotypes, yet we use them all the time. In the United States in particular a deep chasm exists between its fundamental individualistic ideology and the harsh facts of racial and ethnic stereotyping, which sees not individuals but instances of a group. Paradoxically, ethnic writers face precisely this tension: can, should, must, will their ethnic characters, particularly central figures in fictions about growing up, be taken as "representative," as expressive of some distinctively Polish or Chinese or Indian set of characteristics? Few would now argue that such characteristics, *if* they exist at all, are products of one's genetic inheritance. But might they be products of one's 1950s Washington Heights inheritance? Or, to return to Kingston's formulation, are they effects of ethnicity, time and place . . . or the movies?

It can, in fact, be argued that certain central tropes and certain distinctive stylistic features play peculiarly significant roles in different ethnic literatures. Henry Louis Gates Jr. and Houston Baker Jr., for example, have called attention to the importance of the Signifying Monkey and of the call-and-response pattern in African American cultural productions of many kinds. As Gates puts it, "the Signifying Monkey exists as the great trope of Afro-American discourse, and the trope of tropes, his language of Signifyin(g) is his verbal sign in the Afro-American tradition." "Signifyin(g)" is the practice in black vernacular of using innuendo, needling, ridiculing, parodying a previous statement to put down an opponent, to gain status and attention, or to establish one's voice as potent. Gates links the practice to "the tension between the oral and the written modes of narration that is represented as finding a voice in writing," a central phenomenon of many African American texts. The "call-and-response" pattern, Baker argues, characterizes not only African American religious practice but also many other forms of black "expressive culture." It points to the strong oral and folk elements that inform the most sophisticated and elaborate African American written works. One might also point to the centrality of the theme of struggling for freedom in many African American texts. Indeed, in one of the earliest moments of African American literary production, Phillis Wheatley bases her authority to speak to the students at Cambridge University about democratic responsibility or to the Earl of Dartmouth about liberty on her identity as an African *and* an American.

Among Mexican Americans, the border takes on a particular cultural weight—no surprise given its proximity to where most Mexican immigrants initially lived as well as its overnight transformation after the Treaty of Guadalupe Hidalgo.

Moreover, the role of the border in limiting and controlling workers or enabling them to migrate makes it a constant presence in the experience and thus in the culture of Mexican Americans. But in recent years, the "Borderland" has come to name not just a geographical space but a state of consciousness, a *mestizaje* sense of between-ness. As Gloria Anzaldúa has phrased it, "The new *mestiza* copes by developing a tolerance for contradictions, a tolerance for ambiguity. She learns to be an Indian in Mexican culture, to be Mexican from an Anglo point of view. She learns to juggle cultures." The inhabitant of the "Borderlands" thus comes to represent postmodern hybridity not only in terms of nationality but of gender, sexuality, race, or ethnicity. And the language spoken or written by such a *mestizaje* figure is, not surprisingly, an intermingling of, in this instance, English with Spanish.

In significant numbers of Native American texts, a distinguishing stylistic feature is repetition, and the fundamental trope is one of disease or disorder and efforts to restore or maintain health. In Leslie Silko's (Laguna) novel *Ceremony* (1977), for example, the central figure Tayo participates in a series of ceremonies, old and new, designed to cure him of the anomie, violence, and decline imposed by absorption in white culture, and particularly in war. Analogous patterns emerge in other contemporary Indian fictions, such as Louise Erdrich's (Chippewa) *Love Medicine* (1984) and N. Scott Momaday's (Kiowa) *House Made of Dawn* (1968). But one can trace such patterns of disruption and renewal far back into the oral cultures of many Native peoples, in which highly repetitive chants form part of a purification ritual. Critics have suggested that such a trope reflects not only the need of people living in arid or uncertain natural conditions to renew fertility, but also the role imported disease has played in decimating Native peoples, as well as the pervasiveness of alcoholism in the last two centuries among Indians on and off the reservation. The roots of a trope may thus reach out into mythic and historical, as well as contemporary social and personal, origins, as the structure of Momaday's *The Way to Rainy Mountain* illustrates.

But to what extent might such a trope, or those of the borderland or of the signifying trickster, function across ethnic cultures? Charles Chesnutt, for example, develops a fascinating instance of illnesses being cured by trickster figures in his story "Sis Becky's Pickaninny" (1899). And a large number of recent writers have adopted the border metaphor to talk about gay sexuality, among many other topics. In what degree and in what ways are such tropes or certain stylistic qualities distinctive to particular ethnic groups? Can they be rearticulated in differing contexts, for differing purposes, under differing historical skies? Gates traces the figure of the Signifyin(g) Monkey back to complex African origins, but in what ways is the Monkey distinct from trickster figures such as Coyote who inhabit many Native American oral and written texts? Or the tricksters who are also, maybe, curers in such stories as Malamud's "The Last Mohican" (1958) or "The Magic Barrel" (1958)?

Such questions remain on the agenda for the study of multicultural literatures. So, in fact, does the exploration of such literatures to identify other key tropes or elements of style—if any—common to writers of a particular ethnicity. This is no easy task for a student working within one particular ethnic culture; the difficulties are multiplied when one launches into what we might call "comparative multiculturalism," bringing into conversation two or more traditions. That is so, first, because of significant cultural differences among groups, native or immigrant, within the United States. Class training, levels of literacy, family structures, religious affiliations, among other things, have differed enormously and have thus quite differently promoted assimilation, intermingling, continuing ethnic identification, the very production of art or literature. The expectations and assumptions about ethnic culture one forms from the study of one or two groups may, or may well not, carry over fruitfully into the study of others. And second, as I have suggested, multiculturalism is a youthful field of study, barely 30 years of age, as compared with the 80 or 90 years in which mainly white and primarily male American literature has been studied, and the 150 or so years in which English literature has been formally analyzed. It is only now that the tools critical to our trade are being crafted, and so we look at *Ethnic American Literature* not as the end but as the beginning of our work.

Works Cited

Anzaldúa, Gloria. *Borderlands/La Frontera: The New Mestiza*. San Francisco: Aunt Lutie Books, 1987.

Baker, Houston A., Jr. *Blues, Ideology, and Afro-American Literature: A Vernacular Theory*. Chicago: University of Chicago Press, 1984.

Gates, Henry Louis, Jr. *The Signifying Monkey: A Theory of Afro-American Literary Criticism*. New York: Oxford University Press, 1988.

Kingston, Maxine Hong. *The Woman Warrior*. New York: Random House, 1975.

Lauter, Paul, et al., eds. *The Heath Anthology of American Literature*. Lexington, MA: D.C. Heath, 1990.

Morrison, Toni. *Playing in the Dark: Whiteness and the Literary Imagination*. Cambridge, MA: Harvard University Press, 1992.

AFRICAN AMERICAN AUTOBIOGRAPHY

Any discussion of autobiography involves historical and literary considerations; therefore, it is appropriate at the beginning of this essay to cite important dates in African American history and literature. Africans arrived in the New World as early as 1492 when Pedro Alonzo Nino, who was of African descent, was one of the explorers who sailed with Christopher Columbus. Thirty-four years later, in 1526, the first African slaves arrived in territory that eventually became part of the United States (in present day South Carolina).

Twenty Africans in 1619 arrived in Jamestown, Virginia, as indentured servants and were the first Africans to settle in North America. When did the African American literary tradition begin? Many individuals mistakenly believe that it originated with Phillis Wheatley, author of "On Messrs. Hussey and Coffin" (1767), her first published poem; and *Poems on Various Subjects, Religious and Moral* (1773), the first book of verse published by an African American. However, the African American literary tradition began decades earlier, in 1746, when Lucy Terry, at the age of 16, wrote "Bars Fight," the earliest known work by an African American. Since Terry's poem was not published until 1855, Jupiter Hammon's poem "An Evening Thought," written on December 25, 1760, and published in 1761, is acknowledged as the first poem published by an African American. Yet the first published work by an African American is not a poem; it is an autobiography. *A Narrative of the Uncommon Sufferings and Surprizing Deliverance of Briton Hammon, a Negro Man* (1760) marks the beginning of African American prose and, more specifically, the inception of African American autobiography. Since then, autobiography has maintained an influential position in African American literature as thousands of black men and women have written or dictated their life stories.

Eighteenth- and Nineteenth-Century Autobiographies

Spiritual Narratives

Although it is not known whether Hammon wrote or dictated his 14-page autobiography, his *Narrative* recounts the traumatic events that transpire after his master allows him to go to sea and he is captured by Native Americans; Hammon ends his autobiography praising God. Thus Hammon's *Narrative* blends the theme of slavery and two motifs that were popular in colonial American literature: Native American captivity and Christian conversion. Unlike Hammon, a number of 18th- and 19th-century African American autobiographers focused primarily on sacred concerns. Spiritual narratives were created by former slaves, including *A*

Brief Account of the Life, Experiences, Travels, and Gospel Labours of George White (1810); *The Life, Experience and Gospel Labors of the Rt. Rev. Richard Allen* (1833); and *Memoir of Old Elizabeth* (1863). A number of spiritual narratives were written by African Americans who had never been enslaved; among these works is *The Life and Religious Experience of Jarena Lee, a Coloured Lady, Giving an Account of Her Call to Preach the Gospel* (1836), which is the first autobiography written by an African American woman. Other spiritual autobiographies authored by free blacks include *A Narrative of the Lord's Wonderful Dealings with John Marrant* (1785); *A Journal of the Rev. John Marrant* (1790); *Memoirs of the Life, Religious Experience, Ministerial Travels and Labours of Mrs. Zilpha Elaw* (1846); *A Narrative of the Life and Travels of Mrs. Nancy Prince* (1850); Julia A. J. Foote's *A Brand Plucked from the Fire* (1879); and Daniel A. Payne's *Recollections of Seventy Years* (1888). Spiritual narratives dominated African American literary production in the late 18th century, yet they were eclipsed by slave narratives in the 19th century. Although liberation was a paramount concern in both types of autobiographies, spiritual narrators endeavored to be free of sin, and slave narrators sought emancipation from servitude.

Slave Narratives

Hammon's autobiography is the first **African American slave narrative**. The slave narrative, defined as a first person, written or oral testimony of African American bondage, is the earliest form of African American autobiography. Hammon's *Narrative* was followed by *A Narrative of the Most Remarkable Particulars in the Life of James Albert Ukawsaw Gronniosaw, an African Prince, as Related by Himself* (1772); and the two-volume *The Interesting Narrative of the Life of Olaudah Equiano, or Gustavus Vassa, the African Written by Himself* (1789). Gronniosaw and Equiano provide rare, firsthand accounts of life in Africa prior to their arrival in America, and as their titles reveal, Gronniosaw dictated his life story and Equiano wrote his. Thus Equiano's *Interesting Narrative*, the most widely read 18th-century slave narrative, is apparently the first full-length autobiography written by an African American and is recognized as the prototype of the slave narrative. William Andrews estimates that approximately 70 slave narratives were published as books or pamphlets between 1760 and 1865 and that at least 50 book-length slave narratives were published from 1865 to 1930 ("Slave Narrative" 667–68), whereas Frances Smith Foster opines that the total number of slave narratives written or dictated over the years in formats ranging from interviews of a single page to books is at least 6,000 (ix).

Gronniosaw's *Narrative* begins with the phrase "I was born," a convention that was frequently employed in subsequent slave narratives. James Olney identifies additional definitive features found in many slave narratives including testimonials written by white abolitionists, editors, and so forth verifying the authenticity and accuracy of the autobiographies; memories of "first observed whipping"; descriptions of Christian masters or mistresses; accounts of literacy efforts; details of slave auctions; descriptions of failed as well as successful escape attempts; and selections of new surnames (152–53). Foster has identified "four chronological phases" found in many slave narratives: (1) "the loss of innocence" as one becomes aware of "what it means to be a slave"; (2) "realization of alternatives to bondage and the formulation of a resolve to be free"; (3) "the escape"; and (4) "freedom obtained" (85).

In addition to the autobiographies by Hammon, Gronniosaw, and Equiano, other noteworthy slave narratives include *The Confessions of Nat Turner* (1831); *Narrative of the Life and Adventures of Henry Bibb, An American Slave, Written by Himself* (1849); *The Fugitive Blacksmith; or, Events in the History of James W. C. Pennington* (1849); *Narrative of Sojourner Truth* (1850); *Twelve Years a Slave: Narrative of Solomon Northrup* (1853); *J. W. Loguen, as a Slave and as a Freeman. A Narrative of Real Life* (1859); *Running a Thousand Miles for Freedom; or the Escape of William and Ellen Craft from Slavery* (1860); and Elizabeth Keckley's *Behind the Scenes; or, Thirty Years a Slave and Four Years in the White House* (1868). Three slave narratives have attained the status of classics in African American autobiography: *Narrative of the Life of Frederick Douglass, an American Slave, Written by Himself* (1845); *Narrative of William Wells Brown, a Fugitive Slave, Written by Himself* (1847); and Harriet Jacobs's *Incidents in the Life of a Slave Girl, Written by Herself* (1861).

Narrative of the Life of Frederick Douglass, an American Slave, Written by Himself is the preeminent slave narrative. Although Douglass had escaped to the North by the time his *Narrative* was published, he was still a fugitive slave until his freedom was purchased in 1846. Unlike Brown, Douglass does not identify himself as a fugitive slave in the title of his first autobiography; instead he describes himself as an American slave. Thus *Narrative*'s title contains an indictment against the nation that professed to be the land of liberty while it concurrently enslaved African Americans. Douglass expressed this idea in a more vehement manner in his famous 1852 speech "What to the Slave Is the Fourth of July?" in Rochester, New York. Although *Narrative*'s title also includes the phrase "Written by Himself," many of Douglass's contemporaries doubted that Douglass, who was self-educated, could write such an eloquent autobiography; however, if they heard his speech in Rochester or at any other rally sponsored by abolitionists, they realized that Douglass was an exceptional orator as well. Douglass's *Narrative*, along with autobiographies by Brown, Jacobs, and others, became powerful weapons for abolitionists. In chapters 1 through 9 of the *Narrative*, Douglass shows how a human being is made a slave as he depicts slavery's horrors, including the beating of his Aunt Hester, which he witnesses as a boy and considers his initiation into slavery. In chapter 10, Douglass reveals how a slave is transformed into a man as he resolves, prior to his successful escape in chapter 11, that although his slave status is unchanged, he no longer views himself as a bondman. Douglass provides more details about his life as a slave and as an abolitionist in two additional autobiographies, *My Bondage and My Freedom* (1855) and *The Life and Times of Frederick Douglass* (1881).

Douglass's *Narrative* overshadowed all other slave narratives, including the aforementioned works by Brown and Jacobs. Brown wrote several short autobiographies including the 36-page *Memoir of William Wells Brown, an American Bondman, Written by Himself* (1859), and like Douglass, he also wrote three book-length autobiographies. *Narrative of Williams Wells Brown* ranked second in popularity and sales only to Douglass's *Narrative*. Brown's second book-length autobiography, *Three Years in Europe: Or Places I Have Seen and People I Have Met* (published in London, 1852), was published in Boston as *The American Fugitive in Europe, Sketches of Places and People Abroad* (1855). Brown, with the publication of his second autobiography, followed the tradition established as early as John Marrant, who as previously mentioned, published autobiographies in 1785 and 1790. Unlike Marrant's autobiographies, each of Brown's autobiographies was full-length. Thus Marrant and Brown paved the way for 19th-century African American autobiographers such as Douglass and 20th-century African American autobiographers such as Langston Hughes, W.E.B. Du Bois, **Maya Angelou**, and Chester Himes who published multiple autobiographies. Indeed Angelou has carried Marrant and Brown's tradition into the 21st century as her sixth autobiography was published in 2002. Brown's third book-length autobiography, *My Southern Home, or the South and Its People* (1880), is regarded as a bridge between slave narratives and early 20th-century African American fiction and nonfiction. Jacobs's *Incidents in the Life of a Slave Girl* is not the first American slave narrative by a female; *The History of Mary Prince, a West Indian Slave, Related by Herself* (1831) holds that distinction. Jacobs, who hid in a crawl space for seven years rather than become her master's concubine, wrote the only known full-length African American female slave narrative in order to draw attention to the multitude of African American mothers who were still enslaved. Thus Jacobs, like Douglass and Brown, as well as the other slave narrators, wrote and spoke for the silent, enslaved masses.

The influence of the slave narratives can be seen in the earliest African American novels including William Wells Brown's *Clotel: Or the President's Daughter, A Narrative of Slave Life in the United States* (1853); Frank J. Webb's *The Garies and Their Friends* (1857); and Frances E.W. Harper's *Iola Leroy: Or, Shadows Uplifted* (1892). Evoking themes of slavery is not a convention that is limited to 19th-century fiction. Twentieth-century African American novels such as Arna Bontemps's *Black Thunder* (1936); Margaret Walker's *Jubilee* (1966); **Ernest J. Gaines**'s *The Autobiography of Miss Jane Pittman* (1971); **Alex Haley**'s *Roots* (1976); Octavia Butler's *Kindred* (1979); Barbara Chase-Riboud's *Sally Hemings* (1979) and its sequel, *The President's Daughter* (1994); Sherley Anne Williams's *Dessa Rose* (1986); **Toni Morrison**'s *Beloved* (1987); Chase-Riboud's *Echo of Lions* (1989); Charles Johnson's *Middle Passage* (1990); and Louise Meriwether's *Fragments of the Ark* (1994) are neo-slave narratives that consider slavery's myriad experiences or effects. Early 21st-century neo-slave narratives include Lalita Tademy's *Cane River* (2001); Hannah Crafts's *The Bondwoman's Narrative* (written in the 1850s but unpublished until 2002); David Anthony Durham's *Walk through Darkness* (2002); and **Edward P. Jones**'s *The Known World* (2003).

Twentieth- and Twenty-first-Century Autobiographies

Obviously identity is of paramount concern to African American autobiographers. During the 18th and 19th centuries, slaves produced autobiographies that proclaimed their personhood in a society that primarily viewed them as property. After slavery was abolished, African American autobiography, while continuing to present realistic images of black life in America, began providing a panoramic view of African American life as opportunities for blacks increased and became more diverse with each subsequent decade.

1900–1950

During the first half of the 20th century, the last slave narrative was published— Booker T. Washington's *Up from Slavery* (1901). Washington's autobiography, which details his birth into slavery less than a decade before the Emancipation Proclamation was issued, his founding of Tuskegee Institute, and his Atlanta Exposition Address in 1895, was the most popular African American autobiography until the 1940s. After *Up from Slavery*'s publication, the next two significant African American autobiographies were authored by William Pickens, who encouraged black Americans to ignore Washington's philosophy of industrial education and tolerance of racial discrimination in favor of W.E.B. Du Bois's philosophy of academic education as well as political and civil rights. Although Pickens, who was a college administrator, journalist, orator, National Association for the Advancement of Colored People (NAACP) official, and government official, was not born into slavery, his parents were. Pickens's first autobiography, *The Heir of Slaves* (1911) was expanded into *Bursting Bonds* (1923). James Weldon Johnson, a NAACP colleague of Pickens and Du Bois, wrote his autobiography, *Along This Way* (1933), after readers mistakenly believed that his novel, *The Autobiography of an Ex-Colored Man* (1912), was his life story. Du Bois, the foremost African American intellectual of the 20th century, wrote two autobiographies: *Dusk of Dawn* (1940) and the posthumously published *The Autobiography of W.E.B. Du Bois* (1968). In addition to Du Bois's first autobiography, the 1940s marked the publication of **Langston Hughes**'s *The Big Sea* (1940), **Zora Neale Hurston**'s *Dust Tracks on a Road* (1942), and **Richard Wright**'s ***Black Boy*** (1945). *The Big Sea* begins ironically as the 21-year-old Hughes, on board the S.S. *Malone*, tosses his books into the Atlantic Ocean in an effort to be free of his unhappy past, before the ship sails to Africa. Hughes's autobiography evokes Foster's previously mentioned chronological phases of slave narratives: developing awareness, resolving to be free, escaping, and gaining freedom (85). In part 1 of *The Big Sea*, "Twenty-one," Hughes writes that although he has attained adulthood, others exert too much control over him. In an effort to take charge of his life, he signs on board the ship as a mess boy in order to see Africa, the land of his dreams. In part 2, "The Big Sea," Hughes celebrates his independence as he experiences life's ups and downs. Hughes was not the only member of the **Harlem Renaissance** to publish his autobiography; previously mentioned autobiographies by Johnson and Du Bois as well as Claude McKay's *A Long Way from Home* (1937) preceded his, and Hurston's *Dust Tracks* and Walter White's *A Man Called White* (1948) followed *The Big Sea*. However in the third section of *The Big Sea*, "Black Renaissance," Hughes provides the most detailed written account of the Harlem Renaissance by one of its participants. Hughes focuses on his travels in his second autobiography, *I Wonder* *as I Wander* (1956). Both autobiographies employ the travel motif established in Brown's aforementioned *The American Fugitive*.

Hurston's *Dust Tracks*, along with her works of fiction, has received renewed interest since Alice Walker traveled to Florida in 1973 and placed a marker on Hurston's unmarked grave. Hurston's autobiography is of particular interest to subsequent generations of African American women writers who view her as a literary foremother and to scholars interested in Harlem Renaissance personalities. *Dust Tracks* was not the first noteworthy 20th-century autobiography by an African American woman; Ida Wells-Barnett's *Crusade for Justice* was written in 1928, six years before her death, but it remained unpublished until 1970. *Crusade for Justice* focuses on Wells Barnett's public life as a journalist, social activist, feminist, and antilynching crusader rather than on her private life as a wife and mother.

Wright's *Black Boy*, one of the earliest Book-of-the-Month Club (BOMC) selections by an African American, was the most popular black autobiography since *Up from Slavery*. Indeed the BOMC influenced the autobiography's publication. When the publishing company received Wright's manuscript that was titled *American Hunger*, it submitted the manuscript to the BOMC for selection consideration. The BOMC accepted the book only after the publisher agreed to delete part 2, "The Horror and the Glory," which was an account of Wright's years in Chicago. Thus in 1945, only part 1, "Southern Nights" (later titled *Black Boy* by Wright) was published. "The Horror and the Glory" was published posthumously in 1977 as *American Hunger*, and the complete autobiography was first published in 1991. Like Hughes, Wright opts for a memorable beginning when he describes how as a four-year-old, he sets his house on fire. More importantly *Black Boy* documents how **racism** affects African Americans.

1950–

Three of the most widely read African American autobiographies of the latter half of the 20th century are **The Autobiography of Malcolm X** (1965); **I Know Why the Caged Bird Sings** (1970), by Maya Angelou; and *Having Our Say: The Delany Sisters' First 100 Years* (1993), by Sarah Delany and A. Elizabeth Delany (with Amy Hill Hearth). These three autobiographies were adapted for the screen and stage. Malcolm X's *Autobiography* was made into a feature film in 1992, which Spike Lee wrote the screenplay for, directed, and produced; *Caged Bird* was transformed into a 1979 made-for-television film with a screenplay by Angelou; and *Having Our Say* became a Broadway play that debuted in 1995 and was produced by Camille Cosby and Judith Rutherford James. Malcolm X's *Autobiography*, as told to Alex Haley and published posthumously, traces Malcolm X's childhood, conversion to Islam, and trip to Mecca. *Autobiography* was published ten years after Rosa Parks refused to sit at the back of a bus, ten years after 14-year-old Emmett Till was lynched, five years after African American college students staged a sit-in at a Woolworth's lunch counter, four years after "freedom riders" rode South, two years after Martin Luther King Jr. delivered his "I Have a Dream" speech during the March on Washington, and two years after four little girls were killed in the bombing of the Seventeenth Street Baptist Church in Birmingham, Alabama. Following in the

tradition of Frederick Douglass and Richard Wright, Malcolm X audaciously pro-
tested the abuse of African Americans. Indeed the turbulence of the **Civil Rights
Movement** of the 1950s and 1960s is documented in such African American auto-
biographies as **Anne Moody**'s *Coming of Age in Mississippi* (1968); Coretta Scott
King's *My Life with Martin Luther King, Jr.* (1969); Charlayne Hunter-Gault's *In
My Place* (1992); *Rosa Parks: My Story* (1992, with Jim Haskins); Melba Beals's
Warriors Don't Cry (1994); and Vernon Jordan's *Vernon Can Read!* (2001, with
Annette Gordon-Reed). After Malcolm X's *Autobiography*, arguably the most mem-
orable African American autobiography by a male is Arthur Ashe's *Days of Grace*
(1993, with Arnold Rampersad) where Ashe reveals that living as a black person in
United States was a greater burden than living with AIDS. Additional exceptional
African American male autobiographies published during the second half of the
20th century and beyond include Claude Brown's *Manchild in the Promised Land*
(1965); Eldridge Cleaver's *Soul on Ice* (1967); Adam Clayton Powell Jr.'s *Adam by
Adam* (1971); Chester Himes's *The Quality of Hurt* (1971) and *My Life of Absurd-
ity* (1976); John E. Wideman's *Brothers and Keepers* (1984); Ben Carson's *Gifted
Hands* (1990, with Cecil Murphey); Henry Louis Gates's *Colored People* (1994);
Nathan McCall's *Makes Me Wanna Holler* (1994); Colin Powell's *My American
Journey* (1995, with Joseph E. Persico); Marcus Mabry's *White Bucks and Black-
Eyed Peas* (1995); Dwayne Wickham's *Woodholme* (1995); **James McBride**'s *The
Color of Water* (1996); Kweisi Mfume's *No Free Ride* (1996, with Ron Stodghill
II); Amiri Baraka's *The Autobiography of LeRoi Jones/Amiri Baraka* (1997); James
A. McPherson's *Crabcakes* (1998); E. Lynn Harris's *What Becomes of the Broken-
hearted* (2003); and Andre Leon Talley's *A.L.T.* (2003).

Angelou's first autobiography, *I Know Why the Caged Bird Sings*, ushered in
the contemporary era of autobiographies by African American women. *Caged Bird*
contains many memorable incidents such as the Sunday when an overzealous Sister Monroe hits Rev. Thomas on the back of his head with her purse and Thomas's
dentures land by the young Maya's right shoe. Such humorous events are overshadowed by Angelou's recollections of her innocent uncle hiding in the potato and
onion bins in order to escape a lynching mob and her mother's boyfriend raping
her when she is eight years old. After the rapist is murdered, Angelou refrains
from speaking until Mrs. Flowers encourages her to break her silence. Angelou's
five additional autobiographies are *Gather Together in My Name* (1974), *Singin' and
Swingin' and Gettin' Merry Like Christmas* (1976), *The Heart of a Woman* (1981),
All God's Children Need Travelin' Shoes (1986), and *A Song Flung Up to Heaven*
(2002). Other important autobiographies by African American women include
Nikki Giovanni's *Gemini* (1971), Marita Golden's *Migrations of the Heart* (1983),
Pauli Murray's *Song in a Weary Throat* (1987), Bebe Moore Campbell's *Sweet Sum-
mer* (1989), Jill Nelson's *Volunteer Slavery* (1983), Patrice Gaines's *Laughing in the
Dark* (1994); Veronica Chambers's *Mama's Girl* (1996), Rosemary Bray's *Unafraid
of the Dark* (1998), and June Jordan's *Soldier* (2001).

With the publication of the Delanys's *Having Our Say*, African American middle-
class life is emphasized. Other works that also focus on black middle- or upper-
class lifestyles are Lorene Cary's *Black Ice* (1991), Lawrence Otis Graham's *Member*

of the Club (1995), Gwendolyn Parker's *Trespassing* (1997), and Rebecca Walker's *Black White and Jewish* (2001). Affluent African American life is also represented in the autobiographies of athletes and entertainers. Indeed during the latter half of the 20th century and the beginning of the 21st century, this subgenre of African American autobiography has proliferated and, in addition to the previously mentioned Ashe autobiography, is represented by such works as Muhammad Ali's *The Greatest* (1975, with Richard Durham); Sidney Poitier's *This Life* (1980) and *The Measure of a Man* (2000); Kareem Abdul Jabbar's *Giant Steps* (1983, with Peter Knobler); Diahann Carroll's *Diahann!* (1986, with Ross Firestone); Tina Turner's *I, Tina* (1986, with Kurt Loder); Smokey Robinson's *Smokey* (1989, with David Ritz); Hank Aaron's *I Had a Hammer* (1991); Patti LaBelle's *Don't Block the Blessings* (1996, with Laura Randolph); Eric Davis's *Born to Play* (1999, with Ralph Wiley); and Quincy Jones's *Q* (2001).

Two autobiographies that have gained international attention are *Dreams from My Father: A Story of Race and Inheritance* (1995) and *The Audacity of Hope: Thoughts on Reclaiming the American Dream* (2006), both by **Barack Obama**. Written before he was elected president of the United States, these autobiographies offer candid glimpses into his life and politics. *Dreams from My Father*, a lyrically written and deeply personal narrative, maps Obama's life from childhood to the time he is poised to enter Harvard Law School. *The Audacity of Hope*, on the other hand, is a political memoir that documents the formation of ideological outlook that would provide the foundation for the way the future president will govern the nation.

In conclusion African American autobiography has documented black life from the colonial period to the present time. Although the goal of accurate portrayals of African Americans has remained constant since 1760, each autobiography provides a glimpse into the diversity of the African American experience.

Further Reading

Andrews, William L., ed. *African-American Autobiographies: A Collection of Critical Essays.* Englewood Cliffs, NJ: Prentice Hall, 1973.

Andrews, William L. "Secular Autobiography." In *The Oxford Companion to African American Literature*, edited by William L. Andrews, Frances Smith Foster, and Trudier Harris, 34–37. New York: Oxford University Press, 1997.

Andrews, William L. "Slave Narrative." In *The Oxford Companion to African American Literature*, edited by William L. Andrews, Frances Smith Foster, and Trudier Harris, 667–70. New York: Oxford University Press, 1997.

Andrews, William L., ed. *To Tell a Free Story: The First Century of Afro-American Autobiography, 1760–1865.* Urbana: University of Illinois Press, 1986.

Andrews, William L. "Toward a Poetics of American Autobiography." In *Afro-American Literary Study in the 1990s*, edited by Houston A. Baker Jr. and Patricia Redmond, 78–97. Chicago: University of Chicago Press, 1989.

Andrews, William L., Frances Smith Foster, and Trudier Harris, eds. *The Oxford Companion to African American Literature.* New York: Oxford University Press, 1997.

Braxton, Joanne M. *Black Women Writing Autobiography: A Tradition within a Tradition.* Philadelphia: Temple University Press, 1989.

Butterfield, Stephen. *Black Autobiography*. Amherst: University of Massachusetts Press, 1974.

Davis, Charles T., and Henry Louis Gates Jr., eds. *The Slave's Narrative*. New York: Oxford University Press, 1985.

Dudley, David L. *My Father's Shadow: Intergenerational Conflict in African American Men's Autobiography*. Philadelphia: University of Pennsylvania Press, 1991.

Foster, Frances Smith. *Witnessing Slavery: The Development of Ante-bellum Slave Narratives*. Westport, CT: Greenwood Press, 1979.

Franklin, V. P. *Living Our Stories, Telling Our Truths: Autobiography and the Making of the African-American Intellectual Tradition*. New York: Oxford University Press, 1995.

Nelson, Emmanuel S., ed. *African American Autobiographers: A Sourcebook*. Westport, CT: Greenwood Press, 2002.

Olney, James. "'I Was Born': Slave Narratives, Their Status as Autobiography and as Literature." In *The Slave's Narrative*, edited by Charles T. Davis and Henry Louis Gates Jr., 148–75. New York: Oxford University Press, 1985.

Sekora, John, and Darwin T. Turner, eds. *The Art of Slave Narratives: Original Essays in Criticism and Theory*. Macomb: Western Illinois University Press, 1982.

West, Elizabeth. "From David Walker to President Obama." *American Studies Journal* 56 (2012). np.

Linda M. Carter

AFRICAN AMERICAN DRAMA

African American drama is the second-oldest genre in the African American literary canon. African American drama dates to 1823 when Mr. Brown, a ship steward and West Indian native, produced a play he penned, *The Drama of King Shotaway*, at his Lower Manhattan African Grove Theatre. *The Drama of King Shotaway* recounts the 1795 insurrection of black Caribs of St. Vincent's Island in the West Indies. The play is thought to be based upon Brown's eyewitness account of the rebellion.

The year 1823 was also the time of the African Grove's demise (Brown had founded the theater in 1816), and five decades would elapse before another African American drama would appear on a stage. Between the African Grove's final curtain call and that time, however, there was another important milestone in the African American dramatic tradition: the minstrel show.

Born in 1832, the minstrel show was an extremely popular dramatic form in which white actors donned blackface make-up and parodied African American dress, dance, speech, and song. The typical minstrel show featured "shuffling, irresponsible, wide-grinning, loud-laughing Negroes in a musical rendition of darky life on the Old Plantation" (Woll 1).

The early minstrel shows were popular, perhaps not because of the stereotyped characterization of African Americans, but for the romanticized images of plantation life they depicted. For the white audience, these shows were a nostalgic reminder of those antebellum days of the past. Regardless of the reasons for the minstrel show's popularity, African Americans found them offensive, not only for

LaTanya Richardson, left, Denzel Washington and Sophie Okonedo at the curtain call for the opening night of *A Raisin in the Sun* in 2014 in New York. (Charles Sykes/Invision/AP)

their use of racist **African American stereotypes** such as the coon, Sambo, and Mammy, but for the message they sent: that although free, African Americans yearned for the world of slavery that gave them the security of protection. Thus, many African American activists of the time, such as **Frederick Douglass** and Martin Delany, not only wrote articles and essays to rebut and revise the defamatory images propagated by the minstrel show but also to defend African American character and contentment with freedom.

Despite its controversy, the minstrel show has been credited with launching the careers of many African American actors of the time. After the Civil War, finding the minstrel show as the only mainstream outlet for their stage talent, African American performers developed competing versions of the minstrel show. By 1870 several troupes of African American minstrels billed as "real and original" existed and employed 1,490 African American actors.

Thirty-three years after *The Drama of King Shotaway*, William Wells Brown's penned two plays, *Experience, or How to Give a Northern Man a Backbone* (1856) and *The Escape, or A Leap for Freedom* (1857). The two plays, the former which tells the story of a white preacher who condemns slavery after being sold into slavery and the latter, which relates the story of a newlywed couple who escape slavery when they learn that their master plans to separate them so he can take the wife as his concubine, were never produced. Instead, Brown performed readings of them at abolitionist meetings.

In 1880, Pauline Hopkins's *Peculiar Sam, or the Underground Railroad* (1879) became the second play by an African American dramatist to be produced on stage. Her play was performed in Boston by the Hopkins Colored Troubadours. This play was followed three years later by John Patterson Sampson's *The Disappointed Bridge, or Love at First Sight* (1883) and a play that chronicles Haitian history by dramatist William Edgar Easton. Easton's *Dessalines* (1893) is a semibiography of General Dessalines, who became the first Haitian king after helping the country win its independence. Six years later in 1899, Paul Laurence Dunbar penned two plays, *Robert Herrick*, a comedy of manners about the poet for which the play is named, and *Winter Roses*, a play about a widower who reunites with his first love after many years.

Joseph Seamon Cotter Sr.'s *Caleb, the Degenerate* (1903), a play that examines Booker T. Washington's philosophy, is the first African American drama of the 20th century. In 1910, Katherine Davis Chapman Tillman became the second woman to write a play. Her *Fifty Years of Freedom, or From Cabin to Congress* is a commemoration of the 50th anniversary of the Emancipation Proclamation. William Edgar Easton's *Christophe* (1911) completes his examination of Haitian history; the play dramatizes Dessalines's removal from power. Like Easton, W.E.B. Du Bois penned an homage play. His *The Star of Ethiopia* (1913) pays tribute to the gifts Africa has given to the world.

During the early 1900s social protest plays became a common means for dramatists to voice their antipathy toward the American racial climate. In 1916, Angelina Weld Grimké penned *Rachel*, the first social protest play by an African American female playwright. Hailed as a pioneering work in the use of racial propaganda to enlighten white Americans to the plight of African Americans, *Rachel* is the story of a young woman who during the course of the play's plot becomes increasingly aware of the racial violence and prejudice to which African Americans are subjected.

Alice Dunbar-Nelson used her *Mine Eyes Have Seen* (1918) to voice her objection to the treatment that African American soldiers received after their return from World War I. In the play she extols their loyalty to the war. Like, Dunbar-Nelson, Mary Burrill chose to bring attention to the mistreatment of the African American soldier. Her *Aftermath* (1919) dramatizes the tragic killing of an African American soldier after his return to racist America. She brings attention to a woman's right to access to contraceptives in *They That Sit in Darkness* (1919).

Although Marita Bonner's *The Purple Flower* (1927) is not as critically acclaimed as Grimké's *Rachel*, it, too, calls attention to **race**. It is an allegorical treatment of American race relations in which African Americans are depicted as wormlike creatures living in a valley trying to climb the Hill of Somewhere to reach the purple flower of Life-at-Its-Finest; whites are depicted as sundry devils living on the side of the hill who try to keep the worms from getting to the top of the hill.

In 1923, Willis Richardson's *The Chip Woman's Fortune* (1923) had the distinction of being the first African American drama to be produced on Broadway. The play narrates the attempt of a young man to rob an old woman of her life's savings so that he can rid himself of his debt. Following in Richardson's footsteps were

Garland Anderson, Frank Wilson, and Wallace Thurman. Anderson's *Appearances*, which relates the story of an African American bellhop who is tried and exonerated of killing a white woman, debuted on Broadway in 1925. Wilson's *Meek Mose* (1928), which concerns an African American activist whose community loses faith in him after he is unsuccessful in his attempts to help them retain the land from which they are being forced to move by white citizens who want the land for their own use, was followed in 1929 by Thurman's *Harlem*, which is a sordid depiction of life in Harlem.

In addition to his Broadway play, Richardson also wrote a number of other plays, including *Mortgaged* (1924), *Compromise* (1925), and *The Broken Banjo* (1925). Just as prolific as Richardson was Randolph Edmonds. Edmonds is credited with penning 50 plays; most of them were published in the collections *Shades and Shadows* (1930), *Six Plays for a Negro Theatre* (1934), and *The Land of Cotton and Other Plays* (1940).

Other notable writers of the time period include Georgia Douglass Johnson, Eulalie Spence, and Dr. John Frederick Matheus. Johnson wrote two one-act plays: *Blue Blood* (1926), which is about a mulatto's couple discovery that they have the same father, and *Plumes* (1927), which depicts a mother's decision to use her life's savings to grandly bury her dead daughter instead of using the money for an operation that will save her own life. Spence continues the examination of the family with her plays *Undertow* (1927) and *The Fool's Errand* (1927). The former is the story of a man, his wife, and his lover; the latter is a depiction of the ridicule a young, unmarried woman receives when she is mistakenly presumed pregnant. Matheus is best known for the plays '*Cruiter* (1926) and *Ti-Yette* (1930).

The Great Depression caused a waning in the production of African American dramaturgy. However, because of the efforts of the Federal Theatre Project, many playwrights were able to continue their craft.

As a part of the Roosevelt administration's Works Progress Administration (WPA), Congress created the Federal Theatre Project. The Federal Theatre Project established 16 segregated African American units for the production of plays by or about African Americans. The Federal Theatre Project was instrumental in helping young, emerging African American playwrights; not only did it provide them an opportunity to concentrate on their creative efforts, but it also gave them a chance to participate in stage procedures and productions on a large scale.

Not only did the Federal Theatre Project provide unprecedented opportunities for the playwrights, but it also provided opportunities for the audience as well. The nominal prices charged for tickets made it possible for more African Americans to attend performances, and the increased degree of artistic freedom practiced by the project made it possible for the playwrights to project a new and recognizable image for those African Americans.

One of the project's plays that was especially appealing to audiences was the New Jersey Unit's *The Trial of Dr. Beck*. Written by Allison Hughes, it was so successful that after it closed in New Jersey it did a four-week run on Broadway. In the play, Dr. Beck, a handsome and distinguished-looking mulatto, is accused of murdering his wealthy dark-skinned wife, Amanda, and the play unfolds through the evidence at his trial. *The Trial of Dr. Beck* was hailed by the African American community for its emphasis on the need in the African American community for a reevaluation of its self-image. Many saw it as a daring assault on the fact that a social hierarchy based on skin color had been established in the African American community.

Other noteworthy Federal Theatre Project plays are the New York Unit's productions of Frank Wilson's *Walk Together Children* (1936), a dramatization of the conflict between two African American labor unions; Arna Bontemps and Countee Cullen's adaptation of Rudolph Fisher's *Conjur Man Dies* (1936), an examination of superstitions of Harlem citizens; and J. Augustus Smith's *Turpentine* (1936), which is an exploration of the conditions in Southern labor camps, and *Just Ten Days* (1937), a play about a family's attempt to avoid eviction from their home. The Seattle Unit produced *Go Down Moses* (1937), a depiction of Harriet Tubman's life; *Natural Man* (1937), an account of the John Henry myth; and *Swing, Gates, Swing* (1937), a musical. The Chicago Unit's most significant production was Theodore Ward's *Big White Fog* (1938), a moving depiction of a family who find that the injustice, poverty, and prejudice they hoped to escape when they left the South remain impediments in Chicago.

A number of African American plays were also produced on Broadway during the Depression years. Two plays with Broadway curtain calls were J. Augustus Smith's *Louisiana* (1933) and Hall Johnson's *Run, Little Chillun!* (1933). Both plays concern voodoo and Christianity. Dennis Donoghue's *Legal Murder* (1934) examines the Scottsboro Boys Case, and **Langston Hughes**'s *Mulatto* (1935) is an examination of miscegenation. In addition to *Mulatto*, Hughes penned three additional plays during the Depression years: *Little Ham* (1935), *The Emperor of Haiti* (1935), and *Don't You Want to Be Free?* (1937), the latter play having had 135 performances by its final curtain call.

Like the Depression Era, the 1940s was a decade of decline for African American drama. Because of World War II, a number of writers turned their attention to the war effort instead. In spite of the war, a number of dramatists did continue to write, and during this time one of the most renowned theater groups in African American theater history was founded. In 1940, in the basement of the public library on 135th Street in Harlem, Frederick O'Neal and Abram Hill founded the American Negro Theater. Not only is it recognized for its successful productions of Owen Dodson's *Garden of Time* (1939), Hill's *On Striver's Row* (1940), and their adaptation of Philip Yordan's *Anna Lucasta* (1940)—which set a record when it later played on Broadway for 957 performances—but it is also known for having trained actors Harry Belafonte and Sidney Poitier and actress Ruby Dee. Unfortunately, the American Negro Theatre's success also led to its demise, for its best actors left after having found mainstream commercial work.

By the 1950s, African American dramatists had become more skilled at the technique of writing plays, and this ability was exhibited in the plays. The plays of this decade were more sophisticated in their development of character and theme. Common themes included interracial relationships, poverty, integration, segregation, the African American church, and life in the urban North/ghetto. Because most of the African American community was concerned with these issues, many of the plays explored those subjects in some form. One such play was Louis Peterson's *Take a Giant Step* (1953), which depicts the **identity** crisis of a youth who seeks relationships within the African American community after having grown up in a white neighborhood. Another play is Charles Sebree's *Mrs. Patterson* (1954), which dramatizes an African American girl's desire to become as rich as a white lady she knows. A final play is **James Baldwin's** *The Amen Corner* (1955). This play, which played Broadway in 1965, is a critique of the power the African American church has over its congregants' lives.

The most well-known play of the 1950s is **Lorraine Hansberry's** *A Raisin in the Sun* (1959). Not only was it the first play by an African American woman to have a run on Broadway, but it was also the first noncomical Broadway play to be directed by an African American, Lloyd Richards. Many critics considered *A Raisin in the Sun* to have presented the most realistic exploration of African American domestic life of its time. In its dramatization of the Younger family, *A Raisin in the Sun* gave America a glimpse of the struggles and frustrations of the urban African American family.

Other plays penned by African American women during the 1950s were *Florence* (1950) and *Wedding Band* (1956) by Alice Childress and *A Bolt from the Blue* (1950) by Gertrude Jeannette.

African American dramas of the early 1960s were musical in nature. Two well-known musical satires are Ossie Davis's *Purlie Victorious* (1961), which satirizes white-created African American stereotypes, and C. Bernard Jackson's *Fly Blackbird* (1962), a satire of the sit-in movement. Although not a satire, Loften Mitchell's *Ballad for Bimshire* (1963) provides commentary on the ideas of **racism**, nationalism, and colonialism. The other musicals of the period came from the pen of Langston Hughes. His *Black Nativity* (1961), *Jerico-Jim Crow* (1963), *Tambourines to Glory* (1963), and *Prodigal Son* (1965) are all light-hearted examinations of various aspects African American life.

Despite the proliferation of musicals in the early 1960s, a vast number of nonmusicals were also penned during this time. Adrienne Kennedy's *Funnyhouse of a Negro* (1963) is a traditional drama that narrates the attempts of a young girl to come to terms with her mixed heritage. Likewise, Lorraine Hansberry's *The Sign in Sidney Brustein's Window* (1964); Douglas Turner Ward's *Day of Absence* (1965) and *Happy Ending* (1965); and Lonne Elder's *Ceremonies in Dark Old Men* (1965) are also conventional works. Ward's one-act satirical dramas were produced Off-Broadway on a single bill and set a record for 504 performances. Elder's play was nominated for the Pulitzer Prize for drama, and although it did not win that coveted prize, it did win the Outer Critics Circle and Drama Desk awards.

Beginning in the mid-1960s, a Black Theater Movement, growing out of the civil rights struggle, began to flourish. The founders of the movement called for more positive images in plays by African American playwrights and advocated the use of drama as a weapon in the Black Power struggle. The plays of this movement were controversial, as well as shocking and militant. In addition, they presented confrontation and revolution as the sole means of resolving racial problems.

Despite their militancy, the plays of this decade did more than just advocate African American rights and political activism; they also emphasized the dynamism of African American culture. Like "black power," pride in blackness, too, was a common theme of the plays. To the playwrights involved in the Black Theater Movement, it was essential that African American theater become more black oriented, consciously drawing on African American community culture.

The best-known figure and playwright of the Black Theatre Movement is Amiri Baraka (formerly known as LeRoi Jones), who founded and directed the Black Arts Repertory Theatre and School (BARTS) in Harlem. Not only were Baraka and BARTS instrumental in changing the focus of African American theater from one of racial integration to one of separation, but with plays like *Dutchman* (1964), *The Slave* (1964), and *The Toilet* (1964), Baraka brought an increasing racial consciousness and political militancy to African American theater. *Dutchman* is a warning to African American men who may desire white women. In the play a young African American, Clay, is seduced and murdered by a white woman, Lula. *The Slave* has a newly converted black militant as its protagonist. In an attempt to prove his militancy, the protagonist kills his white wife and children. *The Toilet* dramatizes the brutal beating of a white homosexual by a group of black boys. They beat him because he sends a love letter to the leader of their group.

In addition to Amiri Baraka, Ed Bullins was an instrumental figure in the Black Theater Movement. Like Baraka, Bullins penned a number of plays, including *Clara's Old Man* (1965), *The Electronic Nigger* (1968), and *A Son Come Home* (1968). These dramas, which played Off Broadway on a triple bill, were lauded for their realism. *Clara's Old Man* is an account of African American life in the ghetto; *The Electronic Nigger* is a satire of the African American who refuses to think for himself but allows the white man to think for him; and *A Son Come Home* examines the estranged relationship between a mother and her son.

The Black Theater Movement influenced a number of playwrights, including Ben Caldwell, Ron Milner, and Jimmy Garrett. Caldwell's *The Job* (1966) is a work that enjoins African Americans to protest government unemployment-opportunity projects, and his *Prayer Meeting, or the First Militant Minister* (1967) is the story of a preacher who becomes a militant. Milner's *The Monster* (1968) is about a confrontation between college students and their dean who have divergent ideas, and Garrett's *And We Own the Night* (1967) is a brutal depiction of a militant who kills his mother because he views her as being an adversary of the Black Revolution.

The 1970s were a very high point for African American drama. During the decade an African American play won the coveted Pulitzer Prize for drama.

In 1970, with *No Place to Be Somebody*, Charles Gordone became the first African American to win the Pulitzer Prize for drama. Set in a New York City bar, the play examines the thwarted ambitions of the bar's patrons (which includes hustlers, prostitutes, artists, and ex-cons) and its owner, Johnny Williams. Subtitled "A Black-Black Comedy," *No Place to Be Somebody* was hailed for its brutal and honest examination of the individual and communal struggle for identity.

In addition to *No Place to Be Somebody*, a number of other African American plays received awards during the 1970s. Most notable of those plays are

J. E. Gaines's *Don't Let It Go to Your Head* (1970), Philip Hayes Dean's *Sty of the Blind Pig* (1971), J. E. Franklin's *Black Girl* (1971), Mario Van Peebles's *Ain't Supposed to Die a Natural Death* (1971), Richard Wesley's *The Black Terror* (1971), and Joseph A. Walker's *The River Niger* (1976), all of which received Drama Desk awards in their respected years of production. J. E. Gaines's *What If It Had Turned up Heads* (1971), Paul Carter Harrison's *The Great McDaddy* (1974), Leslie Lee's *The First Breeze of Summer* (1976), and Ntozake Shange's *for colored girls who have considered suicide/when the rainbow is enuf* (1976) were recipients of the Obie Award, and Steve Carter's *Eden* was an Outer Critics Circle Award recipient.

Two Pulitzer Prizes for drama were awarded to African American playwrights during the 1980s. Twelve years after Charles Gordone accepted the Pulitzer for *No Place to Be Somebody*, Charles Fuller accepted it for *A Soldier's Play* (1981).

Set in 1944 at Fort Neal, Louisiana, *A Soldier's Play* is a mystery play that through the course of the plot attempts to uncover the murderer of Sgt. Vernon Waters, the leader of the African American company at the segregated World War II army base. The officer in charge of the investigation initially believes Waters's death is a hate crime, but as the story unfolds he realizes that Waters was killed by one of his own men.

In spite of the critical acclaim *A Soldier's Play* received, it was heavily criticized in the African American community. Many African Americans disapproved of the play because of its portrayal of black-on-black crime. Amiri Baraka, in particular, saw the play as "catering to the desires of the white power structure rather than to the needs of the oppressed blacks." Like *A Soldier's Play*, Fuller's *Zooman and the Sign* (1980) was also criticized. It, too, is an examination of black-on-black crime. In the play, the protagonist, Zooman, terrorizes a neighborhood into silence about his unintentional murder of a neighborhood girl.

The second play to win the Pulitzer Prize for drama during the 1980s is **August Wilson**'s *Fences* (1987). *Fences* focuses on the conflict between Troy Maxson, who is an ex-con and former Negro League baseball player, and his son Corey. Corey wishes to play football but, believing that Corey will suffer the same hardships as he did as a professional player, Troy refuses to allow Corey to "waste" his life on sports. In addition to winning the Pulitzer Prize, *Fences* also won a New York Drama Critics Circle Award and a Tony Award.

Many critics have proclaimed the 1980s as the decade of August Wilson. Other than George Wolfe's *The Colored Museum* (1986), which satirizes the African American experience in America, the two other bright spots of the decade are plays Wilson penned. Wilson's *Ma Rainey's Black Bottom* (1982) launched his career when it opened on Broadway in 1984. His *Joe Turner's Come and Gone* premiered on Broadway in 1988, giving him the distinction of having two plays run simultaneously on Broadway (the play debuted while *Fences* was still enjoying its stint at the 46th Street Theatre). *Ma Rainey's Black Bottom* is a play about a group of musicians and ends in the murder of one of them; *Joe Turner* is a about a group of boardinghouse residents, all who are in search of someone or something.

August Wilson's dramaturgy also ushered in the 1990s. His *The Piano Lesson*, a play about the estranged relationship between a brother and sister, won the Pulitzer Prize for drama in 1990. That play was followed by *Two Trains Running* (1992) and *Seven Guitars* (1996). The former focuses on the disintegration of the city, and the latter is a murder mystery that focuses on the events leading to the protagonist's death.

If the 1980s and 1990s are Wilson's decades, the early 21st century is the decade of Suzan-Lori Parks. In 2002, Parks became the first African American female playwright to win the Pulitzer Prize for drama with her *Top Dog/Under Dog*, a tragic story about two brothers, Lincoln and Booth. Parks followed *Top Dog/Under Dog* with *Fucking A* (2003). In the play Parks focuses on a character type she used in an earlier play, *In the Blood* (1999). Both plays have as their protagonist a modern-day Hester Prynne. *Fucking A* is the story of a female abortionist who has an A branded into her skin according to the law of the community in which she lives; *In the Blood* focuses on a young mother who has five illegitimate children and is daily reminded of her sins by the scarlet As that are painted on the walls of the makeshift home in which she and her children live. In 2005, Parks wrote the screenplay for Zora Neale Hurston's **Their Eyes Were Watching God**. In 2011, she composed an adaptation, with Diedre Murray, an adaptation of George Gershwin's classic *Porgy and Bess*, an opera that was first performed in 1935.

The past 181 years have been a time of metamorphosis for African American drama. The genre has evolved tremendously in every aspect. Because of the universal issues they depict and the refined craft of the playwrights, African American dramaturgy is seen and enjoyed by audiences of all nationalities.

Further Reading

Craig, E. Quita. *Black Drama of the Federal Theatre Era*. Amherst: University of Massachusetts Press, 1980.

Elam, Harry, J. Jr., and David Krasner, eds. *African American Performance and Theater History*. New York: Oxford University Press, 2001.

Euba, Femi. *Archetypes, Imprecators and Victims of Fate: Origins and Developments of Satire in Black Drama*. Westport, CT: Greenwood Press, 1989.

Hatch, James V., and Ted Shine, eds. *Black Theater U.S.A.: Forty Plays by Black Americans (1847–1974)*. New York: Free Press, 1974.

Hay, Samuel. *African American Theatre: A Historical and Critical Analysis*. New York: Cambridge University Press, 1994.

Patterson, Lindsay, ed. *The Anthology of the American Negro in the Theater*. New York: Publishers Co., 1967.

Peterson, Bernard L. *Early Black American Playwrights and Dramatic Writers: A Biographical Directory and Catalog of Plays, Films and Broadcasting Scripts*. Westport, CT: Greenwood Press, 1990.

Sampson, Henry T. *Blacks in Blackface: A Source Book on Early Black Musical Shows*. Metuchen, NJ: Scarecrow Press, 1980.

Sanders, Leslie Catherine. *The Development of Black Theater in America: From Shadows to Selves*. Baton Rouge: Louisiana State University Press, 1987.

Toll, Robert. *Blacking Up: The Minstrel Show in Nineteenth-Century America*. New York: Oxford University Press, 1974.

Williams, Mance. *Black Theatre in the 1960s and 1970s: A Historical-Critical Analysis of the Movement*. Westport, CT: Greenwood Press, 1985.

Woll, Allen. *Black Musical Theatre: From Coontown to Dreamgirls*. Baton Rouge: Louisiana State University Press, 1989.

Young, Harvey. *The Cambridge Companion to African American Theatre*. Cambridge, England: Cambridge University Press, 2013.

Yolanda W. Page

AFRICAN AMERICAN GAY LITERATURE

The heterosexist ideologies of the African American community as well as the **racism** of the white gay community have historically often kept African American gay male literature invisible. Yet African American gay males have a rich literary history in which they have used poetry, fiction, drama, and autobiography to express a proud and resistant **identity** and to render their lives visible. Although African American gay writers have often been asked to identify first as "black" or as "gay," most have highlighted the interconnection between their **race** and sexual orientation. Indeed, many gay male African Americans writers publishing in the 1980s and 1990s have placed their work in the tradition of civil rights activism. They have reimagined themselves as "revolutionaries" who are furthering the work of earlier women and men by remaking history and opening up a dialogue about social values regarding sexuality, gender relations, community life, and family. In addition, these writers have also challenged the authority of "white" models of gay identity in the United States and the long history of eroticizing the black male body from a colonial perspective.

The dating of an African American gay literary history depends on how one defines the marker "gay." Prior to World War II most Americans, regardless of race, did not self-identify as "gay," which was still understood more as a sinful action or a gender "deviance," not an identity based on sexual orientation. The expression of same-sex desire and attraction among black men, however, has a longer history, one that is traceable back to at least 1646 when the "Negro," Jan Creoli, was sentenced to death in New Netherlands (Manhattan) for committing sodomy. In *The Autobiography of a Runaway Slave*, the Cuban Esteban Montejo testifies to homosexuality among slaves and even to loving male couples and families prior to abolition, and his account repudiates homophobic myths that homosexuality was a disease imposed by whites or the result of "dysfunctional" matriarchal families.

The first flowering of a self-conscious expression of homoerotic desire, however, occurred during the **Harlem Renaissance**. The younger generation of bohemian writers, Richard Bruce Nugent, Wallace Thurman, Claude McKay, **Langston Hughes**, Countee Cullen, encouraged by Alain Locke, sought to express the full lived experience of African Americans and challenged the cultural practices among middle-class political leaders to portray only a respectable "New Negro" who would win white acceptance. During the 1920s and 1930s, Harlem had a thriving gay community, and despite the objection of leaders such as W.E.B. Du Bois, who feared the depiction of homosexuality would only reaffirm white society's fantasy of black people as overly sexual primitives, many Harlem Renaissance writers depicted—directly or indirectly—homoerotic scenes. The painter Bruce Nugent published the first known gay short story, "Sadji" (1925), in Locke's landmark New Negro anthology, but he is remembered more for his 1926 story "Smoke, Lilies, and Jade," which appeared in the avant-garde literary journal *Fire!!!* and that narrates an explicit homoerotic celebration of black male beauty.

In contrast to Nugent, most Harlem Renaissance artists referred to homosexuality in coded form. The poet Countee Cullen, who, three months after his marriage to W.E.B. Du Bois's daughter Yolande, escaped to Paris with his best man and friend, Harold Jackman, penned numerous poems with homoerotic undertones, such as "The Shroud of Color," "For a Poet," "The Black Christ," "Tableau," and "Every Lover." Although African American literary critics in the past silenced questions about Langston Hughes's sexuality because of his importance as a father of a "black aesthetic," Hughes also wrote layered poems in which the overt subject of race decoys readers away from the homoerotic subtext, such as in "Young Sailor" and "I Loved My Friend." In his 1951 poem, "Café 3 A.M.," Hughes openly denounces the persecution of lesbians and gays, and in his 1963 collection *Something in Common and Other Stories*, he included a story with gay characters, "Blessed Assurance."

Written after the peak of the Harlem Renaissance, Wallace Thurman's 1932 roman a clef novel, *Infants of the Spring*, offers a fictionalized account of the Harlem Renaissance bohemian crowd who were "in the life," particularly Richard Bruce Nugent, who served as the model for the sexually open artist Paul. In the implied attraction between the main character, Raymond, and the white villager, Stephen, the "bisexual" Thurman discloses his desire to dispense with categories that limit sexual expression. Similarly, Claude McKay's 1928 *Home to Harlem* includes an implied homoerotic subtext in the intimate friendship between the main character, Jake, and the Jamaican-born (like McKay) poet intellectual, Ray, amid what is an otherwise stereotypical depiction of bull dykes and pansies in Harlem. In his later autobiography, *A Long Way from Home* (1937), however, McKay would be much more open about his friendship and cohabitation with a white gay hustler Michael when he lived in Harlem.

The 1940s and 1950s post–World War II period of "integrationist" optimism in African American literature was also a time of strict gender and sexual conformity. Cold war ideologies that linked the threat of communism to homosexuality and the assimilationist tendencies of a rising black middle class pressured many gay writers to adopt once again the mask of invisibility. Bayard Rustin, a key civil rights activist, who was arrested in 1952 on moral charges during a police witch hunt, had to distance himself from **Martin Luther King Jr.**'s Southern Christian Leadership Conference.

Yet, representations of homosexuality did not disappear from African American writing. Indeed, they intensified, appearing in the works of Chester Himes, Willard Motley, William Demby, William Yarby, Owen Dodson, as well as **Richard Wright** and **Ralph Ellison**. Although only the playwright Owen Dodson's semiautobiographical novel *Boy at the Window* (1951) alludes to homosexuality in a positive light, other novels such as Himes's prison potboiler, *Cast the First Stone* (1952), and Demby's novel of small town alienation, *Beetlecreek* (1950), have characters who struggle with internalized homophobia and self-hatred, and thus testify to the lived experience of many African Americans.

During the 1950s also appeared the groundbreaking work of **James Baldwin**, the most defining figure in gay African American literature whose legacy has fostered the writing of so many later voices. While living as an expatriate in Paris, Baldwin wrote the first African American public defense of homosexuality, "The Preservation of Innocence" (1949), for *Zero*, a Moroccan journal. In his first coming-of-age novel, *Go Tell It on the Mountain* (1953), Baldwin's protagonist wrestles with an emerging homosexual awareness, but in his 1956 *Giovanni's Room*, Baldwin wrote openly about the struggle for gay self-acceptance, although choosing white characters as his protagonists. To avoid a critical backlash, Baldwin initially had to deny that *Giovanni's Room* was a homosexual novel, and that he himself was gay. In his novels dating from the 1960s and 1970s, however, Baldwin focused with increasing openness on gay subject matter, depicting the troubled relationship between the bisexual black musician Rufus and the white writer Vivaldo in *Another Country*. His subsequent novels *Tell Me How Long the Train's Been Gone* (1968) and *Just above My Head* (1979) continued to set the groundwork for a subsequent generation of gay writers.

During the civil rights era the struggle to reclaim black manhood often became equated with imitating a heterosexist patriarchal ideal. Gay men within the Black Arts Movement of the 1960s and 1970s often became figures of ridicule who lacked the strength and virility to overthrow an oppressive, white, racist society. Black writers and activists such as Amiri Baraka pointed to homosexuals as figures of an emasculation by white men and, therefore, what "authentic" black men were not. Yet the recurrence of gay "degenerates" in plays such as *The Toilet* (1964) testify to a more conflicted relation to homosexuality, and Baraka's autobiographically based *The System of Dante's Hell* (1965) tells the story of a self-hating black gay man in Chicago who is finally "converted" to heterosexuality by a prostitute named Peaches. Not all African Americans associated with the more radical wings of the Black Power Movement, however, shared this homophobia. Huey Newton, the founder of the Black Panthers, sought to build coalitions with gay activists and to implement a more inclusive understanding of the black community.

Whereas the post-Stonewall era of the 1970s saw the growth of white gay fiction published by large commercial establishments, gay African American writing did not reach a similar level of intensity until the growth of black gay grassroots organizations and gay publishing houses and journals. The New York-based writing collective Other Countries (founded in 1986) put out two anthologies, *Other Countries Journal: Black Gay Voices* (1988) and the Lambda award-winning *Sojourner: Black Gay Voices in the Age of AIDS* (1993). Michael Smith, the founder of Black and White Men Together (BWMT), edited the volume *Black Men/White Men: A Gay Anthology* (1983), though it has subsequently been criticized for its white perspective. Two anthologies, however, have been especially important in giving African American gay males a voice: Joseph Beam's *In the Life: A Black Gay*

Anthology (1986), which announced that "black men loving black men is the revolutionary act of the eighties" and Essex Hemphill's *Brother to Brother: New Writings by Black Gay Men* (1991), which similarly connected art to politics and called for a reconstitution of family, community, and nation that includes black voices. The poet Assotto Saint also founded his own Galiens Press to release, in addition to his work, two seminal anthologies of African American gay poetry, *The Road before Us* (1991) and *Here to Dare* (1992).

For this new generation of gay African American writers, the goal of representing themselves as self-identified gay men required developing their own idiom and aesthetic tradition. Many of the poems, essays, and short stories in *Brother to Brother* were self-avowedly experimental in form and drew on African diasporic oral traditions and black gay subcultural practices, such as SNAP!—the coded act of finger popping to convey a variety of messages. In speaking out about a distinctive black gay selfhood that was not the same as the dominant media image of gays as middle-class whites, these writers also introduced a number of themes that would recur in the fiction of other writers in the 1990s and beyond. Some of these would include, finding a home within the African American community, the complications of a loving interracial relationship, black men's internalization of the values of a white homosexual community, the homophobia of the black church, surviving the tragedy of AIDS, the double lives of many black men concealing their sexuality, the relation between sexuality and patriarchal norms of masculinity, and the fight against heterosexist standards that structure social values.

Although E. Lynn Harris's novels, starting with *Invisible Life* (1991), have been among the most commercially successful works of fictions by an African American gay author, since the 1980s, there has been a wide array of fictional production. A number of novelists have dealt with the possibilities or problems of interracial love. Larry Duplechan's *Eight Days a Week* (1985) and *Blackbird* (1987) deal with the relationship between Johnny Ray and his white gay lover Keith, although critics have been divided on whether the black man's attraction to the white lover is a sign of his colonized mind or a reversal of the racial objectification within colonialism. In addition, Canaan Parker's *The Color of Trees* (1992), which is set on an elite prep school campus, deals with a love that transcends color and class differences, and Melvin Dixon's *Vanishing Room* (1991) focuses on the racism of the white male lover. In contrast, another group of writers has sought to reflect a more black-centered consciousness in which characters live and work amidst a largely black population. James Earl Hardy's B-Boy Blues Series has characters who embrace Afrocentricity as part of black gay self-acceptance. Other novelists have dealt specifically with the homophobia in black families, including Steve Corbin's *Fragments that Remain* (1993) and award-winning author Brian Keith Jackson's second novel, *Walking through Mirrors* (1998), which deals with a gay New Yorker's return home to Louisiana for his father's funeral.

The last two decades have also seen a number of African American gay fiction writers becoming a part of the literary canon. In 1989, Randall Kenan published *A Visitation of Spirits*, an autobiographical-based book of magic realism that recalls James Baldwin's *Go Tell It on the Mountain* in dealing with a young man's troubled relation with a homophobic black church. Many of the short stories in his National Book Critics Award–nominated *Let the Dead Bury the Dead*, such as the often anthologized "The Foundations of the Earth," deal with key themes such as the homophobia in the African American community as well as the losses from AIDS. One of the earliest writers to deal with the problem of AIDS was the innovative science fiction writer Samuel Delany in *Flight from Neveryon* (1985). Even in his earliest works, such as *The Jewels of Aptor* (1962), the short story "Aye, and Gomorrah . . ." (1967), and *The Einstein Intersection* (1967), Delany explored through his outcast characters sexual and gender difference. In his novels *Dhalgren* (1975) and *Tales of Neveryon* (1979), homoeroticism had become directly expressed in his fiction. The writings of Gary Fisher, a graduate student who died of AIDS in the mid-1990s, have been edited by Don Belton, the author of another black gay classic, *Almost Midnight* (1986), into a moving collection called *Gary in Your Pocket: Stories and Notebooks of Gary Fisher* (1996), which has engendered increasing scholarly conversation.

Marlon Riggs's document *Tongues Untied* (1989) and his essay "Black Macho Revisited: Reflections of a SNAP! Queen" have become classics in gender and African American studies courses, and inspired the formation of Pomo Afro Homos (postmodern African American homosexuals), a performance art group that produced *Fierce Love: Stories from Black Gay Life* (1991) and that was the first gay group to be funded (though not without controversy) by the National Endowment of the Arts. In his satirical play, *The Colored Museum*, playwright and director, George C. Wolfe included among his 11 exhibits (or scenes) "The Gospel according to Miss Roj," a spunky black SNAP! queen who talks back to the indifference and oppression of the African American and gay communities.

In recent years there have been an increasing diversity of gay African American literature, demonstrating that there is no single gay African American experience. The 1990s saw the release of a numerous powerful memoirs, such as Gordon Heath's *Deep Are the Roots: Memoirs of a Black Expatriate* (1992), Bill T. Jones's *Last Night on Earth* (1995), Alvin Ailey's *Revelations* (1995), and the drag entertainer RuPaul's *Lettin' It All Hang Out* (1995), and transgendered Lady Chablis's *Hiding My Candy* (1996). Several anthologies have also appeared in the late 1990s and early 2000s giving voice to recognized and little-known writers from the past and the present, such as *Go the Way Your Blood Beats: An Anthology of Lesbian and Gay Fiction by African American Writers* (1996), *Shade: An Anthology of Fiction by Gay Men of African Descent* (1996), and one of the most thorough and scholarly representations of 20th-century African American gay literature, *Black Like Us: A Century of Lesbian, Gay and Bisexual African American Fiction*, edited by Devon Carbado, Dwight McBride, and Donald Weise (2002). Finally the scope of African American literature is broadening to include more transnational voices, such as Jamaican American Thomas Glave who explores the situation of gays and lesbians in Jamaica. *I Rise: the Transformation of Toni Newman*, published in 2011, is the first memoir by an African American member of the transgender community. Don Lemon's *Transparent*, also published in 2011, is a moving memoir of the highly visible television journalist who is gay.

Further Reading

Carbado, Devon, Dwight McBride, and Donald Weise. *Black Like Us: A Century of Lesbian, Gay, and Bisexual African American Fiction*. San Francisco: Cleis Press, 2002.

Chauncey, George. *Gay New York: Gender, Urban Culture and the Marketing of the Gay Male World 1890–1940*. New York: Basic Books, 1994.

Dickel, Simon. *Black/Gay*. East Lansing: Michigan State University Press, 2012.

Nelson, Emmanuel S., ed. *Critical Essays: Gay and Lesbian Writers of Color*. New York: Haworth Press, 1994.

Nero, Charles. "Toward a Black Gay Aesthetic: Signifying in Contemporary Gay Literature." In *Brother to Brother: New Writings by Black Gay Men*, 229–50. Boston: Alyson Publications, 1991.

Reid-Pharr, Robert. *Black Gay Man: Essays*. New York: New York University Press, 2001.

Schwarz, A. B. Christa. *Gay Voices of the Harlem Renaissance*. Bloomington: Indiana University Press, 2003.

Stephen Knadler

AFRICAN AMERICAN LESBIAN LITERATURE

With the **Harlem Renaissance** (1920s), African American literature came into its own, connected to a politics and an aesthetics that were uniquely Negro and deeply American and that looked to stake out not only the humanity and freedom of African Americans but also an identity replete with intellectual and artistic traditions. The literature of the Harlem Renaissance put into fictional form W.E.B. Du Bois's theories about the double consciousness of African Americans. It also celebrated African heritage and its contribution to contemporary art forms such as **jazz**. Famous for its sexual permissiveness, the Harlem Renaissance fostered many authors who explored same-sex desire. These were mostly male authors such as Langston Hughes and Countee Cullen who considered only desire between men. However, one of the most famous literary suggestions of African American lesbianism dates from the Harlem Renaissance: **Nella Larsen**'s *Passing* (1929).

As its title indicates, *Passing* belongs to a common subgenre of African American literature popular in the Harlem Renaissance: the passing novel that tells the tale of light-skinned African Americans who pass for white. Larsen's novella indeed focuses on two light-skinned African American women, Irene who does not pass for white and Clare who does. A possible relationship between Irene and Clare haunts the text. Critics note that the very unclear and unknown quality of desire between women in the novel points to how in the first half of the 20th century African Americans may have passed not only racially but also sexually, asking us not to identify lesbian characters but to think about the many desires and identities that intersect and that mask one another in the first centuries of African American literature and culture.

As the Harlem Renaissance gave way to the protest era with the **Civil Rights Movement**, the Black Arts Movement, and the Black Power Movement, the great focus of the African American community turned to the urgent need to secure equal rights. The fight against **racism**, particularly institutional racism, became the single most important issue in African American politics, culture, and artistic production. The reliance of the Civil Rights Movement on Christian ministers and of the Black Power Movement on Muslim clerics established for both profoundly heterosexist value systems. A fear of taking attention away from the movement's antiracist message blocked serious consideration of the ways that race, gender, sexuality, and class implicate one another, of the ways in which the Civil Rights Movement might not only support but also be supported by women's rights and lesbian rights. Furthermore, throughout African American history the mother stands as the holder of tradition, the connection to Mother Africa, so women who might be perceived as untraditional threaten the entire community. African American lesbian writers found no place to express their sexuality that was not considered marginal or even antithetical to the Civil Rights Movement and the great literature that surrounded it. At the same time, the women's and homosexual movements that emerged in the 1960s prioritized gender and sexuality, respectively, over **race**, ignoring the ways that by virtue of their different races some women experience different oppressions, and refusing to acknowledge the racism within their own ranks. Thus African American lesbian authors often kept their lesbianism hidden in their lives and in their works well into the 1970s.

A certain reticence to identify African American authors or characters as lesbian may also, however, indicate not homophobia or fear of coming out, but rather an attempt to express desire between women outside the category "lesbian" that can be taken to be marked white by its allusion to European history (the Greek island of Lesbos) and by its connection to a predominantly white movement. Perhaps the most important example of this, after Larsen's *Passing*, can be found in **Alice Walker**'s epistolary novel, ***The Color Purple*** (1982). Walker refers to herself as a womanist, a term that for her expresses a primary commitment to women that may take any form, from political activism to erotic relationships, but that also always attends to race. Set in rural Georgia in the early 20th century, *The Color Purple* recounts the troubled lives of sharecropping families through a series of letters written by Celie and her sister Nettie. Although Celie marries, leaves, and then reconnects with Mr.___, she finds herself through a relationship with Shug, a blues singer with whom both she and her husband are in love. To both Celie and Shug, the relationship that they share is of primary importance in their erotic and emotional lives, but to neither is it exclusive nor does it stop both women from having subsequent relationships with men. The relationship between Shug and Celie provides an essential alternative to the sexual violence and abuse that Celie suffers with men, but Celie learns not to turn away from men but to embrace them differently. Celie's relationship with Shug brings her to consciousness about her power as an African American woman and allows her to formulate an identity that cannot be organized by any single marker.

Prior to *The Color Purple*, however, a few novels by African American women had begun to claim lesbianism for themselves. The first novel written by an African American woman with a self-identified lesbian protagonist is Ann Allen Shockley's *Loving Her* (1974), though Shockley did not label her own sexual identity. Over a decade later, Shockley's second novel, *Say Jesus and Come to Me* (1985), depicts African American women negotiating their lesbianism and their Christianity. Rosa Guy's *Ruby* (1976) offers another early portrayal an African American protagonist whose primary love relationship was with another girl, but *Ruby* ends with an apparent universal turn to heterosexual adulthood.

Around the same time, African American lesbian poetry provided a space for much more radical expressions of lesbianism. Pat Parker, in *Child of Myself* (1971), *Pit Stop* (1974), *Womanslaughter* (1978), and *Jonestown and Other Madness* (1985), playfully and explicitly describes lesbian lovemaking, coming out of the closet, and black lesbian feminist politics. Cheryl Clarke has devoted herself to assuring that Parker's work continues to be remembered while also publishing her own poetry. In collections including *Living as a Lesbian* (1986) and *Experimental Loves* (1996), Clarke writes with openness, humor, sensuality, and profanity about lesbianism in a violent, underprivileged, urban environment that is nonetheless marked by hope as well as by struggle.

The most well-known African American lesbian writer, **Audre Lorde**, in her "autobiomythography" *Zami: A New Spelling of My Name* (1982), comes up with a novel way to negotiate the apparent disjoints between African American and lesbian identification. By 1982 Lorde was already an accomplished poet and essayist who in *The First Cities* (1968), *Cables to Rage* (1970), *From a Land Where Other People Live* (1973), *The New York Head Shop and Museum* (1974), *Coal* (1976), and *The Black Unicorn* (1978) expressed herself as an African American lesbian. In *Zami*, she traces how she came to that identity and what it means to her. *Zami* describes Lorde's coming of age in a Granadian immigrant family in New York in the 1950s. Lorde/Zami initially connects to her Caribbean heritage rather than to any African American community or identity. She finds in this community a strong assertion of women's sexuality and power, although not any women lovers. The relative invisibility of African American lesbians in New York in the 1950s also contributes to Lorde/Zami's discovering her sexuality with white women and in the burgeoning lesbian community. After an initial exuberance at the acceptance and exploration of her sexuality, however, Lode/Zami finds the racism of white lesbians as stifling as the homophobia of the African American community. She continues to search for a community and an identity where she can be black and lesbian without needing to prioritize either. This she finally finds with another black lesbian, Afrekete, and also with the change of her name to Zami. "Zami" is a term used in parts of Grenada to refer to lesbians and thus asserts the existence of a historical Afro-Caribbean lesbian community. Furthermore, Lorde argues that the very tradition of black mothering is one of "black dykes," so that even married mothers who never have sexual relationships with other women can be part of a community and a history of Afro-Caribbean and African American lesbians. But as a young African American lesbian in New York in the 1950s, Lorde remains a lonely trailblazer, establishing rather than joining a community. By the time that *Zami* reached the presses, however, and certainly aided by the novel's tremendous critical and popular success, an African American lesbian community did exist. And thanks to Lorde, Walker, Parker, and others a variety of identity positions seem increasingly available to African American lesbian writers.

Also in the 1980s, another lesbian straddling Caribbean and African American communities, **Michelle Cliff**, began to publish semiautobiographical novels and essay and poetry collections. In *Claiming an Identity They Taught Me to Despise* (1980), *Abeng* (1984), *The Land of Look Behind* (1985), *No Telephone to Heaven* (1987), *Bodies of Water* (1990), *Free Enterprise* (1993), and *The Store of a Million Items* (1998), Cliff describes the experiences of an Afro-Caribbean girl discovering her cultural and sexual identities between New York and Jamaica. Cliff's work joins a growing body of not only novels and poetry but also critical and anthological work by African American lesbians. These women brought the issues of African American lesbian literature and its relative absence into the critical debates surrounding feminism and lesbianism and also African American studies. Literary and cultural critics such as Barbara Smith, Ann Allen Shockley, Cheryl Clarke, and Jewelle Gomez wrote about how although women, lesbians, and African Americans made great steps forward in the arenas of civil rights and artistic recognition between the 1950s and the 1980s, African American lesbians still often found themselves in the untenable position of needing to proclaim themselves wither lesbian or African American, as if the two could be separated.

In the 1990s African American lesbian writing again turned away from predominantly lesbian-themed novels but now rather than avoiding explicit lesbianism or the term "lesbian," authors such as Helen Elaine Lee, April Sinclair, E. Lynn Harris, and Sapphire integrate lesbian characters and themes into their treatment of the multiple questions of race, class, gender, place, sexuality, religion, motherhood, and family on which African American literature turns. At the same time, a growing body of literature also focuses on lesbian characters involved not only in staking out a place for themselves to exist but also in negotiating the many parts of their lives as African American lesbians. Jewelle Gomez in *The Gilda Stories* (1991) and *Don't Explain* (1998) plays with history and literary genre in a series of romance–science fiction–historical–vampire stories that consider how to articulate African American lesbianism even as they do so. The first novel by Odessa Rose, *Water in a Broken Glass* (2000), traces a young African American sculptor's coming out in the context of her homophobic family but also in an out and proud African American lesbian and gay community. Laurinda D. Brown's first novel, *Fire and Brimstone* (2001), depicts a relationship between a single mother and a minister as the two explore what it means to be an African American family and to have religion in the South. Fiona Zedde has established herself as the author of multiple novels, such as *Bliss* (2005), *Every Dark Desire* (2007), *Dangerous Pleasures* (2011) and *Desire at Dawn* (2014), which may be termed lesbian pulp fiction. Lesbianism has become not the unspoken and unspeakable shadow but rather one of the many spoken pieces of African American literature.

Further Reading

Carbado, Devon, Dwight McBride, and Donald Weisse, eds. *Black Like Us: A Century of Lesbian, Gay, and Bisexual African American Fiction.* San Francisco: Cleis Press, 2002.

McKinley, Catherine, and Joyce DeLaney, eds. *Afrekete: An Anthology of Black Lesbian Writing*. New York: Anchor Books, 1995.

Nelson, Emmanuel S., ed. *Critical Essays: Gay and Lesbian Writers of Color*. New York: Haworth Press, 1993.

Smith, Barbara, ed. *Home Girls: A Black Feminist Anthology*. New York: Kitchen Table Women of Color Press, 1983.

Smith, Barbara. *The Truth That Never Hurts: Writings on Race, Gender, and Freedom*. New Brunswick, NJ: Rutgers University Press, 1998.

Keja Lys Valens

AFRICAN AMERICAN NOVEL

African American novels, here defined as novels written by African Americans, are often distinct from—while remaining a significant part of—the broader tradition of American novels. Given the history of slavery, Jim Crow segregation, the **Civil Rights Movement**, and persistent systemic racial inequity in the United States, African American writers have had particularly fertile ground for crafting novels of social and political critique. With 18th-century philosophers such as Immanuel Kant, David Hume, and Thomas Jefferson arguing that people of African descent did not have the intellectual capacity to create art or literature, the stakes for producing literature were high for the first African American novelists writing in the 19th century. At a basic level, that early African American literature by its very existence claimed a place for African Americans in the human family. Many African American writers further chose, and continue to choose, racial oppression or racial **identity** as their subject matter and use their novels not only to expose the cruelties and inconsistencies of the U.S. racial system, but also to present African American characters who are at the very least the social, intellectual, economic, or moral equals of their fictional white counterparts. Twentieth-century African American novels often engage intraracial (rather than in*ter*racial) identity, black pride and black power, and a transcontinental connection with people of the African diaspora. Not all African American novels, however, center on **race**. Indeed, African American novels range over a wide spectrum of genres, from science fiction to satire to romance, and engage a plethora of topics restricted only by the limits of the human imagination. Arguably, then, *the* African American novel does not exist, for African American novels are as varied as the authors themselves.

Rising to prominence between the late 18th century and the middle of the 19th century, **African American slave narrative**s such as those by Olaudah Equiano, **Frederick Douglass**, William and Ellen Craft, and **Harriet Jacobs** were the first extended narrative publications written by African Americans to find a wide audience in the United States. These slave narratives played a fundamental role in the abolitionist movement of the mid-19th century by providing firsthand accounts of the experience of the oppressed under the rule of slavery and by evidencing the literary, aesthetic, and intellectual equality of African Americans. The earliest African American novels, published in England because their authors could not find a publisher within the United States, were influenced in both form and content by these popular slave narratives, as well as by sentimental fiction, the genre that produced the first best sellers in the United States. Sentimental fiction usually follows a youthful female protagonist through various adventures to a resolution in marriage. For example, the earliest published African American novel, William Wells Brown's *Clotel; or, the President's Daughter* (1853), is the story of three generations of the mulatto descendants of Thomas Jefferson and his slave, (presumably) Sally Hemings. The novel unfolds through the lives of the women as they move from slavery to freedom and ultimately to marriage. However, throughout the novel, Brown (himself an escaped ex-slave) also incorporates real-life stories of the brutality of slavery, advertisements for runaway slaves, and newspaper accounts of slave escapes and captures, digressions from fiction that link his novel closely to the slave narrative.

Brown's novel is also an early use of the trope of the "tragic mulatto/a," one that figures prominently in African American novels up through the **Harlem Renaissance**. The tragic mulatto/a is a light-skinned African American who, because of his or her "mixed" racial heritage, often passes for white and/or is romantically involved with a white person. He or she usually suffers a lamentable fate due to the vagaries of the U.S. race system and his or her individual struggle with racial, familial, and national identity. Frank J. Webb's *The Garies and Their Friends* (1857), another of the earliest African American novels, offers readers both a male and female tragic mulatto. The Garies move to Philadelphia to escape the racism of the South; however, they find themselves under attack because of their interracial marriage. Marie, the light-skinned female protagonist, dies during childbirth while hiding from an angry white mob that has already murdered her husband. In the novel's second half, the couple's orphaned son passes for white, and as an adult becomes involved with a white woman. White **racism** and greed prove his demise: His racial identity is exposed and he dies, presumably from a broken heart after being rejected by his white fiancée. Both mother and son ultimately fall to racism for challenging the color line that separates "black" from "white."

Because the story is set largely in the North, *The Garies* also has a point in common with another early African American novel, **Harriet E. Wilson**'s *Our Nig; or, Sketches from the Life of a Free Black* (1859). *Our Nig* is the semiautobiographical story of a mixed race little girl abandoned by her white mother in the North. Although Frado is not a slave, the narrative follows a trajectory quite similar to African American slave narratives such as Harriet Jacobs's *Incidents in the Life of a Slave Girl* (1861): Little Frado is treated just as harshly as Southern slaves, and she exits the novel alone and trying to support her child with the proceeds of her novel. Although in many points similar to Jacobs's slave narrative, like *The Garies, Our Nig* primarily exposes white Northern racism and belies the illusion of the North as an emancipatory and benevolent refuge for escaped slaves. These early novels illustrated that African Americans were savvy and courageous enough to critique even the region of the United States touted as a haven because not overtly ruled by the law of slavery.

This tendency toward exposing both racism and prejudice through characters who suffer under their influence survives in many African American novels today. Even in the 1850s, however, not all writers let their protagonists pay the price for the destructive nature of racism. Other writers, such as Martin R. Delany, considered the father of American black nationalism, provided a contrasting model of resistance within the fledging African American novel tradition. In his serialized novel *Blake, or the Huts of America* (1859), Delany fictionalized the leaders of slave revolts embodied by men such as Gabriel Prosser, Denmark Vesey, and Nat Turner, men who led or planned slave revolts in 1800, 1822, and 1831, respectively. The novel thus provides one of the earliest militant black characters willing to risk his life to liberate himself and his people by throwing off the shackles of slavery.

With the dissolution of the Confederacy and the beginning of Reconstruction, the focus of many African American novels shifted. Gone was the abolitionist interest in slave narratives and novelistic representations of slave life. Although African American authors continued to use slavery and the Old South as a backdrop for their fiction, many turned their thoughts forward toward the goal of racial uplift. Their texts were written not only to illustrate the ills of slavery, but as importantly, to emphasize the success of those who had once been slaves. The goal of many African American novels, then, was not just to confirm the basic possession of humanity for nonwhites while denouncing slavery and racism, but to illustrate the refined sensibilities, advanced education, and irreproachable morals of those labeled second-class citizens. African American novelists paid significant attention to representing "the best" in African American life in order to justify their claims for equal rights, equal representation, and equal protection under the law. Although *de jure* slavery was dead, the stakes in these decades continued to be high, as the country was negotiating the relationships between African Americans and whites in a post-bellum, industrializing world.

Between 1883 and 1896, the courts were crystallizing custom into law by establishing the legal rights of Jim Crow segregation. African Americans were struggling for equal opportunities in education and political representation, in addition to legal protection against lynch mobs. This period between the Civil War and the turn of the 20th century saw the publication of many novels written by African American women activists. Believing that African American women would lead the race forward into racial equality, these novelists, including writers such as Frances E. W. Harper, Pauline E. Hopkins, Amelia E. Johnson, and Emma Dunham Kelley, wrote sentimental fiction that presented moral, educated African American families, and, specifically, African American heroines. Johnson and Kelley wrote fiction with a decidedly religious theme for a Sunday school audience: Their novels often followed their heroines, who were not always overtly marked as African American, through their quests for spiritual salvation, a goal usually attainted by novel's end. In comparison, Hopkins and Harper, two of the most well-known African American women of the era and highly public figures in the world of magazine journalism, gave readers heroines who often faced moral sexual dilemmas stemming from the lingering complexities of slavery and the

U.S. race system. Their heroines, ranging from a reincarnated African goddess to a woman who resists the sexual assaults of a string of slave owners, triumph with their sexual virtue intact.

This impulse to exonerate African American women from the charge of lasciviousness arose from the racist belief that African American women were biologically incapable of being sexually virtuous, an idea with roots in the ideology of slavery. In response, African American women novelists offered black and white readers alike representations of moral, virtuous black women worthy of membership in the "Cult of True Womanhood" that held sway at the time, and the marriage of these virtuous women at novels' end was the ultimate evidence of their sexual morality. These female protagonists also further acquitted themselves and set a positive example by working toward racial uplift. For instance, in Harper's *Iola Leroy, or Shadows Uplifted* (1893), the light-skinned Iola rejects the option of passing as white and instead marries a (light-skinned) black man. The two close the novel in wedded bliss teaching and preaching to underprivileged African American children in the South. Similarly, in Hopkins's *Contending Forces* (1900), Sappho, who has been raped and impregnated by her white uncle, ultimately marries the (light-skinned) African American hero of the text; the two set off to Europe to open a university for African Americans. Although the novels of this era (opposed to earlier novels such as *Blake* or *The Garies and Their Friends*) offered virtuous, moral, educated, upwardly mobile African Americans, they have also been criticized for presenting very few positive dark-skinned characters. Many suggest in response that these light-skinned characters, no longer tragic mulattas, serve to remind white readers of the artificiality of the color line and, furthermore, allow whites to sympathize with the characters, an important consideration as a significant portion of the intended audience was white.

African American men writers, too, were open to these charges. Charles Chesnutt, perhaps the most famous African American writer of these decades, often used light-skinned protagonists in his short stories and novels. His novel *The House Behind the Cedars* (1900) shares themes from earlier works: the tragic mulatta, passing, racial uplift, and the evils of the slave system. Rena Walden, the daughter of a white ex-slave owner and a mulatta, passes for white until she is forsaken by her white fiancé when her racial heritage is discovered. Her brother, John, however, succeeds in passing as white and exits the novel unscathed by his racial choice. Another of Chesnutt's novels, *The Marrow of Tradition* (1901), also centers on light-skinned African Americans, but also continues the narrative representation of strong, rebellious African American men who resist racism through violence, here in the Wilmington, North Carolina, race riot of 1898. Like Delany's before him, Chesnutt's novel critiques white hegemonies that continued to oppress African Americans while questioning the method of racial classification in the United States. Although Chesnutt continued to write well into the 1920s, during his lifetime he published no novels after 1905. His style, reminiscent of the local color fiction of the 1880s and 1890s, and his settings isolated him from the new fiction that blossomed in the **Harlem Renaissance**. In short, Chesnutt's work did not represent the politically charged voice of the "New Negro."

The Harlem Renaissance, an explosive period of literary, artistic, and philosophical production that reached its peak in the 1920s, witnessed a new racial consciousness. Many of the themes and tropes in African American novels, however, remained the same. For instance, passing continued as one of the most prevalent tropes in African American novels: Novelists such as Jessie Redmon Fauset, James Weldon Johnson, **Nella Larsen**, and George Schuyler all used the trope. Whereas many early passing narratives centered on protagonists who did not know they were passing (they were raised as white), passing novels of the Harlem Renaissance more often provide readers with characters who pass intentionally in order to challenge Jim Crow segregation. Female passers in these novels often pass to marry white men and hence achieve better socioeconomic positions; others pass for access to better jobs. No matter what impetus spurs these characters to adopt a white identity, passing novels of this period usually condemn passing as an act of self- and racial betrayal. The female characters are often 20th-century versions of the tragic mulatta. Male passers, as well, suffer from their choice to pass. James Weldon Johnson's unnamed male narrator in *Autobiography of an Ex-Colored Man* (1912) feels he has sacrificed his "birthright" for materialistic gains garnered from passing as white. Although he fares better than many of his female counterparts, he struggles with guilt and psychological displacement. In short, these novels expressed the new racial consciousness of the Harlem Renaissance by advocating both a pride in and responsibility for claiming one's blackness no matter what the shade of skin. They thus evince the continued philosophy of racial uplift; indeed, many of these passers would be considered a part of W.E.B. Du Bois's "talented tenth," the educated, culturally and economically successful African Americans who had a responsibility to raise up their racial family. They can only do that by proclaiming their blackness.

Not all authors, however, advocated this racial responsibility or resolved the fates of their passers tragically. Wallace Thurman's *Infants of Spring* (1932) satirizes many of the well-known figures of the Harlem Renaissance, and George Schuyler, in *Black No More* (1931), offers readers a satiric spin on passing that ultimately runs its white supremacist characters into a lynch mob who believes them to be black. By novel's end, it is difficult, if not impossible, to accurately identify any character's "true" racial identity in a world where dark skin has gained the cultural currency previously reserved for whites. Additionally, African American authors of the period grappled with a plethora of other narrative themes, structures, and styles. Claude McKay's *Home to Harlem* (1928) delved into the controversy of primitivism that circulated through the period, and **Zora Neale Hurston** combined her university training in anthropology with her narrative genius as a folklorist and novelist to produce novels such as *Jonah's Gourd Vine* (1934) and ***Their Eyes Were Watching God*** (1937). These novels represented a rural African American life that stood in stark opposition to McKay's urban novel. Diverging from the traditional novel structure, Jean Toomer wrote *Cane* (1923), a combination of poems, vignettes, and musings, that engaged all of modernism's fragmentation and play with language while continuing to focus on themes of racial identity, lynching, and the differences between life in Northern urban centers and Southern rural towns.

The heyday of the Harlem Renaissance and the **Jazz** Age faded with the onset of the Great Depression, and, while African American writers such as Hurston and Langston Hughes continued to write through the 1930s or beyond, a new group of African American novelists grew to maturity. Although these decades produced black women writers such as Ann Petry, who carried forward traditions from the black women writers of the Harlem Renaissance, the period is perhaps better known for its male writers. Indeed, even Petry's *The Street* (1946) is often contextualized in relation to **Richard Wright**'s *Native Son* (1940). Wright, one of the most prominent African American writers of the 1940s and 1950s, is kept company by **Ralph Waldo Ellison** and **James Baldwin**, all at one time expatriates in Paris, although not always friends. Like their predecessors a hundred years earlier, their novels continue to critique racism and racial violence in the United States; however, their social protest evinces a racial consciousness changed radically by the Depression, World War II, and socialism. The novels, variously fusions of urban realism, naturalism, and modernism, offer protagonists who struggle psychologically to find their place in a white-dominated society that sees them, *if* it sees them, as "boys," with only few rights that whites need respect. *Native Son* tells the story of Bigger Thomas, a young black man who tries to improve his condition by working within the Jim Crow system. After Bigger accidentally kills his rich, white employer's daughter, his fate is sealed as he flees from the white mob intent on lynching him. Ellison's masterpiece the **Invisible Man** (1951) offers the story of an unnamed narrator who negotiates the social and psychological invisibility of the black man in the United States. Fleeing the 1940s Harlem riots, the narrator ultimately goes underground, living beneath the city in a room electrified with 1,369 light bulbs powered by stolen electricity. Baldwin's *Go Tell It on the Mountain* (1952) fuses an analysis of the psychological impact of the Great Migration northward and the urban North/rural South split with an investigation of the role religion has played in the African American consciousness. These protagonists all search for identity and independence in a racist world. Chester Himes, another expatriate and best known for his detective fiction, wrote the widely acclaimed novel *If He Hollers Let Him Go* (1945), which highlights another psychological reaction to the pervasive racism of World War II America: The novel's protagonist lives in constant fear of doing or saying the wrong thing in a racist world. His fears are ultimately justified when he is falsely accused of having raped a white woman.

The racial unrest and social protest of the 1940s and 1950s matured in the **Civil Rights Movement** of the following decades. Although African Americans were certainly writing novels during the 1960s, the decade witnessed a stronger wave of black autobiography, essays, and poetry that focused directly on issues of black power, racism, equality, and the failings of democracy. The 1970s, in comparison, birthed novels that not only critiqued the inequity of the American social structure and continued to expose the high psychological and physical costs of racism, but that also reclaimed and rewrote African American history in powerful ways. Margaret Walker's *Jubilee* (1966), an intergenerational account of African American women, ushered in other narrative explorations of history, including **Ernest J. Gaines**'s *The Autobiography of Miss Jane Pittman* (1971), Gayl Jones's *Corregidora*

(1975), and **Alex Haley**'s *Roots* (1976). These texts harken back to the slave narratives of the mid-19th century as they situate contemporary social conditions as developing from America's distinct racial history. This narrative reclamation and exploration of history has continued through the last two decades of the 20th century and includes novels such as Sherley Anne Williams's *Dessa Rose* (1986), a tale of African Americans who went West to escape slavery and Southern persecution; **Toni Morrison**'s *Beloved* (1988), the fictionalized account of the escaped slave Margaret Garner who killed her child; Lalita Tademy's *Cane River* (2001), an intergenerational account of one family's women; and Alice Randall's *The Wind Done Gone* (2001), a parody of Margaret Mitchell's best seller *Gone With the Wind* (1936). Evincing the U.S. public's interest in its racial past, many of these fictionalized histories have been made into major motion pictures and television series. The novelists of these decades, however, were not all concerned with exploring or reframing the past. Many were interested in representing a present replete with new forms of racism, violence, and identity crises. Thus rose "gangsta" literature and authors such as Iceberg Slim and Donald Goines, whose novels focus on the lives of young, black, inner-city youths raised in a world of violence. Goines, who wrote his first two novels in jail, was shot to death in 1974.

The last two decades of the 20th century—the post–Civil Rights era—have witnessed another burgeoning of African American novelists. A substantial black readership and expanded black middle class have allowed African American novelists to broaden their scope. In addition to Nobel and Pulitzer Prize winner Toni Morrison, writers such as **Toni Cade Bambara**, David Bradley, **Paule Marshall**, **Gloria Naylor**, **Alice Walker**, and John Edgar Wideman write what might be classified as "literary" fiction that explores African American identity, the African diaspora, or the complex relationship between race and gender. These novels often experiment with temporal linearity, narrative voice, and poetic language. In another vein, and following in the tradition of George Schuyler, Charles R. Johnson and Ishmael Reed write satiric novels often set in historical periods in ways that reflect upon contemporary racial identity and politics. Octavia Butler and Samuel R. Delany write science fiction, and, continuing in the tradition of James Baldwin, E. Lynn Harris and James Earl Hardy explore black male homosexuality. Walter Mosley writes hard-boiled detective fiction, and Terri McMillan and Elizabeth Atkins Bowman keep romance readers busy. Following the tradition of Iceberg Slim and Donald Goines, writers such as Shannon Holmes, Sister Souljah, Nikki Turner, Carl Weber, and Teri Woods write "hip-hop" novels, a genre attracting many younger readers. Hip-hop fiction, a new "urban realism" with a specific and dynamic link to hip-hop music, offers a dramatic record of street life, drugs, gangs, or coming-of-age difficulties for urban youth. And the passing novel survives still, as witnessed by Danzy Senna's *Caucasia* (1998), Elizabeth Atkins Bowman's *Dark Secret* (2000), and Alice Randall's *The Wind Done Gone* (2001).

Regardless of era, genre, style, subject, or intended audience, taken together African American novels reflect the trope of the "talking book," a trope that connects the written text to the complex oral and musical traditions that circulate in African American culture. Writers, from Harriet Jacobs to **Langston Hughes** to Zora Neale

Hurston to Ishmael Reed to Alice Walker to Sister Souljah, incorporate not only in their dialogue but in the very structure of their novels the rhythms, sounds, values, and traditions of African American storytelling. Furthermore, as Henry Louis Gates Jr. has suggested, African American books "talk" to each other. That is, the stories, themes, and characters in African American fiction carry forward with them what has come before in African American culture and combine it with ever developing styles, structures, and stories. Contemporary authors continue to revise and retell in new settings stories of triumph, defeat, despair, and surviving humanity in the face of continued racism and social inequity, and thus African American novels not only talk to each other, but also talk to contemporary readers of all races, ethnicities, and nationalities.

Further Reading

Carby, Hazel V. *Reconstructing Womanhood*. New York: Oxford University Press, 1996.

Christian, Barbara. *Black Women Novelists: The Development of a Tradition, 1892–1976*. Westport, CT: Greenwood Press, 1980.

Dickson-Carr, Darryl. *African American Satire: The Sacredly Profane Novel*. Columbia: University of Missouri Press, 2001.

Fabi, M. Giulia. *Passing and the Rise of the African American Novel*. Urbana and Chicago: University of Illinois Press, 2001.

Gates, Henry Louis, Jr. *The Signifying Monkey: A Theory of African-American Literary Criticism*. Oxford: Oxford University Press, 1988.

Graham, Maryemma, ed. *The Cambridge Companion to the African American Novel*. London: Cambridge University Press, 2004.

Greene, J. Lee. *Blacks in Eden: The African American Novel's First Century*. Charlottesville: University Press of Virginia, 1996.

Hubbard, Dolan. *The Sermon and the African American Literary Tradition*. Columbia: University of Missouri Press, 1996.

Nelson, Emmanuel S., ed. *Contemporary African American Novelists*. Westport, CT: Greenwood Press, 1999.

Tate, Claudia. *Domestic Allegories of Political Desire: The Black Heroine's Text at the Turn of the Century*. Oxford: Oxford University Press, 1993.

Julie Cary Nerad

AFRICAN AMERICAN POETRY

Historically, the beginning of African American poetry is strongly rooted in the oral traditions of an oppressed people, who were largely denied an opportunity and the occasion to create literary expression. As a resistance to their denial, the earliest voices, from the 18th century to the 21st century, have found ways in which to express their experiences, either by adapting traditional forms to suit their needs or by creating new aesthetic forms, which have allowed for a wider range of creativity and freedom. From the beginning of the 18th century, though, poets have encountered numerous problems, such as choice of subject matter, themes, forms of expression, securing a publisher, authenticating authorship, and appealing to a wider audience. However, by envisioning a world of justice and equality, and by cultivating their own art out of a spirit of human necessity, both old and new voices, with innumerable stories to tell, have created a rich legacy of poetry within the larger context of American culture, spanning over 250 years. The quest for freedom remains a defining theme of this poetic tradition.

Eighteenth-Century Beginnings

New England slave Lucy Terry, who converted to Christianity in 1735, was one of the earliest voices to emerge with "Bars Fight" (1746), a historical account of the Indian raid on Deerfield, Massachusetts, composed in rhymed tetrameter couplet. Though not recognized for its literary merits, Terry's work set the pace for an important poetic tradition. After Lucy Terry, the two early poets of note, whose poetry reflects a strong influence of American Wesleyanism and the revolutionary fervor for liberty ensuing from the radical implications of the American Revolution, were Jupiter Hammon and Phillis Wheatley. Hammon, a slave all of his life and the first African American to publish a poem—"An Evening Thought" (1761), a repetitive shout-hymn with the word "salvation" occurring in every stanza—yearned for salvation from this world, but rather than lose his soul fighting against the system of slavery, accepted enslavement on earth instead. Hailed as the Sable Muse of London society, Phillis Wheatley, a Senegal-born woman who used traditional modes and models such as John Milton, Alexander Pope, John Dryden, and William Blake, wrote, around age 20, the first volume of poetry by an African American, *Poems on Various Subjects, Religious and Moral* (1773), which reflected her New England education and a heavy emphasis on the Bible and the classics. It included several elegies in honor of prominent persons, such as Mr. George Whitefield, odes to political leaders and heroes, such as General George Washington, reflective poems, and more general subjects on nature, religion, education, and biblical incidents. Given her upbringing and training in the Wheatley household, she did not write any protest poetry against slavery, like the poets in the 19th century, but her works do reflect a strong growing social conscience.

Nineteenth-Century Poetry

A more articulate tradition of protest through poetry began to emerge in the 19th century. And although the abolitionist movement had emerged from its comatose state, several poets had a more personal interest in the struggle. Concerned with his own human rights and the struggle against slavery and racism, George Moses Horton, a North Carolinian slave and America's first African American professional poet, expressed his protest in his volume of poems, *The Hope of Liberty* (1829), published in an effort to buy his freedom. Unlike Jupiter Hammon and Phillis Wheatley, Horton's tone is distinctly different, and his poetry is void of their heavy religiosity and pious sentimentality.

Like George Moses Horton, other poets devoted themselves to the cause of abolition. James M. Whitfield, one of black America's most forceful and angry abolitionist poets, makes a scathing indictment of injustices in his best-known work, *America, and Other Poems* (1853), especially in the title poem "America," dedicated to Martin R. Delany, where he states it was a "land of blood, and crime, and wrong" (Barksdale and Kinnamon 223). Frances Ellen Watkins Harper, an abolitionist orator and poet, echoes Whitfield in the "wrong" and injustices done to blacks in her familiar volume, *Poems on Miscellaneous Subjects* (1854), which reveals the inhumane practices and abuses of slavery, as she pleas in the poem "Bury Me in a Free Land" not to be buried "in a land where men are slaves." Other contemporaries such as James Madison Bell, and Albery A. Whitman, continued the protest begun by Horton. John W. Holloway, James Edwin Campbell, James David Corrothers, and Daniel Webster Davis mimicked the dominant stereotypes of the popular plantation tradition with dialect poems. Though not totally oblivious to problems of their day, such poets as Ann Plato, and Henrietta Cordelia Ray, chose the route of romantic escapism and wrote about nature, platonic love, and religious ideals.

With the financial assistance of Wilbur Wright, Paul Laurence Dunbar self-published his first volume of poems, *Oak and Ivy* (1893), and launched his career as America's first black nationally known poet and also as one of America's finest lyricists. *Majors and Minors* (1895) garnered him the favorable attention of literary critic William Dean Howells, who also arranged to have *Lyrics of Lowly Life* (1896) published. Disappointed over Howells's endorsement of his dialect poetry, for which he earned national fame and captured white America with poems exhibiting freshness, humor, and catchy rhythms, Dunbar, unfortunately, spent the last years of his life brooding over the critics' neglect of his poetry in Standard English for that of "a jingle in a broken tongue" (Barksdale and Kinnamon 360). Nevertheless, he published 11 volumes of poetry and is remembered for some of his most anthologized poems, "We Wear the Mask" and "Sympathy," both of which vividly portray the frustrations of the black man's dismal plight, including Dunbar's own.

At the turn of the century, several African American poets adopted a number of popular literary traditions or literary trends of the era and were influenced by experiments with local color, regionalism, realism, and naturalism, rejecting, as did other American poets, sentimentality, didacticism, romantic escape, and poetic diction. In this atmosphere of literary freedom, African American women poets like Angelina Weld Grimké wrote with brevity on nature, loss of love, racial issues, and, sometimes, eroticism. Covering a range of themes, Helene Johnson wrote on Negro pride, culture, love, and the love of **jazz** music, and Gwendolyn Bennett wrote of the nostalgia for Africa, the beauty of black women, and the nurturing practices and traditions within African American culture. Traditional in form, Alice Moore Dunbar-Nelson's poetry explored a woman's heart and was precisely crafted. Called the most modernist, original, and unconventional of her contemporaries, Anne Spencer's poetry focused on nature's beauty, friendship, and love, and she exhibited a command of slant rhymes, sinister rhythms, and obscure symbolism. The spirited, ambitious, dynamic Georgia Douglass Johnson, whose home was one of the greatest literary salons in Washington, D.C., published four volumes of poetry centering on romance (often eroticism) and sociopolitical issues. Though her third collection, *An Autumn Love Cycle* (1928), garnered her critical acclaim, her critical reception, and that of other African American women poets during the first three decades of the 20th century, was sorely diminished.

During such an outpouring from the women, two poets' works emerged as robust, militant racial poetry with a political intent. A native of Chicago, Fenton Johnson, who exhibited a keen racial consciousness, produced three volumes of poetry, *A Little Dreaming* (1913), *Visions of the Dark* (1915), and *Songs of the Soil* (1916), using a lyrical Victorian style, dialect in both personal and traditional idioms, free verse forms, and urban realism. Like Carl Sandburg, Edgar Lee Masters, and other Midwestern authors, Johnson wrote of the despair and fatalism prevalent of his own urban experiences. His poem "Tired" captures his despair and melancholy mood when he states, "I am tired of building up somebody else's civilization . . . I am tired of civilization" (Barksdale and Kinnamon 456). Though a prolific writer, W.E.B. Du Bois, known for his scholarly historical and sociological works and his call for racial equality and social justice, wrote little poetry. His most anthologized work, "A Litany of Atlanta," uses as series of supplications and responses with vivid imagery to dramatize the black's plea for freedom and justice, and provides a valuable link to the existing protest prevalent in both the 1800s and the 1900s.

New Negro Renaissance

First known as the New Negro Movement, African American poetry flourished during the **Harlem Renaissance** of the 1920s, and was enriched by numerous young aspiring talents, who were vocal and interested in new themes, styles, and tones of writing. In *The New Negro* (1925), according to mentor, critic, and interpreter of the Harlem Renaissance Alain Locke, a growing racial awareness among African American writers promoted a new self-awareness in their culture and heritage, uninhibited by fear or shame. So as to influence the prevailing views about themselves and their community through their creativity, these artists moved to urban areas, including Harlem, New York, and Chicago, to produce works that were culturally affirming.

The first and most radical voice to emerge during the 1920s was Claude McKay, and the first great literary achievement during this period was his *Harlem Shadows* (1922). A master of the sonnet, the Jamaican-born poet was most noted for his poems expressing anger and rage, which were rich in animal imagery and metaphors, as in "If We Must Die," composed in the wake of the 1919 race riots. Unlike his contemporaries, Countee Cullen, a romantic poet influenced by John Keats and Percy Bysshe Shelley, wrote mostly nonracial poetry on love, youth, spring, and death. Ambivalent about his own racial identity, the few poems that do celebrate blackness, such as "Heritage," reveal his confusion while exploring the problem of racism and the meaning of Africa, though not apparent from the titles of his collections, *Color* (1925), *Copper Sun* (1927), and *Ballad of a Brown Girl* (1927). Expressing his sentiments at being labeled a "Negro poet" in "Yet Do I Marvel," Cullen was, nevertheless, one of the most prize-winning poets nationwide, one of several to benefit from publishing opportunities for promising writers, and one of the best-known poets of the 1920s.

Other poets who came into prominence during the Harlem Renaissance, celebrating a full expression of their own cosmology and cultural myths, were James Weldon Johnson, Sterling A. Brown, and **Langston Hughes**. Writing works rich in folk heritage, they explored the **blues**, spirituals, tales, proverbs, and sayings. James Weldon Johnson's classic anthologies *The Book of American Negro Poetry* (1922) and *The Book of Negro Spirituals* (1925) are landmarks in the study of African American culture. Beginning as a writer of sentimental poems in black dialect, Johnson, who criticized Paul Laurence Dunbar's use of it, abandons dialect, which he claims "[was] not capable of giving expression to the varied conditions of Negro life in America" (Johnson 42), and became a poet who crafted black folk materials and speech patterns into an art form. Relying heavily upon imagery, rhythm, idiom, and a great sympathy for subject matter, Johnson draws on the stock material of black preachers in *God Trombones: Seven Negro Sermons in Verse* (1927).

Langston Hughes, the most prolific, versatile, and experimental artist of the New Negro Renaissance, was poet laureate of Harlem, and a folk poet, who, unlike James Weldon Johnson, combined work songs, blues, jazz, and ballads to depict the harsh realities of the common man. In his first two volumes, *The Weary Blues* (1926) and *Fine Clothes to the Jew* (1927), Hughes captures the heartbeat of black life and recreates the jazzy, exotic world of Harlem nights in such poems as "The Weary Blues," "Bound No'th Blues," "Lenox Avenue Midnight," and "Jazzonia." Always a poet for the people, Hughes continued to capture the sounds, colors, and rhythms of his people throughout the urban blight of the 1950s and 1960s.

Sterling A. Brown, like Langston Hughes, was a master adaptor of folk forms and experimented with blues, work songs, spirituals, and ballads, combining these forms with folk speech to create a sensitive portrayal of the black experience in the rural South. To create a new poetic language that accurately captured the plight of his people, Brown skillfully uses free verse forms, and fuses the blues song with the ballad to create the blues ballad, as is evident in some of his finest poems, "John Henry," "The Odyssey of Big Boy," and "Ma Rainey" in his significant first work, *Southern Roads* (1932). Of his folk poetry, James Weldon Johnson notes, "He has deepened its meanings and multiplied its implications . . . developed a unique technique . . . and worked it into original and genuine poetry" (247).

Over the next three decades, from 1930 to 1960, the major voices that elevated African American poetry to a new level of consciousness and maturity were Melvin B. Tolson, Robert Hayden, Margaret Walker, and **Gwendolyn Brooks**, joined by Samuel W. Allen, May Miller, Margaret Esse Danner, Dudley Randall, Owen Dodson, Frank Marshall Davis, Frank Horne, and others. Stretching the boundaries of language, they explored the subject of history, and aligned themselves with international affairs and socialistic movements. Melvin Tolson used classical imagery, extensive historical allusions, and racial symbolism in his works, *Rendezvous with America* (1944), which includes his award-winning poem, "Dark Symphony"; *Libretto for the Republic of Liberia* (1953); and *Harlem Gallery* (1965).

An award-winning poet of voice, symbol, and lyricism, Robert Hayden, like Countee Cullen, felt that a poet, whether black or white, should not be restricted to racial themes that would evaluate him as a black poet, and that a poet should be able to make any valid statements about any aspect of a man's experience. To prove how such freedom enriched and deepened his own poetry, Hayden wrote, among others, "**Frederick Douglass**," "Runagate Runagate," and "Middle Passage." Margaret Walker, unlike Hayden, fully embraced her racial material and struck a new cord in the title poem of her first volume of poetry, "For My People." A celebration of black people, Walker's prose poem vibrates with racial consciousness and social protest, energetic movement of language, parallelism of words and phrases, and the absence of major punctuation marks, charting new paths in African American poetry.

Pulitzer Prize–winning poet Gwendolyn Brooks and former poet laureate of Illinois was one of the most prolific poets of the 20th century. She was the author of over 20 works, including her first, *A Street in Bronzeville* (1945); *Annie Allen* (1949), which received the Pulitzer Prize in 1950, the first such prize by a black author; *The Bean Eaters* (1961); *Selected Poems* (1963); *In the Mecca* (1968); *Riot* (1969); and *Family Pictures* (1970). Moving from traditional forms, including ballads, sonnets, lyric stanzas, conventional rhyme, and rhythm of the blues, to unrestricted free verse, her works depict, with brevity, black, ordinary people struggling to survive the harsh realities of the urban North, particularly Chicago.

The Black Arts Movement

During the 1960s, after the advent of Malcolm X's assassination, many of the poets of the Black Arts Movement, inspired by his example, achieved a new black renaissance, while politically, socially, and creatively engaged in the struggle for justice and equality. Fueled by their energy and determination, they helped to sustain the **Civil Rights Movement**, by calling for self-reliance, pride in their black heritage and culture, and reaffirming a racial consciousness utilizing black life as a model for their art, exhibited in their poetic style and diction. Complementing such established writers as Gwendolyn Brooks, Margaret Walker, Robert Hayden, Dudley Randall, and Owen Dodson were Amiri Baraka (LeRoi Jones), Larry Neal, Askia M. Touré (Rolland Snellings), Etheridge Knight, Sonia Sanchez, A. B. Spellman, Haki R. Madhubuti (Don L. Lee), Johari Amini (Jewel Latimore), Nikki Giovanni, David Henderson, and Tom Dent.

Three of the earliest visionaries and revolutionaries of the Black Arts Movement, Amiri Baraka (LeRoi Jones), Larry Neal, Askia M. Touré (Rolland Snellings), capture with vigor and pride the spirit of the struggle for black liberation and equality. An acclaimed poet, activist, playwright, editor, jazz critic, and cofounder of the Black Arts Repertory Theatre/School along with Larry Neal, Amiri Baraka is considered the "Dean of Revolutionary Poetry" (Reid 71) and one of the most influential poets for a whole generation of young black writers. In the late 1950s and early 1960s, he gained a reputation as a poet, editor, and jazz critic among the artists of Greenwich Village. Baraka's first published collection, *Preface to a Twenty Volume*

Suicide Note (1961), reveals his emerging political views, and the poem "Black Art" (1965) served as his poetic/political manifesto of the Black Arts literary movement. In more than 12 volumes of poetry, including *The Dead Lecturer* (1964), *Black Magic Poetry* (1969), *In Our Terribleness* (1970), *It's Nation Time* (1970), *Spirit Reach* (1972), and *Reggae or Not!* (1981), Baraka emerged over the years with a strong, nationalistic, frequently militant voice, utilizing onomatopoeia, obscenity, hyperbolic imagery, rhetorical questions, unusual syntax, and signification. What has resulted is a poetry that is experimental and improvisational, evoking a sense of jazz and explosiveness.

Two other poets of note are Larry Neal and Askia M. Touré (Rolland Snellings). Characterized as a spiritual journeyman of the Black Arts Movement, Larry Neal was one of its most influential critics, scholars, editors, and philosophers. In his manifesto and seminal essay, "The Black Arts Movement," he asserts that the movement is "the aesthetic and spiritual sister of the Black Power concept . . . [and] the Black Arts Movement proposes a radical reordering of the Western cultural aesthetic" (Donalson 926). Utilizing the rhythm of black music, in his two collections of poetry, *Black Boogaloo: Notes on Black Liberation* (1969) and *Hoodoo Hollerin' Bebop Ghosts* (1974), Neal often engages African American history, language, and mythology. Another architect of the Black Arts Movement, poet and political activist Askia Touré, has continued to combine his compassion for justice and artistic expression in such works as his long poem *Juju: Magic Songs for the Black Nation* (1970), *Songhai* (1973), and *From the Pyramids to the Projects: Poems of Genocide and Resistance* (1990).

The political and social upheavals of the 1950s and 1960s brought about by the Civil Rights Movement ushered in an outpouring of African American poetry. The assassination of **Martin Luther King Jr.** inspired poetry from Haki R. Madhubuti (Don L. Lee), Nikki Giovanni, Sam Allen, Mari Evans, and Quincy Troupe. In the wake of the Black Power Movement, with its bold language of racial confrontation, black pride, use of free verse, and unconventional poetic structure, the works of Baraka, Neal, and Touré, along with such eminent poets as Madhubuti, Giovanni, Evans, Troupe, Etheridge Knight, June Jordan, Ray Durem, Sonia Sanchez, and Clarence Major, among others, left no poetic innovation untested and no theme untouched. Speaking of the existing body of poetry written by these poets, Margaret Reid notes, "This poetry written expressively for Black people by Black people . . . defied all traditional standards as poets sought to free themselves artistically and politically from . . . imposed restrictions" (97).

Contemporary African American Poetry

Since the 1970s, contemporary African American poets have produced works that draw heavily upon the blues and jazz, features of call and response, the dozens, the rap, **signifying**, and folktales. Though no longer in the throes of a cultural and political revolution like the 1960s, these poets continued to affirm their blackness, which was transformed into a performance that speaks to the power of black music and speech, as in the works of Haki R. Madhubuti, Sonia Sanchez, Amiri

Baraka, Nikki Giovanni, Askia Touré, Jayne Cortez, Eugene Redmond, and Ted Joans. Whereas the works of these poets absorbed full musical forms, oratory and performance, other poets like Alvin Aubert, Pinki Gordon Lane, and Naomi Long Madgett avoided a prescribed poetic form and enhanced their poetry by more subdued means. Lucille Clifton, **Audre Lorde**, Jay Wright, and Michael S. Harper explored more personal and individualized goals. **Rita Dove** credits the Black Arts Movement for her acceptance in America depicting a message other than a politically charged one in her well-known work, the 1987 Pulitzer Prize–winning *Thomas and Beulah* (1986). During the late 1970s and 1980s, like Dove, who earlier published her first book of poems with a major press, *The Yellow House on the Corner* (1980), a large group of poets also published their first poem, chapbook, or book of poetry, and would go on to become some of the most accomplished poets of the 20th century. Among them were Yusef Komunyakaa, Melvin Dixon, Delores Kendrick, Cornelius Eady, Toi Derricotte, Gloria Oden, Sherley Anne Williams, and Thylias Moss. Writing in the 1990s, the voices of Elizabeth Alexander, Thomas Sayers Ellis, Kevin Young, Sharan Strange, Carl Phillips, Natasha Trethewey, and Harryette Mullen, to name a few, write of both public issues and concerns in contemporary life. Other young poets like Ras Baraka, Kevin Powell, Jabari Asim, and Esther Iverem seek to revisit the ideals of the Black Arts Movement in the language of a hip-hop nation, keeping the spirit of a bygone revolution alive and anew.

At the close of the 20th century, African American poetry has experienced an expansive, renewal phase that some have called the "Third Renaissance." Evidence of such a renewal was obvious at the 1994 Furious Flower Conference, the first of its kind to focus solely on poetry, dedicated to Gwendolyn Brooks and hosted at James Madison University in Virginia, where four generations of poets met to read, discuss, and celebrate black poetry. Such a gathering symbolized the importance of poetic expression as a continuous medium and signaled the dynamics of its future growth and development. Poets who launched their writing careers in the 1960s and early 1970s are continuing to write with such skill and force. First-rate examples are Gerald W. Barrax's *Leaning against the Sun* (1992); Haki R. Madhubuti's *Claiming the Earth: Race, Rage, Redemption* (1994); Sonia Sanchez's *Wounded in the House of a Friend* (1995); Amiri Baraka's *Funk Lore: New Poems (1984–95)* (1996); and Askia M. Touré's *Dawnsong!* (2000). African American poets receiving some of the nation's most prestigious achievements and top honors during this time were Derek Walcott, with his 1992 Nobel Prize for Literature (for his epic poem *Omeros*); Rita Dove's 1993 appointment as Poet Laureate of the United States; and Gwendolyn Brooks's naming by the National Endowment for the Humanities as the Jefferson Lecturer for 1994. A few other poets deserve mention as well. Eugene Redmond is the first and only poet laureate of his native East Saint Louis, Illinois (1976), Pinki Gordon Lane, is the first African American to be named Louisiana's poet laureate, and one of the youngest is Marilyn Nelson of Connecticut.

During this renaissance, a new group of young poets emerged and have been published in such anthologies as *In the Tradition: An Anthology of Young Black Writers* (1992), edited by Kevin Powell and Ras Baraka; *On the Verge: Emerging Poets and Artists* (1993), edited by Thomas Sayers Ellis and Joseph Lease; *Every Shut Eye*

Ain't Sleep: An Anthology of Poetry by African Americans Since 1945 (1994), edited by Michael Harper and Anthony Walton; *The Garden Thrives: Twentieth-Century African American Poetry* (1996), edited by Clarence Major; *African American Literature: A Brief Introduction and Anthology* (1996), edited by Al Young; *Trouble the Water: 250 Years of African-American Poetry* (1997), edited by Jerry W. Ward Jr.; and *Beyond the Frontier: African American Poetry for the 21st Century* (2002), edited by E. Ethelbert Miller. Shaping their work in relation to hip-hop culture, many of the younger award-winning poets published in these works, such as Tony Medina, Jessica Care Moore, Ras Baraka, Ruth Foreman, Kevin Powell, Charlie Braxton, Carl Redux Rux, Suheir Hammad, Saul Williams, and Jacquie Jones, have turned toward popular culture, presenting new challenges for critics in understanding their art. This was never more apparent than at the second historic 2004 Furious Flower Conference, also dedicated to Gwendolyn Brooks and hosted at James Madison University, which ushered in the promise of black poetic expression during the 21st century. Many of these new voices, like the poets in the 1970s and 1980s, have debuted their first poems and books of poetry: Angela Shannon's *Singing the Bones Together* (2003), F. Kelly Norman Ellis's *Tougaloo Blues* (2003), Opal Moore's *Lot's Daughters* (2004), and Geoffrey Johnson's *smells i see: a collection of poetry and prose* (2004), to name a few. As James Weldon Johnson affirms in *The Book of Negro American Poetry* (1922), "Much ground has been covered, but more will yet be covered" (47). Committed to the ideals of beauty and liberation, this "ground" will continue to be "covered" by new voices inspired by the muses of long ago, sounding a clarion call for more humanism, for more critics to understand the beauty of poetic expression, and especially for more readers to understand the power and wisdom of poetry from its earliest conception to the present.

Further Reading

Barksdale, Richard, and Keneth Kinnamon. *Black Writers of America: A Comprehensive Anthology*. New York: Macmillan, 1972.

Bell, Bernard. W., ed. *Modern and Contemporary Afro-American Poetry*. Boston: Allyn and Bacon, 1972.

Bolden, Tony. *Afro-Blue: Improvisations in African American Poetry and Culture*. Urbana: University of Illinois Press, 2004.

Bontemps, Arna, ed. *American Negro Poetry*. New York: Hill and Wang, 1963.

Donalson, Melvin. *Cornerstones: An Anthology of African American Literature*. New York: St. Martin's Press, 1996. 926–37.

Gabbin, Joanne V. "Foreword." In *Dictionary of Literary Biography*. Vol. 41: *Afro-American Poets since 1955*, edited by Trudier Harris and Thadious M. Davis, xi–xv. Detroit: Gale, 1985.

Gabbin, Joanne V. "Poetry." In *The Oxford Companion to African American Literature*, edited by William L. Andrews, Frances Smith Foster, and Trudier Harris, 592. New York: Oxford University Press, 1997.

Hayden, Robert. *Kaleidoscope: Poems by American Negro Poets*. San Diego, CA: Harcourt, Brace & World, 1967.

Henderson, Stephen. *Understanding the New Black Poetry: Black Speech and Black Music as Poetic References*. New York: Morrow, 1973.

Hughes, Langston. *New Negro Poets, U.S.A.* Bloomington: Indiana University, 1964.

Jackson, Blyden, and Louis Rubin. *Black Poetry in America.* Baton Rouge: Louisiana State University Press, 1974.

Johnson, James Weldon, ed. *The Book of American Negro Poetry.* New York: Harcourt, Brace, 1922 [reprint 1931].

Major, Clarence, ed. *The New Black Poetry.* New York: International, 1969.

Redding, J. Saunders. *To Make a Poet Black.* Chapel Hill: University of North Carolina Press, 1939.

Redmond, Eugene B. *Drumvoices: The Mission of Afro-American Poetry.* Garden City, NY: Anchor, 1976.

Reid, Margaret Ann. *Black Protest Poetry: Polemics from the Harlem Renaissance and the Sixties.* New York: Peter Lang, 2001.

Robinson, William Jr., ed. *Early Black American Poets.* Dubuque, IA: William C. Brown, 1969.

Wagner, Jean. *Black Poets of the United States: From Paul Laurence Dunbar to Langston Hughes.* Urbana: University of Illinois Press, 1973.

Loretta G. Woodard

AFRICAN AMERICAN SCIENCE FICTION

African American science fiction is also called AfroFuturism. From its early days as "scientifiction," named in the 1920s by Hugo Gernsback, who was a first-generation American and writer for an electronics magazine, the field of science fiction was dominated by white males writing for a predominantly white male readership. Popularized by the pulp fictions of the early 20th century, by 1970, when the Science Fiction Research Association was founded to expand the study of science fiction, science fiction had already captured a large share of the contemporary fiction market and emerged as a significant genre.

Although there is much critical debate regarding the defining characteristics of the genre, a text is generally viewed as a work of science fiction when the narrative is set in a future time; a futuristic setting is used as a basis for speculation about the application or impact of new science or technology on humankind; travel through time or space is used as a motif or device for discovery of some universal truth; and there is a cautionary social commentary embedded in the narrative that comments on the past, the present, and the future. Typically Martin Delany's *Blake, or the Huts of America* (1857) is considered the first African American science fiction novel when science fiction is broadly defined as either imaginative or speculative fiction, terms made popular by literary scholars interested in expanding the canon of science fiction. However, because the term science fiction did not come into use until the late 1920s, it is perhaps more accurate to say that George Schuyler's satiric *Black No More: Being an Account of the Strange and Wonderful Workings of Science in the Land of the Free, A.D. 1933–1940*, published in 1931, is the first African American science fiction novel.

In Schuyler's novel, a Harlem-based scientist, Dr. Julius Crookman, discovers a way to permanently whiten black skin while researching a cure for vitiligo, a disease affecting skin pigmentation. Crookmans's new scientific process, involving nickel plating and electricity, makes it possible for black Americans to turn themselves white in just three days. As black characters turn themselves white, violence erupts across the country, and to protect the secret of their identities and capitalize on the value of their new white skins, some of those now passing for white join white-supremacy hate groups that participate in **racism** and violence against black men, including lynching, mutilation, and torture. In the end of the novel, white skin ceases to be the final determinant of racial **identity** when scientists discover a genetic indicator showing that the majority of white Americans have, as one of the white characters in the novel puts it, "dusky" ancestors and so, the character concludes, all are "niggers" now.

Schuyler continued to write science fiction under the pen name of Samuel I. Brooks, and his work was serialized in black newspapers. His second and third novels appeared in 63 newspaper installments as the story of a black researcher and scientist, Dr. Beldsidus, who creates a futuristic black utopia in the hidden interior of Africa. Dr. Beldsidus and his army of black geniuses and engineers use sophisticated germ warfare and cyclotrons, a futuristic proton impacting weapon of mass destruction, to ground Euro-American air defenses and render the armies and navies of the world completely without power. Under the guidance of Dr. Beldsidus, Africa emerges as the uncontested supreme world superpower. Primarily remembered in the 21st century as an essayist, Schuyler produced more than 20 such novels before his death in 1977.

Although literary scholars use the term speculative fictions or alternative histories to discuss African American science fiction as part of a larger literary tradition, contemporary African American writers of science fiction prefer Mark Dery's 1993 moniker "AfroFuturism" for the speculative fictions and alternative histories that rely upon the conventions of science fiction. Paul D. Miller, a writer and musician who goes by the professional name of D.J. Spooky, defines AfroFuturism as a "zone" and it is in this zone that "core aspects of African-American identity and it's unfolding in America" are "translated" and "fade in the algorithm of life in the liquid parade of the modern mindstream . . . subtle to the point of formlessness" (413–14). In essence, as a literary and cultural aesthetic, AfroFuturism critiques as it revises, interrogates as it creates, and defines as it redefines the very definition of what it means to be human in the modern world. Both the form of the fiction and the fiction itself are impacted by this postmodern perspective.

In contemporary America, the names most commonly associated with the genre of African American science fiction are those of Samuel R. Delany, Octavia Butler, Steve Barnes, and Charles Saunders. Delany and Butler, in particular, have radically redefined the genre. Delany and Butler populate their worlds with characters that are without fixed racial or gender roles, and identity is determined by a character's words, deeds, and thoughts more than by their physical appearance. The physical body is an extension of identity, not the prime determinant, and the main characters are in conflict with the social structure that seeks to delineate the character's place in the man-made world. The main characters seek to transcend the world made by man.

Additionally, what sets AfroFuturism apart from mainstream American science fiction is an insistence on multi**ethnicity**. Instead of the racial tokenism common to even the best of mainstream American science fiction, African American writers of science fiction create characters with "a plethora of identities," and racial and gender "ambiguity is a positive attribute" (Brooks and Hampton 70). Butler, for example, in her *Parable* series, populates her texts with interracial, bilingual families traveling through an interracial, bilingual dystopia in search of a new beginning. In her *Patternmaster* series, characters can change gender as well. Identity is a composite of experience, memory, and emotion, and a single character can carry the archetypal memories of many races.

As the field of African American science fiction has expanded into para-literary genres such as comic books, graphic novels, and movies, multiethnic mixed-blood characters abound. For example, Milestone Media, an African American–owned comic book company (1992–1996), created a line of science fiction comics with a large cast of characters from a variety of ethnic backgrounds including multiethnic characters. Hardwire, Icon, and Xombi are mutants created by scientific disaster or are humans augmented by new cyborg weapons technology, fighting to create a livable world in the Dakota Universe. Movies such as *Underworld* (2003), in which African American producer, writer, actor, and stuntman Kevin Grevioux played the part of the werewolf Raze, depict a world dominated by vampires who track the increasingly technological werewolves using sophisticated databases and futuristic laptop computers. In turn, the werewolves use genetic research to uncover the truth about a mythological common human ancestor who gave rise to both vampires and werewolves. In *Underworld*, there are black and white vampires and black and white werewolves, and the sexual taboo is the mixing of supernatural species, not colors. Color does not determine identity, and the key event of the movie is a Romeo-Juliet style romance between a werewolf and a vampire that is then played out over the course of a thousand years until individual characters choose to separate themselves from their "group" and act on the basis of their own heartfelt conclusions. Peace is achieved only when the three bloodlines again become mixed as one and the resulting mix is stronger.

African American novels, comics, graphic novels, and movies fit into a pattern of AfroFuturism or African American science fiction that emphasizes the need for self-knowledge and an acceptance of **multiculturalism** that goes beyond the embracing of "otherness" so often found in popular American science fiction. Instead of populating a text with representatives of different **race**s, African American science fiction celebrates the diversity that is part of each person's bloodline. Shared blood is shared history, and the texts' heroes recognize that there are worlds within as well as without. That level of self-knowledge, writer Greg Tate explains, comes from an individual pursuit of self-awareness; one must accept that identity is "not something that's given to you, institutionally; it's an arduous journey that must be undertaken by the individual" ("Black to the Future" 766). In African American science fiction identity is not restricted to a single racial identity, and "the final frontier" is not restricted to "space," as Captain James T. Kirk of *Star Trek* might say. Instead, the real journey—the one that requires true boldness—is the journey within.

Further Reading

Brooks, Wanda, and Gregory Hampton. "Black Women Writers and Science Fiction." *NCTE English Journal* 92.6 (June 2003): 70–75.

Dery, Mark. "Black to the Future: Interviews with Samuel R. Delany, Greg Tate, and Tricia Rose." *South Atlantic Quarterly* 92.4 (Fall 1993): 735–78.

Holden, Rebecca. *Strange Matings*. Seattle: Aqueduct Press, 2013.

Miller, Paul D. "Yet Do I Wonder." In *Dark Matter: A Century of Speculative Fiction from the African Diaspora*, edited by Sheree R. Thomas, 408–14. New York: Warner Books, 2000.

Scholes, Robert, and Eric Rabkin. *Science Fiction: History, Science, Vision*. New York: Oxford University Press, 1977.

Darcy A. Zabel

AFRICAN AMERICAN SLAVE NARRATIVE

The slave narrative is a unique genre of African American literature that has helped both to spur other genres and to bring to public attention the trials and talents of African Americans who were enslaved in the United States for hundreds of years. An autobiographical form, the slave narrative is contingent, as its name suggests, on telling the story of an African American who triumphed over slavery by escaping that historical institution in one way or another. Most slave narratives were written by the former slave himself or herself; in other cases, the former slave being illiterate or semiliterate, a ghostwriter was used to pen the "as-told-to" story. In one particular case, oral histories of former slaves who survived beyond the Civil War years were recorded by workers in the Federal Writers Project of the 1930s in a singular effort to capture those voices before they were silenced forever. Today transcripts of those interviews can be read in the volume *Remembering Slavery*. The voices of those interviewed have been preserved on tape.

There are other instances when a tale that fits closely into the genre of slave narrative is written and marketed as simply an autobiography or even as an autobiographical novel. Such is the case with **Harriet E. Wilson**'s 1859 narrative, *Our Nig*, which tells the story of an African American woman who found herself as an indentured servant throughout her childhood in the North. Wilson's narrative is similar to the typical slave narrative in that it exposes Northern **racism**. Wilson was never legally a slave, however, and she was freed from her indentured servant status once she reached adulthood, which marks a significant difference from those writers who were presumed to have been born into slavery for life.

An Early Narrative

Although the slave narrative dates back as early as 1789 with Olaudah Equiano's *The Interesting Narrative of the Life of Olaudah Equiano, or Gustavus Vassa, the*

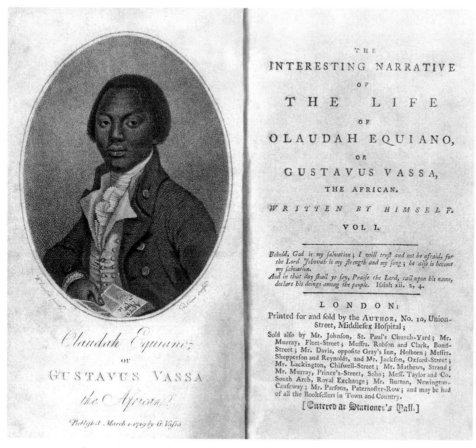

Interior pages from *The Interesting Narrative of the Life of Olaudah Equiano*. (World History Archive/UIG via Getty Images)

African, the majority of slave narratives originate in the 19th century, especially in the decades directly preceding and encompassing the Civil War. Equiano's narrative, however, is extremely important, as it sets the stage for a new genre and as its setting is remarkably different from the standard slave narrative of the century following his. Equiano writes of his actual capture into slavery in his own native Africa and of his subsequent sale to European slave traders. We read in *The Interesting Narrative* of Equiano's miserable experiences on the slave boat, his survival of the infamous Middle Passage, his being sold from one person to another, and finally his ability to purchase his own freedom at the age of 21. Equiano's narrative also conveys the message that human freedom is a basic right and that slavery must be abolished. The fact that Equiano wrote his narrative on his own, and that he wrote it well, served to foster some discussion on inherent racial abilities.

Abolitionism and the Nineteenth Century

The 19th century is the time period most closely associated with the slave narrative. It was during this century that the ugliness and social evils of slavery were taking their strongest hold. Unlike Equiano, the slaves of the 19th century were American born and had been raised in a predominately pro-slavery culture. They had been indoctrinated into Christianity in a twisted way that made slavery seem justified, and they had been raised with the supposition that they were indeed members of an inferior—if not a cursed—race. Still, there existed the basic human desire to be free, to be the master of one's own destiny, and to dream of greater possibilities. It was such a desire that drove some of the enslaved to risk all—including their very lives—and attempt escape. Those who were successful in such attempts often found themselves helped by both black and white abolitionists along the Underground Railroad. It was staunch white abolitionists such as William Lloyd Garrison who encouraged many escaped slaves to tell their stories, largely as a way to persuade other voting members of the United States to join the fight for the abolition of slavery. Some of these escaped slaves were able to write their own stories; some needed assistance. Many were convinced to testify publicly to the truth of their tales. Some became standard members of the antislavery lecture circuit.

The titles of these slave narratives were often long and cumbersome, as well as descriptive. For example, in 1842 Lunsford Lane's narrative was published under the title, *The Narrative of Lunsford Lane, Formerly of Raleigh, N.C., Embracing an Account of His Early Life, the Redemption by Purchase of Himself and Family from Slavery, and His Banishment from the Place of His Birth for the Crime of Wearing a Colored Skin*. Truly, the reader is set up to expect not only a narrative of Lane's life as a slave but also a tale of deeply ingrained racial prejudice.

As the 19th-century slave narrative became more popular and more widely used for the political agenda of the abolitionist groups, the larger readership began to demand proof of the veracity of the tale and proof of the identity of the author. There certainly was the possibility of an unscrupulous white writer fashioning a false slave narrative in the hopes of taking financial advantage of the newest wave of the publishing world.

Beyond that, however, was the biased supposition that a black writer could not automatically be believed. In order to continue to find a steady market for the slave narrative and, in turn, to continue to spread the message of the need for abolition, it became the fashion to include testimonials to the veracity of a given work at the end of the narrative. These testimonials were largely written by white citizens who were considered to be upstanding members of the community. Often a preface written by an especially prominent white citizen was also included; such prefatory statements served as authenticating devices that were intended to validate the slave narratives and testify to their essential truthfulness. All of this set the stage for some of the most important writers of the genre, including **Frederick Douglass**, Harriet Ann Jacobs, Sojourner Truth, and William Wells Brown.

Frederick Douglass

Frederick Douglass became famous with the 1845 publication of his *Narrative of the Life of Frederick Douglass, an American Slave, Written by Himself*. Douglass's book remains one of the most famous of all slave narratives, often being the only text of the genre that appears in a mainstream anthology of literature. Douglass's narrative contains a preface by William Lloyd Garrison and tells the tale of what seemed to many of his contemporaries to be the portrayal of an uncommonly intelligent and industrious African American man. It is precisely this perception that made Douglass's book a best seller in his homeland as well as abroad.

Douglass's story has some similarities to that of Equiano's. Both men are filled with a sense of outrage at their situations, both men are able to procure an informal education, both men are able to learn a trade, and both men find themselves in a position to secure their own freedom. In Douglass's case, this involved saving the money to run North with his wife. Also like Equiano, Douglass was committed to working toward the abolition of slavery. Douglass formally joined the abolitionist movement and became one of its most famous lecturers, even traveling to England to preach against slavery. His narrative became one of the steady tomes of the abolitionist movement.

Douglass presents to the reader tales of the physical brutality of slavery that became pivotal in his fight for the freedom of all. He also presents the human aspects of the enslaved, convincing educated white readers that they had more in common with the black man than they had previously thought possible. This helped to set the stage for further acceptance of future slave narratives.

Harriet Ann Jacobs

When Harriet Ann Jacobs's slave narrative was published 16 years after Douglass's, it marked a critical change in the face of slavery as it was presented to the genteel white readership. Whereas Douglass's narrative illustrates all of the physical brutality of slavery, especially as it touched men's lives, Jacobs's *Incidents in the Life of a Slave Girl, Told by Herself* (1861) forced readers to look carefully at the sexual politics of slavery, something most had refused to do prior to this time. Jacobs exposes the cruelties of repeated sexual harassment and attempted and actual rapes that occurred between the slaveholder and the enslaved woman or even the enslaved girl.

The events surrounding the publication of Jacobs's narrative were also critical to the development of this genre. Jacobs's abolitionist friends certainly urged her to tell her tale, as had the friends of Douglass, but Jacobs did not at first think of writing her own story. She had planned to tell the tale to Harriet Beecher Stowe and let her write it. This plan failed miserably, though, when Stowe decided that Jacobs's tale was unbelievable. After all, who could fathom that a good Christian white man would attempt to abuse sexually a black slave? Stowe went to Jacobs's employer asking for verification of Jacobs's story, which put Jacobs in the uncomfortable position of having her employer hear about this very personal part of her previous life from a stranger, for Jacobs had never revealed this part of her past to her employer. The embarrassment worked out well for the development of African American literature, however, as Jacobs eventually wrote her own story, adding to the growing evidence that intellect and talent were not reserved for members of one racial group alone. With her famous and well-respected contemporaries Amy Post and Lydia Maria Child supporting her efforts, Jacobs found success with the publication of her narrative and also found herself a free woman. Today many scholars see Douglass's and Jacobs's narratives as complementary examples of the slave narrative.

Sojourner Truth

Sojourner Truth's slave narrative represents yet a different style of the genre. Born into slavery as Isabella, Sojourner Truth took on her new name upon her escape from slavery. Though highly intelligent and absolutely committed to doing what she saw as the work of the Lord through her preaching, Truth was illiterate. A physically strong woman who paid for her strength with an unusual degree of physical abuse from her master, Truth had a tale to tell but no means with which to do so on her own. She had survived slavery, she had answered a calling from God, and she had joined the lecture circuit as an outspoken advocate of not only abolition but women's rights as well. When it became evident that Truth's tale must be written down, the white abolitionist Olive Gilbert acted as Truth's ghostwriter. *The Narrative of Sojourner Truth* was originally written in 1850. With the help of other white women friends, Truth continued to work on the narrative until it was reprinted in 1884 under the title *The Narrative of Sojourner Truth; a Bondswoman of Olden Time, with a History of Her Labors and Correspondence Drawn from Her "Book of Life."* As the title suggests, this volume contains much more than Truth's simple slave narrative. It also contains letters and testament to Truth's spiritual journey. The writing of spiritual autobiography was to become yet another important part of African American literature.

William Wells Brown

In 1847, William Wells Brown published his slave narrative, *The Narrative of William W. Brown, a Fugitive Slave*, which, like Douglass's narrative published two years prior, became incredibly successful both in the United States and abroad. Brown's narrative tells of his days of captivity and of his attempts at escape. It also gives the reader a good understanding of what happens to a slave who is caught attempting to escape. Of course, Brown did eventually succeed in escaping. Like Douglass and Truth, he began to lecture against slavery, and, like Jacobs, he eventually had his freedom purchased for him through the help of friends.

The difference between Brown and most of the other writers of the slave narrative is that he saw himself as a creative writer as well as a reporter on the conditions of the enslaved. Brown went on to write several books, including the well-known novel *Clotel; or, the President's Daughter* (1853). He also published drama, a travel book, and history books focusing on African Americans in U.S. history. Brown is considered to be the first African American novelist, playwright, and travel writer in the United States. Brown's slave narrative set the stage for his later works. It also opened the door for other African Americans to see themselves as creative writers and as true literary figures rather than simply as vehicles for the abolitionist movement.

Reconstruction and Beyond

Although slavery technically ended in the United States with the Civil War, the genre of the slave narrative did not. Several former slaves penned the tales of their days as slaves. Among these writers was Elizabeth Keckley, who had worked in the Lincoln White House as Mary Todd Lincoln's dressmaker. These works began to take on a different focus than had the antebellum slave narratives, however. Keckley's *Behind the Scenes, or Thirty Years a Slave and Four Years in the White House* (1868) includes a good deal of the intimacy of the Lincoln household to which she was privileged, bringing her a somewhat different audience than her predecessors had had.

Another post–Civil War slave narrative is Booker T. Washington's famous *Up from Slavery* (1901), which has the dubious distinction of significantly changing the focus of the slave narrative. Washington's premise is that, as slavery is dead, the African American must embrace his or her possibilities and go cheerfully forth, trying to assimilate smoothly into an already established society. Washington's style was unthreatening to his white audience, and he was rewarded for such with much praise, so much so that other writers of the slave narrative attempted to follow his lead.

Today much discussion revolves around how useful Washington's narrative actually was to the cause of true freedom and equality, with many scholars taking the view that Washington may have done more harm than good to the social causes of his race.

Of course, there are also the oral histories of former slaves compiled by the writers of the Works Project Administration. Although these remain a fascinating study, it is interesting to note the near desperation that seems to come from some of the former slaves as they craft their words carefully so as not to offend. Although slavery had officially ended, these former slaves well knew that racism was far from over and that it was perfectly possible to endanger their own lives and those of their families by saying the "wrong thing."

Overview

African American literature is still in a place of discovery. New texts by African American writers are still being recovered, and among these are possible samples of slave narratives, such as Hannah Crafts's *The Bondswoman's Narrative*, a 19th-century work that has recently been brought to publication by literary scholar Henry Louis Gates Jr. What exists in the way of slave narratives at this point in time is a rich variety of personal styles and personal concerns, coupled with a common need to tell the true tales of slavery so that slavery will first be ended and then be kept dormant forever. The reader sees the personality of the author and the uniqueness of the author's situation in the slave narrative. The careful reader, though, is also cognizant that some slave narratives were altered significantly by the white editors who were attempting to help get the narrative published. Lydia Maria Child, for instance, convinced Harriet Ann Jacobs to delete a chapter she had devoted to the infamous slave rebellion of Nat Turner. Child also convinced Jacobs to rearrange her chapters so that the book ended on a more optimistic note. The wise reader of the slave narrative keeps in mind the political situation of the 19th-century United States.

The slave narratives teach much about history. They also served historically to prove the point that African Americans could indeed read, write, think, and calculate as well as could any other people. In addition, they helped the cause of abolition, and, after the Civil War, they underlined the arguments for equal rights for all. As we look beyond the 19th century, we also see the slave narrative as an important step toward the type of **African American autobiography** that emerged in the 20th century.

Further Reading

Andrews, William L. *To Tell a Free Story: The First Century of Afro-American Autobiography, 1760–1865*. Urbana: University of Illinois Press, 1986.

Davis, Charles T., and Gates, Henry Louis, Jr. *The Slave's Narrative*. New York: Oxford University Press, 1990.

Foster, Frances Smith. *Witnessing Slavery: The Development of the Ante-Bellum Slave Narratives*. Madison: University of Wisconsin Press, 1994.

Terry D. Novak

AFRICAN AMERICAN STEREOTYPES

From the first attempts to categorize human beings several hundred years ago, simplified perceptions of racial difference have plagued society. The "scientifically" sanctioned concept of **race** both enabled and encouraged individuals to manufacture certain assumptions and stereotypes about African Americans. With the notable exception of an enlightened few, most spurned the notion of racial equality. Even Thomas Jefferson, who proclaimed in the Declaration of Independence "that all men are created equal," did not truly believe that African Americans were inherently equal to whites. Like many of his contemporaries, Jefferson believed that an indelible color line had been drawn between the two races. In his acclaimed *Notes on the State of Virginia* (1787), Jefferson asserted that African Americans' physical, mental, and moral characteristics offered indisputable evidence of their innate inferiority.

In the hands of Southern apologists for slavery, Jefferson's pseudoscientific theories were substantive proof of African Americans' suitability as slaves. Some advocates of slavery went so far as to suggest that the differences between the two races were so insurmountable that white society was doing "the Negro" a favor by enslaving him. These and other champions of the "positive good" theory argued that slavery was not, as the abolitionists would have everyone believe, an incomprehensible evil but an essential good. In short, they depicted slavery not as the "peculiar institution" it was reputed to be, but as a mutually beneficial relationship between slave owners and their slaves.

Repudiating the "positive good" theory, Harriet Beecher Stowe's *Uncle Tom's Cabin* (1852) sought to portray the African American as the unfortunate victim of a barbarous system. Unfortunately, her stereotypical portrayal of Tom and other slaves as "simple" and "childlike" served to legitimize the prejudice and limited views of those already convinced of the inferiority of African Americans. In her attempt to subvert the stereotype of the African American as lazy, shiftless, and uncivilized, Stowe, inadvertently, created a pejorative tag that survives to this day. Whereas the hero of Stowe's immensely popular novel was the embodiment of forbearance and goodness, the name "Uncle Tom" came to represent something very different. Uncle Tom became a trope, the incarnation of a shiftless, unscrupulous character who catered to whites and betrayed his black brethren.

Not surprisingly, the character (or, more accurately, caricature) of Uncle Tom became a mainstay on the minstrel circuit, which was famed for its patronizing portrayals of African Americans. Drawing on popularly held stereotypes of blacks, minstrel performers exaggerated what they considered to be "the Negro's eccentricities." Donning flashy clothes, and using greasepaint or burnt cork to darken their skins, the actors hammed it up for their white audiences. The handbills and posters advertising the minstrel shows—with their monstrous images of African Americans with protruding lips and misshapen heads—underscored the physical and intellectual differences between blacks and whites to an even greater degree. The figure depicted in these advertisements, and on the stage, was a grotesque caricature of the African American—freakish and inhuman. Although minstrel troupes thought nothing of caricaturing slaves, they were, however, more conscientious in their depictions of the institution of slavery. Playing to the Southern crowd, the performers were careful to limit their portraitures to contented slaves, which would explain their fascination with the character of Uncle Tom, the "happy darkie."

Like *Uncle Tom's Cabin*, Mark Twain's *Adventures of Huckleberry Finn* (1885) sought to expose the perils of slavery. Despite his efforts to the contrary, Twain, like Stowe, failed to fully dignify the slave. Although Twain endowed Jim with many consummate qualities, he nonetheless reinforced the stereotype of the slave as a gullible, superstitious creature. In addition, Jim's placid acceptance of the young Huck's absolute authority over him cemented the slave's status as an indiscriminate piece of property.

However their works were interpreted, Stowe and Twain endeavored to humanize African Americans, not further degrade them. The same cannot be said for Thomas Dixon's *The Clansman* (1905)—the anti–African American novel upon which the film *Birth of a Nation* (1915) was based. A former Baptist minister, Dixon envisioned the novel as an evangelical effort to revolutionize the African American stereotype. Scandalized by American society's acceptance of Stowe's positive rendering of Uncle Tom, Dixon felt it was time they heard the whole truth. Dixon's version of the "truth," as depicted in *The Clansman*, characterized the African

American male as a vicious brute, unable to control his animal urges. With its unflattering portraits of African Americans and its valiant portrayals of the Ku Klux Klan, *The Clansman* provided a strong impetus for the forces of racial bigotry. By Dixon's own admission, the explicit purpose of *The Clansman*, and *The Leopard's Spots* (1902) before it, was to sway public opinion against the African American. As the catalyst for the hugely successful film *Birth of a Nation* Dixon's novel did just that.

Woven into the social fabric by writers whose works were fervently devoted to degrading African Americans, racial stereotypes resonated deeply in the American psyche. The myths perpetuated by the media advocated the continued exploitation and oppression of African Americans. Eminent magazines like *Harper's, Scribner's, Century*, and *The Atlantic Monthly* were replete with epithets such as "nigger," "darkey," "coon," "pickaninny," "mammy," "buck," and "yaller hussy." At the same time, reports of rape and other alleged crimes perpetrated by African Americans leapt from the inflammatory headlines of local and national newspapers. Even when the stories proved to be unfounded, the newspapers, concerned more with increasing circulation than ascertaining the truth of what they printed, never bothered with retractions.

The influx of immigrants during the latter half of the 19th and early 20th centuries also contributed to many Americans' disdain for African Americans. With the number of immigrants rapidly increasing, Americans became that much more conscious of the multiple racial populations within their midst. What aided the immigrants in their **assimilation** into American society was their positioning of themselves against members of the African American community. With the proliferation of the anti–African American sentiment they encountered from the moment of their arrival, it did not take long for the newcomers to figure out that ascension up the social ladder was best accomplished by stepping firmly on the lowest rung.

At the turn of the century, a strong opposition to racial determinism and inequality was launched by the African American intellectual community. Repudiating the oft-recited allegations of "Negro" inferiority, W.E.B. Du Bois and his contemporaries ardently insisted that African Americans had important contributions to make to American society. Du Bois's efforts to uplift members of his race made a significant impact on Alain Locke and other seminal figures of the **Harlem Renaissance**. Intent on proving that African Americans were not intellectually or culturally inferior to whites, they sought to establish a new image for their people—one that both challenged and subverted the old. Through self-confidence and self-actualization, the "New Negro" hoped to shrug off the image of subservience and submissiveness that had characterized the "Old Negro." Only then could members of the African American community hope to emancipate themselves from the chains of bigotry that continued to bind them.

Determined to reclaim the image of the African American from the mire of racist literature, writers like **Richard Wright** took pleasure in undermining the all-too-familiar stereotypes. An indictment of Stowe's classic novel, Wright's *Uncle Tom's Children* (1938) offered a stark look at racial oppression and its ravaging effects on the African American community. Published two years later, *Native Son* (1940) reinvented the character of the African American male in Bigger Thomas, a crude, violent man, who lashes out at a society that has persecuted him. As a protest writer, Wright took issue with African American writers who, in his mind, continued to pander to white audiences. In a biting critique of **Their Eyes Were Watching God** (1937), Wright rebuked **Zora Neale Hurston** for perpetuating the very stereotypes that African Americans had been struggling against their whole lives. Likening Hurston's "quaint" portrayal of "Negro" life and lore to a literary minstrel show, Wright dismissed the novel as unworthy. So obsessed was he with purging stereotyped images from African American culture that Wright failed to appreciate the intrinsic value of Hurston's elegantly written and enormously influential work.

Like their African American foremother, Zora Neale Hurston, **Toni Morrison** and **Alice Walker** also came under fire for failing to eradicate racist stereotypes from their literary works. Morrison's depiction of Cholly Breedlove in **The Bluest Eye** (1970) and Walker's portrayal of Mr. ___ in **The Color Purple** (1982) were said to reinforce the stereotype of the African American male as archetypal rapist. What was most disturbing to Morrison's and Walker's detractors was that the once "spoiler of white women" was now preying on members of his own race, and, even worse, his own family. What such critics failed to appreciate was that these male characters were themselves victims of a racist society.

Recognizing how stereotypes negatively influence people's perceptions of "otherness," the African American community continues to wage a war against reductive notions of race. Fortunately, the battle has not been at the expense of its rich literary tradition.

Further Reading

Baker, Lee D. *From Savage to Negro: Anthropology and the Construction of Race, 1896–1954.* Berkeley: University of California Press, 1998.

Franke, Astrid. *Keys to the Controversies: Stereotypes in Modern American Novels.* New York: St. Martin's Press, 1999.

Fredrickson, George M. *The Black Image in the White Mind: The Debate on Afro-American Character and Destiny, 1817–1914.* New York: Harper & Row, 1971.

Gossett, Thomas, F. *Race: The History of an Idea in America.* New York: Oxford University Press, 1997 [orig. pub. 1963].

Jordan, Winthrop D. *White over Black: American Attitudes toward the Negro, 1550–1812.* Chapel Hill: University of North Carolina Press, 1968.

Lively, Adam. *Masks: Blackness, Race and the Imagination.* Oxford: Oxford University Press, 2000.

Newman, Judie. "Slave Narratives and Neo-Slave Narratives." In *The Cambridge Companion to the Literature of the South,* edited by Sharon Monteith, 26–38. Cambridge, England: Cambridge University Press, 2013.

Toll, Robert C. *Blacking Up: The Minstrel Show in Nineteenth-Century America.* New York: Oxford University Press, 1974.

Carol Goodman

AFRICAN AMERICAN YOUNG ADULT LITERATURE

Historically, most critics of literature for young people have focused on literature by white American authors and illustrators that represents African Americans. However, whether the representations of African Americans in literature by white artists are well rounded and accurate or stereotyped and deceptive, the audience for these books is multiracial. African American young adult literature is best described as a body of literature for ages 10 through 18 produced by African American authors and illustrators that is appreciated by a multiracial audience from many age groups.

Young people have always appropriated narrative, oral and written, for their entertainment, but literature for children and young adults emerged as a distinct and independent form only in the late 18th century. This genre blossomed in England and the United States in the 19th century; it encompasses a wide range of work that appeals to all ages of young people and includes acknowledged classics of world literature, picture books, and easy-to-read stories, poetry, novels and short fiction, and the lullabies, fairy tales, fables, folk songs, and folk narratives from oral tradition. It is only since the 1960s that this genre has been studied and taught as two distinct but overlapping categories: children's literature as meant for preschool and elementary school children, and young adult literature designed for readers approximately 10 through 18 years of age.

African Americans began to publish for children during the so-called Golden Age of children's literature, when a profusion of books designed specifically for a young audience were published in the late 19th century. Despite their abundance, however, these works represented only a portion of the literate youth in America. There were few depictions of African American children in textbooks, periodicals, stories, and poems, and very few of these were unbiased. Mrs. A. E. Johnson's *Clarence and Corinne; or, God's Way* (1890) could be seen as the first African American young adult novel because its author was African American, but the book features white teenagers. More properly seen as the first African American book for young people, Paul Laurence Dunbar's *Little Brown Baby* (1895) is a germinal text in the genre. A collection of dialect poems that celebrate African American folk culture, *Little Brown Baby* is neither didactic nor religious. Intending to delight his young readers, Dunbar also placed African American people and culture in a positive light. After the turn of the century, African American young adult literature expanded with the development of an educated African American middle class. W.E.B. Du Bois's visionary magazine *The Brownies' Book* (1920–1921) offered African American children an entertainment alternative to *St. Nicholas* (1873–1945), the prevailing popular magazine for children, which featured a poem titled "Ten Little Niggers" as late as 1920. Recognizing the urgent need for characters black children could respect and emulate, Du Bois, the only black founder of the NAACP and the editor of that organization's *The Crisis* (1919–1926), experimented with "Children's Numbers," an annual children's issue of *The Crisis*. These issues were so successful that in 1920, Du Bois, along with business manager Augustus Granville Dill and literary editor Jessie Redmon Fauset, established a new magazine aimed specifically at children aged six to sixteen. Incorporating a variety of popular forms, such as fiction, folk and fairy tales, poetry, drama, biography, and photography and illustrations by African American artists, *The Brownies' Book* offered nonreligious, nondidactic entertainment that inspired self-esteem, confidence, and racial pride.

Du Bois and Dill also published two biographies for children, Elizabeth Ross Haynes's *Unsung Heroes* (1921) and Julia Henderson's *A Child's Story of Dunbar* (1921), and thereby pioneered another important form of African American young adult literature. Haynes published 22 biographies, and many of them introduced children to African Americans rarely depicted in their school texts, figures that are now well known, like **Frederick Douglass** and Harriet Tubman. Several African American writers, among them Arna Bontemps, Shirley Graham, and Carter G. Woodson, published biographies of notable African Americans. Committed to educating African American youth about and for the advancement of their race, Woodson founded the Associated Press, which continues today. He published a significant number of African American collections of poetry and folklore, readers, biographies and histories for young adults. Like Woodson, librarians, classroom teachers, and postsecondary educators have worked to ensure that African American young adult literature flourishes and reaches an audience. During her 37-year career with the New York City Public Library as a children's/young adult librarian, storyteller, and administrator, Augusta Baker (1911–1998) added appropriate books to the library's collection, encouraged authors and illustrators, and worked with publishers to get this literature produced and distributed. Following Baker, African American members of the American Library Association Glyndon Greer and Mabel McKissack established the Coretta Scott King Award for African American authors and illustrators of books for children and young adults in 1969. Also in the late 1960s, the Council on Interracial Books for Children began holding contests in order to identify and support promising young artists. These awards have garnered wide professional and public recognition for many of their winners; for example, the first winner of the Council Award, Kristin Lattany's *The Soul Brothers and Sister Lou* (1969), sold over a million copies.

With the growing support of educators, librarians, and publishers, African American young adult literature became an established and expanding tradition that reflected contemporary social and cultural consciousness. **Langston Hughes** collaborated with Bontemps on the short novel *Popo and Fifina* (1932), and Hughes's *The Dream Keeper* (1932) is a classic collection of poetry for young people. Bontemps created an extensive body of work, including biography, fiction, and poetry. The poetry anthology he edited, *Golden Slippers* (1941), includes poetry by respected authors such as Dunbar, Hughes, Countee Cullen, Claude McKay, and James Weldon Johnson. **Gwendolyn Brooks**'s poetry collection *Bronzeville Boys and Girls* (1956) was also an important book for African American young adults. These books gained wide popularity in part because of their literary quality and in part because they offer authentic portrayals of African Americans engaged in the daily life of their society and culture. They are, however, exceptions, since most African American young adult literature from the 1930s through the 1950s offered an integrationist approach to racial difference and the problems of bigotry. Jesse Jackson's *Call Me Charlie* (1945) and Lorenz Bell Graham's *South Town* (1958) and *North Town* (1965) are some of the many books about African American experiences written for young adults of all races. These novels tried to instill a social conscience that afforded awareness and tolerance of racial difference without taking into account cultural difference.

In the 1960s this "social conscience" literature promoting an ideology of assimilation gave way to more culturally conscious young adult literature that reflects African American social and cultural traditions and experiences. Since the late 1960s, African American young adult literature is most often "culturally conscious," with its focus on African American perspective and setting. Over the last 30 years, dozens of African American writers have gained wide popularity through a variety of works that present the range of African American experiences. They offer a tradition of resistance to **racism** and discrimination even as they provide aesthetic experience; they entertain and educate even as they engender racial pride. These books cover multiple forms and genres and are joined by magazines such as *Ebony Jr.* (1973–1985), which offered positive representations of African Americans in art and literature and provided a forum for young writers to publish their work, and *Footsteps*, which has been published since 1999 and includes a variety of art and text, such as reprints of Jacob Lawrence's work or an interview with baseball great Hank Aaron.

As with these illustrated magazines, illustrated texts for young adults are popular and serve a variety of purposes. Illustrations are able to depict African Americans as individuals with a rich and diverse culture. Ashley Bryan's linecut illustrations for his four volumes of African folktales and his collections of African American spirituals, *I'm Going to Sing* (1976) and *Walk Together Children* (2 vols. 1974, 1982), and Brian Pinkney's illustrations for Patricia McKissack's collection of African American folktales, *The Dark Thirty* (1992), are notable examples. Illustrated collections of African American poetry are also important in this genre, such as Romare Bearden's collages of poems by Langston Hughes in *The Block* (1995) and the many titles by Arnold Adoff, among them *All the Colors of the Race* (1982) illustrated by John Steptoe. Illustrated books provide readers of all ages with positive images of African Americans and the rich diversity of their history and culture, and offer a literary experience that can aid in the understanding and interpretation of life experience.

African American literature for young adults also plays important educational and cultural roles. The adolescent years are timely years for dealing with issues of discrimination, prejudice, and cultural differences since adolescents often perceive themselves as a "culture" apart from the mainstream. Authors of young adult fiction who deal with themes of diversity in race, religion, gender, or class can touch young readers in a profound way. Since the 1960s African American young adult fiction has grown into a vast and diverse body of work read by a wide audience. African American writers of young adult literature offer stories of the inner city and rural America, such as Walter Dean Myers's stories about Harlem in *Fallen Angels* (1989) or June Jordan's urban landscape in *His Own Where* (1972), and Mildred Taylor's continuing saga of the Logans, set in rural Mississippi. African American young adult writers set their fiction in the past, the present and the future, such as Julius Lester's slave narrative *To Be a Slave* (1968), Virginia Hamilton's realistic novel *M. C. Higgins the Great* (1974), or Octavia Butler's futuristic fantasy *The*

Parable of the Sower (1993). These writers deal with themes about and alongside racism, such as Rosa Guy's exploration of a lesbian relationship between two black teenagers in *Ruby* (1976), Sharon Bell Mathis's *Listen for the Fig Tree* (1973) about the experience of a blind girl, or Joyce Carol Thomas's short stories representing the African American teenager in the midst of various ethnic groups in *A Gathering of Flowers* (1990). Further, poets and novelists who write mainly for adults are widely read by young adults and taught in their classrooms, among them **Maya Angelou**, **Alice Walker**, **Toni Cade Bambara**, **Lorraine Hansberry**, **James Baldwin**, Lucille Clifton, and **Zora Neale Hurston**.

Young adult novels written by and about African Americans provide one method for beginning to break down barriers created through culture and **ethnicity** even as they generate respect for those cultures and ethnic backgrounds. Now more than a century old, African American young adult literature is a tradition that performs essential functions in the growth and development of its readers, and its benefits go far past simply making visible the formerly absent African American, or countering negative portrayals of African Americans with positive ones.

Further Reading

Baker, Augusta. "The Changing Image of the Black in Children's Literature." *Horn Book* 51 (February 1975): 79–88.

Bontemps, Arna. "Special Collections of Negroana." *Library Quarterly* 14 (July 1944): 187–206.

Harris, Violet J. "African American Children's Literature: The First One Hundred Years." *Journal of Negro Education* 59.4 (1990): 540–55.

Johnson-Feelings, Dianne. *The Best of "The Brownies' Book."* New York: Oxford University Press, 1996.

Johnson-Feelings, Dianne. *Telling Tales: The Pedagogy and Promise of African American Literature for Youth*. Westport, CT: Greenwood Press, 1990.

Kutenplon, Deborah, and Ellen Olmstead, eds. *Young Adult Fiction by African American Writers, 1968–1993: A Critical and Annotated Guide*. New York: Garland, 1996.

Rollins, Charlemae. "Promoting Racial Understanding through Books." *Negro American Literature Forum* 2 (1968): 71–76.

Sims, Rudine. *Shadow and Substance: Afro-American Experience in Contemporary Children's Fiction*. Urbana, IL: National Council of Teachers of English, 1982.

Tolson, Nancy. "Making Books Available: The Role of Early Libraries, Librarians, and Booksellers in the Promotion of African American Children's Literature." *African American Review* 32.1 (1998): 9–16.

Roxanne Harde

ALEXIE, SHERMAN JOSEPH, JR. (1966–)

Sherman Alexie is a poet, novelist, screenwriter, essayist, and comedian. Alexie's writing is highly regarded for its precision in representing the experience of being American Indian in the contemporary moment. In his work, Alexie scripts the confrontation of pain, poverty, and alienation alongside the ability to access laughter, humor, and comedy. Alexie's representations of the tragic through the comic, through the capacity to laugh in the midst of hostility overtly link up much of Alexie's work with narratives of resistance rooted in other ethnic cultural traditions, from the African American **blues** in *Reservation Blues* (1995) to the safe space of the basketball court in *Ten Little Indians* (2003).

Alexie was born in Spokane, Washington, to a father from the Coeur d'Alene tribe and a mother with ancestors from the Spokane, Flathead, and Colville tribes. Registered Spokane/Coeur d'Alene Indian, he was raised on the Spokane reservation in Wellpinit, Washington. As a teenager, he traveled some 15 miles off the Native American reservation to attend a white high school, before returning to a reservation that was hamstrung by chronic alcoholism, poverty, and other material effects of an institutionalized **racism**. Alexie attended college at Gonzaga and Washington State universities in eastern Washington. His mentor, poet Alex Kuo, encouraged Alexie to write his first collection of stories and poetry, *The Business of Fancydancing*, which was first published in 1992. Since leaving Washington State University in 1991, Alexie has published some 20 works of fiction, poetry, screenplays, and essays, including the critically acclaimed *The Lone Ranger and Tonto Fistfight in Heaven* (1993) and *Reservation Blues* (1995).

Clear in much of Alexie's writing is that any understanding of American Indian life must grapple with the bloody history of the American continent's conquest by white folk. Embedded in so many of Alexie's narratives are the losses experienced after Christopher Columbus's "discovery of the new world" in 1492, puritan preacher and educator Cotton Mather's sermons of "America's God-given rights" in the late 1600s, the implicit and explicit policies of Manifest Destiny in the early 19th century and the Indian wars later in that century, and the debilitating conditions of reservation life into the contemporary era. Precisely because this history of conquest—and resistance and resilience of many kinds—is embedded in his work, not only does Alexie's writing speak to other ethnic American literary traditions, but it also resonates with literatures produced in other colonized contexts, from South Asia to sub-Saharan Africa, the Caribbean, and the Spanish Americas.

The Lone Ranger and Tonto Fistfight in Heaven is Alexie's first sustained prose work. The collection of 22 short pieces follows Victor Joseph and Thomas Builds-the-Fire, two friends coming of age on the Spokane Indian Reservation. Thomas proudly embraces his Indian heritage and sees his existence as built through the sum total of stories passed down by his ancestors. His role—indeed his only means of living in the world—is to continue the storytelling tradition. Thomas states plainly, "I learned a thousand stories before I took my first thousand steps. They are all I have. It's all I can do." Victor, on the other hand, finds himself in the middle of what he sees as two opposing worlds, unable to fully identify with either. He cannot fully ground himself in a purified Indian worldview of an idealized heritage; but he is also increasingly uncomfortable in identifying with the capitalist-driven popular culture of the Brady Bunch and rock and roll. Victor's struggle to resolve this tension highlights the ways in which neither world can be purified of its opposite; rather, these forms of identification are always relational and contaminated.

Thomas and Victor reappear in Alexie's first conventional novel, *Reservation Blues*. The narrative here follows the short-lived career of an all-Indian rock band calling itself Coyote Springs. Each chapter opens with an epigraph composed of lyrics from one of the band's songs, and the content of the lyrics—grappling with familial and tribal heritage, poverty, desolation—resonate with the various themes found in the narrative. One of the comedic and fanciful elements of the narrative is found in the novel's opening. A black man appears on the reservation for the first time in its history. The man turns out to be Robert Johnson (1911–1938), the famous guitarist from the early 1900s, widely regarded as one of the musicians who gave birth to the modern blues. In the story, Johnson looks for and receives spiritual salvation in the tribe's maternal figure, Big Mom. The mixing of ethnic traditions here is expanded upon when Thomas finds Johnson's guitar and pledges to "change the world with it." Thus the African American tradition of using music to grapple with the daily terrors of enslavement and racism is imported into Indian culture.

Since 1995, along with publishing several novels and short-story collections, much of Alexie's work has been in other media. He recorded the lyrics from the *Reservation Blues* epigraphs with singer–songwriter Jim Boyd on a critically acclaimed album of the same name. In 1998, the film adaptation of *Lone Ranger and Tonto* was released and distributed across the United States. Titled *Smoke Signals* (director Chris Eyre), the film is understood to be the first major motion picture written, directed, starring, and produced by American Indians. And in 2003, Alexie directed a small video production of an adaptation of *The Business of Fancydancing*. Alexie has also moved into the realm of live performance. For four consecutive years (1998–2001), Alexie was crowned the World Heavyweight Poetry Bout champion and during these years focused some energy on the genre of stand-up comedy as well.

With Alexie's multifaceted work, one finds the importance of seeing how traditional fixed identities are enmeshed in shifting social contexts, how the comic is enmeshed in the tragic. His growing corpus of work leads a new generation of American Indian voices into wider national critical and cultural discourses. These discourses ask incisive questions about the centrality of histories of conquest, resistance, and resilience, and provide frames for representing racial and ethnic difference in new and profoundly moving ways. (*See also* Native American Novel; Native American Poetry)

Further Reading

Coulombe, Joseph L. "The Approximate Size of His Favorite Humor: Sherman Alexie's Comic Connections and Disconnections in *The Lone Ranger and Tonto Fistfight in Heaven*." *American Indian Quarterly* 26.1 (2002): 94–115.

Evans, Stephen F. "'Open Containers': Sherman Alexie's Drunken Indians." *American Indian Quarterly* 25.1 (2001): 46–72.

Lee, Robert. *The Native American Renaissance: Literary Imagination and Achievement*. Norman: University of Oklahoma Press, 2013.

Keith Feldman

ALVAREZ, JULIA (1950–)

Julia Alvarez is a Dominican American novelist and poet, born in New York City and raised there for part of her childhood as well as in the Dominican Republic. She is one of the most popular Latina authors in the United States and is the first Dominican American to have her work accepted for publication by a major publisher.

Alvarez's family arrived in the United States from the Dominican Republic before she was born and then, homesick, returned to their native land when Alvarez was only three months old. After Rafael Trujillo's dictatorship began to divide the country, making it unstable for thousands of Dominicans, Alvarez's family returned to the United States. For Alvarez's father, flight from the Dominican Republic was crucial, because he was directly involved in attempts to overthrow Trujillo's government. Upon arriving back in the United States, Alvarez found a world that was far from welcoming to new immigrants, especially those who spoke a different language or did not look "American." Many of her experiences are captured in her first novel, *How the Garcia Girls Lost Their Accents* (1991), which is based on four sisters who come from the Dominican Republic to the United States. The sisters go through life having to balance the cultural demands and expectations at home with the norms in the United States. They have difficulty appeasing their parents, particularly their father, who believes in the values of the Old World Generation (i.e., the Dominican Republic). The sisters find that while they adapt to customs in the United States, they cannot get entirely away from their father's parental grasp. Even as older women, they struggle with the demand to treat him with a respect that is consistent with the way that he would be treated in the Dominican Republic. But, of course, it is not just parent–child conflicts that help define the process of **assimilation**. Alvarez's portrayals of other conflicts that arise as a result of assimilation are brilliantly captured in her novels, poetry, and her prose.

The Woman I Kept to Myself (2004), an autobiographical collection of poems, each 30 lines long, closely examines Alvarez's life as a writer and expounds on her internal struggle to keep stories to herself as her mother would have preferred. It also discusses her own career choice of becoming a writer. Within this collection, one can find descriptions of the pain and sacrifices that she and her family had to go through in the United States as they made decisions on everything from schooling to which neighborhoods in which to live. She details, for example, the taunts from children who made fun of her in and out school when she was growing up. Likewise, in *Homecoming* (1984; 1996), she explores similar themes of how immigration often results in some type of loss, whether in the form of identity or in one's connection to their family's ancestry. Not surprisingly, she has also written extensively about this subject in her collections of essays, *Something to Declare* (1998). In the work, she discusses the influence that English and Spanish have had on her life. English opened up a new world for her, helping her understand her parents' secret conversations and eventually allowing her to become a best-selling author. Meanwhile, Spanish permitted her to become more creative in her own writing. Although she writes in English, she attributes the verbal rhythm and word choices to her knowledge of the Spanish language.

Alvarez's novels provide a dignified look at Latinas. The Garcia girls rebel, no doubt, but they rarely do so without some reasoning that the reader cannot understand. This is one of Alvarez's great gifts as a writer—she is able to depict characters as full, well-rounded individuals who do not base their decisions on hasty judgments, but rather on an oftentimes complicated cultural labyrinth. *¡Yo!* (1997) continues to portray the strong-willed character, Yolanda, who was introduced in *How the Garcia Girls Lost Their Accents*, and who provides a commentary on many issues pertaining to women. In her two historical novels, *In the Name of Salome* (2000) and *In the Time of the Butterflies* (1994), Alvarez pays homage to women who have become cultural icons in Dominican history. The former is based on the life of Salome Urena, a mulatto woman who becomes the Dominican Republic's most famous poet, and her daughter, Camila, a professor at Vassar College who upon retirement decides to leave the United States and go to Cuba. The latter novel is based on the Mirabal sisters—Las Mariposas—who become involved in clandestine efforts against the government and regime, and one day are brutally murdered. Alvarez's children's books also center on gender, though on a lesser scale. *How Tia Lola Came to (Visit) Stay* (2001) looks at the role of women in an extended family, while *The Secret Footprints* (2000) tells of a mythical female creature, Guapa, who boldly ventures into the world of human beings.

Alvarez's works have appeared in such major publications as *The New Yorker, Ploughshares, American Poetry Review*, and *The New York Times Magazine*. The New York Public Library selected Alvarez as one of 50 poets included in its exhibit, *The Hand of the Poet: Original Manuscripts by 100 Masters, from John Donne to Julia Alvarez*.

She has received numerous awards, including the Hispanic Heritage Award in Literature, the Jessica Nobel-Maxwell Poetry Prize from *American Poetry Review*, and Woman of the Year by *Latina Magazine*. She has been a finalist for the National Book Award, a Robert Frost Poetry Fellow at the Breadloaf Writers' Conference, and has been a recipient of a grant from the National Endowment for the Arts. She is a writer-in-residence at Middlebury College. (*See also* Dominican American Novel)

Further Reading

Contiello, Jessica Wells. "'That Story about the Gun': Pseudo-memory in Julia Alverez's Autobiographical Novels." *MELUS* 36.1 (2011): 83–108.

Jacques, Ben. "Julia Alvarez: Real Flights of Imagination." *Americas* 53.1 (January–February 2001): 22–29.

Rosario-Sievert, Heather. "Anxiety, Repression, and Return: The Language of Julia Alvarez." *Readerly/Writerly Texts: Essays on Literature, Literary/Textual Criticism, and Pedagogy* 4.1 (Spring–Summer 1997): 125–39.

Rosario-Sievert, Heather. "Conversation with Julia Alvarez." *Review: Latin American Literature and Arts* 54 (Spring 1997): 31–37.

Jose B. Gonzalez

AMERICAN BORN CHINESE

A young adult novel in graphic format by Gene Luen Yang, *American Born Chinese* was published in 2006; it became the first graphic novel to be nominated for a National Book Award. Though accessible in form and content, the novel has a sophisticated narrative architecture. It is made up of three seemingly unrelated parts, which converge dramatically at the end to become a unified tale.

The first part of the novel retells the hugely popular legendary Chinese story about the Monkey King. He goes to attend a dinner party hosted in the heavens for various deities but is turned away because he has no shoes. The gatekeeper tells him that though he maybe a king he is still a monkey. Humiliated by the insult and harboring profound self-hatred for his perceived inadequacy, the Monkey King returns to his kingdom and learns various martial arts to prove to others that he is more than a monkey. His new skills make him proud and the Creator punishes him by placing him under a rock for five hundred years until he is liberated from his imprisonment by a monk. The liberation comes from his healing self-acceptance of who he is.

The second segment of the novel focuses on Jin Wang, an American-born Chinese teenager who feels alienated from his peers because of his ethnic difference. His sense of nonbelonging, which is linked to his ethnicity, engenders in him a sense of self-loathing and discomfort with his Chinese heritage. His internalized racism not only leads to self-loathing but hostility toward other Asian students who remind him of his own otherness.

The final section of the novel, much of which is framed as a television show with canned laughter, deals with Danny, a blond American boy, and his Chinese cousin, Chin-kee, who comes to visit him and attend the same school. Chin-kee is a daring and risky character that Yang has created because he is an embodiment of a variety of Chinese stereotypes. He has a comically thick accent, has pigtails, and wears traditional Chinese clothes; he is academically brilliant; he is seemingly asexual yet paradoxically a sexual predator as well. Danny is embarrassed by his cousin and tries to distance himself from him. At the end the three seemingly unrelated parallel narratives of the book converge in a dramatic fashion. Danny, we realize, is actually Jin Wang; he is Wang's *Doppelganger*. Uncomfortable under his own skin, he imagines himself to be a blond all-American teenager. During a confrontation with Chin-kee, Danny knocks Chin-kee's head off and Chin-kee's true identity is revealed: he is the Monkey King in disguise. The Monkey King teaches Wang about the healing power of self-acceptance and the importance of living authentically.

An ethnic *Bildungsroman*, Yang's novel is a coming-of-age narrative; it is the story of Jin Wang's maturation, his psychological and moral development. It is also a fable, a story that includes anthropomorphized mythical figures and animals that ultimately teach a moral lesson. It is a parable about liberating self-acceptance.

Yang's creation of the character Chin-kee has caused some unease among readers. The character's name itself resembles a racist epithet; a variety of stereotypes are embedded in him. It is important note, however, that Yang comically exaggerates the stereotypes in order to collapse them. In other words, Yang appropriates and then destabilizes the stereotypes. It is also important to note that when the real identity of Chin-kee is revealed, we realize that he has merely been *performing* the stereotypes. That the stereotypes are not real but only performative is further reinforced by the fact that the panels in which Chin-kee appears are presented in the format of a sitcom. Those stereotypes, then, are nothing more than fictions, created and circulated in popular culture.

Further Reading

Davis, Rocio G. "Childhood and Ethnic Visibility in Gene Yang's *American Born Chinese.*" *Prose Studies* 35.1 (2013):7–15.

Song, Min Hyoung. "'How good it is to be a monkey': Comics, Racial Formation, and *American Born Chinese.*" *Mosaic* 43.1 (2010): 73–93.

Emmanuel S. Nelson

ANAYA, RUDOLFO (1937–)

A Mexican American novelist, essayist, and emeritus professor of English at the University of New Mexico, Anaya is renowned for his first work, *Bless Me, Ultima* (1972), a best-selling Chicano novel that remains on high school and college reading lists. *Bless Me, Ultima* was awarded the 1971 Premio Quinto Sol (Fifth Sun Award) and is the first of what Anaya considers his New Mexico trilogy, followed in 1976 by *Heart of Aztlán* and in 1979 by *Tortuga*. In addition to these and other novels, he has written essays, short stories, plays, poetry, and children's books, and edited several anthologies. In 2001, Anaya received the National Medal of Arts, one of the highest civilian awards.

The Trilogy

Bless Me, Ultima

Bless Me, Ultima is a coming-of-age novel in which the child, Antonio Márez Luna of Guadalupe, New Mexico, struggles to reconcile two conflicting heritages: the land-loving farmers on his mother's side, and the wandering *vaquero* (cowboy) men of the *llano* (plains) on his father's side. Ultima, the "last" one, comes to live with the family in the year before Antonio begins first grade in the local Anglo school. She is a *curandera*, or folk healer, also called "*la Grande*," or "the great one." Her powers to heal seem mysterious to the very people she cures; though she is deeply respected she is also somewhat feared. Ultima is an essential element in these formative years for Antonio. She teaches him how to gather and use herbs; she encourages him to respect the earth, whether farmland or *llano*; and she helps him to understand the dreams interspersed throughout the text. Indicated by italicized print, Antonio's dreams express his fears or presage the future, but they sometimes recall events that he remembers only subconsciously, such as his birth.

In the nearly two years that pass in the novel, Antonio faces four deaths, two of them violent and one of them the drowning of his own young friend Florence.

He begins school and must speak English for the first time in his young life. He learns to read and becomes successful academically, fueling his mother's hopes that he will be a priest, a learned man. He studies the catechism and receives his first communion, but he also learns the legend of the golden carp, a god-become-fish, a pagan god.

Bless Me, Ultima contains many dichotomies: Catholic/pagan; witchcraft/folk healing; farms/plains; Spanish/English; moon (Luna)/oceans (Márez, or "*mares*"). Narrated from the young Antonio's perspective, but with the retrospection of the adult Antonio, some critics have criticized the novel for a worldview that at times seems rather sophisticated for a seven-year-old boy. Nevertheless, *Bless Me, Ultima* remains an essential text of the Chicano novel of **identity**.

Heart of Aztlán

The second novel of the trilogy, *Heart of Aztlán*, portrays one year in the life of the Chávez family, comprising the father, Clemente; the mother, Adelita; and four of their five children, Jason, Benjie, Juanita, and Ana. They move from their homeland of rural Guadalupe to urban Albuquerque. The fifth son, Roberto, already lives in the Chicano neighborhood of Barelas with his wife. The loss of the family land, sold off to pay debts, initiates the difficult transition from rural to urban, traditional to modern. Clemente gets work at the railroad, replacing a dead worker, and later becomes embroiled in the struggle for workers' rights. The daughters find work to help support the family, and quickly become more independent than tradition allows, undermining Clemente's authority as the patriarch. The *pachuco* or Chicano dude identity attracts both Benjie, who joins a gang and becomes a drug seller and user, and Ana, who drops out of high school. Adelita adapts more readily to change than her husband, who temporarily loses his way, after losing his job and seeking solace in drinking.

Just as Antonio had Ultima as his guide, Clemente has a guide in Crispín, a blind poet-seer who plays a magical blue guitar. Crispín tells Clemente that only by returning to the true "heart of Aztlán" can he find himself and help his people, whether his family, his barrio neighbors, or his abused coworkers at the railroad. The myth of Aztlán is the myth of origin, a kind of Aztec Paradise. Chicanos, or Mexican Americans, trace their heritage to the comingling of the Spanish conquerors and the Aztec Indians. Aztlán is the holy land of origin for the Aztecs, who were instructed by the gods to find their homeland by searching for a cactus upon which an eagle would be mounted, holding a serpent in his beak. That same image is on the Mexican flag today, but for Clemente, Aztlán represents the true source of knowledge and identity, in contrast to the confusion of modern, capitalistic life.

Myth is central to *Heart of Aztlán*, but here myth is used to tell the story of a people, "*la raza*," or "the race." Whereas *Bless Me, Ultima* relates the development of a young boy from a first-person perspective, *Heart of Aztlán* uses a third-person narration to tell the story of the Chávez family, and relates that story to the larger socioeconomic context of many Chicanos. *Bless Me, Ultima* is an early novel of individual Chicano identity; *Heart of Aztlán*, though less popular and less well executed, is one of the earliest novels to deal with the theme of the Chicano movement, and Chicano group identity.

Tortuga

Tortuga (Turtle) completes Anaya's New Mexico trilogy, returning to the first-person narration so successful in *Bless Me, Ultima*. Tortuga is the nickname of the 16-year-old protagonist, so called because his paralyzed body is enclosed in a cast reminiscent of a turtle's shell. This may be Anaya's most autobiographical novel: as an adolescent he was paralyzed instantly when he dove into an irrigation canal and hit the bottom, fracturing two vertebrae in his neck. Like his protagonist Tortuga, Anaya suffered through months of therapy.

Tortuga's physical journey is a short one, from his home across the New Mexican desert to the Crippled Children and Orphans Hospital where he meets other crippled children. Among them is Salomón, a paralytic mute who communicates telepathically with Tortuga, serving as Tortuga's guide, instructing him through visitations to his dreams. Salomón also introduces Tortuga the paralyzed teenager to Tortuga Mountain, a "magic mountain" near the hospital, known for its holy water with healing powers. Tortuga's spiritual journey is longer and more arduous than his physical one. He must overcome his alienation and enter fully into life. Human nature and nature herself provide his path to illumination. Tortuga's experiences with the other patients in the hospital reveal the possibility of true friendship, and the mountain exercises its magic on him. According to Native American legend, Tortuga Mountain is a turtle who once swam freely in the waters that originally covered the desert. One day the waters will return and the turtle will again swim freely. Nature and myth are powerful forces in Anaya's work, and here the connection between the two Tortugas is clear. The protagonist will "swim" free, and he does.

Near the end of the novel Tortuga's identity is revealed—he is 19-year-old Benjie from *Heart of Aztlán*, the alienated adolescent who fell from a tower. The connection between the two novels is reinforced when the cured Tortuga receives a package as he prepares to leave the hospital. It is Crispín's blue guitar, willed to Benjie, suggesting that Benjie's journey of enlightenment will eventually take him to the role of seer once held by Crispín.

Other Works

Short Stories

The Silence of the Llano: Short Stories (1982) is a collection of ten short stories, three of which were first published as sections of chapters in each of the novels of the trilogy. "The Christmas Play" originated in *Bless Me, Ultima*, "El Velo-rio" ("The Wake") in *Heart of Aztlán*, and "Salomón's Story" in *Tortuga*. Of the remaining seven stories, two deal with the theme of incest and four treat the theme of myth-making.

Serafina's Stories (2004) is a Chicano version of *A Thousand and One Nights*, with Serafina, a mission-educated Pueblo Indian, as the Scheherezade whose mesmerizing tales will save her life and the lives of the Indians imprisoned with her.

Novellas
The Legend of the Llorona: A Short Novel (1984) is a retelling of the Llorona, or wailing woman, myth. *Lord of the Dawn: The Legend of Quetzalcoatl* (1987) retells the legend of Quetzalcoatl, the feathered serpent confused with the Spanish conqueror, Hernán Cortés. *Jalamanta: A Message from the Desert* (1996) follows the return of an exiled prophet who brings new wisdom to his village.

The Alburquerque Quartet
Spelled like the original name of the town, which purportedly lost the "r" because an Anglo stationmaster couldn't pronounce it, *Alburquerque* (1992) begins in April, thus beginning a seasonal cycle continued in *Zia Summer* (1995), which begins in June, and *Rio Grande Fall* (1996), which begins in October, and completed by *Shaman Winter* (1999), which begins in December. *Alburquerque* contains characters familiar to readers of Anaya's earlier novels. Benjie and Cindy from *Heart of Aztlán*, appear as adults, Benjamin Chávez and Cynthia Johnson, the biological parents of the protagonist, Abrán González. Abrán is a fair-skinned boxer who discovers he is adopted and goes on a quest to find his natural parents. Sonny Baca is a minor character in the first novel of the tetrology, but the central character of the remaining three novels, which are sometimes referred to as the Sonny Baca mysteries. *Zia Summer* deals with Sonny's detective work to uncover a conspiracy headed by Raven, leader of the Zia cult and perpetrator of ritual murders. In *Rio Grande Fall* Sonny undergoes a ritual cleansing by a *curandera* and again contends with his "dark twin," Raven. In *Shaman Winter* Sonny must again struggle against Raven, this time confined to a wheelchair after a fierce battle with his archenemy. As in his earlier novels, the action alternates between dreams, or dream time, and real time.

Travel Writing
A Chicano in China (1986) is a travel journal that recounts Anaya's month-long visit to China in 1984 and attempts to make connections between his observations of Chinese life and his own Chicano upbringing.

Children's Books
Anaya has published five children's picture books, *The Farolitos of Christmas* (1995), *Maya's Children* (1996), *Farolitos for Abuelo* (1999), *The Roadrunner's Dance* (2000), and *The Santero's Miracle: A Bilingual Story* (2004), as well as *My Land Sings: Stories from the Rio Grande* (1999), a collection of 10 stories for young adults. Like his other works, his children's books are grounded in the culture and legends of New Mexican life.

Plays
Several of Anaya's plays have been produced, but only two have been published: *Who Killed Don José?* and *Billy the Kid*. The former was first published in *New Mexico Plays* in 1989, and both were included in *The Anaya Reader* in 1995.

Poetry

The Adventures of Juan Chicaspatas (1985) is an epic poem about Aztlán and Chicano culture, and the *Elegy of the Death of César Chávez* (2000) memorializes the life of the great labor organizer, founder of the United Farm Workers union.

Edited Works

Anaya has translated, edited, and coedited an impressive number of works, attesting to his central role as a Chicano author and visionary. In 1980, he published *Cuentos: Tales from the Hispanic Southwest*, an English translation of Hispanic folktales. A coedited anthology of short stories, *Cuentos Chicanos—A Short Story Anthology*, followed in 1984. He edited *Voces, An Anthology of Nuevo Mexicano Writers* and coedited *Aztlán, Essays on the Chicano Homeland* (both 1987), and in 1989 edited *Tierra, Contemporary Short Fiction of New Mexico.*

Despite his immense and constant production of work in a range of genres, and the popularity of his Sonny Baca mysteries, Anaya's reputation remains most firmly grounded on his first novel, *Bless Me, Ultima*, and on his role as one of the founding fathers of Chicano literature. He remains one of the most vigorous and influential voices of Mexican American literature, culture, and identity.

Further Reading

Black, Debra B. "Times of Conflict: *Bless Me, Ultima* as a Novel of Acculturation." *The Bilingual Review* 25 (May–August 2000): 146–62.

Dick, Bruce, and Silvio Sirias, eds. *Conversations with Rudolfo Anaya.* Jackson: University of Mississippi Press, 1998.

Fernández Olmos, Margarite. *Rudolfo A. Anaya: A Critical Companion.* Westport, CT: Greenwood Press, 1999.

González-T., César A., ed. *Rudolfo A. Anaya: Focus on Criticism.* La Jolla, CA: Lalo Press, 1990.

Hunt, Alex. "In Search of Anaya's Carp: Mapping Ecological Consciousness and Chicano Myth." *Interdisciplinary Studies in Literature and Environment* 12.2 (2005): 179–206.

Linda Ledford-Miller

ANGELOU, MAYA (1928–2014)

Maya Angelou was an African American author, autobiographer, poet, playwright, editor, and educator. Originally named Marguerite Johnson, she is particularly well known for her autobiographical novels, which deal with the complexities of racial, economic, and sexual oppression. She wrote numerous volumes of poetry and received national honor when she read her poem *On the Pulse of Morning* at the inauguration of President Bill Clinton in 1993. Angelou enjoyed a multifaceted career and worked as a dancer, singer, actress, director, producer, feminist, political activist, talk-show guest, and lecturer. She also received many awards and honorary degrees for her outstanding contributions.

Maya Angelou, 1993. (AP Photo/Mark Lennihan)

Angelou was born on April 4, 1928, in St. Louis, Missouri, and was the daughter of Bailey Johnson and Vivian Baxter. She lived in California until the divorce of her parents and was then sent to live with her paternal grandparents in Stamps, Arkansas. While in Arkansas, she experienced the trials of discrimination and segregation in the pre–civil rights South, but she also witnessed the strength and fortitude of the black community. After several years, Angelou moved to St. Louis where she lived with her mother's family. She was raped by her mother's boyfriend when still just a young girl, and she dealt with the subsequent beating to death of her perpetrator by becoming mute. She eventually returned to live with her grandparents in Arkansas and developed a passion for reading. In 1940, Angelou moved with her mother to San Francisco where she graduated from high school and gave birth as an unwed mother to her son, Guy Johnson. She married Tosh Angelos in 1952 and was divorced soon after. Angelou took private music lessons; studied dance with Martha Graham, Pearl Primus, and Ann Halprin; and studied drama with Frank Silvera and Gene Frankel. During the 1950s, as her career began to flourish, Angelou performed in Off Broadway plays such as *Calypso Heatwave* in 1957 and Jean Genet's *The Blacks* in 1960. In collaboration with Godfrey Cambridge, she produced, directed, and performed in *Cabaret for Freedom* (1960). She was also nominated for an Emmy Award for best supporting actress for her role in the television adaptation of **Alex Haley**'s *Roots*.

Angelou was involved as a leader and activist. During the 1960s, she served as northern coordinator for the Southern Christian Leadership Conference, a responsibility she was encouraged to accept by **Martin Luther King Jr**. Angelou married Vusumzi Make, a civil rights activist, and the couple lived in Cairo where Angelou was an associate editor of the *Arab Observer*. After her relationship with Make dissolved, Angelou moved to Ghana, where she worked as an assistant administrator and teacher at the School of Music and Drama at the University of Ghana and as a feature editor of the *African Review*. Angelou returned to the United States where she was appointed by President Gerald Ford to work on the American Revolution Bicentennial Council. She also received the appointment by President Jimmy Carter to serve on the National Commission on the Observance of International Women's Year. During the 1970s, she married the British writer Paul Du Feu, but this union also ended in divorce. In 1981, she became the first Reynolds Professor of American Studies at Wake Forest University in North Carolina, which is a lifetime position.

Angelou published her first autobiography, **I Know Why the Caged Bird Sings**, in 1970, and wrote five subsequent books on her life. *I Know Why the Caged Bird Sings* deals with her childhood, the rape, her mute period, the many moves she experienced during her younger years, and the birth of her child. Her intense yet lyrical story presents issues regarding gender, **race**, class, power, poverty, sexuality, education, and familial relationships. Her second autobiography, *Gather Together in My Name* (1974), covers the next segment of her life when she works at miscellaneous jobs, such as a cook, cocktail waitress, brothel owner, and dancer. During this dark period in her existence, she experiments with drugs, deals with the kidnapping of her son by a babysitter, and struggles to find meaning in life. In the third addition to her autobiography, *Singin' and Swingin' and Gettin' Merry like Christmas* (1976), Angelou is torn between the responsibility of motherhood and the desire to further her career. She decides to leave her son in the care of her mother, Vivian Baxter, while she goes on a multination tour with *Porgy and Bess*. Throughout the text, the universal theme of motherhood versus career haunts her as she experiences feelings of guilt for not being home with her son. In *The Heart of a Woman* (1981), the fourth autobiography, Angelou continues to fret over her role as a mother. Although her son is now living with her, she continues to leave him on occasion for various opportunities to work. One of the intense passages in the text deals with the trauma of seeing her unconscious son after he has been injured in a car accident. In the fifth autobiography, *All God's Children Need Traveling Shoes* (1986), the theme of motherhood continues, but another important focus is that of Africa, the home of her ancestors. Angelou acquires a stronger sense of personal identity when she realizes that some of her own traditions correlate with those of Africans. Her connection with Africa helps her to better understand and appreciate her role as a mother. In the final and sixth autobiography to date, *A Song Flung Up to Heaven* (2002), Angelou discusses her return to the United States after having lived many years in Africa. She writes of her association with historical figures such as Malcolm X and Martin Luther King Jr., and with icons such as **James Baldwin**. She also tells of beginning to write *I Know Why the Caged Bird Sings*, and says: "I thought if I wrote a book, I would have to examine the quality in the human spirit that continues to rise despite the slings and arrows of outrageous fortune" (212). Angelou's autobiographies draw the reader into the deep pain and struggle of her existence. They chronicle her development as a human being, her familial and personal relationships, and the blossoming of her career. These works also contribute substantially to both black autobiographical tradition and serial autobiography.

Many of Angelou's books of poetry include *Just Give Me a Cool Drink of Water 'fore I Diiie* (1971), *Oh Pray My Wings Are Gonna Fit Me Well* (1975), *And Still I Rise* (1978), *Shaker, Why Don't You Sing* (1983), *Now Sheba Sings the Song* (1987), *I Shall Not Be Moved* (1990), *On the Pulse of Morning* (1993), *The Complete Collected Poems of Maya Angelou* (1994), *Phenomenal Woman: Four Poems for Women* (1995), *A Brave and Startling Truth* (1995), and *From a Black Woman to a Black Man* (1995). Her poetry emerges as a response to a difficult and challenging childhood and provides lessons and wisdom gained during her life of struggle and hardship. She incorporates simple, short lines to make bold statements on social and political issues. In many poems there is a theme of survival and of overcoming oppressive and seemingly overwhelming obstacles. There is also a sense of hope, optimism, and encouragement regarding the possibilities and potential of both men and women on this earth and their ultimate capacity to live together in harmony.

Some of Angelou's other works include plays, screenplays, essays, and children's books. Among her plays are *Cabaret for Freedom, The Least of These* (1966), *Ajax* (1974), and *And Still I Rise* (1976). Her screenplays include *Georgia, Georgia* (1972), for which she also wrote the musical score, and *All Day Long* (1974). Her personal essays can be found in *Wouldn't Take Nothing for my Journey Now* (1993) and *Even the Stars Look Lonesome* (1997). Some of her children's books include *Life Doesn't Frighten Me* (1993), *My Painted House, My Friendly Chicken and Me* (1994), and *Kofi and His Magic* (1996).

Angelou met obstacles and challenges with perseverance and dignity. Rather than allowing negative and difficult trials to weigh her down, she has, on the contrary, risen and met them head on. The theme of survival is prevalent in her work, as are concerns for **identity**, displacement, motherhood, oppression, and imprisonment.

In her writing, she continues the black tradition of storytelling, and she does so with honesty and frankness combined with wisdom, lyricism, and humor. In addition, her narratives follow the structure of a journey in which she moves from place to place in pursuit of self-understanding, knowledge, and self-identity. During the course of her life, she successfully drew upon personal experience, both negative and positive, and channeled it in creative output that has enlightened, encouraged, and enriched society. (*See also* African American Autobiography)

Further Reading

Bloom, Harold, ed. *Maya Angelou*. Philadelphia: Chelsea, 2002.

Braxton, Joanne M., ed. *I Know Why the Caged Bird Sings: A Casebook*. New York: Oxford University Press, 1999.

Jaquin, Eileen O. "Maya Angelou." In *African American Autobiographers: A Sourcebook*, edited by Emmanuel S. Nelson, 10–28. Westport, CT: Greenwood Press, 2002.

Lupton, Mary Jane. *Maya Angelou: A Critical Companion*. Westport, CT: Greenwood Press, 1998

Mickle, Mildred, ed. *I Know Why the Caged Bird Sings by Maya Angelou*. Pasadena, CA: Salem, 2010.

Moore, Lucinda. "A Conversation with Maya Angelou at 75." *Smithsonian* 34.1 (April 2003): 96–99.

Deborah Weagel

ARAB AMERICAN AUTOBIOGRAPHY

In the Arab world, the autobiography genre has been traditionally popular, especially those of esteemed writers such as Taha Hussein, author of the three-part autobiography *The Days* (1926) and Fadwa Tuqan, author of *A Mountainous Journey* (1985). Among Arab American writers, the genre is still developing and is often marked by its stretch of poetic license, illustrated by the fact that the authors rarely tell their story directly, but opt for a more creative narrative and chronology.

Furthermore, the political scene in the last two decades can be seen as a primary force behind the very recent emergence of this genre in Arab American literature in the 1990s. Undoubtedly, the American involvement in the Arab-Israeli crisis, especially in the 1987 and 2000 Intifadas, and in the 1991 and 2003 Gulf wars in Iraq, created a need among Arab American writers to discuss and explain their lives to an American audience that was increasingly curious.

Leila Ahmed's *A Border Passage* (1999) is probably the most traditional Arab American autobiography published to date. Narrated in a direct, chronological style, the book traces Ahmed's life from her childhood in Cairo to her current role as a professor and a writer in the United States. She weaves her personal experiences with intersecting world and national events, and she highlights the ways in which her journeys and experiences in the Middle East, in Europe, and in the United States shaped her **identity**. She concludes that the world has constructed images of Arabs that are false and misleading; she believes that, as a woman and as a Muslim, she can elucidate and clarify the Arab identity and mentality.

The most controversial autobiography published to date has been Edward Said's *Out of Place* (1999) in which the now-deceased Columbia University professor recounts his childhood in Palestine and his family's exile to Cairo, Egypt, after 1948, the year that hearkened the creation of the state of Israel. The title of Said's book succinctly captures the theme popular among Arab American memoirists, the feeling of being a perpetual outsider in one's adopted homeland. In *Out of Place*,

Said, a professor of literature and the author of several seminal works of literary criticism and political analysis such as *Orientalism* (1978) and *The Question of Palestine* (1979), does not cover his entire life, nor even half of it. Instead, he ends the memoir at the point where he is a very young man, focusing mainly on his parents and childhood memories.

He discusses the consciousness of an exile. The person who finds himself in exile will struggle all his life to reconcile his identity, but Said's case is complicated further by the controversy caused in identifying himself as a Palestinian. Because the West Bank and Gaza Strip are Israeli-occupied territories and the crux of the Palestinian-Israeli conflict, this is interpreted as a political statement and not simply a statement of fact.

Out of Place was itself the crux of a controversy, the result of an essay titled "'My Beautiful Old House' and Other Fabrications by Edward Said" by Justus Reid Weiner (*Commentary*, September 1999). Weiner claimed to have spent several years investigating and researching Said's past, and he concluded, in his essay, that Said had crafted a public image as a refugee from Palestine, although he came from a privileged background and lived among Cairo's elite as a young man. Indeed, Weiner even questioned Said's Palestinian roots. The overall point of the essay, as interpreted by many in the Arab American academic and literary community, was to cast doubt upon the portrayal of Palestinians as exiles, as people displaced from their homeland—a central tenet of the Palestinian American identity, which is the Palestinian experience of suffering. As such, many academics and writers leapt to Said's defense, publishing articles that emphasized the right of Palestinians to assert this identity, but the impact was still deeply felt: that the Arab identity is, essentially, a political one because of the unrest in the region.

Fay Afaf Kanafani's autobiography also tells the story of how Palestinian life was impacted in 1948, but from a woman's perspective. *Nadia, Captive of Hope: Memoir of an Arab Woman* (1999) covers Kanafani's difficult childhood in Beirut, Lebanon, including years of sexual abuse at the hands of her own father and the deafening silence of her mother. In fact, the memories were so painful that Kanafani took creative license and chose to write about herself under the name of Nadia—a way to create some distance from these memories in order to recount them truthfully and completely.

Kanafani's memoir is significant because she recounts her emerging awareness of feminism. In the memoir, as unjust actions are taken against her, Nadia rebels from an inner sense of empowerment. For example, she was forced into a marriage with a cousin, and moved to Palestine during the tumultuous 1930s and 1940s; in protest, she refused to consummate the marriage. She was eventually raped by her husband, but the crime solidified her understanding of male–female relationships and inequities.

Nadia, Captive of Hope is considered remarkable because of the fact that Kanafani's feminism was not adopted by interactions with other feminists, especially Western feminists. Middle Eastern feminists hear the common accusation that they are being misled or deceived by Western feminist ideology and that Middle Eastern women should resist feminism as another form of western colonialism. However,

Kanafani's autobiography is a testament to the insistence by Middle Eastern women's rights activists that their feminism is not imported, but arose from the real need to address the flaws of patriarchal society.

Elmaz Abinader's book *Children of the Roojme: A Family's Journey from Lebanon* (1991) is an unusual, but highly artistic, family autobiography. Considered Abinader's seminal work, *Children of the Roojme* traces the history of the Abinader family and their immigration from the Middle East to the United States. The book traces the lives of four generations of her family and offers detailed, rich descriptions of life in Lebanon and the necessary **assimilation** into the culture of the United States. Furthermore, she details the sorrows endured by the Lebanese who suffered through the various wars in the region, poverty, and other crises. It is important for Abinader to paint a portrait of life in the Middle East, to give her readers a sense of the background and experiences of immigrants before they arrive on American shores.

The most nontraditional autobiography to be penned to date by an Arab American writer is *Drops of This Story* (1996), by Palestinian American poet Suheir Hammad. Hammad first made her appearance on the literary scene with a poetry collection, *Born Palestinian, Born Black* (1996), in which the poet, who was born in a Palestinian refugee camp and moved to New York at the age of five, identified her voice with those of African American and other ethnic writers. In her memoir, Hammad uses a fusion style of Arab themes and hip-hop tone, making her one of the first Arab American writers to make a link to other ethnic literary and musical movements. Her writing style is terse and brief with powerful statements delivered in a no-nonsense style. She reflects on her childhood growing up in a New York neighborhood. She also discusses how difficult it was to form and develop the Arab American identity, as well as the specific challenges of being a Palestinian in the United States.

Many of autobiographies by Arab American writers, including those by Said, Ahmed, Kanafani, and even Abinader, focus on the lives of Arabs in the Middle East, then recount the shock of immigration and the ensuing shifts in cultural perspective. Hammad's *Drops of This Story* is one of the first to focus on Arab American life growing up in the United States and the necessary negotiations made between two cultures. (*See also* Arab American Stereotypes)

Further Reading

Armstrong, Paul. "Being 'Out of Place': Edward W. Said and the Contradictions of Cultural Differences." *Modern Language Quarterly* 64.1 (March 2003): 97.

Cherif, Salwa Essayah. "Arab American Literature: Gendered Memory in Abinader and Abu-Jaber." *MELUS* (Winter 2003): 207–28.

Cockburn, Alexander. "Defending the Integrity of Edward Said." *Los Angeles Times* (August 29, 1999): A5.

Crossette, Barbara. "Out of Egypt, A Border Passage." *Migration World Magazine* 28.3 (March 2000): 50.

Fleischmann, Ellen. "Women: *Nadia: Captive of Hope. Memoir of an Arab Woman*." *Middle East Journal* 54.2 (Spring 2000): 325.

Handal, Nathalie. "Drops of Suheir Hammad: A Talk with a Palestinian Poet Born Black." *Al Jadid* 3.20 (Summer 1997): 19.

Hassan, Wail. "Arab-American Autobiography and the Reinvention of Identity: Two Egyptian Negotiations." [Special Issue: *The Language of the Self: Autobiographies and Testimonies*] *Alif* 22 (2002).

Susan Muaddi Darraj

ARAB AMERICAN NOVEL

The novel genre, along with that of poetry, has been highly popular among Arab American writers. However, many critics agree that there is not yet an established canon of Arab American novels, although such works are starting now to amass and distinguish themselves in theme and style. Most of the first novels by Arab American authors tend to be autobiographical either in whole or in part, as are most early novels. Among the themes that are explored in Arab American novels, **identity** is by far the most common. Characters in the novels struggle with a hyphenated identity, attempting to reconcile both their Arab and American cultures. It is commonly agreed that the Arab American identity, more so than the identities of African American, Latino/a, Asian American, and others, is not just a social and cultural construct, but an intensely political one as well.

Some novels have been written in Arabic, by authors living in America, and then translated into English; some are even written in English and then translated into Arabic for Middle Eastern audiences; most, however, are written in English primarily for the English-speaking audience. Some of these novels have found their way into the American mainstream, such as those penned by Diana Abu Jaber, Rabih Alameddine, and Naomi Shihab Nye.

It is generally acknowledged that the first Arab American novel is *The Book of Khalid* (1911) by Ameen Rihani, widely regarded as the father of Arab American literature. Born in 1876 in Lebanon, Rihani emigrated to the United States when he was only 12 years old with his father and his uncle. He attended a New York school but was pulled out so that he could help the family business, namely keeping records and writing letters and transactions in English, the basics of which he had mastered by that point. Without a formal education, Rihani turned to English books, and among his favorite writers were William Shakespeare, Percy Shelley, and Victor Hugo. After several years, he attended law school, but dropped out due to his poor health; his father sent him to Lebanon to regain his health. In Lebanon, Rihani studied Arab literature and soon became fluently bilingual. In this sense, he was truly an Arab American writer, one who read and wrote in both languages. Rihani lived in an age marked by orientalism (an image, first definitely described by Edward Said, of the Arab world by the West that viewed the Arab and Muslim world as inferior in terms of religion, civilization, and culture). Rihani considered it part of his mission to explain the values of Arab culture and literature to his Western readers; thus, he was aware, as his successors would be, of the political facet of the Arab American identity. He returned to New York in 1899 but continued to travel back and forth between America and the Middle East for the rest of his life.

The Book of Khalid is the first novel to be written by an Arab or by an American of Arab descent in English. It is considered remarkable not for its artistic merit, but rather for its scope: Largely autobiographical, the novel describes the trials of its protagonist, a young man named Khalid, who seeks his identity between East and West. The novel is infused with philosophical and political undertones, making reference to Islam, the Baha'i faith, Christianity, capitalism, life in the Arab world, and related themes. The novel inspired many other Arab American writers of his generation, as well as those who succeeded him. *Jahan* (1917) is the title of another novel Rihani wrote in English, and he also authored several works of fiction in Arabic.

Etel Adnan's *Sitt Marie Rose* (1978) is another novel that gained widespread popular recognition, propelling the Lebanese American writer to the crest of the American literary scene. Like Rihani, Adnan's identity is complex and consists of more than one culture; she grew up in Lebanon, speaking French, English, and Arabic. Her main language, however, was French, and she has written about the fact that she regrets not being able to compose in Arabic. She emigrated to the United States to pursue her college education, settling in California. Like the writing of Rihani and other Arab Americans, Adnan's work has a pronounced political undertone; she also incorporates feminist themes into her novel, emphasizing the way in which women especially suffer due to political games and wars.

Sitt Marie Rose, which focuses on the tragedy of the Lebanese civil war, was translated into six languages. It focuses on Sitt Marie Rose, a young Christian Lebanese teacher. During the Lebanese civil war, she sympathizes with the many Palestinian refugees who live in Lebanon, feeling connected to them and their plight. Her sympathies, however, are viewed as traitorous and she is kidnapped and executed, in a brutal, vicious manner, before her students. *Sitt Marie Rose* demonstrates the brutality of war in general while specifically exploring the fate of women in a patriarchal society as well as the ways in which the Israeli-Palestinian crisis has affected the Middle East.

Naomi Shihab Nye's *Habibi* (1997) also focuses on the Israeli-Palestinian crisis, but from a very different perspective. *Habibi* is widely acknowledged as the first young adult novel by an Arab American novelist and depicts the crisis from the point of view of a 14-year-old Palestinian American girl. Liyana Abboud, the novel's young protagonist, moves to Jerusalem for one year with her Palestinian father, her American mother, and her younger brother. There she learns about Palestinian culture and society and comes to love it; her Palestinian grandmother, whom she addresses as Sitti, proves to be a warm and wise mentor for the young teenager. Liyana also begins to understand the Israeli-Palestinian conflict when she befriends and falls in love with Omer, a Jewish boy. The novel is extraordinary, handling difficult scenes of Israeli-Palestinian violence with grace and skill, highlighting the common humanity that persists in the face of hatred. Nye, one of the most widely recognized and prolific Arab American writers, is herself the daughter of a

Palestinian father and an American mother who moved to Jerusalem for one year when she was a teenager. *Habibi* is partly autobiographical and it also exemplifies the manner in which politics fundamentally tends to inform the themes of many Arab American novels.

Rabih Alameddine's *Koolaids: The Art of War* (1999) also deals with politics, although it tackles both Arab and American politics—specifically, the Lebanese civil war and the American AIDS epidemic. The two events are compared because both are senseless, result in the deaths of thousands of innocents, and force people to contemplate their mortality. Alameddine, a painter and artist, tackles two very difficult subjects in a novel whose form is experimental and new for Arab American literature, especially in its adoption of homosexuality as a major theme. The protagonist, Mohamad, arrives in the United States as a teenager; he lives with an uncle, and is supposed to be finishing his studies, but instead decides to become an artist—a decision his father rejects. In defiance, Mohamad remains in the United States, where he is able pursue his chosen profession. He contracts the AIDS virus and eventually dies. But even when he is seriously ill his parents refuse to associate with him; Mohamad's sense of loss of his family, complicated by the deaths of family members in the Lebanese civil war, is overwhelming, finding expression in his art and in his dreams.

Alameddine, who was born in Jordan but lived in Kuwait and Lebanon, is a painter as well as a writer. His second novel, *I, the Divine: A Novel in First Chapters* (2001), features a female protagonist, Sarah Nour El-Din, who wants to write the story of her life but cannot begin. Thus, Alameddine pens various drafts of her first chapters, which the reader pieces together to form a more complete picture of Sarah's troubled life. The novel is exceptional in its form and in its male author's depiction of a convincing female protagonist.

Diana Abu Jaber's *Arabian Jazz* (1993) is also controversial because it offers a humorous look at the crisis of identity many young Arab Americans feel: her main character, Jemora Ramoud (Jem), is the daughter of a Jordanian father and an American mother. Her mother, however, died when Jem and her sister were young, and they were raised by Matussem, their father, who can only express his grief by playing in his **jazz** band. Jem, who is approaching her 30th birthday, feels unsatisfied with her life and struggles to reconcile her identity. Is she an American or an Arab? Should she marry or pursue a career? Should she move to Jordan and seek her identity there or remain in the United States with her family? A visit by a distant cousin, who has grappled with similar issues, helps Jem to realize that home is wherever she chooses to spend her life, and that one is not born with an identity, but must craft it.

Arab American literature in general, the novel in particular, has elicited considerable attention from mainstream publishers in the last decade and especially after the terrorist attacks on the World Trade Center on September 11, 2001. The ensuing war with Iraq that began in March 2003 has also sparked curiosity about Arab civilization at large as well as the culture and lives of Arab Americans. It is to be expected that the political environment, both national and global, will continue to shape Arab American art.

Further Reading

Castro, Joy. "Nomad, Switchboard, Poet: Naomi Shihab Nye's Multicultural Literature for Young Readers: An Interview." *MELUS* 27.2 (Summer 2002): 225–28.

Gabriel, Judith. "Emergence of a Genre: Reviewing Arab American Writers." *Al-Jadid: A Review and Record of Arab Culture and Arts* 7 (Winter 2001): 4–7.

Kohl, Martina. *Arab American Literature and Culture.* Heidelberg, Germany: Universitatsverlog, 2012.

Susan Muaddi Darraj

ARAB AMERICAN STEREOTYPES

By repeatedly disallowing their subjection to negative stereotypes, various ethnic communities, including African Americans, Jewish Americans, and Italian Americans, among others, have succeeded in drastically curtailing the racial and ethnic stereotypes that minority groups have historically faced in the United States. Arab Americans, however, remain somehow outside such antiracist awareness and consequently continue to be subjected to increasing levels of derogatory stereotypes. Accepted by the U.S. public as true, these stereotypes engender feelings of hate toward Arabs living in the United States (both as citizens and otherwise) as well as those living in the Arab world. Arabs are often characterized as cheats, liars, dangerous terrorists, and irrational fanatics, and these stereotypes, disseminated widely by the media and other cultural productions, enter into higher levels of circulation in the United States at moments of national crisis, examples of which include the attacks of September 11, 2001, and the subsequent invasions of Afghanistan and Iraq. Even though the inconsistency in the naturalization of the first wave of Arab immigrants in the early 20th century culminated in the U.S. Census Bureau classifying Arab Americans as white or Caucasian, this group's racial categorization is not stable. Deeply affected by U.S. foreign policy in the Middle East (examples of which include the 1967 Arab-Israeli war and the 1973 oil embargo), Arab Americans still occupy an ambiguous position in terms of **race** and citizenship.

Negative portrayals of Arab Americans have their roots in 18th- and 19th-century European depictions of the Orient, by which the East becomes "the other," replete with subjugated women living in harems and mysterious and romanticized settings harboring a "heathen" population. Such images are handled at length by Palestinian American critic Edward Said in his groundbreaking book *Orientalism* (1978), which questions the foundations upon which the West has constructed its representation of the East as other. This Western outlook, Said believes, is propagated in the current cultural stereotyping of, and prejudice against, Arabs generally and Muslim Arabs particularly, in the West.

Drawing on a repertoire of stereotypes revolving around fanatic killers, oil-rich sheikhs, and an unfamiliar religion set against a desert background, cultural representations of Arabs and Arab Americans disregard the diversity of Arab **identity**, whether in cultural, religious, ethnic, or national aspects. The dangerous confluence of Arab and Muslim identities in the U.S. national consciousness (whereby all Muslims are Arab and all Arabs are Muslim) is one example of the extremely limited and simplistic understanding of Arab and Arab American identity. Statistics show that the majority of the Arab American population is Christian and that the majority of Muslims worldwide are located in Indonesia, India, and Malaysia (Shaheen 3, 4).

Starting in 1967 with the Association of Arab-American University Graduates (AAUG), several organizations have been founded by Arab Americans to promote a better understanding of their community and to fight against Arab American stereotypes and discrimination. Such organizations include the National Association of Arab Americans (NAAA), the American-Arab Anti-Discrimination Committee (ADC), and the Arab American Institute (AAI), formed in 1972, 1980, and 1985, respectively. By focusing on issues affecting the representation and the civil rights of Arab Americans, such as negative stereotypes permeating the media, racial profiling, and hate crimes, these groups ensure that Arab Americans retain an important role in their self-representation as U.S. citizens.

Arab American writers repeatedly address their individual and communal subjection to negative stereotypes that not only relegate them to the margins of American society, but also render them invisible. A host of Arab American writers, such as Joanna Kadi, Lisa Suhair Majaj, and Nada Elia, has focused on this issue of invisibility, noting the manner in which it permeates the various areas of Arab American identity, encompassing the social, cultural, and literary arenas. Poetic challenges to the negative stereotyping of Arab Americans are exemplified in the works of Suheir Hammad and Mohja Kahf, who arm themselves with a distinct ethnic, religious, and racial identity that questions the ambiguity inherent in the current racial categorization of Arab Americans. By featuring in their work the derogatory labels and negative stereotypes targeting Arab Americans, other writers such as Lawrence Joseph and Diana Abu Jaber call attention to the false assumptions upon which such stereotypes are constructed, thus reinforcing the need for their eradication. Barbara Nimri Aziz, Arab American journalist and cofounder of the Radius of Arab American Writers Inc., emphasizes the importance of self-representation through writing, thus calling for Arab Americans to emulate other ethnic communities such as Italian Americans, whose writers' association had as one of its doctrines: "Write or be written." Such an act is elemental for Arab Americans because, as Aziz states, "the histories we learn in school, the tales we hear in the street, the claims made on our behalf, all somehow miss the point. Or simply get it wrong. We are really not how others write us. At best we are invisible. What we witnessed and were taught was not and is not our heritage" (xii).

Further Reading

Aziz, Barbara Nimri. "Foreword." In *Scheherazade's Legacy: Arab and Arab American Women on Writing*, edited by Susan Muaddi Darraj, xi–xv. Westport, CT: Praeger, 2004.

Elia, Nada. "The 'White' Sheep of the Family: But *Bleaching* Is like Starvation." In *This Bridge We Call Home: Radical Visions for Transformation*, edited by Gloria E. Anzaldúa and Analouise Keating, 223–31. New York: Routledge, 2002.

Ghareeb, Edmund. *Split Vision: The Portrayal of Arabs in the American Media*. Washington, DC: The American-Arab Affairs Council, 1983.

Hammad, Suheir. *Born Palestinian, Born Black*. London: Writers & Readers, 1996.

Kadi, Joanna, ed. *Food for Our Grandmothers: Writings by Arab-American and Arab-Canadian Feminists*. Boston: South End Press, 1994.

Majaj, Lisa Suhair. "Arab-Americans and the Meanings of Race." In *Postcolonial Theory and the United States: Race, Ethnicity, and Literature*, edited by Amritjit Singh and Peter Schmidt, 320–37. Jackson: University Press of Mississippi, 2000.

McCarus, Ernest, ed. *The Development of Arab-American Identity*. Ann Arbor: University of Michigan Press, 1994.

Shaheen, Jack G. *Reel Bad Arabs: How Hollywood Vilifies a People*. New York: Olive Branch Press, 2001.

Terry, Janice J. *Mistaken Identity: Arab Stereotypes in Popular Writing*. Washington, DC: The American-Arab Affairs Council, 1985.

Carol Fadda-Conrey

ASSIMILATION

Broadly defined as the conformity of a minority or immigrant group to the customs and attitudes of the dominant culture, assimilation is a common theme in American literature. While often implicating ethnic or cultural **identity**, assimilation may also refer to other differences from the dominant group, such as religion, language, or sexuality. It is a process that varies depending upon the community in question, the historical moment, and differences *within* groups such as generation, gender, and class, for example. We can view assimilation positively as a means for cultural integration despite ethnic differences from the majority or more negatively as the rejection of one's ethnic community and ancestry through complete absorption into the prevailing culture. It may be most helpful to consider assimilation as collections of choices made by minority groups within contexts delimited by national, regional, and local authority, as well as by popular sentiment. Assimilation in American literary history has meant hope and disappointment, accommodation and resistance, and gratitude and rage in complex relationship to one another.

Official policy and public opinion regarding the assimilability of different ethnic groups in the United States has been inconsistent, resulting in unique symbology depending upon the historical circumstances and the ethnic groups in question. During World War I, for example, there were heightened tendencies to view new immigrants as suspicious foreigners due to fears of divided loyalties for European Americans, resulting in policies intended to ensure conformity rather than ones that might encourage unique identities for different groups. In *Theories of Ethnicity: A Classical Reader* (1996), Werner Sollers refers to this attitude toward assimilation, prevalent in American policy especially from 1914 to 1918, as "Anglo-conformity." In fact, institutions such as schools, health care providers, and law enforcement became agents of assimilation to American culture, or "Americanization."

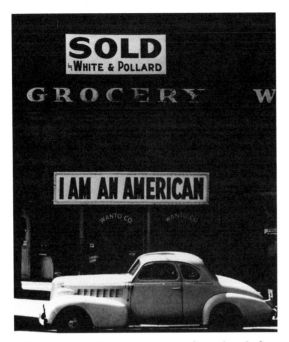

A Japanese American grocery store front days before the internment. (Corbis)

The short-lived experiments in Americanization from this period included many ethnic groups, and, in 1913, the Commission of Immigration and Housing began to develop strategies for transforming immigrant values and to ease the integration of such groups as Mexican American women into labor markets in places like California.

In response, writers such as Norwegian American Waldemar Ager, in published essays in his journal *Kvartalskrift* (1916–1920), and Jewish American Abraham Cahan, particularly in the novel *The Rise of David Levinsky* (1917), became among the first to criticize the expectation that immigrants would discard their cultural histories and practices in favor of new American identities. In later 20th-century writing published by Latin American and pan-Caribbean authors, it is clear that, even when assimilation projects are not so systematic as in this earlier period, almost all aspects of immigrants' cultural practices come under scrutiny, including accents and linguistic practices, culinary habits, and work ethics. In this regard, members of other, supposedly "model" minority groups have ironically been praised for achieving the American dream through hard work and have been used as examples to chastise other minorities who have not experienced upward mobility in the same way. South Asian American writers, including **Bharati Mukherjee** in her novel *Jasmine* (1989), examine the "benefits" of such thinking for immigrants from countries like India, who may seem assimilable because they are considered unthreatening and perhaps also because they fulfill exotic fantasies of the "East."

In the context of historical differences in perceptions of immigrants and racial minority groups, writers from many different backgrounds in the United States have grappled with the questions of if, how much, and with what consequences do immigrants assimilate to the cultural expectations of governing forces, even British immigrants in the 18th and 19th centuries. For example, John Harrower, whose diary (1773–1776) is included in Tom Dublin's *Immigrant Voices: New Lives in America 1773–1986* (1993), describes his transition from a sojourner—an indentured servant who emigrated to the United States because of dire poverty—to a man with grander aspirations and the aim of his wife becoming a true Virginian lady by following him across the ocean. Immigrants like Harrower had hope that they might improve their lots in life and be integrated into the preexisting societies of British colonialists; we must not forget, however, that they faced discrimination as newcomers and that their individual experiences were affected by differing gender roles that generally ascribed greater authority and mobility to men than women.

Through marriage and other familial connections, British immigrant women *might* yet have had the opportunity of assimilating to mainstream culture, but this was not often the case for the indigenous groups already present when Europeans settled the continent. Indeed, Native Americans have long been the subjects of heated disagreement among members of Congress and other governmental groups attempting to ascertain their place in the American nation. While colonial policies such as the Northwest Ordinance of 1787 guaranteed "decent" treatment of Indians, subsequent legislation such as the Indian Removal Act of 1830 and the creation of reservations in the 1870s and 1880s resulted in coercion, often military in nature, to restructure tribal patterns to favor the interests of whites. Literary depictions of Native American histories include accounts of forcible assimilation to Western education, religion and spirituality, and mores about land use and ownership, to name a few. In 1936, D'Arcy McNickle, an adopted member of the Flathead tribe and a man of Cree and white parentage, published *The Surrounded*, revealing the pressures to assimilate to white America that alienated Native Americans from their own communities.

Themes in D'Arcy's writing have been reiterated by other prominent Native American writers including **Navarre Scott Momaday**, James Welch, and **Leslie Marmon Silko**. In her novel *Ceremony* (1977), for example, Silko narrates the return of the half-Indian protagonist Tayo from World War II and Japanese imprisonment to a persistent malaise, or "white smoke," that makes him feel invisible and unable to connect with the people around him or the expectations of daily living. Eventually, he participates in a traditional Laguna Pueblo ceremony and achieves a reconciliation of his multiple cultural influences. Silko thus challenges expectations of Native American assimilation, through the enactment of supposedly lost cultural practices that she shows can still "heal" individuals of this minority community in the United States. More recently published Native American writers such as **Sherman Joseph Alexie Jr.** continue to invoke, while simultaneously problematizing, the symbol of the "the rez" for Native American experiences of assimilation *and* exclusion.

In African American literary traditions, meanwhile, tensions have existed between possibilities for true integration into dominant culture, on the one hand, and the potential *necessity* for a separate black nation on the other. These tensions are a result of the paradox of assimilation within a nation that historically denied basic liberty and humanity to blacks through the institutions of slavery; furthermore, even after the Emancipation Proclamation of 1863, conditions for many African Americans continued to be defined by rampant **racism** and bigotry. Literary debates about black separatism have taken dramatic form, such as in exchanges between Booker T. Washington and W.E.B. Du Bois. Whereas Washington in his autobiography *Up from Slavery* (1901) advocated acceptance of American exclusion of blacks and suggested that blacks construct their own separate programs for racial uplift, Du Bois used the metaphor of "double consciousness" in his *The Souls of Black Folk* (1903) to suggest that such plans only colluded with racist traditions. Du Bois contended that African Americans internalized the negative views of themselves held by whites in power—views that persisted, for example, even after blacks fought for the American cause in the Revolutionary War.

African American writers have historically weighed the different sides of this question, noting throughout the possibility of some African Americans to "pass" for white. In her novel from 1900, *Contending Forces*, Pauline Hopkins narrates the choice of a mixed character, Jesse Montfort, to live as a black man within a black community rather than choosing to take advantage of his ability to be presumed white. In this and later works of African American literature, authors narrate a wide range of responses taken by characters facing pressures to assimilate by "passing," or through other means. During the **Harlem Renaissance**, writers such as **Langston Hughes**, **Zora Neale Hurston**, and Claude McKay focused on a search for shared black cultures in America rather than advocating inclusion in white America. Hurston's ***Their Eyes Were Watching God*** (1937) is considered significant for her depiction of a black character within all-black contexts rather than in relation to white America, although this choice was the subject of controversy among other African American writers of the time. Some readers considered the author's use of black dialect in the novel to be an affirmation of white people's **African American stereotypes**, but others saw it as a refusal to assimilate to particular expectations of American literary form.

African American writers took even more militant stances after World War II, when blacks fought for United States but found that they were still denied the supposed benefits of assimilation. Novels including those by **Ralph Waldo Ellison** and **Richard Wright**, as well as poetry by Amiri Baraka, Nikki Giovanni, and Sonia Sanchez, reflected black demands for racial justice and equality, problematizing earlier requests for the chance to assimilation to white norms. Ellison's ***Invisible Man*** (1952), for example, traces the narrator's search for a viable black **identity** among mentors who advocate everything from grateful submission to white cultural expectations to revolutionary and violent upheaval. Later in the 20th century, these issues continued to shape African American literature, notably in a work like **Toni Morrison**'s ***The Bluest Eye*** (1970), the story of the existential damage done to Pecola Breedlove by the dream of assimilation when she becomes convinced that a pair of blue eyes will solve the tragedies of racism and poverty that structure her life.

As Morrison does in *The Bluest Eye*, Asian American writers have questioned if assimilation is even possible, given the visible differences of some ethnic minorities from hegemonic cultural traits. In particular, the "Yellow Peril" and "inscrutable Asian" phenomena of the late 19th and early 20th centuries reflected a popular perception that Asian immigrants, especially Chinese and Japanese male laborers arriving in the country in significant numbers in these periods, were too culturally different to ever be fully incorporated into the mainstream. This influenced policies such as the Chinese Exclusion Act of 1882 and the National Origins Act of 1924 prohibiting Japanese immigration at the same time that European immigrants were allowed into the country, albeit with specified quotas. In the early 20th century, Sui Sin Far captured such attitudes in her autobiographical writing in "Leaves from the Mental Portfolio of an Eurasian" as well as in her fictional stories, collected in *Mrs. Spring Fragrance and Other Writings* (1995). In these, she reported that North Americans doubted that Chinese immigrants were humans like themselves with equivalent spiritual depths beneath their supposedly stolid expressions.

Such perceptions and accompanying exclusions led to the development of ethnic enclaves such as Chinatowns, as well as to the relocation of particular Asian Americans under certain international contingencies. Fae Myenne Ng's *Bone* (1993), for example, describes bachelor hotels in San Francisco's Chinatown, similar to those created in several American cities when Chinese female immigration was restricted so as to limit family reunification and the growth of this community. Meanwhile, sentiments about Asian inassimilability led to the creation of relocation or **internment** camps beginning in 1942 for Japanese Americans when the United States found itself at war with Japan in World War II, after the bombing of Pearl Harbor. Stories such as those collected in Hisaye Yamamoto's collection *Seventeen Syllables and Other Stories* (1988) describe the fractured existence of Japanese American families during this period, revealing how precarious the possibility of actual inclusion in the American nation has been for some Asian groups at particular historical moments.

In the 21st century, assimilation continues to be a concern for American writers, for immigrants of all backgrounds, as well as for ethnic minorities. Previous models of wholesale Americanization, such as Israel Zangwill's "melting pot" from his play of the same name (1909), have come under considerable scrutiny and criticism by writers because of the implicit assumption that all differences will be eradicated and transformed into one (white) uniform culture. Problematizing the notion of a homogeneous American cultural norm, decades of multiethnic American literature has called for more nuanced and hybridized understandings of identity. (*See also* Ethnicity; Race)

Further Reading

Antin, Mary. *The Promised Land*. Boston: Houghton Mifflin, 1912.

Chu, Patricia P. *Assimilating Asians: Gendered Strategies of Authorship in Asian America*. Durham, NC, and London: Duke University Press, 2000.

Freedman, Jonathan. *The Temple of Culture: Assimilation and Anti-Semitism in Literary Anglo-America*. Oxford: Oxford University Press, 2000.

Overland, Orm. "From Melting Pot to Copper Kettles: Assimilation and Norwegian-American Literature." In *Multilingual America: Transnationalism, Ethnicity, and the Languages of American Literature*, edited by Werner Sollers, 50–63. New York: New York University Press, 1998.

Sanchez, George J. "'Go After the Women': Americanization and the Mexican Immigrant Woman, 1915–1929." In *Unequal Sisters: A Multicultural Reader in U.S. Women's History*, edited by Vicki L. Ruiz and Ellen Carol DuBois, 284–97. New York: Routledge, 1994.

Sollors, Werner. *Beyond Ethnicity: Consent and Descent in American Culture.* Oxford: Oxford University Press, 1986.

Anupama Jain

AUTOBIOGRAPHY OF MALCOLM X, THE

The *Autobiography* (1965), "as told to **Alex Haley**," remains the core text to the work and life, significantly inseparable, of African American activist Malcolm X. The book, dictated to Alex Haley over the course of three years, reveals the discipline, rhetorical force, and unflinching honesty that characterized Malcolm X's devotion to the cause of African American unity. The book revolves around two key transitions in Malcolm's life: his conversion, in prison, to Islam, and his later break from the Nation of Islam and its leader Elijah Muhammad. Thus, a central theme of the book is redemption; also, however, Malcolm's life story reveals the connections between action and social responsibility.

Alex Haley used the impetus of a 1962 interview with Malcolm to propose the autobiography. While highly suspicious of the media and skeptical about the project, Malcolm agreed, and eventually he and Haley developed a working relationship that allowed Malcolm to reveal details of his criminal past in forthright detail, while demonstrating that experience can, and should, lead to self-awareness and, eventually, personal enlightenment.

The book breaks, roughly, into three sections: Malcolm Little's penurious childhood and criminal life; Malcolm's arrest and imprisonment, conversion to Islam, and his life as Elijah Muhammad's disciple; and his split with Elijah Muhammad, his *hajj* and, taking the name El-Hajj Malik El-Shabazz, the reformulation of his segregationist politics and his focus on unity among African Americans, resulting in his formation of the Organization for Afro-American Unity. The book concludes with the circumstances, still somewhat mysterious, surrounding Malcolm X's assassination on February 21, 1965.

Alex Haley wisely remains transparent in the narrative, giving the book the force of Malcolm's own eloquence. Though Malcolm retained the right of final approval of all material, he corrected little of the manuscript; Malcolm never mitigated his criminal life, or the depths of his own debasement, before his religious conversion. In allowing the record to stand unencumbered by conventional narrative strategies of the ghostwriter, the text remains intense and still relevant. Malcolm agreed to let Haley compose an epilogue, without his editorial approval, to be attached to the text. This epilogue allows Haley to emerge as Malcolm's transcriber and further asserts Malcolm's desire that the book reveal his true life as an activist, father, husband, and faithful Muslim.

The Autobiography of Malcolm X became a best seller, selling 50,000 copies in hardback and about five million paperback copies and became required reading in many college courses. The assassination of Malcolm X increased interest in the text and helped it gain wide readership. The book is still perceived as a formative text in the **Civil Rights Movement**, and a profound description of a man's struggle to reclaim his African **identity**. The book was successfully filmed by director Spike Lee in 1992. (*See also* African American Autobiography)

Further Reading

Bloom, Harold. *Alex Haley's and Malcolm X's "The Autobiography of Malcolm X."* Philadelphia: Chelsea House, 1996.

Lee, Spike. *By Any Means Necessary: The Trials and Tribulations of Making Malcolm X.* London: Vintage, 1992.

Terrill, Robert. *The Cambridge Companion to Malcolm X.* Cambridge, England: Cambridge University Press, 2010.

Bill R. Scalia

B

BALDWIN, JAMES (1924–1987)

An African American novelist, essayist, autobiographer, dramatist, scriptwriter, poet, speaker, and civil rights activist, James Baldwin's life and work brought him an international reputation by the early 1960s. Although his legacy has not been without its detractors, there is no doubt his eloquent and incisive critique of the national character, as it has been formed and distorted by questions of **race**, sexuality, and religion, make his work important to the entire enterprise of American literature as well as to the shape of African American literature in the second half of the 20th century. The theme that most differentiates Baldwin from **Richard Wright** and **Ralph Waldo Ellison**, the most prominent African American novelists when Baldwin began writing in the 1950s, is Baldwin's insistence on the fundamental connection between racial and sexual oppression in American experience. More than any other writer of his time, Baldwin challenged the national discourse around race from its preoccupation with "the Negro problem" to an analysis of "the white problem," which Baldwin described as a false "innocence" that involved various levels of denials, collective and individual, of both history and the self. In fiction and nonfiction Baldwin explored the ways in which blacks have paid the price for white denial by becoming symbols of both deviance and desire in the white imagination, and also the ways that whites have paid a price for self-deception. Baldwin's work, however, is not only important for its challenges to white racial ideology but also just as important for its representations of intraracial experience within black families and black communities. In her eulogy, **Toni Morrison** credited Baldwin with making "American English honest—genuinely international" while making it available for black people to express "our lived reality" and "our complicated passion" (Troupe 76).

Major Themes

The complexity of Baldwin's life and work and the politically charged atmosphere in which he wrote have posed significant challenges to scholars and critics, who have frequently emphasized one aspect or period of his work while ignoring or disparaging others. Much of Baldwin's complexity results from his ability to articulate certain seemingly paradoxical positions and themes. Baldwin insists on both the aesthetic and the political value of art, describing the artist as both lover and disturber of the peace. He is severely critical of the Christian church for hypocrisy and for its historical role in the subjugation of blacks, but, at the same time, he shapes his moral vision in the Old Testament language of the Jeremiad and in New

Testament images of revelation and salvation. He draws on both interracial themes and subjects and on black nationalist concerns, and thus critiques some of the limitations of both integrationist and segregationist positions in American race relations. He writes openly and movingly about homosexual love, while arguing against the idea of a homosexual identity. He consistently critiqued categories of identity, white and black, gay and straight, as denying the complex reality of individual experience and as creating and maintaining power relationships.

Early Life

James Baldwin was born August 2, 1924, in Harlem, New York, to Emma Berdis Jones, a young, single woman. Three years later Berdis married David Baldwin, and eventually James became the eldest of nine children. David Baldwin, a former preacher who had come North during the Great Migration looking for work and for escape from Southern violence, was the deacon of a Pentecostal church. The struggle to support his large family in conditions of acute poverty and racial discrimination took its toll. He was harsh and judgmental. Baldwin said that his father had scared him so badly that no one else could scare him again. When Baldwin learned as a teenager that David Baldwin was not his biological father, this knowledge helped explain his father's hostility and rejection of him. Baldwin's troubled relationship with his stepfather is central to the semiautobiographical first novel, *Go Tell It on the Mountain* (1953), and to the early essay "Notes of a Native Son" (1955). Baldwin came to see his father's self-destructive rages as an object lesson—what happens when a black man believes the white world's judgment about himself. All of Baldwin's work blends autobiography and social commentary. He presented his life metaphorically—his illegitimacy symbolic of the condition of being black in the New World, "a kind of bastard of the West."

Influences

Important early influences that informed Baldwin's art and subject matter included the church, his reading, his family, and mentors. When Baldwin was fourteen he experienced a religious conversion and became a child preacher. He would fictionalize this experience in *Go Tell It on the Mountain* in one of the most powerful descriptions of a religious conversion in American literature. At the climax of the novel, the protagonist John Grimes falls to the threshing floor in the Temple of the Fire Baptized and undergoes a religious crisis that is both a reaction to and a temporary solution for the conflict with his father and with his feelings of dread and guilt over his awakening sexual desires. Ten years later Baldwin spoke directly about the psychological and social forces that drove him into the church in *The Fire Next Time* (1963). Despite his negative assessment of the church, he also testified to the enduring power of spirituals and gospel music that came from the black church and that would always be present in Baldwin's literary language, especially as titles, epigraphs, and allusions. From early childhood, Baldwin was an avid reader. Harriet Beecher Stowe's *Uncle Tom's Cabin* made a particular impression on him. In

"Everybody's Protest Novel" (1949), the controversial early essay that would serve as Baldwin's literary manifesto, Baldwin compares *Uncle Tom's Cabin* with Richard Wright's *Native Son* as protest novels, which, he argued, do more to shore up the status quo than to change it because they deny the complexity of Negro life in America by representing blacks as either victims or socially constructed monsters. Baldwin's favorite 19th-century novelist was Henry James, whose influence can be seen in Baldwin's style and in his subject of the American abroad.

Important people in young Baldwin's life included his mother, who was a source of spiritual and moral strength, and his siblings, whom he helped raise. Strong female characters, close relationships between siblings, particularly between brothers, and the importance of the family in the struggle to resist oppression and to achieve self-expression are important subjects of his later fictions *If Beale Street Could Talk* (1974) and *Just Above My Head* (1979) and of his widely anthologized short story "Sonny's Blues" (1957). Baldwin was recognized as a precocious child from the time he was in elementary school. A white teacher, Orilla Miller, took him under her wing and introduced him to theater and movies. Fascinated by theater and film from an early age, Baldwin would go on to write two plays, *Amen Corner* (1954) and *Blues for Mister Charlie* (1964); a screen play of the life of Malcolm X, *One Day When I Was Lost* (1972); and a cultural critique of American film, *The Devil Finds Work* (1976). The hero of his fourth novel, *Tell Me How Long the Train's Been Gone* (1968), is an internationally known actor who becomes a spokesperson in the **Civil Rights Movement**. At Frederick Douglass Junior High, Baldwin received invaluable guidance from two African American male teachers, the poet Countee Cullen, and Herman Porter. During high school, Baldwin met Beauford Delany, an African American artist who became a surrogate father and lifelong friend. Delany introduced Baldwin to secular black music and taught him how to see light and shadow with the eye of the artist.

Transatlantic Commuter and Activist

As a young man Baldwin lived in Greenwich Village and began writing book reviews for the *Nation* and *New Leader*. In 1948, *Commentary* published his first major essay, "The Harlem Ghetto," and the short story "Previous Condition." Also during this period Richard Wright helped Baldwin win a Saxton Foundation Fellowship after reading an early draft of *Go Tell It on the Mountain*. *Another Country* (1962) draws from Baldwin's years in the village. The novel follows the lives of seven characters whose interracial and bisexual relationships suggest the limits and the possibilities of healing the divisions of race and sex through intimate encounters. In November 1948, Baldwin left for Paris with $40 in his pocket to escape the pressures of life in New York where he felt targeted as a black and a homosexual. The next 10 years were immensely productive. Baldwin wrote all the work that gained him an international reputation while living abroad. *Go Tell It on the Mountain* was completed in a tiny Catholic village in the Swiss mountains where he went with his lover Lucien Happersberger. This village, where none of the residents had ever seen a black person before Baldwin's arrival, also became the subject of an important essay on the relationship of the American Negro to European culture, "Stranger in the Village" (1953). Baldwin's first collection of essays, *Notes of a Native Son*, was published in 1955. Baldwin's second novel, *Giovanni's Room* (1956), about homosexual love between a white American, David, and an Italian, Giovanni, who meet in Paris, has become a foundational text for gay and lesbian studies. Initially Baldwin's agent told him to burn the novel because he was a Negro writer and it would alienate his audience, but Baldwin refused to be limited by stereotypes of the role of a Negro writer. David, the first-person narrator whose ancestors "conquered a continent," represents Baldwin's interpretation of the flaws in white American society. David flees to Europe trying to escape himself and the American version of masculinity only to betray his lover Giovanni. This betrayal is part of a larger failure of love that Baldwin understood to be endemic to American society.

In 1957, Baldwin returned to the United States to travel south, interviewed Dr. **Martin Luther King Jr.**, and reported on the Civil Rights Movement. Over the next decade, Baldwin became an important figure in the movement, describing himself as a witness rather than a spokesperson. His years in the pulpit had trained him well as a powerful and eloquent speaker. Now his impressive rhetorical skill was put to use appealing to the American conscience to transform race relations in the United States. In 1963, a watershed year in the struggle for civil rights, Baldwin published *The Fire Next Time*, met with Attorney General Robert F. Kennedy, and appeared on the cover of *Time* magazine. Calling himself a "transatlantic commuter" rather than an expatriate, Baldwin returned to Europe and to Istanbul to write because he found it impossible to work in the United States. By the late 1960s and early 1970s, after witnessing the worsening conditions in American ghettos and the murder of key black leaders, Medgar Evers, Malcolm X, and Martin Luther King, Baldwin became increasingly disillusioned with the American government and the will of the people to bring about social change. His work published after the mid-1960s reflects his disillusionment and anger, but it also reflects his interest in the revolution of black consciousness taking place and his increased willingness to represent homosexual themes in a black context, especially in his last novel *Just above My Head*.

Baldwin's oeuvre includes six novels, seven collections of essays, two plays, two collections of poetry, a collection of short stories, a photo text, a children's story, a screenplay, and many published interviews and dialogues. About three years before his death, Baldwin said, "I certainly have not told my story yet" (Miller 10), which poignantly suggests the extent to which he understood his work as a continuous and unfinished autobiographical project. Baldwin died December 1, 1987, at his home in Saint Paul-de-Vence in southern France. (*See also* African American Autobiography; African American Novel)

Further Reading

Francis, Conseula. *The Critical Reception of James Baldwin, 1963–2010*. Rochester, NY: Camden House, 2014.

Harris, Trudier, ed. *New Essays on "Go Tell It on the Mountain."* New York: Cambridge University Press, 1999.

Leeming, David. *James Baldwin: A Biography*. New York: Alfred A. Knopf, 1994.

McBride, Dwight A., ed. *James Baldwin Now*. New York: New York University Press, 1999.

Miller, Quentin D., ed. *Reviewing James Baldwin: Things Not Seen*. Philadelphia: Temple University Press, 2000.

Porter, Horace. *Stealing the Fire: The Art and Protest of James Baldwin*. Middletown, CT: Wesleyan University Press, 1989.

Scott, Lynn Orilla. *James Baldwin's Later Fiction: Witness to the Journey*. East Lansing: Michigan State University Press, 2002.

Troupe, Quincy, ed. *James Baldwin: The Legacy*. New York: Simon and Schuster, 1989.

Lynn Orilla Scott

BAMBARA, TONI CADE (1939–1995)

Toni Cade Bambara was an African American writer and activist. Born Miltona Mirkin Cade in Harlem, New York City, this fiction writer is most well known for her attention to specifically African American modes of expression—from dialect to oral traditions of storytelling to African American musical forms such as **jazz**. The diversity in the settings of her stories and novels, which range from the urban North to the rural South to the seas near Vietnam, matches the diversity of her creative output as a fiction writer, screenwriter, and documentary filmmaker. Bambara's screenwriting credits include *The Bombing of Osage Avenue* (1986), the documentary on the Philadelphia police bombing of the activist organization MOVE in 1985, and part 3 of the series *W. E. B. Du Bois: A Biography in Four Voices* (1995). Her espousal of the Black Aesthetic Movement's move away from the dominant cultural modes of representation also plays a role in the style and message of her fiction. Beyond writing and film, Bambara was also a professor at Rutgers, Duke, and the City College of New York, an artist in residence at Atlanta's Spelman College, and an activist in feminist and black liberation movements. She died of cancer in 1995.

Bambara published her first story, "Sweet Town," in *Vendome* magazine after graduating from Queens College in 1959 with a BA in English and theater. She completed her master's degree in modern American fiction at the City College of New York while working as a social worker in Harlem and a coordinator of social programs in Brooklyn. From there, she edited two anthologies: *The Black Woman* (1970), containing short stories, poems, and essays by black women writers and activists; and the collection of juvenile fiction *Tales and Stories for Black Folks* (1971), a collaborative project with her students at Rutgers University. Her first solo publication, *Gorilla My Love* (1972), contains 15 short stories written between the years 1959 and 1972. The stories, whose locales range from urban to rural settings and whose characters encompass all ages, are unified by the use of first-person narration and Bambara's attention to the specifics of African American dialect and experience. Four of the stories, "My Man Bovanne," "Gorilla My Love," "Raymond's Run," and "Happy Birthday," are also united in the recurrence of different characters named Hazel. As with the stories in *Gorilla My Love*, the

10 short stories in her next collection, *The Sea Birds Are Still Alive* (1977), focus most often on female protagonists (notable exceptions are "The Tender Man" and the multiplicity of voices in the title story), but here Bambara's expansions in terms of locale reflect her travels to Cuba and Vietnam and her move to Atlanta in 1974. In the title story, for example, the reader drifts on a boat with refugees lost near Vietnam.

The Salt Eaters (1980), the only novel Bambara published during her lifetime and the recipient of an American Book Award, is set in the fictional town of Claybourne, Georgia. The title refers to the African myth that slaves who ate salt couldn't fly back to Africa (Wilentz 62), and also to the faith-healing belief that eating salt can cure poison (Walker 181). The protagonist, former activist, Velma Henry seeks healing at the infirmary after an attempted suicide. Her story is told by a mixture of flashbacks, omniscient narration, and the perspectives of multiple characters. The novel's settings include the Southwest Community Infirmary, the nearby Academy of Seven Arts, a local bus, and the Avocado Pit Café. In her prominence in the resolution of the novel's engagement with cultural and spiritual sickness, the faith healer Minnie Ransom comes to symbolize folk wisdom and communities of women as the key to recovery, over the technology of the male-centered medical community represented by Doctor Meadows (Butler-Evans 182).

After Bambara's death, her friend and editor, novelist **Toni Morrison**, published two additional works by Bambara. *Deep Sightings and Rescue Missions* (1996) contains six previously unpublished short stories and a group of six essays, movie reviews (including a chapter on Spike Lee's *School Daze* [1988]), cultural criticism, and interviews. One interview, "How she came by her name," gives modern readers a clear glimpse into Bambara's early life and her philosophy about the relations between politics and art. In this interview conducted by Louis Massiah, Bambara labels herself not as a writer but rather as "a community person who writes and does a few other things." She also traces the journey that moved her from the name given to her by her father who named her after his employer to the discovery of the name "Bambara" while traveling with her mother to visit her grandmother's grave in 1970. Bambara connects herself with novelist Toni Morrison and poets **Maya Angelou** and **Audre Lorde** as sisters in the "spiritual practice" of gaining independence through choosing one's own name.

After Bambara's death, Toni Morrison edited and published a long manuscript for a novel she considered to be Bambara's greatest life's work. Bambara worked on the novel *Those Bones Are Not My Child* (1999) for 12 years before her death. *Those Bones Are Not My Child* is a carefully researched novel about the search of Marzala Rawls Spencer for her missing child, Sonny. For her story, Bambara draws on interviews and journalistic accounts of the Atlanta child murders of 1979–1981 in which more than 40 children, most young black boys, became victims. Bambara also wrote about these murders in the short story "Madame Bai and the Taking of Stone Mountain" published posthumously in *Deep Sightings and Rescue Missions*.

Bambara and her works play a part in several communities of African American writers, artists, and activists. Her work relates to the community of artists and critics in the Black Aesthetic Movement (also known as the Black Arts Movement) arising in the 1960s and 1970s. Members of this movement, such as Amiri Baraka, Larry Neal, and Ron Karenga, sought to create a "counter-discourse" of black consciousness and to incorporate politics and community engagement into art (Butler-Evans 20, Perkins 154). In her attention to concerns and moments of healing among African American women, Bambara's work is compared with that of **Alice Walker** and Toni Morrison. For Bambara, the social function of art was most often healing. In the essay "Salvation Is the Issue," Bambara ends by saying, "I work to produce stories that save our lives" (Bambara 47). (*See also* African American Novel)

Further Reading

Bambara, Toni Cade. "Salvation Is the Issue." In *Black Women Writers (1950–1980): A Critical Evaluation*, edited by Mari Evans, 71–84. New York: Anchor, 1984.

Butler-Evans, Elliott. *Race, Gender, and Desire: Narrative Strategies in the Fiction of Toni Cade Bambara, Toni Morrison, and Alice Walker*. Philadelphia: Temple University Press, 1989.

Hull, Akasha (Gloria). "What It Is I Think She's Doing Anyhow: A Reading of Toni Cade Bambara's *The Salt Eaters*." In *Home Girls: A Black Feminist Anthology*, edited by Barbara Smith, 124–42. New Brunswick, NJ, and London: Rutgers University Press, 2000.

Perkins, Margo V. "Getting Basic: Bambara's Re-Visioning of the Black Aesthetic." In *Race and Racism in Theory and Practice*, edited by Berel Lang, 153–63. Lanham, MD: Rowman & Littlefield, 2000.

Walker, Melissa. *Down from the Mountaintop. Black Women's Novels in the Wake of the Civil Rights Movement, 1966–1989*. New Haven, CT, and London: Yale University Press, 1991.

Wall, Cheryl. *Savoring the Salt: The Legacy of Toni Cade Bambara*. Philadelphia: Temple University Press, 2013.

Wilentz, Gay. *Healing Narratives: Women Writers Curing Cultural Dis-ease*. New Brunswick, NJ: Rutgers University Press, 2000.

Melissa S. Shields

BELOVED

Remarkable for its thematic complexity and stylistic brilliance, **Toni Morrison**'s fifth novel, *Beloved* (1987), earned her a Pulitzer and no doubt paved the way for the Nobel Prize in Literature. Employing techniques of flashback and multiple points of view, this nonlinear novel confronts the painful and avoided history of. With great specificity it chronicles the racial, sexual, and psychic violence endured by African American ancestors. Dedicated to the "sixty million or more" who perished in the of the trans-Atlantic slave trade, the novel urges us to remember . . . and then, to move on.

The novel is based on a true story of Margaret Garner, a fugitive slave from Kentucky, who when hunted down by slave catchers in 1856 intended to kill her children and herself rather than be returned to slavery; she was prevented from doing so after she took the life of her daughter. Modeled after Garner, Sethe is the

Toni Morrison, 1987. (AP Photo/David Bookstaver)

novel's central character who flees the Kentucky plantation ironically called "Sweet Home" and when facing captivity kills her baby daughter named Beloved.

The novel opens in post–Civil War Ohio with Sethe's sad and haunted house 18 years after Beloved's death. Ostracized by the black community for the infanticide, Sethe and her lonely daughter Denver put up with the restless ghost of Beloved. The spiteful ghost that drove Sethe's two sons to flee their home is driven out by Paul D, a fellow-fugitive from "Sweet Home" who returns to Sethe's life after 18 years. His return stirs Sethe's memories and the two recount to each other their traumatic memories: Sethe's abuse as a mother reproducing for the plantation; the madness and death of her husband, Halle, whose spirit is broken by the brutality of School Teacher, the plantation overseer; wistful memories of her long-suffering but valiant mother-in-law, Baby Suggs; Paul D's chain gang experiences in Alfred, Georgia.

Paul D and Sethe's companionship is short-lived as an intruder who answers to the name of Beloved occupies Sethe's house and takes over her life. Sethe believes this homeless young woman is the ghost of her baby daughter Beloved coming back for reparation. But Beloved is hard to appease. After she seduces and drives out Paul D, who is alienated from Sethe when he learns of the infanticide, Beloved cannot have enough of Sethe's attention. Increasingly isolated, wracked by guilt and remorse, Sethe withdraws into herself. Her adolescent daughter Denver is forced to venture out of the house in search of help from the community. Eventually the community of black women rescues Sethe from her torment. Beloved leaves, vanishing mysteriously. Paul D, wiser, comes back to befriend Sethe, who is finally released from her past into the present.

Beloved takes up literally and metaphorically the theme of possession and exorcism. Constructed by different characters recalling their difficult pasts, these collective narratives of "rememory" take us into the very heart of slavery: the gendered nature of the oppression of black men and women and their resistance to it; the intergenerational impact of the pervasive loss and suffering; and the necessity of healing for both the individual and the community by remembering and working through this trauma.

Further Reading

Andrew, William L., and Nellie Y. McKay, eds. *Toni Morrison's Beloved: A Casebook*. New York: Oxford University Press, 1999.

Bloom, Harold. *Modern Critical Interpretations: Beloved*. Philadelphia: Chelsea House Publishers, 1999.

Grewal, Gurleen. *Circles of Sorrow, Lines of Struggle: The Novels of Toni Morrison*. Baton Rouge: Louisiana State University Press, 1998.

Montgomery, Maxine. *Contested Boundaries: New Critical Essays on the Fiction of Toni Morrison*. New Castle upon Tyne, England: Cambridge Scholars, 2013.

Peterson, Nancy J. "Toni Morrison and the Desire for a 'Genuine Black History Book'." In *Against Amnesia: Contemporary Women Writers and the Crises of Historical Memory*, 51–97. Philadelphia: University of Pennsylvania Press, 2001.

Gurleen Grewal

BILINGUALISM

On a basic level, bilingualism in U.S. ethnic literature entails the systematic use of two distinct languages in a given piece of literature as a way locating the author (as well as the characters) in a particular position in relation to mainstream culture. More generally, bilingualism can be seen as a means of expression that has been an important and ever-present element in the production of ethnic literature in the United States. In addition, bilingualism in the United States can be described as a literary practice aimed at documenting a (sub)culture, and as a way of using a subordinate language to contest (fight) the imposed (and imposing) constraints of the monolingual, mainstream (and thus, dominant) culture. In particular, bilingualism in ethnic literature documents the process(es) by which determined communities change/adapt to and learn or negotiate their new lives or realities. Theoretically, bilingualism also serves as a bond or a bridge between immigrant groups and those of the same heritage who have lived in the United States for generations. By the same token, bilingual literature in the United States also documents the clashes between the new immigrants, those who have lived in the United States for one or more generations, and the mainstream Anglo culture. In the end, bilingualism contests mainstream efforts to eradicate the mother tongue from those communities. Or in many cases, that which has become the second tongue, as second and third generations of U.S.-born minorities oftentimes learn their parents' and grandparents' mother tongue as a second language. In any case, U.S. ethnic writers from different backgrounds have countered for decades (purposely or not) "English only" efforts and initiatives by unabashedly expressing themselves in their literature with words that are "foreign" to the English language, but are reflective of their ethnic backgrounds (i.e., see the works of Puerto Rican writers Esmeralda Santiago and Sandra Estévez or Chinese American **Maxine Hong Kingston**) and ways of thinking (i.e., see the works of Chicana writer Cherríe Moraga where she argues that Spanish, beyond a way of communicating, is a way of living). In many cases authors write entire texts in a bilingual format (e.g., see the works of Chicana writer Gloria Anzaldúa, more specifically, her book *Borderlands/La Frontera*).

As a practice, bilingualism signifies a moving in and out of determined linguistic structures in order to communicate a personal state of mind and a collective reality. (Something to remember here is that culture—whatever that culture may be—is learned and transmitted through language). Language (in this case bilingual language) serves as conduit by which an oftentimes hybrid culture is expressed. Indeed it is precisely this cultural reality that differentiates a U.S. ethnic author using Spanish or Chinese or Ebonics from an Anglo author using Latin or French to spice up their texts or make them seem more sophisticated. Moreover, U.S. ethnic literature provides a unique perspective (unique to a particular community) by using English in conjunction with another distinct language and by sometimes merging both languages, as in the case of Spanglish. For instance, Chicano/a and U.S. Puerto Rican authors use English and Spanish (and in many instances Spanglish) in their pieces as a way of positioning the author (and those like her/him) in the interstices of mainstream Anglo culture and Puerto Rican or Chicano/a culture. In many cases the texts are written primarily in English with some passages in Spanish. In these cases the words in Spanish used by the authors are meant to establish two specific links: (1) a connection with a specific ethnic group at a personal level (and thus establishing a particular heritage); and (2) a broader cultural connection between the author, the community to which he or she belongs, and their heritage. For instance, on a personal level, **Piri Thomas** uses Spanish words in his autobiography ***Down These Mean Streets*** to establish an overt connection with his Puerto Ricanness, even though the book narrates the struggles he faced as an American "of color" in the United States. On a cultural level, however, the use of those words in Spanish (mainly quotidian expressions) was a conscious effort of connecting himself and his community (Spanish Harlem) to a Puerto Rican ethos that is symbolized by the island in the Caribbean and that can only be expressed in one language—Spanish. Some examples of the expressions used by Thomas are: "Dios mío," "hijo," "caramba," "muchacho," "sí," and "suerte." Though the majority of these expressions have linguistic equivalents in English (i.e., "my God," "son," "darn," "kid," "yes," and "good luck"), there is an element of cultural baggage that is claimed by using them in Spanish—a baggage that would be lost if the expression were to be written in English. As Ana Castillo argues in her book *Massacre of the Dreamers*, "Words reflect conceptions of reality and do not simply translate literally" (221). Those conceptions of reality (whatever they may be) are the ones to which bilingual authors seek to remain loyal by keeping them as they are expressed (in this case, in Spanish). Thus, it is not necessarily a refusal of the author to translate, but rather a necessity to conveys specific cultural meaning.

Bilingualism, consequently, serves to highlight the paradox by which these authors belong to two distinctive cultures (e.g., Anglo and Puerto Rican in the case of U.S. Puerto Ricans or Anglo and Mexican in the case of Chicanos/as), yet they also belong to neither. This point is brilliantly illustrated by Sandra María Esteves in her poem "Puerto Rican Discovery #3 Not Neither."

In addition to establishing a direct link to a specific (sub)culture and the ethos of a country, bilingualism in U.S. ethnic literature also documents the creation and maintenance of a new hybrid culture that communicates using a "new" language, a language that reflects the experiences of this in-between culture. An illustration of this phenomenon is the poetry of Lorna Dee Cervantes. In her poem "Poema para los californios muertos" (Poem for the dead Californios), Cervantes weaves English and Spanish, using Spanish mainly to emphasize the historical commotion and sense of loss of the original Mexican settlement in the state of California. For instance, she uses Spanish when talking about the land: "Husbands de la tierra" (husbands of the land) and "tierra madre" (mother land). She also uses it when talking about ancestors and their struggles.

Regardless of the reason for the "other" language, each bilingual text (and bilingual literature in general) must be studied as a whole—not just the English in it, or the "other" language, or the combination of both, but the content as a solid unit. As Judith Hernandez Mora writes, "I wonder if we could think of [bilingual ethnic literature] as an interpretation, a cultural translation of the English [with another language]" (196, my translation). This cultural translation becomes a language code that allows the authors to (re)invent themselves as members of a subordinate group with a rich culture and distinctive experiences living by the rules of a dominant group. Paradoxically the experiences narrated by the authors are similar to the experiences lived by the members of each group (i.e., subordinate and dominant). However, the fact that the authors are simultaneously living the experiences of two different groups makes their experiences unique. For instance, in her memoir *Almost a Woman*, Esmeralda Santiago writes, "Four days after my twenty-first birthday, I left Mami's house, the rhyme I sang as a child forgotten. . . . Martes ni te cases ni te embarques, ni de tu familia te apartes." The cultural code of this old saying (which she wrote in Spanish) would be lost had Santiago translated it into English. At the same time, the reference to her 21st birthday is also important for it marks a rite of passage within Anglo culture—a culture with which she is painfully familiar as a Puerto Rican, who was raised in the United States. Both sets of codes work in this piece to position the author within both cultures. Finally, bilingualism (as a practice in U.S. ethnic literature) provides a tool by which the lives of the members of ethnic communities are highlighted and the reality they live within the broader society is problematized.

Further Reading

Castillo, Ana. *Massacre of the Dreamers: Essays on Xicanisma*. New York: Plume, 1994.

Esteves, Sandra María. *Contrapunto: In the Open Field*. New York: No Frills Publication, 2001.

Hernandez Mora, Judith. "La literature Chicana: Mas alla del ingles y el espanol." In *Double Crossings: Entrecruzamientos*, edited by Mario Martin Flores and Carlos von Son, 193–98. New Jersey: Ediciones Nuevo Espacio, 2001.

Moraga, Cherríe. *Loving in the War Years: Lo que nunca pasó por sus labios*. Cambridge, MA: South End Press, 2001.

Carmen R. Lugo-Lugo

BLACK BOY

Richard Wright's *Black Boy* (1945 [expurgated], 1991 [unexpurgated]) is one of the most distinguished autobiographies ever written by an American author. Its plot centers on the author's experiences from childhood to early adulthood, as those experiences were shaped and interpreted by Wright's powerful imagination. As a child growing up in a family abandoned by his father, Wright relied largely on himself to fight off a world that tried to control him. For instance, he took his father's words to make a cat that was keeping him awake shut up literally, to gain a victory over someone who was more powerful than he, but his mother cited hellfire as a possible punishment for his deed. Also particularly notable in the early part of the book are: his jumping ahead 25 years to report that he did not turn out like his father (an ignorant sharecropper in Wright's view); his insulting his maternal grandmother by telling her to kiss his ass; his rejection of her Seventh-Day Adventism; his early efforts at becoming a writer; his experiences at an optical factory; and his brief sexual adventure with Bess Moss in Memphis, Tennessee.

Part 2, perhaps less inspired than the first part, concerns Wright's experiences in Chicago, where he joins the Communist Party and begins his writing career in earnest. He is surprised when a Jewish couple he works for is hurt when he lies about why he was absent one day—in the South his white employers would have expected him to lie. In another job, after witnessing the Finnish cook spit in the soup, he debates with himself whether he should report it or not, and then decides to tell a young black woman who also works at the restaurant to report the incident, because he knows she is more likely to be believed than he is. Crucial to Wright's literary development during the early stage of his career is his joining the John Reed Club, which provided him with a sympathetic audience for his early work and also espoused a political philosophy, communism that embraced racial equality. Unfortunately, the Communist Party began telling the young author how to write, which eventually led to his resignation from it.

Major themes in *Black Boy* include his struggle for selfhood against the white and the black communities—Wright accepted very little external authority, particularly when it was contrary to his own desires or based on something other than truth. For example, he rejected the authority of his maternal grandmother's church because he felt it was based on wish fulfillment rather than evidence. He rejected his relatives' authority because it was based on tradition. Perhaps the presiding theme in the book is hunger (it was originally titled *American Hunger*), hunger not only for food but also for life itself—knowledge, love, experience, travel, friends, language, education. Because so much in his environment thwarted these desires, Wright was constantly struggling to satisfy what it did not. Another key theme is literacy, which he early realized, as so many other black writers have, would greatly increase his leverage on the white world. An unfortunate subconscious theme is the author's concern that his white readers not identify him with poor black people, whom he sometimes seems to see through white eyes; that is, he sometimes looks *at* rather than *with* poor black people, especially poor black women. Another key theme is his complete rejection of the white South's construction of him as subhuman; it claimed to know him but it misconstrued his silence as agreement on Wright's part, whereas it was only a survival strategy.

Black Boy has had a profound impact on subsequent writers. In particular Wright's condemnation of the black community early in chapter 2, although placed within parentheses in two paragraphs, has drawn comment from other writers, including **Ralph Waldo Ellison** and Houston A. Baker Jr., both of whom have taken strong issue with Wright. Ellison pointed out that he found the black community a rich source for his own writing; Baker also challenges the accuracy of Wright's view. In any case, Wright's autobiography is well worth reading and is in many ways his best book. (*See also* African American Autobiography)

Further Reading

Andrews, William, and Douglas Taylor, eds. *Richard Wright's "Black Boy": A Casebook*. New York: Oxford University Press, 2003.

Fabre, Michel. *The Unfinished Quest of Richard Wright*. 2nd ed. Urbana: University of Illinois Press, 1993.

Felgar, Robert. *Student Companion to Richard Wright*. Westport, CT: Greenwood Press, 2000.

Robert Felgar

BLANCO, RICHARD (1968–)

A Cuban American poet, memoirist, and essayist, Richard Blanco was born on February 15, 1968, in Spain, to parents who were exiles from Cuba and the family immigrated to the United States when Blanco was an infant. He grew up in Miami in the close-knit Cuban exile community, an experience that would profoundly shape his sense of self. Blanco received his undergraduate degree in civil engineering and a master's degree in creative writing from Florida International University. While he has worked as an engineer for several years, he has also taught creative writing at several universities. He became a national figure on January 21, 2012, when he was invited by President **Barack Hussein Obama** to read a poem at his second presidential inauguration. Blanco became the fifth poet in American history to read a poem at a presidential inauguration; more significantly, he became the youngest poet, the first immigrant writer, the first Latino artist, and the first openly gay man to receive that rare public honor and recognition.

Blanco is a lyric memoirist. Confessional in nature, much of his poetry is exploration of self, family, and community. Blanco's first collection of poems titled *City of a Hundred Fires* was published in 1998. He describes the collection as a cultural coming-of-age story that explores his early life growing up in an exiled Cuban family that is surrounded by other Cuban exiles with nostalgic attachment to the island home that they had left behind. He grows up bilingually and biculturally and some of the poems explore the tensions and duality inherent in inhabiting transcultural and translingual spaces. Some of the poems are elegiac: poems for his father who died in 1990 and for the lost homeland of his parents' nostalgic imagination. Collectively the poems offer a poignant portrait of a child of immigrant parents awakening to his cultural inheritance and while accommodating his American present.

Directions to the Beach of the Dead, published in 2005, is a collection of beautifully crafted poems that explore the themes of home and exile from an international perspective. Written during and after extensive travels through Europe and Latin America, the poems are as much about actual journeys as they are about internal voyages, psychological odysseys, and interior quests. As in the previous volume, family too is a palpable presence; there are many intimate portraits of family and community members. Sexuality, which was a muted subject in the earlier volume, surfaces more visibly but only in his most recent collection—*Looking for the Gulf Motel* published in 2012—it becomes representationally prominent.

Looking for the Gulf Motel consists of three segments, each an exploration of a distinct stage in Blanco's life. In the first segment Blanco returns to his familiar territory: his early life in the Cuban exile community and matters of cultural **identity**. In the second section the subject of sexual identity, especially as it overlaps with his ethnocultural identity, dominates. Many of the poems in the third section thematize evanescence: change, fluidity, and impermanence. Family, a familiar presence in Blanco's poetry, is a subtle presence in all sections.

The poem that Blanco is best known for, however, is the inaugural poem that he delivered to the nation on January 21, 2013. Titled "One Today," this occasional poem written in fluid free verse, yet remarkably disciplined and polished, offers a sweeping vision of the United States over one day from dawn to dusk. Made up of nine stanzas, approximately 550 lines long, it is distinctly Whitmanesque in form and tone. The theme that anchors the poem is unity and oneness, a particularly apt theme as he addresses a diverse nation that is deeply divided along political lines. While it is a public poem, Blanco manages to create within a memoirette: woven into the poem is a miniature portrait of the poet and his family. Of his presence on the inaugural stage and his delivery of the poem to his nation, Blanco has said that he finally felt that America was "home."

Further Reading

Cordova, Steven. "Richard Blanco." In *Encyclopedia of Contemporary LGBTQ Literature of the United States*, edited by Emmanuel S. Nelson, 79–80. Santa Barbara, CA: ABC-CLIO, 2009.

Emmanuel S. Nelson

BLUES, THE

A form of African American vocal music, the blues started out rural but later turned urban. As its name suggests, the general character of this music is sad and mournful. Because the blues reflect the uniqueness of the African American experience, they have exercised a profound influence on black literature. Poets have written blues poetry, fiction writers and dramatists have used blues musicians as characters, and critics have developed a "blues aesthetic."

Form

The following is the first verse of the "St. Louis Blues" (1914) written by an anonymous composer at a time when the blues were still a form of folk music. The melody and words were first transcribed by the black cornet player and bandleader W. C. Handy.

> I hate to see de ev'nin' sun go down,
> Hate to see dat ev'nin' sun go down,
> "Cause ma baby, he done lef" dis town.

This verse illustrates the standard 12-bar blues pattern consisting of three lines (AAB), with the first line repeated with a slight variation and the third line resolving or explaining the first two. Early blues also came in two other forms, some in an 8-bar AB pattern and some in a 16-bar AAAB pattern; but all blues shared a call-and-response structure, that is, 2-bar vocal statements alternating with 2-bar instrumental responses. Originally, the instrumental responses were played by the blues singers themselves on their guitars; in later blues they were played by accompanying musicians on their horns.

Melodically the two unique traits of the blues are a standard chord progression and the use of so-called blue notes. All 12-bar blues follow the same basic chord progression, which in the key of C looks like this:

C / C / C / C7 / F / F / C / C / B-flat / B-flat / C / C

Blues singers and instrumentalists tend to stress "blue notes" to give the blues their mournful character. They are the flatted third and flatted seventh notes of a diatonic scale. In the key of C, they are E-flat and B-flat. Moreover, blues musicians like to squeeze these notes so that they wind up either a quarter step sharp or flat.

The themes of the blues fit the mournful character of the music. Early country blues deal mostly with unhappy love and personal misfortune, while later urban blues often reflect social injustice and white oppression. For example, the first urban blues ever recorded, Mamie Smith's "Crazy Blues" (1920), begins like a typical unhappy love number with the singer saying that she can't sleep at night because the man she loves doesn't treat her right. But this blues ends with a vision of racial violence because in the next-to-last verse the singer releases her frustration by fantasizing that she might get herself crazy on hop (opium), get herself a gun, and shoot herself a cop.

Although the lyrics of Mamie Smith's "Crazy Blues" reveal black people's dislike of the white police, they do not refer to any particular social injustice. However, many blues do. An example is Bessie Smith's "Poor Man Blues" (1928). The singer of that blues addresses a rich man who lives in a mansion but pays his workers so little that they are practically starving. She reminds the rich man that the poor man fought in World War I for him, and she ends by asking, "If it wasn't for the poor man, mister rich man, what would you do?"

History

In their early development, the blues were intimately connected with **jazz**; in fact, the first recorded blues was the instrumental "Livery Stable Blues" (1917) by the Original Dixieland Jazz Band. Moreover, classic blues singers were usually accompanied by jazz musicians, and to this day instrumental blues continue to be an important part of jazz. Nevertheless, vocal blues and jazz eventually parted company.

Musicologists believe that the first blues were sung in the 1890s by itinerant male musicians who accompanied themselves on guitars. However, this kind of country blues was not recorded until the late 1920s. Major early blues figures were Charlie Patton, Blind Lemon Jefferson, and Huddie Ledbetter. In the early 1920s, most of the recorded vocal blues were sung by female singers. The blues now became very popular; in fact, during the late 1920s and early 1930s, a veritable blues craze swept the country, and singers such as Ma Rainey, Bessie Smith, and Ida Cox sold millions of records. Bessie Smith even appeared in an early sound movie. But in the middle 1930s, big band Swing music became the new fad, and the blues lost much of their popularity. However, the black big bands of Jay McShann, Fletcher Henderson, and Count Basie continued to feature "blues shouters" such as Jimmy Witherspoon, Jimmy Rushing, and Joe Turner who mostly sang up-tempo blues.

During the 1940s when Swing turned into Be-Bop, vocal blues separated from jazz and turned into rhythm and blues. Over the years the rhythm and blues designation has been applied to a number of different kinds of popular black music. The originators of rhythm and blues were the former jazz musician Louis Jordan and his Tympany Five whose trademark sounds were a stomping beat, a wailing electric guitar, and a screeching saxophone. Other early rhythm and blues musicians were Fats Domino, Little Richard, and Chuck Berry. Their music had a great influence on Elvis Presley, Jerry Lee Lewis, and other white musicians who transformed black rhythm and blues into white rock and roll. This is why we can find 12-bar blues patterns in many songs of later rock and roll bands such as the Beatles, the Rolling Stones, and even the Beach Boys.

When the more popular forms of black music in the 1960s and 1970s—soul, funk, and Motown—moved far away from the blues, musicians such B. B. King and Muddy Waters tried to keep the traditional 12-bar blues alive. This was not easy. B. B. King reports that at a 1960s concert, when he was opening for the rhythm and blues star Jackie Wilson, the black audience tried to boo him off the stage. They simply had no interest in traditional blues because they considered them a backward form of music. But since the 1980s and 1990s, there has been a small revival of the blues. Black blues musicians can again find work in small clubs, both black and white, but at blues concerts, the audiences are mostly white.

The Blues and Literature

Unlike the African American community at large, black literary artists have always been aware of the cultural importance of the blues. Beginning in the 1920s and

1930s, the poets **Langston Hughes** and Sterling Brown have tried to create interest in the blues by writing blues poetry. Both wrote poems that have the classic three-line AAB format with an AAA rhyme scheme, and they also developed two other stanza forms. One of them breaks up each of the traditional three lines into two parts for a six-line stanza with an ABABCB rhyme scheme. For another stanza form, Hughes and Brown eliminated the repetition of the first line in the traditional blues, and broke up the remaining two lines into two parts each. This resulted in a four-line stanza with an ABCB rhyme. In some poems, Hughes and Brown used both the four-line and the six-line stanza forms, and they also inserted blues stanzas in some longer poems whose overall structures are not patterned after the blues. This happens in Langston Hughes's "Weary Blues" (1926) and in Sterling Brown's homage to the blues singer "Ma Rainey" (1931).

Because of the pioneering work of Langston Hughes and Sterling Brown, the blues have become an important part of African American poetry. There is hardly a black poet who has not used the word "blues" in the title of at least one poem. In addition, during the second half of the 20th century many poets have written blues poems in three-, four-, or six-line formats. Among them are Henry Dumas, Michael Harper, Robert Hayden, LeRoi Jones (aka Amiri Baraka), Don L. Lee, Sterling Plumpp, Sonia Sanchez, A. B. Spellman, and Al Young.

The blues have also influenced African American fiction. Many stories and novels of black writers have a blues feeling to them, and some actually employ characters who are blues singers. For instance, in **Ralph Waldo Ellison's** *Invisible Man* (1952), the protagonist has an encounter with a blues singer who identifies himself as Peter Wheatstraw, an actual person who has over 160 records to his name; in **Alice Walker's** *The Color Purple* (1982), the protagonist's best friend Shug Avery is a blues singer; and in Albert Murray's *Train Whistle Guitar* (1974), Gayl Jones's *Corregidora* (1976), and Clarence Major's *Dirty Bird Blues* (1996), the protagonists themselves are blues singers.

African American drama is tinged with the blues as well. In LeRoi Jones's *Dutchman*, the central character makes this observation about the anger that he thinks smoldered inside the blues singer Bessie Smith: "If Bessie Smith had murdered some white people she wouldn't have needed that music." (35). A friend of LeRoi Jones's, the playwright Ed Bullins likes to specify that blues music be heard in the background of his plays (e.g., see *How Do You Do*, 1968); and **August Wilson**, who wrote a play about blues singer Ma Rainey that was produced on Broadway (*Ma Rainey's Black Bottom* [1984]), has said about himself that even though he doesn't play an instrument, he is "cut from the same cloth" as the great blues musicians.

The Blues Aesthetic

All along, black scholars have stressed the cultural importance of the blues, and they eventually developed a concept that has been called the "blues aesthetic." This is the idea that the blues express the racial feeling and vision of life that arises out of the collective life experiences of the African American community.

The most eloquent early expression of the blues aesthetic occurs in a 1945 essay by the novelist Ralph Ellison titled "Richard Wright's Blues." In that essay, Ellison says, "The blues is an impulse to keep the painful details and episodes of a brutal experience in one's aching consciousness, to finger its jagged grain, and to transcend it, not by the consolation of philosophy but by squeezing from it a near-tragic, near-comic lyricism" (90). This notion is expanded and given the status of an indigenous American aesthetic by Ellison's good friend, the scholar and novelist Albert Murray in his book *The Blue Devils of Nada: A Contemporary American Approach to Aesthetic Statement* (1996).

Another influential study of the blues aesthetic is Houston Baker Jr.'s *Blues, Ideology, and Afro-American Literature*. Baker gives a semiotic twist to the blues aesthetic when he says that "the blues . . . exist, not as a function of formal inscription, but as a forceful condition of Afro-American inscription," that is to say, "as a code radically conditioning Afro-America's cultural signifying" (3–4). Baker demonstrates how this code operates by analyzing prose works from *The Narrative of the Life of Frederick Douglass* (1845) to **Toni Morrison**'s *Song of Solomon* (1977).

More recently, Barbara Baker has studied manifestations of the blues aesthetic in the fiction of four Southern writers, three of them black and one of them white. In her book *The Blues Aesthetic and the Making of American Identity in the Literature of the South* (New York: Peter Lang, 2003), Baker includes the white antebellum humorist George Washington Harris because she believes his white characters can be understood only in terms of their interaction with African Americans. They therefore illustrate "the convergence of racial identification inherent in the national character" (5). Baker claims that her work extends a concept developed earlier by Ralph Ellison and Albert Murray. That concept is the "diffusion of blackness within whiteness which Ellison and Murray argue that blues music reflects" (5).

Further Reading

Baker, Barbara. *The Blues Aesthetic and the Making of American Identity in the Literature of the South*. New York: Peter Lang, 2003.

Baker, Houston, Jr. *Blues, Ideology, and Afro-American Literature*. Chicago: University of Chicago Press, 1986.

Davis, Angela. *Blues Legacies and Black Feminism*. New York: Pantheon, 1998.

Ellison, Ralph. *Shadow and Act*. New York: Signet, 1964.

Jones, LeRoi. *Blues People: The Negro Experience in White America and the Music that Developed from It*. New York: Morrow, 1963.

Jones, LeRoi. *Dutchman*. New York: Morrow, 1964.

Oakley, Giles. *The Devil's Music: A History of the Blues*. New York: Taplinger, 1977.

Tracy, Stephen. *Langston Hughes and the Blues*. Urbana: University of Illinois Press, 1988.

Eberhard Alsen

BLUEST EYE, THE

The first novel by Nobel Laureate **Toni Morrison**, *The Bluest Eye* (1970), scrutinizes the influence of a white-dominated culture and its politics of **racism** on the life of a young African American girl. Intent on exposing the absurdity of one group's imposition of unrealistic "beauty" standards on a community that can never measure up to such a benchmark, Morrison underlines the destructive notion inherent in a criterion that spurns "difference." Pecola Breedlove's obsession with blue eyes stems from her belief that if her eyes were "different, that is to say, beautiful, she herself would be different." Ironically enough, the "difference" Pecola longs for is, in fact, "sameness," a sameness that will enable her to escape the "ugliness" of the African American community and be absorbed into the "sanctity" of the dominant culture.

The Bluest Eye opens with an excerpt from a grade school primer painting a Rockwellean portrait of the perfect nuclear family. But as the passage is repeated, the ideal becomes distorted, the illusion broken. The lack of punctuation and spacing reflect just how far removed the black family is from the white experience. As the novel progresses, the disparity between the primer world and Pecola's own becomes glaringly obvious. In stark contrast to the "pretty" green and white primer house, the Breedlove house is an abandoned store littered with old furnishings. Pecola's mother, Pauline, is the antithesis to Jane's "nice," happy mother. Contrary to Jane's mother's idealized contentment, Pauline never laughs and her self-hatred is projected onto her daughter. Pecola's detachment from her mother is exemplified by the fact that she calls her "Mrs. Breedlove," even though the little Fisher girl affectionately refers to Pauline as "Polly." A far cry from the "strong," protective father figure of the primer, Pecola's father, Cholly, uses his strength to brutalize the innocent child he is supposed to shield from abuse. Raped and impregnated by her father, Pecola turns inward, and in her madness is convinced that she has been granted the gift of blue eyes.

Pecola's self-hatred and the African American community's rejection of her, Morrison contends, are symptomatic of a much larger issue—internalized racism. Taught to believe that the dominant culture is superior to their own, African Americans such as Pauline and Geraldine disparage anyone who does not typify the white ideal. So indoctrinated into white culture is Geraldine that she makes fracturing distinctions between members of her own **race** based on such spurious attributes as skin pigmentation and demeanor. The one character in the novel who does not internalize such false judgments is Claudia MacTeer.

Unlike Pecola, Frieda, and other characters in the novel, Claudia does not fall under the spell of white America. Not only does she resent the blue-eyed Shirley Temple's association with the African American Bojangles, but her hostility towardX all little white girls culminates in her desire to torture their soft, pink flesh in childish retribution for the affection adults shower upon them and not her. Similarly, the young black girl is plagued by a need to dismember her white baby doll in an effort to discover its "dearness," to find in it the beauty that seems to elude only her. What Claudia discovers, however, is that the doll's beauty is, in fact, an illusion. Despite her young age, Claudia recognizes that the contempt she feels for the doll and all white or light-skinned girls is dictated by forces beyond her control. It is, in fact, Claudia's unmasking of the evils of the dominant culture, coupled with her tenacious and defiant nature, that enable her to escape Pecola's tragic fate.

Further Reading

Bouson, J. Brooks. *Quiet as It's Kept: Shame, Trauma, and Race in the Novels of Toni Morrison*. Albany: State University of New York Press, 2000.

Otten, Terry. *The Crime of Innocence in the Fiction of Toni Morrison*. Columbia: University of Missouri Press, 1989.

Carol Goodman

BORDER NARRATIVES

A term used to describe the writings of those immigrant groups who have come to feel caught between their native cultures and the culture of their new home country—they are tied to both, but do not properly belong to either. The term border narrative may be applied equally to photojournalism, short story, essay, novel, poetry, or cinematic genres. Oftentimes there is a crossing over and blending of genres. These narratives generally display a tension between the past, present, and future as the ancestral ties to the native culture become severed and the ties to the adopted country become stronger. Frequently there is also a strong generational gap—the immigrants' offspring often do not have a direct connection with the culture within which their parents were raised. Social, economic, political, historic, and cultural themes are common among border narratives.

In the United States the term is applied to much of the writing of Mexican and Mexican American authors living along the U.S.-Mexico border. Their writing is characterized by a conscious blending of English and Spanish languages and to a lesser degree traditional Aztec vocabulary. Like the lives of those who write these narratives, the writings are a product of American and Mexican societies coming together to form a new and distinct culture, which has elements of the others but which cannot be precisely termed either.

The Treaty of Guadalupe Hidalgo of 1848, signed by the United States and Mexico to end their war, ceded roughly 55 percent of Mexico's land (present-day Texas, Arizona, New Mexico, parts of California, Colorado, Nevada, and Utah) to the United States in exchange for $15 million as reparations. Mexico's new northern border would from that point forward follow the following route: from the Gulf of Mexico starting at the Rio Grande, up the Rio Grande to the southern border of New Mexico, westward along the southern border of New Mexico, then north following the first branch of the Gila River, then along the Gila River until its intersection with the Colorado River, and then westward following the Spanish-Mexican division of Upper and Lower California. Articles eight and nine of the treaty included provisions for the protection of the property and civil rights of Mexican nationals who would be in U.S. territory after ratification of the treaty. Furthermore it offered Mexican nationals up to a year to decide whether they wished to retain the Mexican citizenship or to become U.S. citizens. If after a year's time any of those Mexican nationals had not responded, they were to automatically become citizens of the United States. However, the reality of the treaty did not match up with what the document stated legally, as evidenced during the Gold Rush, during which time many former Mexicans living inside the new U.S. boundary were evicted from their lands due to lack of physical deeds to the land they claimed as their own. Many Mexican nationals living in the new U.S. territories were questioned as to whether they actually had been living in these areas prior to the signing of the treaty or if they had immigrated there illegally.

Border narratives often describe the "in-between-ness" of those living on the border, the dangers of living there, the hazards of crossing the border, and the instability often felt by those living along the border. Although not exclusively applied to the U.S.-Mexico border region, border studies, a branch of cultural studies, looks strongly and actively at the U.S.-Mexico border to gain insights into the new culture being created there.

Much of what is currently happening in the literature and culture of these groups is a transformation of the border. The border as a dividing line between cultures is giving way to the border as the connection, the one place where two cultures are connected or even fused. For instance, the line that runs from southern California to Texas is the one place that the United States and Mexico are constantly joined. This is perhaps the largest departure from previous (pre-1970) studies of the border. Liminality, the theoretical concept developed by anthropologist Arnold van Gennep, as a theoretical construct allows cultural theorists to probe some of the dynamics disallowed by other modes of research. To take one example, the Tejano culture, established along the Mexico-Texas frontier, is a culture that is no longer Mexican nor is it properly mainstream American. These are its parents, but Tejano culture has its own rules, codes, and traditions taken from and blended with elements of native Mexican and Texan societies and cultures.

Some of the authors associated with border narratives include Américo Paredes, a journalist, creative writer and scholar; Gloria Anzaldúa, a scholarly writer, children's book author, and frequent speaker on border studies whose book *Borderlands/La frontera* is a classic in Chicano/Chicana studies; Oscar Martínez, a scholarly writer of life on the border; Devon Gerardo Peña, whose book *The Terror of the Machine: Technology, Work, Gender, and Ecology on the U.S.-Mexico Border* is a border study about the working conditions of border residents, particularly women working in the infamous *maquiladoras*, factories along the U.S.-Mexico border that have gained much attention due to their sometimes abusive and inhumane working conditions; **Sandra Cisneros**, a Chicana poet and writer; **Julia Alvarez**; Adriana Ocampos; and **Tomás Rivera**, a Mexican American author, whose book *. . . y no se lo tragó la tierra/ . . . And the Earth Did Not Devour Him* details the life of a 1950s Mexican American family who work as migrant workers as seen from the perspective of a boy.

Mexican American border narratives often employ the use of multiple genres, including prose, poetry, photography, paintings, and drawings. These narratives are equally rife with the triumphs of coming to grips with an unstable social **identity** as they are with the troubles associated with living on the border—run-ins with the Border Patrol, poor economic conditions, abuse at the workplace, struggles to balance traditional family customs, and practices with a modern world and many other similar issues.

There are geographic centers along the U.S.-Mexico border that serve as nuclei for particular border groups (Tejanos and Chicanos to name just two) and these typically spring up in and around the larger U.S. and Mexican cities along the border. Each of these border groups maintains its own cultural norms (dress, speech, codes of conduct), but what unites them all is the struggle to gain a sense of identity where one is fleeting, a struggle to find a home in a region between two countries that could embrace them as their own, but instead reject them as wetbacks in the United States and pochos in Mexico.

Traditionally focusing on the geographic border region between the United States and Mexico, recently border studies scholars have begun to use the term "border" more loosely, applying it wherever a large group of Mexican Americans settles and begins hybridizing within the community. For example, many border scholars look at the Mexican American population of Chicago. The border there is seen to be carried with their culture, even though the actual U.S.-Mexico frontier is geographically quite distant.

Further Reading
Anzaldúa, Gloria. *La frontera/Borderlands*. San Francisco: Spinsters/Aunt Lute, 1987.
Cisneros, Sandra. *The House on Mango Street*. Houston: Arte Público Press, 1985.
Cisneros, Sandra. *Women Hollering Creek and Other Stories*. New York: Vintage Books, 1992.
Henderson, Mae, ed. *Borders, Boundaries, and Frames: Cultural Criticism and Cultural Studies*. New York: Routledge, 1995.
Hernández, Irene Beltrán. *Across the Great River*. Houston: Arte Público Press, 1989.
Michaleson, Scott, and David E. Johnson, eds. *Border Theory: The Limits of Cultural Politics*. Minneapolis: University of Minnesota Press, 1977.
Paredes, Américo. *Between Two Worlds*. Houston: Arte Público Press, 1991.
Rivera, Tomás . . . *y no se lo tragó la tierra/ . . . And the Earth Did Not Devour Him*. Trans. Evangelina Vigil-Piñón. Houston: Arte Público Press, 1987.
Ulibarrí, Sabine. *Tierra Amarilla: Stories of New Mexico/Cuentos de Nuevo México*. Trans. Thelma Campbell Nason. Albuquerque: University of New Mexico Press, 1971.
Valdés, Gina. *There Are Madmen Here*. San Diego: Maize, 1981.
Vila, Pablo. *Crossing Borders, Reinforcing Borders: Social Categories, Metaphors and Narrative Identities on the U.S.-Mexico Frontier*. Austin: University of Texas Press, 2000.
Villarino, José, and Arturo Ramírez, eds. *Chicano Border Culture and Folklore*. San Diego: Marin Publications, 1992.

Alexander Waid

BROOKS, GWENDOLYN (1917–2000)

Gwendolyn Brooks was an African American poet, novelist, and autobiographer. A prolific poet and an important force in Chicago's black community for more than 50 years, Brooks wrote verse recording the experiences of this community where she lived all her life. The first African American of either gender awarded the Pulitzer Prize for poetry, she served as poet laureate of Illinois from 1968 until her death.

Brooks's dedication to the community that served as her central source of inspiration has been manifest throughout her career. She had little formal training in writing but was encouraged by her working-class parents when she expressed a love for words from early childhood. As a teenager she wrote to the African American writers James Weldon Johnson and **Langston Hughes**, both of whom generously responded and with whom she met in person. Remembering the importance of this encouragement, she taught writing workshops and gave readings for aspiring writers of all ages in prisons and other unconventional locations as well as in schools. She sponsored numerous poetry competitions, often donating her own money

Gwendolyn Brooks. (Library of Congress)

as prizes. The tribute volume *Say That the River Turns* (1987), containing the poetry of young writers inspired by Brooks, testifies to her impact as a mentor.

In 1967, when Brooks was already a highly established and celebrated poet, the experience of attending a black writers' conference at Fisk University prompted her to fundamentally alter her view of race in America, moving from a belief in integration toward a celebration of black culture. The first part of her autobiography, *Report from Part One* (1972), movingly details how her interactions with young writers influenced by the Black Power Movement shaped this transformation. Her continued dedication to these goals can be seen in her support for black institutions such as the Detroit-based Broadside Press and the Chicago-based Third World Press and David Press as well as her own Brooks Press, all of which published her work for many years. She has been cited as a kind of literary mother to the Black Arts poets, especially Don L. Lee (later Haki Madhubuti) and Walter Bradford. Her own work can be understood as bearing an important relation both to this tradition and to the work of Afro-Modernist poets like Robert Hayden and Melvin Tolson. Her work also contains important commonalities with that of black women poets and writers who have gained increased critical attention since the 1970s, including Mari Evans, **Audre Lorde**, **Alice Walker**, and Ntozake Shange.

It would be a mistake, however, to see this transformation as delineating a "before" and "after"' in Brooks's work. Her dedication to recording the daily lives of those around her forms a common thread throughout her work. Although later poems make less use of certain forms such as the sonnet and the ballad, her dedication to craft remains paramount. She has been particularly successful in writing poetry that is both intricately complex and accessible to a wide audience, including those not accustomed to reading poetry, although she has sometimes described the difficulty of doing so. She has remained specifically committed to the black audience, insisting that black artists work on their own terms and not overly concern themselves with criticism from outside. The titles of her collection *Primer for Blacks* (1980) and anthology *Blacks* (1987) underscore her belief in the value of black culture ("black" being a term she feels speaks more to cultural **identity** and pride, as well as to an international identity, than the label "African American") and her desire that it not be dissolved in the name of integration or universality.

An overview of some of Brooks's most acclaimed work reflects these continuities. Her first collection of poetry, *A Street in Bronzeville* (1945), began the portrait of Chicago's black community that would continue to develop throughout her career. Although rooted in the particular geography of the neighborhood, Brooks has noted that her poems begin less with places than with people. Indeed, the reader of *A Street in Bronzeville* is left with the vivid image of the title characters of poems such as "the mother," who in fact never becomes a mother because of multiple abortions, "the preacher: ruminates behind the sermon," whose thoughts wander to the loneliness of God, and "Sadie and Maud," women who make opposite choices with ambiguous results.

Annie Allen (1949), the work for which Brooks won the Pulitzer Prize, offers an imaginatively rendered depiction of black experience during World War II. Using the unusual genre of mock epic, Brooks explores her title character's longings and dissatisfaction, using the language of fairy tale to see how family life, romance, and marriage are not only interrupted by war but disappoint in and of themselves. Like much of her work, *Annie Allen* links the experiences of its central figure to a wider context, suggesting the possibilities of transformation available to the larger community of which Annie is a part. Brooks continued her experiments with form in her novel *Maud Martha* (1953). In this work Brooks uses her own highly poetic prose to tell a coming-of-age story that draws heavily on her own experiences, with a particular emphasis on marriage and motherhood, themes that recur throughout her work.

Although published before Brooks's experience at the Fisk conference, *The Bean Eaters* (1960) marks a turning point in her work and anticipates much that was to come. The collection, which Brooks has noted that she prefers to the prize-winning *Annie Allen*, contains many memorable poems that mix the everyday with a wider context, beginning with a dedicatory poem to her father. "We Real Cool" succinctly distills the swagger of young pool players and is perhaps Brooks's most famous poem, while "The Lovers of the Poor" humorously sends up delicate do-gooders. In "The Last Quatrain of the Ballad of Emmet Till," Brooks turns her attention to the historical figure of a young boy killed in a racist attack and attempts to imagine a mother's grief.

In the Mecca (1968) continues this concern with important black historical figures with "Medgar Evers" and "Malcolm X," both of which turn the poet's eye for detail onto these larger-than-life figures while retaining a sense of awe in their presence. The collection draws on Brooks's experience of working for a "spiritual advisor" in a large Chicago housing complex as a young woman during the Depression. The title poem is a long weaving together of the stories of residents of the Mecca, the form emphasizing the difficulty and claustrophobia but also the possibility of these lives. Later sections include a sequence evoking the Blackstone Rangers, a street gang with whom Brooks herself had conducted writing workshops; dedications at two very different Chicago locations; and the first and second variations on "The Sermon on the Warpland," direct addresses Brooks has continued to rework throughout her career. Her poetic concern with specific historical events and figures continued in *Riot* (1969), which addressed the national crisis that followed the assassination of **Martin Luther King Jr.**, and in later works including *Mayor Harold Washington and Chicago, the I Will City* (1983), *The Near-Johannesburg Boy and Other Poems* (1986), and *Winnie* (1988), a long poem dedicated to Winnie Mandela, wife of South African leader Nelson Mandela and in Brooks's estimation an estimable freedom fighter in her own right. (*See also* African American Poetry)

Further Reading

Gayles, Gloria Wade, ed. *Conversations with Gwendolyn Brooks.* Jackson: University Press of Mississippi, 2003.
Mickle, Mildred, ed. *Gwendolyn Brooks.* Pasadena, CA: Salem, 2010.
Mootry, Maria K., and Gary Smith, eds. *A Life Distilled: Gwendolyn Brooks, Her Poetry and Fiction.* Urbana: University of Illinois Press, 1987.

Laura Tanenbaum

C

CANON

Until modern times, the word "canon" was used exclusively in an ecclesiastical context. The canon is still the set of rules, assumed divinely ordered, by which the church (primarily the Christian church in its various embodiments) governs itself. Compare the application of this denotation with the Pali canon, which forms the doctrinal foundation of Theravada Buddhism. Appropriated from the ecclesiastical use to define tenets of practitioners in genres or communities in many areas of the fine arts, such as music, the word is used in literature to denote a list of books accepted by most of a given community as definitive of the rules and mores of that group. Therefore any group of recognizable qualities may, in the field of literature, give rise to a canon. For example, by examining the elements of the type of 18th-century novel labeled Gothic, that is, by looking for the supernatural or for horror within the text, we may recognize this kind of narrative in English literature and be able to replicate the genre, if necessary, in the future. Although a contemporaneous replication of that novelistic form (using the Gothic as an example) would not share in the actual historical canvas against which this genre was first written, our new renditions would carry the patina of our particular experience. We may recognize the influence of this specific genre on 20th-century writers such as Octavia Butler, the science fiction writer, whose novels, such as *Kindred*, although not strictly Gothic, contain elements of the supernatural. This transference of the elements of a particular genre and, therefore, the elements of the respective canon into the literature of another period admits of one paradox of the canon as a grouping: the canon should not, indeed cannot, be closed. Elements of one literary expression flow into those of a later literary and historical period.

In the case of the United States, given the present emphasis on diversity and **multiculturalism**, there is an impetus toward inclusion that is driving the reexamination of the canon. It should seem obvious that the canon as it is conceived is also a reflection of literacy, literary theory, and socioeconomic factors. Pronouncements such as Harold Bloom's tome, *The Western Canon: The Books and School of the Ages*, add to the ongoing question as to who controls the canon. And as Trevor Ross writes in *The Making of the English Canon: From the Middle Ages to the Late Eighteenth Century*, "canons make clear the values of great literature and valued modern work" (92). He also joins the commentary that current tradition and definition of self form part of the impetus for the production and control of literature. Clearly there are aspects of power in this state of affairs. Questions of value and valuation arise, particularly in a system such as this where there is no guideline as to who can decide what is of value or not. An example of this occurred at a major university toward the end of the last century. In a debate concerning the list of writers to be studied in its English Department, voices representing new paradigms were raised. George Sweeney reported on September 22, 1997, in the *Daily Bruin* of the University of California at Los Angeles (UCLA), that Ali Behdad, professor of postcolonial studies, stated the English canon was not invented for England. It was invented as part of colonization, in order to shape and form a certain culture in India and other British colonies. Indeed the jingoism of the poetry of Rudyard Kipling and the cautionary precepts in the so-called folktale "Little Black Sambo," which were dispersed through reading texts to areas of the British Empire as various as the Caribbean, South America, and Australia, were indicative of two sides of the imperialist coin: on one hand, the fortitude of the colonizers was being upheld and on the other, the childlike comicality of the colonized was being reinforced. Arguments at academic institutions such as UCLA contended that the subscribed canon, seen as primarily Western and imperialistically dictated, has traditionally been exclusive and has resisted the influx of multicultural literature. As a result the two forces of traditional literature and new 21st-century literature are trying to find a balance. Nevertheless the question remains as to the identities and qualifications of those who compose the body that chooses and inserts texts into the canon.

To write about the contents of the canon is then fraught with indecision and redolent of the old imperialist structure. In any contention against the inclusion of, for instance, the rhymes of jingoism and adventures of Little Back Sambo, that same tendency to imperialism would surface, as, through the designation of the canon, the community is told how to act, what to read, and what to believe from a set of books that purports to define excellence for the entire community. Irving Howe comments that this is all balanced by teachers who are allowed to speak freely. Thus teachers are assigned the role of arbiter and arbitrator in a system that is already slippery by context, in a country in which, by constitutional definition, all opinions carry the note of validity. And this system, by an unwritten process of checks and balances, identifies writers who appeal to a broad societal base without necessarily questioning old inclusions like "Little Black Sambo." A version of the canon emerges.

To be chosen for the canon is to be anthologized by one of the major presses, such as Norton or Oxford, and thus have one's works placed before a public as the arbiters of literary excellence. These are the writers whose works are important, who have something to say. This list of writers and their works is then perpetuated of itself and, as may be deduced, remains highly dependent on the selection committees of such lists. Therefore, for example, if one considers the works of Rosa Guy one would find that she is memorialized as an insightful, searing young adult fiction novelist. This characterization would be one of her claims to fame since she is seen as a pioneer in the exploration of adolescent feelings in an urban setting. These are universal themes. Compare her *Ruby* with Goethe's *Suffering of Young Werther*, in which, although the latter protagonist is not as young as Guy's Ruby, the struggle for self-definition and the exploration of a youthful psychological landscape share commonalties and appear in print at a fortuitous moment in a community's history. In contrast, a dramatist-poet, such as Owen Dodson, may be avoided as an exponent on adolescent or young adult soul searching and discovery, although his autobiographically based *Boy at The Window* was hailed by respected critics as sensitive and honest.

There is the question then of how to resurrect the dead or distinctive works without discrimination and to do so not just during an Asian Heritage Month or African American Heritage Month celebration. Through what mechanism does anyone in a community find those narratives that are important to and for the culture of the United States, at the same time inserting new voices and retaining the others? The canon wars, aided by the publication of Harold Bloom's afore-mentioned text containing its impressive appendices, Sven Birkerts's anthology *On Literature: The Evolving Canon* (1995), and even the Modern Library's list of the 100 best books of the 20th century, smack of **whiteness** and deservedly created an uproar. Each of these promulgated an idea of the superiority of literature produced by white writers, with some tokenism by inclusion of writers such as **Toni Morrison**. These were the writers who were touted as representative of the thought and experience of the community. Completely ignored was that subtext, and the implications of that subtext, to the canon: literacy. For literacy to thrive, the reader has to be engaged. In 1997, one of a series of researches proposed that students became more active and thorough readers if they were given texts that reflected their own experience. The typical reading list of a public school district would admit a text such as Carolivia Herron's critically acclaimed children's story, *Nappy Hair*, and have it trounced. Careful examination of so-called relevant texts for the young, and this is where the canon making with its effect does start, has revealed that stereotyping and some degree of lessening of self-esteem are reinforced by these texts (Grice and Vaughn, 1992). This is an argument dismissed by Howe. Howe, in his introduction essay on the subject of the canon, questions whether the function of the humanities is to inculcate self-esteem. The canon of children's literature, one of the many subcanons, starts a student's educational road. What the student reads in school is important. If one reads "Little Black Sambo," or *Nappy Hair*, or if one reads the slave narratives, one is exposed to their characterizations, and their language, tone, and action. This statement, of course, takes any other outside reading encouraged by parents or other interested parties into consideration. By the time the student is likely to graduate, the choice of books may have impacted his or her life. The question is to what degree and to what purpose. Outdated texts, denigrating texts, all have their impact on the future. Thus, for example, if the student is familiar with Nathaniel Hawthorne's work, "The Maypole of Merry Mount," and all that the celebration of spring connotes, he or she is learning about the culture of those who colonized modern North America. If he or she is not exposed simultaneously to the Juneteenth festival, then a valuable part of the African American experience and, therefore, the American fabric is pushed into the background. And it is this consideration of the American experience that currently is influencing thought on the literary canon as it is delineated in the United States. The American version, to be inclusive, must acknowledge simultaneously its Western stratum and those other components derived from the history of movement into and within the country politic.

There is the danger of stretching the literary experience and output too thin and this is why judiciousness is necessary in this area of openness and diversity in America. Many an excellent writer, not promoted, has waited to be discovered. Many others have flamed and died without fulfilling their promise, and others with no talent have flourished owing to astute marketing. We cannot ignore the impact of the large press, or the importance of wealth in the process of the canon composition. Significant publishers, such as Norton, influence by their magnitude and imposition of texts and not necessarily by their correctness or relevance of choice. The writer has to be published to be read, read to be appreciated, and appreciated in order to be considered for inclusion in the canon. Even in the area of poetry, by tradition the most declaimed of words, the poem written is more permanent and less subject to change than the poem spoken. A poem that answers the needs of the community enters libraries, school texts, and the marketplace and assumes a place in the status quo, its place concretized by the multiplicity of sensibilities to which it appeals. Thus, with multiculturalism, diversity, and ethnic differences on the forefront of educative political programs, the canon is beginning to reflect the works of the several constituents of the American community. With publishers such as Arte Público Press and Griffon House Publications, with the proliferation of independent printing via the Internet, and with book festivals and reading groups, writers and critics such as Molefi Asante Jr., **Maxine Hong Kingston**, **Edwidge Danticat**, and Oona Kempadoo are placed on reading lists and mentioned in a one or more versions of what, combined, serves as the literary canon.

Further Reading

Anzaldua, Gloria. *Borderlands/La Frontera: The New Mestiza*. San Francisco: Aunt Lute Books, 1987.

Baker, Houston, Henry Louis Gates Jr., and Joyce A. Joyce. "The Black Canon: Reconstructing Black American Literary Criticism." *New Literary History* 18.2 (Winter 1987): 335–44.

Bloom, Harold. *The Western Canon: The Books and School of the Ages*. New York: Harcourt Brace, 1994.

Eliot, T. S. *The Sacred Wood: Essays on Poetry and Criticism*. London: Methuen, 1920.

Ervin, Hazel Arnett. *African American Literary Criticism*. New York: Twayne, 1999.

Fetterley, Judith. *The Resisting Reader: A Feminist Approach to American Fiction*. Bloomington: Indiana University Press, 1978.

Gates, Henry Louis, Jr. "The Master's Pieces: On Canon Formation and the Afro-American Tradition." In *Conversations*, edited by Charles Moran and Elizabeth Penfield, 55–75. Urbana, IL: National Council of Teachers of English, 1970.

Grice, Mary Oldham, and Courtney Vaughn. "Third Graders Respond to Literature for and about Afro Americans." *Urban Review* 24.2 (June 1992): 149–64.

Howe, Irving. "The Value of the Canon." *New Republic* 204.7 (1991): 40+.

Jay, Gregory. *American Literature and the Culture Wars*. Ithaca, NY: Cornell University Press, 1997.

Lauter, Paul. *Canons and Contexts*. New York: Oxford University Press, 1991.

Morrison, Toni. *Whiteness and the Literary Imagination*. Cambridge, MA: Harvard University Press, 1993.

Peters, Cynthia. *Deaf American Literature: From Carnival to Canon*. Washington, DC: Gallaudet University Press, 2002.

Ross, Trevor. *The Making of the English Literary Canon: From the Middle Ages to the Late Eighteenth Century*. Montreal and Kingston, Canada: McGill-Queens University Press, 1998.

Wimsatt, W. K., and Cleanth Brooks. *Literary Criticism: A Short History*. London: Routledge and Kegan Paul, 1970.

Juliet A. Emanuel

CARIBBEAN (ANGLOPHONE) AMERICAN AUTOBIOGRAPHY

Much Caribbean American literature takes the form of loosely autobiographical coming-of-age novels, from **Paule Marshall**'s *Brown Girl, Brownstones* (1959) to **Jamaica Kincaid**'s *Lucy* (1990). **Audre Lorde** speaks to the blurring of lines between autobiography and fiction in Caribbean American literature in the subtitle, "autobiomythography," of her novel *Zami: A New Spelling of My Name* (1982). The story of the author's life, Lorde conveys, combines the tales inherited from her ancestors, the events that she experienced first-hand, and the fictional lives that she has imagined for herself. This blended form of autobiography points to how any autobiography must rely in some way on imagination well as on fact, but also indicates some of the unique features of Caribbean American autobiography. While the autobiography traditionally tells the story of a single and singular self, the one "I" who writes her or his own story, Caribbean and Caribbean American literature remains committed to understanding the individual as always part of a community (a family, a village, a nation, etc.). Thus, autobiographies that blend the protagonist with various other real or imagined people offer an autobiographer whose story is always also that of a community. Nonetheless, the form of the conventional autobiography where a single first-person narrator is clearly identified with the author and faithfully represents the author's biography also serves a number of Caribbean American authors.

Because the Caribbean American community is relatively recent and still in the process of establishing itself, many Caribbean American autobiographies tell the story of coming to America or else remain deeply marked by the parents' arrival. They belong to a tradition of American immigrant literature and to a tradition of African American literature. Like African Americans, Afro-Caribbeans suffered the Middle Passage and slavery, but in the Caribbean, during and after slavery, blacks represented the majority of the population. At the same time, after slavery, Afro-Caribbeans remained the colonial subjects of the British crown often until they immigrated to the United States. Some Caribbean Americans such as Claude McKay and Audre Lorde became major players in African American politics and letters, although others such as **Michelle Cliff** and Jamaica Kincaid continue to understand themselves more as Afro-Caribbeans in America than as African Americans.

Born in Jamaica, McKay immigrated to the United States in 1912 and soon became a major figure in the **Harlem Renaissance** with novels such as *Home to Harlem* (1928) and *Banana Bottom* (1933). Like many writers of the Harlem Renaissance, McKay not only lived in Harlem but also traveled extensively. McKay wrote two autobiographies: *A Long Way from Home* (1937) and *My Green Hills of Jamaica* (1979). *A Long Way from Home* follows McKay's 12 years of wandering the globe and his return to Harlem. In his second autobiography, however, written toward the end of his life, McKay returns to his childhood in Jamaica and to an idealized Caribbean past.

To the second generation, the Caribbean is still an ideal but it is only a distant, almost mythic memory. Marshall's *Brown Girl, Brownstones* portrays a girl growing up in the Barbadian immigrant community in Brooklyn between the two world wars. Selina must negotiate the close-knit Barbadian community that is nonetheless deeply committed to the American dream, her father's nostalgia for Barbados, and her own entry into the multicultural world of New York. In *Zami, A New Spelling of My Name*, Audre Lorde similarly describes her childhood as the daughter of immigrants, in her case from Grenada, although the family does not maintain deep ties to any Grenadian community in New York. Lorde/Zami depicts her young adulthood in the 1950s and her coming to terms with her lesbianism in the context of the lesbian and feminist movements, of the African American community, and of her Grenadian heritage.

While second and especially third-generation Caribbean Americans increasingly identify with African American communities, newer waves of Caribbean immigrants continue to arrive in the United States. Still living between Caribbean and American identities, Michelle Cliff, Jamaica Kincaid, and Patricia Powell continue the Caribbean American autobiographical tradition with novels that blend their own stories with those of their families. Cliff, like Lorde, explores what it is to be a Caribbean American lesbian. In *Abeng* (1984) and *No Telephone to Heaven* (1987), Cliff narrates her forced departure from Jamaica as a child and her struggles to understand her racial, cultural, and sexual difference in the United States and in Jamaica. All of Kincaid's many works retell the stories of her childhood and of her family's past. *Annie John* (1985) and *Lucy* (1990) depict a young girl who grows up in Antigua, comes to the United States to work as a nanny, and discovers herself as an artist. The title of Kincaid's subsequent book, *The Autobiography of My Mother* (1996), foregrounds the complicated identification of the author with the main character of the story. *The Autobiography of My Mother* speaks to the importance of the mother to the identity of the daughter in Caribbean traditions, but it also sets up the autobiography as the story of the person in contrast to whom the author defines herself. Patricia Powell's autobiographical novel *Me Dying Trial* (1993) similarly tells the story of a mother with whom the daughter does not identify.

Mothers also feature prominently in the semiautobiographical short stories and novels of **Edwidge Danticat**, *Krik? Krak!* (1996) and *Breath, Eyes, Memory* (1998). Danticat is from the Francophone Caribbean (Haiti), but writes in English. Her work marks the way in which it becomes increasingly difficult in the American context to separate between Anglophone, Francophone, and Hispanophone

Caribbean authors. Indeed, not only Danticat, but also writers of Cuban, Puerto Rican, and Dominican heritage, increasingly write autobiographical novels in English that share many of the characteristics of Caribbean American autobiographies.

Further Reading

Condé, Mary, and Thuronn Lonsdale. *Caribbean Women Writers*. New York: St. Martin's Press, 1999.

LeSeur, Geta. *Ten Is the Age of Darkness*. Columbia: University of Missouri Press, 1995.

Paquet, Sandra Pouchet. *Caribbean Autobiography*. Madison: University of Wisconsin University, 2002.

Keja Lys Valens

CARIBBEAN (ANGLOPHONE) AMERICAN NOVEL

Because most Anglophone Caribbeans belong to the African diaspora, Caribbean American novels stand at the crossroads of Caribbean novels and African American novels. Authors born in the Caribbean and residing in the United States may be categorized as both Caribbean and Caribbean American, while authors of Caribbean heritage born in the United States may be claimed as both Caribbean American and African American. Close attention to the novels themselves only supports the blurry lines between the different categories, as Caribbean American novels draw on and participate in Caribbean and African American literary traditions. And because both Caribbean and African American literary traditions are themselves composite of African, Euro-American, and many other traditions, it is difficult even to establish hybridity as a mark particular to the Caribbean American novel. A survey of Caribbean American novelists and their works reveals, however, a trend from integration into the **Harlem Renaissance**, the Black Arts Movement, and the **Civil Rights Movement** to, in the last quarter of the 20th century and into the new millennium, greater assertion of ties to the Caribbean and of difference from the African American community.

Jamaican-born Claude McKay (1889–1948) wrote the first novel of the Harlem Renaissance to become a best seller. *Home to Harlem* (1928), based in part on McKay's own experience, exemplifies the Harlem Renaissance as it recounts the story of a working-class black man in Harlem in the 1920s. *Banjo* (1929), McKay's second novel, tells of another important aspect of the Harlem Renaissance: the black American community in France. It is only with *Banana Bottom* (1933) that McKay writes explicitly of the Caribbean. The Caribbean often becomes for both first- and second-generation Caribbean Americans a place that exists primarily in memory, linked to childhood or to family pasts in ways that are easy to idealize, and *Banana Bottom* offers a typically utopic portrayal of Jamaican village life.

A Caribbean American novelist was also at the center of the Black Arts Movement, to which the Harlem Renaissance gave way. Rosa Guy (1928–2012) was born in Trinidad and moved to Harlem before she was 10 years old. Guy cofounded the Harlem Writer's Guild. Her first novel, *Bird at My Window* (1966), charts the struggle of a young black man to hold onto his sanity in the face of a tortuous relationship with his mother and of an increasingly impoverished and polarized Harlem where the Civil Rights Movement is still only a dream. In the 1970s, Guy traveled to Haiti and Trinidad, and when she returned to the United States, began to write novels for young adults, including *The Friends* (1973) and *Ruby* (1976), with West Indian themes. Guy has since published numerous young adult novels, most recently *My Love, My Love, the Peasant Girl* (2002), which follows in the tradition of rewriting Euro-American classics as it resets Hans Christian Andersen's "The Little Mermaid" in the Caribbean, with the major difference between the young lovers being not sea- or land-life, but skin color.

Audre Lorde (1934–1992) was born in New York to West Indian immigrant parents, but although Barbadian traditions permeated Lorde's home, like Guy, she grew up in Manhattan surrounded by African American rather than West Indian families. Lorde's novel, *Zami, a New Spelling of My Name* (1982), reflects a deep connection with the African American community and a distant longing for a Caribbean family past. Allusions to the Caribbean frame *Zami*, and the Caribbean stands in the novel as the ideal source of and home for her black lesbian identity, but the great majority of the novel focuses on Audre's coming of age as a black lesbian in the African American and lesbian scenes in New York in the 1950s and 1960s.

With *Brown Girl, Brownstone* (1959), **Paule Marshall** (1929–) became the first Caribbean American writer to focus her work on the growing Caribbean American community that remained largely separate from the African American community. The largely autobiographical coming-of-age novel follows a young girl growing up in Brooklyn's Barbadian neighborhood. The protagonist finds herself caught between her father's nostalgia for the islands, her mother's intense desire to achieve the American dream of so many immigrants, and her own growing awareness of the African American community. Marshall's subsequent novels, including *The Timeless Place, The Chosen People* (1969), *Praisesong for a Widow* (1983), and *Daughters* (1991) continue to treat the intersection of Caribbean and African American communities and themes. *The Timeless Place* is set on a composite Caribbean island, but in *The Timeless Place* the Caribbean is so rife with the contradictions of its rich and troubled history and its neo-colonial relationship with the United States and Britain that it cannot become a utopia. *The Timeless Place* draws heavily on themes and techniques common to Caribbean literature, highlighting the role of the maroons and finding ways to represent time outside of a linear flow. *Praisesong for a Widow* leans more toward the African American genre of a roots novel, featuring a woman who travels to the Caribbean in search of some sort of connection to her African heritage. But by locating the endpoint of the journey in the Caribbean rather than in Africa, *Praisesong* emphasizes the importance of the Caribbean as a middle point of connection between Africa and African America.

The novels of Elizabeth Nunez also center on Caribbean American characters. Born in Trinidad, Nunez moved to the United States as a teenager. She draws on her own experience to write novels about Caribbean immigrants in the United States.

As she writes of love affairs between Caribbean immigrants, African Americans, and Africans, Nunez brings out the differences and also the similarities of their experiences and of their attitudes. *Grace* (2003) and *Beyond the Limbo Silence* (1998) both explore relationships between Caribbean immigrants and African Americans, and *Discretion* (2000) depicts cross-cultural liaisons in New York by focusing on the rekindled love of a married African diplomat for a Trinidadian-born artist.

Although they align themselves less with African American or even Caribbean American communities, many of the most important Caribbean authors of the 20th century have spent significant parts of their lives living in the United States. Trinidadian Earl Lovelace (1935–), for example, spent more than 20 years of his life studying and teaching in the United States, but all three novels that he wrote during that period, *The Schoolmaster* (1968), *The Dragon Can't Dance* (1979), and *The Wine of Astonishment* (1982), are set squarely in the Caribbean and deal with the classical Caribbean themes of village life and carnival. Lovelace's long residence in the United States, and that of others, such as Belizean novelist Zee Edgell, represent less a desire to become American or to write Caribbean American novels than they do the political and economic realities that force so many people from the Caribbean to leave their island homes.

Other Caribbean authors who have spent the majority of their lives in the United States and see little chance of returning permanently to the Caribbean still maintain primary identification as Caribbean authors but, like Marshall, write novels where the Caribbean becomes a place that has been left behind both in space and in time. The two semiautobiographical novels of Jamaican-born **Michelle Cliff** (1946–), *Abeng* (1985) and *No Telephone to Heaven* (1987), follow the story of a young girl who is forced to move to the United States as a child and who longs to return to Jamaica. In her novels *Annie John* (1986), *The Autobiography of My Mother* (1996), and *Mr. Potter* (2002), **Jamaica Kincaid** (1949–), who left her native Antigua as a teenager, revisits her life and that of her parents in the Caribbean, but in *Lucy* (1990) and *My Brother* (1997), she also describes how life in the United States deeply marks her and her characters' perspectives on family and on the Caribbean. *Me Dying Trial* (1993), the first novel of Jamaican-born Patricia Powell (1966–), details the process of a woman's leaving Jamaica and settling in the United States. After a second novel, *A Small Gathering of Bones* (1994), set in the contemporary Caribbean, with *The Pagoda* (1999), Powell writes a Caribbean historical fiction.

The Caribbean settings and the Caribbean vernaculars of many Caribbean American novels of the late 20th century and early 21st century assert their ties to the Caribbean. But these novels also employ American settings. They continue to parallel African American novels in their connection to the African diaspora even as they also join with the novels of other recent immigrant populations to detail the negotiation of divergent cultural traditions and values. Historical periods and generational differences mark various trends in Caribbean American novels. It remains to be seen if many second- and most third-generation Caribbean American novels will continue to merge into the African American **canon**, or whether changing times will lead to the development of more numbered generations of Caribbean American novelists.

Further Reading

Booker, M. Keith, and Dubravka Juraga. *The Caribbean Novel in English*. Portsmouth, NH: Heinemann, 2001.

Nelson, Emmanuel S. "Black America and the Anglophone Afro-Caribbean Literary Consciousness." *Journal of American Culture* 12.4 (1989): 53–58.

Paquet, Sandra Pouchet. "Caribbean Fiction." In *The Columbia History of the American Novel*, edited by Emory Elliott, Cathy N. Davidson, Patrick O'Donnell, Valerie Smith, Christopher P. Wilson, 586–606. New York: Columbia University Press, 1991.

Keja Lys Valens

CARIBBEAN (ANGLOPHONE) AMERICAN POETRY

The United States has served as both a home for immigrant writers from the Caribbean and as a site of literary production for writers who maintain their Caribbean **identity** and focus even as they live outside the region's geographical boundaries. As the Jamaican novelist and poet **Michelle Cliff** has noted, the Caribbean exists all over the world; Caribbean literature is notable for the number of major authors who have made their homes outside the Caribbean itself. Like other genres of Caribbean American literature, then, Caribbean American poetry can be divided into two major categories: the poetry of Caribbean writers living in the United States and the poetry of American writers of Caribbean descent. This distinction may seem slight, but it remains of critical importance.

Whereas London, during the 1950s and 1960s, was the locus of literary activity for Caribbean writers outside the Caribbean, the United States has in recent decades offered Caribbean writers a host of opportunities, notably academic appointments. Meanwhile, the Hart–Celler Immigration Act (1965) made it easier to enter the United States from the Caribbean. The period since 1965 has consequently seen the biggest influx of Caribbean immigrants to the United States.

Of the Caribbean writers in "exile" in the United States, Derek Walcott (1930–) is certainly the most prominent. The St. Lucian poet, playwright, and essayist, winner of the Nobel Prize in 1990, has taught at several American universities, including Boston University and Harvard University. Walcott's *The Arkansas Testament* (1987) derives largely from the poet's experience of living in the United States. The epic poem *Omeros* (1990) is set primarily in St. Lucia, but includes long passages set in North America; the poem is also notable for its critique of American tourism and industry in the Caribbean. Both works address the correspondences between the experience of slavery in the United States and in the Caribbean. Walcott is also fond of noting the ironic relation between American democracy and slavery. (Dionne Brand, a Trinidadian Canadian poet, has similarly critiqued the American military interventions in the Caribbean.)

There are other notable examples of contemporary Caribbean writers at home in the United States. The distinguished Barbadian poet (Edward) Kamau Brathwaite (1930–), for example, teaches at New York University; he has previously taught at Boston University, Yale, and other American universities. Michelle Cliff

(1946–) was born in Jamaica, but has lived variously in the United States and London as well as in her country of birth. Her writing depicts the experience of growing up in a colonized country, and frequently addresses themes of racial and sexual inequality. Although much of her life has been spent outside Jamaica, her writing, as in *Land of Look Behind: Prose and Poetry* (1985) assumes a Jamaican perspective.

If we expand the definition of poetry to include popular forms, Caribbean poetry has no doubt had its most widespread impact in the United States through the reggae songs of Bob Marley, whose music and Rastafarian beliefs have been absorbed into American popular culture.

It is essential to remember, however, that although these works engage with American culture, they form part of the American literary tradition only tangentially. The borders between national and regional literatures are certainly not fixed, and indeed Caribbean poets draw on American traditions. Yet the cosmopolitan Brathwaite and Walcott are resolutely Caribbean writers despite their time spent in the United States.

In contrast, Claude McKay (1889–1948) came from the Caribbean and became absorbed into the American and African American canons. McKay left Jamaica for the United States in 1912 to further his young poetic career. He became a leading figure in the **Harlem Renaissance** and a founding member of the Black Writers Guild. Prior to his emigration, he published two collections of folk poetry, *Songs of Jamaica* (1911) and *Constab Ballads* (1912). Both works are written primarily in dialect; the former depicts peasant life in Jamaica and the latter draws on McKay's own experience as a policeman. Although he was also known as a prose writer in the United States, he continued to publish poetry, including *Harlem Shadows* (1922). His *Selected Poems* appeared posthumously in 1953. Jamaican poet Louise Bennett, who works in the folk tradition that McKay belongs to, has lived in New York (1953–1955); she now resides in Toronto.

Caribbean American poetry also includes second-generation writers. **Audre Lorde** (1934–1992), for example, was born in New York to parents from Grenada. Although she was a native-born American, hers was a Caribbean immigrant household. Lorde published her first collection, *The First Cities*, in 1968. Her interests in the African diaspora and African mythology are particularly apparent in *The Black Unicorn* (1978).

The poets mentioned thus far all have their origins in the Anglophone Caribbean. But the category of Caribbean American poetry must also include writers from the Spanish Caribbean. New York became an important center in the 1960s for Puerto Rican poets who identified themselves as **Nuyorican**s or Neo-Ricans, that is, first-generation or second-generation Puerto Ricans born or raised in the United States. The Nuyorican Poets' Café, located on Manhattan's Lower East Side (or *Loisaida*), served as a home for writers in this community and produced an anthology, *Nuyorican Poetry* (1975), edited by Miguel Algarín and **Miguel Piñero**. Moreover, poets such as **Judith Ortiz Cofer** and Aurora Levins Morales show that poets of Puerto Rican descent living in the continental United States are not based exclusively in New York.

New York has also provided a home to Cuban American poets writing in Spanish, English, or both. The Spanish-language anthology *Poetas Cubanos in Nueva York* (1986) included, for instance, Reinaldo Arenas, who is also known for his poetry in English. Miami, too, has been an important center for **Cuban American poetry**.

Further Reading

Baker, Houston A. *Reading Black: Essays in the Criticism of African, Caribbean, and Black American Literature*. Ithaca, NY: Africana Studies and Research Center, Cornell University, 1976.

Balderston, Daniel, and Mike Gonzalez, eds. *The Encyclopedia of Latin American and Caribbean Literature, 1900–2003*. London: Routledge, 2004.

Burnett, Paula, ed. *The Penguin Book of Caribbean Verse in English*. London: Penguin, 1986.

Nicholas Bradley

CHINESE AMERICAN AUTOBIOGRAPHY

Although **Maxine Hong Kingston**'s *The Woman Warrior: Memoirs of a Girlhood among Ghosts* (1976) was not the first work of Chinese American autobiography, it generated an interest in the genre that, in effect, established the genre as an area of academic interest. Kingston's book is a collection of five narratives, each of which provides a sense of the hazards of being both Chinese and female. In "No Name Woman," Kingston tells the story of an unmarried aunt on her father's side of the family who became pregnant and was so denigrated by her own family and by the other people in her village that she eventually drowned herself. Simply by writing the narrative, Kingston is violating her family's absolute silence on an episode in the family history that they have been determined to forget, as if the act of forgetting can eventually eradicate history and even her aunt's existence. In offering this memoir as an alternative to forgetting, Kingston seems to be highlighting the irony that the oxymoronic concept of deliberate forgetting is itself an assertion of memory. In "White Tiger," Kingston relates a Chinese folktale about a girl named Fa Mu Lan who becomes an unlikely warrior and defeats the enemies of her village. "Sharman" describes how Kingston's own mother became a doctor, violating just about every expectation of a young woman in her cultural milieu. "At the Western Gate" is another moving narrative about one of Kingston's aunts. In this instance, the aunt travels to America to be reunited with her husband only to discover that he has married another woman and started another family. Finally, in "A Song for the Barbarian Reed Pipe," Kingston describes her own struggles to adapt to America and to synthesize the Chinese and American aspects of her **identity**. The "ghosts" of the title may be understood in multiple ways: they are, at once, the dead ancestors, the people whose stories have been forgotten or repressed, the people who have been left behind in China and are now "alive" to the immigrants only as memories, and the immigrants themselves who feel a profound sense of dislocation and move among their new countrymen with a sense of unbelonging, with the feeling that their presence has at most an ephemeral impact on the American political, economic, social, and cultural landscape.

In *China Men* (1980), Kingston examines the experiences of three generations of men in her family and in the process provides a social, economic, and cultural history of Chinese Americans on the West Coast during the 20th century.

One of the first widely read Chinese American autobiographies was American-born Jade Snow Wong's *Fifth Chinese Daughter* (1950). The book presents a thoughtful account of her lifelong efforts to find a satisfactory balance between the Chinese and the American elements of her heritage and her experience. The sections dealing with her upbringing are noteworthy not only as a sensitive narrative of maturation but also for the intimate details they provide about Chinese American life in the 1920s and 1930s. Interestingly, Wong's second autobiographical book, *No Chinese Stranger* (1975), was published the year before Kingston's *Woman Warrior*, and so despite the quarter century between Wong's two volumes, it cannot be said that she was attempting to cash in on Kingston's success. *No Chinese Stranger* concerns Wong's adulthood. The centerpiece of the narrative is the account of her family's trip to China shortly after it was opened to Western tourists.

In *Nine Hundred Years in the Life of a Chinese Family* (1988), Chinese American journalist Francis Ching locates his own experiences within a truly expansive and exhaustive family history. In *Beyond the Narrow Gate: The Journey of Four Chinese Women from the Middle Kingdom to Middle America* (1999), Leslie Chang chronicles the passages of her mother and three of her mother's friends from the political turmoil and warfare that convulsed China in the 1930s and 1940s to very sedate lives in suburban America. At root, Chang is trying to understand how her bicultural identity and her behavior have been shaped by her often very limited understanding of the experiences that created very different needs and expectations among the women of her mother's generation.

A naturalized American citizen, Katherine Wei-Sender has had an impressive career in corporate management. With the novelist Terry Quinn, she wrote the memoir *Second Daughter: Growing Up in China, 1930–1949* (1984). Inevitably, the story of her maturation provides a very personalized corollary to the titanic historical events that completely transformed China during those two decades. Ironically, despite the terrible turmoil of those years, Wei-Sender's narrative is tinged with nostalgic sentiment both for her lost youth and for the China that disappeared with the Communist victory.

Primarily known as a writer of self-help nonfiction titles, former fashion model Aimee E. Liu has explored the theme of survival in an autobiographical volume and a family history. In *Solitaire* (1979), she describes her own recovery from a severe eating disorder, and in *Cloud Mountain* (1997), she traces the stories of her grandparents, a politically radicalized Chinese scholar and an American woman who met during the disastrous San Francisco earthquake of 1906. The couple spent most of their married life in China, negotiating a series of great political upheavals from the overthrow of the Manchu rule to the Communist takeover under Mao.

In what amounts to a subgenre of these autobiographies, Chinese Americans have recounted their experiences in China during the Cultural Revolution. In *Life and Death in Shanghai* (1987), Nien Cheng offers a vivid account of her extended persecution at the hands of the Red Guards. Cheng had worked for Shell Oil at the time of the Communist takeover of mainland China in 1949, and she had never found a way to eliminate suspicions that she privately maintained bourgeois attitudes. Because of those suspicions, the Red Guards held her in solitary confinement for more than six years. In *Single Tear: A Family's Persecution, Love, and Endurance in Communist China*, Ningkum Wu explains how as a University of Chicago professor, he responded to a request by the Communist government and returned voluntarily to China to teach. For the next three decades, he and his family would be subjected to recurring periods of persecution that came to a terrible climax during the Cultural Revolution.

In *The Winged Seed* (1995), the poet Li-Young Lee recalls his family's escape from China when he was still a very young boy and their subsequent passages through Hong Kong, Macao, Japan, and Indonesia before they secured visas to enter the United States in 1964. Because he has written compelling poems about his family's experiences in Indonesia, Lee has sometimes been identified with a growing group of Chinese American authors with roots in Southeast Asia. Raised in Malaysia, Shirley Geok-lin Lim has written creditably in three genres—poetry, the short story, and the novel—while establishing herself in an academic career, producing influential literary criticism, and editing a number of widely used anthologies of literature from East Asia and the Pacific region. In *Among the White-Moon Faces: An Asian-American Memoir of Homelands* (1996), Lim presents a candid account of a tough childhood and adolescence—her mother deserted the family and her father had a harsh personality and fixed expectations of his only daughter. She found an avenue of escape in academic success and pursued it with an almost relentless determination, earning scholarships to universities first in Malaysia and then in the United States. Throughout this time, she often experienced an uneasy awareness of her foreignness and an unsettling sense of dislocation. In response, Lim has embraced the "warrior" persona defined by Maxine Hong Kingston.

In *Falling Leaves: A True Story of an Unwanted Chinese Daughter* (1998), Adeline Yen Mah describes her troubled relationship with her stepmother, a woman with some French ancestry who had, from the beginning, nothing but antipathy toward Mah. Mah's father was a millionaire, and with his wife and all of his children except Mah, he managed to escape from China just ahead of the Communist takeover. Subsequently raised in the relative isolation of a Shanghai boarding school, Mah, like Shirley Geok-Lin Lim, channeled all of her energies into her studies, and after several fortuitous turns of circumstance, she ultimately set up a medical practice in California as an anesthesiologist. As her parents aged, Mah reconciled with them and even helped to care for them, and yet, when her father and then her stepmother died, Mah was betrayed again when she was pointedly denied any share of the inheritance. So Mah's autobiography provides a sort of purgative testimony, permitting her to have the last word on a relationship in which she was always an unequal party. Ironically, her siblings have spurned Mah because of the book, feeling that her chronicle of their stepmother's betrayals has been itself a betrayal of the family's privacy. In the end, *Falling Leaves* is as much about the continuities and the changes within the Chinese family in the mid-20th century as it is about the eccentricities of this particular Chinese family.

Further Reading

Lee, Jid. *From the Promised Land to Home: Trajectories of Selfhood in Asian-American Women's Autobiography*. Las Colinas, TX: Ide House, 1998.

Leydesdorff, Selma, Luisa Passerini, and Paul Thompson, eds. *Gender and Memory*. New York: Oxford University Press, 1996.

Madsen, Deborah L. *The Woman Warrior and China Men*. Gale Study Guides to Great Literature, Vol. 9. Detroit: Gale, 2001.

Wong, Sau-ling Cynthia, ed. *Maxine Hong Kingston's "The Woman Warrior": A Casebook*. New York: Oxford University Press, 1999.

Martin Kich

CHINESE AMERICAN DRAMA

Prior to the 1960s, theater created by Chinese Americans was scarce, generally confined to the occasional revival of classical Chinese operas or the educational theater practices seen in schools and universities, particularly in Hawai'i. With the establishment of the first Asian American theater in 1965 (the East West Players in Los Angeles), the Asian American theater movement began in earnest, offering new opportunities for Chinese Americans interested in playwriting, directing, acting, and design. Since this time, Chinese American playwrights have made significant contributions to the Asian American theater movement, a fact that reflects the community's history of early immigration to the United States and its standing as the largest Asian American population today.

Chinese American playwrights garner a number of "firsts" in the broad vision of Asian American theater. For instance, Gladys Li (1910–) was the first Asian American playwright of record in the United States. Writing during the early 20th century, Li, a Hawaiian-born Chinese American, proved an active advocate for Asian American theater and film during her lifetime, winning both an Academy Award for her documentary film *Kukan* and a Bicentennial Woman of the Year Award by the National Association of Women Artists of America. Writing many years before the Asian American theater movement began, Li emerged from the educational theater venue, writing three plays during her college years at the University of Hawai'i. All of her works, *The Submission of Rose Moy* (1925), *The White Serpent* (1927), and *The Law of Wu Wei* (1928), received production at the Arthur Andrews Theatre of the University of Hawai'i and were published by the school literary magazine *Hawai'i Quill Magazine*.

One of the chief themes of Li's plays is the irreconcilable difference between traditional Chinese and modern American cultures. For example, in *The Submission of Rose Moy*, a young Chinese American woman struggles between her desire for a western education and her parents' wish that she follow the traditional domestic path for Chinese women. Rose Moy finds that there can be no compromise between her quest for American independence and her filial obligations as a Chinese daughter. At the end of the play, she submits to her Eastern ancestral traditions, fainting to the ground as she concludes that there can be no true meeting between East and West. *The Law of Wu Wei* echoes similar sentiments about the conflict between traditional Chinese filial obligations and the Western value of personal freedom. In this play, Li details the failed romance between a Chinese man, bound by family to marry a woman in China, and the Chinese American woman who he prefers.

This assumption that Eastern and Western cultures are eternally separate is echoed in the early dramatic work of Shih-I Hsiung (1902–1991). Though Hsiung was born in China and spent his writing career in Hong Kong and London, he reveals a strong kinship to Li in his awareness of the stark cultural divide between China and the West. His plays, *Lady Precious Stream: An Old Chinese Play Done into English According to its Traditional Style* (1934) and *The Romance of the Western Chamber* (1935), were devised to educate Western audiences in the appreciation of the Chinese culture. Toward this end, he created English-language plays based on classical Chinese dramatic traditions, hoping to instill his audience with a respect for the artistic traditions of a "foreign" society.

The first significant wave of Chinese American playwrights rejected Li and Hsiung's assumption of an eternal East–West cultural divide. Emerging during the early 1970s, this generation of playwrights promoted a new vision of the Chinese American **identity**, an ethnic identity that was a unique blending of Chinese and American cultures. Building on the ethnic consciousness-raising of the 1960s, Chinese American dramatists explored the complex and multifaceted experiences of Chinese Americans, often seeking to uncover the lost narratives and invisible lives of their parents, grandparents, and great-grandparents. This initial period of Chinese American playwriting, therefore, is notable for its focus on immigration, early life in the United States, the changing Chinese American family, Chinese American identity and cultural traditions, and the issue of assimilation into the white American culture.

Furthermore, Chinese American playwriting, as well as Asian American playwriting in general, can be defined in part by its strong consciousness of "otherness," the ethnic stereotyping and abjection enforced by the dominant culture's media and national identity. Responding to these social phenomena, many of these plays attempt to define the Chinese American identity in positive and human terms, often relying on theatrical realism to help develop a sense of on-stage authenticity and realness.

Again, in the broad vision of Asian American theater, Chinese American playwrights may claim numerous "firsts." Frank Chin (1940–), a member of the first wave of Chinese American playwrights, is the first Asian American playwright to have received national attention for his dramatic writing. His play, *The Chickencoop Chinaman*, produced by the American Place Theatre in New York in 1972, proved an angry and rebellious investigation into the plight of the socially displaced Chinese American male. His second major play, *Year of the Dragon* (1974), offered a provocative and unsettling view of life in an American Chinatown. Chin, who has worked extensively as an editor, fiction writer, and advocate for Asian American literature and theater, has rallied against what he views as the **assimilation**ist tendencies of some of his fellow writers. Chin has, however, also been subject to sharp criticism for the chauvinism, anger, and offensive language expressed in his plays. A colorful figure in the early stage of Asian American theater, Chin's rise to public attention signaled the beginning of a more public presence for Asian American theater artists.

David Henry Hwang (1957–), another member of the first wave of Chinese American playwrights, is the first Asian American playwright to win a Tony Award for Best Play (1988). A leading playwright in the contemporary theater scene today, Hwang based his groundbreaking play, *M. Butterfly*, on a real-life incident of international espionage and sexual misidentification. In this work, Hwang severely critiques the imperialistic fantasies of Western men toward Asian women, embodying his argument in the relationship between a French diplomat and a Chinese opera singer. Though the French diplomat pursues an oppressive romantic relationship with the Chinese opera singer, who he believes to be the "ideal" woman, the singer is ultimately revealed to be a man.

M. Butterfly is not only Asian American theater's best-known play, but is also one of its most controversial. Given Hwang's characterization of the leading Chinese character Song Liling as a seductive transvestite homosexual, one who is also an undercover Communist spy, Hwang has been accused of reinstating negative stereotypes of Asian males. While Hwang's aim is to deconstruct Western views of Asian gendered identities in the blurred identity of Song Liling, his use of conventional assumptions about Chinese secrecy and sexual exoticism troubles some spectators and scholars seeking more positive depictions of Asian peoples. This ongoing controversy reflects both the political complexity of Hwang's drama and the difficulty in representing Asian characters on Western stages. Made into a feature film starring Jeremy Irons and John Lone in 1993, *M. Butterfly* has been the most widely publicized and discussed of Asian American plays to date.

Less controversial than either Chin or Hwang, Genny Lim (1946–) is representative of many first-wave playwrights in her steady quest to uncover the lost narratives of early Chinese immigrants. Known for her careful studies of late 19th- and early 20th-century Chinese immigration and for her unique research at Angel Island, Lim has written two significant works, *Paper Angels* (1978) and *Bitter Cane* (1989). Both plays investigate the hardships and personal difficulties suffered by early Chinese immigrants, offering spectators meaningful insight into the immigration process, labor and work conditions, and the isolated living environments of first-generation Chinese immigrants.

As a genre, Chinese American drama has proven highly diverse, fostering not only traditional plays but also visual-movement work, solo performance, and dramatized fiction. Theater artists such as Ping Chong (1946–) and Dan Kwong (1954–) have explored the boundaries and processes of theatrical performance, developing nationally recognized pieces in "theater of images" and solo narrative, respectively. Mainstream stage-versions of successful Chinese American novels such as *The Flower Drum Song, The Woman Warrior*, and *The Joy Luck Club* also merit inclusion in the genre of Chinese American drama. Of particular note, the original musical version of *The Flower Drum Song* (based on a novel by C. Y. Lee) was reworked by David Henry Hwang in 2002 to address a more contemporary perspective of Chinese American life, particularly in the area of female gender roles.

Chinese American drama benefits from the continued emergence of new writers. Chay Yew (1966–), a self-proclaimed member of the second wave of Chinese American playwrights, is one of the leading new voices in American theater. Known for his innovative stylistic invention, Yew, a Singapore-born Chinese, has achieved international acclaim for *Porcelain* (1992) and *A Language of Their Own* (1994), two dramas that investigate the complexities of gay intercultural romance. In his short career, Yew has presented characters with diverse racial and national identities, as well as with differing class backgrounds, sexual orientations, and cultural histories. This dynamic dramaturgy reflects Yew's own transglobal experience and identity.

In many ways, Yew's work is representative of the developing **canon** of second-wave Chinese American playwrights. In this new phase of writing, issues of ethnic identity are often superseded by concerns about the Chinese American experience in a multicultural society and the ethics of the post–ethnic-identity political sphere. Clearly, as the Chinese American identity grows and evolves on the intercultural global stage, Chinese American dramas will reflect these changes.

Further Reading

Eng, Alvin, ed. *Tokens*. Philadelphia: Temple University Press, 1999.

Lee, Josephine. *Performing Asian America, Race and Ethnicity on the Contemporary Stage*. Philadelphia: Temple University Press, 1997.

Moy, James S. *Marginal Sights, Staging the Chinese in America*. Iowa City: University of Iowa Press, 1993.

Kimberley M. Jew

CHINESE AMERICAN NOVEL

The Chinese American novel emerged as an aesthetic response to a set of specific historical, social, and political circumstances. Like the larger novel tradition, which developed out of an array of genres, such as romance, history, autobiography, and popular journalism, the Chinese American novel assimilates elements of history, autobiography, and myth. Its crowning achievement lies in the imaginative brilliance of **Maxine Hong Kingston's** widely read novels, ***The Woman Warrior: Memoirs of a Girlhood among Ghosts*** (1976), *China Men* (1980), and *Tripmaster Monkey: His Fake Book* (1989), a corpus that transcends conventional generic boundaries. Although *Tripmaster Monkey* is regarded as unequivocal fiction, both *The Woman Warrior* and *China Men* are largely autobiographical, narrating history through family stories.

The case of Chinese Eurasian sisters Edith Eaton and Winnifred Eaton, arguably the first Chinese—and Asian—North American writers, exemplifies the complex ways in which literary form shapes and is shaped by the audience, cultural values, and political climate. Edith Eaton wrote primarily short stories and journalistic pieces about Chinese life in the United States and Canada. Although she penned her essays under her given name Edith, she invariably published the fiction under the Chinese nom-deplume Sui Sin Far (narcissus). Eaton's authorial identifications suggest a canny awareness of her audiences and a process of self-legitimation: In fighting for the rights of Chinese North Americans in articles published in mainstream newspapers, she invokes the cultural authority of "Edith Eaton"; but when writing her short fiction she lays claim as "Sui Sin Far" to ethnic authenticity and insider knowledge of Chinese life.

Edith Eaton's sister Winnifred Eaton engaged in similar performances of identity, exploiting the prevailing cult of japonisme—the West's interest in Japanese culture and art—in order to market her interracial romances. Curiously, as the earliest known Chinese American novelist, she adopted a fictional Japanese persona and wrote books populated with Japanese, Caucasian, and Eurasian characters, but no Chinese. As Onoto Watanna, Winnifred Eaton published more than a dozen novels, one of which, *A Japanese Nightingale* (1901), was adapted for Broadway in 1903. Unlike her sister Edith, who heroically embraced her Chinese ancestry and asserted the rights of the Chinese in the face of rampant Sinophobia, Winnifred, it is argued, exploited the exoticization of the Japanese and sold out her heritage for the ethnic hierarchies of the marketplace. Certainly, the punitive terms of the 1882 Chinese Exclusion Act, which prohibited the entry of most classes of Chinese to America, in comparison to the relatively benign 1907 Gentlemen's Agreement (curtailing Japanese immigration), would argue for Edith's political stature as a writer who refused to pass. But this approach is perhaps overly simplistic and diverts attention from both sisters' ingenious negotiation of their audiences and a patriarchal publishing industry through ethnic affiliation. Winnifred Eaton's successful performances reflect the importance of sociopolitical context in the literary marketplace—the mirror of cultural taste and value—a circumstance subsequent generations of Chinese American novelists responded to in different ways.

Early Chinese American writers, like the Eaton sisters, confronted a culture that viewed the Chinese as unassimilable aliens. In the face of such pervasive xenophobia, they strove to promote positive images of the Chinese. The changing fortunes of the Chinese during the World War II era witnessed the emergence of the modern Chinese American novel tradition. The Chinese alliance with America and the advent of Pearl Harbor on December 7, 1941, reversed the traditional attitudes toward the Japanese and Chinese: as Japan came to be reviled, Chinese stock rose, along with an increased interest in Chinese culture. The Chinese Exclusion Act was repealed in 1943, although the 1924 quota of 105 remained in place. The new geopolitical alliances and Americans' newfound interest in the Chinese enabled the popular reception of the two most noteworthy works of the period, Pardee Lowe's *Father and Glorious Descendant* (1943) and Jade Snow Wong's *Fifth Chinese Daughter* (1950). In both autobiographies, tradition collides with modernity as the second generation's embrace of mainstream myths of individuality confronts the stiff resistance of the old world embodied in the patriarchal authority of the father.

Jade Snow Wong's *Fifth Chinese Daughter* is an especially compelling testimony to the myth of possessive individualism because of its legacy for future generations of female Chinese American novelists. Born into working-class scarcity in San Francisco's Chinatown, Wong became a scholarship student, successful potter and writer, and cultural emissary for the United States in Asia. Wong's achievements are all the more remarkable given her subordinate status as a woman in a traditional Chinese household, a daughter whose education the father would not support. Her sense of being alienated from agency is epitomized in the title, *Fifth Chinese Daughter*, which is not only her name but also the way she thinks of herself, an identity so subordinate that she does not lay claim to an "I." The irony of an autobiography written from a third-person perspective has not gone unnoticed by Maxine Hong Kingston, who argues for the importance of Wong as a literary model and of the specifically feminist elements of Wong's narrative.

In 1924, Congress passed an Immigration Act that specifically barred Chinese women, wives, and prostitutes, and established an annual quota of 105. This law was dramatically effective in curtailing the Chinese population by eliminating reproduction and led to the unique demographic character of Chinatowns—enclaves of aging Chinese bachelors cut off from their families in Canton province, China, the origin of the Chinese diaspora. H. T. Tsiang's *And China Has Hands* (1937) is an early fictional treatment of this bachelor society, but the genre did not achieve fruition until Louis Chu's brilliant novel, *Eat a Bowl of Tea* (1961). Central to the plot is the impotence of Ben Loy, a second-generation Chinese American veteran who is unable to produce an heir with his war bride Mei Oi. Ben Loy's impotence functions as a metaphor for New York's Chinatown, a community of aging, impotent bachelors desperate for new blood. Matters are brought to a head when a rogue seduces and impregnates Mei Oi, but the initial furor and consternation over this transgression give way to celebration when a son is born. Liberated from the oppressive expectations of the parents, Ben Loy and Mei Oi head to San Francisco to begin a new life. A realistic, humorous portrait of a Chinese American community, Chu's *Eat a Bowl of Tea* approaches greatness in its rendition of Cantonese English, an ebullient vernacular that captures the flavor of New York's Chinatown without degenerating into rude caricature.

Chinatown as a specific sociohistorical space functions as the setting for many Chinese American novels; in others, however, Chinatown and its associated history become virtual characters in the novels themselves. These works—which include Lin Yutang's *Chinatown Family* (1948), C. Y. Lee's *Flower Drum Song* (1957), Gish Jen's *Typical American* (1991), Fae Myenne Ng's *Bone* (1993), Sigrid Nunez's *Feather on the Breath of God* (1995), and Canadian Sky Lee's *Disappearing Moon Cafe* (1991 [set in British Columbia and Vancouver's Chinatown])—examine the social and psychological dimensions of place and its connection to Chinese American **identity**. C. Y. Lee's *The Flower Drum Song* was a *New York Times* best seller and was adapted for Broadway by Rodgers and Hammerstein in 1958; in

2001 David Henry Hwang revised the musical to glowing reviews, and in 2002, forty-five years after its initial publication, Penguin Books reissued the novel. Lee's *The Flower Drum Song* introduced mainstream audiences to the social issues of San Francisco's Chinatown and remains as relevant for contemporary audiences as it was in 1957.

The heady liberationist movements of the late 1960s and early 1970s witnessed the emergence of Chinese America's two most influential writers, Frank Chin and Maxine Hong Kingston. American-born contemporaries, the dialogue between Chin and Kingston has become foundational to an understanding of Chinese American literature. For both novelists "writin' is fightin'." But ironically, this belief in the power of the written word to effect change has become a bone of contention between them, centering in particular on the significance of myths: for Chin, the essence of myth is its stability over time; for Kingston, however, myths must be renegotiated continually in order to remain relevant. Chin has criticized Kingston for her liberal treatment of received Chinese myths—the story of Fa Mu Lan for example—an orientation that makes her putative autobiographies "fake." But for Kingston the reinterpretation of myths is an important feminist strategy to assert women's agency.

Fifth-generation Chinese American Frank Chin, the first Asian American playwright to be produced off-Broadway, is perhaps best known for his plays, short stories, and as the lead editor of *Aiiieeeee!* (1974), an early and influential anthology of Asian American writing expanded and published as *The Big Aiiieeeee!* in 1991. That he came to the novel late in his career is understandable given his scathing critique of **Chinese American autobiography**, a genre that he feels has perpetuated a feminized, Christianized, and **assimilation**ist tradition of Chinese American writing ("This Is Not an Autobiography" *Genre* 18 [Summer 1985]: 109–30). Chin attempts to rehabilitate Asian American manhood by appropriating the discourse of black nationalism and by excavating heroic images from a Chinese American context, drawing on an epic history of railroad building.

In the late 1980s Chin undertook a transpacific swerve, replacing Asian American cultural nationalism with a Chinese version of cultural nationalism founded on three Chinese classics—Luo Guanzhong's *The Romance of the Three Kingdoms* (14th century), Shi Nai'an's *Water Margin* (14th century), and Wu Cheng'en's *Journey to the West* (16th century).

Abandoning the autobiographical orientation of much Chinese American writing, Chin's novels focus instead on cultural critique, the way that American history and the media construct demeaning images of Asian Americans. Hence, the very titles of his two novels, *Donald Duk* (1991) and *Gunga Din Highway* (1994), exploit images from popular culture to suggest the construction of Chinese America in the American imagination as well as the epic antidote he prescribes. Set in San Francisco during Chinese New Year, *Donald Duk* narrates how the eponymous 12-year-old protagonist overcomes his alienation from Chinese culture—a self-contempt resulting from pernicious representations of the Chinese in history books and the media—and learns to embrace it. Donald's rehabilitation eventually comes full circle: in his dreams Chinese mythology comes to life on the American frontier as the epic warrior-poet Kwan Kung merges with intrepid Chinese railroad workers.

Chin's second novel riffs on Rudyard Kipling's ballad about the Indian water boy who helps the British defeat his own people. Gunga Din thus functions as an image of Chinese America disseminated through popular culture and symbolizes all those Chinese American writers who promote fake but marketable images of the Chinese to white audiences. In this novel Chin concentrates on Hollywood's construction of Charlie Chan—humble, docile, asexual—as an image of America's racist love. Ironically, the father figure in the novel, Longman Kwan, is lampooned for his naïve aspiration to be the first Chinese American actor to play Charlie Chan, an unworthy ambition because he would be purveying racist stereotypes rather than debunking them. It remains for the aptly named son, Ulysses S. Kwan, to challenge popular stereotypes and introduce enabling images of the Chinese into the American imagination.

Chin himself has identified Louis Chu as a literary forefather, suggesting a masculine tradition of the Chinese American novel inherited by contemporary writers such as Shawn Wong and Gus Lee. In *Homebase* (1979), Wong narrates the story of fourth-generation Chinese American Rainsford Chan, who, orphaned at 15, strives to recover a sense of his parents' love and the history of his male ancestors. *American Knees* (1995), Wong's second novel, examines the pitfalls of interracial romance from the perspective of 40-year-old Chinese American Raymond Ding. Gus Lee's autobiographical first two novels, *China Boy* (1991) and *Honor and Duty* (1994), dramatize the experiences of Chinese American Kai Ting as a youth growing up in San Francisco's rough-and-tumble Panhandle and as a West Point cadet.

If the civil rights era and the legacy of ethnic consciousness raising accents Frank Chin's cultural nationalism, Maxine Hong's oeuvre exhibits the influence of second-wave feminism in the articulation of a Chinese American consciousness and voice. Kingston's *The Woman Warrior* remains among the most widely read texts on university campuses today. One of the work's intriguing features is the way that it revises the genre of autobiography, mingling history, myth, and fiction in a discontinuous narrative in order to dramatize the way that Chinese and family history influence Kingston's contemporary identity. Divided into five sections, the novel dramatizes the subjection of women both in China and America: an aunt's suicide over an adulterous pregnancy; Moon Orchid's (the mother's sister) deterioration into insanity when her husband abandons and rejects her for a younger Chinese American woman; the mute Chinese girl, Kingston's mirror image, whom she bullies. But these examples of Chinese women's oppression are balanced by images of feminine power and autonomy: Fa Mu Lan, the woman warrior; Kingston's mother, the shaman, at once warrior, medicine woman, exorcist, and storyteller who defeats a ghost and liberates a slave girl; Ts'ai Yen, the woman who lived among barbarians for a dozen years and wrote poems about her experience for posterity. That Kingston concludes the novel with an image of Ts'ai Yen in "A Song for a Barbarian Reed Pipe" suggests the blending of the martial Fa Mu Lan with the figure of the artist-poet, the woman warrior who fights through language and art. *The Woman Warrior* itself dramatizes this act of feminist self-realization, moving from the opening vignette of the aunt's tragic suicide to the concluding image of Ts'ai Yen's triumph over bondage and her achievement of a lyric voice. Through *The Woman Warrior* Kingston speaks not only for herself, but for her literary mother Jade Snow Wong and all Chinese women forced into silence.

With her second work, *China Men*, Kingston offers a balancing perspective by dramatizing the history of Chinese men's migration to America, the Gold Mountain. *China Men* begins with a brilliantly comical vignette, "On Discovery," detailing sojourner Tang Ao's feminization in the land of women, a fate that foreshadows the emasculation of Chinese men in America. Simultaneously an analysis of family and a narrative of the nation, *China Men* imagines the stories of her forefathers' migration to the Gold Mountain, the most immediate story being that of her father, whose presence in America is shrouded in silence and mystery. Hence Kingston constructs two different tales of his immigration: in one story, he is the father who immigrates legally according to the laws of the land; in the other, he is smuggled in. Of note is a brief chapter titled "The Laws," which details the history of Chinese exclusion in the United States and provides a stark depiction of the intimate connection between Chinese identity and immigration policy.

If *Woman Warrior* remains Kingston's most popular work, *Tripmaster Monkey* is, incontestably, her most sophisticated text. Set in the heady insurgent milieu of 1960s San Francisco, the novel remythologizes Frank Chin as the **signifying** yellow hipster Wittman Ah Sing—a clear reference to Walt Whitman—in a brilliantly allusive synthesis of Chinese and American culture. Wittman embarks on a journey to narrate the tale of his tribe, a quest that recapitulates the manifold quest-romances of American and Chinese literature. As a playwright, Wittman imagines a play that will transform an exclusively black and white landscape with a signifying Chinese American difference. Significantly, by the end of the novel, after waging the art of war through epic Chinese American theater, Wittman gives up his imaginative identification with the great warrior-poet Kwan Kung and is transformed into a pacifist.

Just as Frank Chin functions as a conduit between Louis Chu and contemporary Chinese American men's writing, Maxine Hong Kingston's influence has paved the way for a new generation of writers who continue to articulate the issues first raised by Jade Snow Wong, including **Amy Tan**, Gish Jen, Fae Myenne Ng, and Sigrid Nunez. Tan's four novels—*The Joy Luck Club* (1989), *The Kitchen God's Wife* (1991), *The Hundred Secret Senses* (1995), and *The Bonesetter's Daughter* (2001)—dramatize the cultural and emotional estrangement that plagues the relationships among various generations of Chinese women. Thematically, Tan's work is traceable to Kingston's *The Woman Warrior*, and the two writers share the imperative to reinvent received myths so as to shatter conventional representations of Chinese women.

In contrast, Gish Jen's *Typical American*, Fae Myenne Ng's *Bone*, and Sigrid Nunez's *A Feather on the Breath of God*—three highly regarded novels—take up the troubled father–daughter relationship that Kingston examines in *China Men*, a lineage traceable to Jade Snow Wong's *Fifth Chinese Daughter*. In *Typical American*, Jen analyzes the experience of the first generation's immigration to America from the early 1940s to the 1950s, suggesting that while the new world liberates Chinese women from the strictures of traditional Chinese culture, it poses a more ambiguous, potentially mortifying challenge for the father. *Mona in the Promised Land* (1996), Jen's second novel, continues the saga of the Chang clan from the late 1960s to the 1990s; this novel is noteworthy because it portrays the making of second-generation Chinese American identity as a construct mediated through the Jewish experience rather than through an ethnocentric return to roots. In *Bone* Ng connects the broader history of Chinese exclusion in America to its destructive impact on the Leong family: the middle daughter's suicide is symptomatic of the absence of love between father and mother, a condition brought about by the father's humiliating status as an illegal alien, a mere paper son. Similarly, in *A Feather on the Breath of God* Nunez narrates a young woman's poignant struggle to come to terms with her Chinese Panamanian father, a man whose silence symbolizes his feelings of impotence. Having fought as an American soldier in World War II, he returns home with a German war bride only to confront **racism** and disenfranchisement.

For writers like Ng and Nunez, the struggle to come to terms with this traumatic paternal legacy is facilitated through storytelling, the process by which their female protagonists develop a sense of agency and empowerment. By telling their family stories, they assume control over their lives and are able to break with an oppressive past. Leila, the eldest daughter and narrator of *Bone*, comes to recognize that her mother does indeed love her husband, and this knowledge ultimately liberates her from the stifling confines of Chinatown and the history that threatens to suffocate her. Likewise, the nameless narrator of *Feather* works toward a sense of identity through art. By imagining a different father for herself, a parent capable of loving his own daughter, she creates a family story that she can truly inhabit, one fueled by love and desire.

Further Reading

Kim, Elaine. *Asian American Literature: An Introduction to the Writings and Their Social Context*. Philadelphia: Temple University Press, 1982.

Li, David Leiwei. *Imagining the Nation: Asian American Literature and Cultural Consent*. Stanford, CA: Stanford University Press, 1998. 21–43.

Wong, Sau-ling Cynthia. "Chinese American Literature." In *An Interethnic Companion to Asian American Literature*, edited by King-Kok Cheung, 39–61. New York: Cambridge University Press, 1997.

Andrew Shin

CHINESE AMERICAN POETRY

Chinese American poetry consists of multiple and heterogeneous poetic traditions and vastly different, idiosyncratic poetic styles. These characteristics in part reflect the historical conditions, geographical differences, and demographic changes that have shaped the emergence and development of poetry by Chinese Americans.

Although the term "Chinese American literature" emerged only during the early 1970s, in the wake of **Civil Rights Movement** and the beginning of multicultural movement, recent scholarship has traced the origins of Chinese American literature to the 1850s when Chinese immigrant communities were established in the United States, especially on the West Coast, and had begun to publish bilingual and Chinese-language newspapers that frequently printed fiction, satire, poetry, and popular Cantonese vernacular rhymes and songs.

San Francisco, also known as "Gold Mountain" among the Chinese, was a gateway of early Chinese immigration, and San Francisco Chinatown became a dynamic economic and cultural center of Chinese American communities. In 1854, according to the estimation of a San Francisco–based bilingual paper, *The Golden Hills' News*, no less than 40,000 to 50,000 Chinese had arrived in "Gold Mountain" from China. The number of Chinese immigrants continued to grow over the following two decades partly due to civil war in China and partly because of the Gold Rush and the post–Civil War demand of labor in the United States. The Chinese population declined in the late 19th century and remained static for about half a century as a result of anti-Chinese **racism**. Singled out as scapegoats during a period of labor unrest, Chinese Americans became targets of discriminatory laws and racial violence. With the completion of the transcontinental railroad in 1870, the anti-Chinese movement intensified, and eventually led to the 1882 Chinese Exclusion Act, which banned immigration of Chinese laborers to the United States and prohibited Chinese from becoming naturalized citizens on the grounds that they were not "white." Not until 1943 did Congress repeal the Chinese Exclusion Act, establishing an annual quota of 105 people for Chinese immigration to the United States and allowing Chinese "aliens" previously barred from citizenship to have naturalization rights. In contrast to the predominantly working-class immigrants to the United States during the 19th century and early 20th century, many of the Chinese immigrants who arrived during and after World War II belonged to the well-to-do, well-educated, or elite class and were able to attend universities and have professional careers in the United States. In 1965, the Immigration and Naturalization Act replaced the national-origin quotas with hemispheric quotas, resulting in a rapid population growth and profound demographic changes in Chinese American communities. These changes became even more dramatic after the normalization of the Sino-U.S. diplomatic relationship following Nixon's visit to China in 1971 and after China's open-door policy began in the 1980s.

The earliest collections of Chinese American verse were written in the local vernacular of the southern province, Guangdong (Canton), where the majority of early immigrants to the United States had lived. *Taishan Geyao Ji* (1919, a collection of Taishan [dialect] songs and rhymes) and *Meizhou Guangdong Hau Quiao Liuchuan Geyao Huibian* (1970, a collection of popular songs and rhymes of Chinese Americans from Guangdong) were published in Chinese, but selections from two volumes of *Jinshan Geji* (Songs of Gold Mountain) were translated by Marlon K. Hom and published as *Songs of Gold Mountain: Cantonese Rhymes from San Francisco Chinatown* (1987). The first volume of *Songs of Gold Mountain*, consisting of 808 rhymes, was published in 1911, and the second volume, consisting of an additional 832 songs, was published in 1915. Of those 1,640 pieces, Hom selected 220 for the 1987 volume. All of these rhymes are written in the regulated Cantonese folk song format of 46 syllables divided into eight lines—5-5-7-7-3-5-7-7—with each line ending in the same consonant or vowel syllable. The predominant themes of these songs are the loneliness of the wives left behind in China, the pain of separation from loved ones, the hardships and struggles for survival in the United States, disappointment at the rarity of chances for of success in the United States, and the disillusionment with the Gold Mountain dreams.

Another important collection of early verses by Chinese immigrants is the bilingual anthology *Island: Poetry and History of Chinese Immigrants on Angel Island, 1910–1940* (1980), translated and edited by Him Mark Lai et al. These poems were written or carved on the wooden walls of the detention barracks on Angel Island (in San Francisco Bay), which between 1910 and 1940 was used as an immigration station, where Chinese immigrants were interrogated and examined to screen out the illegal and undesirable aliens. While waiting for the results of their appeals or orders for their deportation, the detainees expressed their anguish, anger, frustration, humiliation, and disillusionment by writing or carving poems on the walls of the detention center. These poems of various lengths are written in variations of five- and seven-syllable lines and are loosely modeled on the regulated forms of classical Chinese poetry.

The first collection of poems written by Chinese Americans in English, *Chinese American Poetry: An Anthology* (1990), edited by L. Ling-chi Wang and Henry Yiheng Zhao, is a landmark that shows the explosive diversity and development of Chinese American poetry. It consists of selected works by 22 poets of two generations with different backgrounds, works addressing a wide variety of thematic concerns in various poetic forms and styles. Poems included in this anthology range from traditional lyrics such as those by Diana Chang to difficult conceptual poems by Mei-mei Berssengrugge, from Nellie Wong's capacious, meditative lines about Chinese American experience to Marilyn Mei Ling Chin's distinct voice of a passionate feminist, from Li-Young Lee's engaging autobiographical lyric to Arthur Sze's multicultural sequence collage poems, from Wing Tek Lum's love poems that evoke Chinese poets to John Yau's surrealist, postmodern language poems. In addition to their thematic and formal heterogeneity, the geographical locations of those poets—San Francisco, New York City, Chicago, Los Angeles, Santa Fe, Portland, Seattle, and Honolulu, among others—and their prominent poetic careers indicate that Chinese American poetry is no longer contained within Chinatown or circulated among Chinese American communities only. Chinese American poets no longer live in the geographically bounded margins of mainstream American society and culture. However, the multicultural aspects of these Chinese American poems are not simply a direct reflection of the poets' **ethnicity** or social positions. Rather, the formal and stylistic characteristics of Chinese American poetry, like its thematic concerns, are the result of the poets' negotiations with multiple poetic traditions in resistance to assimilation by Eurocentric culture, in search of new ways of using language and form to engage with social issues and to reinvent poetry. Poems collected in *Paké: Writings by Chinese in Hawai'i* (1989), edited by Eric Chock and

Darrell H. Y. Lum, show that Chinese American poets in Hawai'i have contributed to the diversity of Chinese American poetry by incorporating local color, including pidgin, into their poems.

Given that *Chinese American Poetry* was published in 1991 and that any selection necessarily involves exclusion, it is not surprising that many contemporary Chinese American poets are not included in the anthology. Some of these poets are recent immigrants such as Ha Jin, Wang Ping, and Bei Dao; some are openly gay or lesbian poets such as Timothy Liu, Justin Chin, and Sharon Lim-Hing; some are diaspora poets such as the Malaysian-Chinese American poets, Hillary Tham, and Shirley Geok-lin Lim; and some are innovative poets such as Tan Lin and Ho Hon Leung, whose poems do no overtly deal with Chinese American experience per se.

Despite the large number of well-published and award-winning Chinese American poets and the rich variety of poetry they have produced, the 1991 *Chinese American Poetry* remains the only anthology of poetry in English by contemporary Chinese Americans. This phenomenon is perhaps largely due to the efforts to establish pan ethnicity in the formation of Asian American literary traditions. Poems by Chinese American poets are collected in anthologies such as *Dissident Song: A Contemporary Asian American Anthology* (1991), *The Open Boat: Poems from Asian America* (1993), *The Very Inside: An Anthology of Writings by Asian and Pacific Islander Lesbian and Bisexual Women* (1994), *Premonitions: The Kaya Anthology of New Asian North American Poetry* (1995), *Quiet Fire: A Historical Anthology of Asian American Poetry, 1892–1970* (1996), *Take Out: Queer Writing from Asian Pacific America* (2000), and *Asian American Poetry: The Next Generation* (2004). These anthologies provide a larger context for reading Chinese American poetry, most of which is published as the works of individual poets. In spite of their vast differences, Chinese American poets share some important similar characteristics among themselves and with other Asian American poets in their resistance to cultural **assimilation**, in their exploration of identities of race, gender, class, culture, and sexuality, and in their insistence on engaging with social issues through commitment to formal, aesthetic innovations.

Further Reading

Chang, Juliana. "Reading Asian American Poetry." *MELUS* 21.1 (1996): 81–98.

Hongo, Garrett. "Introduction." In *The Open Boat: Poems from Asian America*, edited by Garrett Hongo, xvii–xlii. New York: Anchor, 1993.

Tabios, Eileen, ed. *Black Lightning: Poetry-in-Progress*. New York: Asian American Writers' Workshop, 1998.

Uba, George. "Coordinates of Asian American Poetry: A Survey of the History and Guide to Teaching." In *A Resource Guide to Asian American Literature*, edited by Sau-Ling Cynthia Wong and Stephen H. Sumida, 309–31. New York: Modern Language Association of America, 2001.

Wong, Sunn Shelley. "Sizing Up Asian American Poetry." In *A Resource Guide to Asian American Literature*, edited by Sau-Ling Cynthia Wong and Stephen H. Sumida, 285–308. New York: Modern Language Association of America, 2001.

Zhou Xiaojing

CHINESE AMERICAN STEREOTYPES

As one of the earliest, and largest, groups of Asian immigrants to the United States, people of Chinese descent have had a long history of both troubled and successful attempts at integrating themselves into the larger American populace. Stereotypes purporting to illuminate their "exotic" racial traits and cultural preferences bear witness to the reluctance with which the public greeted these attempts. These surprisingly tenacious images continue to impact Chinese American life via their depictions of gender, family, work, and citizenship.

The first Chinese immigrants to the United States left their villages in order to escape political conflict and hardship. Their arrival in California coincided with that of Anglo workers from the Eastern seaboard, drawn by the promise of the Gold Rush (1849). Thus, international immigration and national migration placed two groups lacking a common language into territory known for its economic opportunity. The competition that ensued fueled nationalist desires for racial homogeneity, resulting in an assertion of insuperable difference between Americans and Chinese. This enabled the "natives" (i.e., earlier generations of European Americans) to limit immigrant access to opportunity. California moved to institute a foreign miners' license tax in 1852 that required nonnatives to pay a monthly fee to roaming tax collectors. Made nervous by the continuing influx of immigrants, the federal government later passed the Chinese Exclusion Act of 1882, which both ended immigration of Chinese laborers and denied naturalized citizenship to those already in the country. Though many of these immigrants were men, such legal actions also affected women: the 1875 Page Act prevented the immigration of prostitutes, but was enforced in such a way as to curtail national entry by virtually all females, regardless of profession. As a whole, these acts were designed to halt the threat of the so-called "Yellow Peril": the idea that, given the chance, the Chinese would quickly engulf a white majority population.

In spite of widespread and systematic anti-Chinese sentiment, however, a more positive characterization of the Chinese developed at the same time. This was based on the growing necessity for Chinese labor in agricultural and railway expansion. Many immigrants had left farms behind in China, and thus came to the United States prepared to share their agricultural and engineering expertise. Irrigation and botanical advice made Chinese laborers valuable assets but fostered an image of them as subordinate/servile. Their involvement with the Central Pacific Railroad (1865) reinforced this idea. Specifically recruited because they had proven equal to the arduous physical tasks demanded by the railroad's path (e.g., driving steel, blasting passages through mountains), the Chinese accepted tasks for which the company had difficulty obtaining white labor. Nevertheless, Leland Stanford, Central Pacific president, praised Chinese workers far less for their courage and endurance than for their passivity and reliability (Takaki 91–92).

Images of the subservient, passive Chinese persisted throughout the 19th century, operating in conjunction with growing competitive and nativist sentiments. Local and national media responded with representations of the Chinese that both grew out of and contributed to these perceptions. Minstrel performances (often associated exclusively with racist characterizations of African Americans) included the figure of "John Chinaman." From the 1850s onward, this "comedic" caricature embodied a host of devious desires and dangerous designs (stealing jobs from white Americans, "overrunning" the country, etc.), as well as numerous cultural differences marking him as utterly foreign and "other" (eating various vermin and domesticated animals, speaking English with a ludicrous accent). Writer Bret Harte's enormously popular poem "The Heathen Chinee" (1870) immortalized such poisonous imagery. Here, Ah Sin, the main character, is repeatedly identified as "childlike" while at the same time he is cheating white men at cards and leaving them "ruined by cheap Chinese labor" (Takaki 105). The accompanying illustrations also underscore conventional stereotypes of Chinese physiognomy. In these, Ah Sin retains his queue, is much smaller than real (white) men, and possesses eyes that are mere slits. Similar visual tropes appear in illustrations for Mark Twain's *Roughing It* (1872), illustrations which portray Chinese men in non-Western dress and lacking pupils. From the beginning, then, 19th-century representations of Chinese immigrants offered little aside from caricatures of physical difference as indicative of negative character traits and dangerous desires. Such caricatures solidified into stereotypes over the course of the century.

In the early 20th century, a number of popular media highlighted racial differences with reference to specific Chinese and Chinese American characters in many ways comparable to Harte's Ah Sin. Comic strips like "Terry and the Pirates" (1934) and "Flash Gordon" (1934), for example, both feature evil Chinese villains—The "Dragon Lady" and "Ming the Merciless," respectively—who instantiate the stereotypical characteristics reminiscent of John Chinaman. The same period also saw depictions of the passive, hardworking Chinese Americans epitomized by the character Charlie Chan. With his elliptical, piecemeal English, the Honolulu detective foiled criminals in numerous movies (1926–1949). The onset of World War II helped ease American fears about the Yellow Peril (the post–Pearl Harbor Japanese assumed the role of preeminent Asian threat), which gave rise to idyllic images of Chinese American **assimilation**. The film *Flower Drum Song* portrayed an all-American community thriving in Chinatown. Using two Chinese American female characters to play out the drama (Mei Li, a "traditional" immigrant woman illegally entering the United States, and Linda Low, a native-born exotic dancer), the film popularized a persistent stereotype. As a dyad, the two women exemplified the opposing images of Chinese American women: one innocent and demure, the other hyper-sexualized. The theme of assimilation, however, continued to circulate in the popular imagination and reappeared in the political sphere late in the century. While the "model minority" stereotype (hard working, passive, intelligent) attaches to virtually all Asian American groups, President Clinton singled out Chinese Americans specifically in a speech welcoming Gary Locke, governor of Washington, into the legislature.

Sometimes atavistic, often pernicious stereotypes insistent upon the "otherness" of Chinese Americans bear witness to the 125-year history of their involvement with and integration into mainstream American society.

Further Reading

Lee, Robert. *Orientals: Asian Americans in Popular Culture*. Philadelphia: Temple University Press, 1999.

Ma, Sheng-Mei. *The Deathly Embrace: Orientalism and Asian American Identity*. Minneapolis: Minnesota University Press, 2000.

Takaki, Ronald. *Strangers from a Different Shore: A History of Asian Americans*. Boston: Back Bay Books, 1998.

Kim Middleton

CISNEROS, SANDRA (1954–)

Sandra Cisneros is a Mexican American novelist and poet. One of the foremost Mexican American writers today, she has garnered critical and popular acclaim for her genre-defying prose narratives about the life experiences of Mexican American women. Her first work of fiction, ***The House on Mango Street*** (1984), explores the sexual and racial oppression, poverty, and violence experienced by a young Mexican American girl. Praised for its unique voice and deft fusion of poetry and prose, *The House on Mango Street* is a staple in today's multicultural literary **canon**. Cisneros's second work of fiction, *Woman Hollering Creek and Other Stories* (1991), contains stories narrated by adult women as well as children exploring similar themes; it was excerpted in *The Norton Anthology of American Literature* in 1998. Her most recent novel, *Caramelo* (2002), traces three generations of a Mexican American family; it was dubbed a landmark work by one reviewer. Cisneros's poetry, which provocatively challenges the restrictions on Mexican American female sexuality, has also gained recognition in recent years.

Sandra Cisneros was born in Chicago to a Mexican father and Mexican American mother, the only daughter among seven children. Her parents divided the family's time between Mexico and the United States; and Cisneros observed the conflicts of cultural loyalty and feelings of alienation her family experienced as they crossed and recrossed the border. While attending the University of Iowa's Writers Workshop after college, Cisneros realized that her childhood experiences differed significantly from those of her classmates. Thus she created the distinctive voice of Esperanza, the narrator of *The House on Mango Street*, to explicate life in the barrio for Mexican American women. Written as a series of vignettes, each never more than a few pages in length, Esperanza's observations are painfully honest and stunningly acute. Seen from the burgeoning consciousness of a girl hovering between childhood and adulthood, the barrio is not a nurturing place for women. Instead, women are restricted by poverty, domestic and sexual violence, and racial prejudice. Although it is often the men who hold them back, these women can imagine escape only with the help of another man. Esperanza's classmate Sally, for example, marries young in order to flee her abusive father, only to discover her husband is equally violent and controlling. The lovely Rafaela is locked in her apartment by her husband, but she daydreams about meeting another man who might offer her a different kind of life. It is Esperanza who questions the traditional Mexican categories for women—virgin, wife and mother, or whore—as she begins to imagine new possibilities for the lives of Mexican American women. By the end of the book, Esperanza realizes that to develop her individuality and artistic creativity, she must live independently of men. Thus in the penultimate vignette, she yearns for her own house: "Not a man's house. Not a daddy's. A house all my own." Esperanza's desires for an independent life are echoed by Cisneros in the author note at the end of the Vintage paperback edition, in which Cisneros is described as "nobody's mother and nobody's wife." *Woman Hollering Creek and Other Stories* continues Cisneros's exploration of women's lives on both sides of the U.S.-Mexico border. Divided into three sections, this book chronicles the stages of female maturation, portraying the exuberant chatter of young girls and the newly awakened sexuality of adolescents, as well as the sharply cynical and fiercely independent voices of mature women. Cisneros keenly captures the vicissitudes of emotion prevalent in each stage of life. In the first section, she writes unerringly in the voice of the preternaturally wise children who document both the individual and communal struggles of Mexican American women. In "Eleven," the protagonist Rachel is humiliated to tears when she is mistakenly identified as the owner of a smelly, raggedy sweater found in her classroom's cloakroom; and thus Rachel's Anglo teacher is subtly indicted for not distinguishing between her Mexican American pupils. Cisneros paints equally vividly the girlish joy of discovering nearly new Barbie dolls sold cheaply at a sidewalk sale and the deep-set contentment of being carried to bed by one's father after falling asleep in a movie theater. In the second section of the book, Cisneros considers the emergent sexuality of teenaged girls, a theme only briefly developed in *The House on Mango Street*. "One Holy Night" chronicles the very real danger of sex for a girl who falls in love with a man who visits her pushcart. Calling himself Chaq after the Mayan god of love and life, the man seduces and then abandons her. While pregnant with his child, the girl sees a newspaper photo of Chaq in handcuffs. Her lover, she learns, is a middle-aged drifter with no Mayan blood, and a serial killer of young girls. This story dramatizes the negative consequences of premarital sex for young women in the Mexican American community; but here the expected outcomes of social martyrdom and single motherhood are eclipsed by the real potential of death at the hands of a murderer. Cisneros's focus on female sexuality continues in the stories of adulthood in the last section of the book. In particular, she demonstrates the limited opportunities available to women to experience fulfilling adult relationships in this patriarchal society. In "Eyes of Zapata," Inés must content herself with the sporadic visits of her lover, the father of her two children, rather than demand his fidelity or his presence in her house, lest he leave her entirely. In the title story, Cléofilas anticipates in her marriage the passionate romance she sees on television shows; instead, her husband consistently beats and verbally abuses her. Ultimately, Cléofilas must rely upon another woman to help her and her children return to the safety of her father's house across the border in Mexico. Here and in other stories, Cisneros questions the primacy of marriage and motherhood in Mexican American culture that undermines any other potential accomplishments by women. In *Woman Hollering Creek*, Cisneros writes longer, more plot-centered narratives, though her poetic style of prose writing follows the arc of *The House on Mango Street*. She liberally sprinkles Spanish words within these stories, leaving the reader to comprehend the phrases as best she may. Yet any disconcertion the reader may feel from this **bilingualism** is countered by the concurrent exploration of cultural displacement experienced by Cisneros's characters; those readers unfamiliar with Spanish can thus empathize with the women who struggle with their dual Mexican and American legacies.

Cisneros's novel *Caramelo* is both her longest and most plot-centered work of fiction. Cisneros writes what she calls the archetypical Mexican love story: the deep ties between parents and children, rather than husbands and wives. Drawing upon the details of her own family history, she explores the tangled relationships between the doting Mexican mother Soledad and her adoring son Inocencio, Inocencio and his American-born daughter Celaya, and Celaya with Soledad, whom the girl dubs "the Awful Grandmother." Cisneros examines the role of storytelling in family histories and the legacies of one's ancestors in forming the individual self. Celaya, for example, has trouble comprehending her grandmother's seemingly irrational demands upon her children until she learns about the traumas of her grandmother's youth that led her to require such devotion and respect from her children. Celaya then better understands "the Awful Grandmother," as well as her own position as the daughter of a Mexican father.

Playing with the conventions of form and narrational integrity, Cisneros includes within the larger plot conversations between the Awful Grandmother and the narrator Celaya, where Soledad objects to her granddaughter's portrayal of the family history. Cisneros also uses multiple footnotes to explicate aspects of Mexican history and culture or to digress from her primary storyline with additional detail about minor characters. Ultimately, *Caramelo* both educates its readers and celebrates the vibrant wealth of Mexican American culture.

Though best known for her fiction, Cisneros has also published several books of poetry, including *Bad Boys* (1980), *The Rodrigo Poems* (1985), *My Wicked, Wicked Ways* (1987), and *Loose Woman* (1994). Cisneros regards her poetry as more personal than her fiction, as it taps deep into her dreams and subconscious; indeed, many of her poems were never intended for publication. Her poems challenge patriarchal limitations placed on female individuality and sexuality, questioning the negative judgments made against women who behave similarly to men. Her poetic style is raw but playful, with short lines and stanzas that emote powerful sentiments. Ultimately, Cisneros's poetry, as well as her fiction, urges a revision of traditional Mexican American female **identity**, one that boldly questions the constraints set again women's psychological and social growth, while also honoring the history and traditions of Mexican American culture. Already the recipient of such prestigious awards as the MacArthur Fellow, Sandra Cisneros is a pioneering figure in Mexican American literature, as well as an essential writer of the American experience. (*See also* Mexican American Poetry.)

Further Reading

Hartley-Kroeger, Fiona. "Silent Speech: Narration, Gender and Intersubjectivity: Two Young Adult Novels." *Children's Literature in Education: An International Quarterly* 42.4 (2011): 276–88.

Madsen, Deborah L. *Understanding Contemporary Chicana Literature*. Columbia: University of South Carolina Press, 2000.

Robin E. Field

CIVIL RIGHTS MOVEMENT

For about 15 years, from the mid-1950s through the late 1960s, the United States experienced an effort by many of its citizens to overturn the long-standing body of law and custom that relegated African Americans to second-class citizenship and to require the United States to offer full civil and political rights to all the country's citizens, regardless of **race**. Through its early years, the movement focused on the American South, where a system of racial oppression and exploitation that dated to slavery kept African Americans poor and living in caste-like circumstances. Once the reality of race relations and living conditions in northern cities gained wider attention, however, it broadened to include the rest of the country. After 1965, the movement was weakened by its successes, which included passage of laws guaranteeing access to public facilities and voting. It was weakened, too, by the Vietnam War, which sapped the country's spirit and resources; the assassination of important leaders, including **Martin Luther King Jr.**; and a backlash against black militancy and against social activism generally. By the early 1970s, the nonviolent protest that had characterized much of the Civil Rights Movement was only a memory, and the coalition of blacks, labor leaders, educators, clergy, and various other liberals that waged a unified campaign for broader civil rights through the mid-1960s was gone.

Historian Harvard Sitkoff writes that, as with revolutions generally, the Civil Rights Movement was nourished by anger and born of hope. The anger came from the continuing degraded existence of African Americans through years when civil and political rights were being pushed as ideals at home and abroad. The term "Jim Crow," shorthand for American racial segregation, hides the humiliation and despair that characterized blacks' experiences and feelings through the middle of the 20th century. But whence any hope? It came from a government beginning to recognize the extent of blacks' oppression (as it trumpeted freedom in the escalating cold war) and an African American population expecting progress following a global war against a racist tyrant. The federal government at mid-century was leaning toward taking on racial discrimination, one might say, just when African Americans were growing increasingly inclined to give government a shove.

And shove they did, beginning in December 1955, in Montgomery, Alabama, in an already charged atmosphere. In May 1954, the U.S. Supreme Court had declared unconstitutional, in *Brown v. Board of Education*, the long-held "separate but equal" doctrine that allowed segregation and inequality in public schools. Almost immediately, white southerners organized to resist the decision's implementation (which the court decreed should occur "with all deliberate speed") and defend their racist way of life. Further raising tensions was the August 1955 murder of 14-year-old Chicagoan Emmett Till, visiting in the Mississippi Delta, for whistling at a white woman, followed by the acquittal of two white men accused of the crime. So when Rosa Parks refused to relinquish her seat on a Montgomery bus and the city's African American population boycotted the bus lines, it made big news. The boycott's success, ending segregation on the city's busses a year later, made bigger news still. Blacks across the South and beyond saw the grit and bravery of Montgomery's black community and recognized the strength ordinary African Americans could command if organized and determined.

The young minister who led the Montgomery boycott, King, soon formed the Southern Christian Leadership Conference (SCLC) to plan further nonviolent, civil rights activities, but the organization's speed was almost as deliberate as the *Brown* decision's enforcement. Thus, the late 1950s witnessed little more than the integration of one Little Rock, Arkansas, high school, facilitated by federal soldiers, and congressional passage of one weak civil rights bill. As the 1960s dawned, few recognized any concerted movement for civil rights underway.

Young African Americans would change this circumstance almost overnight. On February 1, 1960, four students from all-black North Carolina A & T College, in Greensboro, kept their seats after being refused service at a downtown lunch counter. The next day, 27 others joined them, and before the month was out, similar "sit-ins" were occurring in cities across the South. Barely two months later, like-minded youth formed a Student Non-Violent Coordinating Committee (SNCC) to lend organization and planning to the escalating protests. King's SCLC scurried to keep up. Southern whites marshaled their forces to resist pressures for change, too, so by the summer of 1960, battle lines were drawn. Often below the radar in each skirmish would be the movement's soul, the local African Americans, who were tired of the way they were forced to live and ready to take risks to change it.

The protests of the early 1960s fell into patterns. A "Freedom Ride" of blacks and whites riding busses across the South in 1961 to call attention to segregation in interstate commerce resulted in burned busses, injured riders, and prison sentences, but little integration. One year later, a shooting war broke out in Oxford, Mississippi, over the admission of African American James Meredith to the state's university. Civil rights organizations marshaled their forces in 1963 in Birmingham, Alabama, one of the South's most segregated cities, seeking jobs for blacks and integration. Birmingham's director of public safety, Eugene "Bull" Connor, determined to stand firm and the result was scenes of brutality: police dogs biting, and water from fire hoses nearly drowning, peaceful demonstrators. King and city officials eventually reached a compromise that pleased few who had risked life and limb. In August 1963, at the March on Washington, King continued to speak in pacifist tones, but weeks later a bomb killed four African American girls awaiting choir practice in Birmingham's Sixteenth Street Baptist Church, and before the year was out, President John F. Kennedy, who had been moving toward supporting legislation to end discrimination, was assassinated in Dallas, Texas. As the country mourned its fallen president, blacks lamented that a century after Emancipation, many descendants of slaves still could not exercise a citizen's rights.

Kennedy's successor, President Lyndon B. Johnson, knew Congress's back halls and worked them to insure passage, by July, of the Civil Rights Act of 1964, which outlawed segregation of public facilities. Not resting on this success, SNCC was involved in a "Freedom Summer" for Mississippi, which involved volunteers educating black Mississippians on the intricacies of voting. The June 21st murder outside Philadelphia, Mississippi, of volunteers James Chaney, Andrew Goodman, and Michael Schwerner did not deter others, and under their direction a Mississippi Freedom Democratic Party formed and sought acceptance in the Democratic National Convention in August. In denying the Freedom party anything beyond token representation at its convention, the Democratic Party showed its true colors, which in Mississippi remained white.

The Civil Rights Act of 1964 dealt with segregation, leaving disfranchisement as the focus of efforts in 1965. Aware that violent opposition to their nonviolent tactics gained attention, civil rights leaders selected Selma, Alabama, for a voting rights campaign. There, Sheriff Jim Clark had an unruly posse with a reputation for being quick with the nightstick. Clark's men played their role with full brutality on "Bloody Sunday," March 7, riding in on horseback, clubbing demonstrators who knelt in prayer after crossing Selma's Edmund Pettus Bridge. It was a ghastly sight on the evening news. After federal intervention, demonstrators marched the 50 miles from Selma to Montgomery, bringing their protest to the state capital, where Alabama Governor George C. Wallace blustered and stalled. That night, Ku Klux Klansmen shot and killed Detroit housewife Viola Liuzzo, drawn to Alabama by the struggle against injustice. Later in the month, Johnson sent to Congress a bill authorizing federal examiners to register black voters, and on August 6 he signed this Voting Rights Act of 1965.

Liberals everywhere celebrated this second major piece of civil rights legislation in successive years, but their joy may have prevented their recognizing signs of the movement's disunity. As early as the "long, hot summer" of 1964, young blacks had begun rethinking their goals and tactics, slowly distancing themselves from King's nonviolent efforts to achieve integration and moving toward a more militant approach to gaining control of their own destiny. While King was in Montgomery in 1965, describing the moral universe in optimistic terms, SNCC's James Forman was inviting African Americans to knock the legs off of any table where blacks were not allowed to sit. A year later, noting that power was the only thing respected in the world, SNCC leader Stokely Carmichael advised blacks to get power "at any cost." Moderate black leaders shied away from Carmichael's Black Power stance. Meanwhile, less than a week after Johnson signed the voting bill, blacks in the Watts district of Los Angeles waged a six-day riot that required 14,000 National Guard troops to bring order and left 34 dead. Blacks in America's cities, who suffered from lack of jobs, poor education, and the social effects of their culture of poverty, had grown angry at all the attention on the plight of African Americans in the South. The man who some urban blacks looked to for guidance, the enigmatic Malcolm X, had been gunned down by Black Muslim opponents in early 1965. Watts was the first big manifestation of urban blacks' frustrations; many more would occur in coming summers.

The fractured Civil Rights Movement after 1965 simply never healed. More moderate African Americans hoped to work with their allies in labor unions, the

Democratic Party, and government generally to build on their success and bring greater opportunity to black Americans. Johnson's Great Society programs held potential for improvement—his encouragement of employers to take "affirmative action" to make up for past injustices and hire more African Americans became standard practice in federal hiring—so long as the momentum continued. King, who might have remained the leader of moderates, was distancing himself from them and from government supporters with his criticism of the Vietnam War and his emphasis on economic change to help the nation's poor. More radical elements listened to Huey Newton, Bobby Seale, and Eldridge Cleaver of the Black Panther Party for Self-Defense, who encouraged inner-city blacks to arm themselves and take control of their own affairs. The Federal Bureau of Investigation, whose leader, J. Edgar Hoover, considered such activity un-American and dangerous, took on the Black Panthers, killing and incarcerating some and driving others underground or out of the country. By the time of King's assassination in Memphis on May 3, 1968, it was too late for anyone to reunite the movement's various elements. The November election of Richard M. Nixon as the country's president signaled an electorate that was tired of political and social activism. By then, the United States was also a country with a full-blown foreign war on its hands, drawing the attention of many former civil rights demonstrators as casualties mounted.

The Civil Rights Movement's legacy is more than two sweeping pieces of legislation and heightened awareness of the wrongs dealt to Americans of African descent. Out of the effort came a consensus on the legitimacy of civil rights as an issue worthy of national attention and a body of law that continues to be useful in guaranteeing civil, political, and human rights to all Americans. From the movement, too, came greater awareness of women's issues and growth in efforts to insure equal rights on the basis of gender. The movement's shortcomings are evident as well, however. A half-century after the *Brown* ruling, many schools are still segregated, and African Americans remain poorer as a group than American whites. Late in their lives, King and Malcolm X were in agreement that in a capitalist economy, those lacking capital were destined to remain at a disadvantage. The movement tackled the legal basis of segregation and political discrimination, but it failed to alter the economic circumstances, still in existence, that make it difficult for the descendants of former slaves to enjoy equal economic opportunity nearly a century and a half after slavery's end.

Further Reading

Dittmer, John. *Local People: The Struggle for Civil Rights in Mississippi.* Urbana: University of Illinois Press, 1994.

Sitkoff, Harvard. *The Struggle for Black Equality, 1954–1992.* Rev. ed. New York: Hill and Wang, 1993.

Weisbrot, Robert. *Freedom Bound: A History of America's Civil Rights Movement.* New York: Penguin Books, 1990.

Donald R. Wright

CLIFF, MICHELLE (1946–)

Michelle Cliff is a Jamaican American novelist, prose poet, short-story writer, and literary and cultural critic. Growing up Caribbean amid a confusion of cultural influences distorted by colonial and postcolonial sociopolitical realities, Cliff had to negotiate a complex web of privilege and oppression to recover suppressed Amer-Indian and African lines embedded in her family's genealogy. Sexist and heterosexist prejudice also presented formidable obstacles to the adolescent lesbian's determination to claim all her identities in writing. In the face of these ambiguities and challenges, Cliff has seized the possibilities for affirming difference and worked out an aesthetics equal to the task. In particular, three remarkable novels—*Abeng* (1984), *No Telephone to Heaven* (1987), and *Free Enterprise* (1993)—have secured Michelle Cliff an important place in postcolonial Caribbean and African American literature. These novels advance Cliff's project of rewriting "official" histories that have erased or distorted colonized and oppressed people's stories of damage, survival, and resistance. Cliff invests her own conflicted experiences of racialized oppression and privilege in Clare Savage, the Jamaican protagonist of *Abeng* and *No Telephone to Heaven*.

Cliff was born a light-skinned creole of European and African descent in Jamaica, still a British Crown Colony in 1946. At age three, Cliff moved with her family to the Unites States, where the light-skinned Cliffs often passed for white but still experienced difficulties assimilating into U.S. culture. In 1956, the family returned to Jamaica and enrolled Cliff at a private girls' school, where she received an Anglo-centric colonialist education until 1960, when her family moved back to New York. Anne Frank's diaries inspired Cliff to begin writing despite her family's ridicule, and a New York women's writing group encouraged her to launch her writing career with "Notes on Speechlessness" in 1978. In *Claiming an Identity They Taught Me to Despise* (1980) and *The Land of Look Behind* (1985), Cliff experimented in prose poetry and short fiction, honing her craft and courageously exploring her multiple, conflicted identities. Formal study of languages, comparative history, women's studies, and politics also contributed to Cliff's commitment, in her teaching and her writing, to redressing the misrepresentations of history and educating others in the damaging effects of **racism** and other oppressions.

The bildungsroman *Abeng* enacts Clare Savage's journey to politicized consciousness through experimental layered narratives that recover her maternal AmerIndian roots, and claim legendary Jamaican woman-warrior Nanny as foremother of postcolonial resistance. *No Telephone to Heaven* continues migrant Clare's journey to the Unites States and England, then back to Jamaica and revolutionary action. Her story converges with those of other "crossroads" characters—crossing boundaries of nation, **race**, class, and gender—who unite in rebellion, even if the climactic act is tragically compromised. Influenced by **Toni Morrison**'s *Beloved* (1988) and its fictional reconstruction of untold stories of bondage and resistance, Cliff wrote *Free Enterprise*, set in slave-era and turn-of-the-century United States. Mary Ellen Pleasant, African American entrepreneur and rebel, stands at the center of the novel's layered narratives. Ghosts past, present, and future of the African Americas are raised, scattered images and voices of resistance and complicity from disparate times and cultures are collected together to tell a provocatively different black American history of slavery and its aftermath. Cliff's most recent book is *The Store of a Million Items* (1998), a collection of short stories featuring characters in revealing cross-cultural encounters. (*See also* Caribbean (Anglophone) American Novel)

Further Reading

Agosto, Noraida. *Michelle Cliff's Novels: Piecing the Tapestry of Memory and History. Caribbean Studies.* Vol. 1. New York: Peter Lang, 2000.

Backes, Nancy. "Growing Up Desperately: The Adolescent 'Other' in the Novels of Paule Marshall, Toni Morrison, and Michelle Cliff." In *Women of Color: Defining the Issues, Hearing the Voices. Contributions in Women's Studies*, edited by Diane Long Hoeveler, Janet K. Boles, and Toni-Michelle C. Travis, 147–57. Westport, CT: Greenwood Press, 2001.

Elia, Nada. *Trances, Dances, and Vociferations: Agency and Resistance in Africana Women's Narratives.* New York: Garland, 2001.

Garvey, Johanna X. K. "Passages to Identity: Re-Membering the Diaspora." In *Black Imagination and the Middle Passage*, edited by Maria Diedrich, Henry Louis Gates Jr., and Carl Pedersen, 255–70. *W. E. B. Du Bois Institute Series.* Oxford, UK: Oxford University Press, 1999.

Gifford, William Tell. *Narrative and the Nature of the Worldview in the Clare Savage Novels of Michelle Cliff. Caribbean Studies Series.* Vol. 4. New York: Peter Lang, 2001.

Gourdine, Angeletta K. M. *The Difference Place Makes: Gender, Sexuality, and Diaspora Identity.* Columbus: Ohio State University Press, 2003.

Macdonald-Smythe, Antonia. *Making Homes in the West Indies: Constructions of Subjectivity in the Writings of Michelle Cliff and Jamaica Kincaid. Literary Criticism and Cultural Theory Series.* London: Routledge, 2001.

Cora Agatucci

COLOR PURPLE, THE

Published in 1982, presented with the Pulitzer Prize and National Book Award in 1983, and adapted into a major Hollywood film directed by Steven Spielberg in 1985, *The Color Purple* is **Alice Walker**'s third and most controversial novel. In its creative engagement with the epistolary form, the book shows how a poor, uneducated African American woman endures pain and hardship to become, through the nurturing of communal black womanhood, a fully constituted subject of strength, self-confidence, and desire.

The narrative begins with 14-year-old Celie's revelation to God that she is physically and sexually abused by a man, Alphonso, who she believes to be her natural father. He later gives away the two children she has by him. When Celie is married off to Mr.___, she worries that her younger sister, Nettie, will have to endure similar abuse from their Pa. Nettie comes to live with Celie and Mr.___, but his intense jealousy over their tight-knit relationship forces Nettie to leave the house and subsequently move to Africa. Incredibly, the missionaries in whose custody Nettie is placed happen to adopt Celie's two children.

Mr.___ only perpetuates the cycle of violence that typified Celie's life with Alphonso, (who later turns out to be her stepfather). Mr.___ also withholds psychic and affective comfort from Celie by hiding the numerous letters Nettie mails to her from Africa. The downtrodden Celie internalizes feelings of abjection and worthlessness to the point where she convinces her stepson, Harpo, to beat his own wife, the defiant and physically imposing Sofia Butler, into submission, which he does not succeed in doing.

The turning point in the narrative comes with the arrival of Shug Avery, also known as "The Queen Honeybee," a spirited, sexy, and flamboyant **blues** singer who lives by her own rules and refuses to obey the dictates of patriarchal authority; the latter, as embodied by Mr.___, is deflated by his submission to her demands. Though an occasional lover to Mr.___, it is Celie with whom Shug eventually develops a deep and meaningful bond. In their emotional exchanges and sexual encounters, Shug enables Celie to recognize her own beauty and self-sufficiency and thus to leave Albert. The couple settles in Memphis, where Celie makes a living by tailoring personalized, seemingly ungendered, pants for those she loves. Imbued with self-determination, Celie later visits a distraught Mr.___, whose first name is revealed to be Albert, upon her stepfather's death. A momentous reunion occurs when Nettie and the children return from Africa; a corresponding reconciliation has Celie and Albert agreeing to be friends.

Walker's novel has elicited vituperative reactions in both academic venues and the popular media. The sections on Africa have been deemed culturally biased; the frank depiction of lesbian sexuality has been summarily censored on moral grounds; and the putatively "harsh" treatment of black men, especially in the film, has been construed as an indication of Walker's selling out to the white establishment. That the book sparked such fiery, if not sometimes misguided, debate underscores the invaluable discursive effect it has had on black women's writing, African American literature, popular culture, and **race** relations in the United States. (*See also* African American Lesbian Literature; African American Novel)

Further Reading

Gates, Henry Louis, Jr. "Color Me Zora: Alice Walker's (Re)Writing of the Speakerly Text." In *The Signifying Monkey: A Theory of Afro-American Literary Criticism*, 239–58. New York: Oxford University Press, 1988.

Harris, Trudier. "On *The Color Purple*, Stereotypes, and Silence." *Black American Literature Forum* 18.4 (1984): 155–61.

Hernton, Calvin C. "Who's Afraid of Alice Walker? *The Color Purple* as Slave Narrative." In *The Sexual Mountain and Black Women Writers: Adventures in Sex, Literature, and Real Life*, 1–36. Garden City, NY: Anchor, 1987.

hooks, bell. "Writing the Subject: Reading *The Color Purple*." In *Reading Black, Reading Feminist: A Critical Anthology*, edited by Henry Louis Gates Jr., 454–70. New York: Meridian, 1990.

LaGrone, Keven, and Michael Meyer, eds. *Alice Walker's The Color Purple*. Amsterdam: Rodopi, 2009.

Kinohi Nishikawa

COOPER, J. (JOAN) CALIFORNIA (1932–2014)

African American short-story writer, novelist, and playwright. Since the early 1970s, J. California Cooper has written six collections of short stories, three novels, and seventeen plays. Her play *Strangers*, also known as *Ahhh, Strangers* (1978), won Cooper the Black Playwright of the Year Award, and her second collection of short stories, *Homemade Love* (1986), won an American Book Award. Cooper's works are late-20th-century manifestations of the folk traditions of African American literature; they display a unique mix of oral-tradition immediacy with the importance of family, feminism, Christianity, critique of class inequalities that doesn't deny personal responsibility, and a "**blues** sensibility" of optimism under hardship.

It is this unusual, and sometimes quirky, mix of elements conveyed in a quiet intimacy—an intimacy characterized as like listening to a story told by a friend as you and she sit on a porch and snap beans—that has most attracted many readers. Through misspellings, malapropisms, fragments, and other devices, Cooper connects oral intimacy to the vernacular tradition of providing an insider's view of communities whose "nonstandard" languages indicate educational, economic, and political marginalization, yet also a resilience and insightful "folk wisdom" that calls the imputed "superiority" of a "standard" into question. Cooper manifests the African American vernacular tradition of telling seemingly simple stories that show how disenfranchised communities not only survive but can inspire and educate those willing to pay attention.

These characteristics situate Cooper's work as descending from the spirituals, work songs, and folktales that promote African American vitality and coherence while countering the rhetoric of **racism**. To this tradition, Cooper adds both a consistent feminist critique of patriarchy and occasional graphic depictions of sexuality. These depictions range from celebrations of women's sexuality to scenes of degradation. The tone Cooper takes toward women in degrading scenes, however, remains matter-of-fact, maintaining a sort of documentary "distance" that refrains from judging these actions. Cooper's reticence to judge, acknowledges that poverty, racism, and patriarchy sometime leave women with few socially admirable options. What Cooper's stories do not refrain from judging, however, are people's motives, and this sometimes results in a rather old-fashioned moralizing that some critics find heavy-handed.

Criticism has been leveled at Cooper's optimism and belief in the agency of the individual that situates Cooper in the Booker T. Washington tradition of unduly minimizing the effects of the racism and poverty into which many African Americans have been—and continue to be—born. From this view, Cooper's emphasis on hard work, frugality, honesty, and belief in God lets the dominant "white" society off too easily. In Cooper's defense, however, her characters are not blind to class and racial injustices, and the "successes" of her characters are often limited. In many ways, Cooper expresses the blues tradition of turning hardship and loss into success, but success that never leaves sorrow behind.

Cooper's work argues that although African Americans struggle under the injustices of racism, and although women struggle under the injustices of patriarchy, individuals cannot be reduced to categories, and the complexities and possibilities of individuals are beyond capture. From this comes an appreciation of others *as individuals*, an appreciation of their quirks and their potentials and a connecting with others as part of an empathy that Cooper calls "love."

Love in Cooper's work intertwines with Christian faith while sympathizing with those disregarded or rejected by society. This is already apparent in her earliest works. The plot, for instance, of Cooper's *How Now?* (produced in 1973 by the Black Repertory Group of Berkeley, which produced most of Cooper's early plays) details the conflict between a disabled girl who wants to continue her education and the girl's mother who wants her daughter to become pregnant to qualify for welfare benefits. *The Unintended* (ca. 1983) tells about the love that unexpectedly results when a 35-year-old virgin's need for money leads to her sexual involvement with a hunchback.

Cooper's work not only shows the value of paying attention to—and ultimately empathizing with—those ignored by society, but also shows how things are often not as they seem. We find this in the short-story version of Cooper's play *Loved to Death* (date unknown), which appeared under the same name in Cooper's first collection of short stories, *A Piece of Mine* (1984). The 10-page title story is quintessential J. California Cooper. It is conveyed in a modified oral tradition of a narrator speaking to "Mr. Notebook." The narrator is an "all crooked" woman whose sister, Zalina, has the apparent luck of great beauty. But her father tries to rape Zalina, who leaves home and marries; then the white boss of her husband rapes Zalina and kills her husband. Zalina returns home and later dies of alcoholism. The narrator raises Zalina's children and also experiences sex with a local man who had initially come to visit Zalina but then switched to the narrator. In this "oral" story Cooper packs class, **race**, gender, feminist critique, oral sex, the Bible, the importance of education, physical disability, and a counterintuitive understanding of beauty, and then ends with the "blues optimism" of the narrator going outside to run with one of Zalina's children.

Although Cooper has spent much of her adult life in California, many of her stories seem to take place in rural Texas (Marshall) where she lived for a year as a child and for eight years as an adult. Cooper refuses to divulge her age, is vague about how many times she has been married, and is generally reticent with personal information. The broad arc of her work has tended toward increasing "Christian moralizing," but this predominates mainly in Cooper's second novel, *In Search of Satisfaction* (1994).

Cooper's short stories have received more acclaim than her novels, but Cooper's more extended analyses of people and motives in, for instance, the novels *Family* (1991) and especially *The Wake of the Wind* (1998) are historically grounded studies of the horror and complexity of slavery and its aftereffects. Both novels add to our understanding of some of the more difficult aspects of African American life since the mid-to-late 1800s. With Cooper's sixth short-story collection, *The Future Has a Past: Stories* (2001) Cooper remains a unique, engaging, and underappreciated ethnic American voice.

Further Reading

Bryant, Cynthia Downing. "'How I Got Over': Negotiating Whiteness in California Cooper's *Family*." *CLA Journal* 50.4 (2007): 436–57.

Carroll, Rebecca. "J. California Cooper." In *I Know What the Red Clay Looks Like*, 63–80. New York: Crown, 1994.

Marshall, Barbara Jean. "Kitchen Table Talk: J. California Cooper's Use of Nommo—Female Bonding and Transcendence." In *Language and Literature in African American Imagination*, edited by Carol A. Blackshire-Belay, 91–102. Westport, CT: Greenwood Press, 1992.

Kevin M. Hickey

CUBAN AMERICAN AUTOBIOGRAPHY

Due to the relatively recent arrival of tens of thousands of Cuban exiles since the onset of the Cuban revolution in 1959—the largest exodus in the island's history—Cuban American authors have only lately embraced the quintessentially American genre of ethnic autobiography. Out of sixteen single- and multiple-authored autobiographical works noted in this entry, only two were published before 1990. The first of these, *A Book* (1976), by Cuban entertainer Desi Arnaz, describes the vicissitudes of the protagonist upon his arrival in the United States after fleeing civil violence in Cuba in the 1930s—a period that also witnessed Cuban migration to the United States—and his eventual, successful career in the entertainment industry, including his stint as co-protagonist in the comedy series *I Love Lucy*. The second, *Contra viento y marea* (Against All Odds, 1978), is not an autobiography per se, but testimonial literature by young Cuban Americans who returned to the island in the late 1970s with the intention of reconnecting with their native land. Influenced by the antiwar and **Civil Rights Movement**s of the late 1960s and early 1970s, these sons and daughters of exiled Cubans sought to experience Cuban society firsthand, and wrote about their positive impressions in this book, the recipient of the prestigious Casa de las Américas award.

The bulk of Cuban American autobiographical narratives began to appear toward the end of the millennium, authored by a second generation of Cubans who came of age in the United States. Unlike the authors of *Contra viento y marea*, however, they emphasize the failed policies of the Cuban revolution. Written in English, these narratives evince the authors' position of straddling two cultures.

The autobiographies of Carlos Eire, Pablo Medina, and Virgil Suárez are growing-up narratives largely circumscribed to the island. Eire, a professor of religious studies and history at Yale University who uses figurative language like an accomplished poet, offers a poignant tale of a privileged, if vulnerable, childhood in *Waiting for Snow in Havana: Confessions of a Cuban Boy* (2003), winner of the National Book Award for nonfiction. The son of a municipal judge, Eire left Cuba at the age of 11 with his brother through the Peter Pan Airlift in 1962 and never saw his father again. Written in just four months with the urgency of a liberating confession, the book highlights the uplifting magic of childhood as well as the painful consequences of depravity, separation, and exile. A novelist and poet, Pablo Medina also writes about an elitist upbringing in *Exiled Memories: A Cuban Childhood* (1990), while Virgil Suárez, who left Cuba in 1974, delves into growing up in a middle-class home during the revolution in his autobiographical books *Spared Angola: Memories from a Cuban-American Childhood* (1997) and *Infinite Refuge* (2002). Especially for authors such as these who have not returned to their native land, memoirs offer a means of symbolically connecting the past with a present that is an unlikely outcome of that past.

Second-generation Cuban Americans Gustavo Pérez Firmat, Román de la Campa, María del Carmen Boza, Emilio Bejel, and Rafael Campo have also written autobiographies. Published shortly after his celebrated *Life on the Hyphen: The Cuban-American Way* (1994), Pérez Firmat's memoir, *Next Year in Cuba. A Cubano's Coming-of-Age in America* (1995), nominated for a Pulitzer Prize in nonfiction, dwells on the dilemma of a young man torn between his family's obsession with an advantaged past on the island and his need to engage his American surroundings. Laying claim to a hyphenated identity, Pérez Firmat (currently David Feinson, professor of humanities at Columbia University) illustrates the personal dislocations occasioned by exile, presenting at the same time a sympathetic portrait of the beginnings of the Cuban enclave in Miami's Dade County, the author's hometown. Román de la Campa's *Cuba on My Mind: Journeys to a Severed Nation* (2000) focuses on the author's reevaluation of the Cuban regime after an initial period of empathy that led him to participate in the Cuban progressive movement. Another subject he addresses is the role of Cuban Americans within the Latino community. María del Carmen Boza's *Scattering the Ashes* (1998), the only book-length narrative by a single woman writer, revolves around an ambivalent father–daughter relationship.

With his openly gay perspective, cultural critic, poet, and professor Emilio Bejel adds a spin to Cuban American autobiography in *The Write Way Home* (2003), a first-person account on the need to come to terms with one's sexual identity and sense of family. Also assuming a homosexual **identity** in *The Poetry of Healing* (1997), Rafael Campo, a medical doctor and published poet, underscores the healing power of medicine and poetry, as well as its limits, in the midst of the AIDS epidemic. A different approach to gay themes is displayed in Reinaldo Arenas's autobiography *Antes que anochezca* (Before Night Falls, 1992), made into a popular film by Julian Schnabel in 2000. What is emphasized in this book, published posthumously, is Arenas's fallout with the Cuban government due to his unconventional behavior. Arenas lived the last 10 years of his life in New York City where, having contracted the HIV virus, he committed suicide in 1990.

Acknowledged by critics as relevant are a number of autobiographical essays written in the 1990s by Ruth Behar and Eliana Rivero, women who, because of their feminist perspective, have contributed to diversify the white, male, heterosexual, and upper-middle-class viewpoint only seemingly prevalent in Cuban American autobiographical writings. These writers identify with other Latinas with whom they share many concerns as women of color.

Reinaldo Arenas. (Sophie Bassouls/Sygma/Corbis)

Furthermore, women have figured prominently in testimonial writing akin to the testimonial literature that has flourished throughout Latin America since the 1980s. Within this tradition in which individuals bear witness to experiences worthy of public attention, three recent books deserve to be mentioned: *Bridges to Cuba/Puentes a Cuba* (1995), edited by Ruth Behar and Juan León; *ReMembering Cuba* (2001), edited by Andrea Herrera O'Reilly; and *By Heart/De memoria* (2003), edited by María de los Angeles Torres. The three books convey the worldviews of diverse sectors of the Cuban American community. In an effort to overcome the historic divide between Cubans on either side of the Florida Straits, Behar and Torres also obtained the collaboration of Cubans on the island with an interest in building bridges.

Finally, Evelio Grillo's *Black Cuban, Black American* (2000) reminds us that Cuban migration to the United States harks back to the mid-19th century. The son of dark-skinned cigar workers who had migrated from Cuba, Grillo grew up in the early 20th century in a black neighborhood in Tampa, Florida. Foremost among Grillo's apprehensions is the racial binary in U.S. society, which urged him to forge an alliance with African Americans. This memoir, with its emphasis on **race**, stands in evidence of the diverse circumstances that have given rise to Cuban American autobiography.

Further Reading

Alvarez Borland, Isabel. "Autobiographical Writing. Negotiating an Identity." In *Cuban-American Literature of Exile. From Person to Persona*, 61–87. Charlottesville and London: University Press of Virginia, 1998.

López, Iraida H. *La autobiografía hispana contemporánea en los Estados Unidos: a través del caleidoscopio*. Lewiston, NY: Edwin Mellen Press, 2001.

Iraida H. López

CUBAN AMERICAN NOVEL

One of the striking features of what might be called the "history" of the Cuban American novel is its stark refusal to correspond directly to, or in any way simply "represent," what are conventionally taken to be the "histories" of either the Cuban American community, or of some larger Cuban diasporic entity that might include populations both on and off the island that is still called Cuba. That latter history usually traces the conventional line of cause and effect, from the 1959 Cuban Revolution to the consequent exodus of that movement's enemies into a decades-long self-styled exile, primarily concentrated in Miami, Florida. The exiles, in turn, found themselves, in spite of their own most dearly held intentions, both assimilating and establishing themselves in a decidedly "Americanized" context, which, by the 1980s, certainly had taken a significant and defining turn away from that initial "exile" to a more familiar "immigrant" mentality, from which was finally born the identifying category of Cuban American. The history of the production and publication of long prose narrative works of literary fiction, either by U.S.-based writers of Cuban descent, or on the theme of U.S. based Cuban experience, or both, bears little correspondence to that familiar narrative, even when that narrative itself becomes a central trope or point of elaboration in many of the texts collected under the rubric in question.

The starting point for this history of the genre could be, for example, the moment in the late 1980s when two significant publishing events occurred within two years of one another: the appearance in 1987 of *The Doorman* (*El Portero*), Cuban novelist Reinaldo Arenas's only major fictional work to be set entirely in the United States; and the publication in 1989 of Cuban American novelist Oscar Hijuelos's *The Mambo Kings Play Songs of Love*, which that same year became the first novel by a U.S. Latino writer to win the Pulitzer Prize for fiction. The critic Isabel Alvarez-Borland, in 1998's *Cuban-American Literature of Exile* (one of the very few book-length studies of post-1959 off-island Cuban writing), suggests that there is very little novelistic production of note in the Cuban American community before this period. What is striking, therefore, about the phenomenon defined by the near-simultaneous appearance of Arenas and Hijuelos's titles is their utterly tangential relation to the "official" version of Cuban American history. The very openly gay Arenas, for example, had only left Cuba some years earlier as part of the 1980 Mariel boatlift; he was already an established, though severely persecuted, writer in Cuba, and when he finally escaped the country he opted to settle in New York City rather than Miami primarily because of the political and sexual intolerance he saw prevailing in that capital of Cuban America. *The Doorman*, written originally in Spanish and set in late-1980s New York, is bitingly critical of not only Cuban Miami, but also of the United States in the age of Ronald Reagan and AIDS.

The Doorman, stylistically consistent with the fantastical, experimental qualities of Arenas's major, Cuba-based fiction, suffered considerable overshadowing from the flashier success of Arenas's 1992 memoir, *Before Night Falls*. Hijuelos, on the other hand, was born in New York City in the early 1950s to Cuban parents, lived his entire life in the United States, and set the events of his prize-winning novel primarily in the Cuban musical club-land of 1950s New York, hence before the revolution and well outside the frame of reference of exile-dominated Miami. *Mambo Kings*, which was Hijuelos's second novel, set the standard for Cuban American literary expression in English, demonstrating the appropriateness of this adopted language for the narration of a decidedly lasting, increasingly institutionalized immigrant experience.

While Arenas and Hijuelos were enjoying the privilege of seeing their work appear under the imprints of major New York–based publishing houses (Arenas at Grove Press, Hijuelos at Farrar, Straus, and Giroux), at least one other Cuban American novelist of note was beginning to publish at the same moment but at the much more modestly positioned Arte Público Press of Houston, Texas. This was Roberto G. Fernández, whose satiric 1988 novel *Raining Backwards* both corrects and completes some of the complicated representational tendencies in the work of the other two writers. Fernández, like Arenas, was born in Cuba, though he left at a much younger age, in the early 1960s, and settled with his family in Miami, where he grew up. His first literary publications were primarily in Spanish. *Raining Backwards*, Fernández's first novel in English, is set in the heart of early 1970s exile Miami; it therefore reflects in its every detail the writer's intimate familiarity with the qualities of political and cultural life in that community, but it mostly exploits that familiarity to satirize those qualities with a degree of incisiveness that only an insider could manage. In *Raining Backwards* and its follow-up (1995's *Holy Radishes!*, also from Arte Público), Fernández strikes a precarious balance between a deep fondness toward and an equally deep cynicism about the community in which he grew up, and which he continues to write about, from his perhaps safer current position as teacher of creative writing at Florida State University in Tallahassee. Since the late 1980s Arte Público Press has been instrumental in publishing a good deal of work by other, less prominent but also quite talented and even prolific Cuban American novelists, including Elías Miguel Muñoz (see 1988's *Crazy Love*, 1991's *The Greatest Performance* and 1998's *Brand New Memory*, for example), Virgil Suárez (1995's *Havana Thursdays*, 1999's *The Cutter*), and Himilce Novas (1996's *Mangos, Bananas, and Coconuts*). The proliferation of writers and titles issuing from just one small press reflects something of the vitality and urgency of the movement inaugurated by Arenas, Hijuelos, and Fernández in those pivotal years between 1985 and 1990.

Of the novelists to appear on the Cuban American scene in the 1990s, perhaps none has received as much attention and acclaim as Cristina García, whose *Dreaming in Cuban* (1992) marked the appearance of the first major fictional work by a Cuban American woman writing on Cuban American themes. *Dreaming in Cuban* therefore both builds on and corrects the work begun by the established male writers in this nascent tradition by augmenting their already profoundly critical fictive interventions into the business-as-usual of telling Cuban American history by a profound, and profoundly feminist, reconstitution of that history. Born in Cuba, raised in Brooklyn, and based in Los Angeles, García too, like Hijuelos and Arenas before her, embodies a history with no direct correspondence to the Cuban-Miamian-American line. Across her three existing novels (including, after *Dreaming in Cuban*, 1997's *The Agüero Sisters*, and 2003's *Monkey Hunting*), García devotes very little space to direct representations of life in Cuban Miami (which mostly occur in the second novel) while she devotes extraordinary energy to reimagining life in Cuba at various stages of its history. In general, her favored American setting, of significant importance in all three novels, is New York City. Of the three, *Dreaming in Cuban* remains perhaps García's best regarded and certainly most studied; its narrative, across three generations of the women in the del Pino family, also manages to re-narrate Cuban American history across most of the 20th century. Her most recent, *Monkey Hunting*, expands García's range considerably, both historically and culturally. Beginning in the mid-19th century, it tells the story of three generations of a Chinese Cuban family, beginning with the patriarch who arrives in Cuba from China only to be sold into slavery, and ending with his Afro-Chinese Cuban American grandson serving the United States in Vietnam.

Perhaps the most telling counter to both García's literary and political ambitions can be found in the work of the mystery writer Carolina García-Aguilera, who, since the mid-1990s, has been producing an impressive series of pulp-style detective novels featuring a recurring detective figure named Lupe Solano. García-Aguilera's titles, which include *Bitter Sugar* (2002), *Havana Heat* (2000), and *Bloody Waters* (1998), are all unapologetically set in the heart of Cuban Miami, and her garrulous, engaging protagonist/narrator Lupe Solano functions very effectively as an informal cultural informant into the defining mentalities of 21st-century Cuban Miami, a community that manages uncannily to reflect historical changes (like the end of the cold war and the influx of non-Cuban Latinos to Florida) at the same time that it clings tenaciously to its anti-Castro politics as though the revolution had only happened yesterday. *Bloody Waters*, for example, uses the impact of the Mariel Boatlift on Miami's Cuban community as an active factor in the otherwise conventional plot of murder, blackmail, and mayhem with which any reader of postmodern detective fiction would be immediately familiar.

A number of emerging novelists at the turn into the 21st century prove that the Cuban American novel has a bright future, one that will continue the work of already-established figures, both major and minor, and in addition will take on new themes, and new strategies, as the political and cultural conditions defining Cuban America continue to shift. In addition to continuing significant work by writers as important as Hijuelos and García, the new century has seen the publication of new work by writers as disparate as Achy Obejas (who followed 1996's *Memory Mambo* with 2001's *Days of Awe*), José Raúl Bernardo (who followed 1996's *The Secret of the Bulls* with 2003's *Wise Women of Havana*), Ernesto Mestre (who followed 1999's *Lazarus Rumba* with 2004's *Second Death of Unica Aveyano*), and Ana Menendez (see 2003's *Loving Che*). Obejas's *Days of Awe* appeared earlier than García's *Monkey Hunting*, but together they embody the rich, challenging cultural and historical complications informing the ongoing elaboration of Cuban American **identity**. As *Monkey Hunting* explains why there are Cubans of Chinese ancestry, *Days of Awe* explains why there are Cubans of Jewish ancestry; together these novels establish in important, compelling ways how inadequate the national term alone (even when hybridized as Cuban American) can be for the articulation of the always complex, always simultaneous operations of history and identity. Little besides a common interest in the various and complex ways that history can condition identity, especially in the specifically Cuban American context, binds these writers and their works to one another. Their biographies are as various as their literary predilections, and their approaches to the act of narrative are as various as their distinct senses about how exactly history and fiction can and should most productively inform one another.

It is worth noting that significant novels devoted to Cuban American themes have also been produced by some interesting non-Cuban writers, including 1990's *The Perez Family* (by Christine Bell), 1991's *Los Gusanos* (by filmmaker John Sayles) and 1995's *Cuba and the Night* (by journalist Pico Iyer), each of which in its own way evinces the same impatience with the neatness of the "line" of official Cuban American history, and which together suggest that the questioning of the authority and logic of that line may be of value to more than just the Cuban American "community" it claims to name, and to define.

Further Reading

Alvarez-Borland, Isabel. *Cuban-American Literature of Exile: From Person to Persona*. Charlottesville: University of Virginia Press, 1998.

García, María Cristina. *Havana USA: Cuban Exiles and Cuban Americans in South Florida, 1959–1994*. Berkeley and Los Angeles: University of California Press, 1996.

Pérez-Firmat, Gustavo. *Life on the Hyphen: The Cuban-American Way*. Austin: University of Texas Press, 1994.

Smorkaloff, Pamela Maria. *Cuban Writers On and Off the Island*. New York: Twayne, 1999.

Ricardo L. Ortiz

CUBAN AMERICAN POETRY

The literature of the Cuban exile enjoyed a long history in the United States well before the generation of the Cuban Revolution of 1959. The notable poetry of 19th-century exile, for example, includes José María Heredia's **canon**ical ode "Niágara" (1824), the anthology *El laúd del desterrado* (1858), Bonifacio Byrne's patriotic "Mi bandera" (1899), and José Martí's four books of poems, *Ismaelillo* (1882), *Versos sencillos* (1891), and the posthumous *Versos libres* (1913) and *Flores del destierro* (1933). The Recovering the U.S. Hispanic Literary Heritage project has been instrumental in providing current access to this historical period of U.S.-Cuban literature. The project issued a new edition of *El laúd* (1995; ed. Matías Montes-Huidobro) and the first bilingual edition of Martí's complete *Versos sencillos/Simple Verses* (1997; trans. Manuel A. Tellechea). The two compilations that have come out of the first decade of the recovery project, *Herencia: The Anthology of Hispanic Literature of the United States* (2002) and *En otra voz: antología de la literatura hispana de los Estados Unidos* (2003), are indispensable resources on the literature and literary history of Cuban exile in the United States. For the most part, however, this body of exile literature is not relevant for an Anglophone readership (with the possible exception of Martí, who has acquired a place in comparative 19th-century American letters). The Cuban American literature that is most integral to ethnic American literature began with the first generation of exiles following the revolution of 1959, continued after the Mariel boatlift of 1981, and extends into the 21st century with the children of both generations. Numerous literary magazines have given a voice to these writers over the years, including *Areíto, Escandalar, Exilio,* and *Linden Lane Magazine.* Cuban American literature also has received broad distribution through Arte Público Press, Bilingual Press/Editorial Bilingüe, and Ediciones Universal, the three leading publishers of Spanish language and bilingual literature by Latino writers in the United States.

The first generation of Cuban American poets wrote primarily in Spanish and in response to the historical circumstance of their exile from Cuba following the revolution, as opposed to the Chicano and Puerto Rican writers (with whom they are often categorized as the three principal groups of U.S. Latino writers), who found their initial literary expression through the repercussions of the **Civil Rights Movement**. Also in contrast to the English-dominant Chicanos and Puerto Ricans, Spanish was the language of choice for Cubans in the United States in the 1960s and 1970s. As a result, Cuban poetry in the United States of this early period is more likely to be considered Cuban or Cuban exile literature rather than a discrete branch of the growing corpus of multiethnic American literature.

The Cuban American literature anthologies of these two decades reflect such choices of language preference and national allegiance. Early primary and secondary sources confirm that virtually all the poetry of this period was both written in Spanish and regarded as Cuban national literature. These books include two anthologies of exile poets, Angel Aparicio Laurencio's *Cinco poetisas cubanas, 1935–1969* (1970) and Ana Rosa Núñez's *Poesía en éxodo: el exilio cubano en su poesía, 1959–1969* (1970); Matías Montes Huidobro and Yara González's dictionary, *Bibliografía crítica de la poesía cubana (exilio: 1959–1971)* (1972); Orlando Rodríguez Sardiñas's *La última poesía cubana: antología reunida (1959–1973)* (1973); and José B. Fernández and Roberto G. Fernández's *Indice bibliográfico de autores cubanos (diáspora 1959–1979)/Bibliographical Index of Cuban Authors (Diaspora 1959–1979)* (1983). Four of the *Cinco poetisas*—Rita Geada, Ana Rosa Núñez, Pura del Prado, and Teresa María Rojas—appear in Rodríguez Sardiñas's *La última poesía cubana* and in subsequent compilations over the years (Núñez and Prado as late as the 1990s, in English translation). *La última poesía cubana,* one of the earliest compilations of this type, likewise anthologizes several other prominent Cuban exile writers, including José Kozer, Dolores Prida, and Isel Rivero. Most of these poets have continued to write in Spanish (Kozer is especially prolific), although at least one turned to English and even other genres (Prida writes bilingual drama). Still other poets in *La última poesía cubana* (Angel Cuadra, Belkis

Cuza Malé, and Heberto Padilla) went into exile in the United States long after the publication of the anthology. More recently, the practice of bringing together island and diaspora writing has continued in León de la Hoz's *La poesía de las dos orillas: Cuba (1959–1993): antología* (1994). Hoz's alphabetical arrangement of poets presumes the primacy of a national-literature focus rather than the geographical fact of residency either in Cuba or in exile in the United States, the "other shore."

Silvia Burunat and Ofelia García's *Veinte años de literatura cubanoamericana: antología 1962–1982* (1988) is the single best source of poetry and fiction of those years. (Published by Bilingual Press/Editorial Bilingüe, it is also the most accessible.) The thematic organization illustrates both ongoing connections to island concerns (the opening section treats Afro-Cuban **identity**) as well as the tendency to explore—in Spanish—issues of identity, exile, and immigration as part of a nascent Cuban American experience. Especially noteworthy in *Veinte años* are the contributions of Lourdes Casal, Uva Clavijo, José Kozer, and Juana Rosa Pita. Despite the rich tradition represented in all anthologies of this kind and in the dozens of discrete volumes published by these poets, however, the language factor has precluded the inclusion of this literature in English-language books. Ultimately, this early Cuban American poetry remains largely invisible to the general reader of multiethnic American literature.

By the 1980s and 1990s, several factors combined to allow broader recognition of Cuban American poetry. English had become the language of choice and these younger Cuban American poets, unlike the first-generation writers, were writing squarely within American literature. They were publishing in mainstream literary magazines like *American Poetry Review, Blue Mesa Review, Kenyon Review*, and *Prairie Schooner*, as well as in the Latino publications *Americas Review, Bilingual Review*, and *Linden Lane Magazine*. Cuban American poets also were included alongside other Latinos in groundbreaking anthologies such as *El Coro: A Chorus of Latino and Latina Poetry* (1997; ed. Martín Espada) and *Paper Dance: 55 Latino Poets* (1995; ed. Victor Hernández Cruz, Leroy V. Quintana, and Virgil Suárez). Contemporaneous Cuban American anthologies reflect these changed circumstances. Carolina Hospital's *Cuban American Writers: Los Atrevidos* (1988) features the poetry of 10 Cuba-born writers who are "daring" for choosing English even as they identify implicitly and explicitly with both the exile experience and Cuban literature (16–17). Hospital, for her part, is equally daring as an anthologist, not only for asserting a place for such writers in Cuban and U.S. literature, but also for bringing together the breadth of these exile and immigrant traditions in a later anthology, *A Century of Cuban Writers in Florida: Selected Prose and Poetry* (1996; coed. Jorge Cantera). The writer and scholar Gustavo Pérez Firmat has called these writers born in Cuba but raised and educated in the United States the "one-and-a-half" generation. Many of these daring "one-and-a-halfers" (Jorge Guitart, Pablo Medina, Ricardo Pau-Llosa, and Hospital and Pérez Firmat themselves) also appear in Delia Poey and Virgil Suárez's *Little Havana Blues: A Cuban-American Literature Anthology* (1996); still others (Sandra Castillo, Adrián Castro, Silvia Curbelo, and Dionisio Martínez) in Hospital and Cantera's Florida anthology. Together these editors have identified a corpus of poets who depict not only the exile experience, but also more universal aesthetic and thematic considerations. The literary criticism by scholars of this generation—such as Isabel Alvarez Borland's *Cuban-American Literature of Exile: From Person to Persona* (1998) and virtually all of Pérez Firmat's work on Cuban and Cuban American literature and culture—invariably illuminates the development of Cuban American poetry, even though the studies may not directly or exclusively treat poetry per se.

Further Reading

Cantera, Jorge, and Carolina Hospital. "Florida and Cuba: Ties That Bind." In *A Century of Cuban Writers in Florida: Selected Prose and Poetry*, edited by Hospital and Cantera, 1–28. Sarasota, FL: Pineapple, 1996.

Cortina, Rodolfo J. "History and Development of Cuban American Literature: A Survey." In *Handbook of Hispanic Cultures in the United States: Literature and Art*, edited by Francisco Lomelí, 40–61. Houston: Arte Público; Madrid: Instituto de Cooperación Iberoamericana, 1993.

Hospital, Carolina, ed. *Cuban American Writers: Los Atrevidos*. Princeton, NJ: Ellas-Linden Lane, 1988.

Kanellos, Nicolás. "An Overview of Hispanic Literature in the United States." In *Herencia: The Anthology of Hispanic Literature of the United States*, edited by Kanellos et al., 1–32. New York: Oxford University Press, 2002.

Lindstrom, Naomi. "Cuban American and Continental Puerto Rican Literature." In *Sourcebook of Hispanic Culture in the United States*, edited by David William Foster, 221–45. Chicago: American Library Association, 1982.

Maratos, Daniel C., and Marnesba D. Hill. *Escritores de la diáspora cubana: manual biobibliográfica/Cuban Exile Writers: A Biobibliographic Handbook*. Metuchen, NJ: Scarecrow, 1986.

Poey, Delia, and Virgil Suárez. "Introduction." In *Little Havana Blues: A Cuban-American Literature Anthology*, edited by Poey and Suárez, 9–15. Houston: Arte Público, 1996.

Wall, Catharine E. "Latino Poetry." In *Critical Survey of Poetry*. 2nd rev. ed. 8 vols. Edited by Philip K. Jason, 4825–32. Pasadena, CA: Salem, 2003.

Catharine E. Wall

CULTURE CLASH

Culture Clash is a Latino performance/comedy troupe. A comedy trio, it has amassed acclaim from mainstream theater critics as well as scholars of Chicano/Latino theater and performance. The group is an offshoot of Comedy Fiesta, a performance/comedy troupe born in 1984 that consisted of Richard Montoya, Ric Salinas, Herbert Siguenza, Jose Antonio Burciaga, Monica Palacios, and Marga Gomez. By 1988, Comedy Fiesta had become Culture Clash and had been whittled to its present core of Montoya, Salinas, and Siguenza. The influence of the Marx Brothers, Buster Keaton, and Mexican comic actor Cantinflas can be seen in the wit and slapstick that characterize Culture Clash's work. In addition, Culture Clash's use of satire and comedy to comment on an array of social and political concerns reflects the inspiration the trio has drawn from the politically motivated teatro of the Chicano Movement. Armed with intelligence, political astuteness, a sense of humor, a sense of urgency, and a Brechtian sense of theater's potential to raise audiences' consciousness, Culture Clash has consistently managed to provoke critical thinking about various issues.

The group's first two plays, *The Mission* (1988) and *A Bowl of Beings* (1991), brilliantly engage the subjects of Chicano **identity** and the racist organization of the American entertainment industry. In *The Mission*, three Latinos' inability to break into television, film, and stand-up comedy reflects the limited opportunity that is available to aspiring Latino entertainers. As Richard, Ric, and Herbert, the eponymous characters of this quasi-autobiographical play, look for work, they discover their potential for success circumscribed by the fact that only stereotypical and caricatured roles are available to them. *A Bowl of Beings*, Culture Clash's follow-up piece, consists of a series of sketches that dramatize the difficulty of defining Chicano identity. Through a panoply of characters that includes history's first Chicano, a wannabe Chicano revolutionary, a Chicano in the midst of a mental breakdown, and a Chicano-turned-stoner, Culture Clash maps the ways that the cultural and racial hybridity of Chicano identity complicate efforts to define this identity.

After *A Bowl of Beings*, Culture Clash staged a number of productions that explore the history and social relations of specific locations. The first of these productions, *S.O.S.—Comedy for These Uncertain Times* (1992), examines the ailments that Los Angeles communities and families had to confront in the early 1990s: the beating of Rodney King by Los Angeles police officers, the Los Angeles riots, racial tensions, homophobia, and AIDS.

Amid this distressed condition of Los Angeles, *S.O.S.* functioned as a call for change and healing. For *Radio Mambo* (1995), *Bordertown* (1998), *Nuyorican Stories* (1999), and *Mission Magic Mystery Tour* (2000), Montoya, Salinas, and Siguenza interviewed residents of Miami, San Diego, New York's Lower East Side, and San Francisco's Mission District, respectively. In each of these shows, the members of Culture Clash assume the personas of their interviewees in order to provide an insightful snapshot of the various personalities that occupy particular locales. As audiences come face to face with the idiosyncratic individuals of these communities, they realize the dignity and pathos of each one. In addition, the unique challenges that stand in the way of these communities' harmony become apparent vis-à-vis the revelation of the conflicts that haunt them. More generally, Culture Clash has managed, through their site-specific pieces, to foreground the fear, anxiety, animosity, and uncertainty that suffuse contemporary American society and that must be negotiated.

Other pieces by Culture Clash include *Carpa Clash* (1993), a tribute to Cesar Chávez; *The Birds* (1998), a musical adaptation of Aristophanes's work; and *Anthems: Culture Clash in the District* (2002), a site-specific show that explores Washington, D.C. *Chavez Ravine* (2003) has been Culture Clash's most successful piece. This musical exposes the political story behind the construction of Dodger Stadium by unearthing the human history beneath it. As *Chavez Ravine* portrays the deals that resulted in the bulldozing of Mexican immigrants' houses for the sake of building a southern California home for the Brooklyn Dodgers, the show challenges audiences to acknowledge the shady political machinations that have built Los Angeles. Ultimately, *Chavez Ravine*, like many of Culture Clash's other works, lays out for audiences the unfair ways that power, as it is unequally distributed in the United States, encroaches on individual lives and individuals' dignity. (*See also* Mexican American Stereotypes)

Further Reading

Glenn, Antonia Grace. "Comedy for These Urgent Times: Culture Clash as Chroniclers in America." *Theatre Forum* 20 (Winter–Spring 2002): 62–68.

Kondo, Dorinne. "(Re)Visions of Race: Contemporary Race Theory and the Cultural Politics of Racial Crossover in Documentary Theatre." *Theatre Journal* 52.4 (2000): 81–108.

Phillip Serrato

D

DANTICAT, EDWIDGE (1969–)

Edwidge Danticat is a Haitian American short-story writer, novelist, and essayist. She eloquently portrays the depths of human experience in concise, lyrical prose. In her stories, novels, and nonfiction, she combines a breathtakingly expansive sensibility of what it means to be human with a sharp focus on the particularity of her individual characters. Haiti, where she lived from birth until age 12, has been a constant source of inspiration in her work, which deals with life in Haiti, as well as the Haitian diaspora.

Born in Port-au-Prince in 1969, Danticat was raised by an aunt and uncle while her parents struggled to improve the family's living conditions. Her father left Haiti for New York when she was two, and her mother followed when she was four. Remaining with her brother in Haiti, Danticat was fascinated by the special bond between the older women in her family, a fact reflected clearly in much of her work. However, the young Danticat also had a close relationship with her uncle, a Baptist minister who lost his ability to speak after having a laryngectomy. At age 10, she became an extension of her uncle's voice by learning to read his lips and translating his words into spoken language.

An avid reader as well as a listener, Danticat attributes her vocation as a writer to the many stories, both oral and written, that she was exposed to as a young child. In Haiti, she learned to speak Creole and write in French. She acquired English after joining her parents in New York at age 12 and began writing at an early age. In fact, the idea for her first novel had its beginnings in an autobiographical essay about her experience as an immigrant, written only a few years after her arrival in the United States. She studied French literature at Barnard College and received an MFA from Brown University. While distinctive and personal, her writing style has benefited from a close familiarity with Haitian, United States, and French literary traditions. Among her many literary influences are writers such as **Paule Marshall**, **Toni Morrison**, Jacques Roumain, Jacques Stephen Alexis, Marie Chauvet, Maryse Condé, **Jamaica Kincaid**, **Amy Tan**, and **Alice Walker**. Danticat also credits the time she spent listening to the conversations of women in her family as a profound influence on her creative development.

Danticat's first novel, *Breath, Eyes, Memory* (1994), is narrated by Sophie Caco, a young girl who leaves Haiti at age 12 to join her mother in New York. Sophie leaves behind her Tante Atie and her grandmother to start a new life, but cannot free herself from her family's traumatic past. Her mother, Martine, is haunted by the rape that left her pregnant with Sophie as a young woman. Despite tragedy and separation, Sophie comes to understand the strength of the bonds she shares with her female family members after she herself becomes a mother.

Danticat continues to explore the bonds between mothers and daughters in her first collection of short stories, *Krik? Krak!* (1995). The book takes its name from the call-and-response tradition of Creole storytelling in which the storyteller calls out "Krik?" before beginning and the active listener demonstrates enthusiasm and readiness by responding "Krak." The collection adeptly addresses the incredible losses experienced by so many, as well as the hopes and dreams of Haitians, both within and beyond Haiti's borders. One story, titled simply "Nineteen Thirty-Seven," explores multigenerational bonds among women through the trauma of the 1937 massacre that occurred under the brutal regime of Dominican dictator Rafael Leónidas Trujillo.

Danticat's second novel, *The Farming of Bones* (1998), also deals with the 1937 massacre. Here, however, the events become much more than a historically significant backdrop to the underlying narrative. This is a complex and well-researched portrayal of the 1937 massacre, incited by the Dominican government, in which tens of thousands of Haitians (as well as many Dominicans suspected of being Haitians) were murdered on the Dominican side of the aptly named Massacre River. Although other prominent writers, including Jacques Stephen Alexis, **Rita Dove**, and Freddy Prestol Castillo, have explored the 1937 massacre, Danticat's novel is peerless in its finely shaded, though never romanticized representation of the terror suffered by those living under Trujillo's rule.

Danticat's first extended work of nonfiction, *After the Dance: A Walk through Carnival in Jacmel, Haiti* (2002), is a rich meditation on the history, culture, and people of the city of Jacmel in southern Haiti. During her stay in Jacmel, Danticat reflects on the meanings of specific carnival legends and traditions while also engaging in broader meditations on topics such as the social significance of masks. In fact, after participating in the celebration, Danticat ends her journey with the surprising revelation that "as others had been putting on their masks, just for one afternoon, I had allowed myself to remove my own."

In *Behind the Mountains* (2002), Danticat, who was raised in the Bel-Air neighborhood of Port-au-Prince, explores what it might be like for a young girl to emigrate from rural Haiti and move to New York in the year 2000. The novel, which is part of Scholastic's First Person Fiction series, is written in the form of a diary kept by a young girl named Celiane Espérance from Beau Jour, Haiti. The first half of the diary describes Celiane's life in Haiti with her mother and brother, and the second explores her life in New York after the family is reunited with her father. Danticat's second book for young readers, *Anacaona, Golden Flower*, to be published in 2005, recounts the story of Anacaona, a Taino princess who inhabited the island of Hispaniola before the arrival of Christopher Columbus. Both warrior and artist according to legend, Anacaona, who is mentioned often by Danticat in interviews and essays, is a figure greatly admired in both Haiti and the Dominican Republic. Danticat's new book will be a welcome addition to the scarce existing literature available in English on the life and legend of Anacaona.

Danticat's most recent publication is *The Dew Breaker* (2004), a collection of interrelated stories. The title pays homage to Jacques Roumain's 1944 masterpiece of Haitian literature, *Gouverneurs de la rosée* (*Masters of the Dew*). More specifically, however, the term "dew breaker" is a translation of the Haitian Creole "chokèt laroze," which refers to a violent regional leader or authority figure. Male characters play a much larger role in this collection than in Danticat's previous works. All nine stories intersect through the figure of the dew breaker, a man who has fled from his past as a henchman of the Duvalier regime to start a new life in the United States with his family. Although not physically present in each story, the sense that a dew breaker has directly or indirectly affected the lives of Danticat's characters is maintained throughout the collection. Once again, Danticat succeeds in breathing life into carefully nuanced characters who must all find their own ways of dealing with the past. The questions her characters face daily regarding the meaning of family, forgiveness, and healing lead the reader to consider the intensely personal effects of torture on both the perpetrators and their victims.

In addition to her writing, Danticat has also edited collections of other writers' works and taught creative writing at the university level. Her stories have appeared in over 20 periodicals, and her work has been widely anthologized. She won an American Book Award for *The Farming of Bones* and is also the recipient of numerous other awards. Her collection *Krik? Krak!* was a National Book Award finalist, and *Breath, Eyes, Memory* was chosen as an Oprah Book Club selection. In 1996, *Granta* named her "one of the 20 best young American novelists." Today, her invitingly clear prose and moving characters continue to draw both popular and critical attention. Indeed, Danticat is well on her way to becoming one of the most talented writers in the United States today. Nevertheless, the most striking testament to her success as a writer may be found not in the critical accolades or strong sales figures, but in her ability to inspire readers to contemplate the complexity of immigrants' experiences and to learn more about Haiti.

Further Reading

Francis, Donette A. "'Silences Too Horrific to Disturb': Writing Sexual Histories in Edwidge Danticat's *Breath, Eyes, Memory*." *Research in African Literatures* 35.2 (2004): 75–90.
Hausmann, Shea. "The Dangerous Job of Edwidge Danticat." *Callaloo* 19.2 (1996): 382–89.
Shemak, April. "Re-Membering Hispaniola: Edwidge Danticat's *The Farming of Bones*." *MFS Modern Fiction Studies* 48.1 (2002): 83–112.

Sara Scott Armengot

DIAZ, JUNOT (1968-)

Junot Diaz is a fiction writer born in the Dominican Republic, and is considered one of the most promising contemporary authors. Although his success is fairly recent, Diaz has established himself as one of the most gifted Latino writers in modern times. He has the distinction of having been named one of the twenty writers for the 21st century by *The New Yorker*.

Diaz's breakthrough short-story collection, *Drown* (1996), was an instant hit and earned him praise for its lyrical prose. Almost immediately after its publication, *Drown* drew comparisons to **Piri Thomas**'s ***Down These Mean Streets*** (1967), a best-selling autobiographical work that paved the way for Latino writers. Like Thomas, Diaz drew upon the harsh realities of inner-city life, portraying dark worlds and desperate characters in the Dominican Republic, New York, and New Jersey. Diaz's characters are at times part of an ugly but real life—from the ghettoes and rough streets—yet they also represent with brutal honesty the daily struggles that many impoverished immigrants' experience. For example, the short story, "Ysrael," about a young boy in the Dominican Republic whose face is eaten by a pig, is inevitably about the separation between a young child from his parents, who live in the United States. Such situations are not uncommon in Latin American countries where families live off the money that individuals send back home. Similarly, in "Negocios," we experience the angst of a character whose father leaves the family in the Dominican Republic so that he can earn money in the United States, only to remarry. Throughout his short stories, one can find a touch of humor, often dark, but nevertheless effective in helping us appreciate the barriers that so many Dominican families face. In "How to Date a Browngirl, Blackgirl, Whitegirl, or Halfie," the protagonist provides advice on how to seduce women of various ethnic backgrounds, in the end concluding that they must not see government cheese in a refrigerator. Diaz's fiction has frequently been referred to as autobiographical. Having been born and raised in the Dominican Republic and in New Jersey, Diaz certainly was able to learn firsthand about the sometimes tragic but often inspirational lives of many of the characters he depicts. But aside from partly serving as inspiration, the events in his life are separate from the ones in *Drown*. This, of course, isn't to say that events in Diaz's life could not have shown such cruelty as the one depicted in his writing, but that he is a very creative artist whose skills make his stories appear real.

Diaz's work has appeared in such notable publications as *Story, The New Yorker*, the *Paris Review, Time Out, Glimmer Train, African Voices*, and *Best American Short Stories*. He has earned such honors as the Pushcart Prize, a fellowship from the John Simon Guggenheim Memorial Foundation and the National Endowment of the Arts, the Eugene McDermott Award, a Lela Acheson Wallace *Readers Digest* Award, and a Pen/Malamud Award. He is a fellow at the Radcliffe Institute for Advanced Study at Harvard University and is an associate professor at the Massachusetts Institute of Technology. (*See also* Dominican American Novel)

Further Reading

Cespedes, Diogenes, and Torres-Saillant, Silvio. "Fiction Is the Poor Man's Cinema: An Interview with Junot Diaz." *Callaloo* 23.3 (Summer 2000): 892–907.

Torres, Lourdes, and Carina Vasquez. "Junot Diaz." *Dialogo* 15.1 (2012): 29–35.

Wood, James. "*Drown*: Book Review." *The New Republic* 215.25 (December 16, 1996): 39.

Jose B. Gonzalez

DOMINICAN AMERICAN NOVEL

It is not an exaggeration to say that were it not for the growing body of work produced by **Julia Alvarez**, the Dominican American novel would probably not warrant attention as a distinct subcategory of Hispanic American or Caribbean American literature. The most significant wave of Dominican immigration into the United States has occurred over the last three decades. Alvarez's emergence as a major new voice in American letters has provided a cultural marker for the sudden visibility of Dominican Americans in politics, business, entertainment, and many other arenas. In addition, her achievements in several genres have clearly inspired other Dominican American writers to explore what it means to be both Dominican and American at the close of the 20th century and the beginning of the 21st century.

The terrors that eventually touched almost all Dominicans during the long dictatorship of Rafael Trujillo have been the focus of many of the recent Dominican American novels. Nominated for a National Book Award, Alvarez's *In the Time of the Butterflies* (1994) is based on the true story of the Mirabel sisters who were murdered when their plan to undermine Trujillo's rule was discovered by his agents. In *How the Garcia Girls Lost Their Accents* (1992), Alvarez chronicles the experiences of a family that flees the Dominican Republic as Trujillo's hold on power is beginning to unravel. Her novel for young adults, *Before We Were Free* (2002), provides a parallel story about a Dominican family that remains in the Dominican Republic during the deepening crisis.

Like *How the Garcia Girls Lost Their Accents*, Loida Maritsa Perez's *Geographies of Home* (1999) focuses on a Dominican family that has escaped Trujillo's regime and settled in New York. This family, however, includes fourteen children. Their story is told by Iliana, the second youngest of the children and the first to attend college. In the midst of her studies, she returns home to try to resolve at least some of the crises that seem to have erupted at the same time in the lives of her parents and just about all of her siblings. Indeed, the family's past in the Dominican Republic increasingly seems an almost idyllic alternative to its current turmoil.

In Marisela Rizik's *Of Forgotten Times* (2004), the Dominican dictator is called "Iron Fist," and the protagonist is Herminia, the dictator's young wife, who is descended from slaves who had founded a Santerian-style cult around their claim of special access to the supernatural. The best-selling novel in history within the Dominican Republic has been Viriato Sencion's *They Forged the Signature of God* (1993), which darkly satirizes the pervasive corruption of Dominican society under Trujillo and his successor Balaguer.

Trujillo's regime has also been the subject of several important novels by non-Dominicans. Haitian American **Edwidge Danticat**'s *The Farming of Bones* (1999) treats Trujillo's campaign of terror against Haitian visiting workers during the late 1930s. Peruvian Mario Vargas Llhosa's *The Feast of the Goat* (2003) juxtaposes the events leading up to his assassination, with the later return of one of his victims to the Dominican Republic.

The Rizik novel might be categorized as a multigenerational saga, a genre popular among Dominican American novelists. Alvarez's *In the Name of Salome* (2000) fictionally juxtaposes the life stories of the 19th-century Dominican poet Salome

Urina and her daughter Salome Camila. In an unusual strategy, Alvarez presents the mother's story chronologically, but works backward through the daughter's story—so that the novel ends with the mother's death, which becomes her three-year-old daughter's earliest and most formative memory. Nelly Rosario's *Song of the Water Saints* (2003) describes the divergent experiences of three generations of Dominican women whose lives span the 20th century.

Increasingly, Dominican American novelists have focused more exclusively on the issues defining the lives of Dominican Americans struggling to transcend the hard realities of everyday life in urban America, and in particular, the greater New York area. In *Soledad* (2001), Angie Cruz explores the emotional strains on a young woman who has escaped the tough "ethnic" neighborhood in which she was raised and now must return to it to care for her ailing mother. Although the basic situation of this novel parallels that in Perez's *Geographies of Home*, the Dominican past serves as mere background detail than as a dramatic backdrop to the events of Cruz's novel. The same is true of the stories in **Junot Diaz**'s celebrated collection *Drown* (1996). Although the young boys on whom the stories focus are just old enough to have nostalgic memories of life in the Dominican Republic, the emphasis is on their experiences and adjustments while growing up in northern New Jersey. Unified by narrative voice, recurring motifs, and complementary themes, the collection is novelistic in the same way that Sherwood Anderson's *Winesburg, Ohio* and William Gass's *In the Heart of the Heart of the Country* transcend the usual boundaries between the genres.

Alvarez's *Yo!* (1997) is a sequel to *How the Garcia Girls Lost Their Accents*. The youngest, Yolanda, has become a novelist, and this novel presents the story of her successes and failures from multiple points of view but not Yolanda's own. Each chapter is narrated by a different character, and the narrative forms as well as the narrative voices are varied accordingly. The narrators include the members of her family, her friends and personal acquaintants, her former husbands, her students, her critics, and her readers, including a fan who has stalked her for more than a decade. Yolanda is haunted by the lost possibilities in her family's exile from the Dominican Republic, but, for all of the reminiscences, the novel is ultimately much more forward-looking than reflective.

Recent political thrillers featuring Dominican American characters include Manuel Vazquez Montalban's *Galindez* (1998) and Sarah Pemberton Strong's *Burning the Sea* (2002). Mystery–suspense novels in the same vein include Nick Carter's *Dominican Affair* (1982), April Smith's *Be the One* (2000), and Adrian McKinty's *Dead I May Well Be* (2004).

Further Reading

Bramen, Carrie Tirado. "Translating Exile: The Metamorphosis of the Ordinary in Dominican Short Fiction." *Latin American Literary Review* 26 (January–June 1998): 63–78.

Molina, Sintia E. "Duality and Displacement in the Dominican Literature in the United States." *Latino Studies Journal* 9 (Fall 1998): 65–84.

Martin Kich

DOMINICAN AMERICAN POETRY

Dominican poetry in the United States narrates the reality of a people in transition. Throughout the 20th century, Dominicans experienced political and economic hardships that forced them to leave their homeland. The first wave of these islanders arrived in the United States between the 1930s and 1960s, a period in which the Dominican Republic endured the fierce dictatorship of Rafael L. Trujillo. To this first wave of political refugees belong two of the most prolific Dominican poets in the United States today: Rhina P. Espaillat (1932–) and **Julia Alvarez** (1951–). Impelled by economic pressures, the second and largest wave came in the 1980s and 1990s. As the Dominican community increased and organized in the United States, a boom of writers emerged.

Gifted in the art of poetry, Rhina P. Espaillat was inducted into the Poetry Society of America at the young age of 16. She published her work in a number of journals and anthologies, as well as in three books of her own: *Lapsing to Grace* (1992), *Where Horizons Go* (1998), and *Rehearsing Absence* (2001). Espaillat migrated to the United States at a time when Latino immigrants struggled to participate and understand their role in a more politically stable country, but where women and ethnic groups were still marginalized from mainstream society. Learning English was a matter of survival for Spanish speakers, since during the 1930s their language and customs were not as widespread as they are today in many cities of the United States. Education for immigrants like Espaillat was strictly given in English. This meant carrying on with two different realities, the one that was lived in the privacy of the home—where culture and heritage governed—and the one that was demanded by the public domain—where immigrants had to negotiate with a society that required change and integration.

Encouraged by her circumstances, Espaillat mastered the English language, becoming bilingual. However, the majority of her poetic work is written in English. Among other things, in her poetry she writes about the trivial and significant moments that are equally important in shaping our daily lives. With metaphors and other poetic artifacts, she reveals "casual moments" as the richest sources for all kind of poetry, and at the same time she opens a dialogue with family, love, death, and memories. Throughout her career, Espaillat has won many poetic awards, among them the 1998 T. S. Eliot Prize for *Where Horizons Go* and the 2001 Richard Wilbur Award for *Rehearsing Absence*.

Dominican women have made a significant contribution to the ethnic literature of the United States. Julia Alvarez, the most prolific and recognized Dominican writer in this country, presently has approached poetry from a more political angle than Espaillat. Alvarez, who also belongs to the first big wave of Dominican immigrants, left her country at the age of nine. Upon her arrival in the United States, she encountered a society struggling to change a tradition of separatism. The politically charged climate of the 1960s is reflected in her poetry, which has shown a particular interest in class struggle and in the politics of womanhood and family. As an exile, her poetry has expressed the "homesickness" that is often found in the literature of immigrants. Moreover, her poems are, in many ways, accounts of the dilemma between parents and their bicultural children, of the power struggle between men and women, as well as between women themselves. Alvarez is a writer about the complexity of *being* before and after the transnational experience. She has published three books of poems: *Homecoming* (1984), *The Other Side: El Otro Lado* (1995), and *The Woman I Kept to Myself* (2004). In addition, her poetry has appeared in the *New York Times Magazine, The New Yorker*, and *The American Poetry Review*. She is the winner of numerous awards, including the Jessica Nobel-Maxwell Poetry Prize in 1995 and the Hispanic Heritage Award in Literature, 2002.

The topic and style of Dominican poetry continued to diversify in the 1980s and 1990s. In these two decades, a great deal of the poetry was written either in Spanish and English, or only in Spanish. The topics and issues that are addressed in these works are inspired by the experiences of Dominicans in the current world, regardless of where they reside. The uncertainty of the present and the future is a theme that incites the imagination of Marianela Medrano (1964–). This introspective poet finds a place in poetry to question issues of **race**, marginality, and tradition. She has published four books, *Oficio de Vivir* (1986), *Los Alegres Ojos de la Tristeza* (1987), *Regando Esencias* (1998), and *Curada de Espantos* (2002).

There are many Dominican poets in the United States that write their poems in their mother tongue. Some of these writers publish their work in the Dominican Republic, while others publish their material in both countries. The poetic interests and endeavors of these second-wave writers are broad, but a number of them have recurrent themes. Norberto James (1945–), for example, frequently writes poems that allude to sadness, solitude, innocence, *el pueblo*—the people. Social awareness is also a common element in his poems. This topic reoccurs in the verses of Diógenes Abréu (1959–), who writes poems to the metropolis of New York and to the masses of workers that walk its streets. Poetry, as an act of awareness, has a particular twist in the hands of Isabel Espinal (1964–), Yrene Santos (1963–), Isabel P. Hernández (1958–), and Miriam Ventura (1957–). These writers have self and identity as focal points in their poetry. Espinal's awareness of the pressures of being a female and a Latina in society is articulated by Santos from the role of women in a more intimate setting. Awareness of womanhood for Santos is found in the daily demands that family places on women, in their strength and sensuality, as well as in the feeling of emptiness and fragmentation they sometimes endure. For Hernández, this sense of fragmentation is at the core of **identity**, and awareness is just brief moments of clarity. The micro-poems of Miriam Ventura are a keen representation of the ephemeral aspects of awareness.

Alexis Gómez Rosa (1950–) is a poet who distances himself from the morally correct. With a baroque language, his verses follow the path of desire and excess, to uncover pleasure in the act of eating, drinking, and other delights of life. Another poet who focuses on desire is Jorge Piña (1959–), but in the context of dreams, fantasies, and the unconsciousness. However, the expression of desire through the carnal and the erotic is the expertise of Diogenes Nina's *Apricina: Bestia del Paraíso* (1987). Desire in the realm of romanticism is a defining characteristic of the work of Teonilda Madera (1961–) and the already mentioned Yrene Santos.

In the works of Franklin Gutierrez (1951–), readers find history as the object of inspiration. This is especially evident in his collection of poems *Inriri* (1984). Another poet that can be included in this line of historical poetry is Juan Mato (1956–), with his collection of poems *Azúcar, Cayo y Puerto* (1997). Dagoberto López (1955–), on the other hand, finds poetry in the popular, which for him can range from a place, like a small village left behind, to a subject, like the socially marginalized prostitute. Both place and subject are impacted by a capitalist reality. An author who also evokes the popular, but with a personal touch, is Josefina Báez. This creative poet makes the content and the context of her poems one single dance. Báez's *Dominicanish* is an example of a performance-poetry that uses rhythm to capture images of the surroundings. Her poetry is an ode to motion, to the neighborhoods, and people in the mist of the urban. Maitreyi Villamán Matos in *B x 15* finds the popular in the places and characters of these city neighborhoods and uses them as sources of inspiration to speak of the present and the here, the ground for new identity.

Further Reading

Abréu, Dió-genes, and Dagoberto López-Coño. *La palabra como cuerpo del delito.* Santo Domingo, Dominican Republic: Biblioteca Nacional, 2001.

Cocco De Filippis, Daisy. *Tertuliando: Hanging Out.* Vol. 1. Santo Domingo, Dominican Republic: Comisión Permanente de la Feria Nacional del Libro, 1997.

Sagás, Ernesto, and Sintia E. Molina, eds. *Dominican Migration: Transnational Perspectives.* Gainesville: University Press of Florida, 2004.

Torres-Saillant, Silvio. "La literatura dominicana en los Estados Unidos." In *Cruzando Puentes: Antología De Literatura Latina.* Vol. 3. Edited by Luis Leal and Victor Fuentes, 40–45. Santa Barbara, CA: Ventana Abierta, 2001.

Karina A. Bautista

DOUGLASS, FREDERICK (1818–1895)

Frederick Douglass was an African American abolitionist and autobiographer, champion of civil rights and women's rights, orator and circuit lecturer for the Massachusetts Anti-Slavery Society, newspaper editor and journalist, organizer of black combat units for the Union army, marshal of the District of Columbia, recorder of deeds, District of Columbia, and U.S. minister to Haiti. From 1847, when he started his newspaper *North Star*, to the end of his life, he was the undisputed leader of his **race**, first fighting for their freedom from slavery, and after their freedom fighting for their equal citizenship rights. Douglass's major works include three autobiographies, *Narrative of the Life of Frederick Douglass* (1845), *My Bondage and Freedom* (1955), and *Life and Times of Frederick Douglass* (1881, 1892); a historical novella, *The Heroic Slave* (1853), based on the true story of Madison Washington's uprising on the slave ship *Creole*; and electrifying speeches that range from "What to the Slave Is the Fourth of July?" (1853) to "Not Benevolence but Simply Justice" (1865), and from "The Color Line in America" (1883) to

Frederick Douglass. (Library of Congress)

"The Lessons of the Hour" (1894). A self-made man, Douglass inspired his people to fight against **racism**, slavery, segregation, discrimination, and injustice, and has been a beacon of inspiration for oppressed people everywhere.

Born to a slave, Harriet Bailey, and an unknown white man at a farm in Tuckahoe, Maryland, Frederick Douglass was named Frederick Augustus Washington Bailey by his mother. Harriet Bailey was a slave of Captain Aaron Anthony, who managed the vast plantation of Colonel Edward Lloyd V, who had been Maryland governor (1809–1811), and twice U.S. senator (1811–1815; 1819–1825). Grandparents Betsy and Isaac Bailey raised Douglass because Master Anthony assigned Douglass's mother to work on a distant farm. Grandpa Bailey was a freeman who worked as a sawyer, but Grandma Bailey was Captain Anthony's slave. Douglass's relatively carefree life abruptly came to an end when one day, in 1824, Grandma Bailey took him to Captain Anthony's plantation house, which was 12 miles away from where they lived, and left after telling him to play with other children. Douglass did not see his grandmother again.

At Captain Anthony's plantation house, Frederick Douglass gradually learned the harsh realities of slave life. At first, he was assigned only light duties and was spared physical abuse; however, he witnessed the abuse suffered by other slaves. One night he was startled out of sleep by a woman's screams and was astonished to find Captain Anthony mercilessly whipping Aunt Hester. On another occasion, Douglass saw his badly beaten cousin Betsey imploring Captain Anthony in vain for protection from the sexual advances of the drunken overseer Plummer. Douglass's mother passed away when he was only seven years old, and he was not even allowed to attend her funeral. In *Life and Times*, he regrets that he knew his mother very little.

In 1826, at the age of eight, Douglass was sent to Baltimore to live with Hugh and Sophia Auld to care for their two-year-old son Tommy. Douglass lived in Baltimore for seven years. Hugh Auld was the brother of Thomas Auld, who had become Douglass's new owner after the death of Thomas Auld's father-in-law, Captain Anthony. Sophia Auld, who had never before had a slave, treated Douglass kindly. She began to teach him how to read, but she stopped all instruction when her husband angrily told her that education would make him unfit to be a slave.

The hunger for learning was aroused, and Douglass sought other means of receiving instruction. When sent on errands, he would stuff his pockets with bread, which he would exchange for lessons in reading from poor white children. At night, he would copy out words written by Tommy in the blank spaces left in the used copybooks. At the age of 11, Douglass was hired out to work at the shipyard as a general assistant. He would copy out letters written on the lumber by carpenters to indicate their position in the vessel. Douglass tells in his *Narrative* that it was after many years' hard work that he finally learned to write. In 1831, at the age of 13, Douglass bought himself a used copy of the *Columbian Orator* for 50 cents, which he had earned by blacking boots. The speeches in that book seemed to give "tongue" to his thoughts on human rights.

In March 1833, Douglass went back to his owner Thomas Auld, who then lived in St. Michaels, Caroline County, with his second wife Rowena, his first wife having passed away. Finding Douglass too independent, Thomas Auld hired him out as a field hand to the notorious Edward Covey "to be broken." Covey would mercilessly beat Douglass till he felt broken in body and spirit. However, one day in August 1834, Covey pushed him too far. Working at the threshing machine in sultry heat, Douglass collapsed. After he failed to get up, Covey bashed him on his head with a hickory board, leaving him bleeding. Douglass trekked seven miles to report the matter to Master Auld, but he sent him back to Covey. Upon his return, Covey tried to tie him with a rope, but Douglass resisted. After a lengthy fight, Covey retreated. This fight proved to be a turning point in his life as a slave. Standing up to Covey, Douglass felt that he could not be a slave anymore. In the remaining five months he worked for Covey, he was never beaten.

In 1836, Douglass was sent back to Hugh Auld in Baltimore, who put him to work as a caulker, with the wages Douglass earned going to Auld. While working, Douglass planned his escape. On September 3, 1938, dressed in a sailor's suit and carrying a free black seaman's identification paper borrowed from a retired sailor, he assumed the name of Frederick Johnson and boarded the train to New York City and to freedom. In New York, David Ruggles, the Underground Railroad agent, met him at the station and took him home. His fiancée, Anna Murray, who was a free black woman eight years his senior, had financed his escape. She joined him in New York, where they were married. Within hours, they left for New Bedford, Massachusetts, where Douglass changed his surname to Douglass to hide his **identity**. Even as a free man in Massachusetts, Douglass could not be hired as a caulker, so he worked as a general laborer. Anna Douglass helped the family by taking in washing and doing domestic work. The couple had five children—two daughters, Rosetta and Annie, and three sons, Lewis, Frederick Jr., and Charles.

Douglass's career as an abolitionist began in August 1841, when at a Massachusetts Anti-Slavery Society convention, Douglass appeared as an unscheduled speaker and gave such a stirring account of his life as a slave that the society hired him as a lecturer. He served in that position for four years. However, while his audience admired him as a speaker, they could not believe that someone with his deportment and oratorical skills could ever have been a slave. In order to satisfy such skeptics, Douglass took time off from his lecturing duties in the winter of

1844–1845 to write his *Narrative of the Life of Frederick Douglass, An American Slave, Written by Himself*. His *Narrative* appeared in May 1845 and was an instant success. However, his revelation put him in danger of being arrested by slave catchers. In August 1845, he sailed for the British Isles, where he spoke at antislavery rallies to acclaim. British abolitionists led by two Quaker sisters Ellen and Anna Richardson raised money with which they purchased Douglass's freedom in December 1846, paying his owner Thomas Auld 150 pounds sterling. When he left for the States in April 1847, his British friends also gave him a purse containing $2,175 to start a newspaper. Despite opposition from William Lloyd Garrison who feared competition for his own newspaper *The Liberator*, Douglass launched his weekly newspaper, *The North Star*, in 1847. He published it in Rochester, New York, where he had moved, renamed it as *Frederick Douglass' Paper* in 1851, and continued publication until 1860. In 1858, Douglass also launched *Douglass' Monthly*, especially for his British readers, and it continued publication until 1863, the year of the Emancipation Proclamation. Douglass's newspapers were the most successful of the antebellum black-owned newspapers.

Douglass pressed President Abraham Lincoln to make the Civil War a crusade against slavery. He closed his newspaper to help recruit black soldiers for the Union army. Two of his sons, Lewis and Charles, served in the 54th Massachusetts colored regiment. In August 1863, Lincoln invited Douglass for a private conference at which Douglass sought equal pay, promotion, and protection for black soldiers. After President Lincoln's assassination, Mrs. Lincoln sent Douglass the president's walking stick as a token of her husband's regard for Douglass.

During the reconstruction era, Douglass demanded voting rights for blacks, and became a prominent Republican orator. In 1872, a mysterious fire destroyed his Rochester home, and Douglass moved to Washington, D.C. Douglass campaigned vigorously for the enactment of the civil rights amendments to the constitution. In 1878, Douglass bought Cedar Hill, a 15-acre estate with 20 Victorian rooms that once belonged to General Robert E. Lee. Douglass's preeminent status as a national leader won him many political appointments.

In 1882, Douglass's wife Anna died. Two years later, Douglass married Helen Pitts, a white woman who had worked as his secretary when he was the recorder of deeds. Douglass was criticized by some for his interracial marriage, but he dismissed his detractors, remarking that his first wife was "the color of his mother," and his second, "the color of his father." Douglass had a long affair with a German journalist, Ottilie Assing, who became so distraught when Douglass married Helen that she committed suicide. Douglass died of cardiac arrest on February 20, 1895, having spent the day attending a meeting of the National Convention of Women.

Douglass's *Narrative* is the most critically acclaimed of the fugitive slave narratives. Unrivalled in its depiction of the horrors of slavery, it owes its tremendous appeal to its authentic storyline, dramatic brilliance, and impassioned rhetoric. It describes Douglass's arduous journey from slavery to freedom, with the felt immediacy of his personal experience. In the dramatic encounter with the "slave-breaker" Edward Covey, Douglass brings out the dehumanizing effects of slavery and the struggle of slaves to assert their humanity: "You have seen how a man was turned a slave, and you shall see how a slave was made a man." He gives us a peep into the hell of slavery as he shows the slaveholders mercilessly whipping enslaved women. Douglass's *Narrative* invites comparison with two earlier influential works—*The Interesting Narrative of the Life of Olaudah Equiano*, or *Gustavas Vassa, the African, Written by Himself* (1789) and David Walker's *Appeal to the Colored Citizens of the World* (1828). Although Equiano doesn't blame the slaveholders—instead he holds the transatlantic slave trade responsible—and does not attempt to escape to freedom, Douglass abhors the slaveholding Christians and shudders at the prospects of living as a slave for life. Like Walker, Douglass denounces slavery as hideous evil, but he does not endorse Walker's philosophy of "kill or be killed" in the pursuit of freedom.

Douglass's second slave narrative—*My Bondage and My Freedom* (1855), which is four times the length of his first narrative—depicts his life as a slave and a freeman. Douglass contends that a slave has no moral responsibility because a slave has no rights. A slave is justified in stealing food from a slave master who keeps him hungry. The second narrative also describes the destruction of the family under slavery in great detail. Slavery does away with fatherhood as well as with family. The warmth of the "domestic hearth" is alien to slavery. The 1855 narrative replaces the earlier narrative's conversion metaphors with secular expressions. In describing his life as a freeman, Douglass tells about his experience of racism. He is sometimes stoned or greeted with racist slurs at his lectures, is thrown out of first-class cars in the trains, and denied entrance to hotels and restaurants.

Douglass's *Life and Times of Frederick Douglass*—twice as long as *My Bondage and My Freedom*—appeared in 1881. Although it adds few new details about his life as a slave except to add the story of his escape from slavery, it describes his role in the Civil War and the post–Civil War era. He proclaims that he would like to be remembered as an individual who tried to "deliver" his people from "superstition, bigotry, and priestcraft," and urged them to practice "self-reliance, self-respect, perseverance and economy." (*See also* African American Autobiography; African American Slave Narrative)

Further Reading

Andrews, William L. *Critical Essays on Frederick Douglass*. Boston: G. K. Hall, 1991.

Diedrich, Maria. *Love Across Color Lines: Otttilie Assing and Frederick Douglass*. New York: Hill and Wang, 1999.

Martin, Waldo E., Jr. *The Mind of Frederick Douglass*. Chapel Hill: University of North Carolina Press, 1984.

Matlock, James. "The Autobiographies of Frederick Douglass." *Phylon* 40 (March 1979): 15–27.

McFeely, William S. *Frederick Douglass*. New York: W. W. Norton, 1991.

Ripley, Peter. "The Autobiographical Writings of Frederick Douglass." *Southern Studies* 24.1 (1985): 5–29.

Stone, Albert E. "Identity and Art in Frederick Douglass' *Narrative*." *CLA Journal* 17 (1973): 192–213.

Harish Chander

DOVE, RITA (1952–)

Rita Dove is an African American poet and playwright. One of the most versatile poets to emerge in the last twenty years, she stands on the cusp of a new generation of African American writers reworking literary and cultural traditions. Drawing on both African American and other poetic traditions and cultures, Dove creates lyrical and tightly constructed verse that finds the extraordinary in the everyday. Dove served as poet laureate of the United States from 1993 to 1995 and currently teaches at the University of Virginia.

Dove's influences are diverse and complex. She has drawn on the work of Afro-Modernists, including Melvin B. Tolson, **Gwendolyn Brooks**, and Robert Hayden, who used the modernist poetic modes of the mid-20th century to depict African American experiences. In 1985, Dove wrote a critical article defending Tolson against charges of writing for a white audience. She has also written in praise of Hayden and Brooks, as well as of the Caribbean poet Derek Walcott, whose work, like hers, crosses boundaries and views and cultural and racial identities as fluid rather than fixed.

As her defense of Tolson suggests, she bears a complicated relationship to the Black Arts poets. These politically active writers, including Amiri Baraka, Nikki Giovanni, and Sonia Sanchez, aimed to reach a large black audience and serve as the cultural wing of the Black Power Movement, rejecting poetic forms deemed European or white. Highly influential with young African Americans when Dove entered college in 1970, the Black Arts Movement appears in a poem from her first collection, *The Yellow House on the Corner* (1980), titled "Upon Meeting Don L. Lee in a Dream." Dove imagines this important Black Arts poet as an ultimately tragic figure, unable to speak, and reduced from rage to silent tears by the end of the encounter. For Dove, the political project of the Black Arts Movement cannot ultimately speak to contemporary experience, yet Dove herself has noted that she found the stylistic innovation of the black arts poets inspirational. It would be a mistake to argue that her work moves away from African American experience toward a universal ideal, as white critics have so often called on African American writers to do. Instead, Dove's work can be seen as reflecting a fluid, open-ended view of African American identity, drawing on numerous events of this history along with other histories, embracing diverse influences, and making the crossing of geographical and cultural boundaries a particular theme. In so doing, Dove's work can be seen as part of a flowering of African American women writers since the 1970s, including **Toni Morrison**, Ntozake Shange, **Audre Lorde**, and **Alice Walker**, all of whom have replied to African American literary traditions in similarly complex ways.

Weaving together diverse poetic traditions, Dove has cited her study of German language and culture as a frequent source of inspiration, with the poets Heinrich Heine and Rainer Maria Rilke serving as particular influences. In line with this range of influences, *Museum* (1983) displays breathtaking historical and geographical scope, with poems dedicated to figures that include the Chinese prince Liu Sheng, the Italian mystic Catherine of Sienna, and the African American scientist Benjamin Banneker. The collection culminates with the stunningly ambitious "Parsley," which tells the story of the 1937 massacre of 20,000 Haitians ordered by

Rafael Trujillo, the dictator of the Dominican Republic, prompted by the failure of the French-speaking Haitians to pronounce the Spanish word *perejil*, or parsley. Dove moves from the point of view of the Haitian workers in the cane fields to the dictator himself, sharply dissecting the whimsy and self-obsession that underlies his cruelty.

Thomas and Beulah (1986), for which Dove won the Pulitzer Prize, draws on the lives of Dove's grandparents to demonstrate the complexity of the everyday experiences of working-class African Americans. This work has been particularly praised for its depiction of these two characters' stories through parallel sequences of poems. Notably, they inhabit largely separate emotional worlds. "Mandolin" focuses on Thomas's migration from the South to Ohio and his alienation from work and his own wife and daughters. "Canary in Bloom," by contrast, presents the intricacies of domestic life along with its disappointments and longings. *Grace Notes* (1989) further elaborates these themes through tightly constructed metaphors and juxtapositions of the lyrical to the everyday to explore themes including memory, childhood, motherhood, and poetry itself.

Greek mythology and tragedy have proved another fertile source for Dove's work. Wishing to cross boundaries of genre as well as culture and geography, Dove wrote the play *The Darker Face of the Earth* (1994) in blank verse. Performed at the Kennedy Center in 1997, this work translates the Oedipus myth to a South Carolina plantation. The child of the white mistress and a slave, Augustus is sent away only to return 20 years later as a slave known for rebelliousness. Believing himself the son of the master of the plantation rather than the mistress, he successfully leads a slave rebellion but cannot avoid the fate of his mythic predecessor. The play explores the familial dynamics of sexual relationships between slaves and slave owners, prevalent throughout the South although technically forbidden. As in the work of Toni Morrison, the themes of Greek tragedy translate and transform themselves to illuminate African American history. Another collection of poetry, *Mother Love* (1995), draws on another element of Greek tradition, the myth of Persephone and Demeter, in a similarly extended fashion to explore motherhood, adolescent yearning, and the particular grief experienced by mothers. Her most recent collection, *On the Bus with Rosa Parks* (1999), turns to figures of African American history and the **Civil Rights Movement** in particular to further explore the questions of freedom, travel, and identity so central to her unique and growing poetic achievement. (*See also* African American Poetry)

Further Reading

Pereira, Malin. *Rita Dove's Cosmopolitanism*. Urbana: University of Illinois Press, 2003.

Sastri, Reena. "Rita Dove's Poetic Expeditions." *Twentieth Century Literature* 58.1 (2012): 90–116.

Van Dyne, Susan R. "Siting the Poet: Rita Dove's Refiguring of Traditions." In *Women Poets of the Americas: Toward a Pan-American Gathering*, edited by Jacqueline Vaught Brogan and Cordelia Chávez Candelaria, 68–87. Notre Dame, IN: University of Notre Dame Press, 1999.

Laura Tanenbaum

DOWN THESE MEAN STREETS

Piri Thomas's *Down These Mean Streets* (1967) inaugurated what is now known as **Nuyorican** literature, the literature of Puerto Ricans in New York. The protagonist and narrator of this semiautobiographical novel is Piri Thomas himself. The novel turns on Piri's coming to terms with his identity, and the plot follows the series of lessons that Piri learns as he moves through different parts of Harlem, the American South, and the jail system. Thomas puts a Nuyorican spin on the coming-of-age novel, using a Nuyorican character to write also about a whole community. Thomas uses the language of the streets of Spanish Harlem, mixing Spanish, black American slang, and standard English in the narration as well as in the dialogue.

Piri is born into a poor Puerto Rican family living in Spanish Harlem. At a young age, he learns that to survive on the streets of Harlem he must assert a masculinity that depends on violence and domination. Piri succeeds in proving, through repeated fistfights with other boys, that he "has heart" and will rise to any challenge to his turf, his person, or his community. But from a young age Piri feels a strange distance from his family that no amount of manliness can erase. When his family moves into a different part of Harlem and then to the suburbs on Long Island, Piri learns why: Although he is Puerto Rican his dark skin also marks his African ancestry. Piri spends much of his adolescence struggling to understand his racial identity. He relates his experiences of racism to those of his African American friends and travels to the South to try to understand the African American experience. Piri slowly realizes that although he shares much with African Americans, he will always also be Puerto Rican. Grasping his racial and ethnic identity does not, however, free Piri from the bonds of poverty, poor education, and prejudice. He turns to drugs and crime as the only possible escape from the hard reality of the streets, but these provide only temporary relief and ultimately land Piri in jail. During his six years in Sing Sing prison and then in Comstock correctional facility, Piri finally learns a new way to be a man, one that involves educating himself, finding some kind of spiritual guidance, and getting ahead through hard work.

For the first several decades after its publication, *Down These Mean Streets* served as the model that most Nuyorican novels followed. Since the 1980s, women Nuyorican writers also provide alternative stories that remind how the Nuyorican experience goes beyond that of violence, despair, and redemption, but even these alternatives respond to *Down These Mean Streets* and confirm its primacy in Nuyorican literature. (*See also* Puerto Rican American Novel)

Further Reading

Flores, Juan. *From Bomba to Hip-Hop*. New York: Columbia University Press, 2000.

Luis, William. *Dance between Two Cultures*. Nashville, TN: Vanderbilt University Press, 1997.

Mohr, Eugene V. *The Nuyorican Experience*. Westport, CT: Greenwood Press, 1982.

Sánchez-González, Lisa. *Boricua Literature*. New York: New York University Press, 2001.

Keja Lys Valens

E

ELLISON, RALPH WALDO (1913-1994)

Ralph Waldo Ellison was an African American novelist, social critic, essayist, short-story writer, editor, reviewer, researcher for the Federal Writers' Project, and Albert Schweitzer Professor in the Humanities at New York University. In addition to a number of book reviews and short stories, Ellison's main works comprise two profound novels—***Invisible Man*** (1952) and *Juneteenth* (published posthumously in 1999)—and two collections of reflective essays—*Shadow and Act* (1964) and *Going to the Territory* (1986). *Invisible Man* won Ellison the 1953 National Book Award. Opposed to using art as a political weapon, Ellison wrote only about the abiding aspects—"human universals"—of the African American experience. Ellison received many national and international honors, including the Medal of Freedom from President Lyndon B. Johnson in 1967 and the Chevalier de l'Ordre des Arts et Lettres from the French minister of cultural affairs, Andre Malraux, in 1970. In public service, he served on the Carnegie Commission on Educational Television, which established the Public Broadcasting Service (PBS) and was partly instrumental in the creation of the John F. Kennedy Center for the Performing Arts in Washington, D.C.

Ralph Waldo Ellison was born on March 1, 1913, in Oklahoma City, Oklahoma, to Lewis Alfred and Ida Millsap Ellison. (It has hitherto been assumed that Ellison was born in 1914, based on the birth date mentioned in the affidavit signed by a family friend in 1943, an affidavit which was used by Ellison to enter the Merchant Marine; however, all other important documents, including the Douglass School transcript and the 1938 Connecticut Certificate of Marriage, indicate 1913 as Ellison's birth year.) His grandparents had been slaves. Ellison's father was a native of South Carolina, and his mother that of Georgia; the couple moved to the frontier state of Oklahoma in search for greater freedom and job opportunities than those available in the Southeast. Lewis Ellison, who was a trader in ice and coal, died of an abscess in his liver on July 19, 1916, when his older son was only three years old. Ida Ellison worked hard as a domestic and custodian in an African Methodist Episcopal church to support herself and her two children. Ellison attended the segregated **Frederick Douglass** School in Oklahoma City from 1920 to 1932. In 1933, Ellison entered the Tuskegee Institute (now Tuskegee University) on a music scholarship from the state of Oklahoma. In Tuskegee he found the atmosphere more repressive for blacks than in Oklahoma, so he spent most of his time in the library and practicing music. At the end of his junior year, Ellison was forced to leave college because his scholarship money ran out. He decided to seek a summer job in New York to make money to bear his college expenses for his senior year.

In July 1936 he arrived in New York. There he worked at various jobs, such as a waiter, receptionist, janitor, freelance photographer, and once as a trumpeter, but he could not raise sufficient funds to meet his college expenses. Consequently he did not return to Tuskegee and stayed on in New York. In New York he came to know **Langston Hughes** and **Richard Wright**, and both encouraged him to write. Ellison's first review, "Creative and Cultural Lag"—a review of E. Walters Turpin's *These Low Grounds*—appeared in the fall 1937 issue of *New Challenge*. Ellison also reviewed Wright's "Uncle Tom's Children" and Hughes's *Big Sea* for *New Masses*. In his essay, "The World and the Jug," included in *Shadow and Act*, Ellison objects to Irving Howe's view that Wright had significantly influenced Ellison's writing and points out that he found Wright's vision of reality to be limited. In the winter of 1937, Ellison left New York to be with his ailing mother in Dayton, Ohio, where she had moved after her marriage to John Bell. While living in Dayton, he read Ernest Hemingway not only to lead a bird in flight, but also to study his sentence structure and organization of his stories. Other writers who influenced Ellison include Fyodor Dostoyevsky, Herman Melville, Mark Twain, T. S. Eliot, Henry James, William Faulkner, and Andre Malraux. His mother died, and in April 1938 he returned to New York. Back in New York, he began to work for the Federal Writers' Project. As a project writer, he wrote profiles of prominent black New Yorkers and collected African American folklore. In 1939, he published in the September issue of *Direction* his first short story, "Slick Gonna Learn." The story deals with colorblind camaraderie among union men, which saves a black man named Slick from police revenge for his assault on a police officer who had called him a racial epithet. In 1942, Ellison resigned from the Federal Writers' Project to become the managing editor of the *Negro Quarterly*. However, the magazine folded after only four issues. In 1943, he joined the U.S. Merchant Marine to contribute to the war effort against fascism, serving for three years as a cook on a ship taking supplies to U.S. troops in Europe. In 1944, he wrote three of his most important short stories, "Flying Home," "King of the Bingo Game," and "In a Strange Country," all of which have the common theme of a black protagonist seeking to control his own destiny, but who fails due to the limitations imposed by the white establishment. In 1944, he also met Fanny McConnell, an Iowa University graduate, whom he married in 1946. This was Ellison's second marriage. He married his first wife, Rose Poindexter, in 1938, but that marriage soon ended in divorce when his in-laws persuaded their daughter to leave her husband because he would not accept a job in the post office.

In the summer of 1945, while he was staying with a friend in Vermont, on sick leave from the Merchant Marine, Ellison wrote the words, "I am an invisible man." This statement contained the germ seed of Ellison's classic novel, *Invisible Man*. The novel slowly evolved over a period of seven years and was published in 1952, winning immediate acclaim. In 1955, he began to work on his second novel. He lost a substantial portion of the manuscript in a fire in 1967, published nine excerpts from the novel over the years, but died of pancreatic cancer on April 16, 1994, without finishing it. However, John F. Callahan, Ellison's literary executor, edited the unfinished manuscript and published it as *Juneteenth* in 1999.

Invisible Man is a portrait of an African American artist as a young man. The unnamed protagonist has to deal with various false identities that other people and organizations try to impose on him, until he finds, in an epiphany, his individual **identity** as an artist. He is also at the same time a representative figure of the depersonalized and deprived of all **race**s. The novel ends with the rhetorical question: "Who knows but that, on the lower frequencies, I speak for you?"

Growing up in the South, the protagonist finishes high school and goes to a black college on a scholarship. He is expelled from the college and packed off to the industrial North because he inadvertently brings trustee Norton in contact with Jim Trueblood who relates his story of incest to the trustee. Working in New York first at a paint factory and later as a spokesperson for the Brotherhood, a protocommunist organization, he is systematically denied his individuality. Caught up in a race riot in Harlem instigated by the Brotherhood, he escapes to an abandoned coal cellar where in a moment of inspiration he burns all his false identities he has been carrying in his briefcase and discovers that "I am nobody but myself." Shorn of all illusions, he is now free from fear and gets the guts to tell the truth about all the people and organizations that attempt to rob him of his individuality. *Invisible Man* is his memoir.

Juneneeth, set in the Washington, D.C., of the 1950s, is an exquisite lyrical narrative that tells of two men's troubled relationship remembered in flashbacks as Alonzo "Daddy" Hickman attends the severely wounded senator Adam Sunraider lying in his hospital room. This senator is in fact the grown-up child, the light-skinned Bliss, who was raised by the born-again **jazz** musician, Reverend Hickman, but who during his adolescence ran away from Hickman. Daddy Hickman had expected Bliss to be a second Abe Lincoln, now uniting blacks and whites. But, he instead became black people's most virulent enemy. As the novel begins, Daddy Hickman has come to see the senator along with members of his congregation to warn him of an impending threat on his life, but the senator's secretary refuses them admission, viewing them as "disgruntled Negroes." Daddy Hickman's fears come true as the senator is shot by a young black man named Severen from the Senate gallery, when the senator is giving a fulminating tirade against black people. From his hospital bed, Bliss/Sunraider calls for Daddy Hickman to be with him. In their conversations and interior monologues, they remember the shared past, going over significant moments of their relationship and important events of their lives. The title of the novel is ironic because it was during a sermon on June 19, or Juneteenth, the day which was supposed to mark the day of collective freedom, when Bliss breaks away from Hickman to pursue a career in movies and politics. The novel has many scenes of high drama, the most poignant of them being the one between Hickman and Bliss's white mother when the latter asks Hickman to rear the baby of her shame as his own child, even though she was responsible for Hickman's brother Robert's lynching on the false charge of rape. (*See also* African American Novel)

Further Reading

Butler, Robert. J., ed. *The Critical Response to Ralph Ellison*. Westport, CT: Greenwood Press, 2000.

Callahan, John F., ed. *Ralph Ellison's "Invisible Man": A Casebook*. Oxford, UK: Oxford University Press, 2004.

O'Meally, Robert G. *The Craft of Ralph Ellison*. Cambridge, MA: Harvard University Press, 1980. Tracy,

Thomas, P. L. *Reading, Learning, Teaching Ralph Ellison*. New York: Peter Lang, 2008.

Tracy, Steven C., ed. *A Historical Guide to Ralph Ellison*. Oxford, UK: Oxford University Press, 2004.

Harish Chander

ERDRICH, LOUISE (1954–)

Louise Erdrich is a Native American novelist, poet, and children's author. Perhaps the most critically acclaimed Native American writer of the last 30 years, she is best known for her series of novels set on and around an Ojibwe Indian reservation in eastern North Dakota. Often praised for its lyrical beauty and skillful handling of multiple perspectives, Erdrich's work makes use of recurring characters and settings, much like the Yoknapatawpha County novels of William Faulkner.

Family and Education

Erdrich, an enrolled member of the Turtle Mountain Band of Chippewa, is of mixed racial heritage. The daughter of a French Ojibwe mother and a German American father, she grew up in Wahpeton, North Dakota, where both her parents taught at a Bureau of Indian Affairs school. Although she did not live on the nearby Turtle Mountain Reservation where her grandfather had once been tribal chairman, Erdrich spent a great deal of time there as a child. She left North Dakota in 1972 to attend Dartmouth University, graduating with a BA in English in 1976. She received her MA degree in creative writing from the Johns Hopkins University in 1979. In 1981, Erdrich married Michael Dorris, a professor of anthropology and Native American studies at Dartmouth, who was to become a close collaborator in her writing for the next 15 years. As a single man, Dorris had adopted three Native American children, at least one of whom suffered from fetal alcohol syndrome, a devastating disease caused by a mother drinking too much alcohol during pregnancy. A year after the marriage, Erdrich formally adopted these children as well. The couple would go on to have three biological daughters together.

Early Writing Success

Erdrich's first published novel, *Love Medicine* (1984), grew out of several prize-winning short stories she wrote about the lives of Ojibwe Indian characters in North Dakota. The novel explores the intertwined lives of several members of the Kashpaw, Lamartine, and Morrissey families, shifting points of view from chapter to chapter and weaving back and forth in time over 50 years, from 1934 to 1984. It opens with a chapter describing the death of June Kashpaw, a hard-living Ojibwe woman, once vibrant and beautiful, but now caught in a sad web of alcoholism and sexual promiscuity. June's death prompts other characters' memories and those characters' eventual return home to the reservation. Despite dealing with the legacy of hundreds of years of oppression—suicide, alcoholism, cultural **assimilation**—the novel is finally not tragic; images of rebirth and survival counter the hard lives many of the characters live and offer hope for the future. *Love Medicine* was critically well received, winning the National Book Critics Circle Award for Fiction in 1984. Erdrich also published her first volume of poetry, *Jacklight*, that same year, again to critical acclaim.

Erdrich's next several novels continued to explore the settings and characters first introduced in *Love Medicine*. *The Beet Queen* (1986), set mostly in the small town of Argus, North Dakota, near the reservation of Erdrich's first novel, shifts focus from Erdrich's Ojibwe heritage to her father's German American background. The book follows the lives of brother and sister Karl and Mary Adare, who are abandoned by their mother, Adelaide, when she flies away with a stunt pilot at an air show. Karl and Mary ride a boxcar to Argus, where Adelaide's sister, Fritzie, runs a butcher shop with her husband, Pete. The novel contrasts the charming, temperamental, and flighty Karl, a traveling salesmen who can't stay in one place, with the stolid and practical Mary, who settles in Argus and eventually forms a family with her best friend, Celestine James, and Dot, Celestine's daughter by Karl. *Tracks* (1988), the third novel in what various critics have termed the *Love Medicine* cycle or the Matchimanito novels (after the mythic lake which is part of their setting), returns to mostly Ojibwe characters and concerns. Set in the early part of the 20th century, *Tracks* serves as a prequel to *Love Medicine*. The novel opens in 1912 after a devastating tuberculosis epidemic and near-starvation have ravaged the native community. Narrated alternately by two very different narrators—wily, humorous tribal elder Nanapush, and the young, possibly mentally disturbed young woman Pauline Puyat—*Tracks* depicts the cultural dissolution of the Ojibwe in the face of increasing white intrusion and landgrabs by greedy logging companies.

Both *The Beet Queen* and *Tracks* appeared on the *New York Times* best-seller list and helped solidify Erdrich's reputation as one of the best young writers of contemporary American fiction. Erdrich showed her versatility by publishing a second volume of poetry, *Baptism of Desire*, in 1989, the year after *Tracks* appeared.

Literary Stars

During the 1980s, Erdrich and her husband, Michael Dorris, gave numerous joint interviews in which the two discussed their collaborative writing method, detailing how all their books were jointly produced—they'd invent characters and situations together, read their work aloud to each other, and edit every word carefully. Dorris himself was gaining an increasing literary reputation during this period. His first novel, *A Yellow Raft in Blue Water* (1987), received good critical reviews, but he became nationally famous with the publication of his award-winning nonfiction book, *The Broken Cord* (1989), which details his struggles to raise his adopted son, Abel, who suffered from fetal alcohol syndrome. The book was later made into an

ABC TV movie starring Jimmy Smits. By 1991, when Erdrich and Dorris published the jointly authored *The Crown of Columbus*, a novel written to commemorate the quincentennial anniversary of Columbus's 1492 arrival in the Americas, the couple were considered rising stars by the literary community. They were good-looking, deeply in love, and critical darlings, admired not only for the quality of their work, but also for their unique writing relationship. *The Crown of Columbus*, however, did not receive the glowing reviews of Erdrich's and Dorris's earlier works—critics tended to find it somewhat contrived and considered it more of a "potboiler" than a work of serious literary fiction.

Continuation of the *Love Medicine* Cycle

Despite the lukewarm critical response to *Crown*, the early 1990s continued to be very productive years for Erdrich. In 1993, she published a new, expanded version of *Love Medicine* that included four and a half chapters not found in the original novel. She also continued the *Love Medicine* cycle with *The Bingo Palace* (1994) and *Tales of Burning Love* (1996). *The Bingo Palace* takes place after *Love Medicine* and focuses on the hapless Lipsha Morrissey who is in love with powwow dancer Shawnee Ray Toose. Yet Shawnee is also involved with Lyman Lamartine, Lipsha's uncle and the cunning entrepreneur who owns the bingo palace of the title. The book, like many of Erdrich's novels, is both comic and tragic. She deflates Native American stereotypes as her Ojibwe characters participate in tribal traditions as well as contemporary American life, whether going on a vision quest with a talking skunk, getting into food fights at Dairy Queen, or vying over a ghostly Chevy Thunderbird. *Tales of Burning Love* centers on a very minor character from *Love Medicine*: Andy, the mud engineer who has a one-night stand with June Kashpaw the night of her death. In *Tales*, readers discover that "Andy" is really Jack Mauser, part Ojibwe himself. The novel begins with Jack's four ex-wives returning from his funeral. When their car becomes stranded in a blizzard, the four women keep themselves warm by relating tales of their experiences with Jack, in the spirit of Chaucer's *Canterbury Tales*, a work that some critics believe the novel is modeled after. Jack himself seems to be a male version of Chaucer's five-times married wife of Bath. Lusty and unapologetic like Chaucer's wife, Jack, like several of Erdrich's characters, is also a **Native American trickster** figure, getting in and out of trouble, fooling others and being fooled himself, yet loveable and appealing despite his flaws.

Family Tragedy

The 1990s, despite bringing continued writing success for Erdrich, were also filled with personal tragedy. The couple's oldest adopted son, Abel, the subject of Dorris's book, *The Broken Cord*, was struck by a car and killed while the television-movie version of the book was in production. In addition, the storybook romance between Erdrich and Dorris was crumbling. The two quietly separated in 1995, keeping the dissolution of their marriage secret from their many admirers.

Dorris's shocking suicide in April of 1997 amid allegations of child abuse, however, generated intense media scrutiny into the couple's previous life together. For the next several years, Erdrich would try to keep herself and her family out of the public eye as much as possible. Although limiting her public appearances, she continued to publish. Her seventh novel, *The Antelope Wife*, appeared in 1998. Moving away from the characters and settings of the Matchimanito novels, *The Antelope Wife* begins with the story of a 19th-century cavalry officer, Scranton Roy, who is following a dog with a baby strapped to its back on the Western prairie. The novel's main action depicts the descendants of both Roy and an Ojibwe character named Blue Prairie Woman in present-day Minneapolis. The novel uses the metaphor of Native American beading to depict the lives of its contemporary characters, who, like beads off a broken necklace, come together to form new patterns, new designs.

Children's Literature

Erdrich is also an accomplished children's and young adult author. In 1996, she published *Grandmother's Pigeon*, a children's book about a fantastical grandmother who rides off to Greenland on the back of a porpoise, leaving behind for her grandchildren three eggs that hatch into passenger pigeons. *The Birchbark House*, a novel for young adults published in 2002, was a finalist for the National Book Award. It tells the story of Omakayas and her family, a group of Ojibwe Indians living on Madeline Island in Lake Superior in the mid-19th century. The first in a series of novels intended as a companion and corrective to Laura Ingalls Wilder's *Little House on the Prairie* series, *The Birchbark House* consciously attempts to retrace Erdrich's own family history, as researched by her mother and sister. In 2002, Erdrich also published another children's book, *The Range Eternal*, which focuses on a family cooking stove and the light, warmth, and good food it brings the family.

Erdrich in the Twenty-first Century

In addition to publishing her two books for young readers, Erdrich returned to her *Love Medicine* cycle in 2002, publishing *The Last Report on the Miracles at Little No Horse*, which focuses on the character of Father Damien Modeste from her previous work. The report of the title is written by Damien to sum up his investigation into the possible sainthood of Sister Leopolda (Pauline Puyat from *Tracks*). But, as in many of Erdrich's novels, *Last Report* changes readers' perceptions of characters introduced previously. We discover here that Father Damien is actually a woman who has disguised herself as a man and lived among the Ojibwe undetected for over 50 years. Critically well received, the book was commended for its humorous set pieces, especially the death of old Native American trickster figure Nanapush, as well as for its lyrical language and arresting images. Erdrich's most recent novel is *The Master Butchers Singing Club* (2003), which tells the story of Fidelis Waldvogel, a German soldier who returns home from World War I to marry the pregnant widow of his best friend. Immigrating to America, Fidelis and his wife, Eva, settle in Argus, North Dakota, where he opens a butcher shop. They befriend Delphine Watzka, a former circus performer who takes a job in the Waldvogel's shop. A finalist for the National Book Award, the novel explores the complex ties of love and friendship that bind the characters together over a 35-year period. Louise Erdrich currently lives in Minneapolis, where she continues to write, and where she runs an independent bookstore, The Birchbark, with her daughters. (*See also* Native American Novel)

Further Reading

Beidler, Peter G., and Gay Barton. *A Reader's Guide to the Novels of Louise Erdrich*. Columbia: Missouri University Press, 1999.

Chavkin, Allan, ed. *The Chippewa Landscape of Louise Erdrich*. Tuscaloosa: University of Alabama Press, 1999.

Chavkin, Allan, and Nancy Feyl Chavkin, eds. *Conversations with Louise Erdrich and Michael Dorris*. Jackson: University Press of Mississippi, 1994.

Sarris, Greg. *Approaches to Teaching the Works of Louise Erdrich*. New York: Modern Language Association, 2004.

Stookey, Lorena L. *Louise Erdrich: A Critical Companion*. Westport, CT: Greenwood Publishing Group, 1999.

Susan Farrell

ETHNICITY

The origin and definition of ethnicity is complicated by its interrelations with **race**, nation, culture, geography, by migration, immigration, discrimination, dominance and control, and by historical and cultural values of the times. The Greek *ethnikos*, the adjective of *ethnos*, refers to a people or nation, largely a tribal group set apart from the nation-state and sharing common language, culture, and territory. *Oxford English Dictionary* (OED) defines the ethnic as "a subgroup in a larger society distinguished by commonly shared racial, cultural, religious, or linguistic origins and whose group **identity** is officially recognized." These definitions interweave the ethnic into the fabric of race, nation, and culture and reflect the nature of much of the scholarly work on ethnicity in the 20th century.

Ethnic groups were used long before the word ethnicity came into existence. In the United States, the "ethnic" characterizes different peoples who have come to America as a result of immigration and forced or voluntary labor. Yet, prior to the first quarter of the 20th century, the concept of race was used to determine the interactions and relationships among the peoples of America. Ethnicity did not become an established social and cultural expression of group identity until the early 20th century. Since colonial times, white Anglo-Saxon Protestant Americans (WASPs) have identified themselves as a superior race and have assumed dominance and control in every aspect of the nation's life. The chief racial divide was characterized by white **racism** against the blacks, the institution of slavery, and racial segregation after the Emancipation. Other white Americans such as Italians, Jews, Irish, Germans, and Central and Eastern Europeans were regarded as inferior to the WASP race; so were Mexicans, Chinese, and others. The belief in the superiority of the Anglo-Saxon race justified slavery, economic exploitation, political deprivation of "colored races," the conquest of American Indians and Mexicans, and the 1920s anti-Chinese immigration laws.

The assumption of race and color as a basis for citizenship, national identity, and equal rights characterized the political ideology and social, economic, and cultural practice until well into the 20th century. In his 2001 *Whiteness of a Different Color*, historian Matthew Frye Jacobson traces the nation's first legislation as alleging whiteness to citizenship. Mae M. Ngai, in his 2003 "Race, Nation, and Citizenship in Late Nineteenth-Century America, 1878–1900," observes that the racist view "opposed incorporating additional backward races into the nation." In the early 20th century, the Ku Klux Klan unleashed racist violence against blacks; nativism and evangelical Protestantism militated against Catholics and Jews. In their 2003 "Changing Racial Meanings: Race and Ethnicity in the United States, 1930–1964," Thomas A. Guglielmo and Earl Lewis remark that the race ideology, often through legal means, restricted nonwhite Americans' from equal access to quality education, housing, employment, citizenship rights, union membership, land ownership, trial by jury, and interracial marriage.

Influential philosophical, scientific, and social science research of the 1930s and 1940s led to a dramatic shift in American conceptions about race and the rejection of racism as a justified system of human classification and institutional practice. Philosopher John Dewey advocated a pragmatism that equalized all human beings as capable of growth and self-realization. Anthropologist Franz Boas challenged the validity of the idea of race by replacing genetics with the concept of culture and environment. Works of leading social scientists of the time continued to challenge racial thinking, including the rise of Nazi racism in Europe. They asserted the unity among humanity and disqualified race as an indicator of intelligence, psychology, or character. These exemplary works included Ruth Benedict's *Race: Science and Politics* (1940), Ashley Montagu's *Race: Man's Most Dangerous Myth* (1942), and Gunnar Myrdal's *An American Dilemma* (1944).

During and since the World War II, "ethnic" and ethnicity emerged as new social scientific categories, sometimes differentiated from and sometimes connected with race. W. Lloyd Warner was credited as the first American social scientist to use the word ethnic in *The Social Life of a Modern Community*, which he published with Paul S. Hunt in 1941. Lloyd Warner also made a distinction between racial groups and ethnic groups in his 1945 publication, *The Social Systems of American Ethnic Groups*, defining the latter as recent European immigrants to America and lower class, with the promise of joining the American mainstream culture. Steven Fenton, in his *Ethnicity* (2003), credited Max Weber for predating American sociologists in his examinations of ethnicity. Weber discussed three elements of ethnic identity: the *belief* in common origin rather than common descent, ethnic identity as based on cultural and physical differences, and the idea of an ethnic group as the basis of political action. Fenton placed Weber's ideas close to "political ethnicity" of the

1960s America where groups were mobilizing shared ethnic origin for political activism.

Is ethnicity "invented" or "authentic"? Is ethnicity "changing" or "timeless"? Werner Sollors in the introduction of his edited book, *The Invention of Ethnicity* (1989), argued for pluralism versus **assimilation**, branding the blandness of melting pot, mainstream, and majority culture as the "foe of ethnicity." He viewed ethnicity as a "process" and as a "modern and modernizing feature of contrasting feature" rather than "an ancient and deep-seated force surviving from the historical past." In the same vein, Fredrik Barth's *Ethnic Groups and Boundaries* (1969) identified "boundaries" as the central feature of ethnic divisions and focused on a definition of ethnicity as the emergence of ethnic consciousness rather than survival.

Other notable works examined the survival and persistence of ethnic identities despite assimilation. Abner Cohen's *Urban Ethnicity* (1974) examined the emergence of ethnic distinctions in the context of power relations and applied ethnicity to the description of both dominant and dominated groups. Nathan Glazer and Daniel P. Moynihan revealed that ethnic identities persisted among the different groups in their *Beyond the Melting Pot: The Negroes, Puerto Ricans, Jews, Italians, and Irish of New York City* (1963). Like Max Weber, they identified an ethnic–class correlation in residential concentration, occupation, and class and asserted ethnicity as a basis of "political and social action." Glazer and Moynihan popularized the term ethnicity in a collection of essays they edited in 1975: *Ethnicity: Theory and Experiences*. The authors argued that ethnicity challenged, sometimes replaced, or was used interchangeably with race. In their approach, ethnicity marked a new social science research category and was applied to all groups in a society characterized by distinctiveness, consciousness, and identity based on culture and origin.

The successes of the **Civil Rights Movement** have not only altered American thinking about race and ethnicity but also dramatically changed the social, economic, and political structures founded on race. Inspired by and joining forces with African Americans, various ethnic groups in the United States aligned under the banners of pan-ethnicity—as Asian and Pacific Islander American, Hispanic American (or Chicano/a), and Native American—and asserted their presence and demanded their equal access to American opportunities. In his *Postethnic America: Beyond Multiculturalism* (1995), David Hollinger named these newly ethnically conscious groups as "the five great ethno-racial blocs." He further called attention to the fact that these ethno-racial categories were used not merely in the census but as instruments of public service programs, allocation of resources, and measures of equality.

It is significant to note that ethnic movements since the 1960s have made racial-ethnic groups as identities of inclusion in American life rather than discrimination and exclusion as it was in the earlier part of American history. Race, ethnicity, and **multiculturalism** are intricately connected and used interchangeably in intellectual discourse as well as in personal identity definitions despite social scientists' efforts to disengage them. As a result of interracial, interethnic marriages, America sees the emergence of multiethnic and multiracial groups and identities. Jonathan Brennan's edited collection, *Mixed Race Literature* (2000), explored the notion of "ethnic eclecticism" and "complementarity" and cited that the 2000 census, for the first time, gave Americans the opportunity to "designate themselves as being of more than one ethnic-racial stock." Ishmael Reed in his 1997 *Multi-America: Essays on Cultural Wars and Cultural Peace* wrote that a new definition of culture is possible through the inclusion of ethnic histories and cultures with European cultures. Naomi Zack, in her foreword to *Mixing It Up: Multiracial Subjects* (2004), defines race as a human identity and uses the presence of racially mixed people to deconstruct the very notion of race. At the dawn of a new century, American thinking about ethnicity broadens to embrace diverse cultures, races, and peoples. It offers the hope of a place in the world for interracial, interethnic, multiracial, and multiethnic peoples of the world.

Further Reading

Bayor, Ronald H., ed. *Race and Ethnicity in America: A Concise History*. New York: Columbia University Press, 2003.

Brennan, Jonathan, ed. *Mixed Race Literature*. Palo Alto, CA: Stanford University Press, 2002.

Daniels, Roger. *Coming to America: A History of Immigration and Ethnicity in American Life*. New York: Harper Collins, 1990.

Fenton, Steve. *Ethnicity: Racism, Class, and Culture*. London: Macmillan, 1999.

Hollinger, David A. *Postethnic America: Beyond Multiculturalism*. New York: Basic Books. 1995.

Jenkins, Richard. *Rethinking Ethnicity: Arguments and Explorations*. London and Thousand Oaks, CA: Sage, 1997.

Pedraza, Silvia, and Ruben G. Rumbaut, eds. *Origins and Destinies: Immigration, Race, and Ethnicity in America*. Belmont, CA: Wadsworth, 1996.

Sollors, Werner, and Henry and Anne Cabot. *Theories of Ethnicity: A Classical Reader*. New York: New York University Press, 1996.

Wong, Paul, ed. *Race, Ethnicity, and Nationality in the United States: Towards the Twenty-First Century*. Boulder, CO: Westview Press, 1999.

Jie Tian

EUROCENTRISM

Understanding oneself and one's culture in ways that both emphasize and empathize with what is near and familiar are common, if not universal, human tendencies. What is most noteworthy about the European-centered thinking known as "Eurocentrism" is thus not so much the privileging of a certain area's dominant beliefs but the global scope and impact of what is frequently referred to as "Western thought." Over the last five centuries, this thought has developed with an increasing material exploitation that has strengthened Western domination vis-à-vis other regions and, for many, worked to confirm not just the material "superiority" but the "truth"—and thus inherent justice—of Western thought and actions. These actions have included enslavement, forced migration, and indoctrination, all seen as a justified part of Europe's "civilizing mission." From this Eurocentric perspective, the non-European heritages of ethnic Americans have qualified such Americans as essentially non-Western and thus deserving treatment similar to that of those colonized by Europe. Ethnic American writers have responded to this with three basic strategies that can be summarized with the words hypocrisy ("white" America doesn't practice what it preaches), blindness (Eurocentrism maintains faulty perceptions and conclusions), and hybridity ("European" ideas improve with, and sometimes should be replaced by, "non-European" ideas).

Because ethnic Americans have found some ideals promoted by Western thought attractive and potentially advantageous, they have emphasized the hypocrisy of Europeans and Euroamericans who act contrary to those ideals. This response has predominated with groups in particularly subservient positions. We see this, for instance, in the early African American writings of Olaudah Equiano (1745–97) and David Walker (1785–1830). Equiano, in *The Interesting Narrative of the Life of Olaudah Equiano, or Gustavus Vassa, the African* (1789), embraces such Eurocentric tenets as Christianity and capitalism but denounces Europeans as hypocrites who promote not Godliness and competition but cruelty. Walker uses Eurocentrism to castigate Euroamerican hypocrisies in his U.S. Constitution—echoing *David Walker's Appeal in Four Articles; Together with a Preamble, to the Coloured Citizens of the World* (1830). Outside the African American tradition, an important early (albeit more narrowly focused) critique of hypocrisy is the Native American argument in *The Cherokee Nation vs. The State of Georgia* (1831).

Until the end of the 19th century, prominent ethnic American critiques of Eurocentrism derive from African American writers. Native American and other ethnic American literatures largely develop during the 20th century. During the early 20th century, ethnic American writers largely shifted their focus from hypocrisy to the "blindnesses" of Eurocentrism—what Eurocentric thinking doesn't understand and "gets wrong." We see this in Black Elk's (1863–1950) *Black Elk Speaks* (1932) (with John G. Neihardt), which criticizes Eurocentrism's disregard for nature. During the **Harlem Renaissance** (1919–1940), African American writers take a similar tack by arguing that they can provide white Anglo-Saxon Protestant America with much needed sensuality and spirituality.

This ethnic American focus on the problems, especially the violences, of Eurocentrism eventually interpenetrated the 20th-century philosophical movement known as poststructuralism, helping produce postcolonial theory and that theory's preeminent text—Palestinian American Edward Said's *Orientalism* (1978). Such works as V. Y. Mudimbe's *The Idea of Africa* (1994), Emmanuel Eze's *Postcolonial African Philosophy* (1997), Susan E. Babbitt and Sue Campbell's *Racism and Philosophy* (1999), John McCumber's *Metaphysics and Oppression* (1999), Jacques Derrida's *Writing and Difference* (1978), and Robert Young's *White Mythologies* (1990) look at how Eurocentrism's foundational ideas promote violence. Unlike the argument of "hypocrisy," which essentially lauds Eurocentric ideals but lambastes European actions, the "blindness" argument perceives problems even with Western thought's "purest" philosophies.

This opens Eurocentrism to critique at both its heretofore "unassailable" Judeo-Christian and Classical Greek foundations and at its Cartesian, Kantian, and Hegelian "heights." Such postcolonial critiques do not reject Western thinking tout court, nor do they propose some pure and holy alternative way of thinking with which to replace what Samir Amin, in *Eurocentrism* (1989), describes as a worldview that "present[s] itself as universalist," the repository of all answers for all peoples. It does, however, make space for other voices and demands critical self-reflection.

Out of this "blindness" argument has developed the third main ethnic American response to Eurocentrism—hybridity. Hybridity is here defined as the idea that Western thought and culture are neither universal (a position acknowledged in the very word "Eurocentrism") nor sufficient even for "Europeans." It is also the position that all cultures and ideologies are, to varying degrees, hybrid (a position acknowledged in this entry by the quotation marks around "European"). Important to this position is African American W.E.B. Du Bois whose *The Souls of Black Folk* (1903) argued that we must cultivate and embrace the best that each culture offers.

This is the hybridity of the African and European musical traditions that produced **jazz**. Caribbean writer Derek Walcott acknowledges this hybridity in his poem "A Far Cry from Africa." This hybridity is central to both Native American Lori Arviso Alvord's discussion of Native American and Eurocentric medical traditions in *The Scalpel and the Silver Bear* (with Elizabeth Cohen Van Pelt, 1999) and to Native American **Navarre Scott Momaday**'s *House Made of Dawn* (1968). Chicana writer Gloria Anzaldúa embraces hybridities sexual, ethnic/racial, economic, and national in *Borderlands/La Frontera: The New Mestiza* (1987).

"Hypocrisy," "blindness," and "hybridity" have, of course, always been themes of ethnic American literatures, and there are ethnic American responses to Eurocentrism that do not fit neatly into these categories. But the vital point remains that Eurocentrism in many ways created ethnic American literature as a category *other* than Western, and ethnic American literatures have played a vital role in highlighting the artificiality of that category whose legacy has included fear and violence. If we accept that Western thought professes ideals of conviviality, beauty, and justice, then it is ironic that the peoples excluded from this "enterprise" are those whose ideas seem most likely to move Eurocentrism toward its own impossibility of universality. (*See also* Racism)

Further Reading

Amin, Samir. *Eurocentrism*. Trans. Russell Moore. New York: Monthly Review Press, 1989. Trans. of *L'eurocentrisme: Critique d'une ideologie*. 1988.

Eze, Emmanuel Chukwudi, ed. *Race and the Enlightenment: A Reader*. Oxford, UK: Blackwell, 1996.

Kevin M. Hickey

F

FILIPINO AMERICAN NOVEL

Filipino American literature can be defined most broadly as writing by immigrants from the Philippines and by Americans of Filipino descent, which generally engages the intersections of American and Filipino cultures. We need to acknowledge, however, a critical connection between Philippine literature in English and Filipino American literature on both thematic and contextual levels. Writing by Filipinos in English and Filipino American writing began at about the same time—after the colonization of the Philippines by the United States, the propagation of American-style education in the early 1900s, and the subsequent arrival of the first wave of Filipino immigrants to the United States. Further, because many of the earliest writers such as poet José Garcia Villa and novelists such as Bienvenido Santos and N.V.M. Gonzalez lived in both countries, the links were reinforced.

The first wave of Filipino immigrants to the United States produced works that engage two central thematic concerns: first, the Filipino immigrant's process of adaptation to America; second, Philippine history and politics. Interestingly, the first two Filipino American novels set the stage for these parallel recurring literary themes. The earliest known novel is Carlos Bulosan's fictionalized autobiography, *America Is in the Heart* (1947), which describes his boyhood in the Philippines, his journey to America, and his years as an itinerant farmer who participated actively in the foundation of early labor unions. Bulosan immigrated in 1930 at the age of seventeen, and his perspective on America is not simplistic or uncritical: He simultaneously describes the **racism** suffered by Filipino Americans as well as the kindness of persons who helped him when he spent years in the hospital with tuberculosis. Though the text is subtitled *A Personal History*, it must be read as the collective history of early immigrants, who had to deal with the American ideals of tolerance and liberty and the reality of racism and social ostracism. Another writer who creatively engaged the life of Filipino immigrants is Bienvenido Santos, whose novels and short stories foreground the lives of the *manongs* (the early Filipino immigrants), trapped in a limbo of nonbelonging. Solomon King, the protagonist of *The Man Who (Thought He) Looked Like Robert Taylor* (1983), feels a psychic link to the actor Robert Taylor, a connection no one but himself perceives. This imagined bond is a metaphor for the Filipino's alliance with American culture. In *What the Hell for You Left Your Heart in San Francisco* (1987), Santos portrays the Filipino immigrant community of San Francisco as seen through the eyes of a recent immigrant who uncovers the Filipino lives hidden in the streets of the city. Santos explores a culture of contrasts, the spectrum of Filipino immigrants in San Francisco: the oldtimers for whom the city is both home and not home, weighed down by separation from their homeland; the professional immigrants who, moved by the American dream, came to work and set down roots; and of the second generation, for whom America is birthplace but not native land, who hover uncomfortably between two cultures.

The second Filipino American novel, Stevan Javellana's magnificent *Without Seeing the Dawn* (1947), exemplifies the narrative that recalls the Philippine past and deals imaginatively with its history of repeated invasions and colonizations. Published two years after the author's immigration, it is the story of a farmer-turned-soldier during the Japanese invasion of the Philippines that centers on the devastation that war brings to a small town. Other novels that deal with constitutive events of Philippine history—the Spanish and American colonizations, the Japanese invasion during World War II, and the Ferdinand Marcos Dictatorship—include Linda Ty-Casper's *Awaiting Trespass: A Pasion* (1985), *Wings of Stone* (1990), and *Dream Eden* (1996), which narrate the nightmares and violence of corruption and dictatorships; Ninotchka Rosca's complex *State of War* (1988), which foregrounds the enduring effects of colonization and imperialism on persons and communities; and *Twice Blessed* (1992), a satire based on Marcos and his wife. Rosca, an exile from the Marcos dictatorship, stresses in her narratives the dangerous repetitions of history and how foreign interventions have corrupted contemporary society, leading to a perpetual cycle of violence and suffering. Cecilia Manguerra Brainard's *When the Rainbow Goddess Wept* (1994, originally published as *Song of Yvonne*, 1991) focuses on the Japanese occupation from the perspective of a young girl, Yvonne Macaraig, whose archetypal journey from innocence to experience, merges the horrors of war with the recognition of the liberating possibilities of myth and traditional stories. Brainard's *Magdalena* (2003) narrates the intersecting histories of three generations of Filipino women, focusing on their emotional and social conflicts and on the class and racial divisions in Philippine society.

Similarly, Paulino Lim Jr.'s trilogy, *Tiger Orchids on Mount Mayon* (1990), *Sparrows Don't Sing in the Philippines* (1994), and *Requiem for a Rebel Priest* (1996), deal with political turmoil in the Philippines. Tess Uriza Holthe's *When the Elephants Dance* (2002), based on her parents' recollections of the war, presents the Filipinos as pawns of the invaders, and stresses the importance of stories for personal survival and maintaining community. The novel uses multiple perspectives—a 13-year-old boy, his older sister, and a guerilla leader—to convey the brutality of occupation and teach a message of resistance and hope. Three of Santos's novels also deal with family histories, politics, and corruption in the Philippines: *The Volcano* (1965), *Villa Magdalena* (1965), and *The Praying Man* (1982). A posthumously published Bulosan novel, *The Cry and the Dedication* (1985), focuses on a group of seven Filipino peasants, men as well as women, who struggle against Spanish colonization and American occupation.

The second wave of immigrants from the latter part of the 20th century, as well as American-born Filipinos, began to introduce questions that dealt more specifically with recent immigration, changing Philippine politics, and the racial and cultural issues faced by the younger generations. The most notable of the new generation is Jessica Hagedorn, whose *Dogeaters* (1990) is a depiction of Filipino

Jessica Hagedorn. (Anthony Barboza/Getty Images)

society during the Marcos regime. Presenting a wide spectrum of society—from high-class women and politicians to adolescent girls and male prostitutes—she uses a postmodern episodic structure and images from film and popular culture to convey problems of perspective and realities of daily life. The title of the novel comes from a pejorative term for "Filipinos," though the narrative also suggests that politics is a dog-eat-dog world. Her second novel, *The Gangster of Love* (1996), focuses on adjustment as immigrant Raquel (Rocky) Rivera lives a hippy-like adolescence in San Francisco and later moves to New York with her band. Hagedorn's recent *Dream Jungle* (2003) uses the story of the famous hoax in the 1970s of the discovery of a Stone Age tribe, the Tasadays, to reflect on contemporary Filipino cultural identity. The title of Sophia Romero's *Always Hiding* (1998) plays on the

Filipino expression for illegal immigrants who are condemned to live concealed from the authorities.

Novels by second-generation writers explore complex issues about transcultural identity. In Peter Bacho's *Cebu* (1992), a Filipino American priest travels to Cebu to bury his mother, and undergoes a dramatic cultural and spiritual crisis, leading to a tragic death. Brian Ascalon Roley's *American Son* (2001), set in Southern California in the 1990s, narrates the story of biracial brothers, Tomas and Gabe O'Sullivan, who deal differently with their ambivalent feelings toward their Filipina mother and their reality of escalating violence. Bino Realuyo's *The Umbrella Country* (1999) is an unsentimental coming-of-age story of a Filipino boy in a poor Manila neighborhood that concludes with his emigration to the United States. Recent novels that challenge traditional representations of Asians and stress interethnic relations include R. Zamora Linmark's *Rolling the R's* (1995), which centers on a group of 10-year-old fifth-graders who are considered outcasts in the poor community of Kalihi in 1970s Hawai'i and Han Ong's *Fixer Chao* (2001), the story of a young gay Filipino man who, taking advantage of the average American's incapacity to make distinctions among the various Asian ethnicities, poses as a Chinese Feng Shui expert and enters a life of fraud and crime. Linmark uses Pidgin, the local Hawaiian dialect, creatively to illustrate these children's negotiation of identity—racial, cultural, class, sexual—in the context of multicultural American society, while Ong exposes Orientalist attitudes toward Asians and shows how these preconceived ideas can be subverted. These novels attest to the growing variety of Filipino American writing, as these increasingly sophisticated narratives negotiate important cultural and literary concerns and dialogue with the wider context of American writing.

Further Reading

Campomanes, Oscar. "Filipino in the United States and Their Literature of Exile." In *Reading the Literatures of Asian America*, edited by Shirley Geok-lin Lim and Amy Ling, 49–78. Philadelphia: Temple University Press, 1992.

"Filipino American Literature." [Special issue.] *MELUS* 29.1 (Winter 2004): 5–296.

Gonzalez, N.V.M., and Oscar V. Campomanes. "Filipino American Literature." In *An Interethnic Companion to Asian American Literature*, edited by King-Kok Cheung, 62–124. Cambridge, UK: Cambridge University Press, 1997.

Rocío G. Davis

G

GAINES, ERNEST J. (1933–)

Ernest J. Gaines is an African American novelist and short-story writer. Perhaps the best known and most widely taught of contemporary African American writers, Gaines has achieved an unprecedented prominence in American letters. Born the son of sharecroppers on a Louisiana plantation, he has received numerous awards and accolades, including a Guggenheim Fellowship in 1973 and a MacArthur Foundation "genius grant" in 1993. Two novels, *The Autobiography of Miss Jane Pittman* (1971) and ***A Lesson Before Dying*** (1994), were nominated for the Pulitzer Prize, and *A Lesson Before Dying* received the National Book Critics Circle Award. His novels and short stories represent his career-long exploration of the complexities of 20th-century race relations in the South, as well as his preoccupation with history and folk culture. Reflecting his connection to rural south Louisiana and the influence of such writers as William Faulkner and Ivan Turgenev, all of Gaines's stories and novels take place in his mythical world of St. Raphael Parish, Louisiana, and its county seat, Bayonne, which were modeled on Gaines's birthplace and first home, Point Coupée Parish and Oscar, Louisiana. This rich, diverse fictional universe gives Gaines the freedom to examine the racial and ethnic tensions between blacks, whites, Cajuns, and Creoles, as well as the conflicts stemming from differences in class and gender. In addition to his deeply rooted sense of place, Gaines's writing illustrates his persistent thematic concerns—the search for human dignity in an entrenched, racist social system, the possibility of love within such an environment, the conflict between generations in their response to **racism** and racial violence, and the potential for individual transformation and positive social change.

Gaines's first novel, *Catherine Carmier* (1964), manifests many of the themes and literary techniques present in his later works. The main character, Jackson Bradley, returns to his plantation home after living for 10 years in California. As an outsider and an insider, Jackson becomes aware of the changes that have taken place in his absence. His former friendship with Catherine Carmier blossoms into love, despite the opposition of her father. Catherine, a light-skinned black woman, is a Creole, and her mixed racial heritage serves to separate her from both whites and the blacks. Her father, Raoul, refuses to accept her relationship with Jackson, illustrating the internal **racism** within the African American community. Torn between her love for Jackson and her responsibility, loyalty, and love for her father, Catherine is in an impossible situation, which is reflected in the novel's ambiguous, indeterminate ending. In this novel, Gaines also introduces the racial and economic conflict in south Louisiana between blacks and Cajuns, a conflict he develops in more depth in later novels. The Cajuns are supplanting the black tenant farmers, and increased mechanization and racial violence threaten a traditional African American way of life.

Gaines shifts his point of view in his second novel, *Of Love and Dust* (1967), using the first-person narrative perspective that characterizes his later work. In Jim Kelly's narration and the voices of other characters, Gaines captures the rhythms of colloquial Southern speech, a hallmark of his fiction and one of his greatest strengths. Kelly tells the story of Marcus Payne, a young black man arrested for murder, who is released and awaiting trial in the custody of Marshall Hebert, a white plantation owner. As he did in his first novel, Gaines develops the multiple racial and ethnic conflicts between whites, Cajuns, and blacks. Marcus is defiant and rebellious, and Hebert, intent on breaking his spirit, leaves this task to his brutal, uneducated Cajun overseer, Sidney Bonbon. Jim Kelly, a black man who works on the plantation, has learned to negotiate his way through passive acceptance, which is challenged by his promise to look after Marcus. Against this backdrop, Gaines explores love between blacks and whites in a racially polarized community. Bonbon's sexual liaison with Pauline, his black mistress, grows into real love, as does Marcus's affair with Bonbon's wife, Louise. Precipitated by these two interracial relationships, the tragic ending reveals the destructive power of racial division and hatred, only somewhat relieved by the possibility of change evident in Jim Kelly's ultimate understanding of Marcus's heroic spirit.

Bloodline (1968), a collection of five stories, expands on Gaines's themes and initiates a narrative technique he uses to later advantage in *A Gathering of Old Men* (1983), creating multiple narrative voices in a single work. The effort to achieve and maintain personal dignity in the face of racial oppression and the struggle for manhood emerge as common themes in "A Long Day in November," "The Sky Is Gray," "Three Men," and "Bloodline." "Just like a Tree" signals Gaines's experimentation with multiple narrators, a strategy influenced by Faulkner's *The Sound and the Fury* and *As I Lay Dying*. Using 10 different narrators, Gaines tells the story of Aunt Fe, the aged matriarch of a rural black plantation community, whose family decides to move her up north to avoid the racial violence of the early 1960s. Each narrator adds to our understanding of the complex web of social relations, often crossing racial lines, and to our understanding of the pain and loss that come with social change.

The Autobiography of Miss Jane Pittman, his best-known work, established Gaines's literary reputation. In depicting the life of his 110-year-old narrator, he blends history, folk culture, and a powerful speaking voice to paint a vivid picture of African American experience in the 20th century. Modeled on Gaines's great aunt, who helped raise him, Miss Jane begins her long life in slavery and ends in triumph, demonstrating her perseverance, pride, and wisdom. In contrast to the more pessimistic vision of his next, less successful novel, *In My Father's House* (1978), this "folk biography" (Carmean 59) focuses on the power of the individual to achieve heroic stature.

The difficulty black men face in achieving manhood in a racist, oppressive society is Gaines's predominant theme in *A Gathering of Old Men* and *A Lesson Before*

Dying. In the former, each chapter has a different narrator, charting the events following the murder of Beau Boutan, a Cajun farmer, by a black man, and forging a communal history of the plantation where the action takes place. As the old black men confess to murdering Beau, they gain the manhood denied them by racial injustice. The real murderer, Charlie Biggs, finally achieves manhood by accepting responsibility for his actions and refusing to run in fear. *A Gathering of Old Men* ends optimistically, emphasizing the interdependence of blacks and whites and depicting hope for the future. Gaines turns to the past in *A Lesson Before Dying*, examining the historic mistreatment of African Americans and the ongoing legacy of institutionalized racism. Set in 1948, this novel focuses on two men: Jefferson, a young man wrongfully condemned to death, and Grant Wiggins, the narrator, a teacher who counsels Jefferson as he awaits his execution. Jefferson's six-month education in what it means to be a man reveals the potential inherent in those who have been systematically disenfranchised and dehumanized; his determination and courage inspire and change both the narrator and the reader.

Gaines's contribution to American literature is profound and multifaceted, weaving together a powerful history of 20th-century African American experience, a valuable record of folk culture, and an imagined world of richly varied characters and situations. (*See also* African American Novel)

Further Reading

Babb, Valerie Melissa. *Ernest Gaines.* Boston: Twayne, 1991.

Carmean, Karen. *Ernest J. Gaines: A Critical Companion.* Westport, CT: Greenwood Press, 1998.

Estes, David, ed. *Critical Reflections on the Fiction of Ernest J. Gaines.* Athens: University of Georgia Press, 1994.

Young, Reggie Scott. "Ernest Gaines: A Portfolio." *Callaloo* 30.3 (2007): 694–713.

Michelle S. Ware

GALARZA, ERNESTO (1905–1984)

Ernesto Galarza was a writer, scholar, teacher, labor organizer, and community activist born in the village of Jalcocotán, Mexico, in the state of Nayarit. When the Mexican revolution of 1910 began, Galarza's mother and her two brothers embarked on a three-year trip, first to Tepic and then to Mazatlán, Sinaloa, before finally immigrating to Sacramento, California, where they lived at Dodson's Rooming House for four years while Galarza attended Lincoln Elementary. Because of a teacher's encouragement while Galarza was in high school, he received a scholarship to Occidental College. He also received a master's degree from Stanford University and a PhD from Columbia. Galarza studied political science, Latin American history, and economics. He wrote more than a dozen books and numerous articles, reports, and studies on a variety of fields. Among his most important works are *Merchants of Labor: The Mexican Bracero Story* (1964), *Mexican Americans in the Southwest* (1969), *Spiders in the House and Workers in the Field* (1970), and *Farm*

Workers and Agri-Business in California 1947–1960 (1977). He wrote about many subjects, including life in the United States, Mexico, Bolivia, and Argentina; he also published children's stories and poetry.

However, Galarza's most enduring work has been his autobiography, *Barrio Boy* (1971), which richly details his life up through junior high and for which he was the first Mexican American to be nominated for a Nobel Prize in literature. Since Galarza married an Anglo-American woman, Mae Taylor, part of the impetus for the autobiography was to teach his daughters, Karla and Eli-Lu about his Mexican origins. The book begins with an epigraph from Henry Adams, which serves as a disclaimer: "This was the journey he remembered. The actual journey may have been quite different. . . . The memory was all that mattered." It is important to remember that the book was published when Galarza was 66 years old, yet much of the story details his earliest years. No doubt some of his earlier "memories" were actually culled from stories told by his mother and uncles. *Barrio Boy* also pays homage to his mother, uncles, and some of his kindly schoolteachers—all of whom are now immortalized in prose.

The autobiography is divided into five sections: the first carefully depicts his earliest life in the small village of "Jalco" where life was communal; the second narrates his family's "Peregrinations" to Tepic and Mazatlán, where his eyes are opened to a larger world; the short third section details the journey from Mazatlán to Sacramento; and the fourth recounts his family's adjustments in the United States. In the final, and saddest, section, his family makes a down payment on a house and moves to the outskirts of town, where his uncle Gustavo and then his beloved mother, "Doña" Henriqueta, die of influenza. Ernie, just 12 years old, goes to live with his uncle José in a basement room in their old neighborhood.

This autobiography has several strengths; it is an important and dramatic story worth telling for historical reasons. The revolution of 1910 was responsible for the deaths of some 900,000 because of war, drought, famine, and disease. Readers learn of Mexican President Porfirio Diaz and his feared *rurales* and of the "revolutionary" Francisco Madero. During this time many Mexicans immigrated to the United States, and Galarza depicts the appalling working conditions of migrant laborers, although this is a minor part of the book. Furthermore, Galarza attentively describes life and customs in a quaint Mexican village of a bygone time. He is also a sensitive and literate writer who gracefully employs metaphor and figures of speech—making the narrative memorable.

On the other hand, Galarza glosses over some important events. We are told nothing about his Lutheran father (after whom he was named). In terms of the divorce, Galarza writes that it "was a simple matter"; this was *not* the case in traditional Mexico. We are never told if Ernesto ever met his father or attempted to make contact. Another major gap occurs when Galarza's mother marries a Chicano in Sacramento; the event and the fact that Galarza soon has half-sisters are barely mentioned. The death of his mother is similarly understated because Galarza does not over-sentimentalize the event or seek our pity. Finally, there is no mention or even hint of Galarza's later academic successes. Arguably, the book ends prematurely—before he even begins high school.

Despite these minor quibbles, the book makes one of the strongest, most authentic contributions to the field of **Mexican American autobiography**. Galarza's life story has historic, anthropological, psychological, and social value and especially, literary value.

Further Reading

Flores, Lauro. "Chicano Autobiography: Culture, Ideology and the Self." *The Americas Review* 18.2 (Summer 1990): 80–91.

Marquez, Antonio C. "Self and Culture: Autobiography as Cultural Narrative." *The Bilingual Review* 14.3 (1993): 57–64.

Saldívar, Ramón. *Chicano Narrative: The Dialectics of Difference*. Madison: University of Wisconsin Press, 1990.

Paul Guajardo

GARCÍA, CRISTINA (1958–)

Cristina García is a Cuban American novelist. García's most important contribution to Cuban American literature is her complex remapping of Cuban and Cuban American cultural landscapes. Having come to the United States from Cuba as a young child, García she sees herself and others like her as uniquely positioned to write about the experience of exile and the complex identities that it creates. Steeped in magical realism and poetic language, García's novels evoke a mystical connection between Cuba and her people as they tell the stories of multigenerational families fractured by politics and events from their pasts.

García's critically acclaimed first novel, *Dreaming in Cuban* (1992), was a finalist for the National Book Award. Its success brought Cuban American literature to a wider reading audience and established García as one of the most well-known Cuban Americans today. Set in the 1970s, the novel traces the lives of three generations of women in the del Pino family through the stories of Celia, the matriarch, her daughters Felicia and Lourdes, and her granddaughter Pilar, all of whom are, in different senses, estranged from Cuba and yet obsessed with it as a homeland. Although husbands, lovers, and sons also figure in the novel, these four women are at its heart. For Celia, a supporter of Castro's revolution, Cuba is a place in which she can create and maintain memories of the past she desires to live in, enabling her to exist outside of the progression of time. Felicia recognizes that the revolution has brought positive changes by providing food and medical care for the masses, but she also knows that it cannot sustain them emotionally or spiritually. The victim of a violent and unfaithful husband, Felicia retreats into a surreal world shaped by her devotion to *Santeria*, Beny More records, and her son. For the anti-Castro Lourdes, Cuba is static, trapped in the negative past created by the revolution. Lourdes moves to New York and seeks to redefine herself as American, but she can never fully escape her homeland. Lourdes's teenage daughter, Pilar, looks to Cuba as a spiritual and emotional home. Cuba exists for Pilar largely as an imagined space, however, because she was so young when her family left the island. Although Cuba exists more as a myth than a reality for these characters, García's novel suggests that the construct is what is important for each of these women.

Dreaming in Cuban preserves the many Cubas that exist for the del Pinos through García's use of Pilar as narrator. Pilar adopts the voices of her family members in order to record their stories. Filtered through her eyes, her relatives' experiences of exile appear at turns mystical, humorous, and heartbreaking, but each woman's experience is presented with an empathetic vision that does not privilege one experience over another. Thus *Dreaming in Cuban* recognizes the ways in which multiple visions of a time and place can coexist without contradiction.

García's second novel, *The Agüero Sisters* (1997), was highly praised by critics for its lyric language and rendering of the complexities of family relationships, although some readers objected to García's depiction of Miami as a city decaying under the weight of nostalgia. Set in the 1990s, the novel places less emphasis on politics than *Dreaming in Cuban* does, but it continues to develop García's themes of family bonds, the power of memory, and the need to understand the past. The Agüero sisters, Constancia and Reina, are the daughters of Blanca Agüero, a Cuban naturalist. The novel opens with a startling prologue in which Blanca is murdered by her husband Ignacio, also a naturalist and Constancia's father. Constancia and Reina are told different but equally unsettling stories about their mother's death, an event that affects them both profoundly. Much of the novel is devoted to their attempts to reconcile with the past. As in her other works, Garcia moves the narrative between the present and the past, in this case by interweaving the stories of the sisters and their children with excerpts from Ignacio's diary.

Constancia, the elder sister, has lived in the United States for 30 years. She is a Miami entrepreneur who sells her "Cuerpo de Cuba" line of beauty products to help Cuban women recapture their youth and revel in memories of home. Constancia is a petite and feminine woman, faithful to her husband, dedicated to her business, and oddly invested in omens. Reina is a freelance electrician living in Havana. Described as Amazonian, she exists for sensual pleasure and revels in her sexual encounters with multiple partners. After years of division, the sisters reunite when Reina is struck by lightning and has cosmetic surgery to reconstruct her face. She becomes a literal patchwork of her relatives' donated skins, reminding her of the importance of family to identity, and comes to America to find her sister. Constancia is reminded of her own connection to family when she wakes up one morning with her mother's face. She can no longer ignore the past that she has suppressed for most of her life. As both sisters come to realize how deeply they have been affected by their mother's death and their parents' failed marriage, they draw closer together in a search for the truth about their past. In their reunion, García depicts the possibility of unity between different worlds and hope for the future.

García's third novel, *Monkey Hunting* (2003), again considers family, history, and memory, although it departs from her emphasis on families divided between Cuba and America. *Monkey Hunting* traces the story of Chen Pan, a Chinese farmer who comes to Cuba in 1857, dreaming of opportunity and a better life. Chen Pan thinks that he will make his fortune working in sugarcane, but instead he is enslaved for 10 years. When he escapes, he is determined to remake his life, and he opens a secondhand shop in Havana's Chinatown. He also purchases, frees, and falls in love with Lucrecia, a mulatto slave, with whom he has three children. García skillfully interweaves their story with the stories of their children, grandchildren, and great-grandchildren as the narrative shifts from Cuba to New York to China to Vietnam over the course of a more than a century. Although many members of the family are sketched in the text, Chen Fang, Chen Pan's granddaughter who is educated in China and raised as a boy, and Domingo Chen, his great-grandson who flees Cuba with his father to escape Castro and is later plunged into the Vietnam War, emerge as prominent figures. García uses her sweeping narrative to comment on the complexities of **identity** for those who exist between cultures. Coming from a mixture of Chinese, African, Cuban, and American backgrounds, her characters search for the places of belonging and happiness that seem to elude them.

In an interview with Bridget Kevane and Juanita Heredia, Cristina García commented that "the more you can encompass the complexity of a situation, the closer to the truth you get, not the other way around" (76). This idea permeates each of her novels as she deconstructs singular notions of Cubanness and exile and acknowledges the influence of historical forces on families and individuals. (*See also* Cuban American Novel)

Further Reading

Borland, Isabel Alvarez. *Cuban-American Literature of Exile: From Person to Persona*. Charlottesville: University Press of Virginia, 1998.

Kevane, Bridget, and Juanita Heredia. *Latina Self-Portraits: Interviews with Contemporary Women Writers*. Albuquerque: University of New Mexico Press, 2000.

Payant, Katherine. "From Alienation to Reconciliation in the Novels of Cristina García." *MELUS* 26.3 (2001): 163–84.

Amanda M. Lawrence

HALEY, ALEX (1921–1992)

Alex Haley was an African American biographer, journalist, and novelist. He was born on August 11, 1921, in Ithaca, New York; both of his parents were graduate students at that time, his mother at Ithaca Conservatory of Music and his father at Cornell University. His parents sent him to Henning, Tennessee, while he was an infant, and he was raised largely by his grandmother and aunts. After attending college in Mississippi and North Carolina, Haley enlisted in the U.S. Coast Guard. He began as a mess boy and 20 years later retired as chief journalist.

In the 1960s Haley began his civilian career as a freelance journalist and gained considerable public attention because of his high-profile interviews with Malcolm X, **Martin Luther King Jr.**, and Elijah Muhammad of the Nation of Islam, among others. Malcolm X, impressed by Haley's journalistic skills, invited him to collaborate with one of the most influential works in American literature: *The Autobiography of Malcolm X* (1965). Malcolm X acted as the informant; Alex Haley served as the amanuensis: one provided the raw material while the other shaped the narrative. Gathering information from informal conversations, extended interviews, dictations, and diaries, Haley meticulously reconstructed the life of Malcolm X. A runaway best seller, *The Autobiography of Malcolm X* has sold millions of copies internationally and remains a central text in the canon of African American life writing.

Shortly after the publication of that autobiography, Haley began researching his own family history. The research lasted nearly a decade. The result was *Roots* (1976), a quasi-historical, semi-fictional narrative of the story of his family. Nearly an epic in scope and design, *Roots* chronicles seven generations of Haley's family that began with Kunta Kinte, a rebellious young slave who was captured in Gambia, West Africa, brought to the United States, and sold into slavery in 1767. According to Haley, Kunta Kinte fathered Kissy, who gave birth to George. George fathered eight children; one of them, Tom, married Irene, who was part African and part Native American. One of their children was Cynthia, and Haley claimed that she was the grandmother who raised him, told him stories about her ancestors, and inculcated in him his genealogical curiosity.

Roots won dozens of awards, including the Pulitzer Prize. When a miniseries based on the book was shown on American television in 1976, it drew an estimated 120 million viewers. This unprecedented cultural event made Haley one of the preeminent writers of his generation. Though he published a short historical novel titled *A Different Kind of Christmas* in 1988 about a shareholder's son who rejects his family to become an advocate of abolition, *Roots* remains Haley's magnum opus.

Alex Haley, 1974. (AP Photo)

Haley's distinguished career, however, was marred by charges of plagiarism. Margaret Walker, herself an eminent African American poet and novelist, unsuccessfully sued him for copyright infringement. However, the charges of plagiarism brought up by Harold Courlander—the author of *The African* (1968)—were successful: Haley was forced to pay Courlander half a million dollars.

Further Reading

Athey, Stephanie. "Poisonous Roots and the New World Blues: Rereading Seventies Narration and Nation in Alex Haley and Gayl Jones." *Narrative* 7.2 (1999): 169–93.

Moore, David Chioni. "Routes: Alex Haley's *Roots* and the Rhetoric of Genealogy." *Transition* 64 (1994): 4–21.

Emmanuel S. Nelson

HANSBERRY, LORRAINE (1930–1965)

Lorraine Hansberry was an African American playwright, activist, journalist, and editor. One of the most distinguished American playwrights, Hansberry was born into an affluent family in Chicago on May 19, 1930. Her father, Carl A. Hansberry, was a real estate broker and banker; her mother, Nannie Perry Hansberry, was a schoolteacher and community activist. Among their family and friends were some of the most prominent members of the African American elite, such as Paul Robeson, **Langston Hughes**, W.E.B. Du Bois, and Duke Ellington. After graduating from Chicago's Englewood High School in 1947, Hansberry attended the University of Wisconsin at Madison for two years and then moved to New York City, where she studied briefly at the New School for Social Research. During that time she worked as a journalist and served as one of the editors of *Freedom*, a periodical founded by Paul Robeson. In 1953, she married Robert Nemiroff, a Jewish American activist with whom she shared a passionate commitment to progressive politics. Sadly, Hansberry died of pancreatic cancer at the age of 34. By then, however, she had earned her reputation as one of the best American playwrights.

Hansberry's reputation rests primarily on her magnum opus: *A Raisin in the Sun* (1959). A compact and conventionally structured three-act play, *A Raisin in the Sun* remains an American classic. The play is an aesthetically pleasing vehicle that nevertheless carries a provocatively sharp political message. Hansberry's characters are memorable, the dialogue revealing, and the plot engaging. As the play begins, the Younger family awaits a check for $10,000 from an insurance company; the money is a material legacy left to the family by the recently deceased Walter Younger Sr. The check precipitates conflicts among the members of the Younger household: the mother, Lena Younger, wants to make a down payment on a house with the money; the daughter Beneatha, wants the money to attend medical school; and the son, Walter Younger Jr., wants to invest the money in a liquor store in order to get rich quickly. These conflicts along gender and generational lines are resolved when the family confronts a common enemy: Karl Lindner. Mrs. Younger had made a down payment of $3500 on a house in Clybourne Park, a middle-class white neighborhood. Lindner, a representative of that neighborhood, makes the Youngers an offer: The Clybourne Park residents will give the Youngers more money than what they had invested in their prospective new home; in return, the Youngers would give up their claim to the house and not move into the all-white neighborhood. Walter Younger Jr.'s response to Lindner's offer remains one of the most emotionally charged moments in American theater.

Aside from the subject of integration—a subject resonant and urgent in 1959 when the play was first performed—Hansberry's play deals with a web of other themes as well: the relevance of Africa to the construction of contemporary African American cultural identities; class conflicts among African Americans; **assimilation** versus integration; radical questioning of traditional gender roles; the North versus the South; and the importance of family and ancestry. What makes her play enduring, however, is her effortless universalizing of the struggles and triumphs of an African American family living on the South Side of Chicago in the 1950s. The drama won her the New York Drama Critics' Circle Award for Best Play of the Year (1959); she was the youngest and the first black playwright to win that recognition. In 1961, the play became the basis for an immensely popular Hollywood movie, starring Sidney Poitier, Ruby Dee, and Claudia McNeil. In 1973, the play was adapted into a musical titled *Raisin*, and it won a Tony Award.

In the 1980s critics began to recognize the elaborate intertextual links between Hansberry's *A Raisin in the Sun* and **Richard Wright**'s *Native Son* (1940). Hansberry plants several clues in her play to alert the readers that she is engaged in a subversive dialogue with Wright's classic novel. Both works, for example, are set in the South Side of Chicago; both works begin with the sound of an alarm; the families in both works are originally from the South; neither family has a father; the mothers in both texts are domineering, deeply religious women; the protagonists in both works are chauffeurs; and the title of Hansberry's play, taken from a poem by Langston Hughes, rhymes with the title of Wright's novel. After alerting the readers to the intertextual intentions, Hansberry proceeds to offer two sharp challenges—one philosophical, the other political—to Richard Wright. As a naturalist, Wright argues that environment *is* destiny and that the outcome of his protagonist Bigger's life is predetermined by his circumstances. Hansberry, by locating her protagonist in not so dissimilar surroundings, rejects Wright's naturalistic philosophy: Her protagonist magnificently rises above his limiting environment. Hansberry's political disagreement with Wright is equally insistent. In Wright's novel, the women characters are presented in an unrelentingly negative light. Bigger's mother is an irritating nag; his girlfriend, Bessie, is an alcoholic; and the victims of the novel's two spectacularly brutal murders are women. In Hansberry's play, however, most of the strong characters are women. While women act as obstacles to Bigger's growth in Wright's novel, Hansberry presents women as enablers of Walter's painful journey toward maturation and manhood. Thus Hansberry, who was only 29 years old when she published her play in 1959, offers a daringly feminist challenge to the sexism inscribed in *Native Son*, a novel by a man who was seen as an unassailable legend in the African American literary scene during the 1950s.

Though Hansberry wrote a few other plays before her untimely death, none of them matches the aesthetic elegance and emotional power of her debut play. In 1960, she wrote a short, and still unproduced, play titled *Drinking Gourd* about slavery and its social arrangements. *What Use Are Flowers?* (1961) is Hansberry's response to *Waiting for Godot* (1952), an absurdist classic by Samuel Beckett. That work too has never been performed. Despite a diagnosis of terminal cancer in 1963, Hansberry continued to write. Her second play to be produced, *The Sign in Sidney Brustein's Window*, was staged in October 1964. A philosophical play set in Greenwich Village, it maps the incremental politicization of its titular character, Sidney Brustein—an instinctively liberal but largely uncommitted Jewish intellectual. When Hansberry died in January of 1965, she left behind a nearly complete manuscript, *Les Blancs*, which was adapted for stage in 1970 by Robert Nemiroff. A meditation on colonialism as well as its ideological and psychological underpinnings, it is an overtly political play that reflects Hansberry's increasingly global vision. It also reveals her growing impatience with the slow pace of progress in race relations in the United States and decolonization in Africa: the play suggests that violent revolution might be the only viable solution to racial injustice.

To Be Young, Gifted, and Black: A Portrait of Lorraine Hansberry in Her Own Words (1969), available in video form, offers its audience fascinating glimpses into the extraordinary life and achievement of Hansberry, who ranks among other great American playwrights, such as Eugene O'Neill and Tennessee Williams. (*See also* African American Drama)

Further Reading

Carter, Steven R. *Hansberry's Drama*. New York: Penguin, 1993.

Cheney, Anne. *Lorraine Hansberry*. Boston: Twayne, 1984.

Washington, J. Charles. "*A Raisin in the Sun* Revisited." *Black American Literature Forum* 22.1 (1988): 109–24.

Emmanuel S. Nelson

HARLEM RENAISSANCE

The Harlem Renaissance, or the "Negro Renaissance" as it was known during its heyday, designates a moment of unprecedented artistic flowering in African American literary culture. Social changes stemming from the Great Migration, a massive influx of African Americans from the rural South to the urban North, paved the way for more strictly cultural activities. Although African American writers and critics began calling for a cultural renaissance at the dawn of the 20th century, most scholars now agree that the Harlem Renaissance took shape during the so-called **Jazz** Age, beginning with the armistice in 1918 and ending around the time of the Great Depression in the 1930s.

Formulations of the movement's ideals vary almost as widely as the intellectuals who guided the Harlem Renaissance, but a few merit special attention for their centrality to our understanding of African American literary history. *The New Negro* (1925), a collection of essays, poetry, fiction, and visual art edited by Alain Locke, is widely recognized as a key record of the ideals and creative expression central to the movement. In important ways the phrase "Harlem Renaissance" can be misleading: in *The New Negro*, Locke, a Harvard-educated philosopher and critic who taught at Howard University, emphasized the artistic vitality, the youthful energy, and the national scope of the movement. Locke, together with W.E.B. Du Bois, Jessie Redmon Fauset, James Weldon Johnson, and a handful of additional critics, cemented the notion that an avant-garde of accomplished artists might pave the way for a broad program of social uplift. As Johnson optimistically put it in his famous preface to *The Book of American Negro Poetry* (1922), "The world does not know that a people is great until that people produces great literature and art. No people that has produced great literature and art has ever been looked upon by the world as distinctly inferior" (vii). The Harlem Renaissance, then, might be seen as a quest by African American writers and artists to achieve greatness, for themselves and for others.

In many instances the discussion about African American cultural expression took the shape of a debate between those (such as Locke) who valued art above all else and those (such as Du Bois) who insisted that art must first serve the propaganda needs of a downtrodden people. Still other debates ensued concerning the extent to which "racial" properties found their way into African American expression. The most famous example, in the Left-leaning *Nation* magazine in 1926, pitted George S. Schuyler's "The Negro-Art Hokum" against **Langston Hughes's** "The Negro Artist and the Racial Mountain." In effect, the two argued over the "blackness" of African American art, with Schuyler suggesting that African American culture was a variety of regional expression and Hughes insisting on an intrinsic, working-class African American identity. Richard Wright signaled the end of the Harlem Renaissance in his "Blueprint for Negro Writing" (1937), in which he laments the extent to which African American writers pandered to the bourgeois interests of a middle-class white readership.

Wright's scathing assessment of Harlem Renaissance cultural production, though debatable, does indicate a need to study the roles played by the intraracial and interracial dynamics of the Jazz Age literary marketplace. Any survey of the myriad institutions behind literary production during the Harlem Renaissance must begin with the numerous salons organized in virtually every major urban center in the United States. Famous salons, which drew now-canonical figures along with less-accomplished literary pretenders, were held in New York, Washington, D.C., Atlanta, and elsewhere, and from these gatherings emerged a vision of what was possible for African American artists, as well as the energy needed to guide the movement forward in the form of literary contests and journals. The latter ranged from predominantly white publications with an interest in cultural nationalism such as the *Survey*, which published a famous "Harlem" issue edited by Locke in 1925 (and later expanded into *The New Negro*), to journals published by African American social advocacy groups such as the National Association for the Advancement of Colored People (which published *Crisis*, edited by Du Bois) and the National Urban League (which published *Opportunity*, edited by Charles S. Johnson) to limited circulation avant-garde magazines such as *Fire!!*, edited by Wallace Thurman along with a who's who of Harlem Renaissance figures. These journals typically paid very little (if at all), but often they provided young African American writers with their first public venues, with a chance to be heard. Several sponsored regular contests for up-and-coming talent, and the lavish awards banquets at the Civic Club in Manhattan are now the stuff of legend.

A number of Harlem Renaissance intellectuals would eventually attribute the movement's shortcomings to the seduction of African American writers by white readers and publishers interested in a facile cultural primitivism. Although it remains possible to locate well-known examples of such work, the assessment is not wholly fair to the many pathbreaking individuals and firms supporting African American writing. As George Hutchinson has demonstrated, an ambitious new crop of publishers determined to reshape American letters—especially the so-called Young Jews of New York: Albert and Charles Boni, Benjamin Huebsch, Alfred Knopf, and Horace Liveright—took the Harlem Renaissance under its wing. Not only did the new publishers offer African American writers an opportunity to have their voices heard, but they also challenged the genteel publishing establishment centered in Boston by putting out titles now considered classics of Euro-American modernism.

The earliest Harlem Renaissance titles published were almost exclusively collections of poetry. Harcourt put out James Weldon Johnson's *Book of American Negro Poetry* anthology, and this was quickly followed by several key titles in quick succession. During the 1920s, Countee Cullen was widely considered the reigning "Negro Poet Laureate." His verse, collected in several volumes, including his first and most famous book, *Color* (1925), set the standard for formal achievement and intelligence, although today many critics take issue with his steadfast adherence to traditional forms and themes. Cullen made every effort during his short career to establish credentials as a universal (rather than a racial) poet; ironically, his most memorable verse, including "Heritage" and "Yet Do I Marvel," addresses the paradox of African American artistry in a white-dominated world. Cullen also left his impression as an editor; his *Caroling Dusk* (1927) provided a timely update to Johnson's collection, already dated a mere five years after its publication. In addition to his important role as editor of African American poetry, James Weldon Johnson was a poet of the first order in his own right. His several-decades-long career (which included work as a lawyer, a Tin Pan Alley songwriter, and political activist) reached its height of literary achievement in *God's Trombones* (1927), a collection of seven Negro sermons in verse. The poems embody the aesthetic aim espoused by Johnson in several locations, namely, the elevation of folk elements into poetic form. This challenge was taken up by a number of younger poets, such as Sterling Brown, Claude McKay, and Jean Toomer.

Several women—including Gwendolyn Bennett, Angelina Weld Grimké, Georgia Douglas Johnson, Helene Johnson, and Anne Spencer—also made their mark as poets during this time. Although older than most of their Harlem Renaissance counterparts, Grimké, Georgia Douglas Johnson, and Spencer (all born in the 1880s) achieved long careers that were in full bloom during the Jazz Age. They produced spare and often haunting verse that ranks them among the most "modernist" writers of the era. Bennett and Helene Johnson moved among younger and more obviously avant-garde circles, but they recognized their place in a long and rapidly expanding tradition of African American poetry. Bennett's "To a Dark Girl" (1927) and Helene Johnson's "Sonnet to a Negro in Harlem" (1927), for example, pay homage to centuries-old formal models and, arguably, to the more recent work of Langston Hughes.

Today's students of the Harlem Renaissance widely agree that Hughes was its most important writer based on his poetry alone. He first came to the public's attention with "The Negro Speaks of Rivers" (1921), published in the *Crisis* while Hughes was living in Mexico with his expatriate father. In several volumes, including his most famous collections, *The Weary Blues* (1925), *Fine Clothes to the Jew* (1927), and *Montage of a Dream Deferred* (1951), Hughes established a place during his lifetime as the most accomplished poet in African American literary history, all the while experimenting with vernacular forms inspired by **blues** and jazz. But Hughes was also a novelist, an accomplished memoirist (*The Big Sea* [1940] yields some of the most memorable anecdotes to come out of the Harlem Renaissance), a Broadway-produced playwright, and a gifted short-story writer. *The Ways of White Folks* (1934) offers a wide range of short fiction, from relatively conventional to avant-garde and from lightly humorous to scathingly critical of U.S. society.

With the recent publication of several Harlem Renaissance anthologies, it has become increasingly clear how important a role short fiction played in the movement. Some writers, such as Richard Bruce Nugent and Eric Walrond, show flashes of brilliance that drew mixed responses from their contemporaries. Others, such as

Zora Neale Hurston and Jean Toomer, have long been acknowledged as masters of the short-story craft. (Toomer's genre-bending, experimental *Cane* [1923] is often credited with launching the Harlem Renaissance; despite its thin sales, the book was widely and often favorably received by white and black reviewers.) As with the poets, Harlem Renaissance fiction writers gained some measure of attention by publishing their work in small-circulation venues, often parlaying the notice into contracts for full-length novels.

For a variety of reasons, two women novelists went largely unrecognized during their lifetimes, but now they rank as the greatest fiction writers to emerge from the Harlem Renaissance. **Nella Larsen**, in a short and troubled career, produced what are often regarded as the most-accomplished novels of the movement: *Quicksand* (1928) and *Passing* (1929), novels that have been fittingly compared to the fiction of Henry James and Edith Wharton. Since her rediscovery by **Alice Walker** in the 1970s, Zora Neale Hurston has been one of the most often anthologized and most widely read writers in the history of American letters. Hurston, who trained as an anthropologist with Franz Boas, collected folklore in the South and often incorporated her findings into her nonfiction and fiction alike. *Their Eyes Were Watching God* (1937), set in Hurston's native Florida, has become a staple of U.S. high school and college classrooms and has generated a wealth of scholarly analysis during the last three decades.

The only novelist who ranks near Hurston and Larsen is the Jamaican-born Claude McKay, whose *Home to Harlem* (1928) set off a storm of controversy among black intellectuals for its unabashed treatment of New York's wilder side. Still, several additional novelists produced creditable work that continues to draw readers inside and beyond the academy. Jessie Fauset, literary editor at the *Crisis* for many years, wrote four important and well-received novels between 1924 and 1933 (a period roughly coterminous with the Harlem Renaissance). George Schuyler's *Black No More* (1931) and Wallace Thurman's *Infants of the Spring* (1932) offer hilarious send-ups of Harlem social and intellectual life. W.E.B. Du Bois, Rudolph Fisher, and Walter White produced fiction that may be of greater historical than aesthetic value, but critics are still coming to terms with their work. Yet others associated with the Harlem Renaissance wrote novels that precede or post-date the movement, including James Weldon Johnson's *The Autobiography of an Ex-Colored Man* (1912) and Dorothy West's *The Living is Easy* (1948).

The Harlem Renaissance stands apart as the most thoroughly historicized and theorized movement in African American cultural history; still, much work remains to be done in this area of research. Just as feminist scholars in the 1980s and 1990s repositioned women writers at the forefront of the movement, in the 21st-century literary critics and historians have only just begun to take stock of key issues. These include the transnational dimensions of African diaspora cultural and social networks and the cosmopolitan rhetoric inspired by dialogue across national borders; the connection between performance (onstage and off) and social identity; the role of gay and lesbian writers on the Harlem Renaissance margins and in its mainstream; and, as Hughes and Hurston were right to insist decades ago, on the role of popular forms in the African American imagination. No doubt tomorrow's students of African American literature will explore as yet-unimagined avenues for scholarly inquiry. What is clear is that the Harlem Renaissance will remain at the front and center of African American studies for the foreseeable future.

Further Reading

Baker, Houston. *Modernism and the Harlem Renaissance.* Chicago: University of Chicago Press, 1987.

De Jongh, James. *Vicious Modernism: Black Harlem and the Literary Imagination.* Cambridge, UK: Cambridge University Press, 1990.

Favor, J. Martin. *Authentic Blackness: The Folk in the New Negro Renaissance.* Durham, NC: Duke University Press, 1999.

Huggins, Nathan Irvin. *Harlem Renaissance.* Oxford, UK: Oxford University Press, 1973.

Hutchinson, George. *The Harlem Renaissance in Black and White.* Cambridge, MA: Harvard University Press, 1995.

Johnson, James Weldon, ed. *The Book of American Negro Poetry.* New York: Harcourt, 1922.

Lewis, David Levering. *When Harlem Was in Vogue.* New York: Knopf, 1981.

Schwarz, A. B. Christa. *Gay Voices of the Harlem Renaissance.* Bloomington: Indiana University Press, 2003.

Soto, Michael. *The Modernist Nation: Generation, Renaissance, and Twentieth-Century American Literature.* Tuscaloosa: University of Alabama Press, 2004.

Spencer, Jon Michael. *New Negroes and Their Music: The Success of the Harlem Renaissance.* Knoxville: University of Tennessee Press, 1997.

Watson, Steve. *The Harlem Renaissance: Hub of African-American Culture, 1920–1930.* New York: Pantheon, 1995.

Michael Soto

HAWAI'I LITERATURE

As with many places in America's colonized imperium, Hawai'i faces numerous issues that link its literature to its shifting geopolitical status. Territorialization by the United States impacted the concept of "Hawaiian," which made for an awkward transition for literary studies that has utilized such terms as "indigenous," "local," and "regional." This awkwardness produces much anxiety in terms of how one approaches a body of writing. Some scholars have relied on a sociohistorical approach (Hamasaki, 1993; Kwon, 2003), but others have adopted genre- or topic-related guidelines (Sumida, 1991; Morales, 1998). Another distinct avenue is conveyed in the focus on ethnic or racial communities, as is seen in writers' participation in defining Native **Hawaiian literature** (Apo-Perkins, 1980; Balaz, 1989; Kawaharada, 1994; Trask, 1999) and local literature (Hiura, 1979; Sumida, 1986; Chock and Lum, 1986, 1998). Yet, any method entails compromise. History itself represents a challenge to the creation of any timeline as differing perspectives do not culminate in synchronous definitions of literary epochs and movements; this is clear when anthologies of African American literature are compared to those of "traditional" American or other ethnic canons. Genres, likewise, present a distinct disadvantage as they often reimpose established Western standards of literary merit. Specifically, "poetry" and "prose" cannot convey the wide spectrum of Hawai'i's literature, which includes chants, dances, genealogies, oral storytelling, and artistic crafts. Similarly, highlighting divisions based on ethnicity may oversimplify the degree to which Hawai'i's population is intermarried and interrelated. For clarity, this study will engage an historical timeframe—though it should be clear that this does not constitute an evolutionary process.

Hawai'i's literature begins with the indigenous peoples of the islands. Their oral traditions, collectively called *orature*, are now understood as the first major body of "literary" merit. With the creation of a written form of Hawaiian in the 1820s, literacy rates skyrocketed, and many Native Hawaiians quickly adopted the newspaper serial format as an outlet for writing, historical and creative. The rest of the century evolved into an era of intense and prolific publication on the part of noted individuals such as David Malo, Samuel M naiakalani Kamakau, John Papa 'Ī'ī, and S. N. Hale'ole. Concerns about the loss of cultural knowledge and the threat to national independence spurred literary production—King Kal kaua produced *The a Myths and Legends of Hawaii* (1888), and Queen Lili'uokalani offered to the public an English translation of the monarchy's genealogy, *The Kumulipo* (1897). Annexation did not hinder publication; in fact, Nakuina's *Moolelo Hawaii o Pakaa a me Ku-a-Pakaa, na Kanu Iwikuamoo o Keawenuiaumi, ke Alii o Hawaii, a o na Moopuna hoi a Laamaomao* (translated as The Wind Gourd of La'amaomao) of 1902 and John Sheldon's 1906 rendition of the tale of Ko'olau, the leper victim who resisted deportation to a quarantines colony, were directed at the Hawaiian people with the express purpose of supporting the Hawaiian nation and criticizing the provisional and territorial governments.

Unfortunately, the growing domination of Westerners in the islands led to the further expansion of agriculture (sugar and pineapple), massive importation of foreign labor of mainly Japanese and Filipinos, and the beginning development of the tourism industry. Such changes coincided with the belief that Hawaiians were a dying **race** and simultaneously heralded the depreciation of indigenous material, which became branded as subjects for anthropological study. Although credited with the establishment of academic arenas, some of these scholars entertained racially hierarchical notions of artistic and scholarly merit. One such researcher, Nathaniel B. Emerson, translated previously published Hawaiian texts and transcribed other oral sources in *The Unwritten Literature of Hawaii: The Sacred Songs of the Hula* (1905) and *Pele and Hiiaka, A Myth of Hawaii* (1909); however, his 1903 translation of David Malo's *Mo'olelo Hawai'i* includes an introduction that mourns the inability of the Native Hawaiian author to appreciate the value of his own work and that "only of a foreign and broadly cultivated mind to occupy the stand-point necessary to such an appraisal."

For the next 60 years, literary authority lay with those who subscribed to or were thought to have best represented this ideological perspective. Under the guidance of University of Hawai'i English professors A. Grove Day and Carl Stroven, a specific academic definition of Hawai'i's literature emerged with the publication of *The Spell of the Pacific* (1949), an English-language collection featuring selections from James Cook's journal, excerpts from Isabella Bird's travelogue *The Hawaiian Archipelago* (1875), an abridged version of Charles Warren Stoddard's *The Lepers of Molokai* (1885), Robert Louis Stevenson's short piece "The Bottle Imp" (1893), Genevieve Taggard's semiautobiographical tale "The Plague" (1927), Austin Strong's vignette "His Oceanic Majesty's Goldfish" (1944), and William Meredith's poem "Lines Written but Never Mailed from Hawaii" (1946); these works were used to represent an American vision of "Hawai'i."

As critics later point out, the omission of certain names and texts points to a bias on the part of academia. For example, *The Spell of the Pacific* fails to mention one of the most prominent woman writers whose series of works were quite popular in their day. The 1920s were dominated by the novels of Armine von Tempski, the island-born daughter of a ranch manager on Maui. Her romance, *Hula* (1927), is said to have provided the storyline for the Clara Bow film of the same title of the same year. However, Tempski is best remembered for her poignant and emotional autobiography, *Born in Paradise* (1940), which first recounts her childhood on the slopes of Haleakala and the disruption of that idyll by the subsequent suicides of her parents.

In many ways, early scholarly attempts to define Hawai'i's literature grossly overlooked the grassroots writing that was being printed in newspapers and magazines. For example, in 1945 *Paradise of the Pacific* (which later became known as *Honolulu*) sponsored Philip K. Ige's "Two Boys and a Kite" a short story involving children from a pineapple plantation on Maunaloa, Moloka'i. Born to Japanese immigrants, this second-generation (Nisei) writer is one of the first to publicly employ pidgin English in a noncomical fashion:

> "You think da kite goin' fly?" Yone asked.
> "Sure, da kite goin' fly. What you think we make 'em for?"
> "I know; but—you no think da kite kinda heavy?"
> "Nah-h, no worry, Yone, he goin' fly," Noburo said confidently. (20)

Wishing to address further the "desperate need for a writer or writers who can capture on paper the idiomatic speech, the sights, sounds, and smells of ordinary living in Hawai'i" (24), *Paradise of the Pacific* published three more works: "The Forgotten Flea Powder" by Philip K. Ige, "Grandmother's White Hands" by Fumiko Fujita, and "Hawaiian Tragedy" by Yat Cho Au (24–27). Unlike the stereotypical images and sounds that were captured in such Hollywood films as *Hawaii Calls* (1937) or *Waikiki Wedding* (1937), the emerging literature by these young authors, many attending the University of Hawai'i at M noa, was tied to real experiences of growing up a and living in the islands in often less-than-ideal situations. Furthermore, the experience of Japanese Americans during World War II, an event that led to the rise of anti-Japanese sentiment and **internment** for some in the islands, galvanized this community into producing works that documented their hardships. At the time when Hawai'i was electing prominent Japanese American politicians such as Senator Daniel Inouye (1962–2012), Senator Spark Matsunaga (1976–1990), and Governor George Ariyoshi (1974–1986), Margaret Harada's *The Sun Shines on* *the Immigrant* (1960), Kazuo Miyamoto's *Hawaii, End of the Rainbow* (1964), and Jon Shirota's *Lucky Come Hawaii* (1965) all made their debut.

Nevertheless, the commercial success of James Michener's writing, including his epic novel *Hawaii* (1959), and the anticipation of impending statehood led Michener to approach Day and Stroven to compile a book of "the best writing" that had been done on and in the islands. Such a project had already been drafted by Day and Stroven. As noted in the introduction Michener wrote for this collection, which was published as *A Hawaiian Reader* in 1959. The "good literary judgment" of these two scholars is reflected in their selections from Mark Twain, Robert Louis Stevenson, Rupert Brooke, Jack London, and W. Somerset Maugham.

Though not included, two additional Anglo-American writers are mentioned in the foreword: Oswald "Ozzie" (O. A.) Bushnell and Marjorie Sinclair. O. A. Bushnell, like Day and Stroven, was a University of Hawai'i scholar; after serving in the Army in World War II and working at the Territorial Department of Health, Bushnell became a professor and taught both medical microbiology and medical history. Unlike the editors of *A Hawaiian Reader*, Bushnell was what many would consider "local"—born in Kaka'ako (what is now the industrial area southeast of downtown Honolulu) and raised in the islands. His experience is said to have influenced his novels: *The Return of Lono: A Novel of Captain Cook's Last Voyage* (1956); *Molokai* (1963); *Ka'a'awa, A Novel about Hawaii in the 1850s* (1972); *The Stone of Kannon* (1979); and *The Water of Kane* (1980). Bushnell's *The Water of Kane* is especially noteworthy as it reworks the ancient chant into a modern tale involving Japanese immigrants and the construction of an irrigation system that will bring water and life to central Maui. Marjorie Sinclair was another scholar affiliated with the University of Hawai'i. Originally from South Dakota, Sinclair relocated to the islands in 1935 and immediately immersed herself in Hawaiian culture and history. This interest led to the publication of *Kona, A Novel of Two Generations in Hawaii* (1947), *The Wild Wind* (1950), and *Nahi'ena'ena, Sacred Daughter of Hawai'i* (1976). Her tenure as a professor of English from 1955 to 1980 coincided with her work with the Hawai'i Literary Arts Council. She later received the Hawai'i Literary Award in 1980 and so is included in the ranks of many locally celebrated writers, including O. A. Bushnell (1974), A. Grove Day (1979), Gavan Daws (1980), **Maxine Hong Kingston** (1982), Katherine Luomala (1983), John Dominis Holt (1985), W. S. Merwin (1986), Rubellite Kawena Johnson (1988), Milton Murayama (1991), Cathy Song (1993), Victoria Kneubhel (1994), Eric Chock and Darrell H. Y. Lum (1996), and Edward Sakamoto (1997).

Curiously, Michener's introduction in *A Hawaiian Reader* also notes that "the Orientals did not produce a literature of their own" (Day and Stroven xiv) and that what little indigenous material that is offered—David Malo's account of the *ali'i* (Hawaiian chiefly class), Emerson's translation of "The Water of Kane," P ku'i's recounting of the family lore in "The Marchers of the Night" of 1930, "Martha Beckwith's 1951 translation of *The Kumulipo*, and Katherine Luomala's 1951 historical essay, "Menehunes, the Little People"—is properly relegated to the back of the collection as "the language of these passages is so alien to the modern world that it might have alienated the casual reader" (Day and Stroven xiv). This narrow outlook was amended in 1968 when Stroven and Day released *A Spell of Hawaii*, a companion collection that included only one Native Hawaiian writer, Samuel Mnaiakalani Kamakau, yet gave recognition to local Asian writing, to Milton Murayama's "I'll Crack Your Head Kotson," a short story that would later become the foundation for the now widely circulated *All I Asking for Is My Body* (1975).

Maui-born Murayama used many of the images of the sugar plantation and the Japanese labor camps from his childhood as the setting for *All I Asking for Is My Body*, a novella that recalls the vicious cycle of debt and poverty experienced by many immigrants. It would take more than 15 years for Murayama, who relocated to San Francisco, to complete two more books that further document the trials of the Oyama family. *Five Years on a Rock* (1994) follows the mother's life from her arrival in Hawai'i as a picture bride through her multiple childbirths and declining health, whereas *Plantation Boy* (1998) confronts the inability of later generations to escape "plantation mentality" and the racial hierarchy that lingers despite statehood.

Minor references regarding local and Native Hawaiian writers inevitably encouraged scholars of different backgrounds to rethink the concept of literary merit. Just as the research of Martha Beckwith, Mary Kawena Pukui, Katherine Luomala, Samuel Elbert, and John Charlot helped to maintain interest in Native Hawaiian writers and traditions, the findings of Arnold Hiura and Stephen Sumida aided in the recovery and/or large-scale dissemination of local Asian American texts. Hiura and Sumida's work culminated in the publication of a 1979 annotated bibliography of local Asian American "literature" to be found in newspapers, magazines, high school yearbooks, and college playwriting competitions. Their findings highlighted the literary developments that had gone relatively unnoticed by formal literary scholarship. In fact, part of their bibliography included material from an earlier collection compiled by another University of Hawai'i English professor, Willard Wilson, who taught drama writing and encouraged his students to utilize their own culturally specific backgrounds for material. Spanning 1936 to 1956, Wilson's 10-volume *College Plays* features one- and two-act sketches by such writers as Patsy Saiki and Margaret Kwon Pai. Saiki would go on to become an administrator for the Hawai'i State Department of Education and the author of *Sachie* (1977), a coming-of-age novel that addresses the hardships of a Japanese adolescent girl confronting ethnic and racial politics on the Big Island, while Margaret Kwon Pai, a public high school teacher, penned *The Dreams of Two Yi-Min* (1989), an autobiographical account of the Korean immigrant experience in the islands.

Hiura and Sumida's research in the 1970s coincided with a new homegrown literary movement and with what many call the Hawaiian Renaissance, a reflourishing of pride in Native Hawaiian culture and the arts. At this time when musicians expounded and revived grassroots' sounds and subject matter, scholars fervently recorded and developed a language curriculum with the last generation of native speakers of Hawaiian. This is when John Dominis Holt emerged as a major voice in Hawaiian writing. Descended from American missionaries who had intermarried with the Hawaiian *ali'i* (chiefly class), Holt used his childhood experience of growing up surrounded by racial self-hatred, socially paralyzing anger, alcoholism, and the decline of the family fortune as the basis for his fiction. He and his second wife, Frances Damon, founded Topgallant Press (later to become Ku Pa'a), which would later publish Holt's first novel *Waimea Summer* (1976), the story of an urbanite biracial boy from Honolulu who confronts on a visit to the Big Island a crisis of Hawaiian **identity** that pits the elite, educated, and Americanized class of natives against the rural, poorer, but more traditional families. Other Native Hawaiian writers also began their own independent presses and literary outlets, including in 1976 Seaweeds and Constructions, which featured the poetry of Wayne Westlake. The year 1979 witnessed the emergence of Iron Bench Press by the poet Joseph Balaz, who would later edit and publish *Ho'om anoa* (1989), an anthology devoted entirely to indigenous writers of Hawai'i.

Another major development was the launching of Kumu Kahua Theatre, a project designed to give local playwrights greater opportunity to showcase their work. Efforts to promote and utilize Hawai'i's unique cultural material had been earlier launched by John Kneubuhl, a Samoan Hawaiian who later worked in Hollywood as the screenwriter for such mainstream shows as *Gunsmoke* (1955), *Star Trek* (1966), and *Hawaii Five-0* (1968). However, only the success of Kumu Kahua would guarantee an enduring forum for the expression of discontentment with Americanization, economic development, and the tourism that was emerging. Embodying a rejection of continental mainland expectations of both language and literature, plays such as James Grant Benton's *The Twelf Nite O Wateva* (1974) focused on local and Native Hawaiian images and experiences; *The Twelf Nite O Wateva* in particular features a multiethnic cast including a Native Hawaiian prince, a Filipino count, and a Portuguese maid. The Benton's reworking of Shakespeare's *Twelfth Night, or What You Will*, which even includes a pidgin rendition of Feste's song, may seem an irreverent mimicry of the original text; however, the play "localizes" the universal aspects of this English renaissance performance. The play also elevates pidgin to the level of mainstream artistic expression.

Next came *Talk Story*, a conference on multiethnic literature in the islands that took place in 1978. The subsequent publication of an anthology marked the beginning of the careers of many writers who would go on to become key names in Native Hawaiian, local, and Asian American literary circles. The collection includes: Darrell H.Y. Lum's "Primo Doesn't Take Back Bottles Anymore," Mari Kubo's "Women," Wing Tek Lum's "I Did Not Understand," Cathy Song's "Lost Sister," Martha Webb's "Wet Cave," Eric Chock's "Manoa Cemetery," Edward Sakamoto's "In the Alley," and Dana Naone Hall's "The Men Whose Tongues." The Forward clearly identifies the perspective of the text: "The common thread that runs loosely through these stories, diverse in theme, setting, and tone as they are, is that they all in some way illuminate the 'local experience' in Hawai'i. Somewhere in these stories . . . there is a link with being local in Hawaii" (Chock 12). Hiura and Sumida would themselves edit the Hawai'i island version of Talk Story, which featured Edith Kanaka'ole's "Noho Ana I Hilo," Garrett Hongo's "The Hongo Store," Virgilio Menor Felipe's "Hawaii, Plantation of Destiny," Larry Kimura's "The Legend of Kapalaoa," Kazuo Miyamoto's "Hawaii End of the Rainbow," and Patsy Saiki's "The Unwilling Bride." From these humble beginnings, Eric Chock and Darrell

H. Y. Lum established in 1978 *Bamboo Ridge*, a literary journal that featured such important writers as Lois-Ann Yamanaka, Juliet Kono, Cathy Song, Susan Nunes, Rodney Morales, Dana Naone Hall, and Lee Tonouchi. *Bamboo Ridge* has also published a wide range of materials in special editions: an artistic tribute to Native Hawaiian singer/activist George Helm and activist Kimo Mitchell (Ho'iho'i Hou, 1984); World War II internment camp poetry (*Poets Behind Barbed Wire*, 1984); transcriptions and subsequent translations of Hawaiian newspaper articles from 1834 (*The Four-Footed Animals of Ka Lama Hawaii*, 1985); a collection of mainly indigenous writing on the Hawaiian concept of place (*Mlama: Hawaiian Land and Water*, 1985); an anthology of *hapa* (mixed-race) women (*Intersecting Circles*, 1999); and a collection of Korean American writing in the islands (*Yobo*, 2003).

The emergence of the "local" as a measure of cultural familiarity and literary merit inevitably led to conflicts over legitimacy and representation. In fact, anger toward Anglo-American hegemony in scholarship spread to mainland-raised Asian Americans, as demonstrated in O. A. Bushnell's keynote address at Talk Story, which California native Maxine Hong Kingston notes in her book *Hawai'i One Summer* (1987).

> I was humbled when Ozzie Bushnell, author of Ka'a'awa, said that if "us local kids" don't write the Hawai'i novel, the "outsider" will come in and do it. I guiltily identified with this "outsider." Ozzie is such a strong speaker, talking both standard English and pidgin, that I felt scolded, a Captain Cook of literature, plundering the islands for metaphors, looting images, distorting the landscape with a mainland—a mainstream—viewpoint. (47)

Though Kingston was recognized as a Living Treasure of Hawai'i in 1980 and won the Hawai'i Literary Award in 1982, she and other nonlocal writers were finding themselves excluded from collections such as *Growing Up Local* (1998), which editor Darrell H. Y. Lum saw as an attempt to capture the communal sense of a shared history "rooted in the struggles of the working of Hawai'i's sugar plantations" and the shared goal of resisting "the dominant white culture."

The conflict would not end with the rejection of mainland writers of color. By the mid-1990s, criticism began to appear over the proliferation and domination of certain Asian immigrant narratives. This came to a head at the 1998 annual meeting of the Association of Asian American Studies (AAAS) when protests were lodged over the awarding of Lois-Ann Yamanaka for her work *Blu's Hanging* (1997). For many of the protesters, Yamanaka's continuing use of derogatory Filipino stereotypes was unacceptable as they trace back to her original work, *Saturday Night at the Pahala Theatre* (1992). The first poem of this book, "Kala Gave Me Anykine Advice Especially About Filipinos When I Moved to Pahala," is cited as proof of Yamanaka's long-standing fixation on sexually predatory and degenerate Filipino men as one such character again finds his way into the narrative of *Blu's Hanging* in the form of Paulo, a man who molests his own nieces and rapes the narrator's younger brother, Blu. Criticism against and support for this book led to a fracturing among local scholars, as evidenced in the editorials published by *The Hawaii Herald, Honolulu*, and *Honolulu Weekly*. This controversy also served to reinforce the divide between some local Asian scholars and their mainland counterparts, such as Maxine Hong Kingston, Lawson Fusao Inada, Frank Chin, **Amy Tan**, and Shawn Wong, who all sent letters to AAAS to voice opposition to the rescinding of Yamanaka's award.

To further complicate the matter, Native Hawaiian writers and critics began to question why stories of the plantation, as found in Yamanaka's and others' works, would serve as the ultimate representation of the islands. A clear example of this kind of criticism can be found in Haunani-Kay Trask's "Decolonizing Hawaiian Literature" (1999):

> Contemporary writers who claim, through generational residence in Hawai'i, that they are Hawaiian or representative of what would be a unique national literature of Hawai'i, if we were an independent country, confuse the development and identification of our indigenous literature. Asian writers who grew up in Hawai'i and claim their work as representative of Hawaiian literature or of our islands are the most obvious example. By asserting a special island identity, these local Asian authors . . . hope to separate themselves from Asian writers elsewhere in the American imperium. Their claim to difference is precisely that they are local, that is, they are "from" Hawai'i. This kind of settler assertion is really a falsification of place and culture. (169)

Generally speaking, much of the criticism has been leveled at Bamboo Ridge due to the perception that it excluded Hawaiian writers and promoted works explicating oppression faced by primarily the Chinese and the Japanese, an "experience" that is belied by the sociopolitical ascendance of these communities in the islands.

Whether such sentiments will linger remains to be seen, given the establishment of two Native Hawaiian resources—'*iwi*, a literary and visual arts journal, in 1998, and *Ka Ho'oilina: The Legacy*, a periodical devoted to transcribing and translating archived indigenous writing, in 2002—and increased Filipino representation, through the proliferation of video documentaries such as *Bayanihan* (1995), *Sakada Generation* (1996), and *Aloha Philippines* (1996), and the publication of Virgilio Menor Felipe's *Hawai'i, A Pilipino Dream* (2002). It also remains to be seen what the future holds for writing in pidgin, now that it, too, has been identified as a colonial medium that displaces the native language, though Lee Tonouchi, reverently dubbed by the editors of '*iwi* as "da Pidgin guerrilla," continues groundbreaking work in this medium via formal publication in *Da Word* (2001) and in editing collections for independent presses of up-and-coming young talent (*Stick It to Ya: Peanut Butter and Poetry Jam*, 2003 and *Buss Laugh: Stand Up Poetry from Hawai'i*, 2004). Furthermore, the continuing outflow of local and Native Hawaiians to the mainland for educational and economic opportunities will further impact the discussion of literary merits vis-à-vis cultural familiarity; it would appear that critical discussion will continue to take place on the role of "off-Island" Hawaiian and transplanted "local writers." Such a move may allow the canon to expand and include Kiana Davenport, Kathleen Tyau, Lono Waiwai'ole, Garrett Hongo, Susanna Moore, and Carolyn Lei-Lanilau. In the meantime, local resident writers, such as Chris McKinney (*The Tattoo*, 1999; *Queen of Tears*, 2001), Lois-Ann Yamanaka (*Father of the Four Passages*, 2001), and Cedric Yamanaka (*In Good Company*, 2002) address ethnic identity with regard to the urban experience, with McKinney and Lois-Ann Yamanaka probing the darker side of Honolulu, and Cedric Yamanaka choosing a mixture of nostalgia and poignant humor. (*See also* Hawaiian Literature)

Further Reading

Balaz, Joseph P. *Ho'om noa, An Anthology of Contemporary Hawaiian Literature*. Honolulu: Ku Pa'a, 1989.

Carroll, Dennis, ed. *Kumu Kahua Plays*. Honolulu: University of Hawai'i Press, 1983.

Chock, Eric, et al. *Talk Story: An Anthology of Hawaii's Local Writers*. Honolulu: Petronium Press, 1978.

Day, A. Grove, and Carl Stroven. *A Hawaiian Reader*. Honolulu: Mutual, 1959.

Kingston, Maxine Hong. *Hawai'i One Summer*. Manoa: University of Hawai'i Press, 1998 [reprint edition].

Monaghan, Peter. "Asian-American-Studies Group in Turmoil over a Rescinded Book Award." *The Chronicle of Higher Education* (July 10, 1998): A13.

'Oiwi, a Native Hawaiian Journal. Honolulu: Kuleana 'Oiwi Press.

Sumida, Stephen. *And the View from the Shore: Literary Traditions of Hawai'i*. Seattle: University of Washington Press, 1991.

Trask, Haunani-Kay. "Decolonizing Hawaiian Literature." In *Inside Out: Literature, Cultural Politics, and Identity in the New Pacific*, edited by Vilsoni Hereniko and Rob Wilson, 167–82. Lanham, MD: Rowman & Littlefield, 1999.

Seri Luangphinith

HAWAIIAN LITERATURE

One of the difficulties scholars studying Hawaiian literature grapple with is the confusion over what exactly constitutes "Hawaiian." For some, Hawaiian literature is geographic in nature, meaning any and all literature coming out of Hawai'i. For others, Hawaiian literature is thematic, meaning literature referencing Hawai'i or Hawaiian culture. Today, because of the renaissance in Hawaiian culture and national consciousness, Hawaiian literature is more accurately defined as the writing produced by *Kanaka Maoli* (Hawaiians, Native Hawaiians), the indigenous inhabitants genealogically connected to the archipelago of Pacific islands known to the world as Hawai'i. Hawaiian literature can be broadly categorized into three general time periods: pre- and early-contact "orature" or oral traditions (0 A.D.–1820s), post-contact "traditional" literature (1820s–1950s), and post-contact "contemporary" literature (1960s–present).

The basic distinction between traditional and contemporary Hawaiian literature is language based. Traditional Hawaiian literature is writing produced by Hawaiian writers from the 1820s through the 1950s. More importantly, these compositions were penned almost exclusively in the indigenous Hawaiian language. With the rare exception of Queen Liliʻuokalaniʻs autobiography *Hawaiiʻs Story by Hawaiiʻs Queen* (1898) and Emma Nakuinaʻs *Hawaii, Its People, Their Legends* (1904), Hawaiian was the dominant language of expression and medium of composition for Hawaiians for over a century.

First contact between Hawaiians and the Western world occurred in 1778, when British captain James Cook accidentally stumbled upon the islands. For nearly 2000 years prior to Cookʻs arrival, Hawaiians thoughtfully composed, carefully memorized, and painstakingly passed down countless chants (*oli*), songs (*mele*), dances (*hula*), genealogies (*moʻokuʻauhau*), and stories/histories (*moʻolelo*) from one generation to the next. Before the introduction of a writing system to Hawaiʻi, all Hawaiian composition was strictly oral in nature. In 1820, American Calvinist missionaries arrived in Hawaiʻi with the intention of converting Hawaiians to Christianity. In order to accomplish this, they needed to teach Hawaiians to read and write. Once literacy was established, Hawaiians took advantage of the new technology of writing, which enabled them to record and retrieve information in new ways. They wrote prolifically, transforming vast amounts of their oral traditions into literary ones. As the 19th century progressed, Hawaiʻi became one of the most literate nations on earth, second only to Scotland.

The first newspaper in Hawaiʻi was published in 1834. In the span of a century, over 75 Hawaiian-language newspapers, containing over one million pages of information—mostly literature, stories, poems, histories, biographies—was produced. In 1861, the first newspaper independent of missionary or government control, *Ka Hoku o ka Pakipika* (The Star of the Pacific) was published. The inaugural issue (September 26, 1861) featured the initial installment of a serialized and important traditional story set in print for the first time, "He Moolelo no Kawelo" (The Legend of [the Hero] Kawelo). At this time, Hawaiians felt it was important to take control of the presses in order to counteract negative stereotypes being put forth by influential foreigners, namely *haole* (white) missionaries and businessmen who saw their way as the only way to act and live. The independent papers asserted Hawaiian pride in self and culture by publishing literature that was affirming to the Hawaiian populace.

Soon after, S. N. Haleoleʻs *L aʻieikawai*, a love story of an ancient Hawaiian princess of the same name, appeared. First published as a serial in a rival newspaper, *Ka Nupepa Kuokoa* (The Independent), by 1863 it was published as a book and is now widely acknowledged as the first Hawaiian novel. In 1919, this story was translated into English for a wider audience to enjoy.

One of the most significant events in Hawaiian history, which forever transformed Hawaiian society and literature, is the 1893 overthrow of Queen Liliʻuokalani and the native government. Composed entirely of *haole* males with a distinctive colonial and anti-Hawaiian mentality, the new "provisional" government enacted a ban against the Hawaiian language, outlawing it as a medium of instruction in all public schools. Thus, Hawaiian literature, which was composed for centuries in the Hawaiian language, began to die a slow but systematic death. By the mid-20th century, both oral and written Hawaiian language compositions significantly dwindled.

Although the goal of the new government was to "civilize" the Hawaiian nation by making English the official language, because of a changing population and resistant social forces, a new language, "pidgin" (today called HCE or Hawaiʻi Creole English), arose. The language developed as a way for Hawaiians, new ethnic immigrants to the sugar plantations (Chinese, Japanese, Filipinos, Puerto Ricans, Portuguese), and others to communicate across ethnic and linguistic boundaries. As an oral, "living" language, HCE evolved over the decades, each generation of speakers reflecting different social, linguistic, and cultural influences. Yet despite being the predominant language of communication among the working class, HCE was not popularized as a literary language until the contemporary period. Part of the reason for this is the stigma attached to it by the *haole* ruling class, who looked down on all but their standard of English. Although the battle between an amorphous "standard" English and HCE continues today, HCE has gained immense popularity in contemporary Hawaiian writing. One reason is that it is the language most spoken by the people. Another reason is that it is the new language of resistance to colonial domination and oppression.

After the overthrow of the Hawaiian government, traditional Hawaiian language-based literature continued to be produced for a period of about 20 to 30 years, a period during which the last generations of Hawaiians educated in the indigenous Hawaiian language came of age. Once cut off from their native tongue, a lull in Hawaiian literary production occurred during Hawaiʻi's pre- and early territorial period (1940s–1950s). The few Hawaiians publishing at this time, such as Mary Kawena Pukui, Bernice Piʻilani Irwin, and Charles W. Kenn, primarily wrote or translated ethnographic materials based on personal experiences. Some, most notably Pukui, were employed as native informants for *haole* scholars and researchers. A revered cultural icon, Pukui was rarely listed as the primary author of the hundreds of publications she is associated with, despite the fact that culturally important and definitive works such as the *Hawaiian Dictionary* (1957) and *Native Planters of Old Hawaiʻi* (1972) could not have been published without her tremendous insight and knowledge.

It is conceivable that the lack of literary production on the part of Hawaiians and the emphasis on Western-based ethnography of the culture and traditions of the "ancient" Hawaiians during the decades immediately preceding and following World War II are not coincidental. Rather, it reflects the "success" of the systematic colonization of Hawaiians that began with first contact and methodically continued throughout the 19th century. The middle of the 20th century reflects the degree of success of this colonial process, as Hawaiians of that era worked to assimilate to the dominant American culture, and, for the most part, temporarily leaving their own language, culture, and traditions behind.

Native Hawaiian literature developed from the 1960s to the present is considered "contemporary Hawaiian literature." It contains many of the same themes as traditional literature, such as *aloha ʻaina* and *kuʻ*, incorporates many of the same genres of traditional literature, and expresses the same desire to dispel negative stereotypes about Hawaiians. Unlike traditional Hawaiian literature, however, contemporary Hawaiian literature is composed primarily in English, HCE, to a lesser extent Hawaiian, and typically a combination of two or all three languages. With a growing number of skilled Hawaiian-language speakers, however, this is slowly changing.

The 1960s signifies an important transition in Hawaiian culture, marking a period of social and political activism and renewed interest in Hawaiian arts and culture known today as the "Hawaiian Renaissance." This era of concerted resistance and backlash against colonialism also signifies an attempt to reconnect to, uphold, and perpetuate Hawaiian cultural practices that include creative writing. The **Civil Rights Movement** of the 1960s is commonly acknowledged as the inspiration for the "Hawaiian movement" that continues today, as Hawaiians continue their fight to regain their native land base and native political power through sovereignty and self-determination initiatives, regrow their 'olelo 'oiwi (Hawaiian language) through the establishments of *kula kai puni* (Hawaiian language immersion schools), and reinvigorate their cultural arts such as dance, chant, music, and literature.

A foundational Hawaiian author of the contemporary period is John Dominis Holt (1919–1993). One of the first Hawaiian voices of the Renaissance, Holt is also one of the most prolific, authoring over 20 titles in a span of 30 years. Holt's *Waimea Summer* (1976) distinguishes him as the first contemporary Hawaiian novelist. A coming-of-age novel set in the mid-20th century, Holt's part-Hawaiian protagonist, Mark Hull, grapples with understanding the sacred traditions of his Hawaiian heritage and its role in his "modern," Americanized life. Thirty years later, Holt still stands out as one of the only Native Hawaiian novelists, and his *Waimea Summer* as a landmark Hawaiian novel.

It is both strange and inevitable that there are very few Hawaiian novelists in the contemporary period. One reason seems to be that although fed a staple of Western genres for generations, Hawaiian writers are perhaps more familiar and thus more comfortable with traditional poetic genres; although our novelists are almost nonexistent, the number of Hawaiian poets is virtually endless.

Contemporary poetry draws from two traditions: Native Hawaiian oral traditions going back centuries, and foreign influences, from Shakespearean sonnets to spoken word. Poets such as Joe Balaz, Pualani Burgess, Ho'oipo DeCambra, Dana Naone Hall, Mahealani Kamau'u, 'maikalani IKal hele, Leialoha Apo Perkins, Haunani-Kay Trask, and Wayne Kaumuali'i Westlake are some of the earliest voices of the Hawaiian Renaissance whose powerful words still resonate and strongly influence younger generations of Hawaiians today. Although contemporary poets tend to write primarily in the English language, each has a unique style. For example, Joe Balaz's collection of "amplified poetry," a CD recording titled *Electric Laulau* (1998) showcases his pidgin poetry in a way difficult to capture in print. 'maikalani Kal hele's collection *Kalahele, Poetry and Art* (2002) includes his own stylized pen and ink drawings to illustrate his thought-inspiring work. Most noted for her political activism, Haunani-Kay Trask's *Light in a Crevice Never Seen* (1999) and *Night Is a Sharkskin Drum* (2003) are two breathtaking collections of contemporary Hawaiian poetry that exquisitely capture modern Hawaiian expressions of *aloha 'aina* and *ku*'.

As rap and hip-hop have influenced spoken-word poetry, new Hawaiian writers/performers, such as Katana, have become popular. Some spoken-word artists such as Lopaka Kapanui, eschew print media altogether, preferring to release CD audio recordings of their work, such as *Poetry without a Net* (2001).

Because of its connection to performance and oral traditions, Hawaiian playwrights have also enjoyed success. Dramatists such as Alani Apio, Tammy Hailiʻpua Baker, Lee Cataluna, and Victoria Kneubuhl have produced powerful works that poignantly capture the triumphs and tribulations of the modern Hawaiian experience. A recent anthology, *He Leo Hou: A New Voice—Hawaiian Playwrights* (2003), includes some of the best works of these important Hawaiian writers. Baker's work is particularly of note, as she writes and produces Hawaiian-themed plays almost exclusively in the Hawaiian language.

Where Hawaiian language newspapers were the primary repositories of Hawaiian literature throughout the 19th and early part of the 20th centuries, literary journals and anthologies have been the mainstay of Hawaiian literature since. Hawaiian writers do get published in literary magazines, anthologies, and journals, and some publish their own books. Books of particular note are *Hoʻom noa* (1989), an anthology of Hawaiian literature edited by Joe Balaz, and *ʻOiwi: A Native Hawaiian Journal* (1998–present). Established by founding editor M healani Dudoit, *ʻOiwi* is the only contemporary publication dedicated to exclusively publishing the art and writing of Native Hawaiians. Many, however, express frustration at the difficulty of getting published because of cultural differences in literary aesthetics—what editors and publishers consider "good" literature worthy of publication.

Vibrant and complex, Hawaiian literature has continued to evolve and grow with time and outside influences. Reflecting both values of the ancient past and thoughts of the modern era, it holds a unique place as an ethnic "American" literature. Not a part of the North American continent, Hawaiʻi is "American" only because a non-Hawaiian ethnic minority lobbied for Hawaiʻi's annexation to the United States, which occurred illegally in 1898, despite strident Hawaiian protest. As such, Hawaiian literature continues to reflect ancient themes expressing *aloha ʻaina*—love and patriotism to a beloved land base, celebration of traditional cultural beliefs both ancient and modern—and *k ʻ*—resistance to American colonialism, as Hawaiians continue to assert themselves as indigenous Pacific people seeking self-determination and political independence. (*See also* Hawaiʻi Literature)

Further Reading
Holt, John Dominis. *Waimea Summer*. Honolulu: Kupaʻa, 1998.
Hoʻomanawanui, Kuʻualoha. "He Lei Hoʻoheno no na Kau a Kau: Language, Performance and Form in Hawaiian Poetry." *The Contemporary Pacific* (Fall 2004): 29–82.
Kal hele, ʻmaikalani. a I *Kalahele, Poetry and Art*. Honolulu: Kalamaku, 2002.
Liliʻuokalani. *Hawaiʻi's Story by Hawaiʻi's Queen*. Honolulu: Mutual Publishing, 1990.
Trask, Haunani-Kay. "Writing in Captivity: Poetry in a Time of Decolonization" and "Decolonizing Hawaiian Literature." In *Inside/Out: Literature, Cultural Politics, and*

Identity in the New Pacific, 17–26, 167–82. Lanham, MD: Rowman & Littlefield, 1999.

Wat, John H.Y., and Meredith M. Desha. *He Leo Hou: A New Voice—Hawaiian Playwrights.* Honolulu: Bamboo Ridge Press, 2003.

Kuʻualoha Hoʻomanawanui

HOSSEINI, KHALED (1965-)

Khaled Hosseini is an Afghan American writer and physician. Hosseini's first novel, *The Kite Runner* (2003), is at once a personal journey, an expose of diabolical class separation, a concise history of the demise of Afghanistan, and a devastatingly sad novel about sins and atonement. Amir, the narrator, is fascinated by the concept of sinning from the time he is a little boy and routinely contemplates its meaning while assessing his own sins.

Amir grows up in Kabul, the privileged son of Baba, a powerful, intelligent, yet remote *Pashtun*. While in fifth grade, a teacher of Islamic doctrine identifies drinking alcohol as a sin. Confused, Amir reports this lesson to his father as his father is mixing himself a cocktail. Baba tells Amir that there is only one sin: theft. All sins, he explains, are simply a variation of theft, including lies and murders, because someone is robbed of something.

Although Afghan class protocol demands that *Hazaras* remain servile to the *Pashtuns* who employ them, Hassan, the son of Ali, Baba's *Hazara* servant, and Amir are nearly inseparable. Their favorite pastime is reading tales from *The Shahnamah* (the Persian *Epic of the Kings*), which Amir must read to Hassan because he is illiterate.

Khaled Hosseini, left, with Marc Foster at the premiere of *The Kite Runner* in 2007. (AP Photo/ Matt Sayles)

The boys' characters reflect their social status. Hassan, the humble servant, is honorable, forgiving, and resilient. Amir, the coddled son, is weak, easily intimidated, and subject to jealousy that, at times, causes him to behave reprehensibly. During a kite-running tournament, Amir commits the sin—failing to rescue Hassan from Assef, the neighborhood bully—for which he spends his life atoning. Amir's guilt is so profound that during any crisis, he vomits, attempting to purge his sin. Throughout his life, Amir accepts his grave emotional losses as his penitence.

When Amir returns to Kabul 20 years after fleeing from the Russian invasion, he learns that he and Hassan are half-brothers, a stunning revelation because Baba committed the one sin he decried. Ironically, the two men who are the architects of this theft are named Ali and Baba, like the 40 thieves in another Persian epic. In the end, Baba, Ali, and Amir are nearly exonerated. The real crime is the artificial class separation that pits a family against itself.

The almost-too-tidy plot revolves around characters who are Afghan caricatures demonstrating the brutal paradoxes of a harsh, war-ravaged environment. For example, the evil Assef, who idolizes Hitler, grows into a vile, tyrannical Taliban leader who stages stonings in Kabul's arena. And Rahim Khan, Baba's lifelong friend and sage, who declares the Taliban inhumane, puts in motion the chain of events that leads Amir to repent for his sin by becoming a man who fights his own battles. These two characters are the opposite poles between which all hapless Afghan citizens are tossed.

Further Reading
Aubrey, Timothy. "Afghanistan Meets the Amazon: Reading The Kite Runner in America." *PMLA* 124.1 (2009): 25–43.

Suzanne Hotte Massa

HOUSE ON MANGO STREET, THE

Sandra Cisneros's fictional account of a Chicana growing up in an urban Hispanic community is inspired by her own experience of growing up in a barrio in Chicago. This Mexican American coming-of-age novel is distinguished by its formal experimentation: it is composed of a series of vignettes in first- and third-person narratives, narrated from the vantage point of childhood and early adolescence. Together, these stories create a composite picture of a Latino immigrant community. The naïve point of view and simple diction are disarming. What this early-adolescent perspective enables is a fresh and searing critique of the hierarchical world built on various exclusions and subordinations.

The narrator is a girl, Esperanza, who attends Catholic high school and whose family's desire for the American dream house is compromised by the limitations of class. They can afford only a small and shabby house on Mango Street. Esperanza learns firsthand the alienation of those who do not belong to the norm or the dominant group: she experiences the discriminations of gender (being a girl in a male-dominant culture); **race** (being brown in a white-dominant society); **ethnicity** (being Chicana, not Anglo-American); class (being poor, not middle class); and language (being bilingual in an Anglophone society). Through her own and others' experiences she discovers the daily subordination by gender, the process of socialization by which girls learn to become "girls" and boys to become "boys." Esperanza and her friends discover high heels and the function of hips; their innocent play barely disguises the grim script of femininity: girls becoming sex objects, with reproduction as the ultimate justification of womanhood. Sally's and Rafaela's stories of punishing fathers and husbands demonstrate both the pervasive fear of female sexuality and the imperative to control it. The girls and women in Esperanza's neighborhood seem to have adapted to the double standards and limitations of their gendered roles, suffering sexual abuse, domestic violence, and abandonment. Esperanza herself is subject to sexual harassment on her first job, and to date rape.

All of the above factors contribute to her being unhappy with her own **identity** and life—she likes neither her name nor her house. Even though none of these oppressive constructs of race, class, gender, or sexuality are of her making, she experiences shame and self-loathing. Fortunately, she is not silenced; rather, she aspires for change. Like the skinny trees in her neighborhood, she endures and grows. A budding writer, she wants a house of her own (echoing the feminist writer Virginia Woolf's desire for a "room of her own") and, unlike Sally, refuses to be guided by sexist norms. She knows her aspirations will make her leave the world of Mango Street behind. However, she realizes that she owes something to those who do not have the strength and mobility she has. Aware of the privilege of education, she hopes to empower them through her writing. This refusal to forget or dissociate herself from her cultural and class origins distinguishes her from all those who succumb to normative social pressures and assimilate into the dominant world.

Further Reading

Gutierrez-Jones, Leslie S. "Different Voices: The Re-*Bildung* of the Barrio in Sandra Cisneros' *The House on Mango Street*." In *Anxious Power: Reading, Writing, and Ambivalence in Narrative by Women*, edited by Carol J. Singley and Susan Elizabeth Sweeney, 295–312. Albany: State University of New York Press, 1993.

Madsen, Deborah L. "Sandra Cisneros." In *Understanding Contemporary Chicana Literature*, 105–34. Columbia: University of South Carolina Press, 2000.

Olivares, Julian. "Sandra Cisneros' *House on Mango Street* and the Poetics of Space." In *Beyond Stereotypes: The Critical Analysis of Chicana Literature*, edited by Maria Herrera-Sobek, 160–70. Binghamton, NY: Bilingual Press, 1985.

Quintana, Alvina E. "*The House on Mango Street*: An Appropriation of Word, Space, and Sign." In *Home Girls: Chicana Literary Voices*, 54–74. Philadelphia: Temple University Press, 1996.

Gurleen Grewal

HUGHES, LANGSTON (1902–1967)

Langston Hughes was an African American poet, playwright, memoirist, and novelist. With Walt Whitman, Hughes figures as one of America's great poets of the people. His body of work has been quoted and referenced so profusely throughout the culture that Hughes might be said to be a cultural institution. Emerging, while in his late teens, as a key voice of the **Harlem Renaissance** of the 1920s, Hughes went on to produce more than 50 books ranging in genre from poetry, fiction, and drama to children's literature, sociocultural commentary, biography, and autobiography.

Born in Joplin, Missouri, Hughes was the son of James Nathaniel Hughes and Carrie Mercer Langston Hughes. The couple separated when their son was very young. James Hughes, disillusioned with life in the United States, moved to Mexico, where he remained. Langston Hughes only visited him a few times, and the two were never close. Throughout Hughes's childhood, his mother struggled economically and moved frequently. Carrie Hughes, who loved literature and the theater, worked a variety of jobs to make ends meet, leaving her young son for long stretches of time in the care of her mother, Mary Langston, in Lawrence, Kansas. When his grandmother died, Hughes joined his mother, her second husband Homer Clark, and his stepbrother, first in Lincoln, Illinois, then in Cleveland, Ohio, where he attended Central High School, excelling academically and becoming known for his writing ability. His first poem to be published for a national audience, "The Negro Speaks of Rivers," appeared in 1921, shortly following his high school graduation, in *The Crisis*, a magazine edited by W.E.B. Du Bois that, over the next decade, regularly featured the young poet's work.

After staying briefly with his father in Mexico, Hughes arrived in New York City in 1922 to begin studies at Columbia University. According to Hughes's biographer Arnold Rampersad, although financial problems marred Hughes's short-lived career at Columbia, his entry into the Harlem cultural scene was pivotal in shaping the poet's sense of African American **identity** and his desire to render black speech, experience, and musical forms in poetry. He developed contacts and friendships with Du Bois, the novelist Jessie Fauset, Countee Cullen, Arna Bontemps, **Zora Neale Hurston**, and Alain Locke. The latter, an African American scholar and critic, included Hughes's work in *The New Negro* (1925), a multigenre anthology celebrating the depth and variety of the literary work associated with modernism, the Harlem Renaissance, and with the unapologetically black-centered vision of a new generation of writers. Although from 1922 until 1926, Hughes worked several jobs that yielded little stability—including working as a mess-boy on a commercial ship destined for West Africa and living in Paris after jumping ship on a voyage to Europe—these years were significant in the growth of Hughes's pan-African consciousness. Further, these early "wandering" years culminated in the publication of his first book of poems, *The Weary Blues* (1926).

Harlem and Beyond: A New Poetry

Walt Whitman and Carl Sandburg were early poetic influences for Hughes, particularly in their democratic themes, their accessibility, and their expansion of free verse. *The Weary Blues* reflects not only these influences, but also those of the streets and nightclubs of Harlem. The title poem incorporates actual **blues** lyrics into a sketch of a Lenox Avenue bluesman singing and playing the piano until dawn. "Sweet Blues!" the poem exclaims, "Coming from a black man's soul." As a prefatory poem to this widely acclaimed first book, Hughes included the poem "Negro," which both glories in a heritage that long preceded the founding of the American republic and plainly bears witness to that republic's indebtedness to and continued oppression of the race. More "genteel" critics—both black and white—expressed reservations about Hughes's depiction of prostitutes and gin-drinking club denizens (the book was published in the midst of Prohibition), but Hughes, like many modernist poets of the time, was committed to moving poetry out of the parlor and into the thick of life.

Hughes was adamant about the importance of writing from an African American perspective and of embracing both the sacred and profane aspects of identity and experience. "The Negro Artist and the Racial Mountain," an article he wrote for *The Nation* in 1926, amounts to a manifesto refusing the lure of assimilation by Eurocentric cultural traditions. Also in this year, Hughes began studies at Lincoln University, a historically black college in Pennsylvania. While completing his bachelor's degree, he continued to publish his work, including his second book of verse, *Fine Clothes to the Jew* (1927), "his most brilliant book of poems, and one of the more astonishing books of verse ever published in the United States—comparable in the black world to *Leaves of Grass* in the white" (Rampersad 141). Many of the poems, including "Suicide," "Hard Luck," and "Po' Boy Blues," follow the 12-bar blues lyric stanza, and the personae throughout the collection are often workers confined to "Negro" jobs—"Elevator Boy," spittoon cleaner—and women whose energies are sapped by the conditions of their lives and people at the margins, such as the speaker in "Mulatto," who is rejected by the white father with a history of using the bodies of black women like "toys."

The 1930s is viewed as the most politically radical decade in Hughes's career, for he frequently published in left-leaning periodicals such as *New Masses* and *Negro Worker*. During the Cold War years of the 1950s, he, along with Du Bois and actor Paul Robeson, would be accused by conservatives of communist sympathies; Hughes himself had to testify before a subcommittee on subversive activities led by Senator Joseph McCarthy. Indeed, Hughes did use his poetry to directly criticize racial and economic injustice under American capitalism, with such works as the powerful "Three Songs about Lynching," "Let America Be America Again," and "Goodbye Christ." This latter poem, identifying with Marxist atheism and renouncing Jesus on the grounds that self-interested institutions have "pawned [him]/Till [he's] done wore out," alienated Hughes from many of his readers. Hughes published a number of poems on a 20-year case in Scottsboro, Alabama, in which eight young African American men charged with raping two white women had been sentenced to death. In addition, he became actively involved in the Spanish Civil War and the struggle against fascism in that country, reflecting his concerns and experience in poetry and prose.

In 1942, Hughes published *Shakespeare in Harlem*, which explores the ballad tradition while continuing, in poems such as "Ku Klux," to bear witness to injustice. This volume was followed by *Fields of Wonder* (1947) and by *One-Way Ticket* (1949), the latter of which introduced readers to one of Hughes's most-loved personae, Madam Alberta K. Johnson, an African American woman who faces daily problems—such as the phone bill, the rent, and disappointment in love—with attitude and voice. The book's title poem reflects Hughes's disgust with the lack of change in American **race** relations, especially in the Jim Crow South, voicing a desire to move elsewhere.

The famous line "What happens to a dream deferred?" governs the "riffs, runs, breaks, and distortions" of *Montage of a Dream Deferred* (1951), a book-length sequence composed "in the manner of a jam session," as Hughes explained in his preface to the book, and meant to reflect thematically and formally Harlem life in the wake of its **Jazz** Age glory. Bridging longer, more conventional free-verse lyrics like "Theme for English B" with snappy interludes recalling the musical theme, *Montage* also draws on cinematic technique even as it calls into question the film industry's representation of blacks.

With international status as a major American poet, Hughes edited his own *Selected Poems* (1959) and read and spoke all over the world. Hughes's longest poem, published in book form as *Ask Your Mama! Twelve Moods for Jazz* (1961), plays off the African American rhetorical practice of the "dozens," in which insults are traded within certain unwritten limits. Although the text of this poem loosely provides musical accompaniments and lends itself to performance, it is also a highly experimental, even postmodern, text consisting of prose poetry, spatial versification, and syntactic fragmentation. Hughes's final book of poetry, *The Panther and the Lash* (1967), was published posthumously. *The Collected Poems of Langston Hughes*, edited by Arnold Rampersad and David Roessel, appeared in 1995 and includes many previously unseen poems.

Story, Stage, and Newsprint

Hughes was also an accomplished writer of prose fiction. In his late 20s, he published a novel, *Not without Laughter* (1930), to much acclaim; reviewers found the characters and setting of the novel to be true to a kind of American experience seldom seen in the fiction published at the time. Hughes based some of the novel on his own childhood in the Midwest: the protagonist, Sandy Rodgers, is a boy being raised by his mother and grandmother in the fictional town of Stanton, Kansas; in using this setting, Hughes invokes a popular mainstream novel also set in Kansas and also dealing, although from a white perspective, with a young child's hopes and dreams: Frank L. Baum's *The Wizard of Oz*. More frequently, Hughes earned much of his living from short stories; collections include *The Ways of White Folks* (1934), *Laughing to Keep from Crying* (1952), and *Something in Common and Other Stories* (1963). More recently, these and others have been published in a single volume, *Short Stories of Langston Hughes* (1997).

With his love of theater and performance, passed on in part by his mother, Hughes was nearly always involved in writing plays, librettos, and musicals. *Five Plays by Langston Hughes* (1963) includes *Mulatto: A Tragedy of the Deep South*, which was written in 1930 and produced on Broadway in 1935, and *Tambourines to Glory*, a gospel-laced play that Hughes characterized as a "folk ballad in stage form" involving the struggle of good against evil. Perhaps Hughes's greatest and most enduring stage success was *Black Nativity*, which premiered on Broadway in 1961. His activist drama—including the 1932 *Scottsboro Limited*—has been collected in *The Political Plays of Langston Hughes* (2000).

Hughes was a prolific writer of literature for children. *The Dream Keeper* (1932) is a collection of Hughes's more youth-friendly poems, among them the well-known "Mother to Son." His children's books, such as *The First Book of the Negroes*

(1952) and *The First Book of Africa* (1964), both teach and entertain young readers. Hughes also lent his pen to numerous books designed to educate adult readers on the richness of African American contributions to American culture. And, from 1942 until 1966, Hughes wrote a column for the black-owned Chicago *Defender* that frequently featured humorous sketches from the imagined life of Jesse B. Semple, or "Simple," a character who so endeared himself to readers that these columns have been collected into more than five volumes, including the posthumous *The Return of Simple* (1994).

Langston Hughes wrote two memoirs, *The Big Sea* (1940) and *I Wonder as I Wander* (1956). In these, Hughes shares insights into the family, community, culture, and society that alternately nurtured, disappointed, and enraptured him. In a career encompassing both the Harlem Renaissance and the Black Arts Movement of the 1960s, both the Jim Crow era and the Civil Rights Movement, Hughes's prodigious output registers the perceptions, experiences, and dreams of an individual "genius child" who wrote for and from a larger collectivity. (*See also* African American Poetry)

Further Reading

Barksdale, Richard K. *Langston Hughes: The Poet and His Critics*. Chicago: American Library, 1977.

Gates, Henry Louis, and K. A. Appiah, eds. *Langston Hughes*. New York: Amistad, 1993.

Kent, George E. "Langston Hughes and Afro-American Folk and Cultural Tradition." In *Langston Hughes: Black Genius*, edited by Therman B. O'Daniel, 183–210. New York: William Morrow, 1971.

Rampersad, Arnold. *The Life of Langston Hughes*. 2 vols. New York: Oxford University Press, 1986, 1988.

Tidwell, John Edgar, and Cheryl R. Roger, eds. *Montage of a Dream: The Art and Life of Langston Hughes*. Columbia, MO: University of Missouri Press, 2007.

Ellen McGrath Smith

HURSTON, ZORA NEALE (1891–1960)

Zora Neale Hurston was an African American novelist, folklorist, short-story writer, and playwright. A highly visible effervescent personality during the **Harlem Renaissance**, Hurston gathered wealthy patrons, fellowships, and praise for her short stories, plays, and collections of Southern black folklore. She published four novels, two books of folklore, and an autobiography between 1934 and 1948. All received good reviews and sold well, but Hurston's work was dismissed by black male critics as irrelevant, unrealistic, and useless because it did not ideologically further the struggle for black equality or depict the horrors of life in the South for many Negroes. Hurston was a free-spirited artist, not an angry protester of **racism**, and she wrote of life as she knew and observed it. Because she refused to be "tragically black," all of her works were out of print when she died. During the 1970s, however, Pulitzer Prize–winning author **Alice Walker**, searching for the matrilineal ancestors of African American fiction, rediscovered Hurston and reclaimed *Their Eyes Were Watching God* as one of the best novels of the 20th century. The work of Walker and of Hurston's first biographer Robert E. Hemenway gave birth to a new and powerful resurgence in Hurston scholarship. *Their Eyes Were Watching God* is now a standard text in African American literature and women's studies classes. Many readers also are inspired by Hurston's fearless, outrageous, and mesmerizing personality, her thoroughly unconventional lifestyle, and her refusal to compromise her genius to any obstacles, including three very brief marriages, criticism from black authors, lost jobs and fellowships, occasional extreme poverty, and a devastating false accusation of child sexual abuse.

Born in Notasulga, Alabama, Hurston was raised in Eatonville, Florida, a small all-black community 10 miles west of Orlando. Her father John Hurston's powerful presence and speaking voice called him to a career as a preacher, and the family lived for a time an idyllic life described in Hurston's delightfully entertaining autobiography *Dust Tracks on the Road* (1942). The fifth child and second daughter of eight surviving children, Zora's free-spirited, impudent, tomboyish ways angered her father, but were encouraged by her mother.

Hurston's first novel, *Jonah's Gourd Vine* (1934), is a fictionalized retelling of her parents' love and troubles. Her masterful transliteration of Southern black dialect and her unique way of describing even the harshest elements of black life without heavy-handed morbidity made *Jonah's Gourd Vine* a success with critics and readers alike. John Pearson, the main character, rises from rags to riches through his physical strength, intelligence, hard work, and powerful oratorical skills, but his personal magnetism makes him the target of women who boldly try to seduce him before and after his marriage. The rise and fall of this strong, talented, and sincere black preacher who is crowned and then condemned by a black community is beautifully written but did nothing to promote social change. Neither is this a feminist novel, since the good wife endures and dies, while loud, sexually assertive women force themselves on her husband, whose tragic flaw is yielding to them. Hurston presents life as she saw it, with all its complexities and unsolvable mysteries, but offers no answers. Her characters are the salt of the earth, both sinned against and sinning in their own community and unconcerned with the white world. Some, like John Pearson's stepfather, are as unusually striking as Emily Brontë's Heathcliff, and all are described with Hurston's uniquely humorous, droll, and slightly satiric tone. Zora was 14 when her mother died. Her father immediately married a 22-year-old Eatonville girl, leading to the disintegration of the family. Traveling from relative to relative and state to state, Zora went through a series of menial jobs including a one-year stint as lady's maid to an actress in a traveling troupe of white actors, who treated Zora as a novelty and a pet. She managed to complete her high school education by shaving 10 years off her age to enroll in a free Baltimore public school, then attended Morgan Academy, and subsequently began to pursue a degree at Howard University in Washington, D.C.

Urged to come to New York City in 1925 during the height of the Harlem Renaissance by the publisher of her first short stories, Zora arrived with no money but soon met and befriended practically all of the new Harlem Renaissance writers and their wealthy patrons. She also began studying anthropology and received a scholarship to travel to rural black communities in the South and record folktales. *Mules and Men* (1935) is a collection of her gathered folktales that differed so much from academic writing that some critics called it a novel, because a first-person narrator (Zora) describes her situation and the events surrounding the telling of the tales in a most entertaining manner. In 1936, Hurston traveled to Jamaica and Haiti to study Obeah and Voodoo. Using her charm and wit as a ticket into secret ceremonies, Zora fearlessly followed her subjects into backcountry settings, risking her life to learn about, observe, and partake in Voodoo rituals, which are recounted in *Tell My Horse: Voodoo and Life in Haiti and Jamaica* (1938).

While in Haiti, Hurston also wrote *Their Eyes Were Watching God*, a completely different type of work, which was published upon her return to the United States in 1937. The impetus for writing this feminist love story was Hurston's decision to suddenly leave a much younger man with whom she was passionately in love because he demanded more attention than Zora could spare. Writing this man out of her life resulted in Hurston's best written and most widely read work. The style is lyrical, sensuous, poetic, and spare. The main character, 16-year-old Janie, ignores her grandmother's stories about the violent and tragic history of her family and people, because she is too alive in the present to feel burdened by anyone else's past. Forced to marry an ugly old farmer to protect her from predatory men, Janie Crawford, refuses to bow down and become wifely and submissive. She cares nothing for property or security and soon runs away with a passing stranger, Joe Starks, simply because he is heading to new horizons. However, Starks, an ambitious man who becomes mayor and chief property owner in Eatonville, wants Janie to be his "trophy wife" and stay away from the common people (everyone else in town). Janie lives for sensations, not for ideas and books, so she feels trapped and betrayed. When Starks dies, Janie, a wealthy and attractive widow, refuses advances by black men of property and position and falls for a charming drifter named Tea Cake, who is considerably younger, gambles for a living, works only when he needs the money, treats Janie just like a friend, and brings her into the center of life with the "common folk."

Even though Tea Cake once stole all Janie's money, once beat her, and refuses to leave the Everglades in time to avoid a hurricane, Janie would rather die with Tea Cake than live a hundred years without him. When Tea Cake, insane from contracting rabies, tries to kill Janie, she waits for him to pull the trigger on five empty chambers, giving him every chance to come to his senses before she shoots him to save her own life. Even though Tea Cake bites her as he lies dying, she never seeks the rabies antidote that she knows Tea Cake needed. Instead, she returns to Eatonville in her overalls and tells her best girlfriend that she has lived enough in one year to survive on the memories for the rest of her life.

In her riveting romance, Hurston is more critical of patriarchal and bourgeoisie values within the black community than of racism and Jim Crow. Janie seems to be Hurston's alter ego, who would sacrifice everything for love, thrusting aside money, career, education, and reputation. Her unorthodox desire to be one of the poor folk rather than a middle-class wife is a resistance to patriarchally imposed roles that Hurston also embraced. Readers and most critics admired the novel, but influential black male critics such as **Richard Wright** and Ralph Ellison found nothing to praise in Hurston's valorization of the illiterate, improvident, fun-loving black population at the expense of the ambitious and financially successful black middle class. Hurston's fearless portrayal of life as she wanted to live it (for a while) celebrates a woman's desires, her right to choose a man rather than be chosen, and her liberty to follow her dream in search of romantic love or anything else.

Hurston's next novel, *Moses, Man of the Mountain* (1939), is a rewriting of the Exodus story with the Israelites in bondage shown, through their dialect, to be emblematic of black slaves in America. Black Americans have identified themselves with the Israelites in Egypt for centuries, and Hurston wanted to reveal the African tradition of Moses as chief magician, worshipped as a great deity himself in Africa and Haiti. Hurston's characterization of Moses has some strikingly prescient resemblances to **Martin Luther King Jr**. But in representing his tribe of followers, Hurston's satire is harsh. None of those who left Egypt will cross over into the Promised Land because they are an envious, vengeful, ignorant, complaining people who cannot rid themselves of their "slave mentality," expecting the great magician to provide for all their needs and wants. Women are especially petty and envious or selfish and proud. Hurston always charmingly sidestepped her experiences of discrimination and Jim Crow and believed that she was not hindered by a few local laws and ignorant crackers. Moses is similarly critical of everyone, even those with no beauty, charm, or wit, who thinks that freedom can be given as a gift or through legislation. Hurston implies that freedom is a state of mind, and those who don't possess it are weak and undeserving.

Hurston's intent in her last novel, *Seraph on the Sewanee* (1948), is also difficult to judge, because the main character, a "poor white trash" woman who has been trampled on since birth, endures and learns to accept a humiliating and completely subservient role in her marriage to a sexist and brutal husband who nevertheless loves her and she him. Hurston had observed that poor whites in the Florida turpentine camps lived similar lives to poor blacks and spoke a similar dialect, and she wanted to show that a black author could write convincingly about white people. The book received good initial reviews and sold well, but Hurston's arrest on trumped-up child sexual abuse charges shortly after the book was released kept her from promoting it. Hurston was devastated that a black court worker had leaked this libelous and lurid case to the black press, which publicly vilified her.

After being acquitted, Hurston left New York City and spent most of the rest of her life in Florida. She continued to write many articles and stories, worked temporary jobs when she needed the money, and labored on several novels, which were not accepted by publishers. Ironically, her last rediscovery by the general public before her death occurred when she was working as a maid for a wealthy white couple in Miami. When they accidentally realized how famous she was, Zora was not the least embarrassed to be found working as a domestic, and enjoyed the publicity and new literary assignments she received. Hurston could move in and out of work in positions as varied as anthropologist, drama professor, maid, and substitute teacher, leaving as soon as her genius called her back to her writing. She valued her freedom more than money, position, love and marriage, or the security to be found by holding on to any of these. (*See also* African American Novel)

Further Reading

Boyd, Valerie. *Wrapped in Rainbows: The Life of Zora Neale Hurston*. New York: Scribner, 2003.

Campbell, Josie P. *Student Companion to Zora Neale Hurston. Student Companions to Classic Writers Series*. Westport, CT: Greenwood Press, 2001

Hemenway, Robert. *Zora Neale Hurston: A Literary Biography*. Urbana: University of Illinois Press, 1981.

King, Lovalerie. *The Cambridge Introduction to Zora Neale Hurston*. Cambridge, England: Cambridge University Press, 2008.

Barbara Z. Thaden

I KNOW WHY THE CAGED BIRD SINGS

Maya Angelou's *I Know Why the Caged Bird Sings* is her first and most celebrated autobiographical narrative, and its publication in 1970 amounted to an urgent demand for black nationalists and white feminists alike to recognize the singular overcoming of adversity that marks the experiential "lifework" of black womanhood.

Taking its cue from the last stanza of Paul Laurence Dunbar's poem "Sympathy" (1899), Angelou's title refers to the narrator's achievement of empowering self-awareness in the face of personal injury. With the dissolution of their parents' marriage, three-year-old Marguerite Johnson (Angelou's name by birth) and her four-year-old brother, Bailey Jr., are sent from Long Beach, California, to Stamps, Arkansas, to live with their paternal grandmother, Mrs. Annie Henderson, or "Momma." In time Marguerite learns the racist social codes that separate black from white by observing those who patronize or pass by Momma's general store. Tempering the ever-present threat of a Klan lynching is Angelou's account of certain hilarious episodes of overzealous, even violent, worship by the church faithful.

When she is eight, Marguerite and Bailey are taken by their father, Bailey Sr., to stay with "Mother," Vivian Baxter, in St. Louis. Here Marguerite is molested and eventually raped by Mother's live-in boyfriend, Mr. Freeman. Soon after being found guilty of these crimes in court, Freeman is murdered, presumably by Baxter men out for revenge. Traumatized by this series of events, Marguerite returns to Stamps a morose, introverted child. It is Mrs. Bertha Flowers, Momma's educated neighbor and friend, who patiently relieves Marguerite of her silent mourning of innocence lost by encouraging the fragile but motivated girl to read books from her personal library.

Marguerite and Bailey move away from Stamps when they are teenagers to live with Mother in San Francisco. A turning point in Marguerite's life is the harrowing summer she spends with her father in his mobile home in Los Angeles: After being knifed by his live-in girlfriend during a heated argument, Marguerite settles among other abandoned and drifting youth in a junkyard for a month. Her return to San Francisco sees Bailey falling out with Mother, leaving home for good, and Marguerite fighting discriminatory hiring practices to become the first African American to work on the city's streetcars. The narrative ends with Marguerite, pregnant after having consensual sex for the first time, giving birth to her son as a 16-year-old single mother.

Despite offering imaginative and critical insight into black female **identity** formation and American social history more generally, Angelou's autobiography has been the target of censorship in intermediate and secondary schools across the nation. In particular, parents and administrators have objected to its "pornographic" representation of child sexual abuse in the form of Marguerite's rape. What goes unnoticed in such reproof is the main reason why schools took up the book in the first place: Angelou's coming-of-age narrative confronts the often harsh realities of her past as a means of inspiring readers to locate hope, determination, and self-assurance in their own lives. (*See also* African American Autobiography)

Further Reading

Braxton, Joanne M., ed. *Maya Angelou's "I Know Why the Caged Bird Sings": A Casebook.* New York: Oxford University Press, 1999.

Jaquin, Eileen O. "Maya Angelou." In *African American Autobiographers: A Sourcebook*, edited by Emmanuel S. Nelson, 10–28. Westport, CT: Greenwood Press, 2002.

Megna-Wallace, Joanne. *Understanding "I Know Why the Caged Bird Sings": A Student Casebook to Issues, Sources, and Historical Documents.* Westport, CT: Greenwood Press, 1998.

Smith, Sidonie Ann. "The Song of a Caged Bird: Maya Angelou's Quest after Self-Acceptance." *Southern Humanities Review* 7.4 (1973): 365–75.

Kinohi Nishikawa

IDENTITY

Identity, in general terms, relates to the specifics of who, what, and where about the person(s) and includes a series of markers that identify that person in terms of **race**, class, culture, gender, religion, **ethnicity**, and/or nationality. One's identity is an important aspect of self, but its varied representations in all forms of literature, in different genres as well as different time periods ranging from ancient to contemporary settings, delineate how identity reflects and marks up one's culture. The theme of identity or identity-in-the-being is thus a predominant one in literature. Countless examples of thematic exploration of identity can be found in ancient, medieval, modern, and postmodern literature. In the contemporary context of **multiculturalism** and transnational globalization, identity assumes even more significant relevance in cultural and sociological as well as economic terms.

Although each individual may be unique, social distinctions based on one's color, class, shared views, and lifestyle delegate people into distinguishing groups. Those sharing similar traits in a group become identified with that group—sometimes leading to a hierarchy among the groups. Historically, those identified with Euro-Western norms, and racially visible as white, have been ascribed as the standard example of the preferred group in the social hierarchy. All others have been given the label of an "ethnic" group. With the turn-of-the-century globalization, a need for comprehension of ethnicity has increased in life as well as in art.

Ethnic Identity in America

The contemporary multicultural scenario in what was earlier seen to be a world defined by Eurocentric norms now demands that attention is given to non-European interests. As a result, the term "ethnic identity" has come to the forefront in contemporary ethnic literature worldwide. In the U.S. multicultural context, ethnic identity has posited different ways of perceiving ethnicity according to different perceptions about American identity itself. A predominant question about identity in ethnic American literature is whether it is changeable or fixed. For instance, can a non-American become American by just crossing the border or is there more to acquiring an American identity? In terms of literary representation such questions point to the so-called politics of identity. Can a specific ethnicity be represented in only one way or are there other possible ways of representing that ethnic group? When some ethnic writers represent ethnic concerns differently they are seen as attempting to claim Americanism or catering to Western ideology. Likewise if some ethnic writers represent their ethnic group as "too ethnic" they are not fully accepted by "American"/Western readers.

Comprising a history of colonization, enslavement, racial discrimination, and immigration, the United States now epitomizes a conglomeration of diverse cultures and ethnicities amidst a rich mixture of languages, norms, religions, and values and offers the world a "crossroad culture," so to speak. Ethnic identity—the sense of sharing an ethnic heritage comprising common ancestry, shared beliefs, and lifestyles—is valued by many as the core of their sense of belonging. At the same time, living in America, the land of immigrants, and becoming American demands that ethnic identity not be merely exclusionary. It should rather enhance one's cultural heritage than exclude one from other coexisting groups and ethnicities. Thus important questions arise pertaining to how much of one's ethnic background should be abandoned for full acceptance or to become truly American. It becomes equally important to create an identity that is both ethnic and American simultaneously.

Discussions regarding ethnic identity in a North American context center on two existing characteristic models. The first model is commonly identified as the "melting pot" metaphor of **assimilation** that primarily caters to the Eurocentric notion of race mixing. Derived from Israel Zangwill's 1922 play *The Melting Pot*, the term refers to assimilationist urgency wherein old ethnicities are surrendered in favor of a new Anglophone American identity. In this case, the original ethnic identities "melt" and give way to an Americanized identity. The assimilationists thus believe that the minorities in America must discard their inferior racial/ethnic traits in order to be accepted in the American mainstream. A growing awareness of American multiculturalism has caused some Americans to challenge the earlier notions of the nation as a "melting pot" and to reconsider other models of identity that would strive to maintain a balance between one's ethnic identity and one's interaction within the American setting. Consequently, the second model of multiculturalism is based on cultural pluralism and strives to maintain diversity by preserving ethnic affiliations and differences. Commonly identified with the "salad bowl" metaphor, the second model, by preserving differences, hinders complete acceptance in the American culture. The multicultural world of America that tends to portray a melting-pot ideology or a pluralist national identity marks ethnic identity in hegemonic terms of difference and marginality. Thus ethnic identity always remains ethnic in a minimalist way and is different from the normative, mainstream American identity. This has become a kind of struggle for many contemporary writers. For instance, the reason why writers such as **Bharati Mukherjee** and **Richard Rodriguez** protest against their ethnic or hyphenated labeling and instead present themselves as exemplary American writers is that ethnicity (for them) works as a minimalist experience. Such impositions of an ethnic identity become defining terms of subjectivity against which these writers constantly struggle.

Writers of ethnic literature narratively perform, negotiate, resist, and even transgress identities within specific historical contexts. In doing so, these writers pursue the reexamination of available models and methods that shape our understanding of categories like "American," "ethnic," "multiculturalism," and "immigrant sensibility." In one way or another, ethnic literature, especially that written in the contemporary era, thus challenges a unitary concept of identity that defines one essentially as "Self" or as the "Other." Writers define identity in ethnic literature in terms of shared spaces that deal with history, memory, violence, home, and other concepts linked to ethnic discourse. At the same time, such representations also point to our assumptions about ethnic identity as being a prefixed notion and raises questions about ethnic labeling and assimilation in America. The idea that ethnic identity can be a constantly, dynamically changing concept and ultimately no longer exclusively "ethnic," calls our attention to our perception of ethnic identity only in terms of marginality or as a "minority" identity. When some ethnic writers represent such a concept of "Americanization," in which ethnic identity assimilates or acculturates, they are challenged for occluding ethnic origins and even encrypting ethnic identity.

Representations of ethnic identities in American literature are chiefly drawn from historical references and portray a diverse methodology of approaching cultural differences. Literary representations of ethnic identity are thus manifested through historical and sociological factors of the times influencing the experience of people identifying with a particular ethnic or group affiliation. For example, identity in African American literature of the 19th and 20th centuries is portrayed in relation to socially oppressive systems, such as slavery, and racial as well as gender discrimination. Likewise ethnic identity in Asian American literature of the 19th and 20th centuries draws upon the experience of discrimination faced through exclusionary, prohibitive immigration laws, as well as racial and gender discrimination.

Identity in the Context of Diaspora, Exile, and Migration

An understanding of certain key terms such as "diaspora," "exile," and "immigrant" is helpful in understanding the dynamic of the way a particular ethnic identity is represented in ethnic American literature. The word "diaspora" was originally used to refer to the dispersion of Jews outside of Israel when they were exiled to Babylonia. On a broader level, the term now refers to the dispersion of a community of people outside their homeland. The experience of diaspora thus entails a condition of "living" in two spaces at the same time. Expatriate communities who share a common diaspora share similar traits including a collective memory or vision of their ancestral homeland. They feel a sense of alienation and prejudice caused by their view that they will never be fully accepted by the host country where they now live. Their emotional bonds are more with the original homeland as they hope and believe that they will return there eventually. Because of these bonds, they strongly believe in collective commitment to maintenance and prosperity of the original homeland. The condition of "exile" is a more painful and traumatic emotional one when a sense of danger in the original homeland is involved, as it suggests punishment or banishment from one's homeland (although leaving can be voluntary or involuntary). Exile can be a solitary experience compared to diaspora, which is always collective. Thus an exile feels an even more extreme sense of alienation in the host country than a diasporic community does. Such a person feels nostalgic desire and pines for return to the homeland. Although in diasporic communities, the loss of homeland is replaced by collective efforts to maintain a "home outside home" as in ethnic enclaves like Chinatowns and Greek towns, the exiled individual feels a painful sense of homelessness. Such pulls and tugs of cultural as well as geographic dislocations have a considerable impact on one's identity.

The immigrant deals with similar concerns of displacement and cultural dislocation yet has a different outlook on the whole situation. The immigrant does not feel a state of perpetual exile, homelessness, or lifelong commitment to an ethnic affiliation. The term "immigrant" has been used in different ways in third world and minority people's struggles against invasion, colonialism, and political oppression. It seems now that in a rapidly globalizing world, the immigrants themselves conceptualize and express their identities in terms of individuality and choice rather than those of sociology as in the case of exile or diaspora. The immigrants thus learn to see and interact with the world and interpret it rather than relinquish it for the sake of their original homeland. However, the host country sometimes looks at the immigrant with suspicious eyes due to the perpetuation of certain ethnic stereotypes.

Thematically speaking, identity in ethnic American literature is thus represented as an experience of diaspora, exile, or migration. Ethnic American literature deals with issues of identity in flux or movement in relation to an American mainstream. The people in such literature are represented to be desperately seeking meaning as minorities, struggling with their circumstances of cultural displacement, or learning to maintain a balance between an ethnic heritage of the past and their identities adapting to the mainstream culture around them. Whereas ethnic heritage is represented through the shared historical past as in the circulation of myths, folktales, or legends, and the passing on of different familial and cultural values than the mainstream world, the adaptation of identities to mainstream culture is expressed through a multicultural approach that accepts the American ideals also.

Ethnic American writing is commonly categorized based on ethnic identity as in Asian American, African American, Jewish American, Native American, and Hispanic literatures. Respectively these branches of ethnic literature depict struggles and challenges faced by those of a particular ethnic identity. For example, in African American literature the vast range of experiences are drawn from slavery in the slave narratives, the oral transmission of folklore and myths, and the aesthetic of rebellion and protest. African American writing of the **Harlem Renaissance**, the **Civil Rights Movement**, and the modern-day call for acknowledgement of a strong African American identity in multicultural America. Works of **Frederick Douglass**, Charles W. Chesnutt, W.E.B. Du Bois, **Ralph Waldo Ellison**, **Harriet Jacobs**, **Toni Morrison**, **Zora Neale Hurston**, and **Toni Cade Bambara** are notable for their contribution to American literature.

Contemporary ethnic writing in America has greatly contributed to the way we understand ethnicity and multiculturalism. Writers such as Carlos Bulosan, Bharati Mukherjee, **Maxine Hong Kingston**, David Henry Hwang, Gloria Anzaldúa, Cherríe Moraga, **Navarre Scott Momaday**, **Amy Tan**, **Leslie Marmon Silko**, and many others have enriched the American literary scene.

Further Reading

Knippling, Alpana Sharma. *New Immigrant Literatures in the United States*. Westport, CT: Greenwood Press, 1996.

Sollors, Werner. *Theories of Ethnicity: A Classical Reader*. New York: New York University Press, 1996.

Parvinder Mehta

INTERNMENT

In 1942, under Executive Order 9066 issued by President Franklin D. Roosevelt, about 120,000 Japanese immigrants and American-born Japanese were uprooted from their West Coast homes and interned in inland camps.

The internment of Japanese Americans during World War II has been identified as one of the most regrettable events in American history. Officially declared to be a "military necessity," the relocation and incarceration of the West Coast Japanese Americans were really measures based on racial profile. Although the United States was also fighting Germany and Italy, German Americans and Italian Americans did not face the same mass internment as Japanese Americans. Also, although Hawai'i was in close proximity to Japan and the site of the Pearl Harbor bombing, Hawaiian Japanese Americans were spared the mass relocation. As Japanese Americans composed a significant portion of the Hawaiian population and were an indispensable workforce on the islands, they were not interned like their continental counterparts. Thus, the ground to intern Japanese Americans on the West Coast proves to be, not a "military necessity," but **racism**.

In fact the internment symbolizes the climactic point of half a century of anti-Japanese (and anti-Asian in general) sentiment on the Pacific Coast. Long before World War II, many immigration laws were enacted to bar the flow of Japanese (and Asian) immigrants and restrict them from becoming naturalized citizens. The passage of a series of alien land laws, which prohibited "aliens ineligible for citizenship" from buying and owning any real properties, created tremendous difficulties for them to gain a livelihood in America. However, the harsh laws and legislation

A Japanese American internment camp in Manzanar, California, 1942. (AP Photo)

did not repel Japanese Americans. On the contrary, the hardship compelled them to form strong ethnic communities. Although Japanese American communities were strengthened and indeed prevailed, the hostility and resentment of white farmers and workers were also aggravated. The Pearl Harbor incident turned racial prejudice and hatred into hysteria and paranoia.

Of the 120,000 internees, there were about 7,000 American citizens. Many of them were school-age children and elderly people. They were first taken to 16 temporary assembly centers and then further transported to 10 relocation camps in desolate places, including Tule Lake and Manzanar in California, Minidoka in Idaho, Heart Mountain in Wyoming, Topaz of Utah, Postona, Gila River in Arizona, Amache in Colorado, and Rohwer and Jerome in Arkansas. Both assembly centers and relocation camps were hastily installed buildings that resembled army barracks. An average apartment, measuring 20 feet by 25 feet, accommodated a family of four to six persons. It was also insufficiently and crudely equipped with a stove, army cots, and straw mattresses. Internees had to use communal bathrooms and waited in long lines to have their three meals in mess halls. Apart from the poor condition of housing and repressive daily routine, internees were also struggling with tough weather and environs on a daily basis.

The detrimental effects of the internment, which were not only financial and physical, but also profoundly psychological, are reflected in Japanese American writings. Japanese American writers grappled with questions of loyalty, home, and **identity**, in works published in camp magazines such as *Tulean Dispatch* (Tule Lake, California), *The Pen* (Rowher, Arkansas), and *Trek* (Topaz, Utah). In the immediate postwar decade, Mine Okubo's *Citizen 13660* (1946), Yamamoto's "The Legend of Miss Sasagawara" (1951), and Monica Sone's *Nisei Daughter* (1953) focus on Japanese American identity and on internment life and its effect on the characters. Later, the ethnic movement and the redress movement encouraged more writers to reexamine the history and recuperate personal memories. For example, Jeanne Wakatsuki Houston and James Houston's *Farewell to Manzanar* (1973), an autobiographical text, depicts camp life and difficulty with reintegration into American society. Mitsuye Yamada's collection of poems titled *Camp Notes* (1976) also centers on the internment experience and postwar resettlement. In 1982, Yoshiko Uchida, a well-known author of children's literature, published *Desert Exile*, an autobiography chronicling her family's displacement and internment during World War II. (*See also* Japanese American Autobiography)

Further Reading

Chung. *An Absent Presence: Japanese Americans in Postwar American Culture, 1945–1960.* Durham, NC: Duke University Press, 2001.

Takaki, Ronald. *Strangers from a Different Shore: A History of Asian Americans.* Boston: Little, Brown and Company, 1989.

Yogi, Stan. "Japanese American Literature." In *An Interethnic Companion to Asian American Literature*, edited by King-Kok Cheung, 125–55. New York: Cambridge University Press, 1997.

Shuchen Susan Huang

INVISIBLE MAN

Published in 1952 and recipient of the National Book Award in 1953, **Ralph Waldo Ellison**'s *Invisible Man* has been hailed as a masterpiece of African American, American, and world literature. Informed by the epic scope of Herman Melville, the existential vision of Fyodor Dostoevsky, and the **blues** ethos of black cultural expression, the only novel Ellison completed before his death in 1994 is an allegory of the alienated continuity of the black experience in the United States.

The book begins with a confession: "I am an invisible man." Thus are readers introduced to the unnamed black protagonist who says that his narrative will explain why he has been in "hibernation" for so long and why the present is the time for "action." His story is initially set in the Deep South, where he participates in a "Battle Royal" that has black boys fighting each other for the entertainment of whites. The narrator is also subjected to deliberate sexual prohibition when a voluptuous white stripper dances in front of the boys and white men. Left in an abject state of guilt and disgust, he ironically receives a scholarship to attend a college not unlike Tuskegee Institute.

Though his first years at school are promising, the narrator makes an unforgivable faux pas when he takes Mr. Norton, the white benefactor whose philanthropy is more a function of liberal condescension than genuine concern, to see the destitute and incestuous Trueblood family. Norton's exposure to the family rekindles sexual longing for his dead daughter, and condemnation of the narrator is a way to lash out against his own perversion. Dr. A. Herbert Bledsoe, the president of the college, is an ingratiating public figure who caters to white demands in order to secure power and prestige over other blacks; he expels the narrator after the Trueblood episode.

The narrator moves to New York City and there finds a job in the Liberty Paints factory making the aptly named "Optic White." When that predictably suffocating position terminates in a machinery explosion, he returns to Harlem and is quickly enlisted in the Brotherhood, a quasi-communist revolutionary group led by the white, one-eyed Brother Jack. Jack's counterpart is Ras the Destroyer, a militant Garveyite who criticizes the Brotherhood for its patronizing stance toward blacks. The narrator thus finds himself caught between a white socialist and a black nationalist, neither of whom "sees" him for who he is. Tod Clifton, a black activist formerly linked to the Brotherhood, is similarly disillusioned with Harlem politics and resorts to selling Sambo dolls on the street. In search of a scapegoat, the Brotherhood blames the narrator for Clifton's disappearance from its ranks; he responds by going undercover and impersonating a man-about-town. But when Clifton is killed by a white police officer, a full-blown riot erupts in Harlem, and the resulting fracas sees the narrator literally go undercover. In a manhole he suffers a castration fantasy that paradoxically frees him of all "illusion," thereby granting him the resolve to commit his story to paper.

Ellison's is the most compelling novel about psychic estrangement from a sense of social and cultural belonging in postwar American letters. Moreover because it signaled upon publication a definitive break from the African American literary protest tradition, it has enabled countless black authors since to write not necessarily "for" or in the name of their **race** but on terms of their own artistic choosing. (*See also* African American Novel)

Further Reading

Baker, Houston A. Jr. "To Move without Moving: An Analysis of Creativity and Commerce in Ralph Ellison's Trueblood Episode." *PMLA* 98.5 (1983): 828–45.

Callahan, John F., ed. *Ralph Ellison's* Invisible Man: *A Casebook*. New York: Oxford University Press, 2004.

Nadel, Alan. *Invisible Criticism: Ralph Ellison and the American Canon*. Iowa City: University of Iowa Press, 1988.

Warren, Kenneth W. *So Black and Blue: Ralph Ellison and the Occasion of Criticism*. Chicago: University of Chicago Press, 2003.

Kinohi Nishikawa

IRANIAN AMERICAN LITERATURE

Although many Iranians came to the United States prior to the Iranian Revolution of 1979 (ostensibly for higher education and training during the period of close U.S.-Iran relations with the former Shah), the largest number arrived here after the popular uprising that led to the overthrow of Mohammad Reza Shah and the establishment of the Islamic Republic and clerical rule. Approximately three million Iranians left Iran between 1979 and 1985; the largest number of these exiles, refugees, and immigrants settled in the United States and a smaller number settled in Western Europe. Many Iranians temporarily settled in major urban centers such as Los Angeles, Houston, Chicago, and New York, hoping to return eventually to their homeland, but with the outbreak of the Iran-Iraq War, which lasted for nearly a decade, many Iranians made the United States their permanent home.

Expatriate Writing Prior to 1979

Although prior to 1979, Iranians living in the United States did not suffer from the dramatic stereotypes and stigmas associated with the revolution and the taking of U.S. hostages at the American embassy in Tehran, writers of Iranian origin still had to contend with the difficulties of trying to convey their culture to an American audience largely unfamiliar with their background. These writers contributed to a body of work that introduced American readers to ideas about Iranian culture and history, and embodied an expatriate sensibility—that is, they wrote about their individual sojourns as immigrants or rendered in English their memories and experiences of Iran. Early Iranian American writers include novelists Taghi Modaressi (*The Book of Absent People* [1986] and *The Pilgrim's Rules of Etiquette* [1989]), Nahid Rachlin (*Foreigner* [1978], *Married to a Stranger* [1983], and *Veils* [1992]), Manoucher Parvin (*Cry for My Revolution: Iran* [1987]), and Donné Raffat (*The Caspian Circle* [1978]). Ali Zarrin and Bahman Sholevar are among the first published Iranian American poets to write in English. The impetus of these writers is in part to maintain a connection with their homeland and to make sense of the expatriate experience; the novels suggest a kind of "outsiderness" in the United States as well as in their native Iran. Each of these authors had been living outside of Iran for a considerable time before writing their respective novel(s).

Modaressi, Parvin, and Raffat, the three male novelists, have a preoccupation with politics, history, and the social struggles within Iran. Readers are guided through a labyrinth of political and sociological shifts taking place in Iran before and after the revolution: Raffat's *The Caspian Circle* is foregrounded by events surrounding the overthrow of Mohammad Mossadeq; Modaressi's novels deal with the political repression of the Shah and its impact on one family, as well as the tumultuous events of the revolution and its impact on the intellectual elite; and in Parvin's novel, an Iranian student living in the United States has aspirations to overthrow the Shah. These authors articulate a concern with the male discursive realms of politics, history, and social discourses.

Rachlin, on the other hand, who herself immigrated to the United States as a student and married an American, is preoccupied with her status as an Iranian woman trying to negotiate her Iranian upbringing with some of her newfound liberties as a woman in the United States. Rachlin's first novel, *Foreigner*, was, to a great extent, a pathbreaker since it was the first time American audiences had heard directly from an Iranian woman.

Exile, Memory, and Translation—Post-1979 Writing

The revolution and its aftermath made exiles of writers and intellectuals, many of whom experienced their exile as what Hamid Naficy has called a "profound dystopia"—a sense of paralyzing crisis and a nostalgia for home (Naficy 10–15). For postrevolutionary writers, loss of their physical home, their language, culture, and even the audiences with whom they communicated became even more remote with the establishment of the Islamic Republic and the backlash against intellectuals and writers who were perceived as too Western. Being part of the intellectual elite that faced certain censorship or persecution in Iran after the establishment of the Islamic Republic, many disaffected writers and artists settled in the United States after 1979.

For those who did survive the move west and transformed their exile into a literary creation, memoirs and autobiographies were the genre of preference. First-generation Iranian writers often wrote from the perspective of their exile and alienation as individuals, but also presented narratives of collective dissolution. Living outside Iran had both its positive and negative aspects; for women, particularly, exile presented opportunities to refashion themselves against the strict edicts of the new Islamic government preoccupied with dictating women's behavior, dress, and position as part of its attempt to define a new national, Islamic **identity**. But exile also conjures fundamental losses that, despite living in the more liberal West, cannot be healed.

Autobiography, Ethnography, and Exilic Memoirs

Memoir, whether political or literary, represents the most successful example of this emergent literature engaging mainstream interest and acceptance. The memoir form lends itself perfectly to a concern with the past and with personal memory, particularly the period before the Iranian Revolution. A number of political and literary memoirs have also been marketed as "personal accounts" of the "Islamic revolution" or have been cast as counter-narratives to the often simplistic and stereotyped image of Iran and Islamic people that was often portrayed in the U.S. media. These memoirs have presented an opportunity for individual Iranians to speak for themselves and to step outside the rhetoric of politics, particularly the radical poles of Iranian and American official government rhetoric, and to voice an individual subjectivity. Among those memoirs written in the late 1980s and early 1990s are Shusha Guppy's *Blindfold Horse: Memories of a Persian Childhood* (1988) and *Daughter of Persia: A Woman's Journey from Her Father's Harem Through the Islamic Revolution* (1992) by Sattareh Farman Farmaian (coauthored with American writer Dona Munker). Both of these memoirs feature childhood memories of growing up in prominent, aristocratic families and portray a nostalgic and somewhat exoticized image of Iran. These works belong to a category we might loosely label the "exilic memoir"; an autobiographical narrative with an exilic sensibility and a social, political, and cultural relationship to Iran informed by his or her family's political and economic prominence. These "exilic memoirs" are driven less by an interest in literary expression and more urgently on a narrative of past events and ethnographic details that are under threat or lost in the upheaval of the revolution.

Blood and Oil: Memoirs of a Persian Prince (1997), an autobiographical text by another member of the Farman Farmaian family (half-brother of Sattareh), Manouchehr Farman Farmaian, coauthored with his daughter Roxanne Farman Farmaian. *Blood and Oil* can be read as a political memoir since it documents Manouchehr's involvement with the oil ministry of Iran under the Shah's government and his subsequent exile to Venezuela after the revolution.

From Memoir to Iranian American Literature

The memoir form has been central to the development of Iranian American literature in English largely because it has the capacity to encompass both personal and national history—something with which Iranian Americans continue to be very preoccupied as they struggle with their place as outsiders in Iranian culture and in U.S. society. In addition to the three previously mentioned memoirs, two writers of a younger generation offer their perspective of the Iranian Revolution and the forced migration of their families. Both Tara Bahrampour's *To See and See Again: A Life in Iran and America* (Farrar, Straus, and Giroux, 1999) and Gelareh Asayesh's *Saffron Sky: A Life Between Iran and America* (1999) chronicle a return to Iran after a period of absence from the country of their childhood and documents the dissonance between the Iran they grew up in and the Iran that they revisit as grown women long after the revolution. The theme of the return to Iran after a long separation surfaces again and again in much of the recent literature of the Iranian diaspora because it reflects the growing interest of young people, whose life circumstances were affected by the revolution, to travel to Iran but who, because of the nature of U.S.-Iran political relations or Iran's internal difficulties, were unable to visit Iran during the previous 20 years. This geographic, historical, and cultural rupture serves as the backdrop to these more recent memoirs that chronicle the shifting loyalties between Iran and the United States, and document the ongoing attempt to negotiate those divides as both a personal and literary "journey."

These texts describe the return journey to Iran after a period of separation following the revolution—a central theme in the narratives of their divided/bicultural identity. A further difference distinguishing these texts from narratives by exiles is their departure from Iran during childhood; and although the politics of the revolution affected them directly, they were less conscious of how it would shape them. They rely less on nostalgic memories, and instead attempt to negotiate past and present, thus recognizing that their childhood memories, although strong, have been clouded by the experience of having lived a life in America—a life between cultures. Bahrampour's book received considerable attention because her biography reflects a relatively common experience; she is the product of a mixed marriage between an Iranian father and an American mother. *To See and See Again* moves from the nostalgic recollections of her childhood in Iran to her present-day adult perspective when she returns to a pay a visit to her family as a 30-year-old woman.

The Emergence of a Distinct Iranian American Voice

The most recent memoir published to date, *Funny in Farsi: A Memoir of Growing Up Iranian* (2003), inaugurates a different sensibility. Rather than taking life in Iran as the primary focus (as in the previously mentioned memoirs), Firouzeh Dumas writes about her experiences of childhood and some of the cultural dissonance of growing up Iranian in the United States. Her memoir begins with her family's arrival in 1972 (a time when many young Iranian students and professionals were coming to the United States to study or work). Dumas had a comfortable few years in America afforded by her father's professional life. All that changed, however, when the revolution took place and her father lost his position in the National Iranian Oil Company. Like many of her generation, Dumas documents the painful memories of growing up in the United States during the period of the hostage crisis when many Iranians concealed their national identity by declaring themselves Turkish, Russian, or French. This memoir points to one of the themes shared in recent writing by second-generation Iranian Americans—the hostage crisis and its coverage in the U.S. media as the galvanizing moment for Iranian American identity. Although it had the effect of shaming and silence many young children, it also became the impetus for writing.

Many of the pieces in the first anthology of Iranian American writing, *A World Between: Poems, Short Stories, and Essays by Iranian-Americans* (1999), helped to articulate and solidify the literary and cultural concerns of second-generation Iranian Americans. The short stories and personal essays in the collection, like much of the recent fictional work by Iranian American writers, suggest that the preoccupation with a dual perspective—Iran and America, past and present, Iranian and American—are themes that all ethnic groups work through in their literature. Perhaps this duality or in between-ness has been made more pronounced due to the depiction of Iran in the U.S. media and the difficulties of having access to Iran and Iranian culture after the revolution. Because whole families were scattered across the globe and because of the political situation, the war, and the difficulties of acquiring visas to the United States, Iranians have not felt quite settled in their new environment. Writing by this second generation—those who have spent a majority of their life in the United States and who have been cut off from the staples of everyday Iranian culture and customs—articulate the Iranian American identity beyond the memoir form.

A number of novels have also been recently published by Iranian American authors. These include Susanne Pari's *The Fortune Catcher* (1997), Gina Nahai's *Moonlight on the Avenue of Faith* (2001) and *Cry of the Peacock* (2000), and Farnoosh Moshiri's *At the Wall of the Almighty* (1999) and *The Bathouse* (2003). Nahai and Pari both deal with the fallout of the Iranian Revolution and its impact on their respective protagonists. Pari's novel chronicles the return of her hero and heroine, Dariush and Layla, from the United States to a turbulent, postrevolutionary Iran where they secretly marry in 1981 against the wishes of Dariush's fundamentalist grandmother, Maman Bozorg. Nahai's most recent novel weaves a tale of political turmoil but this time from the perspective of Iran's Jewish community. The novel is narrated from the perspective of five female voices and uses magical realism to weave a tale of two places: Tehran and Los Angeles.

Farnoosh Moshiri, who comes from a prominent literary family, fled Iran in 1983 and has been writing in English for a number of years. *At the Wall of the Almighty* addresses the experience of imprisonment in Iran under the Islamic Republic. Unlike the two previously mentioned novels, *At the Wall* is concerned with the brutality of the prison experience after the establishment of the Islamic Republic and the suppression of political dissent.

Moshiri's narrative suggests that although migration may be a large part of the Iranian diaspora experience, the untold stories of the revolution, of brutality, torture, and the struggle to reconcile those stories with the experience of having left that world behind are equally important.

Whence This Emergent Literature?

Iranian American literature, like all literatures of diaspora, is in the process of establishing and articulating a new face and vocabulary on American soil. The fact that this literature has begun to find an audience and is expressing the common sentiments associated with exile, adjustment, **assimilation**, and cultural pride nearly 25 years after the largest population of Iranians arrived in North America is not surprising. Iranian Americans as a group, like many ethnic groups of the United States, initially find their voice in the midst of historical events, stereotypes, and the resurgence of cultural pride after a period of self-concealment and shame.

Further Reading

Davaran, Ardavan, ed. "Exiles and Explorers: Iranian Diaspora Literature since 1980." *The Literary Review* 40.1 (Fall 1996): 5–13.

Karim, Persis, and Mohammad Mehdi Khorrami, eds. *A World Between: Poems, Short Stories, and Essays by Iranian-Americans*. New York: George Braziller, 1999. 21–27.

Karimi-Hakak, Ahmad. "The Literary Response to the Iranian Revolution." *World Literature Today* 60.2 (Spring 1986): 251–56.

Naficy, Hamid. *The Making of Exile Cultures*. Minneapolis: University of Minnesota Press, 1993.

Rahimieh, Nasrin. "The Quince-Orange Tree, or Iranian Writers in Exile." *World Literature Today* 66.1 (Winter 1992): 39–42.

Sullivan, Zohreh T. *Exiled Memories: Stories of Iranian Diaspora*. Philadelphia: Temple University Press, 2001.

Persis Karim

ISLAS, ARTURO, JR. (1938–1991)

Arturo Islas Jr. was a Mexican American novelist, poet, and professor. He was born to Arturo Islas and Jovita La Farga on May 25, 1938, in El Paso, Texas. His parents named him to honor the memory of the first Arturo Islas, who was an intellectual, poet, and hero shot dead by a Federalist bullet in the Mexican Revolution of 1918. In many ways, Islas lived up to this memory, becoming himself a poet, novelist, and intellectual who cleared new paths of expression and thinking in the late 20th century.

Born the first of three sons, Islas (or "Sonny," as his family called him) grew up in a racially divided and divisive El Paso during the late 1930s and 1940s. This was a time when signs stating "No Mexicans Allowed" were posted in shop windows and when the public swimming pool was only open to Mexicans just before emptying and cleaning. The Islas family—especially the paternal grandmother, Crecenciana Sandoval Islas—espoused bicultural Anglo and Mexican values and encouraged bilingual Spanish/English fluency, providing Islas with the tools necessary to side-step prejudice from an early age. So, while many of his Mexican American peers struggled with English-only classes in elementary school, Islas excelled. Although Spanish was spoken at home, Islas became an avid reader and writer in English from an early age. If he wasn't under the great oak at the back of the family's house on Almagordo Street, he was to be found at the library or with this grandmother doing homework. Any spare time he had, he spent as an altar boy at the local parish.

Islas's childhood became even more ascetic after he contracted the polio virus just after turning eight years old and just before returning to school after summer break. The polio was caught early enough to curtail an untimely death, but not fast enough to prevent the uneven growth of his legs; even after a surgery during his teenage years, he would not only have to buy two separate pairs of shoes to match the different sizes of his feet, but he would walk with a decided limp for the rest of his life.

Throughout high school, Islas's passion for knowledge continued unabated; he excelled especially at science and English. Although a shorter left leg left him with a limp, this didn't stop him from dancing a mean jitterbug at school socials. His charm and good looks made him extremely popular. Graduating El Paso High as class valedictorian in 1956, Islas became the first Chicano to attend Stanford on an Alfred P. Sloan scholarship. Although Islas entered Stanford with the idea of becoming a neurosurgeon, by the time he graduated in 1960 with a degree in English and minor in religion (Phi Beta Kappa), it was with the firm conviction that he would pursue literary studies and creative writing. That fall, Islas returned to Stanford to embark on his PhD studies in English. Here he studied with Ian Watt, Wallace Stegner, and Yvor Winters—the most influential of his mentors. However, during the height of the **Civil Rights Movement** and worker and student protests worldwide (Mexico, Paris, and Czechoslovakia), he decided to take some time out of the program to explore life outside the ivory tower. After working for more than a year, including as a speech therapist at the Veterans Administration hospital in Menlo Park where Ken Kesey had also worked, Islas suffered from an ulcerated intestine that led to a brush with death and, after three major surgeries, an ileostomy. After recuperating from his surgeries and learning to live with a colostomy bag, Islas finished his PhD and secured a tenure track position in the English department at Stanford in 1971.

During the next five years on the Stanford campus Islas developed pathbreaking courses on Chicano/a literature, established a Chicano/a literary journal, worked to open scholarly spaces for incoming Mexican American undergraduates, and wrote reams of poetry as well as his first novel, *Día de los muertos/Day of the Dead*. Much of his writing during this period not only textures the experiences of a Chicano, but also absorbs his full exploration of life as a gay man living in a San Francisco bursting at the seams with same-sex exuberance, an exploration that included cruising and the frequenting of S&M clubs and bath houses. In 1976, the university recognized Islas's creative work and tremendous dedication to teaching and his students by promoting him to associate professor. During this period, he dedicated much time to writing, revising, and sending out the manuscript of *Día de los muertos* to try to secure a contract with a New York publisher. By the early 1980s, *Día de los muertos* had been rejected by over 30 different publishers; letters from publishers such as HarperCollins and Farrar Straus & Giroux attest that editors objected to his excessive use of Spanish (a quick glance at the original manuscript shows the contrary) and/or to his too-strong presence of a gay Chicano protagonist. Islas finally published the novel, much transformed, as *The Rain God* in 1984 with a small local publisher, Alexandrian Press in Palo Alto. It immediately achieved a word-of-mouth eminence within university and high school classrooms and journalistic acclaim in such newspapers as the *San Francisco Chronicle* and the *Los Angeles Times*. In a review for the *El Paso Herald-Post*, fellow El Pasoan (and Stanford PhD alumni) Vicki Ruiz celebrates Islas's shaping of fully developed "poignant women characters . . . who live, love and endure," and concludes, "Whether outspoken or shy, these *mujeres* share an inner strength on which they rely to keep their families together." And friend and professor at the University of California at Santa Cruz, Paul Skenazy, writes in his review for the *Oakland Tribune* that Islas's autobiographical fiction transforms "family legend into a subtle, quiet fiction that challenges the assumptions we too often bring to ethnic literature [and whose] protest in the novel is more plaintive than outraged." He also notes that it is a novel that ultimately, "unravels the knotted strands of belief, social experience and cultural myth that become destiny." Yale's Héctor V. Calderón compared the novel to Juan Rulfo's *Pedro Paramo* and García Márquez's *One Hundred Years of Solitude*, championing it (and opposing it to **Richard Rodriguez**'s *Hunger of Memory*) for its delicate and complex expression of the Chicano experience.

Islas had finally realized his dream of publishing a Chicano novel that spoke with great subtlety and nuance not only to the ins and outs of a Chicano family's life, but also to the interiority of a gay Chicano. That the novel did well—it was translated into Dutch as *De Regen God*—spurred Islas on to write the next novel. During a visiting professorship (1986–1987) at the University of El Paso, Texas, Islas wrote a draft of the novel he ultimately titled, *La Mollie and the King of Tears*. In a sharp turn from the mythopoetic voice of *The Rain God*, he uses a fast paced first-person narration told from the point of view of Louie Mendoza—a pachuco-styled musician from El Paso living in San Francisco's mission. Islas employs the noir genre to frame Louie's adventures and his coming to terms with his past (a lost daughter), his brother's queer sexuality, and his internalizing of self-destructive values. When Islas sent the manuscript out, he again met with great resistance. The novel was eventually posthumously published in 1996 by the University of New Mexico Press—a press that had rejected the manuscript when he had first sent it.

While Islas's experience with trying to get *La Mollie* published met with dead-ends, *The Rain God* was selling well; too well, in fact, for the small Alexandrian Press to keep up with demand. Islas knew that he needed to reach back out to New York, so he signed on with famed literary agent, Sandra Dijkstra, who shopped it around for paperback rights and also secured him a contract with William Morrow to write a sequel. With his advance contract (and, later, a contract with Avon to publish *The Rain God* in paperback) in hand, Islas began typing out the story of characters from the fictionalized town of "Del Sapo" (an anagram of El Paso that also playfully translates from the Spanish as "From the Toad") and set earlier (1950s–1960s) than *The Rain God*. Between late 1987 and early 1989, the novel that would be published as *Migrant Souls* took shape. Here, Islas focuses less on the Angel family and the gay character Miguel Chico and more on the women in the family—especially that new generation of women, like Miguel Chico's cousin, Josie Salazar, willing to act and speak against the family's restrictive sexist and racist codes of conduct. The protagonist of *The Rain God* still appears, but less as consciousness that controls the flow of events and more as a secondary figure that can relate to the other outcast characters from the sidelines. Here again, Islas blurs the border between biographical fact and narrative fiction; his intertextual play—ures from *La Mollie* appear as minor characters and French lesbian writer Colette as well as Chicano authors Rolando Hinojosa and Americo Paredes appear in disguised form—serves as a metafictional device that announces its fictionality. Upon publication, *Migrant Souls* proved another success for Islas. It sold out within a month and ranked at the top of *San Francisco Chronicle*'s best-seller list. Anglo and Chicano writers and scholars alike sang its praises. Poets Denise Levertov and Adrienne Rich gave it their seal of approval. Chicano scholar Roberto Cantú identified it as a dramatic move away from an Us/Them understanding of Chicano and Anglo **race** relations. For Cantú, Islas "advances other narrative dimensions to a higher aesthetic level" to open his readers' eyes to different ways of understanding complex social relations and hybrid cultural phenomenon.

Although mostly known for his two novels, *The Rain God* and *Migrant Souls*, Islas's creative drive and output was immense. We see this not only with the posthumous addition of *La Mollie and the King of Tears* to his opus, but also with the many unpublished short stories, poetry, and beautifully wrought scholarly essays that are now published with Arte Público Press. Though Islas's life was radically cut short when he died of AIDS-related pneumonia on February 15, 1991, his impact as a gay Chicano writer, teacher, and intellectual has been tremendous. Many of his former PhD students, including José David Saldívar and Rafael Pérez-Torres, are now leading scholars in Chicano/a studies. His unyielding drive to confront and overcome a bigoted publishing industry and his dedication to crafting rich and nuanced Chicano/a (gay and straight) poetry and narrative fiction has stretched wide the horizon of the American and world literary landscape. (*See also* Mexican American Gay Literature)

Further Reading

Aldama, Frederick Luis, ed. *Arturo Islas: The Uncollected Works*. Houston: Arte Público Press, 2003.

Aldama, Frederick Luis. *Critical Mappings of Arturo Islas's Narrative Fictions*. Tempe, AZ: Bilingual Review Press, 2004.

Aldama, Frederick Luis. *Dancing with Ghosts: A Critical Biography of Arturo Islas*. Berkeley: University of California Press, 2004.

Frederick Luis Aldama

J

JACOBS, HARRIET (1813–1897)

Harriet Jacobs was an African American autobiographer and slave narrator. Jacobs's *Incidents in the Life of a Slave Girl* (1861) is one of a very few existing female slave narratives. She wrote it, as she explains in her preface, "at irregular intervals, whenever I could snatch an hour from household duties," while living as an escaped slave in the North, and published it under the pseudonym "Linda Brent." The autobiography borrows from the genre of sentimental domestic fiction and is often read as a novel; indeed Jacobs's editor, the abolitionist Lydia Maria Child, noted in her preface to the narrative that "some incidents in her story are more romantic than fiction."

Jacobs, however, assures her readers that "this narrative is no fiction." Crafting her autobiography for the cause of abolition, Jacobs used the techniques of the sentimental novel to reach her audience of 19th-century white women. Her appeal to sympathy and use of sentimentality is almost a seduction of the reader. She wanted not only to retain credibility but also make palatable the details of her sexual abuse at the hands of her master and her sexual transgression in taking a white lover. The middle-class Northern mothers might respond to the narrator's repeated depiction of their shared maternal identities—her appeal to them early in the narrative, for example, to "contrast *your* New Year's day with that of the poor bond-woman." But Jacobs feared alienating some whose, as Child put it in her preface, "ears are too delicate to listen" to the stories of a fallen woman. Referring to herself in both the first and third person, she negotiates the tensions between revelation and concealment, public and private, and her individual life and that of a representative "slave girl" as her title has it. Mixing genres, Jacobs opens up significant silences and dwells in the created space between modes.

Her textual gaps are in fact analogous to the famous garret space. The story follows Brent through childhood and into early womanhood, when her master, Dr. Flint, attempts seduction and rape. She chooses to take a white lover, Mr. Sands, in order to reassert control of her body and thwart Dr. Flint. She bears two children, hoping that her lover will purchase and manumit his secret family, but Dr. Flint's refusal to sell them drives her to attempt escape. An aborted flight leads her to inter herself into a crawl space above her grandmother's house for seven years, to wait out Flint. From the tiny garret she manipulates him with letters apparently mailed from the North, almost creating him as a character in an epistolary novel. He had used her literacy against her by writing her vile notes and whispering obscenities in her ear, and now she turns his tools of language against him.

Her "loophole of retreat," as she calls the hiding place, is thus both a prison and a refuge: as a "living grave," so described in *Incidents*, it literalizes the state of slavery, which is to be beyond "the pale of human beings," and is itself a "living death," in Jacobs's words. Like her self-inflicted confinement, the process of telling her story is painful: "she wept so much and seemed to suffer such mental agony," remembered her friend Amy Post in October 1859, and Brent characterizes memory as distressing throughout the autobiography. But Jacobs also locates power and renewal in invisibility. Like **Ralph Waldo Ellison**'s Invisible Man, who retreats to a basement space reminiscent of her attic, she uses her retreat away from society to fashion a subversively *present* absence. A sister of the Victorian "madwoman in the attic," Brent lives in the interstices of the American house divided, embedded in cracks of its institutions, and watches and works for the destruction of the edifice of slavery. The autobiography and the hole, as sites of memory, are ultimately protective and aggressive spaces in the margins of hegemonic discourse, from which Brent emerges, as though from a chrysalis, as the writer Jacobs. (*See also* African American Autobiography)

Further Reading

Carby, Hazel V. *Reconstructing Womanhood: The Emergence of the Afro-American Woman Novelist*. New York: Oxford University Press, 1987.

Green-Barteet, Miranda. "'The Loophole of Retreat': Interstitial Space in Harrriet Jacobs' *Incidents in the Life of a Slave Girl*." *South Central Review* 30.2 (2013): 53–72.

Kaplan, Carla. "Narrative Contracts and Emancipatory Readers: *Incidents in the Life of a Slave Girl*." *Yale Journal of Criticism* 6.11 (1993): 93–119.

Nudelman, Franny. "Harriet Jacobs and the Sentimental Politics of Female Suffering." *ELH: English Literary History* 59 (1992): 939–64

Zoe Trodd

JAPANESE AMERICAN AUTOBIOGRAPHY

The Japanese started to arrive in America in the 19th century, though no Japanese American autobiographies were written until the early 20th century. The first notable autobiographies were written by women, and just as noteworthy more autobiographies thematize the Japanese American **internment** experience in World War II. What follows is a brief discussion of major Japanese American autobiographers and their works produced in the past eight decades.

 Two early autobiographies were written by women. Etsu Inagaki Sugimoto (1874–1950), an immigrant, wrote one of the earliest Japanese American autobiographies, *A Daughter of the Samurai* (1925), which looks back at the narrator's childhood in her home country of Japan while recounting the kind of education she received and the social and cultural customs that the Japanese practiced that she witnessed. The values that she was inculcated in are loyalty, bravery, and honor that characterize the spirit of samurai. The second part of the autobiography focuses on Sugimoto's life in California with her Japanese merchant husband and her forced return to Japan after her husband's death. The narrative ends with her permanent return to the United States with her daughters. Sugimoto makes no mention of **racism** in the United States, though implicit criticism of her adopted country can be found in the autobiography. Another early autobiography is Kathleen Tamagawa's (1897–1979) *Holy Prayers in a Horse's Ear* (1932). The child of a marriage between a Japanese man and an Irish woman, Tamagawa writes about her parents' interracial marriage and her own biculturalism, her acclimation to a life in Japan where her father took his family to Yokohama as a silk buyer, and her own marriage to a white American and the couple's global travels.

Daniel Inouye, 2011. (AP Photo/Luis M. Alvarez)

Monica Sone (1919–2011) published *Nisei Daughter* in 1953. Inspired by the Chinese American Jade Snow Wong's autobiography *Fifth Chinese Daughter* (1945) that narrates a young girl's growth in San Francisco, Sone's autobiography deals with essentially the same time period as its Chinese predecessor, though its geographical locale is mostly set in Seattle where Japanese Americans were ordered to evacuate. Sone recounts almost idyllic memories of her childhood life on the waterfront of Seattle where her parents owned a small hotel, but contrasting this peaceful prewar life are the hardships and humiliating ordeals Sone's family suffered at the concentration camps—first at Puyallup and then at Minidoka. Sone returned to the internment camp to visit her parents a year after her departure for college. Sone wrote the book partly to educate readers about her Japanese American family and their community, partly to denounce the government's racist and oppressive mistreatment of a people, and partly to describe the realization of her bicultural heritage and the development of her own cultural and racial identity. Also scrutinized are the psychological aftermaths of camp life on Nisei Japanese Americans like Sone herself and how they internalized racialized victimization.

Daniel Inouye (1924–2012) wrote *Journey to Washington* (1967), with the assistance of Lawrence Elliott before his reelection to the United States Senate, chronicling the growth of a young Japanese American boy into a war hero and eventually a prominent legislator. The book narrates Inouye's childhood experience up to the point of his entry into national politics. The dominant themes are patriotism, loyalty, and heroism. Inouye expresses an unequivocal American **identity** when

Pearl Harbor called on Americans to join the fight against fascism. A strong sense of determination, resilience, and optimism is clearly conveyed throughout the narrative. Whether faced with racial problems in school or racial hatred following Pearl Harbor or life-threatening situations in World War II, Inouye remains determined to succeed in his American dream through a hard work ethic and belief in American ideals and values.

Jim Yoshida (1921–) collaborated with Bill Hosokawa, himself an autobiographer, in writing *The Two Worlds of Jim Yoshida* (1972). Yoshida's is very different from other Japanese American autobiographies written about Japanese American experiences right before, during, and immediately after World War II, for the majority of them focus upon the evacuation and internment of Japanese on the West Coast. Yoshida's work deals with a unique experience of an American of Japanese origin detained in his ancestral country with which the United States was at war and for which he was forced to serve under its flag. It is the story of a man without a country. When World War II broke out, Yoshida took his father's ashes to Japan where he was drafted to fight in the Japanese Imperial Army in China. The two worlds Yoshida refers to are apparently the United States and Japan, between which he was emotionally torn while physically stuck in Japan. The autobiography delineates two major issues: Yoshida's conscription and service to the Japanese army, and his legal battle with the United States government to reclaim his American citizenship. To atone for what he was forced to do during his Japanese years, Yoshida volunteered his service to his birth country by willingly joining U.S. troops in Korea to fight another war in the early 1950s.

Jeanne Wakatsuki Houston (1935–) and James D. Houston (1934–) started to collaborate on Jeanne's personal experience of internment at Manzanar in the late 1960s and published *Farewell to Manzanar: A True Story of Japanese American Experience During and After the World War II Internment* in 1973. The autobiography presents first-hand accounts of the internment experience at one particular concentration camp during World War II. While the book focuses on the family of the Wakatsukis, it also attempts to include the experience of Japanese Americans beyond the circles of family and friends. As is true of other similar accounts of the wartime incarceration, *Farewell to Manzanar* does not merely recount or denounce the internment, but it takes on the onus of exploring and confronting the role of **racism** in the U.S. government's implementation of a **race**-based decision. The Houstons contrast the different lifestyles that the Wakatsukis lived before, during, and after the internment and the war. Jeanne's story is chronicled in her struggles with her racial and cultural identity as well as in her efforts to assimilate into the mainstream culture. Her struggles are characterized by a desire for acceptance in a racially divided society. The end of *Farewell to Manzanar* stages Jeanne's return to the concentration camp with her husband and their three children, thereby providing both a physical and psychological closure to what she believes to be a shameful experience.

Bill Hosokawa (1915–2007) is known for two autobiographies: *Thirty-five Years in the Frying Pan* (1978) and *Out of the Frying Pan: Reflections of a Japanese American* (1989). Hosokawa's personal experience of internment during World War II, his encounters with racial discrimination, and the Asian American experience in general are the principal concerns of many of his newspaper columns that he eventually collected into *Thirty-five Years in the Frying Pan* and *Out of the Frying Pan*. Hosokawa digs to the bottom of the Japanese American internment that he himself, his wife Alice, and their son Michael endured at Heart Mountain by tracing both the political and racial motivations of the government's decision to incarcerate Japanese Americans. Hosokawa investigates the causes of such mistreatment by scrutinizing the links between race and political status in the United States and the reasons why the Bill of Rights applies to certain citizens and not others like his family and his ethnicity under war circumstances.

Yoshiko Uchida (1921–1992) published an autobiography, *Desert Exile: The Uprooting of a Japanese-American Family*, in 1982, followed by another, *The Invisible Thread: An Autobiography*, in 1991. Both narratives recount the Japanese American internment experience. Desert Exile delves into issues of identity, racial and cultural heritage, and the psychological effects of this racially motivated exile of Japanese Americans. Uchida not only narrates her blissful childhood lived among different ethnic groups and her racially more aware years during college, but also examines her ambivalence about being American in Japan and being Japanese in America. *The Invisible Threat* recaptures the essence of Uchida's first autobiography except that it was written for a younger audience and with new perspectives informed by Japanese Americans' redress movement. In the latter Uchida expresses her positive views of Japan and affirmatively reiterates her Japanese American identity.

David Mura (1952–) is a Sansei poet writing autobiographies. He published *Turning Japanese: Memoirs of a Sansei* in 1991, followed by *Where the Body Meets Memory: An Odyssey of Race, Sexuality & Identity* in 1996. *Turning Japanese* was not first written as a book; it was a collection of essays published previously on various topics such as cultural identity, racial politics, and sexuality from the viewpoint of a Sansei. *Where the Body Meets Memory* delves into basically the same issues that Mura explored in his first autobiography, with emphasis on race, sexuality, and identity, though the book includes stories about his parents and grandparents, which makes it more of a memoir than an autobiography.

Another poet writing autobiography is Garrett Hongo (1951–), who takes the name of his birth village for his narrative: *Volcano: A Memoir of Hawaii*. Hongo left Hawai'i at the age of six and settled down in Los Angeles with his parents—a move that his memoir concentrates on. Hawai'i seems like a paradise lost to the narrator who is now on a quest for self-identity through researching his family history and the land that is the site of that history. Thus history and geography occupy prominent places in the autobiographical narrative.

George Takei (1937–) is an actor writing autobiography. Known as Sulu to fans of the TV series *Star Trek*, Takei wrote *To the Stars: The Autobiography of George Takei, Star Trek's Mr. Sulu* (1994), which reflects his **ethnicity** as well as his career path. Like Frank Chin's novel *Gunga Din Highway* (Takei was cast in Chin's televised play *The Year of the Dragon* in 1974), *To the Stars* examines the important issue of representation of Asians in Hollywood on TV and in films. As a former internee in World War II, Takei also looks into the Japanese American internment and its effects on his parents. Even though Takei's book focuses on the self and his family, his message about subverting Asian American stereotypes and self-representation forms an important theme throughout the narrative.

Further Reading

Ghymn, Esther Mikyung. "Yoshiko Uchida's Positive Vision." In *The Shapes and Styles of American Asian Prose Fiction*, 67–89. New York: Peter Lang, 1992.

Goodsell, Jane. *Daniel Inouye*. New York: Thomas Y. Crowell, 1977.

Holte, James Craig. "Monica Sone." In *The Ethnic I: A Sourcebook for Ethnic-American Autobiography*, 161–66. Westport, CT: Greenwood Press, 1988.

Huang, Guiyou, ed. *Asian American Autobiographers: A Bio-Bibliographical Critical Sourcebook*. Westport, CT: Greenwood Press, 2001.

Lim, Shirley Geok-lin. "Japanese American Women's Life Stories: Maternality in Monica Sone's Nisei Daughter and Joy Kogawa's Obasan." *Feminist Studies* 16.2 (Summer 1990): 289–312.

Okamura, Raymond Y. "Farewell to Manzanar: A Case of Subliminal Racism." *Amerasia Journal* 3.2 (1976): 143–47.

Rayson, Ann. "Beneath the Mask: Autobiographies of Japanese-American Women." *MELUS* 14.1 (Spring 1987): 43–57.

Sakurai, Patricia A. "The Politics of Possession: The Negotiation of Identity in America in Disguise, Homebase, and Farewell to Manzanar." In *Sakurai, Privileging Positions: The Sites of Asian American Studies*, 157–70. Pullman: Washington State University Press, 1995.

Sumida, Stephen H. "Protest and Accommodation, Self-Satire and Self-Effacement, and Monica Sone's Nisei Daughter." In *Multicultural Autobiography: American Lives*, edited by James Robert Payne, 207–43. Knoxville: University of Tennessee Press, 1992.

Yamamoto, Traise. "Nisei Daughter, by Monica Sone." In *A Resource Guide to Asian American Literature*, edited by Sau-ling Cynthia Wong and Stephen H. Sumida, 151–58. New York: Modern Language Association, 2001.

Guiyou Huang

JAPANESE AMERICAN NOVEL

Language, generation, and the periods before and after World War II are useful reference points in Japanese American literature. Before World War II, Japanese writing in English appeared primarily in journalistic forms rather than the literary. In the late 1920s Issei writers published poems and stories in Japanese language newspapers in Hawai'i and on the West Coast of the United States. Issei-owned newspapers such as the *New World-Sun* and *Kashu Mainichi* served as important publishing forums and professionalizing contexts for Nisei writers. These publications enabled the examination of international issues and domestic **race** relations that defined Japanese as a specific ethnic group, and contributed to a growing awareness of generational differences between foreign-born Issei and their American-born Nisei children. Novels of the early 20th century emphasized Japanese culture and generally constructed it as "exotic" and "foreign." According to Elaine Kim, prewar Issei novelists were often members of the Japanese aristocracy, and envisioned themselves as "living bridges" between Japanese and American cultures. A case in point is Etsu Sugimoto's autobiographical novel *A Daughter of the Samurai* (1925), which portrays a romanticized "old Japan" under siege by modernization while simultaneously expressing admiration for American progress and modernity. Some writers from elite backgrounds in Japan focused on Japanese laboring classes in the United States. Yone Noguchi's *The American Diary of a Japanese Girl* (1912) takes the form of a fictionalized diary written in broken English to narrate the story of a young Japanese woman's search for work in the United States.

The evacuation and detention of over 120,000 Japanese Americans during World War II had a particularly strong impact on the Nisei, for whom the **internment** raised troubling questions of racial **identity** and nationality. During the internment Japanese American writings in English appeared in camp newspapers and literary magazines but were censored by government officials. Stan Yogi suggests that Hawaiian Nisei writers took up the novel in their exploration of Japanese American history and culture in the period immediately following World War II (134). He attributes the earlier emergence of the postwar Japanese American novel to the large population of Japanese Hawaiians on the islands who did not experience the displacement and dispossession of internment to the same extent as those in the continental United States and Canada. Postwar Japanese Hawaiian novels, including Shelley Ota's *Upon Their Shoulders* (1951), Margaret Harada's *The Sun Shines on the Immigrant* (1960), and Kazuo Miyamoto's *Hawaii: End of the Rainbow* (1964), offer varied perspectives on immigration, **assimilation**, and internment in Japanese American history.

Nisei writers of the 1950s increasingly took up the bildungsroman, or novel of formation, that conventionally follows an immigrant protagonist's journey of education and enlightenment and culminates with assimilation into the nation and the development of self-knowledge. According to Lisa Lowe, Asian American bildungsroman narrate an immigrant's desire for assimilation and upward mobility, but simultaneously expose the racial and economic contradictions of the incorporation of Asian immigrants into the nation. Lowe further argues that the bildungsroman became an important vehicle for Nisei writers to question celebrations of the postwar period as a triumph of American democracy and gave voice to the **racism** and anti-Japanese hostility that denied full citizenship and the possibility of hyphenation to Japanese Americans. Monica Sone's autobiography *Nisei Daughter* (1953) illustrates how Japanese Americans were encouraged to reject Japanese culture and to internalize the conflation of Japanese **ethnicity** with disloyalty to America. One scene shows her protagonist Kazuko burning her Japanese-language books and expresses the sense of alienation and anger that it produces for her. The novel offers a critical view of the equation of American identity with the negation of Japanese culture, but also refers to feelings of anger and resistance, exemplified by Kazuko's refusal to burn a Japanese doll from her grandmother.

John Okada's *No-No Boy* (1957) is a poignant exploration of the trauma of internment in Japanese American historical memory. For Nisei writers like him, the representation of Issei, Nisei, and Sansei became intertwined with competing inter-pretations of the internment. The novel centers on Ichiro, a "no-no boy" who defies the "loyalty questionnaire," which required Issei and Nisei to renounce loyalty to Japan and to state their willingness to serve in the U.S. armed forces. Okada depicts Ichiro's fraught attempts to accept his decision and rebuild his life in the context of postwar anti-Japanese hostility and the fragmentation of the Japanese community in Seattle. Through interior monologues and characters that represent different sec-tors of society and responses to internment, the novel explores the persistence of the wartime opposition of "Japanese" and "American" identities and its individual and collective impact on Japanese Americans. Okada also uses the figure of Kenji, a crippled war veteran, to question the false conflation of military service with the successful incorporation of Japanese American men into postwar American society.

The **canon**ization of Okada's novel by Asian American writers of the 1970s illus-trates the convergence of the recovery of Japanese American novels with the pro-duction of a tradition of resistance in Asian American writing. Japanese American novels became key to efforts to challenge the Japanese American Citizens League (JACL) position, exemplified by Bill Hosokawa's memoir *The Quiet Americans* (1969), which stressed the willingness of Japanese Americans to prove their loyalty to the United States through internment. During the late 1970s Japanese American groups in the United States and Canada began to explore possibilities for Japanese American monetary reparations, which encouraged Nisei to speak out against the internment. Although writings on internment by non-Japanese, including wartime reports in *Life* magazine and Karen Kehoe's novel *City in the Sun* (1947), were pub-lished during the war, many Japanese American novels were not recognized or widely read until the 1970s. For Asian American writers of the 1970s the intern-ment experience served as a catalyst for artistic production rather than a deterrent. According to the *Aiiieeeee!* anthology editors, the problem was not a lack of writ-ings by Japanese Americans but rather the limitation of publishing forums (xliii).

The recovery of internment novels by Asian American writers of the 1970s coin-cided with the articulation of masculine Japanese American identities. By casting the "no-no boy" as the emblematic figure of Japanese American identity, Asian American writers of the 1970s also generated male-centered models of Asian American literature. In the 1980s Japanese American female novelists took up the theme of "breaking silence" in female-centered representations of internment and its long-term effects. Joy Kogawa's *Obasan* (1981) explores the complexities of Jap-anese American history and memory through notions of speech and silence, com-plicating traditional associations of speaking with resistance and emancipation and silence with repression and shame. The novel narrates the story of three generations of Japanese Canadians through letters, dreams, diary entries, and private memory, and brings together a private trauma of childhood sexual abuse with the public violence of internment. Kogawa's works have also helped to generate discussion on the specificity of Japanese Canadian histories of immigration and racialization. Marie Lo cautions against U.S.-centered accounts of Japanese Canadian literary history, but suggests that Asian Canadian writings need to be considered in terms of both national and transnational histories of racialization and colonialism (99).

The postmodern novel has helped to reconfigure the Japan-United States trajectory as well as the emphasis on the West Coast of the United States. Although the bildungsroman continues to be an important literary model, contemporary writers have looked to other genres for inspiration. In the1980s and 1990s women have primarily authored Japanese American novels, and many have seen critical and financial success in the literary marketplace. Some novels refer to historical themes of internment and dislocation and feature female protagonists and "feminist" themes. Cynthia Kadohata's *The Floating World* (1989) takes up an archetypal "American" genre, the "road novel," to portray the nomadic existence of a Japanese American family during the 1950s. Her second book, *In the Heart of the Valley of Love* (1997), continues to explore the theme of displacement in a futuristic landscape of Los Angeles. Karen Tei Yamashita's magical realist novels explore the Japanese diaspora in Brazil, which emerged in part from the 1924 Oriental Exclusion Act, which barred Asian immigration to the United States. *Brazil-Maru* (1992) is the story of Japanese immigrant laborers on Brazil's coffee plantations. *Tropic of Orange* (1997) is a novel that explores the effects of the North American Free Trade Agreement on both sides of the U.S.-Mexico border. Hiromi Goto's *A Chorus of Mushrooms* (1995) shifts the focus from urban communities to three generations of Japanese Canadian women in a prairie town. Although postwar Japanese American writers tended to downplay Japanese life and culture, some contemporary novelists have made conscious attempts to engage Japan. For example, Ruth Ozeki's *My Year of Meats* (1998) connects Japanese female protagonists in the United States and Japan through excerpts from Sei Shonagon's *Pillow Book*.

Japanese Hawaiian writers have utilized the bildungsroman genre and pidgin English to narrate stories that highlight the "local" context of Hawai'i. Milton Murayama's *All I Asking for Is My Body* (1959) explores racial, ethnic, and class struggle in Hawai'i during the 1930s and 1940s, particularly the complicity of filial obligation with the systematic exploitation of Japanese and Filipino plantation laborers. Like Murayama, Lois Ann Yamanaka contradicts the stereotypical image of Hawai'i as an idyllic paradise, and instead foregrounds the poverty and hard living conditions on the islands. Set on the island of Moloka'i, *Blu's Hanging* (1997) is narrated by the eldest daughter of the Ogata family, who assumes responsibility for her siblings after their mother's death. In June 1998, protests erupted at the Asian American Studies Association (AASA) meeting in Honolulu when the novel was presented with AASA's 1997 national fiction award. Criticism centered on Yamanaka's portrayals of Filipinos and perpetuation of stereotypes of Filipinos as sexual deviants and resulted in the rescinding of the award and the resignation of the Association's executive board. Candace Fujikane argues that local and national medias' focus on the story of censorship has obscured the context of local Filipino protests against systemic local Japanese racism in Hawai'i. For Fujikane the protests need to be understood in relation to ideologies of race and ethnicity that maintain the political and economic dominance of white and local Japanese settlers in Hawai'i (161).

Contemporary Japanese American novelists continue to explore the internment experience and its implications for civil liberties. In response to attacks on the

World Trade Center on September 11, 2001, expanded law enforcement and intelligence legislation has refocused attention on the Japanese American internment. Both critics and supporters seized upon the example of Japanese American internment to counter and justify the targeting of groups and individuals perceived as possible terrorists and threats to national security. Published in the aftermath of the Patriot Act, Julie Otsuka's *When the Emperor Was Divine* (2002) uses notions of loyalty and disloyalty to explore the long-term effects of internment for a single family. Narrated by multiple, unnamed protagonists, the novel diverges from previous narratives that revolve around an individual. As Otsuka suggests, novels continue to provide ways of exploring conflicts and intersections of past and present, identity, and community that continue to trouble Japanese American writers.

Further Reading

Chan, Jeffrey Paul, Frank Chin, Lawson Fusao Inada, and Shawn H. Wong. "An Introduction to Chinese-American and Japanese-American Literature." In *Aiiieeeee! An Anthology of Asian American Writers*, xxi–xlviii. New York: Penguin Books, 1974.

Fujikane, Candace. "Sweeping Racism under the Rug of 'Censorship': The Controversy over Lois Ann Yamanaka's *Blu's Hanging*." *Amerasia Journal* 26.2 (2000): 158–94.

Kim, Elaine H. *Asian American Literature: An Introduction to the Writings and Their Social Context*. Philadelphia: Temple University Press, 1982.

Lo, Marie. "Obasan." In *Resource Guide for Asian American Literature*, edited by Sau Ling Wong and Stephen Sumida, 97–107. New York: Modern Language Association, 2001.

Simpson, Caroline Chung. *An Absent Presence: Japanese Americans in Postwar American Culture, 1945–1960*. Durham, NC: Duke University Press, 2001.

Yogi, Stan. "Japanese American Literature." In *An Interethnic Companion to Asian American Literature*, edited by King-Kok Cheung, 125–55. Cambridge, UK: Cambridge University Press, 1997.

Cynthia Tolentino

JASMINE

Bharati Mukherjee's novel *Jasmine* (1989) occupies a prominent position in South Asian American literature and focuses on a theme central to the tradition: migration and settlement. The novel traces the travels of the eponymous heroine who arrives from India to settle in the United States. Through a series of self-transformations, which are frequently propelled by acts of violent disruption, Jasmine is Americanized. Jasmine's migration from east to west is reproduced in her movement from the East Coast to the West Coast of the United States; it is when she heads out from the Midwest for her last destination, the California frontier and, in particular, the University of California at Berkeley—a symbol in the novel of free thought and untroubled **multiculturalism**—that Jasmine realizes an unfettered American selfhood.

Jasmine's journey may be charted according to the names she adopts along the way. The novel begins with a brief flashback to Jasmine, as Jyoti, during her childhood in Punjab. This early moment is important to the novel's narrative for it establishes a crucial theme: individual will versus fate, where the first signifies the possibility of self-creation and Americanization and the second implies that tradition, **ethnicity**, nationality, and immigrant are essential and unalterable attributes of oneself. When Jyoti is seven years old, an astrologer foretells her widowhood and exile. Jyoti rejects this with a passion, and in doing so, she suffers a wound and is scarred on the forehead. Resisting the notion that her beauty is now marred and that as a woman she will be shunned, she asserts that her scar is a third eye through which she can view invisible worlds.

As a young woman, Jyoti marries Prakash, a political revolutionary who is also a master of creating electronic equipment using odds and ends—similar to how Jasmine will succeed in her journey by creating and recreating herself by building on materials and contexts available to her. It is Prakash who gives her the name Jasmine. Soon Prakash is murdered in an episode of communal violence. Carrying through with Prakash's plan study in the United States, Jasmine follows unpleasant underground routes to the New World, landing upon a Florida shore. She is brutally raped; she kills her rapist, burns her luggage from India, and continues on her way "traveling light." En route, a Quaker woman who befriends and helps her names her Jazzy.

In Manhattan, Jasmine is a nanny to Duff, daughter of a Columbia University professor named Taylor. Taylor renames her Jase; she now leaps into an intellectual, cosmopolitan life where her exoticism is valued. But in order to elude her husband's killer who is pursuing her, Jase flees to a small provincial town in Iowa. She moves in with Bud, an aging banker, and is now Jane, a middle-class housewife downplaying her foreignness. Jane distinguishes herself from other migrants who remain "hyphenated" in contrast to her own "genetic" assumptions of American identity. Bud is shot and left handicapped. Soon after, Taylor and Duff stop on their way to Berkeley. Feeling "greedy and reckless with hope," Jasmine leaves Bud to join them.

Jasmine has enjoyed a wide readership, from the mainstream to professional literary critics. It has been controversial, as well. For some, it offers an optimistic perspective on immigration, where Jasmine rejects marginalization and struggles and alters to secure her place in the New World. For others, the novel does not adequately question the complexities of cultural and class differences, America as a place of possibility and mobility, or the myth of the melting pot. The answer may lie in the age-old dilemma presented initially: Is it our will or destiny that determines our existence? (*See also* South Asian American Literature)

Further Reading

Nelson, Emmanuel S., ed. *Bharati Mukherjee: Critical Perspectives.* Westport, CT: Greenwood Press, 1993.

Ninh, Erin K. "'Gold digger': Reading the Marital and National Romance in Bharati Mukherjee's *Jasmine.*" *MELUS* 38.3 (2013): 146–59.

Ray, Sangeeta. "Rethinking Migrancy: Nationalism, Ethnicity, and Identity in *Jasmine* and *The Buddha of Suburbia.*" In *Reading the Shape of the World: Toward an International Cultural*

Studies, edited by Henry Schwarz and Richard Dienst, 183–201. Boulder, CO: Westview, 1996.

Wickramagamage, Carmen. "Relocation as Positive Act: The Immigrant Experience in Bharati Mukherjee's Novels." *Diaspora* 2.2: 171–201.

Krishna Lewis

JAZZ

An indigenous American music created by the descendants of enslaved Africans, jazz has inspired literary artists because of the legendary lives and personalities of its major musicians and because of trademark elements such as improvisation, poly-rhythms, riffs, and scat singing. Since 1919 many poets have written jazz poetry, and since the 1950s a few poets and musicians have collaborated in recording poetry recitals with jazz accompaniment.

History

Jazz originated during the first decade of the 20th century in New Orleans, Louisiana. It evolved out of four major influences: a style of piano music called ragtime; a type of black folk music, the country **blues**; the call-and-response music in black churches; and the music played by marching brass bands. The first great jazz band was that of Joe "King" Oliver, a band in which the trumpet virtuoso Louis Armstrong got his start. Oliver and Armstrong's music was later named New Orleans Jazz. White musicians copied this music and called it Dixieland Jazz. By the 1920s both kinds of music had spread to Chicago and New York, and in the 1930s jazz evolved into swing, played chiefly by big bands. The best swing bands were the black bands of Count Basie, Duke Ellington, and Fletcher Henderson, but the best advertised and best paid were the white bands of Benny Goodman, Woody Herman, and Artie Shaw.

In response to the white commercialization of jazz, the saxophonist Charlie Parker, the trumpeter Dizzy Gillespie, and the pianist Thelonious Monk created a new and very difficult form of music that white musicians could not easily imitate and exploit. This happened in the 1940s, and the new music was called bebop. Bop was not as popular as swing because it was difficult to dance to. The 1940s also saw a revival of New Orleans and Dixieland Jazz. This very danceable, good-time music became popular with young people not only in the United States but also in Europe before it was eclipsed by rock and roll.

As bebop began to fade in the early 1950s, pianist Dave Brubeck, baritone saxophonist Gerry Mulligan, and other white musicians working on the West Coast developed cool jazz, a serene-sounding music, seemingly more influenced by the baroque music of Johann Sebastian Bach than by the African American jazz tradition. In the mid-1950s, the pianist Horace Silver, the drummer Art Blakey, and other East Coast musicians reasserted the black tradition in jazz by turning bebop into hard bop, which was less complicated, more hard-driving, and more blues-influenced.

Jazz in all its forms reached the peak of its popularity in the late 1950s but then suffered a serious decline in the 1960s. Two things kept audiences away. One was rock and roll, which had become popular when Elvis Presley started recording in 1956 and even more so after successful British groups such as the Beatles and the Rolling Stones spawned similar bands in the United States. The other debilitating development was the emergence of free jazz, a form of music championed by the saxophonist Ornette Coleman. It dispensed with fixed chord progressions and fixed rhythms and was appreciated only by musicians. By the end of the 1960s most radio stations were no longer playing jazz, and most jazz clubs had closed. This crisis drove the trumpeter Miles Davis to collaborate with rock and roll musicians and to create a hybrid form of music called Fusion, which enjoyed brief popularity in the 1970s. Like most rock and roll, Fusion relied heavily on electronic amplification of the sounds of all instruments, even the horns.

Jazz began to pull out of its crisis in the middle 1970s with a return to a hard-swinging acoustic music called straight ahead jazz. This form of jazz is a combination of elements from the swing, bebop, and hard bop eras. One of the driving forces behind this development was the veteran tenor saxophonist Dexter Gordon who had spent the doldrum years from 1962 to 1976 in Europe, where jazz was more popular than in America. Many young musicians enthusiastically embraced straight ahead jazz. Among them were the trumpeter Wynton Marsalis and the tenor saxophonist Joshua Redman. The growing popularity of straight ahead jazz led to a modest resurgence of all kinds of jazz during the 1980s and 1990s. This resurgence was modest because jazz has become high art and is appreciated more by the white middle class than by the African American community from which it originally sprang.

Form

The African heritage of jazz can be heard chiefly in the musicians' use of syncopation and counter rhythms. To this day West African drummers are unequaled at laying down several different rhythmic patterns simultaneously. While this is a skill that only the best modern jazz drummers have been able to master, a more basic skill that even gifted amateur musicians can attain is the ability to make the music "swing"; that is, to create a tension between the basic beat of the tune and the melody they are playing. This is the tension that makes audiences want to tap their feet or snap their fingers. As the title of a Duke Ellington tune says, "It [jazz] don't mean a thing, if it ain't got that swing."

Improvisation, in most jazz forms, is limited by the structure of the tune, called "theme" or "head," and its chord progression or "changes." The most common structures in jazz tunes are 12 bars (AAB), 16 bars (AB or AABA), or 32 bars (AB or AABA). One run-through of such a pattern is called a "chorus." The theme is usually played by the ensemble at the beginning and at the end of the piece, and in between the musicians take turns improvising. Jazz musicians don't just embellish the melody of the theme but also memorize its chord progression and use it to create melodies that have very little to do with the original tune.

Two elements in jazz that have been of special interest to poets are riffs and scat singing. Riffs are short phrases that are repeated—usually by the ensemble, but sometimes also by the soloist—and interspersed in the improvisations. Scat singing happens when jazz singers improvise by singing not words but nonsense syllables such as "shoo-be-doo-be-doo" or "oop-bopsh'bam," the latter being the title of a tune written by the great bebop trumpeter Dizzy Gillespie.

What distinguish the improvisations of jazz musicians from the improvisations of musicians in classical music is not only that their improvisations swing but that they rely heavily on so called "blue notes." In the key of C, these notes are E-flat and B-flat. They are called blue notes because they were the notes emphasized in the old-time country blues, which many consider to be the true source of jazz. An improvisation that doesn't stress blue notes will simply not sound "jazzy."

A trait that jazz musicians share with composers of classical music is their desire to pay homage to those from whom they learned. Thus New Orleans and Dixieland trumpet players like to quote Louis Armstrong phrases, straight ahead musicians keep quoting Charlie Parker's bebop phrases, and contemporary drummers often quote licks from forebears such as Max Roach and Art Blakey.

Jazz and Literature

Many literary artists have used jazz musicians as protagonists in their fiction and treated them as admirable counterculture figures. Perhaps the best-known examples are the piano players in the short stories "Powerhouse" (1941) by Eudora Welty and "Sonny's Blues" (1957) by **James Baldwin** and the blues singer Ma Rainey (an historical figure) in **August Wilson**'s play *Ma Rainey's Black Bottom* (1984). Jazz musicians also figure prominently in a number of novels by contemporary writers, for instance, in John Edgar Wideman's *Sent for You Yesterday* (1984), Xam Wilson Cartier's *Be-bop, Re-bop* (1987), and Nathaniel Mackey's *Djibot Baghostus's Run* (1993).

In jazz poetry there is a closer symbiosis between jazz and literature than in jazz fiction. Jazz poetry began shortly after jazz was first recorded. There are basically two kinds of jazz poetry—one that does not require the cooperation of jazz musicians and one that does.

The first kind is simply poetry about jazz or jazz musicians and attempts in various ways to capture the qualities of the music. An early example is Carl Sandburg's "Jazz Fantasia" of 1919. In that poem the speaker urges a group of black musicians to "batter on your banjos, sob on your cool winding saxophones" and to "go husha-husha-hush with the slippery sandpaper" (probably a reference to a washboard being used as a percussion instrument). In 1926, the black poet **Langston Hughes** set the standard for the use of jazz elements in poetry when he published his collection *The Weary Blues*.

Recordings of the second type of jazz poetry—the kind being recited to jazz music—were first made in the 1950s by the white Beat poets Kenneth Patchen, Kenneth Rexroth, Lawrence Ferlinghetti, and Jack Kerouac. In most of these recordings there is little connection between what the poets are reciting and what the musicians are playing. A notable exception is Jack Kerouac's *Blues and Haiku* (1958). On that recording the improvisations of the saxophonists Al Cohn and Zoot Sims succeed in capturing the mood of the poems that Kerouac is reciting.

In 1958, Langston Hughes, who had been reciting his poems to jazz accompaniment since the 1930s, finally recorded some of his poems. His *Weary Blues* contains some of the finest examples of jazz poetry. These jazz poems stand out both because of the way they capture the quality of jazz and because of the way the musicians interweave their improvisations with the poetry.

Hughes's comments on his jazz poetry provide a good definition of that art form. In the "Introduction" to his book of poems *Montage of a Dream Deferred*, Hughes says that just like bebop his poetry contains "conflicting changes, sudden nuances, sharp and impudent interjections, broken rhythms, and passages sometimes in the manner of the jam session, sometimes the popular song, punctuated by riffs, runs, breaks and disc-tortions [*sic*]." And in the liner notes for his recording of *Weary Blues*, Hughes says about his collaboration with jazz musicians:

> I tell my musicians, and I've worked with several different groups, to improvise as much as they care to around what I read. Whatever they bring of themselves to the poetry is welcome to me. I merely suggest the mood of each piece as a general orientation. Then I listen to what they say in their playing and that affects my own rhythms when I read. We listen to each other.

The most intimate melding of poetry and jazz occurs when there is a match not only of the moods but also of the structures of the poetry and the music. This happens when poets write their poems to fit specific jazz patterns or musicians write jazz tunes to fit specific poems. For one thing many jazz poems follow the standard AAB structure of the 12-bar blues. Also, musicians such as Duke Ellington, Billie Holiday, Charlie Mingus, and Archie Shepp have written poetry to fit jazz tunes of their own. Here the borderline between jazz and poetry disappears, and some scholars argue that such poems are only jazz poetry when they are recited or chanted, but when they are sung, they are jazz lyrics.

Some well-known contemporary poets who have produced jazz poetry are Jayne Cortez, Nikki Giovanni, Michael Harper, Amiri Baraka, Don Lee, Sterling Plumpp, Sonia Sanchez, and A. B. Spellman. Collections of jazz poetry can be found in *Moment's Notice: Jazz in Poetry and Prose*, edited by Art Lange and Nathaniel Mackey, and in the two volumes of *The Jazz Poetry Anthology*, edited by Sascha Feinstein and Yusef Komunyaka.

Further Reading

Feinstein, Sascha, and Yusef Komunyaka, eds. *The Jazz Poetry Anthology*. Bloomington: Indiana University Press, 1992 and 1996.

Hartman, Charles. *Jazz Text*. Princeton, NJ: Princeton University Press, 1991.

Hughes, Langston. *Montage of a Dream Deferred*. New York: Holt, 1951.

Lange, Art, and Nathaniel Mackey, eds. *Moment's Notice: Jazz in Poetry and Prose*. Minneapolis: Coffee House Press, 1993.

Oliphant, Dave. *The Bebop Revolution in Words and Music.* Austin: University of Texas Press, 1994.

Wallenstein, Barry. "Poetry and Jazz: A Twentieth Century Wedding." *Black American Literature Forum* 25.3 (1991): 595–620.

Ward, Geoffrey. *Jazz: A History of America's Music.* New York: Knopf, 2000.

JONES, EDWARD P. (1950–)

Edward P. Jones is an African American fiction writer. His very first book, *Lost in the City* (1992), a collection of fourteen stories, won the PEN/Hemingway Award and was a finalist for the National Book Award. His first novel *The Known World* (2003) was also highly acclaimed. It was listed on the *New York Times* Editor's Choice and won the National Book Critics' Circle Award for fiction. In 2004, he won the Pulitzer Prize for fiction and was one of the recipients of the prestigious MacArthur grants.

Jones, born and raised in Washington, was educated in local public schools, Holy Cross College, Massachusetts, and earned his master's degree in fine arts from the University of Virginia. Despite the publication of several of his stories that were later collected in *Lost in the City*, he continued to work for a financial magazine, writing on the side, and occasionally teaching creative writing.

For *Lost in the City*, Jones drew upon his experiences of growing up in Washington, D.C., to portray often forgotten African American communities. Modeled after James Joyce's *Dubliners, Lost in the City* portrays a wide array of characters, each different from the other, yet all bound by their race and their struggle with their environment against poverty, crime, failed dreams, envy, and false pride. **Racism** is a pervasive fact in their lives, yet not the focus of Jones's stories; he depicts distinct individuals of all ages and temperaments realistically. There are children nurtured by their family and community, young men embroiled in crime, enticing impressionable youth, old people living in precarious conditions in city-subsidized housing, middle-class men and women defeated despite their academic achievements, and vulnerable women hurt in their elusive search for love. Some of these characters truly get lost in the city while others eventually reach their destination. Most of the stories are told in third person, allowing Jones to step back and create the world that he knew well. When a rare first-person narrator is brought in, it is only to emphasize the limited understanding of the character.

In *The Known World* Jones shifts the setting to the antebellum South and explores a little known aspect of slavery, the existence of black slave owners. The novel is set in Manchester County, Virginia, in the 1840s. His imaginatively rendered descriptions and frequent references to the U.S. Census data and other historical scholarly studies create the illusion of a real geographical area, very much like William Faulkner's imagined Yoknapatawpha County.

The fact that a small number of free blacks owned slaves in the South has been confirmed by recent scholarship. Slaves skilled in masonry, carpentry, shoemaking, and other highly prized crafts were often hired to local landowners and businesses and were sometimes helped by their owners to buy their freedom, and with the continuing goodwill of the master eventually bought their own family members. In strictly legal terms, the family members then became the property of the new owner. Some freed slaves, however, bought other slaves as commercial assets. Jones uses this little known historical fact to weave a complex world of the 1840s to the 1860s.

The novel begins with an account of the death of 31-year-old Henry Townsend whose freedom was bought by his father and whose previous owner helped him to set up his own farm. At his death Henry owned 50 acres and 33 slaves. The novel is not centered on his achievements entirely, but focuses primarily on the perni-cious effects of slavery on human relationships. The sprawling world of Jones's novel encompasses not only masters and slaves but also others on the fringes: the spurned white women embittered by their men's extramarital relationships, slave women victimized by their masters, the poor whites barely eking out a living, illit-erate law enforcers asserting their authority over the blacks, conscientious white men uncomfortable with the notion of enslaving another human being yet carrying out the law in the name of their godly duty, Native Americans—a step above the slaves in the social hierarchy, but treated with equal disdain—and new immigrants considered undeserving of justice.

In form and structure *The Known World* draws its inspiration from the Victorian novels. The circuitous plot has looping episodes, shifts from past to present and even a glimpse of the future, and frequent digressions in twelve chapters bearing long titles, each with three sections following the pattern set in chapter 1, "Liaison. The Warmth of Family. Stormy Weather." An omniscient narrator steers the readers through this richly populated world. The genial, controlled, narrative voice intro-duces the characters, informs the readers of their past, and in many instances even lets them have a glimpse of the future; other times the narrator allows the readers to be direct observers of events and even share the thoughts of the characters. Jones creates no stereotypes of blacks or whites. William Robbins, the most powerful man in the county, is replete with contradictions. He guards and treats his property as a typical plantation owner would, yet he dearly loves a slave (freed later) and the two children he has with her. He values Henry yet does not set him free, but lets his father Augustus toil for years to pay for his son's freedom. Sheriff Skiffington, a devout Christian, never questions the cruel punishments of runaway slaves and condones their masters' acts. The novel is peopled with flesh and blood individuals filled with complexity and contradictions.

Power and control, at the core of master–slave relationship, are hard to relin-quish whether the master has white or black skin. Henry, his wife Caldonia, and Fern Elston, an educated free black woman, all may seem enlightened in some ways but continue to own their human property. Henry's lofty aspirations to run a model plantation with slaves living like a family make little difference to those who are in his power.

Jones's controlled tone of quiet outrage, subtle humor and irony, vivid—almost poetic—language creates an emotional effect of the devastation that slavery causes and makes the novel a biting indictment of slavery and its corrupting influence on the lives touched by it. As the epigraph, a line from the spiritual—"My soul's often wondered how I got over"—indicates his book is a tribute to the invincible spirit of his forebears that helped them survive the ordeals of slavery. The success of his novel has established Jones's reputation as one of the best contemporary writers, though *The Known World* remains the only novel he has published so far. In 2006, he published *Lost in the City*, a collection of short stories. Like his 1992 short story collection, this one too focuses on the lives of mostly working-class African Americans in the Washington, D.C., area.

Further Reading

Maslin, Janet. Review of *The Known World* by Edward P. Jones. *New York Times* (August 14, 2003): Section E, 1, 7.

Pierce, John. "Enticing Identities: The Failure of Assimilation in Edward P. Jones's *The Known World.*" *Valley Voices: A Literary Review* 13.1 (2013): 60–68.

Yardley, Jonathan. Review of *The Known World* by Edward P. Jones. *Washington Post Book World* (August 24, 2003): 2–3.

Leela Kapai

JOY LUCK CLUB, THE

Amy Tan's novel *The Joy Luck Club* (1989) remains a landmark in Asian American literature. Tan's book has become a narrative model for other writers to follow. Its complex portrayals of mother–daughter relationships reveal the depth of familial bonds as well as intricate cultural and generational differences. The popularity and critical aftermath of Tan's book have contributed greatly to the recognition and validation of Asian American fiction in American literature.

The novel opens in San Francisco two months after the death of Suyuan, the main narrator Jing-mei's mother. As the central symbol, the "Joy Luck Club" was initiated by Suyuan in Kweilin during the Japanese invasion of China. Four young women took turns hosting parties, serving and consuming foods for good fortune, playing mahjong, and telling stories about good times in the past and hope for the future. Such an extravagance during wartime becomes the means by which these women raise their spirits and keep at bay fear, despair, and miseries. The San Francisco version of the club started in 1949, when Suyuan, An-mei Hsu, Lindo Jong, and Ying-ying St. Clair met at the First Chinese Baptist Church. Over the years the mothers have been hosting and attending the club where they can recall memories of China and talk about their American-born daughters.

Through Jing-mei's framing narrative, Tan's novel covers considerable temporal and geographical territory. Essentially episodic, the chapters allow each character to tell her story in a first-person narrative. The four pairs of mothers and daughters' love for each other, together with their misunderstanding based on cultural and generational gaps, fills Tan's novel with richness and tenderness. The book ends with the reunion of Jing-mei and her twin half-sisters whom Shuyuan lost during her flight to Chungking in war-torn China. At the airport in Shanghai, Jing-mei finally understands her mother's love and hope for her.

Well received with more than four million copies sold, *The Joy Luck Club* has been translated into at least 12 languages. In 1993, a stage adaptation by American playwright Susan Kim was performed in China; a feature film, directed by Wayne Wang, based on Tan's screenplay was released in America. (*See also* Chinese American Novel)

Further Reading

Bloom, Harold. *Amy Tan's "The Joy Luck Club."* Philadelphia: Chelsea House, 2002.

Braendlin, Bonnie. "Mother/Daughter Dialog(ic)s In, Around, and About Amy Tan's *The Joy Luck Club*." In *Private Voices, Public Lives: Women Speak on the Literary Life*, edited by Nancy Owen Nelson, 111–24. Denton: University of North Texas Press, 1995.

Shear, Walter. "Generation Differences and the Diaspora in *The Joy Luck Club*." *Critique* 34.3 (Spring 1993): 193–99.

Shen, Gloria. "Born of a Stranger: Mother-Daughter Relationships and Storytelling in Amy Tan's *The Joy Luck Club*." In *International Women's Writing: New Landscapes of Identity*, edited by Anne E. Brown and Marjanne E. Gooze, 233–44. Westport, CT: Greenwood Press, 1995.

Xu, Ben. "Memory and the Ethnic Self: Reading Amy Tan's *The Joy Luck Club*." *MELUS* 19.1 (Spring 1994): 3–18.

Lan Dong

K

KINCAID, JAMAICA (1949–)

Jamaica Kincaid is an African Caribbean/American short-story writer, novelist, and essayist. She is one of the most important and original voices of Caribbean post-colonialism and postmodernism. Born Cynthia Elaine Potter Richardson, on the tiny island of Antigua (then a British colony) in the West Indies, Kincaid left at age 17 to work as an au pair in New York. Observing the lives of the wealthy, white, privileged "conquerors" of the world, her sense of being one of the conquered, colonized, exploited, and oppressed became acute. She soon began speaking frankly, dressing outrageously, and living fearlessly as a starving freelance writer until she became a staff writer for *The New Yorker* in 1976, where she worked until 1995. She currently lives in Vermont with her husband and two children.

Kincaid began her fiction writing career as the author of "Girl," a one-long sentence short story. Her fiction is set in either Antigua or Dominica, her mother's island of origin. *At the Bottom of the River* (1985), a collection of short stories, brought her to the attention of the reading public. From this first collection to her most recent novel, *Mr. Potter* (2002), Kincaid has continued to blur the line between fiction and autobiography. Her characters are identifiable members of her family—or her employers, in the case of the novel *Lucy* (1991). Events and entire passages are repeated from novel to novel, from nonfiction to fiction, sometimes but not always from different points of view. Kincaid's entire oeuvre is an elaborate creation of a history for a family (her family) and a people (Antiguan descendants of slaves) not part of official history. Her style is unique, characterized by short sentences, frequent repetition of words and phrases, and frequent use of parenthetical expressions. Often approaching her subject obliquely, beginning with a long list of things that it is not, Kincaid also takes on the postmodernist project of revealing the void that language disguises. By acknowledging the impossibility of describing experience through language, by admitting that even those events that truly happened are linguistic creations, Kincaid implies that all histories are linguistic constructions and must be evaluated for their constructive or destructive effects.

Annie John (1985), Kincaid's first (highly autobiographical) novel, describes an unusually strong child/mother dyad that breaks up when the title character approaches adolescence. Her mother's shocking betrayal results in the 17-year-old Annie leaving Antigua for England. The story both describes an intensely intimate mother/daughter relationship and acts as a metonymy for Antigua's dependent relationship with the colonizing British. *My Brother* (1997), a nonfiction account of Kincaid's visits back to Antigua as her youngest brother was dying of AIDS, reveals the source of Annie John's emotional catastrophe in Kincaid's own life as being the birth of her three younger brothers beginning when she was already nine years old. She felt immediately devalued by her mother and stepfather as being only a daughter, and was forced to drop out of school to take care of her young siblings.

As a postcolonial author, among Kincaid's major themes are the devastating long-term consequences of slavery and colonization. Kincaid never flinches at looking straight at her subjects and describing them with a graphic matter-of-factness. In *My Brother*, her portrayal of Devon's AIDS-ravaged body, his nonchalance at spreading the disease to others, and the nonexistent medical care at what passes for a hospital, are vivid laments for the meaningless lives and senseless deaths of the postcolonials who have limited perspective on their own situations. *A Small Place* (1988), a long nonfiction essay, reveals the author's deep, personal, but outspoken hatred toward the slave traders and slave owners, the British colonizers, the present free but corrupt government of Antigua, and the tourists who admire the natural beauty of Antigua but display the cultural blindness and arrogance of first-world colonizers to a people they consider inferior.

Mr. Potter (2002) imagines the life of her father, whom she only met as an adult. Like *My Brother*, it is an indictment of the ignorance and lack of perspective of both the formerly enslaved and colonized and of the European and Middle Eastern immigrants to Antigua. Being poor and illiterate, Mr. Potter knows almost nothing about history, geography, and current events. A Czechoslovak survivor of the Holocaust sees only blank ignorance in Mr. Potter, and cannot fathom any similarities in their situations—and neither can Mr. Potter. Like his own father, Mr. Potter has many children he does not love or even know, with many different women. Lack of paternal and maternal love, a legacy of slavery and poverty, is Mr. Potter's only inheritance and only legacy to his children.

In perhaps her most accomplished novel to date, *Autobiography of My Mother* (1996), the main character, like Mr. Potter, is a spiritual and cultural (as well as actual) orphan, but unlike Mr. Potter, she is acutely aware of her circumstances. Xuela Claudette Richardson experiences the world as composed of only victims and victimizers. As a postmodern subject, she rebels against identifying with any and every dominant discourse. Descended from Carib Indians, African slaves, and European colonizers, she positions herself as one of the disinherited, the disenfranchised, and the defeated and refuses to pass on the legacy by refusing to bear children. She cannot identify with the victors and refuses to become a victim. She sees her self-imposed exclusion and alienation as a victory over history, and although this everlasting "No" has saved her from a false identity created by others, it has restricted her ability to be fully human.

Kincaid's incantatory poetic style and her unflinching, unmasking gaze into the deepest levels of the psyche as a product of history ensure her place as a pivotal Caribbean author of the late 20th and early 21st centuries. (*See also* Caribbean (Anglophone) American Novel)

Further Reading

Bloom, Harold, ed. *Jamaica Kincaid*. Philadelphia: Chelsea House, 1998.

Everett, Julian. "The Postcolonial Orphan's autobiography." *College Literature* 36.3 (2009): 45–65.

Paravisini-Gilbert, Lizabeth. *Jamaica Kincaid: A Critical Companion*. Critical Companions to Popular Contemporary Writers. Series ed. Kathleen Gregory Klein. Westport, CT: Greenwood Press, 1999.

Barbara Z. Thaden

KING, MARTIN LUTHER, JR. (1929–1968)

Martin Luther King Jr. was an African American Baptist minister, civil rights leader of the 1950s and 1960s, orator, essayist, and winner of the 1964 Nobel Prize for Peace. From a family tradition of preaching from both his father's and mother's sides, King was exposed to Christian values and African American Baptist pulpit oratory since his childhood. His relentless struggle for social justice continued a long tradition of protest in African American letters and ensured him a prominent place in the pantheon of American history. In his many speeches and writings, he consistently capitalized on the power of language to effect change and alter the course of history. He potently used strategies of black folk preaching such as call and response, rhythmic and dramatic oratory, and typology at the same time generously invoking biblical figures and ideas, African American history and literature, and world and American political history. These elements are notably reflected in three generally celebrated texts, "Letter from Birmingham City Jail," "I Have a Dream," and "I've Been to the Mountaintop."

King wrote "Letter from Birmingham City Jail" on April 16, 1963, as a reply to an open letter by eight white Alabama clergymen who had called upon his nonviolent resistance movement to let local and federal courts deal with the issues of integration in order to avoid inciting civil unrest. He argued that he was prompted by Christian values in his fight for social justice and that American democracy and morality were at stake. He repeatedly reaffirmed that his struggle was anchored in Christian love, brotherhood, and nonviolence.

"I Have a Dream" is King's most celebrated speech. He delivered it on the steps of the Lincoln Memorial on August 28, 1963. The speech fittingly opens with the invocation of Abraham Lincoln, who signed the Emancipation Proclamation in 1863, King's reminder to America that "one hundred years later" (repeated four times) the promise of the Proclamation has not become a reality for African Americans, who, in spite of the Thirteenth, Fourteenth, and Fifteenth Amendments as well as several civil rights acts and the 1954 Supreme Court decision known as *Brown v. Board of Education*, are still victims of violence, segregation, discrimination, and disenfranchisement. He stresses that his struggle is rooted not in "bitterness and hatred" and violence but in Christian love, brotherhood, and nonviolence even in the face of police brutality, generalized injustice, and fatigue. The "I Have a

Dream" part envisions an America where the "self-evident" truth of equality and the "unalienable rights of life, liberty, and the pursuit of happiness" will also be a reality for African Americans, and where brotherhood, freedom, justice, and Christian love will triumph. Invoking the words of a Negro spiritual ("free at last"), he projects an Edenic vision by reiterating his belief in the "land of liberty" and his dream that one day all God's children, black and white, of all religious creeds, will be united in freedom regained.

In "I've Been to the Mountaintop," a speech he delivered at the Mason Temple in Memphis, Tennessee, on April 3, 1968, King urged African Americans to be Good Samaritans and support the roadside victims—the garbage workers on strike. He called on African Americans to work together to defeat the modern Pharaoh's attempt to keep them enslaved, arguing that the collective power of black Americans could be used to oppose injustice and violence, achieve victory, and effect change in hiring practices by some companies and by the local government. King ended his speech by suggesting that despite threats on his life, he did not fear for his life. In spite of the general apocalyptic tone of the speech, he compared himself with Moses and asserted that he had been to the mountaintop and had seen the glory of God and the Promised Land of liberty, freedom, and justice for all even though he may not get there with the rest of his listeners. He was assassinated the next day.

At a difficult time when other black leaders had given up on acceptance by white America and were instead promoting black nationalism, King's message of love, hope, inclusion, and racial equality inspired the nation and the world, and the words of this prophet of peace still resonate today with the same compelling voice. (*See also* Civil Rights Movement)

Further Reading

Hansen, Drew W. *Martin Luther King, Jr. and the Speech That Inspired a Nation*. New York: Ecco, 2003.

Miller, Keith D. *Voice of Deliverance: The Language of Martin Luther King, Jr. and Its Sources*. Athens: University Press of Georgia, 1998.

Aimable Twagilimana

KINGSTON, MAXINE HONG (1940–)

Maxine Hong Kingston is a Chinese American novelist, creative nonfiction writer, and essayist. She is known for her compelling literary works that incorporate the long ignored history of Chinese Americans along with her remembrances of her family and ethnic community. Kingston is one of the writers whose works help to build up the foundation of Asian American literature and enable it to be acknowledged as a valued part of American literature. Her writing has inspired younger generations of writers to continue to explore individual struggles over **identity** construction, family stories, and community histories. Written in the genres of fiction and nonfiction, her works have inspired discussion about literary genres and have drawn attention to her insightful and comprehensive illumination of immigrant experiences in America. Her innovative writing has demonstrated the possibility to redefine memoirs and fiction through creating an invented form of narrative, empowered by elements of history, biography, memory, legend, folktale, myth, and anecdote. The complexity and multiplicity of Kingston's books resist the categorization of any single genre or traditionally defined classification, thus shedding new light on American literature.

No other literary works by Asian American writers have achieved as wide acceptance from general audiences and acclaim from critics as **The Woman Warrior** (1976). This book is estimated to be "the most anthologized of any living American writer" and is read by "more American college students than any other living author" (Skenazy and Martin vii). Frequently discussed together with works by such prominent Latina, Native, and African American writers as Gloria Anzaldúa, **Leslie Marmon Silko**, and **Toni Morrison**, this book has contributed to the appropriation of oral literature as a medium to inherit, transmit, and invent cultural memory through creating a new American literary form. The debate on the (mis)representation of Chinese tradition and Chinese American culture in Kingston's works has incurred long-lasting interest among scholars and students of ethnic American literature. *The Woman Warrior* and *China Men* (1980) have added the phrase "talk story" into American literary tradition and English vocabulary. Through reshaping the "talk stories" based on her mother's tales, the Chinese community's anecdotes, cultural memory, and Kingston's own experience of growing up with a double heritage, she engages with both her Chinese ancestry and her American presence and seeks for a balance between gender and **ethnicity**. Her writing covers a broad range of themes that are crucial to ethnic literature in particular and hold universal appeal in general. Another book by Kingston that defies categorization is her limited edition work *To Be the Poet* (2002), integrating poetry, essays, and her personalized illustrations.

Born in 1940 in Stockton, California, Maxine Ting Ting Hong was Chinese immigrants Tom Hong's and Ying Lan Chew's first American-born child. Tom was a professional scholar in his home village of Sun Woi, near Canton, before he migrated to America in 1925. In Stockton, Tom worked as manager of a gambling house and then opened his New Port Laundry. His story has been integrated into *China Men*, where Kingston challenges her father's silence through imagining and reshaping his experiences. Shortly after Tom's departure, their two children died young; Chew went to To Keung School of Midwifery in Canton where she received medical training. She later became a doctor and practitioner in her home village. After a 15-year separation, Chew was able to join her husband in America, where she worked hard in different jobs helping to support her family. As the principal storyteller in the Hong household, Chew employed her talk stories to transmit Chinese tradition and moral values to her American-born children. The narratives, together with ethical and pedagogic codes, which Kingston received from her mother in childhood, have been embedded in a variety of forms in her writing.

Because Kingston grew up among Chinese immigrants, her first language was Say Yup, a dialect of Cantonese. The Chinese community in the San Joaquin Valley, where Kingston spent her childhood, was an enclave where people knew one another well and exchanged gossip frequently. The warning against misbehavior, which Brave Orchid emphasizes through her story of the "No Name Woman" in *The Woman Warrior*, provides a mirror image of such a close-knit environment. The communal talk stories thus became a rich source of materials that Kingston could reshape and recreate in her memoirs and novel.

Kingston was barely fluent in English at the beginning of her school life. The wordless Chinese American girl in *The Woman Warrior* and the metaphor of the "black curtain" in her limited edition book *Through the Black Curtain* (1987) reflect the young narrator's anxiety about gaining a voice to break the profound silence for herself and for her community. Kingston earned her BA in English from the University of California at Berkeley, where she participated in protests against the Vietnam War and in other political movements in the 1960s and met her future husband Earll Kingston. The Kingstons moved to Hawai'i in 1967 and remained there for 17 years, leading a life that followed their pacifist ideals. Essays collected in *Hawaii One Summer, 1978* (1987) reflect a variety of aspects in her Hawaiian life. Kingston also embeds her life and thoughts over the years of activism and pacifism in her novel *Tripmaster Monkey* (1989) and her recent book *The Fifth Book of Peace* (2003).

China Men (1980)

If *The Woman Warrior* focuses on female narrative of history, memory, and story, *China Men* appears to be a parallel book that honors the male characters' familial and communal experiences. Although it is not canonized, as is *The Woman Warrior*, *China Men* has gained lavish praise and acceptance from readers and critics, becoming a landmark in Asian American tradition as another book of "mixed genre." It opens in the mid-19th century, roughly the historical period of Chinese immigrants' large-scale arrival in America. In her storytelling and imagination, Kingston portrays the great-grandfathers, grandfathers, fathers, and brothers as heroic characters in order to correct the usually demeaning image of Chinese men in America. By bridging China and America through the history and stories of her family's men, she claims her ancestors' contributions to the development of America and adds another hue to the multicolored portrait of American history.

China Men is composed of six narratives about her male kin, which are interlaced with twelve brief mythical or historical vignettes. "The Father from China" chronicles her father's (BaBa) life as a cherished baby, a smart student, and then a scholar in his home village in feudal China. "The Great Grandfather of the Sandalwood Mountains" is the story of Bak Goong, who works on sugar cane plantations in Hawai'i. "The Grandfather of the Sierra Nevada Mountains" tells the experiences of Ah Goong as a coolie in the transcontinental railroad camps. "The Making of More Americans" portrays a group of male relatives' who have journeyed to America. In "The American Father," BaBa (now called *Ed*) is a laborer doing menial jobs, then a gambling house manager, and finally the owner of a laundry. "The Brother in Vietnam" concludes the odyssey of her kinsmen toward becoming American by recollecting her California-born brother's story as a Vietnam veteran. The brief tales and vignettes interspersed between chapters introduce and contextualize personal, familial, and communal history.

Tripmaster Monkey: His Fake Book (1989)

After two books published as nonfiction, *Tripmaster Monkey* is considered Kingston's first fiction. The reviews and critical responses toward her third book are mostly positive. Diverging from the first-person narrative that dominates her first two books, the story in *Tripmaster Monkey* is told by an omniscient narrator. Shifting from the concern about family and community history, Kingston's novel knits multiple elements around one man's "show." The protagonist, Wittman Ah Sing, a California native and fifth-generation Chinese American in his 20s, seeks his **identity** with his Chinese heritage and American rearing in the roaring political context of the 1960s in San Francisco. The characters who surround Wittman are his mother, Ruby Long Legs (a former Flora Dora Girl); his father, Zeppelin Ah Sing (a theater electrician); his wife-to-be, Taña (a painter); among others, all of whom make up the mosaic of the multicultural environment of the American West Coast at the time. These people become the cast of Wittman's play in the book, a performance of multiculture in theater and reality. Wittman is portrayed as a person dwelling between boundaries: cultural, ethnic, and artistic. He holds a BA in English and is also fluent in Chinatown patois. For him, being bilingual is a symbol of his bicultural identity. The manipulation of language, including storytelling and stage performing, is the medium of Wittman's identity pursuit. The denouement is marked by the antihero's unpunctuated monologue.

Instead of Chinese or Chinese American, Kingston's third book receives literary nourishment from a global context. It is enriched by appropriation of such sources as the Chinese mythological Monkey King, an allusion to American poet Walt Whitman and his "Song of Myself," and the rich symbolism and complex structure based on the works of Latin American author Gabriel García Márquez. Like the Monkey King who is the prominent characterization of rebellion, Wittman, a draft dodger, an actor, a playwright, and unemployed, represents a phenomenal image. The play Wittman is developing throughout the book is reminiscent of stories of the bandits in *The Water Margin* as well as the historical legend of the three sworn brothers of the peach garden from *Romance of the Three Kingdoms*, but his play nonetheless has an innovation style reflecting the 1960s and Wittman's own rumination of identity and **ethnicity**.

The Fifth Book of Peace (2003)

Kingston begins her recent publication with an autobiographical account titled "Fire" that echoes the loss of her fourth book-in-progress, together with her

Oakland house and possessions, in a fire in 1991. The second chapter "Paper" interlaces factual and fictional accounts of the mystical "three books of peace" from ancient China. It is followed by a long section called "Water" that chronicles the adventures of Wittman Ah Sing, together with his wife, Taña, and son, in Hawai'i, demonstrating continuity with and development of her novel. The concluding chapter, "Earth," records Kingston's journey with a group of Vietnam veterans to an international Buddhist community in France where they meet expatriate Vietnamese nuns and monks. Written in a space between fiction and nonfiction, Kingston's new book is concerned with political matters centered on peace that are more universal than ethnic. Another experiment in literary form, it not only traverses the boundaries between autobiography and novel as well as between the journalist and the imaginary, this work also plays with continuity and innovation based on her earlier writing.

I Love a Broad Margin to My Life (2011)

Kingston's most recent publication is a remarkable memoir written in verse. In beautifully crafted poems, Kingston offers a sweeping map of her eventful life. Some of the major characters from her novels resurface and are artfully braided into the fabric of her autobiography. The poems range from her domestic life to her political activism to her career as a teacher and artist. It offers memorable glimpses into a purposeful life. (*See also* Chinese American Autobiography; Chinese American Novel)

Further Reading

Huntley, E. D. *Maxine Hong Kingston: A Critical Companion*. Westport, CT: Greenwood Press, 2001.

Li, David Leiwei. "*China Men*: Maxine Hong Kingston and the American Canon." *American Literary History* 2.3 (Autumn 1990): 482–502.

Linton, Patricia. " 'What Stories the Wind Would Tell': Representation and Appropriation in Maxine Hong Kingston's *China Men*." *MELUS* 19.4 (Winter 1994): 37–48.

Nishime, LeiLani. "Engendering Genre: Gender and Nationalism in *China Men* and *The Woman Warrior*." *MELUS* 20.1 (Spring 1995): 67–82.

Shu, Yuan. "Cultural Politics and Chinese-American Female Subjectivity: Rethinking Kingston's *Woman Warrior*." *MELUS* 26.2 (1987): 199–224.

Skandera-Trombley, Laura E., ed. *Critical Essays on Maxine Hong Kingston*. New York and London: Prentice Hall International, 1998.

Skenazy, Paul, and Tera Martin, eds. *Conversations with Maxine Hong Kingston*. Jackson: University of Mississippi Press, 1998.

Slowik, Mary. "When the Ghosts Speak: Oral and Written Narrative Forms in Maxine Hong Kingston's *China Men*." *MELUS* 19.1 (Spring 1994): 73–88.

Tanner, James T. F. "Walt Whitman's Presence in Maxine Hong Kingston's *Tripmaster Monkey: His Fake Book*." *MELUS* 20. 4 (Winter 1995): 61–74.

Williams, A. Noelle. "Parody and Pacifist Transformations in Maxine Hong Kingston's *Tripmaster Monkey: His Fake Book*." *MELUS* 20.1 (Spring 1995): 83–100.

Wong, Sau-Ling Cynthia. "Necessity and Extravagance in Maxine Hong Kingston's *The Woman Warrior*: Art and the Ethnic Experience." *MELUS* 15.1 (Spring 1988): 3–26.
Woo, Deborah. "Maxine Hong Kingston: the Ethnic Writer and the Burden of Dual Authenticity." *Amerasia Journal* 16.1 (1990): 173–200.

Lan Dong

KOREAN AMERICAN LITERATURE

Between the early part of the 20th century and the mid-1960s, high-profile Korean American literary works were rarely discussed in academic and commercial literary contexts except in certain instances that corresponded to a small number of Koreans who had immigrated to the United States. In the wake of new waves of immigration after 1965, however, Korean American writers have been flourishing not only in their numbers, but also in the breadth and quality of their literary works. No longer constrained within the confines of immigrant experiences, such as basic survival, cultural conflicts, and assimilation, the newest generations of Korean American writers have brought about a "renaissance" of Korean American literature since the mid1990s.

The First Wave of Korean Immigrants and Their Literary Expressions

By 1888, a small number of Korean students, merchants, exiles, and migration laborers began to arrive on American shores, and the first major wave of Korean immigrants was initiated with the Hawaiian sugar plantations laborers during 1903–1905. It was a time of powerful Western imperialistic advances in Asia; moreover, the Korean peninsula was annexed by Japan—a rising Asian power—in 1910. As a result, a number of Koreans were forcibly relocated or voluntarily emigrated. Korean immigrants, as a people without a country, thought of themselves as exiles as well as immigrants. The plight of Koreans during the colonial period (1910–1945), the loss of individual and collective **identity**, and the struggle in adjusting to life in the New World were reflected in early Korean American writing of the age.

Even though *When I Was a Boy in Korea* (1928) by Il-Han New (1895–1971) was the first published Korean American work written in English, Young-hill Kang (1903–1972) is a pioneering figure in Korean American literature. Kang's first book, *The Grass Roof* (1931), is an autobiographical fiction based upon his childhood experiences in a northern region of Korean with extended explanations of Korean culture and realities of his country under Japanese colonial ruling before his immigration to American. Picking up the story where his first book leaves off, Younghill Kang's *East Goes West: The Making of an Oriental Yankee* (1937), a representative Korean and Asian American literary work of the age, depicts a Korean immigrant's struggle to carve out a place for himself. In chronicling the narrator's trials and tribulations, Kang seeks a mediation on the possible modes of harmonizing East and

West through a series of vignettes of American life and Korean immigrants' struggle between their Eastern traditions and Western modern values.

Between the Korean War and 1965

The second wave of Koreans arrived between the Korean War (1950–1953) and 1965 as war orphans or wives of American servicemen who had been stationed in Korea. But the Korean American community still remained small before restrictive immigration laws were lifted in 1965. Although Korean American writers of this period attempted to maintain strong ties to their country of origin politically and culturally, the variations on the familiar themes of Korean immigrants' writings became more diverse, laying the foundation of post-1965 Korean American literature.

Richard E. Kim, who served in the military during the Korean War, represents the group of postwar Korean American writers. Critically acclaimed and gaining worldwide attention, his first novel, *The Martyred* (1964), still remains the only Asian American work ever nominated for a Nobel Prize for literature. Set in the North Korean capital of Pyongyang immediately after the Korean War, *The Martyred* explores the themes of religious belief, salvation, and human nature in the form of a mystery novel. His second book, *The Innocent* (1968), as a follow-up to his debut, deals with moral issues and existential human dilemmas. Despite Kim's contention that the book is not about a historical event itself but about universal human issues, *The Innocent* reminds some readers familiar with Korean history of the 1961 military coup d'état in South Korea and could also be read as a nuanced commentary on the Vietnam War.

Induk Pahk (1896–1980) is a Korean American writer who paved the way for the tradition of women's writing in Korean American literature through her keen awareness of women's voice in family (Induk is typically a name for men in Korea) and immigration experiences in her three autobiographical works: *September Monkey* (1954), *The Hour of the Tiger* (1965), and *The Cock Still Crows* (1977). Her well-known *September Monkey*, covering her life from her birth in Korea to her success as an educator in the United States, provides an intriguing possibility for building a bridge between the two cultures.

Most of the works of Kim Yong Ik (1920–1955), who, like Richard Kim, taught writing at several American universities, are set in Korea including *The Diving Gourd* (1962), *Blue in the Seed* (1964), and *Kim's Love in Winter* (1969), a collection of short stories. His works clearly demonstrate how much the history of Korea's political and economic debilitation during the tumultuous times of war and colonization, and enforced modernization, still obsessed the Korean American writers.

The Post-1965 Korean American Writing and the Future of Korean American Literature

In 1965 the Immigration Act abolished the discriminatory quota system based on national origin that had restricted the numbers of Asians allowed to enter the

United States. The group of new Korean immigrants was relatively well educated and trained in their professions, but language and cultural barriers often forced them to work outside the fields in which they had been trained. The first post-1965 immigrants focused on the basic necessities of finding housing, securing jobs, and providing for their families. As Korean immigrant families began to settle into their adopted country and find relative success, the new generations of Korean Americans have been witness to an especially rich production of Korean American writing. The cultural differences across generations that had become more and more prominent also characterize the Korean American writing of this period. Not only *Il Se* (first generation) and *I Se* (second generation), but also *Il Chom O Se* (generation 1.5) who were born in Korea and moved to the states in their childhood, began to go through a complex process of defining and articulating their own identities from different perspectives that represented each generation's experiences.

One of the Korean American texts widely used in college courses for many years after the Asian American explosion of the late 1970s is *Clay Walls* (1986) by Kim Ronyoung (1951–1982), which draws on conflicting ideas of being Korean in California in the decades between the two world wars. *Clay Walls* calls into question the established boundaries of Korean American identities by presenting multiple character perspectives to the reader. Exploring tribulations of a Korean immigrant family, *Clay Walls* focuses its attention on the meaning of "wall," which is expanded to include the many "walls" between men and women, parents and children, nations, and cultures. The similar theme of bridging "walls" between cultures and generations continues be examined in Ty Pak's collection of short stories, *Guilt Payment* (1983).

With different spins and foci on the lives of Korean immigrants in the United States, the following works partake of the characteristic of autobiographical writing in Korean American literature: Margaret K. Pai's *The Dreams of Two Yi-Min* (1989), *Man Sei!* (1986) and *In the New World* (1991) by Peter Hyun (1907–1993), Sook Nyul Choi's *Year of Impossible Goodbyes* (1991), and Mary Paik Lee's *Quiet Odyssey: A Pioneer Korean Woman in America* (1990). Without an equivalent, *Dictee* (1982) by Theresa Hak Kyung Cha (1951–1982) demonstrates an experimental writing style of merging various genres and disrupting literary conventions along with her unique approaches to the issues of history, identity, language, memory, and feminism. Challenging conventional patterns of historical and autobiographical writing, Cha's *Dictee* opens up spaces in which Korean American women, who have been silenced by their differences of **race**, gender, and language proficiency, are enabled to articulate themselves. Each fragmented story written in different styles makes readers continuously conscious of how the very act of piecing together fragments to make a coherent narrative sometimes oppresses the voices of the people in "margin."

The new-generation Korean American writing also bore fruitful results in poetry writing. A lesbian and women's rights activist and a writer, Willyce Kim attempts to reject the submissive role of an Asian American woman in her two collections of poems, *Eating Artichokes* (1972) and *Under the Rolling Sky* (1976). Cathy Song, a part-Korean and part-Chinese American born in Hawai'i, received the 1982 Yale Series of Younger Poets Award with her first collection, *Picture Bride* (1983).

A touching lyric eulogy to her ancestral roots, *Picture Bride* dramatizes history through the lives of the poet's family in Hawai'i. Myung Mi Kim's *Under Flag* (1991) merges the issue of language fluency with the difficulty of overcoming cultural differences through a young immigrant child's life.

Since the mid-1990s, Korean American literature, an initially marginal literature, has established itself as prominent through a combination of critical recognition in the academy and commercial success. **Chang-rae Lee** is the most prominent Korean American writer currently in the literary mainstream. His debut, *Native Speaker* (1995), captures the issues of identity, **assimilation**, language, and a possibility of political affiliation of immigrant groups through a story of Korean American Henry Park, a narrator who builds his career with a shadowy multinational intelligence firm by spying on notable Asians. *Native Speaker* takes the form of both detective novel and political thriller. As a follow-up to his debut novel, Lee, in *A Gesture Life* (1999), continues to delve into the difficulties of **assimilation** by unearthing main character Franklin Hata's past relationship with a Korean "comfort woman" (women forced into serving the Japanese soldiers sexually) during World War II behind his impeccably judged veneer of his "gesture life."

Nora Okja Keller, a Korean American writer of a mixed heritage, places the comfort women issue in the center of her novel *Comfort Woman* (1997) and discusses the historical and cultural relationship between Korea and the United States through the story of a once-comfort woman and her daughter by an American missionary. Her next novel, *Fox Girl* (2002), set in an "America town" in Korea following the Korean War, continues to look into the inextricable ties between the two cultures and histories as a historical extension of her first novel. In a similar

Chang-rae Lee, 2004. (AP Photo/Daniel Hulshizer)

vein, Heinz Insu Fenkl's *Memories of My Ghost Brother* (1996), based upon the author's experiences as a mixed child of an American soldier father and a Korean mother, traces the experiences of rejected children and their families in a military camp/town in South Korea.

Patti Kim's *A Cab Called Reliable* (1998), Susan Choi's *The Foreign Student* (1998), Linda Sue Park's Newbery Medal–winning *A Single Shard* (2001), An Na's *A Step from Heaven* (2002), and Don Lee's short-story collection *Yellow* (2003) are notable outcomes of Korean American literature of this period that address various issues in Korean immigrants' lives stemming from the demographic and sociopolitical changes in the Korean American community.

Conclusion

Corresponding to the growing recognition of Korean American literature from the academy and various readerships, recent years have seen the publication of anthologies of Korean American literature, such as *Kori: The Beacon Anthology of Korean American Fiction* (2001), *Century of the Tiger: One Hundred Years of Korean Culture in America 1003–2003* (2003), *Echoes Upon Echoes: New Korean American Writings* (2003), *Yobo: Korean American Writing in Hawaii*, and *Surfacing Sadness: A Centennial of Korean-American Literature 1903–2003*. One of the notable trends in the growth of Korean American literature since the 1990s is that neither the country of ethnic origin nor the country of habitation functions as a singular place for identity formation, thereby calling into question the very assumptions and meanings of identity pivoting on inherited cultural tradition and shared histories of deprivation and discrimination. For example, one may find in Chang-rae Lee's *Native Speaker* and Leonard Chang's *Over the Shoulder* (2001) a sly subversion of reader's expectations, which are suggestive of a possibility of the establishment of genre writing in Korean American literature. Chang-rae Lee and Susan Choi have Japanese Americans as central characters in their recent novels. Even the narrator in Chang-rae Lee's newest novel, *Aloft* (2004), is not Asian American. Gary Pak's fictions are deeply rooted in a local Hawaiian tradition and Susan Choi, who views herself more as a Southern writer than as a Korean American writer, exemplify the transformations and divergent claims in Korean American writing and render the definition of Korean American literature quite complex in light of particular contexts and the interest each writer represents. Extended into a larger context of Korean diaspora writing and expanding the boundaries that circumscribe the reading of Korean American writers, Korean American literature is likely to continue to perform ongoing negotiations with various readerships and the competing claims of communities where values and meaning are not always collaborative but even sometimes conflicting in moments of historical transformation.

Further Reading

Han, Jae-Nam. "Korean American Literature." In *New Immigrant Literature in the United States: A Source Book to Our Multicultural Heritage*, edited by Alpana Sharma Knippling, 143–58. Westport, CT: Greenwood Press, 1996.

Kang, Laura Hyun Yi. *Compositional Subjects: Enfiguring Asian/American Women.* Durham, NC: Duke University Press, 2002.

Kim, Elaine H. *Asian American Literature: An Introduction to the Writings and Their Social Context.* Philadelphia: Temple University Press, 1982.

Kim, Elaine H. "Korean American Literature." In *An Interethnic Companion to Asian American Literature,* edited by King-Kok Cheung. 156–91. New York: Cambridge University Press, 2000.

Kim, Kichung. "Affliction and Opportunity: Korean Literature in Diaspora, a Brief Overview." *Korean Studies* 25.2 (2001): 261–76.

Kim, Pyong Kap. "Korean Americans." In *Asian Americans: Contemporary Trends and Issues,* edited by Pyong Kap Kim, 199–231. Thousand Oaks, CA: Sage, 1995.

Lee, Jeeyeon. "Korean American One-Point-Five." In *The Asian Pacific American Heritage: A Companion to Arts and Literature,* edited by George J. Leonard, 143–50. New York: Garland, 1999.

Solberg, S. E. "The Literature of Korean America." In *The Asian Pacific American Heritage: A Companion to Arts and Literature,* edited by George J. Leonard, 515–26. New York: Garland, 1999.

Yu, Pyong-ch'on. "Korean Writers in America." *Korean Journal* 7.12 (1967): 17–19.

Seongho Yoon

L

LAHIRI, JHUMPA (1967–)

Jhumpa Lahiri is an Indian American novelist and short-story writer. Born in London to parents from India and raised in Rhode Island, Lahiri earned her bachelor's degree from Barnard College and her master's degrees in English, creative writing, and comparative studies in literature and the arts, followed by a PhD in renaissance studies from Boston University. A fellowship at the Fine Arts Work Center in Provincetown launched Lahiri's career as a fiction writer. Her short stories have appeared in *The New Yorker, Aging, Epoch, The Louisville Review, Harvard Review*, and *Story Quarterly*. Lahiri has taught creative writing at Boston University and the Rhode Island School of Design. Currently, she lives in New York City.

The recipient of a Transatlantic Review 1993 award from the Henfield Foundation and a fiction prize from *The Louisville Review* in 1997, Lahiri published her first collection of short stories, *The Interpreter of Maladies*, in 1999, going on to receive the PEN/Hemingway award for the best debut of the year. The title story of her collection was selected for both the O. Henry Award and *The Best American Short Stories*. In 1999 *The New Yorker* named her as one of the 20 best writers under the age of 40.

The Interpreter of Maladies, which won her the Pulitzer Prize for Fiction in 2000, is a collection of nine stories, seven of which deal with immigrant lives in the United States. The two exceptions, "The Real Durwan" and "The Treatment of Bibi Haldar," are set in Calcutta. However, the protagonists in these two stories—one a sweeper of stairwells, and the other an epileptic young woman—share the common dilemmas of displacement and marginalization. Lahiri's characters, whether it is Mr. Pirzada in "When Mr. Pirzada Came to Dine" or Mrs. Sen in "Mrs. Sen's," are all caught up in situations that offer few explanations and fewer solutions. In "The Interpreter of Maladies," the bored Mrs. Das, who is visiting India with her husband and children, is another discontented character. She steps out of her apathy only to relapse into it when Mr. Kapasi, the interpreter of maladies, is unable to interpret the cause of her unhappiness, even after she has confessed to him a dark secret of her sexual life. Mrs. Sen, a babysitter, becomes desperate when she can neither hold on to the familiar world she has left behind nor adapt herself to the New World she has come to live in and where she "cannot sometimes sleep in so much silence." "A Temporary Matter," a finely crafted and acutely poignant story, illustrates the alienation of Shoba and Shukumar, whose marriage has come to an impasse. A one-hour power cut for five consecutive evenings draws them into an intimacy they hadn't experienced since their baby's death. The reprieve, however, is lost as soon as the electricity is restored. "The Third and Final Continent" is different from the rest of the stories, for here the protagonist has traveled farther in terms of time and experience. Though he is still bewildered, as he says at the end of the story, "by each mile I have traveled, each meal I have eaten, each person I have known, each room in which I have slept," he is at peace for he has found his "final continent" at last.

Written in a direct, unadorned but lucid prose, the stories stand out as a testament to Lahiri's control of the narrative art where there is not a word out of place, not a situation sentimentalized, and not an emotion exaggerated. In exploring the psychological and physical dislocation of her characters, she manages to negotiate and interpret, too, the differences between Indian and American cultures for her readers. *The Namesake* (2003), Lahiri's first novel, continues with and extends the themes of displacement, alienation, and the search for one's **identity**. Gogol Ganguli, the protagonist of the novel, is born to Indian immigrant parents in Cambridge, Massachusetts. His father names him Gogol after the Russian writer Nikolai Gogol, whom he greatly admired. The boy, however, grows up resenting his name Gogol as much as he hates his Indian culture. Since the given name is neither Indian nor American, the boy changes it to Nikhil in an effort to reinvent himself. He wants to announce to the world, "I'm Nikhil," but realizes that "his parents, and their friends, and the children of their friends, and all his own friends from high school, will never call him anything but Gogol." Obviously, Lahiri uses the name as a metaphor for one's identity and the crises brought on by its indeterminacy. The farther Gogol/Nikhil goes from his family and his heritage, the farther away he travels from himself. It is only toward the end, actually after his father's death, his failed marriage, and his widowed mother's decision to return to India, that Gogol/Nikhil comes to the point of self-realization, from where his growth may begin. For the first time he recognizes the pain his parents must have gone through "leaving their respective families behind, seeing them so seldom, dwelling unconnected, in perpetual state of expectation, of longing. He had spent years maintaining distance from his origins; his parents, in bridging that distance as best as they could." He is finally at home in his body.

The Namesake makes a fine attempt at understanding the immigrant psyche, which involves more than a physical and cultural displacement. "For being a foreigner, Ashima . . . [begins] to realize, is a sort of lifelong pregnancy—a perpetual wait, a constant burden, a continuous feeling of sorts." Lahiri effortlessly weaves into her narrative scenes of Calcutta that range from crowded streets and buses to posh suburbs and quite bungalows. Not a single discordant note is to be found in her dialogue, for she understands the American idiom and uses it deftly. And what is more, she is a good storyteller. Missing from the novel, however, is the intensity and tension the reader finds so fascinating in her short stories, which affects the delineation of characters in the novel as well. The pace of the narrative slows down when Lahiri strains after details of Indian customs created for the benefit of the American reader. But these are minor points in an otherwise fascinating story.

In 2008, Lahiri published a collection of short stories titled *Unaccustomed Earth*. Once again the stories, like those in her previous collection of short fiction *The*

Interpreter of Maladies, focuses on the lives of Bengali immigrants in the United States. A dazzling collection of stories, they offer piercing glimpses in the private lives of older immigrants who are not quite as home in the United States and younger, second-generation Indian Americans share some of their parents' uneasiness but face new challenges of growing up and finding their place.

Lahiri's most recent publication is *The Lowlands* (2013), nearly an epic narrative that offers a sweeping vision of the lives of four generations of Indian and Indian American families. The novel begins in the 1960s Calcutta, a place where political violence is commonplace, and ends in the 21st-century United States where one sees Obama stickers on car bumpers. While reviews have been mostly favorable, many critics suggest that Lahiri is most at home crafting short stories than weaving epic tales.

Jhumpa Lahiri belongs to a newly emerging group of young diasporic writers, such as Monica Ali and Zadie Smith, who write about their peoples back home, about immigrants to the West, and about the mixing of cultures with an ease and unselfconsciousness that places them in the mainstream of English writing. (*See also* South Asian American Literature)

Further Reading

Austen, Benjamin. "In the Shadow of Gogol." *New Leader* (September/October 2003): 31–32.

Bess, Jennifer. "Lahiri's Interpreter of Maladies." *Explicator* 62.2 (2004): 125–28.

Bromwich, David. "The Man without Qualities." *Nation* (October 2003): 36–38.

Dhingra, Lavina, and Floyd Cheung, eds. *Naming Jhumpa Lahiri: Canons and Controversies.* New York: Lexington Books, 2012.

Farnsworth, Elizabeth. Interview. *PBS Online News Hour*. April 12, 2000.

Kakutani, Michiko. "Liking America, but Longing for India." *New York Times* (August 6, 1999): E2.

Lewis, Simon. "Lahiri's Interpreter of Maladies." *Explicator* (Summer 2001): 219–21.

Lynn, David H. "Virtues of Ambition." *Kenyon Review* (Summer 2004): 160–67.

Munson, Sam. "Born in the USA." *Commentary* (November 2003): 68–71.

Rothstein, Mervyn. "India's Post-Rushdie Generation." *New York Times* (July 3, 2000): E1.

Ruddy, Christopher. "Strangers on a Train." *Commonweal* (December 19, 2003): 18–20.

Sen, Mandira. "Names and Nicknames." *Women's Review of Books* (March 2004): 9–10.

Vijay Lakshmi Chauhan

LARSEN, NELLA (1891–1964)

Nella Larsen was an African American novelist and short-story writer. She was born April 13, 1891, and died March 30, 1964. The daughter of a Danish mother and a West Indian father, Larsen at birth was named Nellie Walker. When Larsen was two years old, her father died. Shortly after his death, Nella's mother married Peter Larsen, a white man of Danish descent. Peter Larsen adopted Nellie Walker, who from that time on used the surname Larsen.

When Larsen's mother and stepfather welcomed the birth of their own biological daughter, color discrimination began to occur in the home. Peter Larsen was embarrassed by Nella Larsen's dark skin and made no attempt to hide his embarrassment from his stepdaughter. Larsen therefore spent as much time away from her all-white family as she could. Finding little joy in her home, Larsen turned to books for comfort and for self-education. Her extraordinary knowledge and book learning would later cause most of her literary and professional associates to assume that she was a college graduate, though she never took a degree.

With her sister, Larsen attended private school in Chicago. From 1909 to 1910, she attended Fisk University, where for the first time in her life, similar to W.E.B. Du Bois, she was immersed in African American culture. Unlike Du Bois, however, who upon arriving at Fisk found comfort and embraced his black environment, Larsen did not feel at ease there, or in any other predominantly black community. Leaving Fisk after only one year and moving to Denmark, Larsen audited classes at the University of Copenhagen.

In 1912, Larsen returned to the United States and for the next three years studied nursing at Lincoln Hospital in New York City. She worked in the field of nursing, both as a nurse and supervisor of nurses, for the next six years. First, she was employed at Tuskegee Institute's Andrew Memorial Hospital and later at Lincoln Hospital, where she had received her training in nursing. Larsen also worked for New York City's Board of Health.

In 1920, Larsen's first literary work was published in *The Brownies' Book*, a magazine edited by Jessie Redmon Fauset, a writer with whom Larsen developed a friendship. James Weldon Johnson, Langston Hughes, Walter White, and Carl Van Vechten—all writers of the **Harlem Renaissance**—also befriended Larsen. These friendships began developing in 1922 when Larsen took a job in the Harlem Branch of the New York Public Library.

While Fauset was the individual who first published Larsen, White and Van Vechten were the ones who assisted Larsen in having *Quicksand* (1928) published, which was the first of her two novels. These two men persuaded Alfred A. Knopf publishers to offer Larsen a contract. With the publication of Larsen's second novel, *Passing* (1929), Larsen's standing as a major author of the Harlem Renaissance was firmly established.

The plots of both of Larsen's novels are quite similar in that they both concern women of mixed **ethnicity**. Helga Crane, the protagonist of *Quicksand*, is the daughter of a Danish American mother and an African American father. Helga struggles for acceptance from her family but does not receive it. She constantly moves from city to city and from country to country in pursuit of acceptance and happiness.

In *Passing* Irene Redfield and Clare Kendry, two African Americans who look white, are at the center of the story. Although both women are "passing," meaning that their skin color allows them to live the lives of white women, Irene passes only now and then. Clare, in contrast, having married a white man who does not know that she is an African American, passes one hundred percent of the time.

In 1928, the Harmon Foundation awarded Larsen a bronze medal for fiction. Her two-time nomination for the Harlem Award for Distinguished Achievement among Negroes in the literature section, in 1928 and 1929, meant that she had won the respect and acclaim of her fellow artists. And Larsen won a Guggenheim Fellowship in creative writing in 1930, becoming the first African American woman to win the award in that category.

The year 1930 did bring Larsen honor on the one hand, but brought dishonor on the other. The award-winning novelist was at the height of her popularity when in 1930 she was accused of plagiarizing "Sanctuary," her short story that had been published in January of that year. Although her publishers accepted her explanation that the similarities between her story and "Mrs. Adis" by the British writer Shelia Kaye-Smith could be attributed to sheer coincidence, an emotionally damaged Larsen lacked the motivation to continue her writing. After "Sanctuary" Larsen published nothing else.

On a more personal level, Larsen's marital difficulties may have contributed to her literary silence. She had married Elmer Imes, an African American physicist involved in pioneering work at Fisk. Although the marriage had been troubled for a while, the couple remained together for the sake of Imes's career. His extra-marital affair with a white woman eventually led the couple to divorce in 1933. Imes's involvement with the woman was reported in various black newspapers around the country. Larsen suffered great embarrassment and became despondent. Her embarrassment was exacerbated in 1941 when, after Imes's death, the white woman, carrying the cremated remains of Imes, returned to Fisk and scattered Imes's ashes over the campus.

Mother-in-law issues also plagued the Larsen–Imes marriage. Imes's mother—who looked like a white woman—and Larsen did not get along well. Ms. Imes refused even to visit in the home of her son and daughter-in-law while Larsen was present.

The accusations of plagiarism and the troubles of home undoubtedly had an impact on Larsen's creativity. Larsen's natural tendency toward nervousness and her fondness for privacy may also have made it difficult for her to concentrate and discipline herself for the task of writing.

Some of the biographical details of Larsen's life are difficult to substantiate and others, because of Larsen's unwillingness to discuss the more personal aspects of her life, are difficult to locate. Some sources give 1891 as the year of her birth while others say 1893. Some scholars have speculated that Larsen was elusive about her life quite simply because she felt rejected by her white relatives and found it too painful to discuss her feelings of rejection and sadness. Records from Fisk show that Larsen changed her name from Nellie Marian to Nella Marie, which suggests Larsen's attempt to separate herself from a painful past while also attempting to construct a new **identity**.

Not a particularly friendly woman, Larsen was an outsider. She was different from most of the other women of her time. For example, Larsen wore short dresses, smoked cigarettes, kept her hair short, and subscribed to no organized religion. Her outsider status and her desire for privacy caused her to live her final days alone and to die alone. Larsen died of a heart attack in her Second Avenue apartment in New York. A friend discovered her body almost a week later.

Even though Larsen was one of the most significant novelists of the Harlem Renaissance, she was all but forgotten until the 1960s when the next great African American artistic movement occurred, namely the Black Arts Movement. That movement led to the reprinting of many forgotten African American texts, and *Quicksand* and *Passing* were two of the more popular novels to be rediscovered and reprinted. Since the 1960s, Larsen's novels have continued to be of interest to those studying African American literature, American literature, and women's literature.

Further Reading

Davis, Thadious M. *Nella Larsen, Novelist of the Harlem Renaissance: A Woman's Life Unveiled*. Baton Rouge: Louisiana State University Press, 1996.

Hutchinson, George. *In Search of Nella Larsen: A Biography of the Color Line*. Cambridge, MA: Belknap Press, 2006.

Joyce Russell-Robinson

LAVIERA, TATO (1951–2013)

Tato Laviera was a Puerto Rican American playwright and poet. He was born in Santurce, Puerto Rico, in 1951 and migrated to New York with his family when he was nine years old. Besides having taught writing at Rutgers University, he was deeply committed to helping the community, having worked as the director of the Community Services, served as chair of the board of directors of the "Madison Neighbors in Action," and sat on the board of directors of the "Mobilization for Youth, Inc."

Although younger than poets like Miguel Algarin, Pedro Pietri, Sandra Maria Esteves, and Jack Agueros, Tato Laviera is often catalogued with them as a **Nuyorican** poet. Adopting the name "Nuyorican" as a reference both to the city and to their Puerto Rican origins, these poets were part of the Beat Generation, which produced such figures as Allen Ginsberg and Jack Kerouac. The Nuyorican poets drew their experiences, as did the Beat poets, from bohemian city life. Unlike the poets of the Beat era, however, the Nuyorican writers were truly living a life of deprivation as the children of immigrants who spoke little English and were placed at the lowest rung of the socioeconomic ladder.

Laviera has written eight plays, several of which have been presented in New York, including *Piñones* (1979), *La Chefa* (1981), *Here We Come* (1983), *Becoming Garcia* (1984), and *The Base of Soul in Heaven's Café* (1989). Laviera's plays reveal his interest in what it means to belong to both the Puerto Rican and American cultures. It is with his poetry, however, that Laviera has left an indelible mark on the literary landscape. Laviera straddles both cultures in his poetry, and the title of one of his books, *AmeRícan* (1986), is a reflection of his concept of himself as neither wholly American nor wholly Puerto Rican. His other books of poetry include

Enclave (1981) and *Mainstream Ethics* (1989). His most influential work to date, however, is *La Carreta Made a U-Turn* (1979).

La Carreta Made a U-Turn was the first book published by the now renowned Arte Público Press in Houston, founded by Nicolás Kanellos. The success of the book is evidenced by the fact that it is now in its seventh edition and has sold more than 60,000 copies. It is considered by many literary critics to be the poetic work that best embodies the cultural and linguistic ambiguity that Puerto Ricans living in New York often feel. The book's title derives from Rene Marques's 1953 play *La Carreta* (The Oxcart), which describes the Puerto Rican people's transition and movement from the countryside to the urban areas of the capital and eventually to New York City. Laviera picks up the story where Marques left off, in effect adding a fourth act to the play, which he divides into three distinct sections.

The first section, titled *Metropolis Dreams*, picks up Marques's characters in their urban environment. In poems like "angelito's eulogy in anger," Laviera captures the essence of the bilingual Nuyorican by presenting both an English and Spanish version of the text. Laviera also examines the sometimes confrontational relationship between Puerto Ricans in New York and those on the island. In *Loisaida Streets: Latinas Sing*, the second section of the book, the poet captures the sounds and images of the Lower East Side of Manhattan. In "titi teita and the taxi driver," one of the books' forty-two poems with English titles but Spanish texts, a newly arrived immigrant provides a cab driver with an address in broken English. The cab driver offers to take her, albeit at an outrageous price, and thus begins her journey into what will be a punishing world. Finally, unlike Marques's characters, Laviera's characters do not return home, but instead stay in their New York slums in the third section of the book titled *El Arrabal: Nuevo Rumbon*.

Laviera's poetry has appeared in several anthologies including *Herejes y mitificadores: Muestra de poesía puertorriqueña en los Estados Unidos* (1980), *Aloud: Voices from the Nuyorican Poets Café* (1994), and *The Prentice Hall Anthology of Latino Literature* (2002). The continued success of Laviera's work is demonstrated by its increasing appearance in mainstream anthologies such as these. By employing code-switching and powerful imagery, Laviera provides a vivid picture of a new immigrant whose two distinct identities have merged into one, and his work is sure to be relevant to newer generations of readers. (*See also* Bilingualism; Puerto Rican American Drama)

Further Reading

Bird-Soto, Nancy. "The Playful 'I' in Tato Laviera's Poetry." *Journal of Midwestern Modern Language Association* 46.1 (2013): 1–14.

Flores, Juan, John Attenasi, and Pedro Pedraza. "*La Carreta Made a U-Turn*: Puerto Rican Language and Culture in the United States." *Daedalus* 110 (1981): 193–217.

Luis, William. "From New York to the World: An Interview with Tato Laviera." *Callaloo* 15.4 (1992): 1022–33.

Rodriguez de Laguna, Asela, ed. *Images and Identities: The Puerto Rican in Two World Contexts*. New Brunswick, NJ: Transaction, 1999.

Eduardo R. del Rio

LEE, CHANG-RAE (1965–)

Chang-rae Lee is an Asian American novelist. With just three novels, he has established himself as a major voice in Asian American literature. He is clearly the most prominent Korean American novelist, and it is not an exaggeration to say that the publication of his first novel, *Native Speaker*, in 1995 marked the starting point for the emergence of Korean American literature onto the national scene.

Chang-rae Lee was born in Korea on July 29, 1965. When he was three years old, his parents, Young Yong and Inja (Hong) Lee, immigrated to the United States. They settled in metropolitan New York, where his father established a successful psychiatric practice. In contrast, his mother was a homemaker and never mastered English. Although the family lived first on the Upper West Side of Manhattan and then in New Rochelle, they attended a Korean Presbyterian church in Flushing. So almost from the start, the spheres of Lee's life were defined by paradoxical demarcations—between the lives led by his a professional father and by his homebound mother and between their own family life in prosperous suburban neighborhoods and life in the ethnic, inner-city neighborhoods of most Korean American immigrants.

After graduating from Phillips Exeter Academy, Lee received a BA from Yale University in 1987, worked for a short time as an analyst on Wall Street, and then pursued a graduate degree in creative writing at the University of Oregon, receiving an MFA (Master's in Fine Arts) in 1993. He has since taught in the creative writing program at the University of Oregon.

For *Native Speaker*, Lee received the PEN/Hemingway Award for Best First Fiction and the 1995 Discover Award. In addition, the literary journal *Granta* included Lee in its list of the 50 best American writers under the age of 40.

The protagonist of *Native Speaker* is Henry Park, a relatively young Korean American who works for a shadowy spy-for-hire company specializing in ethnic and racial investigations. At a point when Park's few, fragile personal relationships have come apart, he is assigned to infiltrate the organization of a popular Korean American city councilman from Flushing who is being touted as a New York mayoral candidate. Almost inevitably, Park's **identity** as a spy is revealed, causing him to confront profound questions about his identity apart from his spying. *Native Speaker* has been justly praised for its convincing synthesis of a broad variety of themes. The immigrant's experience is presented as being, at once, archetypically American and marginalizing. The native language is integral to the immigrant's sense of identity, to a feeling of personal continuity and stability in the midst of tremendous changes in circumstance, and yet it is also the major obstacle to **assimilation** and success in America. The difficult transition from one culture to another involves continual compromises between very different expectations and between very different ways of articulating them. On the simplest level, the word "native" becomes itself paradoxical, designating both the immigrant's "native" tongue and the new language that his children need to learn to speak as the "natives" do.

Lee has expressed his concern that a novelist who chooses to focus on his **ethnicity** or region is too readily categorized as "ethnic" or "regional"—with both terms suggesting works with less than universal themes and less than lasting import. Consequently, it is hardly surprising that in his second and third novels he has tackled subjects that are pointedly not "Korean American" but that address some of the same themes of identity and dislocation that he explores in *Native Speaker*.

In *A Gesture Life* (1999), Lee provides a penetrating character study of an aging Japanese American man who seems perfectly assimilated but who harbors a secret that has kept him from being truly contented and that in one way or another has had a corrosive effect on most of his personal relationships: While serving in the Japanese army during World War II, he first fell in love with and then abandoned one of the Korean "comfort-women" that the Japanese military had forced into its brothels.

In *Aloft* (2004), Lee presents the story of a middle-aged Italian American man who is aptly, but in the end, perhaps more ironically, named Jerry Battle. His enjoyment of flying solo in his Cessna becomes symbolic of his deepening alienation from the people closest to him—his longtime girlfriend, his debilitated and yet overbearing father, and his impetuous, self-indulgent son—and, more broadly, from the norms of the suburban community and culture that he has allowed to define him. (*See also* Korean American Literature)

Lee's next novel, *The Surrendered*, was published in 2010. This sprawling novel, written in Lee's characteristically elegant prose, is a harrowing novel about the Korean War, its victims, and survivors. The novel begins in 1950 as June Han, the protagonist now 11 years old, is fleeing from the war that has just begun but quickly moves the 1980s New York, where Han has settled down and is dying of terminal cancer. The novel is often grim, with vivid descriptions of violence and death, but Lee's remarkable storytelling makes the reading of the novel an unforgettable experience.

Further Reading

Chen, Tina. "Impersonation and Other Disappearing Acts in *Native Speaker* by Chang-rae Lee." *MFS: Modern Fiction Studies* 48 (Fall 2002): 637–67.

Dwyer, June. "Speaking and Listening: The Immigrant as Spy Who Comes in from the Cold." In *The Immigrant Experience in North American Literature: Carving Out a Niche*, edited by Katherine B. Payant and Toby Rose, 73–82. Westport, CT: Greenwood Press, 1999.

Engles, Tim. "'Visions of Me in the Whitest Raw Light': Assimilation and Doxic Whiteness in Chang-rae Lee's *Native Speaker*." *Hitting Critical Mass: A Journal of Asian American Cultural Criticism* 4 (Summer 1997): 27–48.

Huh, Joonok. "'Strangest Chorale': New York City in *East Goes West* and *Native Speaker*." In *The Image of the Twentieth Century in Literature, Media, and Society*, 419–22, edited by Will Wright and Steven Kaplan. Pueblo, CO: Society for the Interdisciplinary Study of Social Imagery, University of Southern Colorado, 2000.

Lee, James Kyung-Jin. "Where the Talented Tenth Meets the Model Minority: The Price of Privilege in Wideman's *Philadelphia Fire* and Lee's *Native Speaker*." *Novel: A Forum on Fiction* 35 (Spring–Summer 2002): 231–57.

Parikh, Crystal. "Ethnic America Undercover: The Intellectual and Minority Discourse." *Contemporary Literature* 43 (Summer 2002): 249–84.

Song, Min Hyoung. "A Diasporic Future? *Native Speaker* and Historical Trauma." *Lit: Literature Interpretation Theory* 12 (April 2001): 79–98.

Martin Kich

LESSON BEFORE DYING, A

Winner of the 1993 National Book Critics Circle Award, Ernest Gaines's *A Lesson Before Dying* is a riveting piece of legal fiction that is as much a wrenching story about institutional injustice as it is a compelling human drama of a man who learns to affirm life even as he confronts certain death. Set in a small Louisiana town in the late 1940s, the novel focuses on Jefferson, a young black man who happens to be present during a violent crime that results in the death of a white shop owner. He is arrested and a trial with an all-white jury ensues. During the trial the defense attorney, whose job is to exonerate Jefferson, compares Jefferson to a hog that is incapable of premeditated murder. Jefferson's godmother, Miss Emma Glenn, is deeply wounded by the attorney's comparison of Jefferson to a hog. With the help of Tante Lou she enlists Grant Wiggins, the local black school teacher and Lou's nephew, to speak with the imprisoned Jefferson and help him realize that that he is not what the defense attorney—and many whites like him—believe he is.

A reluctant Grant embarks on what he believes is an impossible mission. A college-educated black in the segregated South, Grant is frustrated by the severely restricted life he leads and wants to flee the South. An atheist, he troubled by the attempts of Rev. Mose Ambrose to spiritually save Jefferson who has been condemned to die on an electric chair between noon and three o'clock on the Friday following Easter. Jefferson initially rebuffs Grant's attempt to reach him but gradually the two men forge a bond. Grant encourages Jefferson to write down his thoughts in a diary as he faces his imminent death. Jefferson learns to face his death with dignity. A man who was dehumanized learns to rehumanize himself and affirms his self-worth even as he faces his extinction. Grant too is transformed by his friendship with Jefferson. Paul Bonin, a white deputy at the jail who witnesses Jefferson's electrocution, is also transformed by what he has seen. The novel ends on a redemptive note of interracial alliance as Paul offers his hand in friendship to Grant and accepts Grant's invitation to come and speak his students one day about Jefferson's heroism.

Gaines's novel can be read as an allegory. The action of the novel begins just prior to Christmas and ends shortly after Easter and thus covers an important period in the Christian calendar—a time period that encapsulates the central drama of Christianity from the birth of Christ to his crucifixion and resurrection. Like Christ, Jefferson is falsely accused, subjected to a trial that is mockery of the judicial process, and sentenced to death. The timing of Jefferson's death too is significant: between noon and three o'clock on a Friday. Like Christ's death, Jefferson's death too has redemptive qualities. Jefferson becomes a rallying point for the African American community, including the school children whom Grant teaches. The diary that Jefferson leaves behind becomes part of his legacy, his final testament. The glimmer of interracial understanding and alliance that emerges at the end of the novel suggests a process of cleansing, the possibility of redemption. Grant, who once wanted to flee the South, now decides to stay and he will be teaching his students more than reading, writing and arithmetic; he will be teaching a generation of young people who are likely to become actors in the impending Civil Rights Movement that will change the South and the nation at large. Thus Gaines takes a tragic tale and transforms it into a story of redemption, a narrative of transcendence.

While two male characters, Grant and Jefferson, seem to dominate the action of novel, a closer look reveals the centrality of the women characters. It is Miss Emma, deeply wounded by the defense attorney's casual comparison of her godson to a hog, who insists that Grant should go and speak with the imprisoned Jefferson who is awaiting death by electrocution. With the active help of Grant's aunt Lou, she is able to achieve her goal. Thus she is not only foundational to the plot but also propels it forward. Grant's girlfriend, Vivian, too is an important presence in the novel; she is instrumental in helping Grant see his social mission and his obligations to his community. She is crucial to Grant's eventual decision to stay in the South.

An onomastic reading of the novel adds rich new layers to the narrative. Jefferson's name, for example, evokes the name of Thomas Jefferson, the third president of the United States, who is widely acknowledged to have fathered several children with Sally Hemings, an enslaved woman on his plantation who was also his mistress for almost 30 years. The white attorney who compares Jefferson to a hog—and many whites like him—is unaware of the mixing of bloodlines and the very real kinship that exists between black and white Americans. This racial intermingling is very much a part of the American experience, yet it is a subject that is generally not talked about. Grant's name is reminiscent of Ulysses S. Grant—the brilliant soldier who helped defeat the Confederate troops, helped end slavery and, as the twice-elected 18th president of the United States, presided over the period of Reconstruction—a period when African Americans made significant gains with expanded civil rights, a period that astonishingly witnessed the election of African American Congressmen from South Carolina and Mississippi. Rev. Mose Ambrose clearly evokes the name of the Old Testament Moses, the man who led his people to the Promised Land. The white deputy, Paul, is not unlike the Paul of the Old Testament: he too is transformed by something he witnesses. Saul, on his way to Damascus, sees Christ who appears before him as a blinding light; this epiphanic moment transforms him and he renames himself as Paul when he reaches Damascus to memorialize his profound change. Paul in Gaines's novel, who is momentarily blinded by the electrocution of Jefferson, too is transformed by his experience and is redeemed by it. Thus, Gaines's purposeful choice of names to his characters opens new interpretive possibilities.

Further Reading

Baker, Sarah E. "Ernest J. Gaines and *A Lesson Before Dying*: The Literary Spiritual." In *Literature and Music*, edited by Michael Meyer, 117–34. Amsterdam: Rodopi, 2002.

Brown, Anne Gray. "Writing for Life: 'Jefferson's Diary' as Transformative Text in Ernest J. Gaines's *A Lesson Before Dying*." *Southern Quarterly* 47.1 (2009): 23–46.

Emmanuel S. Nelson

LORDE, AUDRE (1934–1992)

Audre Lorde was an African American poet and writer. Self-described "black lesbian, mother, warrior, poet," Lorde celebrated the multiple aspects of her **identity** and affirmed the power of difference in her poetry, essays, and prose writing. She refused to be silenced, despite her marginalized position in society, and confronted the injustices of **racism**, sexism, and homophobia with courage, hope, and eloquence.

The youngest of three daughters, Lorde was born in New York City to parents who emigrated from Granada, the West Indies, with the hope of achieving financial success and then returning home. However, the family remained in the United States, creating a sense of dislocation for Lorde, which strongly contributed to her conception of home as a journey rather than as a single geographic locale. Severely near-sighted, Lorde began speaking when she was five years old, and she later described her early communication as a form of poetry. She published her first poem in *Seventeen* magazine after it was rejected by her Catholic high school's student paper.

Audre Lorde, 1983. (Robert Alexander/Archive Photos/Getty Images)

Lorde enrolled at Hunter College in 1951, but did not receive her BA until 1959 because she had to support herself throughout her studies. She worked as an X-ray technician, medical clerk, social worker, and factory employee, among other jobs. During the 1954–1955 academic year, she studied at the National University of Mexico. In 1961, she received an MA in library science from Columbia University and worked as the young adult librarian at Mount Vernon Public Library. The following year she married lawyer Edwin Ashley Rollins. They had two children, Elizabeth and Jonathan, and divorced in 1970.

After receiving a grant from the National Endowment for the Arts in 1968, Lorde left her position as the head librarian at Town School Library in New York City to become the poet-in-residence at Tougaloo College in Mississippi. Her first volume of poetry, *The First Cities* (1968), is an introspective collection that uses natural images to describe the complexities of human emotion. These poems reflect an acute disillusionment with American ideals and anticipate her later exploration of themes such as dispossession, marginalization, and activist rage. In *Cable to Rage* (1970), Lorde explores marital love, personal deception, and child rearing. Using fresh, powerful language, Lorde examines the fleeting nature of love and suggests that betrayal is a result of the human capacity for change. The poem "Martha" contains Lorde's first reference to her homosexuality, a major concern of her later works.

Lorde published most of her critically acclaimed poetry in the 1970s. After receiving a Creative Artists Public Service grant in 1972, Lorde wrote *From a Land Where Other People Live* (1973), which was nominated for a National Book Award. In this collection, Lorde unites political concerns with personal experiences of outrage, discrimination, and self-exploration. Writing about the devastation caused by racism in the black community, Lorde protests the domination of white culture. She also examines her identity as a black woman and describes her relationships with other women.

The New York Head Shop and Museum (1974) is often considered Lorde's most radical poetic work. In stark urban images, she decries the deterioration of the city and expresses her anger in a more aggressive style, which is characteristic of the new black poetry movement of 1960s. In *Between Ourselves* (1976), Lorde again uses poetry as a means of channeling her rage against social injustice and as a way to confront personal conflicts and concerns. She received the Broadside Poets Award in 1975.

Coal (1976) was Lorde's first book to be released by a major publishing house. A compilation of poems from her first two books, this collection was read by a wider audience and helped to bring Lorde to national attention. In *The Black Unicorn* (1978), Lorde uses African mythology to assert her blackness and to express her female identity. She celebrates the land, culture, and people of Africa while also emphasizing the multiple aspects of her identity. Much of Lorde's later poetry addresses the mother–child relationship. Lorde offers conflicted representations of the mother; she is both a repressive force linked to conformity and deception and a figure of comfort, love, and identity.

Lorde's first major work of prose, *The Cancer Journals* (1980), is also the first publication about breast cancer by a black woman. As she describes her struggle with the disease and its aftermath, Lorde writes from a fundamental need to express her pain and to share her experience with others. She confronts her fear, anger, and despair with courage and a passionate will to survive. Lorde's decision not to wear a prosthesis following her mastectomy testifies to her rejection of conventional standards of beauty and to her desire to honor her survival physically. *The Cancer Journals* was the winner of the American Library Association Gay Caucus Book of the Year Award for 1981.

Lorde's second major prose work, *Zami: A New Spelling of My Name* (1982), is a "biomythography" that combines aspects of memoir, poetry, fiction, and mythology to describe her artistic maturation and her search for a home space. As the story of a poet's journey to self and voice, Zami focuses upon the development of Lorde's creative sensibility while also imaginatively rewriting experience. The central metaphors in Zami center on images of the home and body. For Lorde, making a home means fashioning a line of descent composed of women who have contributed to her identity, especially as a poet and an outsider. While affirming the physical embrace of bodies and erotic pleasures, she also writes about her mother as a figure of difference and envisions a cultural heritage that validates her lesbianism.

Despite the success of Lorde's poetry, she has become best known in academic circles for her essays on black feminism and her reevaluation of difference. In her influential collection, *Sister Outsider: Essays and Speeches* (1984), Lorde asserts her lesbianism and argues for the relevance of feminism to the black community. Essays such as "The Master's Tools Will Never Dismantle the Master's House" and "Age, Race, Class and Sex: Women Redefining Difference" explore the role of difference as a dynamic, enriching force, which is too often presented as a threat to social stability. In "The Uses of the Erotic," perhaps her most cited essay, Lorde presents the erotic as a vital source of female power. She argues that the racist patriarchy of American society has oppressed and devalued female creativity. Lorde explains in "Poetry Is Not a Luxury" that empowerment comes from a firm commitment to self-expression.

Lorde combined her socially conscious writing with a strong dedication to community involvement. With Barbara Smith, she founded Kitchen Table: Women of Color Press to promote the writings of feminists. She also helped create Sisterhood in Support of Sisters in South Africa and served on the board of the National Coalition of Black Lesbians and Gays. From 1980 to 1987 Lorde was poet and professor of English at Hunter College where she mentored young feminists and students of color. In 1991, she was named the poet laureate of New York.

Following her death in St. Croix in 1992, women and men all over the world held tributes to her. In eulogies and vigils, they remembered a poet and activist who eloquently protested social injustice and passionately claimed the multiple facets of her identity. Lorde's commitment to self-expression and social consciousness have made a significant impact on black feminist thought and critical discourses on **race**, gender, and sexuality. (*See also* African American Lesbian Literature)

Further Reading

Leonard, Keith D. "'Which Me Will Survive': Rethinking Identity, Reclaiming Audre Lorde." *Callaloo* 35.3 (2012): 758–77.

Steele, Cassie Premo. *We Heal from Memory: Sexton, Lorde, Anzaldúa, and the Poetry of Witness.* New York: Palgrave, 2000.

Wilson, Anna. *Persuasive Fictions: Feminist Narrative and Critical Myth.* Cranbury, NJ: Associated University Press, 2001.

Stephanie Li

MARSHALL, PAULE (1929–)

Paule Marshall is a Barbadian American writer and author of five novels and two short-story/novella collections, *Soul Clap Hands and Sing* (1961) and *Reena and Other Stories* (1983). Marshall's fiction focuses on females of the African diaspora facing conflicts of **identity** and engaging in quests for self. Traveling from America (usually Brooklyn, New York, where her family immigrated during World War I) to the Caribbean, France, and—in memory—to the Sea Islands of South Carolina, or back to America from Europe or the islands, these women find missing parts of themselves and spiritual sustenance.

Marshall is well known for creating compelling characters, large themes focusing on how Barbadians and Barbadian Americans can survive in a materialistic, avaricious white world, and a strong sense of place for all her work. Rows of leaning Brooklyn brownstones, island shacks, palatial hotel rooms, and small, cramped apartments in Paris or Manhattan all reveal the inner lives—triumphs, dreams, disasters—of those that inhabit them. Houses are especially important in her fiction. The attached row houses of her first and most recent book reflect the strong family and community bonds of the Afro-Caribbean in America who lease and own them. Purchasing property becomes the obsession of many who are caught up in chasing white American dreams to their own detriment (loss of culture, loss of self, and loss of an integrated black identity).

Brown Girl, Brownstones (1959) is a coming-of-age novel that takes Selina Boyce from a 10-year-old, listening to the talk of the Barbadian American women sitting in her mother's kitchen (oral language raised to an art form when these women talk to release their immense creativity) and trying to save her father's dreams from her mother's wrathful destruction, to a young adult dancer encountering her first racist insults.

The Chosen Place, The Timeless People (1969) focuses on the vagaries of power when a large-scale American research team, headed by Saul Amron, comes to Bourneville, the poor, black section of a small Caribbean island. The islanders learn ultimately they must save one another and themselves with interracial friendships such as arise between the protagonist, Merle Kinbona, and Saul and with Merle's return to Africa to discover family ties and cultural understanding, in the wake of crisis and disorienting events.

Praisesong for the Widow (1983) focuses on Avey Williams, an affluent African American widow in her 60s, who jumps ship from her Caribbean cruise to become reconciled with her "opposite," Lebert Joseph, an old man she encounters in a rum shop on the beach in Granada (Marshall's literary incarnation of the Yoruba trickster Legba, mediator between gods and humans who serves as agent for Avey's rebirth). The gift she receives from him—psychic, spiritual, and political—and brings back to her native land and her community in White Plains is ancestral storytelling. She will share her cultural awakening with others to bring them to a better understanding of how to deal with the oppressive materialism that she sees shattering the spirit of African Americans.

Daughters (1991) is about Ersa Beatrice MacKenzie, who is the symbolic daughter of Celestine, the family housekeeper and her father's earliest lover, and of Astral Forde, the manager of her father's hotel and his long-term mistress, and the real daughter of Estelle, wife of Primus MacKenzie (also the prime minister), the prime mover encircled by female constellations. In *Daughters*, Ersa is searching for a way to live in America where those who categorize her as immigrant erase half her life.

In *The Fisher King* (2000), Marshall introduces an eight-year-old boy, grandson and namesake of Sonny, a famous **jazz** pianist who, years earlier, fled America for fame—and later neglect—in Paris. Sonny, with Barbadian grandfather, African American grandmother, Barbadian American mother, and African father, begins his own quest as the novel unfolds: trying to mend the fractures of **race** and class in this complicated family. Here, as in *Daughters* and *Praisesong for the Widow*, Marshall uses as her dominant narrative strategy a dense, interweaving of back stories to fill gaps of information and family and social history and to explore themes such as the conflict of the dreamer and doer in marital relationships (aggressive females like Selina Boyce's mother, Silla, and Saul Amron's wife, Harriet, who destroy their husbands' dreams in order to shape and design their lives, or males like Primus MacKenzie and Sonny Payne who keep a circle of females all moving to their designs); the loss of innocence, when female trust or male dreams are shattered or young adults encounter racist, classist, or sexist constrictions; the quest for self in a world that sees the black female in generic rather than individual, personal ways; and the need for knowledge of oneself and one's culture—for taking a spiritual journey into the past—in order to understand how one will face the future.

As an ethnic feminist, Marshall emphasizes women, especially mothers and foremothers of female children, telling stories for the transmission of culture, as Avey remembers hearing from her great-aunt Cuney in South Carolina as a child in *Praisesong for the Widow*. But men also tell stories in Marshall's books. In *Daughters*, Primus MacKenzie tells his wife, Estelle, the story of Congo Jane and Cudjoe, coconspirators in slave resistance and equals in strength and value to one another, a story that Estelle tells Ersa and Ersa tells her lover and friend Lowell, and one that Ersa adopts in her own quest for equity in male–female relations. (*See also* African American Novel; Caribbean (Anglophone) American Novel)

Further Reading

Christian, Barbara. *Black Feminist Criticism: Perspectives on Black Women Writers*. New York: Pergamon, 1985.

DeLamotte, Eugenia. *Places of Silence, Journeys of Freedom: The Fiction of Paule Marshall*. Philadelphia: University of Pennsylvania Press, 1998.

Ferguson, Moira. *A Human Necklace: The African Diaspora and Paule Marshall's Fiction*. Albany: State University of New York Press, 2013.

Pettis, Joyce. *Toward Wholeness in Paule Marshall's Fiction*. Charlottesville: University Press of Virginia, 1995.

Skerrett, Joseph. "Paule Marshall and the Crisis of Middle Years: *The Chosen Place, the Timeless People*." *Callaloo* 6.2 (Spring–Summer 1983): 68–73.

Washington, Mary Helen. "Afterword." In *Brown Girl, Brownstones* by Paule Marshall, 311–25. New York: Feminist Press, 1981.

Wilentz, Gay. *Binding Cultures; Black Women Writers in Africa and the Diaspora*. Bloomington: Indiana University Press, 1992.

Nina Mikkelsen

MCBRIDE, JAMES (1957–)

James McBride is an autobiographer, novelist, journalist, musician, and composer. Born in 1957 to a white Jewish mother and an African American father, he grew up in Brooklyn's Red Hook housing projects. Having never known his biological father, Andrew Dennis McBride, who died before James was born, McBride developed a close bond with his mother. Following the death of her first husband, Ruth McBride married another African American man, Hunter Jordan, who died when James was a teenager. Frustrated by his mother's struggle to raise 12 children on her own, the rebellious McBride turned to alcohol and drugs as a means of escape. Fortunately, his strong upbringing and fear of incarceration encouraged McBride to alter his reckless lifestyle. At 17, he began attending an all-black public school, which cultivated his interests in writing and music. Upon graduation, McBride enrolled in Oberlin College in Ohio, where he received a bachelor of arts degree. After college, he continued his pursuit of higher education and earned a master's degree in journalism from Columbia University.

The recipient of several literary and music awards, McBride oscillates between careers as a writer and a musician. In addition to having worked as a journalist for the *Boston Globe, People Magazine*, and the *Washington Post*, McBride has written for *Essence, Rolling Stone, The Philadelphia Inquirer*, and the *New York Times*. He has also composed music and lyrics for such renowned artists as Anita Baker and Grover Washington Jr. In 1996, McBride published his acclaimed memoir, *The Color of Water: A Black Man's Tribute to His White Mother*, which was awarded the Anisfield-Wolf Book Award for literary excellence. An amalgam of autobiography and biography, *The Color of Water* relates McBride's search for self while attempting to unlock the mystery of his mother's **identity**. The lone white face in a sea of black, Ruth McBride Jordan was respected and admired by her neighbors as a mother who instilled pride and ambition in her children. Her refusal to pigeonhole herself according to **race**, while at times baffling to her young son, offers an intriguing commentary on American society's color consciousness. Following the success of *The Color of Water*, McBride was chosen to coauthor *The Autobiography of Quincy Jones*, which was released in the fall of 2001. Published the following year, McBride's first fictional work, *Miracle at St. Anna*, is an historically based novel that recounts the experiences of four African American soldiers, a band of partisans, and an orphan boy trapped in the Italian foothills during World War II. A tale of hope and courage, *Miracle at St. Anna* speaks to the resiliency of the human spirit and the commonality of the human experience.

McBride published his novel *Song Yet Sung* in 2009. A compelling tale set in Maryland's eastern shore prior to the Civil War and loosely based on historical events, it centers on Liz Spocott, a runaway slave. Wounded in the head by bounty hunters who are determined to capture her, she develops a capacity for visions of the future—visions that delve far into the future to include Martin Luther King and the emergence of urban hip-hop. Though the novel vividly captures many harrowing events, it has a powerful redemptive edge: suffering that is suffused with hope.

In 2013, McBride won the National Book Award for his next novel *The Good Lord Bird*. The setting is again the days before the Civil War. The narrator is Henry Shackleford, an enslaved man who meets John Brown, the famous abolitionist, at a tavern. Together they begin a journey together. Shackelford recalls his meetings with **Frederick Douglass**, Harriet Tubman, and other historical figures. He describes with compelling clarity John Brown's calamitous raid on the Harpers Ferry. Some critics have favorably compared the novel to Mark Twain's *The Adventures of Huckleberry Finn*. (*See also* African American Autobiography)

Further Reading

Harper, Phillip Brian. "Passing for What? Racial Masquerade and the Demands of Upward Mobility." *Callaloo: A Journal of African American and African Arts and Letters* 21.2 (Spring 1998): 381–97.

Carol Goodman

MEXICAN AMERICAN AUTOBIOGRAPHY

In reading a novel we are allowed into the writer's creative mind, but in reading an autobiography we are given privileged access into the writer's very soul. Mexican Americans now constitute the largest minority group in the United States, and since much of their literature is autobiographical, one task is determining what should be categorized as fiction and what can be considered autobiography. Autobiographical literature is found in all genres: novels, essays, short stories, poems, plays, biographies, and oral histories/*testimonios*. Autobiographies range from the lyrical-poetic to the sociohistorical with everything in between.

The origin of Mexican American autobiography depends on how the term *Mexican American* is defined, for some 16th- and 17th-century Spanish explorers like Bartolomé De Las Casas (*A Short Account of the Destruction of the Indies*, 1552) and Bernal Díaz (*The Conquest of New Spain*, ca. 1568) wrote about their travels in the Americas. These works might more accurately be referred to as U.S. Hispanic literature, but even that definition can be problematic. Generally scholars of the

Mexican American autobiography focus on works published after 1848, when the Treaty of Guadalupe Hidalgo was signed and when some 80,000 Mexican nationals became U.S. citizens.

Autobiographical writers often address questions of identity: "who am I?" Increasingly, there are autobiographies written by those who are part Mexican, so **identity** issues abound. Some writers wish to preserve history and leave a record for the younger, often more assimilated generation. Many memoirs focus on coming-of-age experiences, which often include immigration, schooling, language acquisition, **assimilation**, cultural conflict, migrant work, love, sex, and religion. Other narratives are episodic and focus on specific dramatic events; some autobiographies underscore themes of prejudice; a few read like a Chicano rags-to-riches story. More and more, these narratives are written by the moderately famous (actors, politicians, business people, scholars, singers). Memoirs are also produced by war veterans, ex-gang members, gays, prisoners, students, and ministers. Furthermore, Mexico's tripartite identity—Spanish, Indian, and *mestizo* (mixed)—contributes to a complicated sense of identity and loyalty.

Autobiographical works raise questions about truth, exaggeration, embellishment, obfuscation, posturing, and so forth. Since many autobiographies are penned late in the author's life, memory also serves as a significant factor. Some writers record dialogue that may have occurred when they were young, but it is unlikely that they can remember such details verbatim five or six decades later. There is thus the *invention* of words and scenes, though usually these literary conventions are accepted by readers. Sometimes childhood is romanticized or idealized; sometimes past difficulties are exaggerated; important details can be left out or ignored. Writers usually (and sometimes artificially) impose structure, emphasize conflict or change, create themes or resolution, composite characters, and change names (or circumstances) of people. Moreover, in recording a life, the life is not merely explained or presented, but rather a *persona* is developed. Similarly, time and space create restrictions, for it is impossible to record a life in totality: much must, of necessity, be left out. Thus, some of these narratives end while the authors are barely out of their teens, some focus primarily on the latter part of their lives—their successes, some are primarily about their formal education, and some autobiographies give a great deal of background on the lives of ancestors and parents and therefore border on biography.

A few autobiographical works defy genres and are difficult to classify: **Richard Rodriguez**'s works take the form of autobiography, essays, and journalism. Like the work of other Mexican American writers, Floyd Salas's writing is autobiographical, biographical, and fictional. Cherríe Moraga and Gloria Anzaldúa both inventively combine poetry, essays, stories, journal entries, lesbian politics, and autobiography. Anzaldúa, for example, described herself as a Chicana *tejana*–lesbian–feminist writer. Other autobiographical texts are sociological, political, historical, psychological, or anthropological.

Under the rubric of autobiographical fiction—one of the largest categories within Mexican American literature—we have a number of notable works including: **José Antonio Villarreal**'s *Pocho* (1959), **John Rechy**'s *City of Night* (1963),

Tomás Rivera's *. . . y no se lo trago la tierra* (1971), **Rudolfo Anaya**'s *Bless Me, Ultima* (1972), Nash Candelaria's *Memories of the Alhambra* (1977), **Sandra Cisneros**'s *House on Mango Street* (1984), **Arturo Islas**'s *The Rain God* (1984), and Patricia Santana's *Motorcycle Ride on the Sea of Tranquility* (2002); these writers, and myriad others, borrow considerably from their own life experiences.

Early writers of autobiographical narratives include Fabiola Cabeza de Baca, Fray Angelico Chavez, Cleofas Jaramillo, Miguel Otero, Juan Seguin, Leonor Villegas de Magnon, and Luis Perez, among others. In these early writers' works, there is sometimes a romanticized view of the world. Many of these narratives were written by middle-class Mexican Americans who often referred to themselves simply as *Hispanos* or *Mejicanos*—without a hyphen, and there is often considerable class consciousness as well as an attempt to maintain Spanish (as opposed to Mexican or Indian) roots.

One of the most enduring and endearing Mexican American autobiographies is **Ernesto Galarza**'s *Barrio Boy* (1971), which begins in Mexico during the revolution of 1910. Young Ernie migrates with his mother and uncles and eventually settles in Sacramento, California. The subtitle "The Story of a Boy's Acculturation" presents one of Galarza's concerns, for he believes his own experiences are characteristic of thousands of other immigrants who fled the revolution. The book ends before Galarza begins high school, even though he went on to earn a PhD. Like other works in this genre, this is a poignant, somewhat bittersweet, coming-of-age story that relates the difficulties associated with immigration and poverty.

Oscar Acosta's *The Autobiography of a Brown Buffalo* (1972) presents a troubled and complex individual searching for a sense of identity. The autobiographical novel is organized around several trips/quests: Acosta is on an actual road trip, he trips on drugs, and he explores his past via a psychiatrist. These journeys/quests are effectively interwoven within the late 1960s San Francisco counterculture. At the end of the book, in Mexico, Acosta claims to have finally found and accepted himself. The sequel, *The Revolt of the Cockroach People* (1973), chronicles his legal work for the Chicano Civil Rights Movement in Los Angeles. Although at times crude and sexist, Acosta captures the complexities of his culture and his era.

A prominent and controversial book is Richard Rodriguez's *Hunger of Memory*, which was positively reviewed when it appeared in 1981. It is partly a collection of previously published—and carefully crafted—essays that were compiled and edited into book format. As a child, Rodriguez was inadvertently taught to be ashamed of his brown skin, and he once tried to scrape away the dark pigment with a straight razor. Other chapters deal with Rodriguez's assertions that because of his superior education, he is not a disadvantaged minority but rather a middle-class assimilated American. Numerous Chicano scholars think that Rodriguez repudiates his culture, and he has been accused of having a colonized mind. In particular, minorities have been critical of his stance against affirmative action and bilingual education. Despite these critiques, it is acknowledged that Rodriguez is a fine prose stylist. He is an award-winning journalist who has since produced two other collections of essays: *Days of Obligation* (1992) and *Brown* (2002), which discuss topics germane to minorities. One work that might serve as a companion piece to

Hunger of Memory is Ruben Navarrette's *A Darker Shade of Crimson* (1993) about his experiences as a Chicano at Harvard University. He devotes a few pages to discussion of Rodriguez.

Also of particular significance are the two distinguished autobiographies by Francisco Jiménez: *The Circuit* (1997) and *Breaking Through* (2001), in which he chronicles his family's immigration from Mexico to California, their struggles, deportation, and their return. Despite hardship and prejudice, and because of much diligent work, Francisco manages to excel in school and continue to college. Thus, he is able to break through the cycle of poverty and ultimately become a professor.

Gary Soto is among the more prolific producers of personal stories. He has written at least four autobiographical texts, and his background as an award-winning poet lends his writing a richness of imagery and metaphor. His short stories about growing up poor and Mexican in Fresno, California, are full of grace and humor. *The Effects of Knut Hamsun on a Fresno Boy* (2000) is a highly recommended introduction to Soto's autobiographical prose since it borrows from earlier books and presents new work as well.

Surprisingly there are not many autobiographies by women, and Mary Helen Ponce adds the much-needed female voice to this genre. *Hoyt Street* (1993) is a collection of charming stories set in a small town near Los Angeles in the 1940s and 1950s. These stories primarily detail her years up to the onset of puberty. She relates coming-of-age experiences that are typical of Mexican Americans growing up at that time. Another notable work is Elva Trevino Hart's *Barefoot Heart: Stories of a Migrant Child* (1999), a sensitively written account that carefully delineates the wearisome world of migrant work. Although she begins by writing, "I am nobody. And my story is the same as a million others," she went on to earn a graduate degree in computer science/engineering from Stanford University. Michele Serros's *How to Be a Chicana Role Model* (2000) is a funny, hip, contemporary, and loosely autobiographical work set in the Los Angeles area. Other significant works include Norma Cantu's *Canicula* (1995) and Pat Mora's *House of Houses* (1997).

Gang memoirs and prison narratives have increased in popularity, and in this category Luis Rodriguez's *Always Running: La Vida Loca: Gang Days in L.A.* (1993) stands out among the best written. One poet who has recently produced prose about his prison experience is Jimmy Baca, whose *A Place to Stand* (2001) is an exceptionally moving and dramatic story of a boy who is essentially abandoned by his parents, grows up in an orphanage, and eventually goes to prison on drug charges. While there, he teaches himself to read and thus transforms his life. Mona Ruiz, a former gang member, became a police officer and, with the *Los Angeles Times* journalist Jeff Boucher, produced *Two Badges: The Lives of Mona Ruiz* (1997). Ruiz not only renders gang life from the female point of view, but she also presents episodes from an abusive marriage that she is finally able to flee.

Although Chicano/a literature is primarily a working-class instrument, most writers who have penned their life stories ironically have graduate degrees—including PhDs. Recently there have been a number of autobiographies by former college professors and administrators, including *Luis Leal: An Auto/Biography*,

Julian Nava: My Mexican-American Journey, Ramón Ruiz's *Memories of a Hyphenated Man*, and Kevin Johnson's *How Did You Get to Be Mexican?* While many autobiographies are loosely set within the Chicano/a movement of the 1960s and 1970s—and include such themes as poverty, racism, and the migrant experience—increasingly, there are works that lie outside the marginalized-Mexican point of view: writings by Linda Chavez, Julian Nava, David Maldonado, Kevin Johnson, and perhaps Floyd Salas and Miguel Otero are examples. These writers, like some who are part Mexican, such as Anthony Quinn, Joan Baez, John Rechy, Cherríe Moraga, Luis Alberto Urrea, Linda Chavez, and Kevin R. Johnson, do not always identify with traditional Mexican culture.

In contrast, Mexican nationals have come to the United States and written about their experiences, as did Ramon Perez in his depiction of picaresque adventures as an illegal, *Diary of an Undocumented Immigrant* (1989). A more difficult case is Ilan Stavans (*On Borrowed Words*, 2001), a Mexican of Jewish ancestry, now a professor at Amherst College. An eclectic and prolific scholar, Stavans also writes about U.S. Latino literature (among numerous other topics). In a loose sense, some of the work by Perez and Stavans could be considered Chicano literature. When *Famous All Over Town* by Danny Santiago was published, readers thought it was an autobiographical work by a young Chicano, but it turned out to have been penned by an elderly Anglo social worker named Daniel James. Some writers do not fully accept the designation "Chicano," like José Antonio Villarreal or Richard Rodriguez. Furthermore, as Mexican Americans continue to intermarry we will have more complex categories: among the more interesting, Blaxicans (black-Mexican) and Mexipinos (Mexican-Filipino), as well as amalgams of other minority groups.

Memoirs by those somewhat well known have been recorded by Anthony Quinn, Linda Chavez, Julian Nava, Joan Baez, Lydia Mendoza, Maria Hinojosa, David Maldonado, Luis Leal, Bert Corna, Miguel Otero, Ramón Ruiz, and others. And while the working-class immigrant autobiography will continue to be popular, there will continue to be more autobiographies by women, those who are middle class, and those who are not Catholic and by semi-celebrities, politicians, athletes, actors, and scholars. Increasingly, there will be more works that are unorthodox or experimental within the genre—works like Michele Serros's *Chicana Falsa and Other Stories of Death, Identity, and Oxnard* (1993). The accelerated output within Mexican American autobiography will also lead to more scholarly research on the subject, for there is a scarcity of full-length works in the field.

Autobiography is usually literary ground zero for those who wish to write; apprenticeship novels are often based on the writer's life. Though many authors feel that their experiences are not unique, Mexican American autobiographies provide a privileged portal into what it means to immigrate, what it means to be marginalized, what it means to suffer, what it means to love, and ultimately what it means to be human.

Further Reading

Bruce-Novoa, Juan. *Retrospace: Collected Essays on Chicano Literature.* Houston: Arte Público Press, 1990.

Flores, Lauro. "Chicano Autobiography: Culture, Ideology and the Self." *The Americas Review* 18.2 (Summer 1990): 80–91.

Jimenez, Francisco, ed. *The Identification and Analysis of Chicano Literature.* Binghamton, NY: Bilingual Press, 1979.

Lattin, Vernon E., ed. *Contemporary Chicano Fiction.* Binghamton: Bilingual Press, 1986.

Olivares, Julian, ed. *The Americas Review* [Issue on U.S. Hispanic Autobiography] 16.3–4 (Fall–Winter 1988): 3–243.

Padilla, Genaro M. *My History, Not Yours: The Formation of Mexican American Autobiography.* Madison: University of Wisconsin Press, 1993.

Saldívar, Ramón. *Chicano Narrative: The Dialectics of Difference.* Madison: University of Wisconsin Press, 1990.

Shirley, Carl R., and Paula W. Shirley. *Understanding Chicano Literature.* Columbia: University of South Carolina Press, 1988.

Paul Guajardo

MEXICAN AMERICAN CHILDREN'S LITERATURE

Over the past decade, the field of Mexican American children's literature has expanded dramatically. To be sure, publishers' interest in tapping a lucrative market has facilitated this growth. Yet although market dynamics are integral to any understanding of the astounding growth that has taken place in this genre, they do not fully explain why, in particular, authors such as Gloria Anzaldúa, Luis J. Rodríguez, Ana Castillo, **Rudolfo Anaya**, and Juan Felipe Herrera, all already renowned for their "adult" fiction, criticism, and theory, have begun in greater numbers to write for younger audiences. Collectively, Mexican American writers who publish books for children tend to be motivated by a desire to tell the stories of Mexican American lives in order to validate these experiences. In addition, many of these authors seek to intervene, for the better, in the thinking habits of young readers by facilitating critical thinking about various social issues.

Poet Francisco Alarcón, who has published several illustrated collections of poetry for children, suggests the importance of depicting culturally specific experiences when he explains, "When you don't see your own images through the media or in books, you start thinking you're weird, and your self-esteem gets bruised" (Fernandez E3). In collections such as *Laughing Tomatoes and Other Spring Poems* (1997), Alarcón makes poetry out of daily life and out of the immediate physical environment that may be familiar to children. In effect, the people, landscape, and cityscape that surround young people emerge poetic in their own right. Importantly, the apparent simplicity of the poems in terms of their structure, language, and subjects invites young readers to make poetry about their own surroundings and experiences.

The earliest examples of Mexican American children's literature emanate from this basic desire to validate Mexican American identities. Works such as Elia Robledo Durán's *Joaquín, niño de Aztlán* (1972), Graciela Carrillo's *El frijol mágico* (1974), and Nepthtalí de León's *I Will Catch the Sun* (1973) legitimate Mexican American cultural attributes simply by portraying these attributes. As the authors of these texts strategically contradict the erasure and disparagement of Mexican American **identity** and culture, they attempt to counter the shame young people may feel because they are "different" or because they belong to an ethnic group that historically has had a denigrated standing in the United States. Along these same lines, a number of writers have published adaptations and collections of Mexican and Mexican American folktales in an effort to celebrate and sustain these oral traditions.

A number of writers have devoted themselves to telling hitherto untold stories about the children of migrant, farm-working families. For example, bilingual, illustrated books by Juan Felipe Herrera (*The Upside Down Boy* [2000], *Calling the Doves* [2001]) as well as Francisco Jimenez's novel, *The Circuit: Stories from the Life of a Migrant Child* (1997), depict the sometimes warm, sometimes traumatic nature of life for these children. Herrera and Jimenez foreground the family as a space of love and security for these children while school and the public realm in general represent intimidating, alien spaces. Though books such as these hold special significance for children for whom immigration, **racism**, and social marginalization are a part of their own experience, books such as these can also be valuable for children who come from different backgrounds and who are otherwise unfamiliar with such experiences. For such children, the stories told by Herrera and Jimenez can prompt an empathetic understanding of how some children live and thus enable a critical understanding of racism, poverty, and immigration. This is especially true of Gloria Anzaldúa's controversial work, *Friends from the Other Side* (1993). This illustrated book deconstructs figurations of Mexican immigrants as "wetback" others by emphasizing their moral decency and by inviting compassion for Joaquín, an undocumented boy who worries about eluding the Border Patrol and who struggles to support his mother and himself.

The recent surge in literature for children by established Mexican American writers such as Anzaldúa can be best understood via realization that these writers wield an activist desire to inspire positive changes in readers' attitudes, perceptions, behaviors, and sympathies in relation to a range of contemporary issues. To write for children allows writers of an activist orientation to extend the reach of their efforts to raise others' critical awareness. In turn, they manage to more completely fulfill their commitment to contribute to the well-being of their communities.

Ana Castillo, Luis Rodríguez, and Rudolfo Anaya are some of the other noteworthy authors who have crossed over into children's literature. Castillo, who has received acclaim for novels such as *So Far from God* (1993) and *Peel My Love Like an Onion* (1999), offers young readers of *My Daughter, My Son, the Eagle, the Dove* (2000) a re-envisioning of gender roles. In an effort to disrupt the perpetuation of conventional definitions of masculinity and femininity that lead to unhealthy forms of manhood and cripple women's autonomy and self-esteem, Castillo encourages boys to become compassionate men while she asks girls to grow into confident, self-reliant, and brave women. Like Castillo, Rodríguez betrays a special interest in tackling gender issues in his children's books. In *América Is Her Name* (1998), the subjects of racism and the oppression of women and girls within Latino cultures are portrayed critically. In *It Doesn't Have to Be This Way* (1999), Rodríguez interrogates masculinity and gangs. A former gang member himself, Rodríguez suggests that boys can find ways to be men outside of gangs.

To maximize the activist value of their books for children, many Mexican American authors craft their stories so that they provoke both children and adults to think critically about a range of social and cultural concerns. For this reason, some Mexican American illustrated books for children may seem bolder in relation to other illustrated books for children in terms of the issues they engage and their frank manner of engaging them. Ideally, through dual address, both young and old(er) readers can come to better understandings of the problems that haunt their lives and their communities so that they may both participate in the healing of these problems. As children and adults share in the experience of reading about contemporary concerns, they can share with each other their understandings of the issues being addressed and then collaboratively arrive at possible strategies for rectifying them.

Gloria Velásquez is an especially innovative figure within the field of Mexican American children's literature. In her *Roosevelt High School* series (which includes *Juanita Fights the School Board* [1994], *Maya's Divided World* [1995], and *Tommy Stands Alone* [1999]), Velásquez introduces protagonists who tackle the same difficult issues that adolescents face. Issues of discrimination and gender suffuse *Juanita Fights the School Board*, a novel about a girl who is expelled from school for fighting another student who had been hurling racial slurs at her. Although one valuable feature of this first installment in the *Roosevelt* series is its depiction of life for the daughter of farm worker parents, an important feature of the sequel, *Maya's Divided World*, is its depiction of an upper-middle-class Mexican American household. Together, *Juanita Fights the School Board* and *Maya's Divided World* portray diversity among Mexican American families. Maya's mother is a university professor and her father is an engineer, and because of their commitment to their professions, Maya feels neglected. Eventually, she rebels and runs away from home. *Tommy Stands Alone* is a breakthrough novel that portrays the homophobia, parental rejection, and suicidal tendencies that too many gay adolescents endure. With this novel, Velásquez speaks to gay youth by acknowledging their ordeals, and she simultaneously invites others to reconsider homophobia.

Of course, while well-intentioned authors of literature for children pursue particular political agendas, the issue of literacy development cannot be overlooked. Indeed, it is possible to worry that as Herrera, Anzaldúa, Rodríguez, and others explore the political possibilities of children's literature, the capacity of stories to develop literacy risks being forgotten. Authors thus face the challenge of crafting books that strengthen young readers' reading skills, nurture a love of reading, and convey positive lessons about potentially unpleasant subjects. Herrera creatively tries to accomplish this balance with *Super Cilantro Girl* (2003), a story that disarticulates the validity of border policies as it introduces readers to a Chicana superhero. Questions remain, however, as to whether a writer really can ever perform such a careful balancing act. Moreover, ethical questions automatically accompany any efforts to inscribe a political purpose into a book for children because of a fear of such books functioning as nothing less than tools of indoctrination.

Gary Soto and Pat Mora, perhaps the most prolific Mexican American writers of books for children, validate Mexican American experiences and convey positive messages, yet they seem especially concerned with creating enjoyable reading experiences. Relative to some other Mexican American children's books, the works of Soto and Mora tend to be lighter in terms of their politicized content. Soto has in fact professed his commitment to writing short stories and illustrated books that entertain audiences. Indeed, some of his work captures culturally specific experiences, appeals to culturally specific sensibilities, and engages difficult realities, such as racism and poverty. Predominately, however, Soto crafts his works to hold universal appeal. Among his collections of short stories, *Baseball in April* (1990) and *Living Up the Street* (1992) focus on common growing-up experiences. Of Soto's many illustrated books, *Too Many Tamales* (1993) has become a Christmas classic because it amuses readers with its playful narration of a girl's worry that she has unwittingly dropped her mother's wedding ring in tamale dough.

Pat Mora, who has been celebrated for her poetry for adults (*Chants* [1984], *Borders* [1986]), has also produced a number of books for young adults and young children. *My Own True Name: New and Selected Poems for Young Adults* (2000) engages the personal issues young adults must face as it also touches upon various social topics. Illustrated books such as *Pablo's Tree* (1994), *The Desert Is My Mother* (1994), and *Tomás and the Library Lady* (1997) cover themes as diverse as family ties, the beauty of nature, and the excitement that can be found in the library. Thus, in contrast to authors who unflinchingly deal with harsh realities in their books for children, Mora emphasizes the freedom and excitement that can also characterize childhood. Rather than suggesting Mora's naïve insistence on protecting tenuous assumptions about childhood innocence, her books simply reflect her different strategy for participating in child readers' lives.

Diversity in writers' agendas has made Mexican American children's literature a very dynamic genre. A survey of the field reveals a panoply of approaches that writers have followed as they participate in the moral and intellectual edification of young people, encourage cultural pride, and provide young people with amusement. Ultimately, such diversity can be seen as healthy and useful. The existence of so many different approaches to the writing of literature for children means that there are ongoing reevaluations within the genre, and this carries the possibility for more enlightened innovations and developments to occur.

Further Reading

Day, Frances Ann. *Latina and Latino Voices in Literature for Children and Teenagers*. Portsmouth, NH: Heinemann, 1997.

Fernandez, Maria Elena. "A New Chapter on Cultural Pride." *Los Angeles Times* (September 24, 2000): E1+.

Phillip Serrato

MEXICAN AMERICAN DRAMA

The roots of Mexican American drama extend far beyond the physical borders and historical formation of the United States. Theatrical performances by Mexican Americans have occurred for as long as formerly Mexican territories have been part of the United States. Mexican American performance traditions derive from a rich array of cultural performances all over the world, including various indigenous performance styles, colonial Spanish religious dramas, Mexican *carpas* (tent shows), Brechtian techniques, Augusto Boal's theater of the oppressed, and various forms of social protest theater in the United States in the 1960s. Since the start of the Chicano Movement in 1965, many Mexican American theater practitioners have chosen to identify as Chicanas and Chicanos, rather than Mexican Americans. For this reason, Mexican American drama from 1965 to the present is most often categorized as Chicana/o drama. From its inception to the present day, Mexican American drama/Chicana/o drama has been a valuable and active part of American drama as a whole.

The earliest Mexican American theater frequently consisted of Catholic morality plays in Spanish performed throughout the southwestern United States as a means of increasing church membership or teaching lessons from the Bible. Mexican American performances also included secular folk dramas, traveling tent shows in Mexican *carpa* style, and vaudevillian *variedades* (variety shows). Nicolás Kanellos and Elizabeth Ramírez are among the scholars who have written about Mexican American drama before 1965.

The Chicano Movement began with the United Farm Workers (UFW) union's first major act of social protest: the Great Delano Grape Strike of 1965. **Luis Valdez**, the son of migrant farm workers and a native of Delano, convinced the UFW leader César Chávez that theater could be used as a means to further the strike. Valdez founded El Teatro Campesino (The Farmworkers' Theatre) by bringing together a group of unionized farm workers as a company of actors. On the first day of rehearsal, Valdez passed out scripts he had written for a political skit. When he discovered that most of his actors were illiterate, the scripts were tossed aside, and a theater of improvisation was born. Valdez would create scenarios, and the actors would improvise short scenes that encouraged workers to

Luis Valdez, right, with Cesar Chavez. (AP Photo/ Daniel Goodrich)

join the union and support the strike. The *acto* (short political skit) became the signature format of El Teatro Campesino because it was a portable and effective medium of performance. The troupe performed in the fields and on the beds of trucks so that they could reach their target audience and escape quickly if angry growers threatened them.

El Teatro Campesino quickly began performing about issues beyond the strike, and as their popularity grew during the Chicano Movement of the late 1960s and early 1970s, *teatros* (Chicana/o theater companies) began appearing all over the United States. Groups such as Teatro de la Esperanza (Theatre of Hope), Su Teatro (Your Theatre), Teatro de los Pobres (Theatre of the Poor), and many others fed the Chicano Movement by rallying groups of people to various causes associated with the Movement. Chicana/o performances during this time period argued in favor of bilingual and ethnically specific education for Chicana/o students, explored Chicana/o **identity**, and protested against the Vietnam War.

In 1967, El Teatro Campesino broke away from the UFW and began performing longer plays scripted by Valdez. They also began performing in some more conventional theatrical venues, such as college campuses. Other Chicana/o *teatros* also began expanding from the format of the *acto* and created more complex performances with more fully developed characters.

So many *teatros* emerged during the Chicano Movement that in 1971 they formed a national network, known as TENAZ, an acronym for *El Teatro Nacional de Aztlán* (The National Theatre of Aztlán). TENAZ served as a means for *teatros* to stay informed about the activities of other groups, exchange ideas, and hold theater festivals. In Spanish the word *tenaz* means "tenacity," and the word symbolizes the strength of the commitment that these *teatros* made not only to one another but to the production of Latina/o theater. The organization brought together groups from all over the southwestern United States, the East Coast, Puerto Rico, and Mexico. The informal newsletter *TENAZ Talks Teatro*, published quarterly for many years by Jorge Huerta, circulated information about the activities of *teatros* and their productions. The organization technically still exists, and many of its members remain very active in the field of Chicana/o theater. However, members have not held meetings or festivals under the heading of TENAZ since the early 1990s.

In 1974, Teatro de la Esperanza produced the first Chicana/o docudrama. The play *Guadalupe* tells the story of a small town in northern California by the same name. Director Jorge Huerta and musical director Ginger Huerta led a team of undergraduate actors from the University of California, Santa Barbara, as they did research and conducted interviews with the residents of Guadalupe. Students in the town had staged a series of walkouts in protest of the physical and psychological abuse inflicted on Chicana/o students in the local public schools. The parents of the students formed a committee to protest the mistreatment of their children, and many of the committee members were arrested during a peaceful protest at a school board meeting. Teatro de la Esperanza chronicled the struggles of the townspeople in a collectively written musical drama that toured the United States and Mexico. The political message of the play was so effective that audience members in both the United States and Mexico joined their local unions in record numbers after seeing performances of the play.

Another politically charged and notable Chicano docudrama was written in 1979 when playwright Carlos Morton took inspiration from a newspaper article that described the murder of Chicano Richard Morales by a small-town Texas police chief. *The Many Deaths of Danny Rosales* (originally titled *Las Many Muertes de Richard Morales*) uses the setting of a courtroom to tell the story of the murder from several different perspectives. Morton conducted extensive research in the writing of the play. He paid particularly close attention to the ways in which the crime and the trial were represented in the media and used the differing accounts he found to give the characters depth. The title character dies three times during the course of the play, and each time the audience learns something new about the police chief's role in the crime. The play has been rewritten a number of times and has had several different endings. All the versions of the play provide a powerful critique of police brutality and the criminal justice system.

Perhaps the most well-known work of Chicana/o theater opened at the Mark Taper Forum in Los Angeles in 1978. Luis Valdez received a grant from the Rockefeller Foundation to write his landmark play *Zoot Suit*. Like *The Many Deaths of Danny Rosales, Zoot Suit* tells the tale of a murder, a trial, and the grave injustices of a racially biased court. The early 1940s were a time of great social strife for young Chicana/os in Los Angeles, and the press generated widespread and unfounded fear of Chicana/o youth wearing zoot suits and known as *pachucos*. Eventually the racial tension erupted in the now-famous Zoot Suit Riots, but years before the riots began, Henry Leyva and a group of his teenage friends stood trial and were wrongly convicted in the Sleepy Lagoon Murder Trial of 1942. After many years of court battles, all of the young men were eventually exonerated and released.

The play *Zoot Suit* follows the character of Hank Reyna (based on Henry Leyva) through his trial, conviction, and release, but Valdez provides his audiences with special insight into Hank's character and his internal struggles by giving him an alter ego known as El Pachuco. El Pachuco's character narrates the play, at times stopping the action in classic Brechtian fashion to ask the audience to think about the larger social issues the play addresses. Edward James Olmos played El Pachuco in the original production of *Zoot Suit*, the Broadway production in 1981, and the film version of the play. The character became an archetypal role in Chicana/o theater, and Olmos went on to become an iconic figure in Chicana/o popular culture.

The success of *Zoot Suit* opened the doors for Chicana/o plays in the professional theater. It also marked a shift in Chicana/o theater from a time when *teatros* and collectively written plays dominated to a trend toward individually written plays being produced in community, university, and regional theaters. Since the 1980s, many talented Chicana writers have emerged as playwrights, including Cherríe Moraga, Evelina Fernandez, Edit Villarreal, Josefina López, and Milcha Sánchez-Scott, among others. The plays written by these women added rich layers of meaning and perspective to the canon of Chicana/o theater, which had previously ignored many of the contributions of women during the movement.

Cherríe Moraga's *Heroes and Saints* premiered in 1992 at Brava! For Women in the Arts at the Mission Cultural Center in San Francisco, California. Drawing on the early Luis Valdez play *The Shrunken Head of Pancho Villa*, Moraga creates a lead character who has no limbs. Cerezita has been born the victim of pesticides sprayed in the fields where her mother worked while pregnant. Despite her literal and metaphoric incapacitation, she is able to perceive, analyze, and resist the injustices she sees in her community. Cerezita represents the devastation that growers and chemicals have wreaked upon farm workers and their families, while simultaneously embodying the will to resist these oppressions.

Cerezita's family suffers from a variety of social and physical maladies. Cerezita's mother refuses to let her out of the house. Her father deserted the family long before the play begins. Her sister's baby is dying because of birth defects caused by the pesticides, and her gay brother contracts HIV during the course of the play. Moraga has been criticized for addressing too many issues in a single play, but she has also been praised for weaving together deeply meaningful social issues that in reality do have enormous impacts on one another. *Heroes and Saints* examines the corporeality and spirituality of a farm worker community, as the limbless protagonist watches the children around her die. The play addresses life and death with rich metaphors and symbolism melded to urgent social issues.

Just as the sexist tendencies of the early Chicano Movement had previously shut out the voices of women, the homophobia of the movement prevented the voices of queer playwrights from being heard. Guillermo Reyes, Oliver Mayer, Monica Palacios, Cherríe Moraga, and Luis Alfaro are among those who have been writing on queer themes in Chicana/o theater since the 1980s. Though Guillermo Reyes is of Chilean American descent, academics and theater practitioners often include his work in discussions of Chicana/o theater because so many of his characters are Chicanas and Chicanos.

The premier of Reyes play *Deporting the Divas* took place in March of 1996 at the Celebration Theatre in Los Angeles, California. The play's main character is a Chicano named Michael González who works as a U.S. border patrol agent. He also struggles with his homosexuality, especially when he discovers his attraction to Sedicio, an undocumented immigrant who broadens Michael's mind and tolerates his profession. Michael has an ongoing daydream of his ideal mate: a transvestite tango queen named Sirena Angustias. Michael's wanderings between fantasy and reality reflect his fragmented identity as a gay Latino, and the conflicts in the play over immigration issues serve to question labels such as "illegal" and "undocumented" when applied to thinking, feeling human beings who are no less a part of U.S. society and economy than native-born citizens.

Several of the original *teatros* from the 1960s and 1970s remain active today, including El Teatro Campesino and Teatro de la Esperanza. Groups such as the Latino Theater Company, the Chicano Secret Service, and Latins Anonymous have written and produced popular performances in the time since the end of the heyday of Chicana/o *teatros*. However, the three-man *teatro* **Culture Clash** is currently the

Chicana/o theater group that finds the most consistent and widespread commercial success in the regional theaters. Since 1994 Culture Clash has been working on a continuing project they call Culture Clash in AmeriCCa. Regional theaters around the country have commissioned the trio to write interview-based plays about their cities, as a means of exploring interactions between different ethnic and cultural groups in the United States. Using sketches from their first site-specific play, *Radio Mambo: Culture Clash Invades Miami*, and each of the five subsequent plays in the project, they regularly tour the country performing a compilation show also called *Culture Clash in AmeriCCa*.

In a departure from the episodic format of their previous site-specific plays, Culture Clash's most recent research-based play *Chavez Ravine* returns in many ways to the tradition of docudrama in Chicana/o theater. The play had its premiere in the summer of 2003 at the Mark Taper Forum in Los Angeles under the direction of Lisa Peterson. *Chavez Ravine* documents the struggle over land rights in a section of Los Angeles known as Chavez Ravine. The ravine once held generations of Mexican American families who were displaced for the purpose of constructing Dodger Stadium. Actress Eileen Galindo joined Richard Montoya, Ric Salinas, and Herbert Sigüenza of Culture Clash to perform the more than 50 characters in the play. The play blends slapstick humor, historical fact, and deliberate fiction as it retells the history of Los Angeles and its people.

Ultimately, Mexican American and Chicana/o drama is a theater of politics, a theater of community, a theater of social justice activism. Its performance venues and writing styles have changed and evolved significantly, from the religious performances begun during the Spanish conquest to El Teatro Campesino's *actos* of the Chicano Movement to professional productions of Chicana/o plays in theaters all over the country. All of these Chicana/o performance traditions are still practiced today, but the art form continues to evolve and diversify with the community. What has not changed, however, is the pervasive activist spirit and community-oriented nature of the work being done in Chicana/o theater.

Further Reading

Huerta, Jorge A. *Chicano Drama: Performance, Society and Myth*. Cambridge, UK: Cambridge University Press, 2000.

Huerta, Jorge A. *Chicano Theater: Themes and Forms*. Ypsilanti, MI: Bilingual Press/Editorial Bilingüe, 1982.

Kanellos, Nicolás. *A History of Hispanic Theatre in the United States: Origins to 1940*. Austin: University of Texas Press, 1990.

Kanellos, Nicolás. *Mexican American Theatre: Legacy and Reality*. Pittsburgh: Latin American Literary Review Press, 1987.

Kanellos, Nicolás, ed. *Mexican American Theatre: Then and Now*. Houston: Arte Público Press, 1989.

Ramirez, Elizabeth C. *Chicanas/Latinas in American Theatre: A History of Performance*. Bloomington: Indiana University Press, 2000.

Ashley Lucas

MEXICAN AMERICAN GAY LITERATURE

Gay Mexican American (Chicano) writing came into its own in the 1980s. While gay Chicanos were certainly writing before this period, they were largely silenced by homophobic Chicano-nationalist and mainstream publishers; and though post-1969 Stonewall gay/lesbian activism led to the founding of small presses that produced and disseminated larger numbers of white gay and lesbian authors, gay literature of color (Chicano especially) continued to receive scant attention.

The renaissance of gay Chicano literature in the 1980s owes much to the activist–intellectual work of lesbian feminists such as Cherríe Moraga and Gloria Anzaldúa. The 1981 publication by AuntLute Press of *This Bridge Called My Back*, an anthology edited by Moraga and Anzaldúa, marked an important shift in the publishing of Chicano lesbian literature. Their various creative explorations and explosions of the traditionally straight Chicano versus Anglo fiction and poetics that defined a 1970s Chicano **canon** helped pave the way for the arrival of the gay Chicano author.

In 1986, the foremost Chicano literary scholar, Juan Bruce-Novoa, published the seminal essay, "Homosexuality and the Chicano Novel," wherein he naturalized the union of "gay" with "Chicano." No longer could one read, for example, **John Rechy**'s novels as gay sex-shock narrative; one had to read his work as fundamentally Chicano as well. Moreover, Bruce-Novoa remapped the existing straight Chicano/a literary canon, identifying its implicit homoerotic edge. For Bruce-Novoa, to ignore the gay Chicano voice was to miss the "dynamic and exciting" force at the core of Chicano literature.

Largely the result of such scholarly moves toward inclusion and of the hard work of lesbian and gay activist intellectuals and writers—the establishment of independent publishing venues and the struggle to educate a New York publishing world—gay poets, playwrights, and novelists, began coming into their own.

In the area of poetry, we see a range of different voices, including Francisco X. Alarcón (1954–) who blazed new trails with his powerfully gay and indigenous poetic voice as seen in *Ya vas, Carnal* (1984) and *Tattoos* (1984). In both collections, Alarcón uses poetic rhythm and a penetrating, staccato voice to affirm his gay and Chicano **identity** within a racist and homophobic mainstream society. For Alarcón, the black marks on the page were more than just words, they formed images that lashed back at his racist world. In his *Body in Flames* (1991), Alarcón intermixes pre-Columbian myth with his inhabiting of a gay Chicano body in the present; he clears a space for a gay Chicano poetic where mind is no longer forced apart from body. In the mid-1990s yet another important gay Chicano poet arrived on the scene, the late Gil Cuadros. However, rather than unify a mythological past with a gay Chicano present, Cuadros sought to texture his childhood and coming out experience as a teenager in Los Angeles; to capture his feelings of estrangement both from the white gay community that exoticizes his brown body and from his Chicano community that promotes a queer hostile *machismo*, he intermixes poetry and prose in the writing of his memoir, *City of God* (1994)—a powerful testament to his struggle to humanize the gay Chicano experience before his death from an AIDS-related illness.

Gay authors have found solid footing in other genres such as memoir/essay form and drama. For example, one of the first on the drama scene was Los Angeles born and based, Luis Alfaro. A self-identifying queer artist–activist, Alfaro's many performances and plays—*Downtown* (1980), *Cuerpo Politizado* (1996), *Straight as a Line* (2000), to name a few—often employ a sharp, biting edge to express the multiform gay Chicano experience. And gay journalist/essayist **Richard Rodriguez** has made a name for himself nationwide. Though his work for the Pacific News Services deals mostly with issues of **race**, his essayistic memoirs bring together issues of being gay and brown in the United States and Mexico; we see this faintly whispered in his best-selling *Hunger of Memory* (1982) and then more boldly in his *Days of Obligation* (1993) and *Brown* (2003). In *Days of Obligation*, for example, he makes public secrets otherwise kept in the closet by his Chicano upbringing: "to grow up homosexual is to live with secrets and within secrets. In no other place are those secrets more closely guarded than within the family home." In *Brown*, he uses his trademark fast-paced and highly stylized journalese to render visible his experiences as queer and Chicano in so-identified post-Protestant/Catholic, post-colonial Americas.

Gay Chicano novelists have carved paths deep and wide into the Chicano and literary canons. We see this especially in the work of John Rechy, **Arturo Islas Jr.**, and Michael Nava, who have variously used a number of different storytelling techniques and styles—the picaresque, the mystery suspense, stream of consciousness, and mixed media pastiche—to reframe one-dimensional representations of gay Chicanos. We see this, for example, with Rechy's use of the stream of consciousness form to tell the story of Amalia Gómez in his novel, *The Miraculous Day of Amalia Gómez* (1991). Here, Rechy focuses on the psychological transformation of Amalia as she comes to terms with a contemporary racist and violent Los Angeles as well as her son's gay sexuality. And we see in the novels of the late Arturo Islas—*The Rain God* (1984) and *Migrant Souls*—how one can weave with great subtlety the gay voice into the texturing of Chicano family life along the U.S.-Mexico border. Islas complicates his vision of gay Chicano **identity** and experience in his posthumously published novel, *La Mollie and the King of Tears* (1996), where he uses a fast paced first-person voice to tell the story of straight Louie Mendoza, whose discovery of self includes his coming to terms with his own fluid sexuality as well as his brother's gay identity. Author Michael Nava introduced gay Chicano lawyer/detective character, Henry Rios, when he published *The Little Death* in 1986, and he published seven more novels in the series that finally ended in 2001 with *Rag and Bone*. Nava's self-identifying gay and Chicano character, Henry Rios, not only solves grisly murders and crimes but does so while dealing with affairs of the heart and with a constant sense of loss: friends and love-interests lost to AIDS.

Gay novelists, playwrights, and poets like Nava, Islas, Rechy, Alarcón, Cuadros, Rodriguez, Alfaro, and others have influenced many straight and queer Chicano writers. Their creative visions celebrate the triumph of defying the odds while not losing sight of the goal to foster deep human empathy and understanding.

Further Reading

Aldama, Frederick Luis. *Arturo Islas: The Uncollected Works*. Houston: Arte Público Press, 2003.

Bruce-Novoa, Juan. "Homosexuality and the Chicano Novel." In *European Perspectives on Hispanic Literature of the United States*, edited by Genvieve Fabre, 98–106. Houston: Arte Público Press, 1988. Reprinted from *Confluencia-revista hispanica de cultura y literatura* 2.1 (1986): 69–77.

Foster, David William, ed. *Chicano/Latino Homoerotic Identities*. New York: Garland Publishing, 1999.

Frederick Luis Aldama

MEXICAN AMERICAN LESBIAN LITERATURE

Two radical Chicanas exploded Mexican American literature in the 1980s with their explicit treatment of lesbianism. Gloria Anzaldúa and Cherríe Moraga hail from different backgrounds and represent different aspects of the Mexican American community, but the anthology that they coedited, *This Bridge Called My Back* (1981), and each woman's first work, Moraga's *Loving in the War Years* (1983) and Anzaldúa's *Borderlands/La Frontera* (1987), changed the face of Chicano literature and culture. Prior to the publications of these works, Chicano literature had briefly seen the treatment of male homosexuality in **John Rechy**'s *City of Night* (1963) and the explicit treatment of female sexuality from the poems of Bernice Zamora and those of Alma Villanueva. But Anzaldúa and Moraga introduced not only the frank narration of lesbianism but also a careful consideration of its place in Chicano literature and culture. Anzaldúa's and Moraga's works mix the genres of essay, short story, poetry, and memoir; they are radical in their form as well as their content, suggesting that Chicana lesbian literature not only tells a new story, but also offers a new way of telling stories.

In *This Bridge Called My Back*, Moraga and Anzaldúa present Chicana lesbianism in the context of the radical women of color movement in the United States in the 1980s. Radical feminism, anti**racism**, and challenges to the dominance of heterosexuality fit together, the anthology proclaims. Chicana lesbians belong to a whole movement of women who include Chicana feminists like Norma Alarcón and other radical women of color, from bell hooks to Chrystos. These women came together to critique the ways in which patriarchy operates in the guises of colonialism, racism, male dominance, and compulsory heterosexuality to deny women access to the full and free exploration and expression of their sexuality and of their personhood. Under the editorial hand of Moraga and Anzladúa, the anthology staked out a space for Chicana feminists and lesbians who had been previously unknown not only in women of color circles, but also in Chicano circles.

Moraga and Anzaldúa's lesbianism is a Chicana more than a Mexican American lesbianism. It is intimately tied to the Chicano/a movement that, beginning in the late 1950s, asserted Chicanos as not immigrants, not hyphenated Americans, but native people of the Southwest, colonized first by Spaniards and then by North

Americans. They trace their heritage as *mestizos* (mixed people) to include Aztec, Spanish, and Anglo strands. Moraga and Anzaldúa's Xicanisma (Chicanisma) critiques the male dominance and heterosexual order of the Chicano Movement, but from within the movement.

Like the Chicanos, Moraga and Anzaldúa claim their Aztec heritage, although Moraga and Anzaldúa single out La Malinche and La Llorona as their spiritual ancestors. La Malinche was the Aztec woman who supposedly served as Cortez's translator and lover. La Malinche regularly suffers accusations of being a traitor and a whore. But Moraga and Anzaldúa portray her not as the traitor but as the sacrificial lamb to Spanish colonialism, and not as a whore but as the mother of all mestizos. They do not claim La Malinche as a lesbian, but rather as an example of how existing between two supposedly separate identities is a classically Chicana position and also as an example of a Chicana whose sexual life refuses the single two options standard in Chicano culture: virgin (mother) or whore. La Llorona stands as the archetypal bad mother in Chicano folklore, legendary for having killed her own children to wander forever crying and in search of young souls to snatch away. Again, Moraga and Anzaldúa claim not that La Llorona was a lesbian but that she exemplifies the ways in which all Chicana women are expected to become mothers or be forever damned. In La Llorona, they find an ancestor who can be rehabilitated as an emblem of women who stand outside of Chicano sexual and familial mores.

In the essays that make up her memoir-like book, *Loving in the War Years*, Moraga uses an English strongly marked by Spanish, but she also discusses how she was raised monolingually, taught that English was the language of progress. English was also her father's native language, for Moraga is from a half-Chicano, half-Anglo family. For these reasons, Moraga was from a young age acutely aware of concerns about selling out, about losing Chicano culture through an embrace of all things Anglo that, she thought, included lesbianism. Paradoxically, Moraga feels herself to be an outsider both as half-Anglo and as the darkest person in her family. She discusses how skin color as well as sexuality complicate understandings of "the Chicana." For Moraga, a surprising realization was that although male domination serves men, women, and specifically mothers, play a primary role in perpetuating it. She describes how her own mother tried to teach her to be always subservient to her brothers and tried to show her through her own example that an unsatisfactory marriage was preferable to no marriage at all. Moraga refused her mother's lessons in women's oppression just as she refused to believe that lesbianism is by definition foreign and antithetical to Chicano culture. *Loving in the War Years* represents her effort to stake out a space within Chicano history and culture for Chicana lesbians.

Anzaldúa, in *Borderlands/La Frontera*, shares Moraga's project of rewriting Chicano history to include Chicana lesbians and of considering exactly what it means to be a Chicana lesbian. The language of *Borderlands/La Frontera* combines Spanish and English even more than does *Loving in the War Years* and also discusses the different variations of Chicano "Spanglish." In her discussion of language, Anzaldúa writes not only about how languages like Spanish and English become embattled, but also about how tongues and thus bodies and language about bodies and sexuality are subject to policing from both within and without the borderlands. Anzaldúa writes more explicitly than Moraga of women's sexuality both in terms of the sexual violence that all Chicana women risk and in terms of the sexual pleasure that Chicana lesbians can find with other women. *Borderlands/La Frontera* finds the borderlands that are such an important paradigm in Chicano studies to be also the paradigmatic site for Chicana lesbianism: It is indeed a site of contact between tongues, between cultures, and between people. It is the periphery that is the center of Chicana **identity**. But Anzaldúa also advocates for radical change in Chicano and in Anglo culture, a restitution of what she sees as the repressed Indian part of the *mestizo* identity and an accompanying reconfiguration of the roles of women.

Although they remain the most famous and the most radical, *This Bridge Called My Back, Loving in the War Years*, and *Borderlands/La Frontera* are not Moraga's and Anzaldúa's only collaborative or respective works. Moraga has also written a number of plays and short stories and a memoir of her entry into motherhood. Anzaldúa has also edited another radical women of color anthology, *Making Face, Making Soul* (1990), and with Analouise Keating has edited a follow-up to *This Bridge Called My Back, This Bridge We Call Home* (2002).

Nor are Anzaldúa and Moraga the only Chicana lesbian authors. Ana Castillo is famous not only for her lesbian poems and stories, some of which are collected in *My Father Was a Toltec and Other Poems* (1995) and *Loverboys* (1997), where some, but not all, of the lovers are boys, but also for her novels where lesbianism is less explicit, including *So Far From God* (1993), and *Peel Me Like an Onion* (2000). The first traditional Chicana "coming out story" that traces a girl's discovery and declaration of her lesbianism is Terri de la Peña's *Margins* (1991). De la Peña also writes of lesbianism in *Latin Satins* (1994) and *Faults* (1999). Alicia Gaspar de Alba is a Chicana critic and creative writer whose collection *The Mystery of Survival and Other Stories* (1993) considers the importance of history and of memory as well as the inventive possibilities of collaboration between women across cultures and times. Gaspar de Alba's second book, *Sor Juana's Second Dream* (1999), claims this grande dame of Mexican letters as a foremother to Chicana lesbians. Other Chicana lesbian authors include the poets Emma Pérez and E. D. Hernández. As *This Bridge We Call Home* indicates, Chicana lesbians may always be pulled between apparently competing loyalties, but they know that they have a right to claim that liminal space as their own and continue to build their community there.

Further Reading

Anzaldúa, Gloria, and Cherríe Moraga, eds. *This Bridge Called My Back: Writings by Radical Women of Color*. New York: Kitchen Table, Women of Color Press, 1983.

Arredondo, Gabriela F., et al., eds. *Chicana Feminisms: A Critical Reader*. Durham, NC: Duke University Press, 2003.

Ramos, Juanita. *Compañeras: Latina Lesbians*. New York: Latina Lesbian History Project, 1987.

Torres, Lourdes, and Inmaculada Pertusa, eds. *Tortilleras: Hispanic and U.S. Latina Lesbian Expressions*. Philadelphia: Temple University Press, 2003.

Trujillo, Carla. *Chicana Lesbians: The Girls Our Mothers Warned Us About*. Berkeley: Third Woman Press, 1991.

Keja Lys Valens

MEXICAN AMERICAN POETRY

Often referred to as Chicano or Chicana poetry, this body of work gained national recognition in the late 1960s and early 1970s, against the backdrop of the Chicana/o civil rights movement known as *el movimiento*—meaning the movement. The term Chicana/o refers to people of Mexican ancestry who are either born in the United States or who have resided there for an extended period of time. *Movimiento* activists encouraged its usage as a way of affirming a cultural and political resistance to **assimilation**. This is not to say that Mexican Americans did not produce an extensive amount of work before this time. In Chicana/o literary history, critics have traced a continuity from Spanish colonial times to the present, and literary recovery projects throughout the 1990s have brought to light numerous works written since 1848—the year that the treaty of Guadalupe Hidalgo ended the Mexican American war and in the process, annexed nearly half of Mexican territory, a region we now refer to as the southwestern United States. By definition, Chicanas and Chicanos are Americans; consequently, their poetry is also American—it is best understood in the context of U.S. history and culture and of how those elements have shaped the experiences of Mexican Americans.

Just as there is no singular Chicana/o experience, it follows then that poetry written by Mexican Americans is as Cordelia Candelaria describes it, "multiplicitous, wide-ranging, and dynamic," made up of "a diversity of voices, styles, idioms, images and personas" (xiv). This diversity accurately reflects Chicana/o cultural *mestizaje*, meaning mixture. Originally applied to the mixture of bloodlines that were the result of the conquest, *mestizaje* is a concept that is used to articulate the cultural mixture between the Mexican and the American that forms the basis of Chicana/o experience. This notion of hybridity makes singular claims of authenticity impossible; indeed, such claims are always limited and misleading.

The Spanish Colonial and Mexican National Periods (1492–1810 and 1810–1848)

Critics have stressed the imperative of including these two periods in the history of Chicano poetry, making a parallel to the inclusion of English colonial writers such as Anne Bradstreet (1613–1672) and Cotton Mather (1663–1728) within American literary history. Like their Anglo-American counterparts, these writers chronicled their times and reflected on them in various literary genres, including verse. The colonial expedition led by Juan de Oñate (1598–1608) produced the epic *Historia de la Nuevo Mexico* (1610) written by Gaspar Perez de Villagra (1555–1620), which details the brutalities of conquest. During colonial and national periods, literary culture was deeply influenced by ongoing and intense conflicts, first with Native Americans, and later with Anglo-Americans. Despite their relative distance from Mexico City, Southwest Mexicans stayed in touch with culture and news from Mexico and Spain as they were in constant contact with Mexican traders and government officials. As Anglo-American settlers moved west, interactions between Mexicans and Anglos become the norm, through trade as well as intermarriage. By the 1830s, prior to the annexation of Texas, Mexicans there were outnumbered by Anglos, and by the 1840s the Santa Fe Trail connected St. Louis with New Mexico. This interaction was of course, not always peaceful as evinced in the two-year war between Mexico and the United States, which ended in the treaty of Guadalupe Hidalgo that not only annexed nearly half of Mexican territory, but also made guarantees to Mexican land rights, schooling, language, and religion, most of which were gradually eroded during Anglo-American expansion west.

The Nineteenth Century

In the mid-19th century, a considerable amount of writing was devoted to chronicling the American takeover and its political, material, and cultural implications. Prominent figures dictated their memoirs, and a vast amount of poetry appeared in dozens of Spanish-language newspapers in the Southwest. Often these writers were concerned with the identity of a culture in transition, and they frequently viewed poetry as an instrument of political resistance. This attitude toward the social importance of poetry has shaped Chicana/o poetic production to the present day. Indeed, the literature of *el movimiento* assumes this deep interconnection between poetry and politics.

During the colonial and Mexican national periods, this frontier society lacked the social infrastructure necessary to maintain widespread literacy. In scholarly efforts to reconstruct the literary culture of the period, critics have stressed the need to incorporate oral forms, such as oral histories, folktales and songs, and religious dramas, as well as the *corrido* into literary history. The continuities between literary and oral forms are seen most explicitly in the *corrido*, given the ways that it serves to document the struggles of the common people, commemorate historical events, and monumentalize figures of resistance, such as in the "Corrido of Gregorio Cortez." In 1958, Americo Paredes wrote one of the first sustained studies of Chicana/o literary criticism, *With His Pistol in His Hand: A Border Ballad and Its Hero*, an analysis of this *corrido* and its "development out of actual events and of the folk traditions from which it sprang" (1). Paredes posits that the folk base of Chicano literature is the *corrido*, a position that has deeply influenced the ways that critics have read this tradition. Teresa McKenna explains "that Chicano literature proceeds out of a folk base has been a common assumption of most Chicano critics. That it evolves out of an oral tradition is a widely held corollary to this belief" (29). McKenna elucidates the scholarship on the *corrido* by stressing shared and consensual meaning formed in the relationship between the audience and the *corridista*—that *corridos* are narrated is important. They are socially engaged forms of expression that refer outward into the world. This dynamic between the text, the audience/reader, and the world is important to understanding how literature can embody social protest, as well as engender it.

The Early Twentieth Century (Interaction Period, 1910–1942)

According to one of the foremost Chicano literary historians, Francisco Lomeli, this period is characterized by two main factors: "first the adjustment by Chicanos to having to share the Southwest with Anglos; and, secondly an increased influx of Mexican immigrants" (312). Both of these elements are deeply influenced by relationships between the United States and Mexico: primarily the increased need for cheap agricultural labor in the United States following the Chinese Exclusion Act of 1882, the Gentleman's Agreement with Japan in 1907–1908, and the Immigration Acts of 1917, 1921 and 1922, all of which severely limited immigration from other sources (G. Sanchez 19). Large-scale migrations were made possible by the construction of railroads in Mexico, financed largely by U.S. investments. In the first three decades of the 20th century, approximately 1.5 million Mexicans migrated to the United States. According to historian George Sanchez, "immigration restrictions directed against Mexicans were at first consistently deferred under pressure by southwestern employers and then, when finally enacted, were mostly ignored by officials at the border. American administrators, in effect, allowed migrants to avoid the head tax or literacy test—instituted in 1917—by maintaining sparsely monitored checkpoints even after the establishment of the border patrol in 1924" (19–20).

Throughout this period, literary activity became centered in the publications of mutual aid societies such as LULAC (the League of United Latin American Citizens) and La Alianza, which worked for the incorporation of Mexicans into American society and worked against racial discrimination. A few collections of poetry and prose have been recovered, such as Felipe M. Chacon's collection *Poesia y Prosa* in 1924. Jose Ines Garcia published numerous books of poetry in the 1920s and 1930s. Fray Angelico Chavez wrote poetry in a mystical tradition, publishing *Clothed with the Sun* (1939) and *New Mexico Triptych* (1940), among other books. In addition, from 1936 to 1940 The Works Progress Administration in New Mexico collected more than two hundred oral histories, many from Chicana/os.

The Bracero Progam, an agreement between the governments of the United States and Mexico that imported more than 80,000 Mexican migrant workers between 1942 and 1965, is yet another element in Mexican migration to the United States. In this cultural environment of exploitation and discrimination between 1943 and 1964, what Lomeli calls the "Pre-Chicano Period," few Chicana/os made breakthroughs in the publishing world. The Zoot Suit Riots of 1943 have been cited by numerous critics and historians as evidence of widespread discriminatory attitudes of the times. Lomeli cites four major elements in the lack of publication: a negative social stigma that Mexicans could not write, the emphasis given to English at the expense of Spanish, the false illusion of equality after World War II and the Korean War, and perhaps most significant, the "systematic exclusion from any significant educational mobility by a society that needed a ready-made unskilled labor force and labeled [Chicanos] as such" (313).

The Chicano Renaissance (1965–1975)

Coined by Felipe de Ortego y Gasca, this term includes all of the work in every genre of literary and artistic expression that is directly engaged with *el movimiento*, as well as work by other writers addressing the experiences of Chicana/os. Two major influences in this movement were **Luis Valdez** and El Teatro Campesino, which he helped to found in 1965 as an effort to help support the United Farm Workers Union and their organizing efforts. Poetry was one of the major forms of literary and political expression during *el movimiento*, marked by an earnest and prolonged emphasis on self-definition, social justice, and community building. In defining "classic" Chicana/o poetry, that is, a poetry which "evinces a strong narrative or dramatic line," written during and after *el movimiento*, Rafael Perez-Torres lists five major elements: a socioeconomic position of disempowerment, bilingual or interlingual modes of expression, issues of **identity** formation, a variety of vernacular expressions, and an affirmation of indigenous cultural elements (6). During this period, a Chicano cultural nationalism emerged that stressed "barrio themes, a historical uniqueness and [Chicano's] Indian heritage, particularly Aztec" (Lomeli 313). Rodolfo "Corky" Gonzalez's poem "Yo Soy Joaquin" (1967) is a remarkable and historic piece of protest poetry, articulating a Chicano consciousness that was fundamental to *el movimiento*, helping to cement a sense of Chicano identity necessary for social action. Published by the Crusade for Justice in Denver, it was part of a trend of publications and presses that were deeply concerned with the role of literature and publishing within activism. Poetry such as "Yo Soy Joaquin" was frequently read aloud at rallies and distributed in leaflet form. Equally important were the many literary and cultural events such as the Floricanto festivals, which featured the work of writers and artists.

Quinto Sol emerges as a major force in publishing the journal *El Grito*, which showcased such writers as Jose Angel Gutierrez and **Tomás Rivera**. The rise of small presses in Chicano urban communities as well as the rise of presses in Chicano university communities helped to solidify this poetic revolution in print. Poets such as Lorna Dee Cervantes and Juan Felipe Herrera started small presses and published the work of their peers, as in Cervantes's *Mango Magazine* and Herrera's broadside *Citybender*. Chicana/o poetry gained national exposure in the early 1970s though the nationwide circulation and printing of early anthologies such as *El Espejo/The Mirror* (1971), *Literatura Chicana: Texto y Contexto* (1972), *We Are Chicanos* (1973), and *Chicano Voices* (1975).

Major figures in *movimiento* poetry include Alurista, Abelardo Delgado, and Jose Montoya. Alurista is perhaps best known for articulating a profoundly indigenous and Chicano worldview. He is widely acknowledged as the author of "El Plan Espiritual de Aztlán" (1969), which references a mythic Aztec homeland as central to Chicano identity (when geographically located, it is almost always in the Mexican territory lost in the Treaty of Guadalupe Hidalgo), and his poetry is deeply invested in questions of indigenous spirituality and its connection to contemporary Chicano barrios, bilingual and interlingual expression, and social justice: We can see all of these elements at play in his first collection *Floricanto En Aztlán* (1971). Abelardo Delgado's *Chicano: 25 Pieces of a Chicano Mind* (1969) takes a different approach, often articulating anger and frustration at **racism** in the United States, as we can see in the poem "Stupid America," where he clearly connects the importance of creativity to survival. Montoya's early poems voice a "new Chicano sensibility, namely its power to dramatize otherness and to bring readers into electrifying contact with social forms wholly different from Anglo American ones" (Saldivar 10). For example, two of his best-known poems, "El Louie" and "La Jefita," both introduce personas particular to Chicana/o culture, the figure of the pachuco and of the long-suffering mother, respectively. Many of Montoya's early works are elegiac and address questions of social justice as well as the place of Chicano poetry within American literature as in "Pobre Viejo Walt Whitman."

Women too were active in creating poetic works of protest and art during *el movimiento*; it is only recently however, that their work has been published and widely anthologized. Along with Lorna Dee Cervantes, Anita Sarah Duarte and Ana Nieto Gomez wrote critiques of machismo in *el movimiento* while affirming the centrality of women's voices and actions. Bernice Zamora's *Restless Serpents* (1975) has received considerable critical attention for the ways she articulates a distinctively Chicana feminist vision that connects the past to the present, while offering a critique of Western male power.

Pinto poetry—that is, poetry shaped by prison conditions and prison culture—is another important element of the Chicano Renaissance. Abelardo Delgado, Ricardo Sanchez, and Raul Salinas write poems that reflect the dehumanizing aspects of imprisonment, and the violence of the border and the fields is institutionalized within the prison. Jimmy Santiago Baca, according to Perez-Torres, most clearly writes out of the pinto poetic tradition, in a search for transcendence from violence, using the word as a weapon against oppression (119).

After the height of the Chicano Movement in the mid-1970s, publishing shifted to include more women. Marta E. Sanchez's important study, *Contemporary Chicana Poetry* (1985) cites Alma Villanueva, Lorna Dee Cervantes, Lucha Corpi, and Bernice Zamora as authors central to understanding the body of work produced by women during this period. Particularly important is the reinterpretation of mythic female figures, such as *La Malinche*, who goes from traitor to the Mexican nation to a bridge builder and communicator. Since the 1980s many Chicanas, most notably Pat Mora, Naomi Helena Quiñonez, Gloria Anzaldúa, and Cherríe Moraga, have explored in their poetry their relationships to female cultural figures, such as the Virgin of Guadalupe, La Malinche, and La Llorona, as well as a host of Aztec goddesses. After the establishment of a Chicana/o literary tradition, Chicana/o poets began to question cultural nationalist models of expression. Previous ways of imagining a Chicana/o identity that centered on a fixed and authentic origin, such as Aztlán, have been reimagined—Aztlán itself has been reconceptualized as a metaphoric and spiritual place of connection rather than a geographical region. Authors such as Anzaldúa and Guillermo Gomez-Pena have explored the border and "the borderlands" as an important metaphor for understanding the *mestizaje* of Chicana/o experience and identity. Lorna Dee Cervantes and Ana Castillo offer alternative conceptualizations of home that center on their experiences as women and as writers.

The relationship between identity, empowerment, and sexuality is explored extensively in much Chicana/o poetry. Moraga's *Loving in the War Years* (1983) combines poetry and essays to explore questions of racial and sexual identity. Anzaldúa's landmark collection of essays and poems, *Borderlands/La Frontera: The New Mestiza* (1987), articulates the border as the place of belonging for the *mestiza*, and Anzaldúa also theorizes how sexuality, specifically her identity as a *lesbiana*, a Chicana lesbian, has shaped her experience. Numerous collections such as **Sandra Cisneros**'s *My Wicked Wicked Ways* (1987) and *Loose Woman* (1994) and Francisco X. Alarcón's *Body in Flames/Cuerpo en Llamas* (1990) explore the erotic as a potentially empowering site of possibility.

Chicana/o poetry has shaped and been shaped by a distinctly American literary tradition. In Wolfgang Binder's *Partial Autobiographies: Interviews with Twenty Chicano Poets* (1985), many of the poets reflect on the importance of creative writing courses in American universities, such as Gary Soto's connection to his much admired teacher Philip Levine and Sandra Cisneros's experiences at the Iowa Writers' Workshop. We also see the importance of institutionalized support for these writers in grants and fellowships, such as the National Endowment for the Arts creative writing fellowships for Sandra Cisneros, Lucha Corpi, Juan Felipe Herrera, and Gary Soto, and the **Frederick Douglass** as well as the Ford Foundation fellowship awards for Ricardo Sanchez (xii). This sort of recognition signals not only much needed financial support, but also a clear understanding that these poets are of national importance, and their work reflects not only their experiences as individuals and as Chicana/os, but also their experiences as Americans in a multicultural and multiethnic society. Chicana/o poetry will continue to shape the landscape of American letters precisely because of its affinity with hybridity and cultural interaction and the ways in which it highlights relationships between literature and culture. (*See also* Bilingualism)

Further Reading

Arteaga, Alfred. *Chicano Poetics: Heterotexts and Hybridities*. New York: Cambridge University Press, 1997.

Candelaria, Cordelia. *Chicano Poetry: A Critical Introduction*. Westport, CT: Greenwood, 1986.

Lomeli, Francisco. "An Overview of Chicano Letters: From Origins to Resurgence." In *Chicano Studies: Survey and Analysis*, edited by Dennis Bixler-Marquez, et al., 309–17. Dubuque, IA: Kendall/Hunt, 1992.

McKenna, Teresa. *Migrant Song: Politics and Process in Contemporary Chicano Literature*. Austin: University of Texas Press, 1997.

Ortego y Gasca, Felipe de. "An Introduction to Chicano Poetry." In *Modern Chicano Writers: A Collection of Critical Essays*, edited by Joseph Sommers and Tomas Ybarra Frausto, 108–16. Englewood Cliffs, NJ: Prentice Hall, 1979.

Paredes, Americo. *With His Pistol in His Hand: A Border Ballad and Its Hero.* Austin: University of Texas Press, 1958.

Paredes, Raymund. "Mexican American Literature: An Overview." In *Recovering the U.S. Hispanic Literary Heritage,* edited by Ramon Gutierrez and Genaro Padilla, 31–52. Houston: Arte Público Press, 1993.

Perez-Torres, Rafael. *Movements in Chicano Poetry.* New York: Cambridge University Press, 1995.

Saldívar, Jose David. "Towards a Chicano Poetics: The Making of the Chicano Subject: 1962–1982." *Confluencia* 1.2 (1986): 10–17.

Sanchez, George. *Becoming Mexican American.* New York: Oxford University Press, 1993.

Sanchez, Marta. *Contemporary Chicana Poetry.* Berkeley: University of California Press, 1985.

Eliza Rodriguez y Gibson

MEXICAN AMERICAN STEREOTYPES

Between 1836 and the Mexican American War of 1846 to 1848, the United States wrested control of Mexico's northern half, the vast resource-rich territory stretching from Texas to California. This formative act of national territorial expansion produced a significant U.S. minority from the Mexican communities of Texas and the Southwest, a minority augmented by continuing mass migration from Mexico since the early years of the 20th century. Concomitant with the United States' swift evolution as a continental power, the Mexican-origin population became the focus of mass media, popular cultural, and historiographical representations and attitudes that have, since the mid-19th century, functioned as stereotypes about Mexicans in the wider U.S. population.

A contested term, stereotyping generally signifies the production and circulation of clichéd, reductive, and often negative and demeaning ethnic and racial types by which the agents and institutions of a dominant culture claim to identify, represent, and know a particular group or people. The perpetuation of stock Mexican types—for example, the male Latin lover and the female "Mexican spitfire," the lazy greaser, the bandit, the drug runner, the gang member—reflects pervasive and longstanding cultural attitudes in the United States that also affect other U.S. Latinos and, more generally, Latin Americans as a whole. These peoples have been cast variously in the Anglo-American popular imagination as the embodiments of an exotic, dark and sinuous "Latin" sensibility, of irrational and superstitious-cum-magical Catholicism, of heat, spice, emotionality, and musicality, of barely repressed violence, and of potential illegal border-crossing and organized criminality. In the critical literature about such stereotypes, the complex production and circulation of myriad ethnicized "Latin" types in the United States has been called "Latinism" (Berg 4) and "Tropicalization" (Aparicio and Chávez-Silverman). The pervasiveness of "Latin" stereotypes in the United States may also have roots in the Black Legend, an anti-Spanish discourse that emerged in the 16th century in Protestant Europe and in England's American colonies. The legend demonized the Spanish as inhumane, rapacious, and cruel and decried the intermixing of Spanish, indigenous, and African peoples throughout the Spanish empire as proof of those peoples' inherent cultural and racial deficiency. The legend implied that the Spanish-speaking inhabitants of the Americas were less civilized than the peoples and cultures derived from non-Catholic northern Europe.

In the Mexican American case, ethnic stereotyping is intimately related to two resilient, and not necessarily mutually exclusive, discourses of otherness. First, Mexican Americans are often said to form a non-"American" or alien sector, and thus a marginal and expendable one. This "alienizing" discourse has focused on the purportedly foreign signs derived from the "dark" mixed European-indigenous racial history of many Mexicans, as well as the maintenance of the Spanish language. Second, the Mexican American sector is also often treated as a coherent, homogeneous, and readily identifiable constituency, hence the targeting of Mexican Americans, and other Latinos, by the U.S. state as a potentially criminalized and problem sector and by U.S. media and corporate concerns as a lucrative and exploitable consumer market. Both discourses limit the possibility of nuanced representations by ignoring the many complicating factors at work within the diverse Mexican American population: class status, regional location, generational perspective, familial migratory history and lengths of residency, mixed-racial background, gender and sexual differentials, deeply felt commitment to the host society, and bi- or multilinguistic capacities.

For many commentators, the U.S. film industry has been perhaps the most influential perpetrator, both in the United States and beyond, of stock Mexican and Mexican American types. From its earliest days, Hollywood has tended to portray Mexico as a space worthy of U.S. intervention and salvation, as is evident in numerous Westerns that feature Anglo-Americans riding south of the border to rectify injustice and save Mexicans who are unable to look after their own interests. From such films derive a set of globally recognizable Mexican characters: the docile Mexican, propped up against a cactus or saloon wall, sleeping under a highly colored blanket; the dirty, unshaved, and vicious *bandito;* the simple and poor *campesino* or rural worker whose heavily accented English provokes audience laughter; the dark untrustworthy temptress; the slick, macho Latin lover. Hollywood film has also generated its own stock types about the Mexican American community itself. This typecasting is evident in the many films made about the border patrol and border policing, which feature unscrupulous Mexican Americans on the wrong side of U.S. law, thus perpetuating the notion that Mexican Americans are more often than not "illegal aliens." A related criminalizing trend animates the more recent genre of inner-city films that focus on Mexican gangs and urban violence. The corporate world, too, has been a rich source of stereotypes about Mexican Americans, a contemporary example being the Taco Bell chain's deployment of a "Mexican" chihuahua in its advertising campaigns. A notable trend in mass media in the 1980s and 1990s was the rise of an erotic–exotic representational gaze, signified by the ubiquitous chili and soundtracks of salsa music, by which Mexican Americans and other Latinos were portrayed as icons of sensuality and libidinal heat.

Since the 1960s, many Chicana/o critics and cultural producers have been concerned to counter prevalent stereotypes either by critiquing them or by answering back with their own representations of Mexican Americanness. This double ambition has driven much Chicana/o film, documentary, theater, literary, visual art, music and performance work. The self-styled cultural guerilla, Guillermo Gómez-Peña, for example, has consistently mocked stock Mexican types in performances that feature alternative ethnic characters, such as "Mad-Mex" and "El Mexterminator," which are intended to challenge dominant-cultural assumptions and prejudices. This antistereotyping trend has also led to calls for a "Brown out" of the mass media, an attempt to counter the media underrepresentation of Latinos and to insert more positive and reflective portrayals of Latinos in U.S. popular cultural production, notably film and television.

Further Reading

Aparicio, Frances R., and Susana Chávez-Silverman, eds. "Introduction." *Tropicalizations: Transcultural Representations of Latinidad.* Hanover, NH: University Press of New England, 1997.

Berg, Charles Ramírez. *Latino Images in Film: Stereotypes, Subversion, and Resistance.* Austin: University of Texas Press, 2002.

Dávila, Arlene. *Latinos, Inc.: The Marketing and Making of a People.* Berkeley: University of California Press, 2000.

Noriega, Chon A. "*El hilo latino*: Representation, Identity and National Culture." *Jump Cut* 38 (1993): 45–50.

Paul Allatson

MOMADAY, NAVARRE SCOTT (1934–)

Navarre Scott Momaday is a Native American poet, Pulitzer Prize–winning novelist, playwright, storyteller, painter, founding trustee of the National Museum of the American Indian, regents' professor of the humanities at the University of Arizona. Momaday has lectured and given readings internationally, and his articles appear in many periodicals. Major works include *House Made of Dawn* (1968), **The Way to Rainy Mountain** (1969), *Angle of Geese* and other poems (1974), *Owl in the Cedar Tree* (1975), *The Gourd Dancer* (1976), *The Names: A Memoir* (1976), *We Have Been Lovers, You and I* (1980), *The Ancient Child* (1989), *In the Presence of the Sun: Stories and Poems, 1961–1991* (1992), *Circle of Wonder: A Native American Christmas Story* (1994), *The Man Made of Words: Essays, Stories, Passages* (1997), and *In the Bear's House* (1999).

Multicultural Experience and the Pulitzer Prize

N. Scott Momaday was born in Kiowa country in Oklahoma. He grew up among the rich oral traditions of the reservations and pueblos of the Southwest and lived among Navajo, Apache, Hispanic, and Anglo children. This tribal history was

N. Scott Momaday. (Christopher Felver/Corbis)

repeated for his entertainment, but as an adult he recognized the fragile nature of the captivating stories that shape his work. His literary scholarship and painting reflect his desire to preserve this rich cultural experience. Momaday's parents were teachers with artistic interests. His father was a painter and his mother a writer. Like his parents, Momaday's career has integrated writing, painting, and teaching. His credentials reflect interests in political science, law, literature, and language and include a bachelor's degree from the University of New Mexico and an MA and PhD from Stanford.

In the 1960s civil rights and ethnographic studies influenced a new categorization of literary texts. This shift formed a broader concept of literary criticism and increased accessibility of the literary **canon**, opening the way for Momaday's interpretative discourse. Disciplinary viewpoints had previously assigned oral narratives, histories, autobiographies, and similar works to anthropology or labeled them historical documents, but the new canon recognized many of these works as literature, making space for new writers. Benefiting from this shift toward a more inclusive canon, Momaday's Pulitzer Prize–winning first novel, *House Made of Dawn*, received recognition while he was still a relatively unknown writer. Recordings for the Museum of the American Indian, Smithsonian Institute, and National Public Radio, in addition to other national and international events, continue to support and extend Momaday's earlier recognition.

Cultural History, Legend as Art

Through allegory (narratives that dramatize symbolic or abstract ideas), anecdote (short narratives that expose overarching themes), and archetype (recurring cultural symbols, characters, or landscapes), Momaday interweaves history and legend. His art resonates with history, connecting language and the human experience to the natural world, while explicitly translating and celebrating Native American experience. This multicultural approach is recognized by a range of world literature scholars. His gift for storytelling has specifically influenced other Native American writers, including Joy Harjo and **Leslie Marmon Silko**. Momaday's reverence for the physical and the metaphysical is demonstrated in the imagery of Rainy

Mountain Cemetery and of walking among the stones marking the burial site of family members. This vibrant imagery gives voice to his Kiowa heritage and provides a model for other Native American writers.

Momaday's literary models and paintings are windows into the Kiowa culture, praised by critics for their visual power. Matthias Schubnell calls *The Ancient Child* Momaday's most comprehensive commentary on art—his "most painterly work"—and notes that Momaday, like the German expressionist Emil Nolde, rejects the commercialization of art, preferring to search for the "primal, mythic mentality." This connection of **identity** and artistic genius to "myth, place, and the human unconscious" lifts Momaday's work from its Native American boundaries to establish broader cultural commonalities. His character, Set, searches for primitive identity, reflecting the expressionists' concern for artistic substance, authenticity, and intrinsic meaning ("Locke Setman" 468).

Critics call Momaday's approach in *The Way to Rainy Mountain* cinematic. Readers view an ancient Kiowa landmark, a knoll rising out of the Wichita Range on the Oklahoma Plains. This narrative incorporates concepts of time, place, and self. The descriptions of Oklahoma weather include winter blizzards, spring tornadic winds, and summers that turn the prairie into "an anvil's edge." The images of land, trees, and weather conspire to define time and place. Momaday distinguishes the whole from the isolated elements of this land that nurtures his cultural identity. The land looms large, inhabited by "great green and yellow grasshoppers." The land is lonely, and time crawls. The writer's return to Rainy Mountain provokes an interior monologue, linking the history of the southern Plains Kiowas and his grandmother's Montana forebears. He calls the vast continental interior a "memory in her blood," and he calls his grandmother's inherited reverence for the sun and her later Christian faith images of suffering and hope. Aho's house, once a significant site for feasting and activity and a place for viewing the stars, has become a small place inhabited by funeral silence. A strangely enlarged outline of a cricket against the moon and a warm wind mark the culmination of the writer's pilgrimage.

Voice, Language, and Landscape

These autobiographical descriptions the natural landscapes associated with Momaday's Kiowa heritage are a powerful blend of literary methods and traditions. Momaday's observance of the significance of landscape, or "spirit of place," is an essential element of Native American oral tradition. In *In the Presence of the Sun* Momaday conveys his early fascination with language as a creative link to legend, symbolism, and spiritual, or aesthetic objects. The writer selects narrative and lyric forms, fusing genres, for their capacity to fit his pithy style. He blends the qualities of verse and prose, history and imagination, and personal identity and culture to produce an integrated voice for storytelling. In imaginative prose the writer personalizes his exploration of history and culture to produce what he calls "an act of understanding."

In addition to his blending of verse and prose qualities, Momaday also manipulates characterization to preserve in contemporary English his multicultural experience and Kiowa heritage. In *Ancient Child*, his second novel, the protagonist is an adopted Kiowa-Anglo, and in his collection of poems, prose, and paintings, *In the Bear's House*, the healer (Grey) is Navajo, Kiowa, Mexican, French, Canadian, Scotch, Irish, and English, perhaps reflective of his mother's blended heritage. These works are designed to preserve the traditional sacred elements of a culture that Momaday believes may not be transferring effectively to new generations. In *The Man Made of Words: Essays, Stories, Passages*, a recurrent theme is the threatened loss of the sacred narratives that reflect the culture's oral tradition and explain significant tribal events and beliefs.

Momaday considers his distinctive regional work as also fragments of a universal story. Local geography, customs, and speech, subtly and consciously, influence the regional narratives of his childhood. Memoir becomes a microcosm of layered personal reflection and historical imagery. Momaday uses this blended private and public voice in *The Gourd Dancer* and *The Man Made of Words* to dramatically introduce into American literature people and places that are vital to the understanding of Native American culture. For example, the repeated appearance of the bear is a significant literary and cultural symbol. The writer selects strong cultural imagery and allows the contrasting poetic influences of such writers as Emily Dickinson and Frederick Goddard Tuckerman to work in tandem with themes uncharacteristic of Native American culture, such as the Crucifixion, to tell a more inclusive story.

These contrastive investigations of traditional imagery in Native American and Anglo-American culture take Momaday's investigation a step further than some cultural texts go, representing the Native American experience, as Roemer views it, as inherently multiethnic and multicultural. In *House Made of Dawn*, Momaday considers the cultural complexities of young Native Americans who must balance the ancient ways of their ancestors against their own need to survive 20th-century materialism. In Abel, a young Tano Indian, Momaday represents the experience of individuals caught between cultures. Abel returns from World War II and is plunged into a different kind of war, involving his elders' world of ceremonies, the harsh realities of poverty, and the promised abundance of the urban world. The traditional Native American understanding of the psychic self's origins further complicates these contraries. This experience of self, as mythic and tribal, is inherent in the related concept of the sacredness of the land, with brain, bone, and land being integrally connected. For these individuals, leaving the land is not optional. Self is firmly bound to the land, and going from the land initiates a disintegration of self. Returning to the land is returning to self. This homing pattern, essential to the spherical, cyclical nature of tribal narratives and Native American novels, is especially evident in *The Ancient Child* and *House Made of Dawn*.

Culture's Personal Journey

Like the traditional forms of his culture's storytelling, Momaday's themes are frequently circular in structure, with event incorporated into event and basic subtexts expanding into even more complex themes (see Roberson). Momaday's literary connection of personal narrative and history is simultaneously an overview of the corresponding progression of personal and tribal identity development. In *The Way to Rainy Mountain*, by connecting the migration of the Kiowas and his own journey back to Rainy Mountain, Momaday creates a *whole journey*. This experimentation with sensory, metaphorical, and symbolic language provides a successful vehicle for his literary art and cultural narrative, and the blurring of genre boundaries suggests the indistinct boundaries that frequently redefine self and culture (see Schubnell). Momaday also employs selective omniscience and interior monologue to focus the reader's perception and to capture preverbal sentiments. Momaday's effective documentation of the Kiowa cultural identity through his own personal narrative, myth, and history embraces the literary and cultural objectives of both.

Memories of Rainy Mountain Creek and the culture of childhood clearly shape Momaday's art. The home where his father was born was built in 1913 by Momaday's grandfather, Mammedaty. Momaday remembers first hearing the language of his Kiowa forebears and receiving his Indian name in the arbor beside his grandfather's house. He describes the house and arbor as now in disrepair, inhabited only by the songs and prayers of memory. Momaday has been instrumental in establishing the Buffalo Trust, a cultural archive and center designed to assist young Kiowas. The trust's mission is preserving the Kiowa heritage. The buffalo, representing the sun, is the logo of the association and the sacred symbol of the Kiowa Sun Dance. The Buffalo Trust is a public effort to recover and preserve a vanishing culture. The land of the buffalo has changed, but Momaday's art and the Kiowa concept of time merge the past and present, painting everything that represents either reality as existing side by side, conversing to create mutual understanding. (*See also* Native American Novel)

Further Reading

Fox, Richard Wightman, and James T. Kloppenberg. *A Companion to American Thought.* Cambridge: Blackwell, 1995. 464–66.

Isernhager, Hartwig, ed. *Momaday, Vizenor, Armstrong: Conversations on American Indian Writing.* Norman: University of Oklahoma Press, 1998.

Ives, Stephen, director. *The West.* DVD, VHS. Tampa, FL: Warner Home Video, 2003.

Lincoln, Kenneth. "Old Songs Made New: Momaday." In *Sing with the Heart of a Bear: Fusions of Native American Poetry, 1890–1999*, 240–255. Berkeley: University of California Press, 2000.

Roberson, Susan L. "Translocations and Transformations: Identity in N. Scott Momaday's *The Ancient Child.*" *American Indian Quarterly* 22.1. (1998): 31–46.

Roemer, Kenneth M. *Approaches to Teaching Momaday's "The Way to Rainy Mountain."* New York: MLA, 1988.

Roemer, Kenneth M, ed. *N. Scott Momaday: The Cultural and Literary Background.* Literary Conversations Series. Norman: University of Oklahoma Press, 1985.

Schubnell, Matthias, ed. *Conversations with N. Scott Momaday.* Jackson: University Press of Mississippi, 1997.

Schubnell, Matthias. "Locke Setman, Emil Nolde and the Search for Expression in N. Scott Momaday's *The Ancient Child*." *American Indian Quarterly* 18.4 (1994): 468–81

Schubnell, Matthias. *N. Scott Momaday: The Cultural and Literary Background*. Norman: University of Oklahoma Press, 1985.

Stella Thompson

MOODY, ANNE (1940–)

Anne Moody is an African American activist, author, and autobiographer. Moody became aware of America's racial injustices at an early age, and by the time she entered college she was extremely active in national civil rights organizations. In her writing and her public life, Moody has fought for African Americans' human rights, political representation, social equality, and individual freedom from exploitation, discrimination, and violence.

Moody's most famous work, her award-winning autobiography *Coming of Age in Mississippi* (1968), recounts her life as an African American girl who faces **racism** as she develops her self-identity and grows to adulthood in America's Deep South. Moody's autobiography is factual but includes some fictional techniques. The narrative's tone and plot development are novelistic, and she recreates several conversations and events in more detail than she could have remembered. In addition, Moody dramatizes her psychological self-exploration as she struggles against stereotypes and searches for a public voice.

Coming of Age fits into the rich African American tradition of literary autobiographies that began with the narratives of escaped slaves, such as **Frederick Douglass** and **Harriet Jacobs**. A number of famous southern authors and activists, such as Booker T. Washington, Mary Church Terrell, **Zora Neale Hurston**, and **Richard Wright**, contributed their own talents to this literary tradition. Moody, like the previous autobiographers, emphasized the value of education and actively resisted the oppressive attitudes and exploitative institutions of white America. After Moody, other political and social activists, such as Malcolm X and **Audre Lorde**, published their own autobiographies.

Although Moody wrote fiction, such as *Mr. Death: Four Stories* (1975) and several uncollected short stories, she considered herself first and foremost an activist. *Coming of Age* is more than a literary work; it documents how the lives of typical Southern African Americans intersect with America's racial history and the organizations fighting racism. Born in Mississippi to sharecropping parents, Moody is four when her autobiography begins. She depicts racism from a child's perspective, describing plantation life, segregated schools and movie theaters, and daily verbal and physical abuse against her people.

As Moody grows older, she develops a deeper awareness of the hardships and horrors African Americans face in the South. She despises white people for believing they are racially superior and using their position to acquire unfair social privileges. She also despises the apathy within her own community, wishing more African Americans would actively fight for justice, equality, and personal dignity.

Even as a child, Moody disagrees with family members and friends who believed it was not their "place" to protest injustice or even to vote. She becomes angry when her frustrated father runs away from his family instead fighting for social improvements. A teenaged Moody accepts the responsibility of earning money for the family, experiencing bigotry and exploitation first-hand as a maid and tutor.

After high school, Moody enters Tougaloo College, where she succeeds academically and works fearlessly and tirelessly against segregation, discrimination, and lynching in the South. An independent and proud young woman, Moody wants her life to have purpose, so she joins several civil rights organizations: National Association for the Advancement of Colored People (NAACP), Congress of Racial Equality (CORE), and Student Non-Violence Coordinating Committee (SNCC). She speaks out against injustice, registers Southern African Americans to vote, and participates in boycotts, such as the 1963 sit-in to integrate the Woolworth's lunch counter in Jackson, Mississippi. Moody's activism gets her arrested, and several times her life is threatened. She uses her own experiences to teach workshops on self-protection to activists and demonstrators. Finally, Moody expresses both hope and despair for the movement's future as she participates in the 1963 March on Washington, where **Martin Luther King Jr.** gives his famous "I Have a Dream" speech.

Moody's autobiography ends in 1963, when she became disillusioned with the **Civil Rights Movement** and left the South. She had become more militant and no longer believed a grassroots, nonviolent organization could defeat the causes of racism or liberate her people. Moody, however, was not done fighting social problems. In 1964, she moved to Ithaca, New York, to become the civil rights project coordinator at Cornell University. A few years later she moved to New York City to continue writing and serve as counselor for the city's antipoverty program.

Further Reading

Hudson, Angela Pulley. "Mississippi Lost and Found: Anne Moody's Autobiogrph(ies) and Racial Melancholia." *A/B: Auto/Biography Studies* 20.2 (2005): 282–300.

McKay, Nellie. "The Girls Who Became the Women: Childhood Memories in the Autobiographies of Harriet Jacobs, Mary Church Terrell, and Anne Moody." In *Tradition and the Talents of Women*, edited by Florence Howe, 105–24. Urbana: University of Illinois Press, 1991.

Rishoi, Christy. *From Girl to Woman: American Women's Coming-of-Age Narratives*. Albany: State University of New York Press, 2003.

Matthew Teorey

MORRISON, TONI (1931–)

Toni Morrison is an African American novelist, editor, and literary critic. The only African American to win a Nobel Prize in literature, Toni Morrison is a visionary writer who celebrates the rich cultural heritage of black life in sharp, vivid prose. One of the most important American novelists and intellectuals of the 20th century,

Morrison has had a profound impact on a generation of young writers of color and on the development of the African American literary **canon**.

The second of four children, Morrison was born Chloe Anthony Wofford in the small, industrial town of Lorain, Ohio. Morrison's father, George, a hardworking shipyard welder, held as many as three jobs at once and believed in the moral superiority of African Americans. Ramah, Morrison's mother, was more optimistic about the possibility of achieving racial harmony, and instilled in her children a firm belief in self-reliance, community, and family. Morrison grew up listening to her parents spin long, enchanting tales of deceased relatives, ghosts, and powerful dreams. Reading was also a favorite childhood activity for the young writer, who was especially fond of Leo Tolstoy, Fyodor Dostoevsky, Jane Austen, and Gustave Flaubert. Morrison attended integrated schools, where she consistently impressed her teachers. Although only one member of her family had attended college, she was determined to continue her education at the university level. In 1949, she enrolled at Howard University, where she studied English literature and the classics. At Howard, Morrison changed her name to Toni and joined the theatrical group, the Howard University Players. In 1955, Morrison received a master's in English from Cornell University. She wrote her thesis on the theme of suicide in the works of Virginia Woolf and William Faulkner. After working briefly at Texas Southern University, Morrison returned to Howard in 1957 to teach English. The following year she married Harold Morrison, a Jamaican architect with whom she had two sons, Harold Ford and Slade Kevin. Morrison returned to Lorain after her marriage ended in 1964, but soon thereafter she accepted an editorial position with Random House in Syracuse. Alone in New York with her two young children, Morrison began writing as a way to combat her solitude and isolation. In the evenings, she returned to a story she began while teaching at Howard, a brief sketch of a childhood girlfriend who wished for blue eyes. This story would eventually become *The Bluest Eye* (1970), Morrison's first novel.

Although *The Bluest Eye* was not a commercial success, its vibrant prose and courageous exploration of destructive American values attracted critical attention. Exploring the origins and devastating consequences of racial self-hatred, Morrison focused her novel on the most ignored member of society, a poor, black girl who longs for blue eyes. Pecola Breedlove believes herself to be ugly and accepts the beauty and virtue of whiteness. Although Morrison's description of Pecola's descent into insanity offers a pointed critique of white American values, the novel is primarily concerned with the health and responsibilities of the black community.

Morrison was working in New York City when her second novel, *Sula* (1973), was published. Nominated for a National Book Award, *Sula* describes the relationship between childhood friends Sula Peace and Nel Wright. While Nel marries and settles into a conventional life in the Midwestern Bottom community, Sula attends college, travels, and becomes a social rebel. Upon her return to the Bottom, Sula is perceived as evil because she refuses to conform to traditional conventions and patterns of behavior. In this poignant novel of oppositions, Morrison examines the interdependency between good and evil and the complex relationships between black women.

As an editor at Random House, Morrison sought to develop the African American canon by promoting the work of key literary and historical figures. She helped to publish books by **Toni Cade Bambara**, Gayl Jones, Angela Davis, and Muhammad Ali. She also edited *The Black Book* (1974), an anthology of the history of African Americans. During her research for *The Black Book*, Morrison came across the history of Margaret Garner, a slave woman who killed her daughter rather than give her up to her master. This story would provide the inspiration for Morrison's masterpiece, the novel ***Beloved*** (1987).

Morrison's third book, ***Song of Solomon*** (1977), received massive critical acclaim. A national bestseller, it won the National Book Critics Award and was the first African American Book of the Month Club selection since *Native Son* (1940). In *Song of Solomon*, Milkman Dead undergoes an epic quest for **identity**. The privileged son of a materialistic father and a troubled mother, Milkman embarks on a search for gold that becomes a transformative journey for cultural knowledge and understanding. *Song of Solomon* contains some of Morrison's most memorable characters, including Pilate, Milkman's wise aunt, who was born without a navel and converses with her dead father. Drawing upon African American folklore as well as biblical stories, Morrison explores mythic concerns of flight, family, and responsibility while offering a fundamental ethos of hope and love. In 1980, Morrison was named to the National Council of the Arts by former President Jimmy Carter, and a year later was elected to the American Academy and Institute of Arts and Letters.

Following the widely anticipated publication of her fourth novel, *Tar Baby* (1981), Morrison became the first black woman to appear on the cover of *Newsweek*. *Tar Baby* is set on an imaginary Caribbean Island and involves the love affair between Jadine, an educated black model, and Son, a handsome drifter. They meet at the estate of Valerian Street, a retired white millionaire, who is accompanied by his fragile wife Margaret and their black servants, Sydney and Ondine Childs. Although Jadine is the niece of Sydney and Ondine, she occupies a different social circle due to the patronage she receives from Valerian. Some critics found Morrison's exploration of social hierarchies to be overly didactic, whereas others described her portrayal of white characters as shallow and clichéd. Despite these mixed reviews, *Tar Baby* is marked by Morrison's signature lyrical style and her preoccupation with issues of community and identity.

In 1983, Morrison left Random House and began teaching creative writing at the State University of New York in Albany as the Albert Schweitzer Professor of the Humanities. During this time, she began work on the unpublished play *Dreaming Emmett*. In her only work for the theater, Morrison recreates the murder of Emmett Till and the white men who were acquitted of the crime. Till speaks from the dead to describe his brutal death.

Morrison continued to explore voices beyond the grave in her internationally acclaimed bestseller ***Beloved***. Set in Reconstruction-era Ohio, *Beloved* tells the story of Sethe, an escaped slave woman who murders her daughter rather than return to a life of bondage. Morrison describes Sethe's struggle to keep her slave memories from consciousness along with her need to confront the ghosts of her past. Sethe's repression is unsettled by the arrival of Paul D, a man she knew in slavery, and Beloved, a troubling stranger who doesn't seem to know who she is. In this powerful novel, Morrison describes the dehumanizing effects of slavery and the complexities of maternal love. Although most critics praised *Beloved* for its soaring prose, innovative narration, and rich characterizations, controversy erupted after it failed to win the National Book Award and the National Book Critics Circle Award. In response, 48 prominent African American writers and intellectuals, including **Maya Angelou**, **Alice Walker**, and John Wideman, published a letter in the *New York Times* decrying this oversight. Later that year, *Beloved* was awarded the Pulitzer Prize, and it continues to be hailed as a major contribution to American literature.

In 1988, Morrison was named the Robert F. Goheen Professorship of the Humanities at Princeton University, becoming the first black woman to hold an endowed chair at an Ivy League institution. Morrison's appointment was part of a major effort at Princeton to develop its African American studies program. She was joined by such prominent black intellectuals as Cornel West and Arnold Rampersad. While teaching creative writing and working with the African American, American, and women's studies departments, Morrison began work on her sixth novel, *Jazz* (1992). The most technically ambitious of Morrison's books, *Jazz* is narrated by an unnamed and unreliable speaker who demands a collaborative storytelling relationship with the audience. This enigmatic voice describes the violent love triangle between Violet and Joe Trace and a haughty teenager named Dorcas. While recounting the thrilling sense of possibility that New York City offered blacks following the Great Migration of the 1920s, the narrator describes Joe's love affair with Dorcas and his subsequent murder of the young girl. Although *Jazz* received mixed reviews, it confirmed Morrison's commitment to taking stylistic risks in her work and demonstrated her belief in the dynamic nature of storytelling.

In her only work of literary criticism, *Playing in the Dark: Whiteness and the Literary Imagination* (1992), Morrison examines the **racism** in American literature, arguing that historically readers have been constructed as white. She describes a largely ignored but extremely influential "Africanist presence" in texts by such canonical authors as Edgar Allan Poe, Willa Cather, and Ernest Hemingway. Morrison contends that works by white Americans are haunted by a black presence that acts as a repository for anxieties concerning slavery, **race**, and the tenuous construction of American identity. Morrison continued to expand the scope of her critical gaze in *Justice, En-Gendering Power: Essays on Anita Hill, Clarence Thomas, and the Construction of Social Reality* (1992), a collection of essays she edited on the Supreme Court Justice's controversial appointment. Although many critics disagreed with Morrison's contention that Thomas rejected his black identity in order to succeed in white America, the publication of this book along with her growing popularity as a novelist propelled her into the national spotlight. She became a major public figure, offering strong opinions on issues as diverse as the 1992 Los Angeles riots and the American literary **canon**.

In 1993, Morrison received the Nobel Prize for Literature. Her acceptance speech focused upon the power of language and narrative to create identity and community. Morrison has since become an international celebrity, lecturing widely even as she continues to teach and write. Her books have continued to be best-sellers in part because of the support of Oprah Winfrey and her influential book club. In 1998, *Beloved* was made into a film, starring Winfrey. That same year, Morrison published *Paradise* (1998), a novel set in an all-black town in Oklahoma. Exploring issues of exclusion and acceptance, *Paradise* describes the invasion of a local convent by a group of men who believe that the refuge for wandering women has become a threat to their town. Morrison returns to themes of community and the problematic but necessary role of social pariahs in this sweeping novel of a town's rise and fall. Morrison's most recent novel, *Love* (2003), describes the complex relationships of the Cosey family and the decline of their beachfront resort, a once luxurious vacation destination for African Americans. *Love* again highlights the elegance of Morrison's prose and her firm dedication to writing for and about the black community. In her 2008 novel, *A Mercy*, Morrison returns once again the territory that she has imaginatively claimed as her won: slavery in America. The setting of the novel is America in the 1690s. What appears Edenic on the surface is poisoned by enslavement in its many manifestations and violates the human body and spirit. Narrated by many voices, the novel has a complex structure yet has the smoothness and coherence of a skillfully crafted quilt. Morrison's most recent novel is *Home* (2012). Written in dazzling prose, it tells the story of Frank Money, a young African American Korean War veteran who has fought abroad to defend freedom and comes "home" to an unfree land. Many of the themes that Morrison has explored in her oeuvre crystallize in this short novel with stunning clarity. (*See also* African American Novel)

Further Reading

Anderson, Melanie. *Spectrality in the Novels of Toni Morrison*. Knoxville: University of Tennessee Press, 2013.

Conner, Marc C., ed. *The Aesthetics of Toni Morrison: Speaking the Unspeakable*. Jackson: University Press of Mississippi, 2000.

Gates, Henry L., and K. A. Appiah, eds. *Toni Morrison: Critical Perspectives Past and Present*. New York: Amistad, 1993.

McKay, Nellie Y. *Critical Essays on Toni Morrison*. Boston: G. K. Hall, 1988.

Page, Philip. *Dangerous Freedom: Fusion and Fragmentation in Toni Morrison's Novels*. Jackson: University Press of Mississippi, 1995.

Peach, Linden. *Toni Morrison*. New York: St. Martin's Press, 2000.

Royson, Tessa. *The Cambridge Introduction to Toni Morrison*. Cambridge, England: Cambridge University Press, 2013.

Stephanie Li

MUKHERJEE, BHARATI (1940–)

Bharati Mukherjee is an award-winning Indian American novelist, short-story writer, and essayist. Bharati Mukherjee was born on July 27, 1940, in Calcutta,

India, to an upper-class Hindu Brahmin family. Influenced in her early years by Western education in England and Switzerland, Mukherjee was a keen and ardent reader and by the age of eight had already read many Western as well as Bengali classics. After receiving her BA and MA degrees in India, Mukherjee came to America to attend a writing workshop in the Iowa Writers Workshop in 1961. She subsequently earned her MFA in creative writing in 1963 and PhD in English and comparative literature in 1969. Mukherjee's writing career began while teaching at McGill University in Montreal. She has taught creative writing at Columbia University, New York University, and Queens College and is currently a distinguished professor at the University of California, Berkeley.

While studying for the writing workshop at Iowa in 1961, she met fellow student Clarke Blaise—a naturalized American citizen of Canadian origin—and fell in love with him. They got married, and Mukherjee moved with Blaise to Canada after completing their studies. Mukherjee could not assimilate her **identity** in the Canadian terms of mosaic culture. After 14 years of life in Canada, she migrated with her family to United States in 1980 and has vehemently embraced the American multicultural notion of identity. After her naturalization as an American citizen, she has openly declared and celebrated her **assimilation**ist attitude and adoption of an American identity. Her rejection of a hyphenated identity as an Indian American or Asian American writer reveals her demand that she be considered equally at par with the European immigrants who do not feel the need to claim such an identity. She also denounces the labeling of postcolonial writer in relation to her works. Mukherjee insists that she be seen as an American writer following the ideals of the American dream in a heterogeneous, multicultural America.

A predominant theme in Mukherjee's fiction as in other immigrant fiction is the issue of identities that one must learn how to transform in order to survive in contemporary, multicultural America. In the process, sometimes cultures and traditions are deemed to be shed off in favor of new and different ideals that suit such transformation. Mukherjee situates herself in the American tradition and compares herself with writers such as Bernard Malamud and **Maxine Hong Kingston**, who also deal with transformation and forging of new identities in their fiction. She denounces the self-conscious exiles replete with nostalgia and diasporic longings as in the works of other writers of Indian origin such as Salman Rushdie, Amitav Ghosh, and Ved Mehta. She welcomes the maximalist approach of America's new immigrants who have shed all past lives and languages to assume newer, American identities. In "Immigrant Writing: Give Us Your Maximalists" she explains her authorial stance of an immigrant rather than a diasporic, expatriate writer. Her refusal to relate to the exile sensibility is on account of excessive pain and sense of loss endured therein. This does not mean that she avoids the pain that is very much present in the lives of her fictional characters. She refuses to see her own position as an immigrant in terms of loss. Her affirmation of her self-defined identity precludes the experience of pain. Her characters thus learn to grow out from their painful experiences.

Mukherjee's own denial of an exilic position of expatriation demands that her labeling as a writer of exile or postcolonial writer be truncated and that her fiction be seen as representation of American ideals and beliefs. She believes herself to be an ex-colonial who, in the ethnic and gender-fractured world of contemporary American fiction, is able to enter several lives fictionally. Like a chameleon, she discovers her material from her adapted surroundings and is thus able to Americanize herself instead of getting framed by predefined, ideologically charged notions of a minority identity.

Mukherjee writes about the immigrant group that she feels had not been written about in American fiction. Her stories and novels are full of characters that confront their various identities in different geopolitical spaces. Although her earlier writings, such as *Days and Nights in Calcutta* (1977), record her experiences of being a colonial who writes in a borrowed language (English) in an alien country (Canada), her later writings, especially the ones written after her migration to America are celebrated efforts to forge a new identity for herself as well as other immigrants in her fiction.

Her fiction can be seen as representative of showing the evolution of an immigrant from a diasporic, expatriate sensibility. The three stages identifiable in her fiction are those of expatriation, transition, and immigration. In her earlier works she writes as a diasporic writer trying to find her identity in Indian heritage, as in *The Tiger's Daughter* (1971) and *Wife* (1975). Her frustration at the racial intolerance and discrimination faced in her years in Canada is evident in *Darkness* (1985) and *The Sorrow and the Terror* (1987); and finally she claims a status of the American immigrant in works such as *The Middleman and Other Stories* (1988), ***Jasmine*** (1989), *The Holder of the World* (1993), and *Leave It to Me* (1997). Her recent novel, *Desirable Daughters* (2003), seems to accentuate all of these issues in a very subtle manner. Apart from fiction, Mukherjee has also coauthored two books of nonfiction with her husband, Clark Blaise: *Days and Nights in Calcutta* and *The Sorrow and the Terror*.

Mukherjee drew national attention when she won the prestigious National Book Critics Circle Award for best fiction for her collection titled *The Middleman and Other Stories* in 1988. Truly multicultural, the various stories depict the transformation of America in the light of migration and cross-cultural journeys. Beginning with "The Middleman" and ending with her widely anthologized story "The Management of Grief," the collection reveals the intricacies, complexities, as well as dilemmas faced by the new immigrants in America. Coming from diverse backgrounds and different countries such as Italy, Vietnam, Philippines, Afghanistan, and Trinidad, these immigrants reflect dauntless courage in attaining the American experience and identity and learn to survive challenges brought therein. The title story deals with Alfie Judah, an Iraqi-born immigrant who inadvertently becomes a middleman in illegal arms deals to rebel guerrilla groups in South America. Alfie, like other characters in Mukherjee's fiction, learns to survive in multicultural America that is also imperialistic and violent. Another story "Fathering" deals with clash of identities in the life of an American Vietnam veteran named Jason who has to choose between his peaceful life with wife Sharon or to be a father to his Vietnamese daughter Eng who is suffering from the war. "The Management of Grief" deals with the story of a Hindu woman, Shaila Bhave, whose husband and two sons are killed in a plane explosion. She learns to manage her grief in a cross-cultural manner and rebuild her life anew.

A critical survey of some of her novels likewise reveals a trajectory from pessimism to affirmative optimism that is followed by most of her characters. In *The Tiger's Daughter*, the protagonist Tara, an English-educated expatriate visits India and is unable to connect because of being treated as an outcast in Bengali society because of her marriage to an American. The narrator reflects on the decline of Calcutta amidst communist uprisings. Tara feels alienated from her friends and people around her. Her violent rape by an evil politician is symptomatic of the violation and exploitation of innocent peasants in the name of progress. In the end the old world is abandoned when Tara leaves India to be back with her loving husband in America.

Jasmine deals with a story of a young, naïve Indian widow whose illegal entry to America reveals the hidden dangers faced by immigrant women and how she must shed her past and old selves and learn to transform herself to be able to survive in America. She is through the course of the novel Jyoti Vijh, Jasmine, Jane Ripplemeyer, and Jase. She has lived in Punjab, India, New York, Iowa, and in the end leaves for California. She makes her own destiny and seems to succeed in the end. However, this process of making one's destiny is not an easy one. Her initial plan to come to America and commit the ritual of *sati* after her husband's death by terrorist bombing is abandoned when she is raped on the first night of her arrival in America. Her suicidal plan is replaced with her killing of the rapist instead as Jasmine learns to survive in America. Revealing indomitable courage, she is able to choose her own destiny eventually instead of one of loneliness and widowhood as predicted by an Indian astrologer in the beginning of novel. Her relationships with Taylor, an American professor, and Bud, an Iowan banker, reveal different notions about the American experience. Her choice to leave Bud, who is paralyzed, and go with Taylor in the end signifies the pursuit of American dream that seems to promise fruitful choices to her than in life with Bud as a caregiver.

Leave It to Me is another novel that deals with the theme of transforming identities. The narrator Devi is like Jasmine, a woman with multiple identities. She is first introduced as Debby DiMartino, the adopted daughter of Italian American parents living in Schenectady, New York. She learns from her adopted mother about her birth in India and that her mother was an American hippie of the 1970s. Debbie's anxiety about her birth parents progresses the novel ahead and reveals a darker, more violent America. She learns that her father was a Eurasian sex-guru and a serial killer. In search for her biological mother, Debbie changes her name to Devi and like an avenging Goddess incurs violent acts during this pursuit. Her different relations with men end with violent acts as arson and even murder. Through the portrayal of starkly sensational violence, Mukherjee impels the readers to understand how violence, as also was the case in *Jasmine*, becomes instrumental in transforming one's self.

Desirable Daughters deals with the intriguing tale of Tara Bhattacharjee and her two sisters amidst prejudices, ambitions, familial ties, and shocking secrets.

The narrator, Tara, is divorced from her billionaire husband and is raising her teenaged son and living with a Buddhist boyfriend. Comparable to **Amy Tan**'s famous novel *The Joy Luck Club* that also highlights different lives across different generations, *Desirable Daughters* portrays skillfully through the stories of three sisters, Tara, Padma, and Parvati, a complicated portrayal of lives in between cultures in India and America. The novel's beginning depicts Tara's namesake ancestor, who is five years old in 1879 and is married to a tree in a ritual as her husband dies from a snake bite on the wedding night. The narrative moves to Tara's visit with her son to the same forest where her ancestor became a "Tree-Bride." The sudden appearance of a young man who claims kinship to Tara's family unravels the family secrets as Tara is forced to confront her sisters and learn the family's shady past. Chris Dey claims to be the illegitimate son of Padma Mehta and Ron Dey. Amidst secrets, deceptions, and a near-fatal bombing, the novel is a tale of going back to one's roots, past, and history and getting connected with it. Tara learns to accept her past and legacy from which she was separated and reconsiders the choices that she had made in her life in America. *The Tree Bride*, published in 2004, is a sequel to *Desirable Daughters*. It marks a distinct new direction in Mukherjee's oeuvre. Mukherjee, who in Jasmine exuberantly celebrated Americanization, now privileges a transnational identity—one that melds Indianness with being an American. It is a story of Tara, an Indian American, who forges a new understanding of herself by reconnecting with her familial and national history. Mukherjee's most recent novel, *Miss New India* (2011) extends the new trajectory of her work: it is set entirely in contemporary India. It celebrates the new India that has emerged in the last 20 years or so as a result of a booming economy and exciting new possibilities. The portrait of India that emerges in this novel is a vastly different place than the one that the protagonist in *The Tiger's Daughter* (1971) returned to. With the publication of *Miss New India*, Mukherjee's work has come a full circle: from uneasy expatriation to exuberant immigration to a celebration of return "home" to India, a burgeoning new India with immense potential and possibilities.

The critical reception to Mukherjee's works has been mixed. Although it has drawn enthusiastic response from Western critics for her celebration of American identity, her rejection of a hyphenated identity and dismal portrayals of India have drawn harsh criticism from some of the Indian critics. Regardless, Mukherjee's contribution to the American literary scene is significant in its changing perceptions about ethnicity in general. (*See also* South Asian American Literature)

Further Reading

Alam, Fakrul. *Bharati Mukherjee*. New York: Twayne Publishers, 1996.

Nelson, Emmanuel, ed. *Critical Perspectives*. New York: Garland, 1993.

Reddy, Vanita. "Beauty and the Limits of National Belonging in Bharati Mukherjee's Jasmine." *Contemporary Literature* 54.2 (2013): 33–68.

Parvinder Mehta

MULTICULTURALISM

Multiculturalism is the assertion of the value of cultural diversity within Western societies and of the international significance of non-Western cultures. It is a reaction against **Eurocentrism**, **whiteness**, and patriarchy, especially as those perspectives have served as sources of and have provided measures of cultural value. It is an outgrowth of interrelated cultural phenomena: the postcolonial reconstruction of precolonial cultural traditions; the increasing mobility of populations and the resulting pluralism in most if not all societies; the political, social, and economic activism and the cultural self-assertion of minority populations; and the progressive movements promoting the rights of women and of gays and lesbians. As a movement, multiculturalism profited from the great attention given to ethnic heritage and the formalization of ethnic studies programs in the 1960s and the 1970s.

Interestingly, the term *multiculturalism* was coined in the early 1960s in Canada, which to outsiders might seem to be one of the most racially homogenous nations in the world and therefore an unlikely setting for the initiation of a discussion of how diverse cultures interact. When the Canadian federal government began using the term *bicultural* to describe the nation, it intended to appease the French-Canadian activists in Quebec and to diffuse the separatist movement in that province. However, it created another controversy because spokespersons for Canada's Native Americans and significant Asian minority were soon protesting their apparent exclusion from the national dialogue. Gradually, the Canadian government began to use *multicultural* instead of bicultural, except when addressing issues directly related to French Canada. Yet, as the term *multiculturalism* has become more widely used internationally, its definition has become more elastic, and the Canadian government has begun to substitute the phrase *cultural mosaic*.

Stephanie Lherisson, a junior draped in the flag of Haiti, prepares to enter the gym during a performance at the Circus for Diversity 2002 at the Avon High School and Middle School in Massachusetts. (John Tlumacki/The Boston Globe via Getty Images)

In the 1980s, multiculturalism became the catchword for the shift in emphasis within elementary, secondary, and university curricula from the ideas and works of dead white males to those of people of color and other previously marginalized voices. The pedagogical aim was both to broaden the perspectives of those raised on assumptions of cultural privilege and to legitimize the self-expression of those whose cultures had previously been regarded as either inconsequential or inferior. In effect, the promotion of open cultural exchanges among students from diverse cultural backgrounds would also equalize the opportunities for educational achievement for all students, regardless of their cultural heritage. And education is seen as the key to political, economic, and social empowerment.

Proponents of multiculturalism have treated concepts such as **race**, **ethnicity**, and sex as problematic because they presuppose straightforward categories and because they inherently promote preferences and reinforce prejudices. But cultural phenomena such as multiethnic and multiracial ancestries and transgenderism have made the traditional categories seem arbitrary and moot. Thus, proponents of multiculturalism have offered as alternatives the more flexible and adaptable concepts of cultural identity and gender identification.

The United States has long been described as a melting pot, and that cultural conception has been a very important element—if not *the* central mythic element—of the national **identity**. The multicultural concepts of cultural diversity and cultural pluralism would seem compatible with the traditional concept of the melting pot. Critics of multiculturalism—and, in particular, opponents of the emphasis on multiculturalism within education—have argued, however, that the American **assimilation** of cultural variation has not previously meant the celebration of *continuing* cultural differences.

Instead, opponents of multiculturalism have argued that assimilation has traditionally signified the process by which cultural minorities have become largely indistinguishable from the majority and have been absorbed into or subsumed within the mainstream culture. Through this process, even distinctive cultural markers have typically been reduced to rather superficial affirmations of one's cultural heritage—holiday traditions, fashion preferences, and culinary options. Cultural heritage has not remained the primary way to define an assimilated individual's personal or communal identity. Indeed, even those superficial cultural indicators have been mainstreamed in ways analogous to restaurant franchising. Most Americans, regardless of ancestry or geographic location, have fairly ready access to restaurants that offer Italian, Mexican, or Chinese cuisine. Moreover, there is no longer any assumption that the majority of the diners at, say, an Italian restaurant will be Italian Americans or that even the owners of an Italian restaurant will necessarily be Italian Americans. In fact, to extend this line of discussion even a bit farther, much of the menu at an Italian restaurant in an American city is likely to be more American than Italian and would be unavailable at a restaurant in Rome or in another Italian city.

Critics of multiculturalism have complained that its proponents have placed a greater emphasis on continuing cultural difference than on assimilation. These critics have warned of the dangers of cultural balkanization, of the loss of a sense of national identity to the acceptance of increasingly diverse and seemingly competing cultural identities. They have warned against the erosion of the fundamental values on which the national identity and prosperity have seemingly been fashioned.

They have complained most vehemently about the general unwillingness of the proponents of multiculturalism to acknowledge the deficiencies of cultures other than the traditional Western culture. And they have frequently expressed dismay at the paradox that within the supposedly "open exchanges" promised by multiculturalists, pejorative labels such as racist, fascist, and chauvinist have frequently been applied to critics of multiculturalism in order to divert their energies, if not to silence them completely.

Proponents of multiculturalism have countered that Eurocentric, white, and patriarchal values may have largely defined American culture but they have never done so exclusively. Proponents have made the case that Western history, and especially American history, has always been defined by the tension between assimilation and pluralism. In fact, this tension has been a largely positive source of much of the energy fueling the most dynamic political, economic, social, and cultural transformations of Western societies. Furthermore, proponents of multiculturalism have argued that the emphasis on cultural hegemony, rather than on cultural pluralism, has permitted the rationalization of many of the worst injustices within Western societies. Within the United States, these injustices have included the dispossession of Native Americans, the enslavement of African Americans, and the exploitation of unskilled immigrant labor. Clearly, the conflicts over multiculturalism have been as much about the historical interpretation of the past as they have been about shaping the futures of Western societies.

Nonetheless, demographic trends suggest that within the next half-century what are now minority cultures in the United States may replace or reconstitute what has been the nation's majority or mainstream Anglo-American culture. In his article "America's Increasing Diversity" published in the March/April 2004 issue of *Futurist*, Nat Irvin II presents a broad range of statistics that point to the inevitability of this dramatic transition. By 2025 the non-Hispanic white population of the United States will decrease to 60 percent of the total population, and by 2050 it will constitute just under 50 percent of the total. And there is an international corollary to this decline. In 1997, Caucasians accounted for about 17 percent of the world's population, but by 2010 they will constitute only 9 percent of the total. It is not so much the case that white populations are declining but, instead, that nonwhite populations are increasing at a much greater rate. As Irvin points out, between 2000 and 2050, nonwhites will account for more than 90 percent of the growth in the U.S. population. More specifically, according to the latest census data for the 20 fastest-growing U.S. cities, over the last decade the African American population has increased at almost five times the rate for non-Hispanic whites, and the Asian American and Hispanic populations have increased at about fourteen times the rate for whites.

One might think that these trends would make arguments over multiculturalism moot, but, in fact, they have seemingly caused the arguments to intensify not just within the United States, but in the United Kingdom, Australia, Germany, France, and most nations with large immigrant populations. The critics of multiculturalism have generally adopted one of two basic political strategies: either to mandate broad assertions of the continuing efficacy of the traditionally predominant culture or to legislate against specific practices of other cultures. The first strategy would include such actions as the identification of English as the official language in states such as Florida, Texas, and California, where the acknowledgement of **bilingualism** on official forms and street signs has become a salient issue. The second strategy would include the recent ban in France on female students' wearing traditional Muslim head coverings to class.

The proponents of multiculturalism have advanced their cause in a variety of ways. In some instances, the tactics have seemed somewhat trite. For instance, in 1993 the National Education Association designated the third Monday of October as National Multicultural Diversity Day. The designation is something of a redundant tongue twister, which only reinforces the sense of skeptics that it is something being forced onto and perhaps foisted onto American mainstream culture. On the other hand, in 1976 proponents of multiculturalism from academia and publishing created the Before Columbus Foundation, which has provided substantial support for projects that have substantively promoted multiculturalism in the arts and education. To provide just one significant illustration of this work, in 1992, the Before Columbus Foundation sponsored W. W. Norton's publication of a pair of anthologies of multicultural fiction and poetry.

Recent anthologies with a multicultural emphasis have included Robert Pack and Jay Parini's *American Identities: Contemporary Multicultural Voices* (1996), **Rita Dove**'s *Multicultural Voices* (1995), Laurie King's *Hear My Voice: A Multicultural Anthology of Literature from the United States* (1993), Alan C. Purves's *Tapestry: A Multicultural Anthology* (1993), and Elizabeth P. Quintero and Mary K. Rummel's *American Voices: Webs of Diversity* (1997). Anthologies restricted to one literary genre have included James R. Payne's *Multicultural Autobiography: American Lives* (1992), Anne Mazer's *America Street: A Multicultural Anthology of Stories* (1993), Ishmael Reed's *From Totems to Hip Hop: A Multi-Cultural Anthology of Poetry Across the Americas, 1900–2002* (2002), and Maria Mazziotti Gillan and Jennifer Gillan's *Unsettling America: An Anthology of Contemporary Multicultural Poetry* (1994).

In addition, some multicultural anthologies have had a somewhat more specialized focus. Margaret L. Anderson and Patricia Hill Collins's *Race, Class, and Gender: An Anthology* (2003) has a more pointedly political, economic, and feminist slant. In Mary Frosch's *Coming of Age in America: A Multicultural Anthology* (1995) and in Maria Mazziotti Gillan's *Growing Up Ethnic in America: Contemporary Fiction about Learning to Be American* (1999), the immigrant's adaptation to America culture is juxtaposed with the adolescent's gradual adjustment to maturation. David Landis Barnhill's *At Home on the Earth: Becoming Native to Our Place: A Multicultural Anthology* (1999) concentrates on responses to the natural world and environmental issues. Multicultural anthologies with a special emphasis on gender have included Estelle Disch's *Reconstructing Gender: A Multicultural Anthology* (2002), Amy Kesselman, Lily D. McNair, and Nancy Schniedewind's *Women: Images and Realities, A Multicultural Anthology* (2002), Amy Sonnie's *Revolutionary Voices: A Multicultural Queer Youth Anthology* (2000), and Franklin Abbott's *Boyhood, Growing Up Male: A Multicultural Anthology*

(1998). Several notable anthologies of multicultural literature have had a more international focus—for instance, Victor J. Ramraj's *Concert of Voices: An Anthology of World Writing in English* (1994) and John McRae's *Now Read On: A Multicultural Anthology of Literature in English* (1999).

Some terms commonly associated with multiculturalism actually predate it, whereas others have developed in its wake. In the late 1940s, Fernando Ortiz coined the term *transculturation* to designate the dramatic increase in exchanges between cultures and the gradual blending of cultures due in large part to rapid advancements in technologies related to communications and transportation. More recently, *interculturalism* has become the standard term for the promotion of tolerance and the vilification of racism and ethnic prejudice within a particular society. It designates the institutional development of programs that promote the recognition of and the acceptance of cultural diversity. The phrase *identity politics* refers to the attempt to exploit cultural identification or issues related to multiculturalism for political gain. Although initially a descriptive label, the phrase has subsequently acquired generally pejorative connotations.

Further Reading

Amoia, Alba, and Bettina L. Knapp. *Multicultural Writers since 1945: An A-to-Z Guide.* Westport, CT: Greenwood Press, 2004.

Auerbach, Susan, ed. *Encyclopedia of Multiculturalism.* New York: Marshall Cavendish, 1994.

Crowder, George. *Theories of Multiculturalism.* Cambridge, England: Polity, 2013.

King, Laurie. *Hear My Voice: Bibliography: An Annotated Guide to Multicultural Literature from the United States.* Menlo Park, CA: Addison-Wesley, 1994.

Kutzer, M. Daphne, ed. *Writers of Multicultural Fiction for Young Adults: A Bio-Critical Sourcebook.* Westport, CT: Greenwood Press, 1996.

Lee, A. Robert. *Multicultural American Literature: Comparative Black, Native, Latino/a and Asian American Fictions.* Jackson: University Press of Mississippi, 2003.

Long, Robert Emmet. *Multiculturalism.* New York: H. W. Wilson, 1997.

Miller, Suzanne M., and Barbara McCaskill, eds. *Multicultural Literature and Literacies: Making Space for Difference.* Albany: State University of New York Press, 1993.

Miller-Lachmann, Lyn. *Global Voices, Global Visions: A Core Collection of Multicultural Books.* New Providence, NJ: R. R. Bowker, 1995.

Singer, Judith Y., and Sally A. Smith. "The Potential of Multicultural Literature: Changing Understanding of Self and Others." *Multicultural Perspectives* 5.2 (2003): 17–23.

Susser, Ida, and Thomas C. Patterson, eds. *Cultural Diversity in the United States: A Critical Reader.* Oxford, UK: Blackwell, 2000.

Martin Kich

NATIVE AMERICAN AUTOBIOGRAPHY

Defining and discussing the Native American autobiography can be a worthy but complicated task. In Anglo-American culture, the very definition of "autobiography," the story of a person's life written by herself or himself, would seem to eliminate many Native American autobiographies. Examination of the rich history of the Native American autobiography requires an expanded definition of "autobiography" as well as a basic understanding of the Native American culture.

Arnold Krupat, a foremost scholar on Native American literature, explains issues that complicate the study of Native American autobiographies in his works *For Those Who Come After* (1985) and *Native American Autobiography: An Anthology* (1994). First, although Native Americans were telling their stories thousands of years before any ethnographers arrived to do it for them, the stories were related orally. He writes, "Tribal people were oral people who represented personal experience performatively and dramatically to an audience" (Krupat, *Native American Autobiography* 3). For the Native American autobiography to exist in written form, someone else had to write it down in many instances. This leads to issues with authorship and accuracy. Is it an autobiography if it was not written by the person whom the story is about? Many Native American autobiographies were written down by ethnographers, so most scholars agree that an expanded definition of autobiography is necessary to the study of Native American autobiography. But Krupat has created two categories of Native American autobiographies to address this issue: "autobiographies by Indians" (written by the subjects themselves) and "Indian autobiographies" (written down by someone other than the subject).

Second, the principles that guide mainstream ideas about themes that should be present in an autobiography, such as emphasis on the individual's achievements, cannot usually be applied to Native American autobiography because the individual is "always subordinated to communal and collective requirements" (Krupat, *For Those Who Come After* 29). But Krupat and other scholars have, in recent years, worked to provide audiences with a greater understanding of Native American autobiography by examining its history and providing much-needed critical scholarship.

Probably the first Native American autobiography was written by the Reverend Samson Occom in 1768. Occom was a Mohegan who became a well-known Christian minister. His work is reflective of a period of time between the arrival of the white settlers and the Indian removal in 1830. His words reflect the common sentiment of the white settlers of this period when he writes, "I was Born a Heathen and Brought up In Heathenism" (Krupat 106). During this time, Native Americans throughout the country were being converted to Christianity, and some who were converted were taught to write in English. Although there is little evidence of autobiographical writings of the southwestern Native Americans who were also Christianized during this time, there were several northeastern Native Americans who left behind autobiographical records.

The autobiographies of the 19th century would be quite different. The 19th century was the age of Indian war and Indian removal. Native Americans were considered obstacles to western expansion and were treated as such. Native Americans were removed to reservations, and those who resisted were often massacred. Though the U.S. government was ultimately successful in removing Native Americans to reservations, many Native Americans successfully resisted for periods of time. Many non-Indians wanted to help some of the most famous Native American resistors tell their stories. So the Native American autobiographies of this period were mostly collaborations between Native American storytellers and Euro-American recorders.

Perhaps one of the most famous of these collaborations is the collaboration between Black Hawk and Antoine Le Clair. Black Hawk was a traditional war chief of the Sac and Fox tribes who faced a period of imprisonment after resisting removal from his tribal lands. He was defeated in the Black Hawk War in 1832 and was imprisoned in several places before ultimately being allowed to return present-day Illinois. At this time, he expressed interest in narrating the story of his life to Le Clair who was a government interpreter for the Sac and Fox. Le Clair then recruited John B. Patterson to write the autobiography from Le Clair's notes. *The Life of Black Hawk* (1833) was quite popular and went through several editions. In 1882, Patterson revised the work, now titled *The Autobiography of Ma-Ka-tai-me-she-kia-kiak*, but because Black Hawk died in 1838, he had no say in this revision. Although this work is critical in the study of Native American autobiography and scholars are quick to point out that, without Le Clair and Patterson, Black Hawk's story would have been lost, there are clearly issues with accuracy in such a situation. And, unfortunately, no notes or transcripts exist from Le Clair's original interviews with Black Hawk.

Another famous Indian resistor was Geronimo. In 1886, a year before the Dawes Act, Geronimo and his band of about 30 Apache warriors were forced to surrender to an army of 2,500. He, along with the other Apaches from the southwest, was sent to Florida. Like other tribes who were sent far from their homelands, the Apache became very sick, and many died. Later, Geronimo and other survivors were shipped to Fort Sill, Oklahoma. Geronimo would never see his homeland again.

While in Oklahoma, Geronimo met Stephen Melvil Barrett, a superintendent of the schools in Lawton, Oklahoma. Barrett persuaded Geronimo to tell his life story, but officers at Fort Sill objected. Barrett later got the project underway after he wrote to President Theodore Roosevelt, but Barrett was forced to write footnotes disclaiming any government responsibility whenever Geronimo made negative remarks about the army or any government official. Geronimo narrated his story in Apache, which was then translated to Barrett by a third party, Asa Daklugie, a son of an Apache chief. Again, there are no manuscripts of this collaboration. It is important to note that, although Geronimo seems to speak quite impersonally as he relates his story in terms of his entire culture, this is his way of relating the story of himself. *Geronimo's Story of His Life* was published by Barrett in 1906. Geronimo died considering himself a prisoner of war.

Perhaps the most famous Native American autobiography also comes from this period. *Black Elk Speaks* (1932) is a result of the collaboration between Black Elk and John Neihardt. Black Elk was a Sioux medicine man and was present at the infamous Custer fight of 1876 and later joined Buffalo Bill's Wild West Show. *Black Elk Speaks* includes details about Black Elk's great visions, his memories of the Custer fight, and his years with Buffalo Bill, but interestingly he makes no mention of the years he spent as a Catholic catechist.

After the Wounded Knee Massacre of 1890 where over 150 Native American men, women, and children were killed, there was little resistance from any Native American survivors. "The prevailing social Darwinism of the period suggested that the Indian must either step up to the next rung of the evolutionary ladder and become 'civilized' or, quite simply, go the way of the dinosaur and die" (Krupat 237). Now, in order to survive, it was thought that the Native Americans not only needed instruction in Christianity, but they also needed instruction in capitalism. Because the reservations were for the tribes (the group) as opposed to individuals, the U.S. government decided that it was now necessary to destroy the reservations. This was the purpose of the 1887 Dawes Act. It was also during this time that Indian schools began, most of which were abusive. Run by the Bureau of Indian Affairs or various churches, most of the Indian schools (though not all) were notoriously difficult for Native Americans. Native American children were forbidden to speak in their native languages and were beaten if they did so. But there were schools whose teachers at least attempted to provide a positive experience to their students, such as the Santee Indian School; the teachers at this school taught in Lakota as well as English. One positive to come out of this very difficult time is that the Native American autobiographies during this period were written by the subjects themselves. These autobiographies paint a complicated and realistic picture of the lives of many Native Americans. Autobiographies from this period include Gertrude Bonnin's (Zitkala-Ša's) autobiographical essay series published in the *Atlantic Monthly* in 1900. A Dakota Sioux, Bonnin experienced great success with her writing, overcoming both racial and gender oppression to be successful in a white man's world.

It is also at the beginning of the 20th century that professional anthropologists began to interview "ordinary" Native American men and women who were representative of their culture. Influenced by Franz Boas, father of modern anthropology, these anthropologists spent several decades recording life histories of Native Americans. A result of this movement away from recording the lives of famous chiefs and warriors is that more women's autobiographies were recorded. Although there are numerous published examples of the collaborations between anthropologists and Native Americans, "Narrative of an Arapaho Woman" provides strong evidence of the anthropologists' quest during this time to write the stories of "average"

Native Americans. In "Narrative of an Arapaho Woman," the anonymous subject relates the story of her life and, interestingly, makes no mention of whites, even though she would have certainly had encounters with them. "Narrative of an Arapaho Woman" was first published in *American Anthropologist* in 1933 by Truman Michelson.

In 1968, the U.S. Congress passed the Indian Civil Rights Act. Also, during this year, **Navarre Scott Momaday**'s novel *House Made of Dawn* was published, winning the Pulitzer the following year in 1969. These events mark the beginning of what many scholars refer to as the "Native American Renaissance." Momaday's autobiographical **The Way to Rainy Mountain** (1969) is similar to other modern Native American autobiographies in that the text relates his personal story in relation to his quest to understand his ancestors' culture. Momaday, a Kiowa, uses a sparse, lyrical style, clearly influenced by Native American orality, to tell the stories of himself and his family.

Leslie Marmon Silko, another modern Native American author, published her multiform autobiography, *Storyteller*, in 1977. According to Hertha Dawn Wong, Silko, like "other contemporary Native American writers . . . emphasizes how one's land and community, processed by memory and imagination and shaped into language, create one's personal identity" (187). Like Momaday, Silko is also known for her lyrical method of bringing the Native American oral tradition through in her writing.

Scholars agree that the Native American autobiography is an untapped resource for literary critique. The rich, complicated, and sometimes tragic history of the Native American peoples has provided the opportunity for important autobiographies to emerge. And as authors of Native American descent continue to merge cultural traditions, the Native American autobiography will continue to develop down an interesting path into the 21st century.

Further Reading

Krupat, Arnold. *For Those Who Come After: A Study of Native American Autobiography*. Berkeley: University of California Press, 1985.

Krupat, Arnold. *Native American Autobiography: An Anthology*. Madison: University of Wisconsin Press, 1994.

Lee, Robert. *The Native American Renaissance*. Norman: University of Oklahoma Press, 2013.

Wong, Hertha Dawn. *Sending My Heart Back Across the Years: Tradition and Innovation in Native American Autobiography*. New York: Oxford University Press, 1992.

Crystal McCage

NATIVE AMERICAN DRAMA

Oral performance is, of course, a standard feature of Native American oral tradition, but the earliest drama written by Native Americans can be traced to the Cherokee writer Lynn Riggs and his play, *The Cherokee Night* (1936). The full flowering of this genre by Native writers, both Canadian and American, waits until the larger movement called the "Native American Renaissance" of the late 20th century. This movement, starting roughly with **Navarre Scott Momaday**'s Pulitzer Prize–winning novel, *House Made of Dawn* (1969), saw the emergence of many Native American writers in all genres. Although the number of Native playwrights is relatively small, these playwrights have nevertheless emerged as a potent force in Native literature.

Native American drama is a pan-tribal genre, with playwrights coming from many different tribal traditions and from different areas of North America. Thus, the style of Native drama ranges from Native traditionalism to historical pageant, from realism to existentialist drama in the mode of Bertolt Brecht. Thematically, Native drama addresses themes such as tribal loyalty versus individual identity, the effects of cultural stereotyping and cultural encroachment, and the ways in which older traditions can give strength to Native people.

Native American drama, unfortunately, has frequently been treated by critics and scholars less as drama than as ethnography. This is perhaps unsurprising because much Native American drama often consciously uses elements of ritual and per-formance specific to the author's tribal heritage. This view of drama as ethnogra-phy may also arise because of the relative richness of dramatic forms in Native religious rituals. For instance, the Navajo Chantways are intricately "staged" ritual dramas. Because of this, critics may sometimes emphasize the "primitive" nature of Native drama, even to the point of considering contemporary Native American playwrights as shamans or as primitive artists, even as backwater relics, rather than as self-conscious artists who are working in a contemporary medium.

In fact, Native American drama is the product of such a self-conscious, contem-porary movement, albeit one with certain religious, social, even political overtones. In that sense, it is not quite drama that exists for its own sake, as entertainment, but instead is a body of work by diverse playwrights informed by an insistence that its audience take seriously Native North American realities.

Rollie Lynn Riggs (Cherokee) was born in the Oklahoma Territory and knew firsthand the reality of Native North American experience. As a playwright, Riggs's only noteworthy success was *Green Grow the Lilacs* (1930), a non-Native play that was changed by Rodgers and Hammerstein into the popular musical *Oklahoma!* Riggs's *The Cherokee Night* failed to make Broadway, instead being produced first in Rose Valley, Pennsylvania, near Philadelphia, and later at the University of Iowa, directed by Riggs himself. Riggs's themes in *The Cherokee Night* radiate from the slow realization that Cherokees' weakness comes not from being Cherokee but from being insufficiently Cherokee. Their tribal degeneration stems not from their tribal heritage but from forgetting their heritage.

The next significant moment in the history of Native American drama was the creation of a training program for Native American playwrights at the Institute of American Indian Arts in Santa Fe. Begun by Roland Meinholtz, the program recruited young people from all over the United States and enrolled them in a course of study intended to instruct them in dramatic technique and theatrical presentation. Though this program lasted only a few years, it nevertheless created a vanguard group of artists who had been encouraged not just to learn all they could about the theater but who had also written, acted in, directed, and produced experimental theater with Native American actors and tribal themes.

The first professional company to achieve national recognition from this vanguard was the American Indian Theater Ensemble (AITE), a group formed in 1972 as an adjunct of La Mama Experimental Theater Club. As a company-in-residence as La Mama, the AITE group produced experimental plays, one acts, and enactments of tribal myths. Among their productions was *Body Indian*, by Hanay Geiogamah. Geiogamah also has had a number of other plays produced, among them *49* and *Foghorn*. The group also had a European tour.

By 1974 the group had changed its name to the Native American Theater Ensemble (NATE) and had moved to Oklahoma City. Their purpose in doing this was twofold. They wished to take their work into the heart of Indian country, to perform it for the people for whom it was intended. They also wished to draw from the strength of community.

AITE/NATE spawned a number of other theater groups: the Navajo-Land Outdoor Theater (1973), Spiderwoman Theater (1975), and Red Earth Performing Arts Company (1974). In addition, the Institute of American Indian Arts continued to be a launching pad for experimental artists. Spiderwoman Theater, in particular, has been a productive force for three decades, its best-known productions including *Winnetou's Snake Oil Show from Wigwam City* and *Power Pipes*.

As these groups provided support and, in some cases, facilities and feedback for Native playwrights, a number of playwrights rose to prominence in the genre. Among these playwrights are Bruce King (*Evening at the Warbonnet*), Annette Arkeketa (*Ghost Dance* and *Hokti*, among others), and William S. Yellow Robe (*The Independence of Eddie Rose* and *Starquilter*, among others).

In Canada, other groups arose. The most prominent of these groups was Native Earth Performing Arts (NEPA). Native Earth was based in the Native Canadian Centre in order to remain in the Native social context. The first works were collective creations, written and performed by the actors. The first show, *Double Take/A Second Look*, was created in collaboration with Spiderwoman Theatre, an outgrowth of Native American Theater Ensemble, and with Tukak Theatret, a Danish theater comprised primarily of Greenland Inuit, with musical direction by Tomson Highway. It consisted of a set of short scenes examining stereotypes about Native people around the world.

In 1986, Native Earth secured government funding and hired its first full-time staff, including Tomson Highway as artistic director. Also in 1986, NEPA presented its first scripted work, Highway's *The Rez Sisters*. It was a breakaway hit, attracting large audiences across Canada and at the Edinburgh Theatre Festival. Prominent Native Canadian playwrights first produced at Native Earth include Drew Hayden Taylor (*Only Drunks and Children Tell the Truth* and *Toronto at Dreamer's Rock*, among others), Daniel David Moses (*Coyote City*, among others), Billy Merasty, Marie Humber Clements (*now look what you made me do* and *Urban Tattoo*, among others), and Monique Mojica (*Princess Pochahontas and the Blue Spots*).

Further Reading

Brask, Per, and William Morgan, eds. *Aboriginal Voices: Amerindian, Inuit, and Sami Theater.* Baltimore: The Johns Hopkins University Press, 1992.

Darby, Jaye T., and Stephanie Fitzgerald, eds. *Keepers of the Morning Star: An Anthology of Native Women's Theater.* Los Angeles: UCLA American Indian Studies Center, 2003.

Geiogamah, Hanay, and Jaye T. Darby, eds. *American Indian Theater in Performance: A Reader.* Los Angeles: UCLA American Indian Studies Center, 2000.

Geiogamah, Hanay, and Jaye T. Darby, eds. *Stories of Our Way: An Anthology of American Indian Plays.* Los Angeles: UCLA American Indian Studies Center, 1999.

Lee, Robert. *The Native American Renaissance.* Norman: University of Oklahoma Press, 2013.

T. J. Arant

NATIVE AMERICAN NOVEL

The novel form is not indigenous to Native American art or culture; thus, Indian contributions to this genre did not appear until the mid-19th century. As complex containers of often contradictory cultural, ethnic, and national experiences, Native American novels offer rich perspectives on what it means to live Indian in America and to write about that experience in an essentially non-Native form and language.

Although the novel as a genre has evolved over the centuries, in general it describes an extended fictional narrative composed of linked episodes. The Native American novel arose late, virtually disappeared for several decades, and reemerged more abundantly in contemporary times. In general, Indian novels have reflected both their artistic and cultural trends within Indian and American communities during the ebbs and flows of their production. Thus, the Native American novel over time represents a fusion of intercultural traditions and offers commentary on Indians' connections to and distance from mainstream Euro-American society and art. Although earlier novels tended to mimic their white counterparts, later publications show Natives adapting and revising mainstream models to contain their own cultural concerns and traditions. Today, the Native American novel is considered an integral part of the multicultural American literary **canon**, with distinctive indigenous features that set it apart as "Indian."

Early Novels (Nineteenth to Early Twentieth Century)

The first known Native American novel exemplifies both imitation and fusion. Published in 1854, John Rollin Ridge's *Life and Adventures of Joaquin Murieta, the Celebrated California Bandit* is a conflation of European form and Indian content. Ridge's story is a fictional biography of a Mexican American outlaw named Joaquin Murieta, who soon became a lasting cult hero in the American West. The reader's sympathy is evoked for Murieta, also part Indian, as he seeks revenge on the whites who tortured him, his family, and his betrothed, and robbed him of his land. The story clearly evokes Native dispossession, as Ridge himself was a Cherokee Indian, but deals with this matter only indirectly; the book is otherwise wholly Western and has been compared usefully to Byronic and European romances. As a work of American literature, *Murieta* seems to have paved the way for subsequent dime novels and Westerns that became popular in the latter half of the century. Ridge's contribution to national letters, though largely unacknowledged, is an important example of the way Indian writers adopted not just the generic forms but also the subject matter of the dominant culture. Serious meditations on Indian mistreatment and dispossession are sacrificed here in the service of an entertaining, colorful, popular tale.

Ridge's work responds to the concerns of his historical moment, which was still occupied with westward exploration and Indian removal. As expansion continued into the latter part of the century, and along with it, Native restriction to reservations, literary activity among individual tribes was limited. Many Indians remained illiterate, and the publications that did appear tended to be memoirs of the experience of migration, **assimilation** into white culture, or of children being shipped off to white boarding schools. Indians incensed by their unfair treatment at the hands of the federal government began composing treatises, scathing recollections, or defiant collections of tribal history. Sarah Winnemucca Hopkins (Pauite), Charles Eastman (Sioux), and Gertrude Bonnin (Sioux) all gained recognition for their important autobiographies and compilations of folktales around the turn of the century. Although autobiography was by far the most popular mode of Native writing during this period, several Native American poets such as Alexander Posey (Creek) were publishing their works as well. Only one other novel was written by an American Indian in the 19th century: Sophia Alice Callahan's *Wynema* (1891). Callahan's work more self-consciously narrates the gap between Indian and white experience, with its mixed-blood female protagonist and a range of literary and cultural allusions both indigenous and European.

Several decades separated the novels by Ridge and Callahan; another lengthy span of years was to pass before novel writing picked up with fervor. During these transitional periods, Indians were becoming more and more engaged with narrating the terms of their own histories, their tribal memories, and their own identities within the dominant culture. In keeping with increased feelings of Native alienation, loss, and displacement, the novels of the 20th century are more overtly concerned with issues of **race**, culture, land, and memory. The novel form reappeared in Native American letters in the 1920s with *Co-ge-we-a, the Half-Blood* (1927), which represents the first novel written by an Indian woman, an Okanogan named Mourning Dove. Much of the story signals a throwback to the dime-store Westerns of the previous century; so, too, does the 1928 novel *Long Lance: The Autobiography of a Blackfoot Indian Chief* by a Blackfeet Indian named Sylvester Long, which is in fact a fictional adventure story. Long's novel is, however, rich in ethnographical detail that would have been edifying to American readers. Mourning Dove's work, too, represents progress beyond the formulaic, as her concerns are particularly modern: a half-blooded Indian woman struggles to embrace the heritage embodied by both her grandmother and a similarly mixed-blood love interest, whom she ultimately rejects. It seems no coincidence that such Native novels made their return during the decade in which American Indians were finally granted the right to vote with the Indian Citizenship Act of 1924. The long era of political memoir writing, inspired in some way by this surge for recognition as individuals with sovereignty, could now give way to Indians' full participation in the artistic climate of the rest of the country.

This does not mean that these writers were satisfied with citizenship and assimilation, though; on the contrary, Native American struggles for tribal sovereignty, separate from that of the United States, would intensify over the course of the 20th century, and such battles continue today in the political and legislative arenas. The Native American novel thus reflects a population in profound conflict with itself, its own roots, its relationship to American life and culture, and to the Western world at large. It is no coincidence that a substantial number of Native American authors are of mixed blood; this division and ambivalence forms the central theme of much of their literature. This conflict is apparent in the thematic preoccupations during the 1920s and 1930s, as represented in novels of the period by John Milton Oskison, D'Arcy McNickle, and John Joseph Mathews. Mathews's protagonist in *Sundown* (1934) is mixed not only in blood but in his affiliation, as he is unable to find refuge in either his Osage family and tradition or white culture, where he receives education and military training. McNickle, an extensively educated Flathead/Salish Indian, features a part-Spanish Indian whose attempt to reconcile his antagonistic heritages spurs a string of violent episodes. Oskison was the most well known of these writers, and he was also the least Indian: only one-eighth Cherokee. His novels, which include *Wild Harvest* (1925) and *Brothers Three* (1935), reflect Natives' growing ambivalence about associating with the white world, even by individuals with more white blood than Indian.

The "mixed-breed" character will continue to haunt the novels written later in the century. Unfortunately, Native American literature experienced another hiatus in the 1940s and 1950s while the nation's tribes were undergoing traumatic reorganization and termination measures imposed by the Hoover administration in 1949. Attempts to assimilate Indians more comprehensively into American life met with resistance and resentment; consequently, the next generation of writers, resurfacing in the 1960s, struggled even more with issues of hybridity, nationality, and place. Fortunately, their redoubled challenges are answered by an increasing number of Native writers seeking voice and empowerment in literary activism.

Contemporary Novels (1969–Present)

Despite the broad range of prolific Indian authors publishing during the first half of the century, the Native American novel did not receive widespread attention and acclaim until much later. The **Civil Rights Movement** of the 1960s encouraged Indian activism and struggles for sovereignty that continue into the present day, and it created a climate that particularly helped draw interest to marginalized groups generally. White readers and critics, still the major population, became more receptive to such struggles and worked to integrate more diverse voices in the literary canon. The two first and most influential contemporary Indian novelists were **Navarre Scott Momaday** and **Leslie Marmon Silko**. The Kiowa Momaday appeared on the literary scene first with his Pulitzer Prize–winning *House Made of Dawn* (1969). Silko's *Ceremony* (1977) was published eight years later, making her famous as the first contemporary female Indian novelist (some call her *the* first, though this is historically inaccurate). Both Momaday's and Silko's revolutionary novels feature a young male protagonist returning home after war, traumatized by battle but equally distressed about reintegrating into their communities. Thus, their stories become parables for the fractured, violent nature of everyday American Indian existence, the ruptures of assimilation and dislocation, and for Tayo, Silko's protagonist, the negotiation of mixed-race **identity**. Both novels invoke storytelling and tradition as means for healing, on both the individual and communal levels, but neither story ends entirely optimistically. Silko reaches for more universal, good-versus-evil themes that implicate all races and cultures; her art is also integrative, blending both traditional and Western elements into a whole and weave together story, poetry, pictures, and ceremony.

The challenging, unconventional styles of these two works also influenced a great number of writers who came after. Both Momaday and Silko chose complex narrative modes and chronologies, mixing not only genres but temporalities and realities. These qualities are considered uniquely "Indian" in their embracing of nonlinear historical and temporal elements and in their prioritizing of myth as a seamless component of reality; but they are also, in some ways, features typical of modern and postmodern writing generally, which tends to be disjunctive, complex, and experimental. Indeed, Indian authors often use these postmodern qualities to their advantage, reshaping them with Native American features. Ojibwa author **Gerald Vizenor**, for instance, reimagines the "crossblood" individual as a site of multiple cultural and historical experiences, a combination that is distinctly playful and liberating. His characters, embodying urban landscapes but charged with the importance of the past and tradition, have been described as trickster figures much like those indigenous to both Native and African American cultures. Vizenor's huge body of work includes well-known novels such as *The Trickster of Liberty* (1988) and *Heirs of Columbus* (1991).

Although many contemporary Native novelists engage in postmodern textual play, others remain focused on the past, the land, and the families that have lived and struggled there, meditating on their increased importance to contemporary cultural survival. **Louise Erdrich**, for example, a member of the Turtle Mountain Band of Ojibwa, has won unprecedented critical and popular acclaim for her interrelated novels tracing several generations of tribal families, beginning with *Love Medicine* (1984) and followed by *Beet Queen* (1986), *Tracks* (1988), and *The Bingo Palace* (1994). Critics have routinely praised Erdrich for her success in intimately creating a world populated by the peoples, places, and Native experiences she knows so well and, subsequently, bringing them to widespread attention in the American mainstream. Linda Hogan, a mixed-blood Chickasaw from Oklahoma, has extended her own purview still further, writing about several different tribes and their diverse communities and experiences and, in fact, creating fictional tribes as well. The cross-cultural message is similar, though, as Hogan writes extensively about the unifying plight of losing land, tradition, memory, and, along with it, a sense of affiliation and self. Her critical gaze turns on the greed of whites who rape the land and its people for resources and profit, particularly oil, as in her 1990 novel *Mean Spirit*. Her latest novel, *Power* (1998), describes a fictional tribe of Florida Indians and their negotiations between the American judicial system and the ancient laws of tribal governance and ecological balance.

Indeed, although many Native American authors decry the loss and contamination of their way of life to inimical American attitudes and institutions, many still struggle with their own very real connections to the white world. The mixed-blood figure thus remains a significant presence in novels by contemporary writers, as do the themes of assimilation, fragmentation, loss, and despair. Although his later works are less optimistic, James Welch's *Winter in the Blood* (1974) exemplifies the importance of attaining peace and integration, as a Blackfoot Indian in Montana reaches back across memories and generations to come to terms with his own present dislocation and alcoholism. **Sherman Joseph Alexie**'s debut novel, *Reservation Blues* (1995), gestures across racial borders and brings the African American **blues** artist Robert Johnson onto the Spokane Indian reservation in a fictional merging of Native and black American musical forms and cultural experiences. LeAnn Howe's 2001 novel, *Shell Shaker*, fuses multiple temporalities that skillfully interweave the present moment with historical texture and myth, essentially creating a revisionist version of actual events—in this case, the murder of a Choctaw chief by his own people. Louis Owens, another Choctaw, also engages in rewriting history, mixing genres, the real and the surreal, the past and the present, in order to sketch a more accurate picture of complex contemporary Indianism. Perhaps his best-known novel to date, *Bone Game* (1994), is haunted simultaneously by a 19th-century murder and a string of contemporary serial killings; the book's half-Indian narrator, a displaced English professor, must figuratively return to his people and his tradition in order to realize ultimately that the murders are connected. So many Native novels reiterate this nonlinear temporality, reminding readers that the tragedies and triumphs of the past must be recalled and addressed consistently and overtly in order to make sense of—and ultimately to make peace with—the present.

Critical Approaches to the Native American Novel

It is undeniable that American Indian novels, like the Indians themselves, have pervaded and influenced American literature and culture on a number of levels. In its significant departure from the oral tradition that characterized the Indian narrative for countless generations, the novel form itself—not to mention the mainstream English language it adopts—represents a crucial compromise. In many ways, however, Indian authors have made the form their own, tampering with and enriching European tradition in turn. That is, the Native American novel is perceived to have distinctive qualities that derive from these oral and communal traditions: the fluid blending of storytelling and myth into the texture of real life, the focus on multiple generations of individuals within specific tribes, and the nonlinear narrative forms hospitable to such themes.

Along with the increased production of Native American literature came increased efforts on the part of critics to understand and appreciate it. Previously, oral traditions and poetry had been examined mainly on the basis of what they could teach anthropologists and ethnologists about the curious ways of these indigenous peoples. The possibility that these works could represent serious and lasting pieces of literature simply did not occur to most reviewers until the 20th century. Even then, the cultural allure of "primitivism" tended to contaminate even well-meaning attempts to gain knowledge and appreciation of Indian texts, much like the curious whites who flooded Harlem nightclubs in the 1930s seeking an authentic, "primitive" experience. In the 1920s, a critic named Mary Austin became a champion for indigenous American literature, lamenting the fact that mainstream students were likely to learn far more about European history and authors than about the Native inhabitants and artists of their own country. Austin was successful in bringing more sustained critical attention to Indian literatures, but her focus was largely on poetry.

Critical turns to the American Indian novel did not happen seriously until the auspicious coincidence of the Civil Rights Movement and the 1969 publication of Momaday's *House Made of Dawn*. Since then, annual sessions of the Modern Language Association and other major literary conferences and journals have been devoted to the exploration of Native American literature. Moreover, full-length dissertations and books have been written on the subject. Many of these investigations seek to understand the complex relationship between orally transmitted cultures and the bounded, Euro-American literary text. Marxist approaches have been used to analyze the Indian's vexed relationship to the material culture of the United States, which it is both dependent upon and detached from. Freudian models have been invoked to describe the alienation, fragmentation, and general psychological trauma incurred by a people so thoroughly oppressed and disrupted. Others, such as Arnold Krupat, have argued that such Western modes of criticism may be largely inappropriate for examining indigenous texts. One thing is certain: With the current popularity of airing multiethnic experiences and literatures, such discussions and debates about the Native American novel are sure to continue, deepen, and enrich the current **canon**—much as the novels themselves have done. (*See also* Native American Autobiography)

Further Reading

Alexie, Sherman. *Reservation Blues*. New York: Warner Books, 1996.

Allen, Paula Gunn, ed. *Studies in American Indian Literature: Critical Essays and Course Designs*. New York: Modern Language Association, 1983.

Krupat, Arnold. *The Voice in the Margin: Native American Literature and Canon*. Berkeley: University of California Press, 1989.

Larson, Charles R. *American Indian Fiction*. Albuquerque, University of New Mexico Press, 1978.

Lee, Robert. *The Native American Renaissance*. Norman: University of Oklahoma Press, 2013.

Oaks, Priscilla. "The First Generation of Native American Novelists." *MELUS* 5 (1978): 57–65.

Owens, Louis. *Other Destinies: Understanding the American Indian Novel.* Norman: University of Oklahoma Press, 1994.

Wight, Andrew, ed. *Critical Essays on Native American Literature.* Boston: G. K. Hall, 1985.

Melanie R. Benson

NATIVE AMERICAN ORAL TEXTS

It would seem incongruous that nonliterate societies could produce literature. Yet although most Native American tribes had no written languages other than those that were the products of transliteration by ethnologists (notwithstanding the Maya of Mesoamerica, who employed hieroglyphics long before contact with Europeans; many other tribes, including the Kiowa and the Lenape, who used pictographs; and the Cherokee, who after 1819 employed a syllabary invented by mixed-blood Cherokee Sequoyah to write in their language) they all possessed vast bodies of oral literatures, commonly referred to as "folklore," repetitively spinning myths, epics, orations, and ritual dramas into the cultural fabric of their tribes. Unfortunately, serious study of Native American oral literature has too often been precluded by poor translations and the ethnocentrism of scholars who have historically evaluated these works based on the structural and aesthetic criteria established by Euro-American masterworks, as well as their own cultural biases.

Mythology, although undoubtedly an important component of Native American oral literature, is perhaps the least understood and most contentious. Historically, to the ethnologist in whom the tenets of cultural Darwinism were inculcated,

James Willard Schultz. (Underwood & Underwood/Corbis)

a myth was little more than superstition, a tale unraveled by a storyteller to an audience in a technologically or scientifically barren culture to explain natural phenomena. Thousands of these myths were recorded by ethnologists in scores of monographs, related to them by tribal members, with the altruistic desire of the dominant culture to preserve them before the Native culture vanished (that is before it assimilated). This mentality has unfortunately perpetuated the notion that the only true Native cultures are those that are pre-contact, not recognizing that cultures are fluid and adaptable and that change does not negate political or literary viability. Myths therefore were dismissed as quaint artifacts relegated to the past, belonging to a dead people.

To Native peoples, however, a myth is a culturally owned truth, and its retelling and reenactment are vital to the continuation of not only the tribe, but also of the cosmology, and "is ongoing and relevant, not the [remnant] of a vanishing culture" (Womack 27). Contact does not eradicate the myth but rather informs and transforms it. The conflict between ethnographer and Native American is revealed in Vine Deloria Jr.'s *God Is Red*, in which Deloria challenges scientific notions of the arrival of Native Americans via a land bridge across the Bering Strait. Deloria counters the accepted scientific theory with traditional creation stories, such as the Navajo's emergence from an unpleasant underworld or the Creek's emergence from a fissure in the earth. Deloria's point is that these stories should be given credence by non-Native scientists, alleging that the stories are supported by suppressed archaeological evidence that threatens the mainstream theory. Deloria posits that non-Natives cannot consider Native American creation myths as truth because to do so elevates Native peoples to the status of original owners of the land, not as recent newcomers from Asia who can be displaced by other immigrants; blatant disregard for creation myths of Native peoples more importantly disputes their status as sovereign nations by denying that the oral literature comes from living, flourishing cultures and consigning it to ethnography.

Myths might elucidate not only the long distant past and the Creation but also the not-so-distant past in the tribe's history, as does an oral historical epic narrative, not unlike Homer's *Iliad* or the Anglo-Saxon *Beowulf*, epic poems that originated as oral literature. One version of the Muskogean migration legend, for example, tells of the tribe's journey across the Mississippi River to the southeastern United States, led by two brothers, Chahta and Chikasha. A magical red and white striped pole, planted upright at the end of each day, determined the following morning their journey by pointing the direction of that day's route. Upon reaching the southeast, the brothers quarreled and separated, with one brother founding the Choctaw tribe and the other the Chickasaw.

Undoubtedly, the most controversial of the oral historical epic narratives is the Wallamolum, an alleged account of the Lenape people from the time of Creation to the 17th century, which also has the distinction of being recorded in pictograph form. Documented in the Wallamolum is the Lenape's migration across the ice-covered Bering Strait, their subsequent journey along the Rocky Mountains, and their settlement of eastern North America. The Wallamolum details the Lenape's battles with the Tallegwi tribe (recognized by some scholars as the Cherokee) and the Tallegwi's defeat at the hands of the Lenape and the Iroquois. University of Transylvania (in Lexington, Kentucky) professor Constantine Rafinesque received the Wallamolum in 1820 from an enigmatic Dr. Ward, and the pictograph account was preserved with red ink on long-since-vanished sticks, accompanied by verses in the Lenape language describing the drawings. Three translations of the Wallamolum are extant. In the latter part of the last century the authenticity of the Wallamolum came under fire, and some scholars believe that Rafinesque perpetrated a hoax, writing the verses first in English, then translating them into Lenape. Also, Rafinesque may have been skeptical of the recent alleged discovery and translation of golden plates by Joseph Smith and the subsequent formation of the Church of Jesus Christ of Latter Day Saints; Rafinesque may have therefore created the Wallamolum in an attempt to dispel the commonly propounded assertion (one supported by Smith in the Book of Mormon) that the Native Americans were descendants of the Lost Tribes of Israel or to suggest the ease of duping the 19th-century scientific community. If it is an authentic document, however, the Wallamolum is perhaps the most important artifact relating to North American Indian culture.

An almost universal symbol in much of the oral literature of Native America is the trickster, usually characterized by the anthropomorphized Raven, Mink, or Blue Jay in the Pacific Northwest, Rabbit in the southeast (known as Nanabozho in the Eastern Woodlands), or Coyote in California and the southwest. The trickster figure has come to epitomize Native storytelling for Anglo audiences. At once a cultural hero and a cultural threat, the trickster—often depicted as a highly sexed male—serves to reinforce the boundaries of appropriate behavior by demonstrating undeniably inappropriate (and humorous) behavior. The trickster figure is found not only in Native American storytelling but also in oral literatures worldwide. For example, Brer Rabbit stories, which evolved from African trickster hare stories, came to the southern United States with slavery and often share similarities with Cherokee and Creek trickster rabbit stories. These similarities perhaps suggest that the oral literatures of African slaves and Native Americans may have intersected in the American southeast.

Oratory is also a genre of Native American oral literature, and its prominence is indicative of the social status enjoyed by one who could effectively and eloquently communicate. An oration was often political, a means by which sovereignty was demonstrated diplomatically by challenging the rule of the dominant culture. No Indian-language versions of the most famous 18th- and 19th-century orations exist, and most orations first appeared in print years after their initial delivery and only in translation. For example, Rudolf Kaiser retraced the history of the well-known oration of Chief Seattle of the Suquamish and Duwamish Indians of Puget Sound, noting that the speech was made in 1853 and first published in a newspaper account in 1887. This 1887 version accepts the U.S. doctrine of Manifest Destiny and also details things that Seattle did not know about in 1853, such as the transcontinental railroad, while the version that gained prominence in the 1970s warns of "impeding white-caused ecological doom." The lack of a primary source in the original language often allows for editions that publicize current ideologies as well as perpetuate Pan-Indian or dominant-culture perceptions of Native

Americans, such as the noble savage stereotype. Contemporary orations, however, delivered and recorded in Indian languages, and subsequently translated, offer perhaps more truthful Native perspectives of white–Indian relations.

The oral literature of Native America remains the vital expression of thriving cultures. Native American oral literature has also found its way into Native American written literature, in the works of **Louise Erdrich**, **Navarre Scott Momaday**, **Leslie Marmon Silko**, **Sherman Joseph Alexie**, Hanay Geiogamah, Diane Glancy, and Maurice Kenny, among others. As Craig S. Womack writes regarding Creek oral literature, although applicable to all Native American oral literatures: "The oral tradition is a living literary tradition, the standard by which Creek stories, oral and written, are judged. Like any other literary tradition, it consists of a complex body of genres [and structural components], as well as a relationship to larger Creek ceremony, society, politics, and government, that need to be explored in terms of formulating and analyzing approaches to Creek literary texts" (Womack 66). (*See also* Native American Oral Texts; Native American Stereotypes)

Further Reading

Bierhorst, John. *Four Masterworks of American Indian Literature*. New York: Farrar, Straus & Giroux, 1974.

Bright, William. *A Coyote Reader*. Berkeley: University of California Press, 1992.

Deloria, Vine, Jr. *God Is Red: A Native View of Religion*. Golden, CO: Fulcrum Publishing, 1994.

Hymes, Dell. *"In Vain I Tried to Tell You": Essays in Native American Ethnopoetics*. Philadelphia: University of Pennsylvania Press, 1981.

Kroeber, Karl, ed. *Traditional American Indian Literatures: Texts and Interpretations*. Lincoln: University of Nebraska Press, 1981.

Krupat, Arnold. *The Voice in the Margin: Native American Literature and the Canon*. Berkeley: University of California Press, 1989.

Swann, Brian, ed. *Smoothing the Ground: Essays on Native American Oral Literature*. Berkeley: University of California Press, 1987.

Vizenor, Gerald, ed. *Narrative Chance: Postmodern Discourse on Native American Literatures*. Albuquerque: University of New Mexico Press, 1989.

Vizenor, Gerald, ed. *The Trickster of Liberty: Tribal Heirs to Wild Baronage*. Minneapolis: University of Minnesota Press, 1988.

Wiget, Andrew, ed. *Handbook of Native American Literature*. New York: Garland Publishing, Inc., 1996.

Womack, Craig S. *Red on Red: Native American Literary Separatism*. Minneapolis: University of Minnesota Press, 1999.

W. Douglas Powers

NATIVE AMERICAN POETRY

Although it has its roots and inspiration in the oral traditions of American Indian tribes, American Indian poetry, in the very strictest sense, is primarily a 20th-century phenomenon; prior to this time, the written and published works of

Native American authors generally consisted of autobiographical stories and journalistic accounts of tribal life. The American Indian writers who did publish poetry in the late 1800s were better known both then and now for their works in other genres. Cherokee John Rollin Ridge primarily wrote fiction and autobiography, but a volume of his poetry, *Poems* (1868), was published posthumously by his wife. Likewise, Mohawk Emily Pauline Johnson published two volumes of poetry, *The White Wampum* (1895) and *Canadian Born* (1903), but is remembered for her short stories. And Lynn Riggs (Cherokee) published *The Iron Dish* in 1930 but is best known for his play *Green Grow the Lilacs* from which the musical *Oklahoma!* was derived.

Although these poets helped to prepare the way for the mainstream publication of American Indian poets, the true Renaissance of writing by Native authors occurred in the middle 20th century, propelled by two major events. The first was the publication of **Navarre Scott Momaday**'s novel *House Made of Dawn* (1969), which was awarded the Pulitzer Prize. The second was the rise of the America Indian Movement (AIM) and a resurgence of political activism by young Native Americans, resulting in the occupation of Alcatraz, the Trail of Broken Treaties and the occupation of Wounded Knee, South Dakota. These events not only marked an increased interest on the part of non-Indians in listening to the voices and messages of American Indians but also a new determination by Indians to write in their own words about themes that are primarily Indian.

Though American Indian poets write in a form that is primarily Western (generally free and blank verse), they imbue that form with a sense of "Indianness" that makes it unique. What is particularly important for Indian poets is the connection between their writing and oral past of their people. Poets such as **Leslie Marmon Silko** (Laguna Pueblo) and **Simon J. Ortiz** (Acoma Pueblo) insist that their writing is but part of a cultural continuum that stretches back to the oral tales, ceremonies, and songs of their tribes. Ortiz speaks on this in his poem "Survival This Way," suggesting that "the way" of surviving for a Native person is to participate in the cultural traditions of one's tribe, traditions that are passed from one generation to the next. Likewise, Wendy Rose (Hopi/Miwok) suggests that poets participate in the preservation of tribal history by finding new words with which to express the old traditions, thereby grounding their work in those traditions.

A related theme explored by American Indian poets in their writing is **identity**, the struggle to define one's self as an American Indian set against the alienating effects of the modern world and its separateness from traditional lifestyles and beliefs. Many American Indian poets explore what it means to be a part of a people whose ancestry goes back thousands of years and how tribal traditions and events can have meaning in a mechanized society. Because of their focus on cultural traditions, American Indian poets also emphasize the importance of history, both tribal and national; for these writers, making connections between past and the present are key to this dilemma of living as an Indian in the modern world.

Joseph Bruchac, an Abenaki poet and critic, notes that in addition to the awareness of and respect for tribal culture, American Indian poetry generally embodies a deep respect for the earth and the natural world and an understanding of the power of written words. For most American Indian writers, English is different than it is for white Americans because it is either their second language or at least second in significance to the language spoken by their tribe. Because of this, for Native poets, language is never simply ornamental or aesthetic but always powerful and purposeful.

The topic of the importance of words and the necessity of finding the right voice with which to speak is addressed frequently in American Indian poetry, sometimes through the use of voice. Wendy Rose often writes in voices that are not her own, speaking instead for those whose story has not been told or if told, has been misrepresented; in the poem "Truganiny," for instance, Rose speaks with the voice of an aboriginal woman whose stuffed body was put on display as the "last" of her people. When Rose does speak in her own voice, she describes herself not as singing or telling stories but only as making noise, an indication of her own search for the right words to express her meaning.

Language and words are imbued with power and meaning in the poetry of N. Scott Momaday (Kiowa). Though best known for his Pulitzer Prize–winning novel, he also published several volumes of poetry, the most notable being *The Gourd Dancer* (1976). In many of his poems, Momaday uses language as the connecting thread between the traditional past and the present, focusing especially on naming as a source of power even in the modern world. In the title poem, "Gourd Dancer," Momaday emphasizes the significance of a man's name being called in the context of a Giveaway Ceremony. For Momaday, words have power and the ability to recall an image or moment to mind as vividly as if the writer—or the reader—were experiencing the moment first hand. His reverence for language is evident in the lyrical imagery of his poems, which also celebrate the natural world and its importance. Many of Momaday's poems deal directly with images of nature, as in "The Bear," a description of an ancient and scarred bear, or in "Trees and Evening Sky," a pure imagist poem that vividly depicts a sunset. Place is also of key importance to Native writers; in "To a Child Running with Outstretched Arms in Canyon de Chelley," Momaday depicts the child embracing the "spirit" of the natural landscape in this sacred place. For Momaday, his Kiowa past, the natural world, and specific places and histories are all tied together by his use of and reverence for language, because words have the power to make things real.

Language also has power and significance for Simon Ortiz (Acoma Pueblo), but its power goes beyond the single word. For Ortiz, language is tied to the process of speaking and listening; the true meaning of an utterance comes not just from the meaning of a single word but rather in the understanding of the message as a whole. Ortiz uses language to articulate what it means to be Acoma, a people with a 2,000-year-old sense of identity, in the modern world. Part of the answer involves understanding one's past and connecting it to the present. In his collection *From Sand Creek* (1981), Ortiz connects the massacre of Cheyenne and Arapaho referenced in the title to other recent events in American history and in so doing, situates his own Native experience in this country within the continuum of American history in general. For Ortiz, violence in this country's history is a direct consequence of whites having lost this connection to their traditional past. In addition,

Ortiz postulates a reverence for the natural world as a means of coping with the disconnect between traditional Indian life and the modern world; connecting one's self to nature is a means of connecting to a world that is broader in significance than merely the individual objects and inhabitants it contains. In "The Serenity in Stones," Ortiz expresses this clearly as he envisions a piece of turquoise as part of the sky and all that it represents. "A San Diego Poem" explores what happens when an American Indian loses that connection to the natural world: the narrator experiences isolation and fear while airborne because he has lost physical contact with the earth. Even upon landing, the narrator remains lost in the labyrinthine tunnels under the airport, which he describes as distinctly American, metaphorically buried in the concrete maze. Thus for Ortiz, physical and spiritual connection to the natural world is key to Indian identity in a world that contradicts or devalues the traditional way of life; the alternative is either violence or alienation and death.

In contrast to Ortiz, James Welch (Blackfeet-Gros Ventre) often expresses bitterness and anger over the events of recent history and their effects upon Native identity, which Welch sees as devastating. Skeptical of the possibility of retrieving traditions and history because of these dramatic changes, Welch's writing presents reservation life as a series of pointless attempts to defend a way of life that cannot be recovered. His poem "Harlem, Montana, Just Off the Reservation" is a bleak portrayal of life in a reservation border town, where Indians frequent the taverns and the whites are bigoted and ignorant. The setting of Welch's writing is often the bar rather than the natural world, and his characters, isolated by their poverty, are unable to connect with their spiritual past amid the bleak surroundings of the modern environment they inhabit. Even the natural world in Welch's writing is harsh and uncompromising, as can be seen in "Christmas Comes to Moccasin Flats," where the snow is not a cause for celebration but sends people huddling in their cabins and waiting for the next shipment of commodities to help them survive a hostile winter. For Welch, nature remains uncompromising and hostile, rather than a source of renewal and rebirth; there is little hope of repairing the broken connection between past and present.

One writer who does see the natural world as a means of renewal is Joseph Bruchac (Abenaki). For Bruchac, place is key; many of his poems' titles reference specific places, such as "Hawks Above the Hudson In March," an imagist style poem that centers on a lyrical description of hawks circling a frozen river. Bruchac writes with respect for the natural world; in "Bobcat, 1953," he emphasizes the connection between not only the narrator's past, as he remembers a story his grandfather told him, but also between the narrator and the animal, for he is one of the few able to sneak up on the wary bobcat. Bruchac's collection *This Earth Is a Drum* (1973) centers on the concept that planting and working a garden brings a person into close communication with the natural world. Bruchac also uses natural settings to make the connection between the modern-day and the larger cultural tradition of his people by retelling, in his poems, traditional tales of the Abenaki, inspired by a specific location. In "The Spreaders," Bruchac relates an Abenaki folktale about little men who accost unwary travelers in the heavily forested areas of upstate New York. Awareness of these connections, of how place maintains the connection between a traditional past and the chaotic present, is for Bruchac a way of maintaining Indianness and balance. In "Onondaga Lake," a sharp contrast is presented between the lake's pristine past as a watering hole for buffalo and its polluted and gray present. But still, Bruchac notes, the Indian people, despite their poverty and sorrow as represented by the polluted lake, are first to notice the changing of the seasons and the blooming of the flowers, because of their connection to traditional places, which Bruchac sees as key to maintaining an Indian identity.

Identity for Leslie Marmon Silko (Laguna Pueblo) can be found in the songs and stories of the American Indian's past. This is vividly explored in the poetry that intertwines within the pages of *Ceremony* (1977), poems that retell traditional stories of the Laguna and emphasize that the solution to the disconnect brought on by living in the modern world can be found by seeing one's self as part of a continuum of stories that reaches back to the time of creation. In "Toe'Ash: A Laguna Coyote Story," Silko makes this evident by updating the traditional coyote tales, applying the label of "coyote" to present-day politicians and businessmen who, although they attempt to be clever by promising the people food if they vote, end up being tricked themselves. This poem explicitly makes the connection between a traditional past and the modern present; Coyote's presence in the 20th century implies not only a continuum but also the relevance of the old tales, which, Silko suggests, infuse modern life with meaning and promise.

Ray A. Young Bear (Mesquakie) also writes of the importance of maintaining connections between the physical world of his spiritual past, where spirits and animals have as viable a role as humans do, and the contemporary landscape, where the voices of the spirits and the memories of past events are distorted by the hustle and bustle of everyday life. Like Welch, Young Bear speaks of how the lives of traditional storytellers and wise men have changed in the contemporary world, as they appeal to modern technology, such as headphones and radio newscasts, in an attempt to hear the voices of the old gods. This juxtaposition of the traditional and the modern gives Young Bear's poetry a surreal quality that is often seen in the works of America Indian writers.

A similar surreal quality is present in the writings of **Louise Erdrich** (Chippewa). But here, the source of the surreal is located inside the individual, rather than in the natural world. Erdrich explores issues of gender roles and women's needs in her poems, which feature characters such as a woman who makes a "to do" list of things required for her to appease a god who is representative of the disapproving father or husband. Most of the characters in Erdrich's poems are women who seek justification from the male figures in their lives. But Erdrich generally ends her poems by affirming the importance of family and by suggesting that the darker emotions of anger, rage, and hatred can find a more constructive outlet in the energy needed to raise a family. Thus, for Erdrich, families help maintain one's identity.

Paula Gunn Allen (Laguna) also speaks of a struggle for identity, writing as a woman poet in an urban setting, separated from the traditional homeland and her people's history. In "Recuerdo," Allen recalls a moment when, climbing a mountain with her family, she believed she heard the voices of the old gods, voices that, as an adult living away from the sacred lands of the Laguna Pueblo, she now struggles to hear amid the clock ticking and other mechanized sounds of the urban environment. However, Allen insists that urban Indians can maintain contact with their ancestral past, suggesting that doubt, rather than technology, is their true enemy.

Linda Hogan (Chickasaw) also speaks of this doubt as she addresses the problems of living a divided life as, like Allen, an urban Indian who works and lives away from a reservation setting. Hogan most often associates moments of hearing those ancestral voices with images of sunlight and the dawn, so that light becomes equated with truth and belief. But in her more overtly political poems, Hogan inverts this dichotomy, envisioning darkness as the only place where the truth can be told, because in the light, one has to be polite and civil. Ironically, the poet must enter into darkness, where the truth about repression of Native peoples can be told, in order to bring this truth into the light. For Hogan, using language and words to make these stories real is a way of doing just that.

For Joy Harjo (Creek), a search for a confident voice manifests itself in the form of multiple voices speaking within a single poem. Many of the speakers in Harjo's poetry are inarticulate or mute; for them, the language they have available is insufficient to express their message. Even the poet in Harjo's work is often overcome by her inability to express the truth in words of a language that is not her own; in "Anchorage," the speaker is powerfully reminded of the history of Native peoples in North America by her encounter with a silent Athabascan woman, but she cannot find the words to express what she knows. Harjo suggests that there is always the potential for the poet to speak these transformative and clarifying words, and she speculates about the possibility of discovering a new and precise language that would enable her to express her thoughts in a way that English cannot.

Humor can be a way of using language to express the truth, and for **Sherman Joseph Alexie** (Spokane) it becomes a vehicle both for making connections to the past and for coping with the poverty and living conditions on the reservation. Humor enables Alexie to critique both Indians and white people, as he does in "The Native American Broadcasting System," where he suggests that if only one white man remained alive, he would reinvent himself as a Cherokee and create a modern-day Trail of Tears. This poem also expresses the effects of modernization on the traditional way of life by juxtaposing images of technology with icons from the Spokane traditional past.

American Indian writers use poetry, a borrowed form, as a means of addressing the key questions faced by Native peoples in the modern world. Their poems, even in the 21st century, continue to contemplate Indian identity and the importance of traditions, of maintaining connections to the past. For Native peoples attempting to live a balanced life amid the technology of today, this is an important issue that cannot easily be resolved.

Further Reading
Allen, Paula Gunn. *Studies in American Indian Literature: Critical Essays and Course Designs.* New York: MLA, 1983.

Bruchac, Joseph. "Many Tongues: Native American Poetry Today." *North Dakota Quarterly* 55 (Fall 1987): 239–44.

Castro, Michael. *Interpreting the Indian: Twentieth Century Poets and the Native American.* Albuquerque: University of New Mexico Press, 1983.

Lee, Robert. *The Native American Renaissance.* Norman: University of Oklahoma Press, 2013.

Parini, Jay. "Native American Poetry." In *The Columbia History of American Poetry*, edited by Jay Parini, 728–49. New York: Columbia University Press, 1993.

Patti J. Kurtz

NATIVE AMERICAN STEREOTYPES

The arrow-wielding savage and the sexualized Indian princess have been immortalized by Hollywood films, advertising, and sports team mascots. Despite a few exceptions, depictions of Native Americans bear little resemblance to the reality of most Native Americans today. Old stereotypes continue to be perpetuated, yet at the same time Native American film directors and writers today are deconstructing these images. These invented images are not only inauthentic to specific tribes, but they also perpetuate the idea that all Indians are alike and that they are still living in the 19th century.

Hollywood Indians

Hollywood films have had a powerful impact on how most Americans view Native Americans: There have been thousands of films that portray Native Americans since the beginning of the motion picture industry. Yet, although individual Europeans are usually identified as Irish, Polish, or Swedish in films, the over 500 Indian tribes have, until recently, been lumped together. Films before the mid-20th century usually depicted Indians who were identified as one tribe, say Apache, but their rituals were from the Lakota Sioux and their clothes from the Navajo. If we were to come to conclusions about Indians based on *most* Hollywood films, we would think that there were no Indians before 1820 or after 1910. We would think that the "red man" was a Noble Savage, a Faithful Tonto, an exotic, virile barbarian, a Woodsy Christ figure, a druggy hippy, or pure evil, and that all Indian women were princesses and that Indians only speak in monosyllabic words ("How" or "Kemo Sabe").

It was not until the 1960s that Indians began to be portrayed as more fully human, with individual tribal cultures. In 1968, the American Indian Movement (AIM) was established and a series of incidents (the occupation of Alcatraz in 1968 and Wounded Knee Incident in 1973) led to more sympathetic films; however, most movies stayed with historical rather than contemporary settings, and white characters remained the main protagonists (e.g., *Little Big Man, Tell Them Willie Boy Is Here*, and *Thunderheart*). Richard Harris, the star of *A Man Called Horse* (1970), plays an Englishman who takes part in the Sun Dance ceremony and ironically shows the Sioux how to use a bow and arrow. *Dances With Wolves* (1990) was both praised for Kevin Costner's realistic touches (using the Lakota language with subtitles in English) and criticized for regressing to the vanishing Indian theme and the white-man-as-protagonist structure. In the film, the Sioux are treated as individuals; however, the Pawnee are purely evil Hollywood Indians. At the end, the white protagonists leave their Lakota friends to be slaughtered and oppressed by the U.S. government. Other films such as Disney's *Pocahontas* (1995) update the Indian princess stereotype and revise the historical events, much to the horror of many critics.

Yet the biggest impact of Hollywood's focus on mostly 19th-century Indians is the perpetuation of the myth that Indians are extinct, or that those both on reservations and off will soon be either assimilated or will self-destruct. Few Hollywood films have depicted the contemporary Native American. When the film *Pow Wow Highway* (1989), based on the book by David Seals, came out it was immediately a cult classic, especially with Native American viewers, because it was the story of contemporary Indians struggling with both cultural and political issues. Despite casting Indians in most of the roles, the lead role is played by Al Martinez, a non-Indian. But this is one of the first films to show Indians without feathers and loincloths, so despite its flaws it was a start to showing contemporary Indians in Hollywood film. The film also confronts the power of Hollywood movies and stereotypes about the spirituality of Indians when the main character mimics a jail break he watched on television and when an aunt makes fun of her nephew after he asks her to tell him the meaning of life—she just wants to be left alone to watch television.

Sherman Joseph Alexie's film *Smoke Signals* (1998), directed by Chris Eyre and based on Alexie's short story "This is what it means to say Phoenix, Arizona," also depicts young Indians on a reservation in a way that both alludes to and twists Hollywood stereotypes about Indians. Thomas is a storyteller, but his stories don't turn into new age, shamanistic trite sayings, and though Victor is a warrior, he is not a silent one. *Smoke Signals* is a road film, like *Pow Wow Highway*, but updated: it is the first feature film to have been written, directed, and coproduced by Native Americans, with Native Americans in all the lead roles. Alexie has said that the film's theme is loving someone despite his or her faults, a theme that transcends the focus on Indian characters.

Advertising and Sports Mascots

Stereotypes of Indians have been used to sell products so successfully that most consumers recognize the Indian maiden in 19th-century dress on packages of Land O' Lakes butter and the Indian chief on cans of Calumet baking power. And debate over the use of Indian figures as mascots or names of sports teams (the Braves, Indians, Chiefs, and Redskins, to name a few) continues today, with alumni of some universities threatening to stop giving funding if a team's name is changed for "political correctness."

Stereotypes in Literature

Hollywood, advertisers, and the sports world are not alone in creating and maintaining stereotypes about Native Americans. Written stories of Indian savagery were very popular in the 16th and 17th centuries. These "captivity" narratives were often adventure tales, filled with danger and violence. There is usually an exceptional "noble" Indian who establishes a connection with the captive, but for the most part, the Indians are portrayed as savages. In 1682, the best-selling book was *The Narrative of the Captivity of Mrs. Mary Rowlandson*, which pitted a Christian white woman against savage Indians. This theme continued in magazines, paintings, and dime novels well into the 20th century.

In 1826, James Fenimore Cooper's novel *The Last of the Mohicans* established future stereotypical extremes of the Indian: the noble savage and the bloodthirsty savage. Five film versions exist of this novel. Native character Chingachgook is portrayed as a regal character, but he is also one of the last of this breed, beginning the myth of the vanishing Indian. Natty Bumpo, the white frontiersman, is one of the first in a line of Hollywood white frontiersman who is a better Indian than the Indians.

The late 20th century gave rise to what is now called the Native American Literary Renaissance. These writers often explicitly address stereotypes. **Louise Erdrich** addresses the stereotypical Hollywood Indians embedded in American attitudes toward Indians in her 1984 poem "Dear John Wayne" from her collection *Jacklight* (1984). The poem confirms the power of Hollywood even 100 years later as it depicts contemporary Indians growing increasingly uncomfortable while watching a John Wayne movie at a drive-in as the audience cheers when Wayne arrives to avenge the deaths of the white settlers. Other writers who depict the ambiguities of being both American and Native American today include James Welch, Sherman Alexie, Elizabeth Woody, **Leslie Marmon Silko**, and Thomas King, among many others.

Conclusion

Although film and literature may continue to maintain the stereotypes—both sympathetic and hostile—of Native Americans, with the ongoing presence of writers such as Sherman Alexie, who is attempting to challenge stereotypes in both the literary and film worlds, perhaps the stereotypical images of the 19th-century Indian will pass and Americans can begin to learn about the 21st-century realities of the various Indian cultures that have been influenced by and have influenced American culture.

Further Reading

Hirschfelder, Arlene, et al. *American Indian Stereotypes in the World of Children*. 2nd ed. London: Scarecrow Press, 1999.

Kilpatrick, Jacquelyn. *Celluloid Indians: Native Americans and Film*. Lincoln: University of Nebraska Press, 1999.

Purdy, John. "Tricksters of the Trade: 'Reimagining' the Filmic Image of Native Americans." In *Native American Representations*, edited by Gretchen Bataille, 100–18. Lincoln: University of Nebraska Press, 2001.

Reid, T. V. "Old Cowboys, New Indians: Hollywood Frames the American Indian." *Wicazo Sa Review* (Summer 2001): 75–96.

Rollins, Peter C., and John E. O'Connor, eds. *Hollywood's Indian: The Portrayal of the Native American in Film*. Lexington: University Press of Kentucky, 1998.

Stacey Lee Donohue

NAYLOR, GLORIA (1950–)

Gloria Naylor is an African American novelist and anthologist. Alongside such figures as **Toni Morrison**, **Alice Walker**, and **Toni Cade Bambara**, she is a key voice in the rich outpouring of literature by African American women in the 1980s and 1990s. Her novels dramatize issues of community, connection, and **identity**, often through their focus on powerful but careworn women who tend to be the culture bearers for their communities. Orphans and those isolated from family, those seeking identity and community, also frequently people her fictions. Place plays an equally important role, as she tends to create very specific geographies that reflect her narrative structures. Connections interest her, as witnessed by her habit of placing at least one reference in each novel to a character or place or event from one of the others.

Naylor was born January 25, 1950, in New York City to parents who had just moved there from rural Mississippi, where they had been sharecroppers. She grew up in the Bronx and other areas of the city, including Harlem and Queens. A love of New York and of the foibles of its people and its neighborhoods is apparent in her fiction. Equally, however, Naylor displays an intuition for and understanding of the rural South, thanks to her parents' background and the family's frequent visits to family and friends there.

Naylor inherited a love of reading from her mother, who had worked extra hours in the fields in order to afford a library subscription. Naylor's mother also influenced her by joining the Jehovah's Witness during her daughter's adolescence. Upon high school graduation in 1968, Naylor was baptized in that faith, becoming in the process a minister. She began work as a switchboard operator in order to support her ministry. She continued as a missionary in New York, then in Dunn, North Carolina, and finally Jacksonville, Florida, through 1975.

At the age of 25, Naylor broke with the Jehovah's Witnesses and entered college, first pursuing a nursing degree from Medgar Evers College. Deciding her strongest interests dwelt elsewhere, she changed both school and major, receiving a bachelor's degree in English from Brooklyn College, City University of New York, in 1981. Naylor married in 1980 but divorced the next year.

Essential to her development as a writer was the experience in 1977 of reading Toni Morrison's *The Bluest Eye*. She has described discovering for the first time that books were being published about her experiences, her life, and her community. She has said *The Bluest Eye* gave her the authority to develop her own voice and to write the stories she knew. It also motivated her to pursue a master's degree from Yale in Afro-American studies, which she completed in 1983.

Naylor's first publication was a short story, "A Life in Beekman Place," published in *Essence* magazine in March 1980; its editor, Marcia Gillespie, strongly encouraged her to keep writing. It was also at this time in her life that Naylor began traveling outside the United States, visiting Spain and Tangiers in 1983.

Naylor's first novel, *The Women of Brewster Place* (1982), is told through seven interconnected stories, each featuring a different woman who has ended up living on a cul-de-sac that, once home to Irish immigrants, then Italian, is now populated primarily by African Americans. It has come to be a dead-end street, both literally and figuratively. The stories begin with that of Mattie Michael, who comes to Brewster Place as an older woman, having lost her house when she put it up as bond for her son, Basil, who fled rather than face a murder charge. As with each of the stories that follows, Mattie tells us about her years before Brewster Place: growing up with a doting but strict father, being beaten and thrown out by that father when she became pregnant, and taking up residence with Miss Eva, an older woman who eventually bequeaths her a house. Like Mattie's story, each woman's story seems close to an end once we see her arrive at Brewster Place, for the sense of a downward spiral that led them to this place and the poverty it holds mark it as a place of despair, not one of new beginnings.

Through the rest of the stories, Mattie remains as a figure who passes on the lessons she learned from Miss Eva, healing what she can of the pain around her—the fraught relationship of a young black nationalist to her disapproving mother, the rape of one member of a lesbian couple, and, in one of the most notable scenes, a young mother after the death of her child. Mattie thus takes her place as the older African American figure of wisdom who will reappear in Naylor's fictions, just as those figures do in much contemporary writing by African American women. Although there is no sense of an easy or happy ending for the women of Brewster Place, the novel does offer hope through community, as dawn breaks on the day of a block party. *The Women of Brewster Place* was awarded the American Book Award for best first novel in 1983. Oprah Winfrey spearheaded the transformation of the novel into a made-for-television film, broadcast in 1989, with Winfrey in the role of Mattie Michael.

Naylor's Yale master's thesis became her second novel, *Linden Hills* (1985). It also focuses on the dynamics within an African American community but does so in the context of a middle- and upper-class neighborhood. Modeled after Dante's *Inferno*, with a neighborhood arranged in concentric circles leading down to its center and the home of its founding family, and with its Virgil and Dante in the guise of two young men looking for handyman work for Christmas money, *Linden Hills* delivers a stinging critique of materialism and status seeking.

Mama Day, considered by many to be Naylor's most successful effort, appeared in 1988. A love story between George, a "stone city boy" from New York, and Cocoa (also known as Ophelia), from an island off the coast of the Georgia/South Carolina border, it is told in three narrative voices: George, Cocoa, and the communal voice of the island, Willow Springs. George is an orphan raised to believe in an extreme form of self-reliance while Cocoa has behind her generations of the Days, direct descendants of the slave woman, Sapphira Wade, who had wrested possession of Willow Springs from her master. Cocoa was raised by her grandmother and her great-aunt, Miranda "Mama" Day, one of the wise old culture-bearer women with deep knowledge of both the natural and the supernatural worlds. Miranda's given name is one of the many elements of *Mama Day* that put it in dialogue with Shakespeare's *The Tempest*, along with the island setting and the presence of conjurors. Naylor has stated that she found the structure to *Mama Day* while reading William Faulkner's *As I Lay Dying*.

Also in 1988 Naylor received a Guggenheim fellowship, followed by the Lillian Smith Award in 1989. In 1990, she founded One Way Productions, a film company to help bring *Mama Day* to the screen, although that has not yet been accomplished. One Way Productions has brought to the stage various works designed for children.

Naylor continued the magic realism and the multiple narrative voices she established in *Mama Day* with *Bailey's Cafe* (1992). Once again it is a novel comprising the stories of seven people, but this time the structuring principle is music, particularly **jazz** and **blues**. Orchestrated by "Maestro," the proprietor of Bailey's Café whose name we never know, each woman (and one man dressed in women's clothes) takes center stage to tell her or his story at this way station of a café, an in-between place that inhabits nowhere and everywhere. Their stories resonate collectively through a shared element of each person having been defined by her sexuality; in interviews, Naylor has described the novel as a disquisition on the label "whore," demonstrating the various ways the term is used, and that finally no such thing exists. Naylor has also written *Bailey's Café* as a play; it had a successful run at the Hartford Stage in Connecticut in April 1994.

For the next few years, Naylor devoted much of her effort to compiling an anthology of African American writing, published in 1995 as *Children of the Night: The Best Short Stories by Black Writers, 1967 to the Present*. She conceived it as a follow-up to **Langston Hughes**'s 1967 *The Best Short Stories by Black Writers: 1899–1967*. Given that the 37 stories "are recent; we are still within them," she chose to arrange them into topical categories, rather than chronologically, in order to avoid the sense of developmental progression. Her primary goal she describes as the selection of "the best to demonstrate, either thematically or structurally, mechanisms for surviving constant assaults against one's mind and spirit."

In 1998, Naylor returned to the setting of her first novel with *The Men of Brewster Place*, this time, as the title suggests, telling the story of the men who had such an impact on the lives of the women in her first novel (only one of the central characters did not appear in *The Women of Brewster Place*). The question each faces is, "What does it mean to be a man?"; each story shows an aspect of the complicated nature of that question in a society that has tried to deny maturity on the basis of skin color. The male gathering place is the barbershop, although it does not seem to hold out the same sense of power through community as the earlier work. Indeed, the final scene depicts just one man, "one tired warrior . . . one man standing is all that's needed." (*See also* African American Novel)

Further Reading

Awkward, Michael. *Inspiring Influences: Tradition, Revision, and Afro-American Women's Novels*. New York: Columbia University Press, 1991.

Christian, Barbara. "Gloria Naylor's Geography: Community, Class, and Patriarchy in *The Women of Brewster Place* and *Linden Hills*." In *Reading Black, Reading Feminist: A Critical Anthology*, edited by Henry Louis Gates Jr., 348–73. New York: Penguin, 1990.

Felton, Sharon, and Michelle C. Loris, eds. *The Critical Response to Gloria Naylor*. Westport, CT: Greenwood Press, 1997.

Fowler, Virginia C. *Gloria Naylor: In Search of Sanctuary*. New York: Twayne, 1996.

Gates, Henry Louis, Jr., and K. A. Appiah, eds. *Gloria Naylor: Critical Perspectives Past and Present*. New York: Amistad, 1993.

Harris, Trudier. *The Power of the Porch: The Storyteller's Craft in Zora Neale Hurston, Gloria Naylor, and Randall Kenan*. Athens: University of Georgia Press, 1996.

Kelley, Margot Anne, ed. *Gloria Naylor's Early Novels*. Gainesville: University of Florida Press, 1999.

Montgomery, Maxine Lavon. "Authority, Multivocality, and the New World Order in Gloria Naylor's *Bailey's Café*." *African American Review* 29 (Spring 1995): 27–33.

Montgomery, Maxine Lavon. *Conversations with Gloria Naylor*. Jackson: University Press of Mississippi, 2004.

Naylor, Gloria, and Toni Morrison. "A Conversation." *Southern Review* 21 (July 1985): 567–93.

Stave, Shirley A. *Gloria Naylor: Strategy and Technique, Magic and Myth*. Wilmington: University of Delaware Press, 2001.

Storhoff, Gary. " 'The Only Voice Is Your Own': Gloria Naylor's Revision of *The Tempest*." *African American Review* 29 (Spring 1995): 35–45.

Ward, Catherine C. "Gloria Naylor's *Linden Hills*: A Modern Inferno." *Contemporary Literature* 28 (1987): 67–81.

Whitt, Margaret Early. *Understanding Gloria Naylor*. Columbia: University of South Carolina Press, 1999.

Wilson, Charles E. *Gloria Naylor: A Critical Companion*. Westport, CT: Greenwood Press, 2001.

Kathryn West

NUYORICAN

A term used as a proper noun to describe persons of Hispanic (particularly but not exclusively Puerto Rican) descent living in New York City, especially on the Lower East Side. As an adjective it may apply equally to the particular Spanglish dialect spoken by New York City's Hispanic population or to anything created or manufactured by a Nuyorican.

The term is a fusion of the words "New York" and "Puerto Rican." Other Hispanic immigrant groups have come to accept the label as pertaining to them as well, although many reject any and all association with this term. Often seen as politically charged, there are many different perspectives on the word: some see the word as a source of pride in their cultural ancestry, while others see it as evidence that either the Hispanic population is spreading its influence too far or, conversely, that North American culture is eroding the essence of being Latino.

The largest movement of Puerto Ricans from the island to the mainland in the 20th century occurred after World War II. By that point,

Miguel Algarin at the Nuyorican Poets Cafe. (Christopher Felver/Corbis)

every Puerto Rican had officially been declared a U.S. citizen by the Jones Act of 1917, the Great Depression had passed, and industry was doing well in the U.S. mainland. The ease with which Puerto Ricans could travel into and out of the country coupled with the opportunity for wages higher than those offered in Puerto Rico brought many Puerto Ricans to New York. This Puerto Rican workforce could come to New York to earn more money than was possible on the island and could return to their homeland at any point. As many immigrant groups have done historically, the Puerto Ricans coming to New York settled here close to one another; in this case it was the Lower East Side of Manhattan, or "Loisaida," as many call it affectionately.

Linguistically, "Nuyorican Spanish" is a variant of other Spanglish dialects. "Spanglish" is any combination of the English and Spanish lexicons or grammars, although it is mostly associated with the interjection of English words into Spanish syntax, as in, "Voy a chequear el correo." The English verb "to check" is inserted into the Spanish and treated as a regular verb. Nuyorican Spanish includes Spanish of mostly Puerto Rican character but also demonstrates other Caribbean and Central American Spanish influences.

Nuyorican influence in the arts has been most prominent in spoken word poetry, although some Nuyorican influence may be noted in the plastic arts as well. Miguel Algarín, retired English professor at Rutgers University, founded the Nuyorican Poets' Café circa 1973 as a forum for young poets to be heard, especially those whose voices would not otherwise be heard. The Nuyorican Poets' Café has grown to be one of the most critically acclaimed and popular venues for young artists coming from traditionally underrepresented groups. The café hosts nationally famous poetry slams as well as concerts, theatrical performances, and is host to art exhibits and comedy performances as well. The Nuyorican Poets' Café is also involved in many community outreach programs. (*See also* Bilingualism)

Further Reading

Algarín, Miguel, and Bob Holman, eds. *Aloud: Voices from the Nuyorican Poets' Café*. New York: Henry Holt and Company, 1994.

Algarín, Miguel, and Miguel Piñero, eds. *Nuyorican Poetry: An Anthology of Puerto Rican Words and Feelings*. New York: Morrow, 1975.

Morales, Ed. *Living in Spanglish: The Search for Latino Identity in America*. New York: St. Martin's Press, 2002.

Santiago, Esmeralda. *When I Was Puerto Rican*. New York: Vintage, 1994.

Santiago, Roberto. *Boricua: Influential Puerto Rican Writings*. New York: Ballantine, 1995.

Stevens, Ilan. *Spanglish: The Making of a New American Language*. New York: Rayo, 2003.

Teck, Bill. *The Official Spanglish Dictionary*. New York: Fireside, 1998.

Alexander Waid

OBAMA, BARACK HUSSEIN (1961–)

Barack Hussein Obama is the 44th president of the United States, winner of the 2009 Nobel Peace Prize, and the author two best-selling autobiographies. Obama was born in Hawaii to a white mother from Kansas and a black father from Kenya. After his parents' brief marriage ended, his mother married an Indonesian and moved with her son to Indonesia when Obama was six years old. When that marriage too dissolved, his mother moved him back to Hawaii—Obama was 10 years old then—to live with his maternal grandparents. After graduating from high school in Hawaii, he attended Occidental College in Los Angeles for two years and then transferred to Columbia University in New York City from where he graduated. After working as a community organizer in Chicago for three years, he earned a degree in constitutional law from Harvard Law School, returned to Chicago where he practiced civil rights law and taught at the University of Chicago Law School. In 1997, he was elected to the Illinois state legislature, in 2004, he was elected to the U.S. Senate, and in 2008 he was elected to the highest office in the country. The first black president of the nation, Obama was reelected in 2012.

Obama is a gifted writer. At the age of 33 he began to write his first autobiography, *Dreams from My Father: A Story of Race and Inheritance*, which was published in 1995. It received respectable reviews but the sales were modest. However, it was republished in 2004 when Obama became a rising star in the Democratic Party and it became a best seller when he declared his candidacy for the presidency of the United States in 2006. A self-representational text, it offers a glimpse into Obama's personal and political formation; a lyrically penned autobiography, it testifies to his exceptional command of the English language, his piercing intellect, his profound capacity for self-reflection, and his emerging political outlook. The book is foundational to our understanding of the man who stunned the nation and the world by becoming the first African American to win the White House.

Dream from My Father is a *Bildungsroman*, a coming-of-age narrative that maps the moral and psychological development of its young protagonist. It is the story of Obama's maturation. Divided into three parts titled Origins, Chicago, and Kenya, the narrative covers three pivotal stages of Obama's early life. It begins on a dramatic note: a 21-year-old Obama, then a university student in New York City, receives a phone call informing him of his father's death in a car accident in Kenya. More than 400 pages later, it ends on Obama's emotional visit to his father's burial site in Kenya seven years later. As the book's title itself suggests, the father whom he barely knew, is a haunting presence in the narrative. The book, in psychological terms, is a chronicle of Obama's internal journey to find a lost father and thus understand and come to terms with his complex personal inheritance and his mixed racial identity. His birth in Hawaii, a place is that is geographically and culturally marginal to the continental United States, four formative years in Indonesia, and his discovery of the African side of his extended family provide an intriguing picture of the emergence of an international and cosmopolitan identity. Yet his years as a student and as community organizer in large urban centers of the United States, such as Los Angeles, New York City, and Chicago, reveal his increasing identification with black America and his growing awareness of himself as an African American. His marriage to Michelle Robinson, a Harvard-educated attorney from a working-class black family on the south side of Chicago, which he talks about in the book's epilogue, solidifies his personal connection to the black American experience and his integration in a black American community.

The narrative architecture of the book not only reveals Obama's mastery of the craft of autobiographical writing but also the art of fiction. While grounded in autobiographical facts, Obama in his prefatory statement admits that some of the characters in the book are composites of various individuals he knew; that he has deliberately altered the chronological sequence of events; and that the extensive dialogues in the book are fictional approximations. The result is a compelling story with a smooth narrative flow that offers a broad sweep of the narrator's early life. The lyricism and elegance of Obama's prose add to the book's readability.

While *Dreams from My Father* is a deeply personal story, *The Audacity of Hope: Thoughts on Reclaiming the American Dream*, Obama's second autobiographical book, is a much more explicitly political narrative. It is divided into nine chapters that are anchored by a prologue and an epilogue; the chapters are meditations on topics ranging from the U.S. Constitution to race relations and religion. It is more of a political manifesto than an intimate memoir. Obama's prose has occasional flashes of brilliance but on the whole his second book is considerably less compelling than his first.

Obama's third book *Of Thee I Sing: A Letter to My Daughters* was published in 2010. An illustrated children's book, it offers poignant tributes to 13 pioneering figures in American history. Included among the 13 individuals are Abraham Lincoln, Sitting Bull, Martin Luther King Jr., Helen Keller, and Cesar Chavez. The tributes are all the more evocative because Obama frames them in epistolary format and addresses them to his two young daughters.

An essay titled "A More Perfect Union," which Obama delivered as a televised speech to the nation on March 19, 2008, is one of the more widely read short pieces by the president. Prompted by a crisis in his campaign to win the Democratic nomination for the presidency of the United States, Obama decided to address publicly the issue of race relations. As a candidate who had attempted to present himself as a post-racial persona, he was now forced to confront the topic of race. In this essay he frames America as an evolving nation, a work in progress, an unfinished journey toward a more perfect union. He weaves his own life story and situates himself strategically in the narrative: he uses his biracial background and his multicultural upbringing to validate and authenticate his commentary on the subject of American race relations. He then proceeds to explain the roots of black anger as well as white anxiety and urges both blacks and whites to move to a higher level of mutual understanding and recognition of the common ground they share. A rhetorical masterpiece, the essay skillfully blends autobiography, history, and black pulpit oratory to deliver an intensely political yet deeply personal statement on race. He ends the essay with an anecdote that crystallizes the various thematic threads of the essay into a coherent whole.

Further Reading

Banita, Georgiana. "'Home Squared': Barack Obama's Transnational Self-Reliance." *Biography* 33.1 (2010): 24–45.

Carpio, Glenda R. "Race & Inheritance in Barack Obama's *Dreams from My Father*." *Daedalas* (2011): 79–89.

Jones, Laura. "Under the Bus: A Rhetorical Reading of Barack Obama's 'A More Perfect Union.'" *Postmodern Culture* 21.2 (2011): np.

Emmanuel S. Nelson

OKADA, JOHN (1923–1971)

John Okada was a Japanese American novelist. Okada's only published work of fiction, *No-No Boy* (1957), has been recognized at home and abroad as a classic of Asian American literature and widely examined in anthologies, literary histories, Asian American studies, and scholarly journals.

Before the novel was rediscovered by Frank Chin and other Asian American writers in the mid-1970s, John Okada's *No-No Boy* had been ignored for almost two decades. When first published in 1957, the novel was not only neglected by the American dominant public, but also unwelcome in the Japanese American community. Its first edition of 1,500 copies had not sold out when John Okada died in obscurity in 1971. The negative response to the novel surprised its publisher, Charles E. Tuttle, who assumed that the Japanese American community "would be enthusiastic about it." On the contrary, they "were not only disinterested but actually rejected the book" (*Aiiieeeee!* xxxix). In the afterword of the second edition in 1976, Frank Chin, in addition, said that he "got the impression his family was ashamed of the book" (256). After Okada's death, his widow wanted to offer all of his manuscripts to the Japanese American Research Project at the University of California at Los Angeles, but the manuscripts were rejected, and the widow was even encouraged to destroy the papers.

Set just after the end of World War II, *No-No Boy* begins with Ichiro Yamada's return to the Japanese American community in Seattle from a two-year prison term. A 25-year-old Nisei, Ichiro is imprisoned for refusing the draft and answering "No-No" to the two questions on the loyalty oath issued by the War Department in 1943. The first question asks "Are you willing to serve in the armed forces of the United States on combat duty whenever ordered?" The other reads "Will you swear unqualified allegiance to the United States of America and faithfully defend the United States from any or all attack by foreign or domestic forces, and foreswear any form of allegiance or obedience to the Japanese emperor, to any foreign government, power, or organization?" Ichiro's double negative to both inquiries regarding his loyalty and combat duty makes him an outcast in the Japanese American community and a traitor to the country. Moreover, he is labeled a "no-no boy." *No-No Boy* depicts Ichiro's reunion with his family and a rapid sequence of encounters with friends, neighbors, and strangers. The succession of events illustrates Ichiro's step from the trauma of being a no-no boy and his journey to reestablish an **identity** out of fragments.

In the pursuit of a "whole" identity, Ichiro first tries to understand why he said, "No-no." After two years in jail, he is still uncertain about his actions. His probing begins with his reunion with the family. Through examining his relationships with them and tracing his development from childhood into adulthood, Ichiro gradually understands the formation of himself as a no-no boy. Fractured and disjointed by the war, the family includes atypical Japanese: a patriotic and maniac mother, an ineffectual and alcoholic father, and a rebellious and malicious brother. Clinging to her fanatical loyalty to Japan, the mother cannot admit the Japanese defeat in the war. Unable to accept the outcome of the war, the mother isolates herself socially and psychologically. No longer able to live in a fantasy-filled world with Japan's glorious victory and her eventual return to Japan, the mother finally drowns herself in a tub full of water. Although regarding the mother as a crazy woman, Ichiro wonders: Who is crazy? The mother? Or those who were so delirious as to fight for a country that denied them? In contrast to the mother as a "rock" who usurps the head of the family, Ichiro's father is a "round and fat and cheerful-looking" man. He is called by Ichiro "a baby," "a fool," and even "a goddammed, fat, grinning, spineless nobody." Of his father, says Ichiro, "He should have been a woman. He should have been Ma." In addition to the eccentric parents, Ichiro's younger brother, Taro, feels shame for his parents' "Japaneseness" and Ichiro's "no-no" status. On his 18th birthday, Taro waits no longer to join the "American" army to prove his loyalty. In order to show his disassociation from Ichiro's treason and gain acceptance of his peers, Taro betrays his brother, leading Ichiro to be beaten by his friends. Unwilling to be a "Japanese" brother or a "Japanese" son, Taro desires an identity—an American one—separate from his parents' and his brother's.

In the novel not only Japanese Americans but also other ethnic groups suffer from being excluded from the mainstream of America. Blacks, Japanese, Chinese, Mexicans, Filipinos, and Jews all strive for recognition as complete persons, namely Americans. But being American in the novel is characterized by a practice of inclusion and exclusion. As the members of these ethnic groups cannot assume the primary attribute of the dominant culture (i.e., white skin), they can never cross "the unseen walls" to become American. In agonies of unfulfillment, they turn against one another and impose racial discrimination on other groups. In the novel the blacks ask the "Japs" to go back to Tokyo; in turn, the Japanese despise the blacks and feel superior to the "Chins," who may see themselves better Asians since China was America's ally during the war. **Racism** gnaws at the heart of each ethnic American, disfigures the spirit of every community, and finally damages the nation as a whole.

Beginning with Ichiro's return home—the onset of a quest for an identity—*No-No Boy* ends with his still-ongoing search for the meaning of his existence. Constantly examining his "half of self," either Japanese or American, Ichiro is obsessed with recurrent guilt as a no-no boy, worthy of nothing: He turns down two jobs, a chance to go back to the university, and love from Emi. Although concluding on a note of "hope," the novel emphatically depicts Ichiro as a solitary seeker, one still compulsively journeying to an indefinite destination. (*See also* Internment; Japanese American Novel)

Further Reading

Chin, Frank, et al. *Aiiieeeee: An Anthology of Asian American Writers*. Garden City, NY: Doubleday, 1974.

Lawrence, Keith and Floyd Cheung. *Received Legacies: Authority and Identity in Early Asian American Literature*. Philadelphia: Temple University Press, 2005.

Ling, Jinqi. "Race, Power, and Cultural Politics in John Okada's *No-No Boy*." *American Literature* 67.2 (1995): 358–81.

Yogi, Stan. "'You Had to Be One or the Other': Oppositions and Reconciliation in John Okada's *No-No Boy*." *MELUS* 21.2 (Summer 1996): 63–77.

Fu-jen Chen

ORTIZ, SIMON J. (1941–)

Simon J. Ortiz is an Acoma Pueblo poet, fiction writer, essayist, and storyteller. One of the preeminent figures in contemporary Native American literature, Simon J. Ortiz's vast body of work offers consistent testimony to the continuing presence of indigenous Americans in their ongoing struggles against centuries of colonial oppression. While Ortiz became recognized in the 1970s with the publication of his poetry collection titled *Going for the Rain* (1976), no single text marks Ortiz's influence in Native American literature. Rather, it is Ortiz's enduring commitment to writing as an act of decolonization and resistance over decades that has built his reputation as not only a powerful writer and speaker, but as an artist of integrity and heart.

Although Ortiz views himself as a storyteller in all of his literary productions, he is best known as a poet. Ortiz grew up in the small village of *Deetseyamah* (McCarty's) in Acoma Pueblo, New Mexico, and his poetry is firmly rooted in *nuu yuh Aacquemeh hano ka-dzeh-nih* ("the Acoma people's language"). While his poems address themes from Coyote (or trickster) mischief to working in New Mexican uranium mines, their syntax, structure, format, and repetitions emphasize *Aacquemeh* orality, often achieving the breath-paced quality of language chanted or sung. Like most Native writers, Ortiz struggles with the inherent contradiction of attempting to transmit his indigenous oral tradition in written form, a condition that distances language from the intimacy of its spoken and performed context. Especially in more recent works, such as *Out There Somewhere* (2002), Ortiz includes words, phrases, and entire poems in his *Aacquemeh* language. In doing so,

Ortiz simultaneously foregrounds the continuing presence of this precolonial language and demonstrates the Acoma people's abiding resistance to colonial attempts to eradicate the language that forms the very basis of their culture and worldview. In *Aacquemeh* language, Ortiz finds a palpable quality arising from the contours and textures of his homeland and community, in contrast to the abstractions of European languages such as English or Spanish, which easily migrate because they are not rooted in specific sacred geographies. Still, Ortiz believes that all languages possess spiritual energy and life force, a world-making power that demands of writers and speakers great responsibility because words carry with them tangible social and political consequences. Of Ortiz's many collections of poetry, his own favorite volume is *from Sand Creek* (1981), which won a Pushcart Prize. Both autobiographical and historical, *from Sand Creek* is Ortiz's poetic manifesto bearing witness to the brutality of United States' imperialist policies that frame war as righteous at the expense of innocent people slaughtered and also the veterans who return damaged and disenfranchised after fighting for their country. The Veteran's Administration (VA) Hospital in Fort Lyons, Colorado, is the setting of *from Sand Creek*. Fort Lyons was also the military headquarters for the U.S. troops who, along with 700 Colorado Volunteers under the command of reverend Colonel John W. Chivington, massacred and mutilated 105 Cheyenne and Arapaho women and children and 28 men (in an encampment of about 600 people) on November 29, 1864. The Cheyenne leader Black Kettle had been promised peaceful habitation for his people at this site by the U.S. government, and was flying a flag of peace presented by President Lincoln when the massacre took place. In this 45-poem cycle—with one or two brief declarative sentences preceding each untitled poem on the facing page—the VA Hospital becomes the zone in which Ortiz reveals the intimate histories of wounded veterans. These histories include his own, as Ortiz was a patient in the Fort Lyons VA Hospital between 1974 and 1975, where he was treated for alcoholism. In *from Sand Creek*, Ortiz considers his position as a Native, an American, and a veteran within complex cycles of American imperialism against Native peoples, whether on domestic or foreign soil. He explores the layers of innocence, ignorance, and complicity that allow such assaults against human life and dignity to continue, and frames a vision for the future in which love, compassion, historical consciousness, and cross-cultural understanding replace exploitation, hatred, and destruction.

Just as Ortiz's *Aacquemeh* oral tradition finds expression through poetic form, so does the process of oral narrative lend itself to Ortiz's short fiction. *Men on the Moon* (1999) collects the nineteen short stories originally published as *Fightin'* (1983), plus seven additional stories (most published first in the anthology *The Man to Send Rain Clouds* [1974], edited by Kenneth Rosen, and in Ortiz's 1978 collection, *Howbah Indians*). Ortiz has made minor revisions to a few of the stories in *Men on the Moon*, just as a traditional Native storyteller incorporates slight changes in the telling of her or his stories over time. The landscapes of Ortiz's stories include the familiar terrain of his southwest *Aacquemeh* homeland, a lonely migrant work camp in rural Idaho ("Woman Singing"), and the urban strangeness of the streets of San Francisco, where earnest white hippies play at being "real Indians" ("The San Francisco Indians"). Ortiz's direct language and quiet tone amplify the themes of his more political stories involving the abuse of power by colonial authority against Native peoples, such as an incident with a racist policeman ("The Killing of a State Cop") or a young Pueblo man's flight from federal Indian boarding school ("Pennstuwehniyaahtse: Quuti's Story"). Other stories register powerfully in more intimate contexts, as when a Laguna Pueblo couple helps their white Oklahoma neighbors mourn the death of a younger brother, who stepped on an American mine in Vietnam, by giving the Okie couple an ear of white corn and a ceremonial corn husk bundle in traditional Laguna fashion ("To Change Life in a Good Way"). These stories illustrate the small details of life within its epic sweep through human relationships and attempts at understanding, some of which succeed, some of which fail, and many of which remain unresolved and under negotiation. Ortiz has stated that from earliest memory he has always existed inside language, and that language has always existed in the form of stories. In a different manner than his poems, Ortiz's short fiction cultivates a similar narrative intimacy between reader and author that both reveals the values that shape Ortiz's **identity**, and allows readers to be moved.

In addition to his many collections of poetry and short stories, Ortiz has written three children's books and has edited a number of important Native American literary anthologies, including *Earth Power Coming* (1983) and *Speaking for the Generations* (1998). The influence of Ortiz's literary production in subverting mainstream stereotypes of Indians and promoting literature as an act of Native self-determination, resistance against colonialism, and an assertion of cultural and political sovereignty has inspired his own and future generations of Native writers, as well as a wide non-Native literary public. When Ortiz began to write, he knew of few Native American writers, so his curiosity and love of words led him to read everything from Emily Dickinson to the Beat poets. Yet, it is the role of language in oral narrative, song, prayer, and other speech acts within his *Aacquemeh* culture that has laid the enduring foundation for Ortiz's writing. (*See also* Native American Poetry)

Further Reading

Wiget, Andrew. *Simon Ortiz*. Boise, ID: Boise State University Press, 1986.
Wilson, Norma. "Language as a Way of Life: The Poetry of Simon J. Ortiz." *The Nature of Native American Poetry*, 45–64. Albuquerque: University of New Mexico Press, 2001.

Jane Haladay

ORTIZ COFER, JUDITH (1952–)

Judith Ortiz Cofer is a Puerto Rican–born poet and novelist, raised in the United States. She is one of the most versatile writers in the United States and has established herself as a very popular and innovative author. Her work often uses code-switching, alternating between Spanish and English and mixing the two, as a way of reinforcing her Puerto Rican and American heritage and adding artistic value to her writing.

Of all the novels and poetry collections Ortiz Cofer has written, her autobiographical work, **Silent Dancing**: *A Partial Remembrance of My Puerto Rican Childhood* (1990), best showcases her talents. Written as a series of creative nonfiction essays followed by poems that add commentary at the end of each chapter, *Silent Dancing* presents the story of a young Ortiz Cofer and her family's migration from Puerto Rico to the United States, namely to Paterson, New Jersey. Her father, who enlisted in the navy, brought his family to the mainland and struggled against all odds to achieve a better life. Once here, he was immediately made aware of the prejudice he would face, especially among landlords who preferred not to rent to Puerto Rican families and who were used to having Jewish tenants. Still, he strongly believed that the United States was the best place for his family, so he did as much as possible to keep them from being dragged down by the daily grind of living in tenement housing. During the times that her father had to be away for extended periods of time, Ortiz Cofer and her family would return to Puerto Rico, and this, in turn, kept her ties to the island strong. At the same time, this pattern of shifting between two cultures made it more challenging for her to grow up without much cultural conflict. In this way, *Silent Dancing* provides a collage of stories and poems that focus on the many facets of immigrant life that so many Puerto Ricans experience. For example, it details the bicultural, bilingual worlds of Puerto Ricans who, at times, are made to feel like they have no home.

A common theme in Ortiz Cofer's writing is the role of women in Latino/Puerto Rican worlds. Although Ortiz Cofer has claimed that her own grandmother, who had progressively nontraditional views, would have laughed at the idea that she was a feminist, there is no doubt that Ortiz Cofer's work demonstrates a deep awareness and understanding of the challenges that Latinas face in predominantly patriarchal societies. In fact, she has dedicated a significant number of works to this issue; *Woman in Front of the Sun: On Becoming a Writer* (2000), *Sleeping with One Eye Open: Women Writers and the Art of Survival* (1999), *The Line of the Sun* (1989), and *The Year of Our Revolution: New and Selected Stories and Poems* (1998) all concern themselves with women's roles in such spheres as the family, the workplace, relationships, politics, and even literature.

As someone who takes very seriously the importance of storytelling traditions, Ortiz Cofer demonstrates through her writing that women have played a pivotal role in Puerto Rican culture, in keeping that tradition alive. Her works detail how stories about mythical figures, told to young girls, have the effect of serving as warnings to them about how to behave ladylike. Her female characters are strong, often in control of relationships even when the male head of the household earns the wages. One of her most widely acclaimed novels, *The Line of the Sun* (1991), which was nominated for the Pulitzer Prize, looks closely at women who find that their fight for equality can succeed only if it is to be supported by a network of women. Just as she does in other works, Ortiz Cofer draws on the spiritual traditions of the Caribbean with characters who perform Santeria. No doubt inspired by her own upbringing, the novel depicts a young woman who grows up living in Paterson and Puerto Rico. Ortiz Cofer grew up surrounded by relatives and family friends who believed in the supernatural—her grandfather claimed to communicate with spirits. Quite often in her stories, however, females are the ones who are most affected by spiritual and religious practices.

Ortiz Cofer's poetry switches between English and Spanish, in part because so much of her poems center on life in a bicultural, bilingual world. A frequently anthologized poet, Ortiz Cofer weaves Spanish words, expressions, and names in her poems as a way to capture artistic truth. It is not uncommon for her poems to be written almost entirely in English, with the exception of one or two words that stand out and provide important meaning and significance. The poem, "Fulana," for instance, contains only one word in Spanish—the title's namesake. A word that means a female "so and so," *fulana* loses its true connotation in English. Hence, in such a case, and in similar other occasions, Ortiz Cofer's use of Spanish is not only warranted but crucial toward developing a poem that captures the emotions in an experience that takes place in more than simply a monolithic world, but in a world full of bicultural encounters. Such use of Spanish distinguishes her from other Latino poets, many of whom use Spanish as a reflection of dialects and speech patterns that are found in many Latino households. These poets' use of Spanish is much more prevalent, and, to a certain degree, can be said to address bilingual readers. As a result, Ortiz Cofer's writing has been praised by many mainstream critics.

Ortiz Cofer has earned many accolades and awards for her work. She has been the recipient of fellowships from the National Endowment for the Arts and the Witter Bynner Foundation, and has received such awards as Best Book of the Year from the American Library Association, for *An Island Like You: Stories from the Barrio* (1998), a Paterson Book Prize, the O. Henry Prize for Short Story, the Pushcart Prize, and the first Pura Belpre Medal. Her work has appeared in such prominent publications as *Best American Essays 1991, The Norton Book of Women's Lives*, and the *O. Henry Prize Stories*. She has been a featured speaker in conferences, literary festivals, and symposia throughout the United States and is currently a professor of English and creative writing at the University of Georgia. (*See also* Bilingualism; Puerto Rican American Poetry)

Further Reading

Acosta-Belen, Edna. "A *MELUS* Interview: Judith Ortiz Cofer." *MELUS* 18.3 (Fall 1993): 83–97.

Davis, Rocio G. "Metanarrative in Ethnic Autobiography for Children: Laurence Yep's *The Lost Garden* and Judith Ortiz Cofer's *Silent Dancing*." *MELUS* 27.2 (Summer 2002): 139–58.

Faymonville, Carmer. "New Transnational Identities in Judith Ortiz Cofer's Autobiographical Fiction." *MELUS* 26.2 (Summer 2001): 129–57.

Lopez, Lorraine M. and Molly Crumpton Winter, eds. *Rituals of Movement in the Writing of Judith Ortiz Cofer*. Pompano Beach, FL: Caribbean Studies Press, 2012.

Ocasio, Rafael. "Puerto Rican Literature in Georgia?: An Interview with Judith Ortiz Cofer." *Kenyon Review* 14.4 (Fall 1992): 43–51.

Rangil, Viviana. "Pro-Claiming a Space: The Poetry of Sandra Cisneros and Judith Ortiz Cofer." *Multicultural Review* 9.3 (September 2000): 48–51, 54–55.

Jose B. Gonzalez

P

PASSING

Nella Larsen's *Passing* (1929) remains one of the most intriguing novels of the **Harlem Renaissance**. The novel's plot pivots on the relationship between two main characters, Irene Redfield and Clare Kendry, who are light-skinned enough to pass for white. Irene, who is married to a Harlem-based physician, passes for white whenever she can use her pseudo-whiteness to gain social privileges that she would otherwise be denied. Clare, however, is married to a pathologically racist white businessman who believes that his wife is white. So Clare conceals her cultural **identity** and passes for white on a full-time basis.

The novel begins with an accidental meeting of Irene and Clare in a sleek Chicago restaurant after having lost touch with each other for over a dozen years. They reestablish their friendship. Irene feels vaguely tantalized by Clare and her beauty, her toughness and daring, and her casual disdain for upper-class conventions. Yet she also feels faintly uneasy with the emotional intensity that begins to characterize their friendship. In the second section of the novel, Clare visits Irene in New York; the visit, ostensibly, is prompted by her desire to reconnect with her roots but her motives remain ambiguous. And Irene becomes increasingly puzzled by her own fascination with Clare. Irene's feelings become more complicated when she begins to suspect that her husband and Clare might be having an affair. In the final segment of the novel, Larsen stages a dramatic confrontation: Clare's racist husband, in search of Clare, wanders into a glamorous party in Harlem and finds her there. Moments later Clare falls out of a window and dies. Whether her fatal fall is an accident, suicide, or murder is left to the reader's speculation.

A novel of manners, *Passing* offers an articulate critique of the values and foibles of the black upper class of the 1920s. More importantly, Larsen's use of the phenomenon of passing deconstructs the very concept of "**race**" by subverting the presumed rigidity and impenetrability of racial categories. But perhaps the most daring aspect of the novel is its subtle exploration of transgressive sexuality: on the surface it appears to be a conventional novel about two married women, but subtextually it hints at lesbian desire.

Since the mid-1980s *Passing* has generated substantial critical attention. This renewed academic interest is at least partly due to the novel's curiously postmodern sensibility: *Passing* points to the instability, even the performative and fictional nature, of all identities.

Further Reading

Davis, Thadious. *Nella Larsen: Novelist of the Harlem Renaissance*. Baton Rouge: Louisiana State University Press, 1994.

Grayson, Deborah R. "Fooling White Folks, or, How I Stole the Show: The Body Politics in Nella Larsen's *Passing*." *Bucknell Review* 39.1 (1995): 27–37.

McIntyre, Gabrielle. "Toward a Narratology of Passing: Epistemology, Race, and Misrecognition in Nella Larsen's *Passing*." *Callaloo* 35.3 (2012): 778–94.

Wald, Gayle. *Crossing the Line: Racial Passing in Twentieth-Century U.S. Literature and Culture*. Durham, NC: Duke University Press, 2000.

Youman, Mary Mabel. "Nella Larsen's *Passing*: A Study in Irony." *CLA Journal* 18 (December 1974): 235–44.

Emmanuel S. Nelson

PEDAGOGY AND U.S. ETHNIC LITERATURES

The impact of U.S. ethnic literatures on American literary pedagogy has been profound. Curricula and syllabi are more diverse and inclusive and minority writers and texts receive significant scholarly and popular attention. **Canon**ical texts are often approached in new, fruitful ways, focusing on the politics of injustice and the ways ideology shapes discourse. Yet the challenges for instructors and students of U.S. ethnic literature remain. Fortunately, scholar-teachers of U.S. ethnic literatures continue to engage in serious, ongoing reflection about principles, objectives, and practices.

Pedagogy of U.S. ethnic literatures is deeply embedded in multiculturalism, an identifiable ideology, political movement, and educational movement. Built on the recognition that democratic ideals of egalitarianism and justice often go unrealized, **multiculturalism** seeks to redress such injustices and inequities through increased inclusion of racial, ethnic, and other marginalized social groups in cultural, social, educational, and political arenas. But the debate between multicultural and "traditional" educators is ongoing. In general terms, traditionalists charge multiculturalists with politicizing curricula and classrooms through the infusion of multiculturalism, while progressivists argue that curricula and classrooms are and always have been political, biased toward Western, white male experience and knowledge. Progressivists, therefore, seek to include voices and perspectives of previously marginalized groups in curricula. Some who are critical of current multicultural approaches to education countercharge that emphasizing exclusions based on race, class, gender, and sexual orientation does not serve diversity because it divides students. Rather, they see multiculturalism as purely political, defined in terms of what some have called "oppression studies."

In literary studies, culture wars take the form of "canon wars," a term coined by Gerald Graff and William Cain, which indicates controversies over the texts that should be studied, taught, and even appreciated or revered. Traditionalists appeal to the past, to God, to natural laws, or to foundationalist claims to Truth. Revisionists, however, view cultural diversity as America's foundation; curricular diversity,

Protesters gather to support the Tucson Unified School District. Superintendent of Public Instruction John Huppenthal announced on June 15, 2011, that the Tucson Unified School District was violating state law by teaching the Mexican American Studies Department's ethnic studies course. (AP Photo/Ross D. Franklin)

then, not the "Great Books" of Western civilization, form the basis for understanding American society's multicultural composition. Moreover, revisionists tend to subscribe to postmodernist, antifoundational claims to truth, knowledge, and morality; the "Great Books," therefore, provide only one version of truth rather than Truth with a capital "T." By including texts, voices, worldviews, philosophies, and belief systems of previously excluded groups, revisionists claim, the curricula encourages students to develop multiplicity in their approach to knowledge.

Yet many versions of multiculturalism exist, ranging from the "liberal" to the "radical," each representing particular philosophical and political beliefs. Liberal multiculturalisms go by many names: "corporate," "liberal," "boutique," and "institutionalized." They tend to focus on the study of all different cultures and nationalities and the "appreciation" of everything another culture has to offer, at least on the surface. Multiculturalism, according to these versions, is the celebration of different customs, foods, dress, and religious holidays. In the study of U.S. ethnic literature, liberal multiculturalism is manifested in efforts to make curricula and syllabi representative and inclusive; as such, students experience a smorgasbord of ethnic writers as they move their way from one culture to another, often by using one of several available anthologies.

But this approach to U.S. ethnic literature has been criticized on several grounds. First, it may reinforce **assimilation**ist and universalist values through thematic focuses such as "family," "home," and "love." Students are encouraged through a liberal multicultural approach to U.S. ethnic literature to think that except for surface differences, such as where we live or what we celebrate, "underneath we're all alike." Students tend to read unfamiliar texts from their own perspectives, thereby appropriating and erasing difference. **Leslie Marmon Silko**'s short story, "Yellow Woman," for example, is often interpreted as a feminist tale of a woman's break from the mundane domestic sphere, which stifles her imagination and passion. However, when read through the context of traditional Cochiti and Pueblo Yellow Woman tales, Silko's story resists a white feminist perspective.

Similarly, adding or replacing old texts with new ones may lead to diversification but does not transform literary studies. The add-on approach, as many scholar-teachers have called it, forces ethnic texts into white, male ways of reading and teaching. It likewise focuses on diversity at the expense of issues of inequity and injustice; real-world political gains do not inevitably accrue from diversification of the literary canon. Thus many scholar-teachers of U.S. ethnic literatures call for new kinds of teaching approaches that neither eliminate cultural difference nor ignore systemic injustices. For example, it is not enough to add African American writer **Ernest J. Gaines**'s *A Lesson Before Dying* into a course on American literary modernism, even though this text shares some modernist features. Rather, pedagogical approaches to *A Lesson Before Dying* should account for the particulars of **race**, class, and gender as these categories of difference modify or challenge modernist characteristics. Jefferson's efforts to regain his humanity after having been called a "dumb animal" by his defense attorney are deeply embedded in what Grant Wiggins, another character, calls the "black man's burden," dating to slavery.

In response to what are seen by many as liberal multiculturalism's shortcomings, critical multiculturalists address the politics of race and other social categories of difference. Critical multiculturalists advocate a critique of the power relations that work to undermine efforts at equality and attempt to focus on and thus remedy the uneven distribution of goods, power, and access to knowledge. Critical multiculturalisms attend to power, structural inequalities, injustice, discrimination, and hate.

In critical multicultural literature classrooms, students study power dynamics in U.S. ethnic literatures. For example, critical multicultural pedagogies interrogate individualist ideologies that blindly promote notions of equal opportunity and merit-based achievements. Students examine countless topics, including education, advertising, television, family, and literature. Students may, for example, analyze Chicana writer **Sandra Cisneros**'s *The House on Mango Street* and Chicano writer **Tomás Rivera**'s *. . . y no se lo trago la tierra/And the Earth Did Not Devour Him* against the backdrop of individualist ideology as generally articulated in canonical literature, television, and film. Furthermore, critical pedagogists have moved away from a focus on literary interpretation to what has been called a "politics of interpretation." That is, critical multiculturalists ask students to consider the ways their reading practices are shaped by cultural forces, such as race, class, and gender, and how they might try on unfamiliar ways of reading.

Objectives

The conflicts between liberal and critical multiculturalisms impact pedagogical objectives of U.S. ethnic literatures. Why do we teach texts by U.S. ethnic writers? Do we teach these texts to foster understanding of cultural difference, to promote aesthetic appreciation, to sharpen awareness of language use, or to hone socially just attitudes? Do we teach ethnic literature so that our minority students can see themselves in American literary history and thus develop or reaffirm self-worth? These important questions remain largely unresolved, except that many scholar-teachers assume all are important, even if difficult to include together in any one course.

In particular, for many instructors, multiethnic literary studies should engage issues of justice and equity and prepare students for active democratic participation. Many instructors have thus made their literature classes sites of antiracist, antisexist, anticlassist social change, spaces for cultural critique. For some of these instructors, U.S. ethnic texts are powerful vehicles for conveying how oppression and discrimination harm individuals and cultural groups. While acknowledging that transformations in politics and ethics do not usually occur through one or two semesters of literature study, these instructors nonetheless view reading literature by ethnic writers as an important first step toward social engagement and change.

Other teacher-scholars, however, question such motives and objectives, usually along two lines. First, is it fair or appropriate, they ask, to impose an instructor's moral and political agenda on students? Are teachers of U.S. ethnic literatures hypocritical in their refusal to accept students' conservative viewpoints when multiculturalists advocate respect for and acceptance of difference? Additionally, some instructors worry about how to grade fairly students whose politics are disagreeable to themselves and their disciplinary claims. Moreover, when an instructor's viewpoint dominates classroom dialogue, how will students participate in knowledge making? Some opponents of what has been called "politicized teaching" argue that students may merely mimic the teacher to please her.

For others, the emphasis on politics belies aesthetic appreciation. Efforts to broaden the canon to include diverse, previously marginalized voices were conducted with recognition of the socially constructed nature of literary excellence. As a result, criteria for constituting literary "greatness" became increasingly nebulous. Some scholar-teachers believe that a further consequence has been the privileging of "political" U.S. ethnic literatures– those texts that advance social justice agendas–at the expense of considerations of a text's aesthetic dimensions. Recently, however, multiculturalists have begun to acknowledge that aesthetics and politics are often inseparable, and efforts to more clearly identify and invent ethnic aesthetics are underway, particularly in African American, Chicano/a, Asian American, and Native American literary critical communities.

Teaching Multiculturally

Among the most crucial pedagogical questions for U.S. ethnic literatures is *how* these texts should be read and, subsequently, taught. Should these texts simply be added to an instructor's standard or familiar course syllabus, fit in as the instructor deems appropriate? What about the cultural, ethnic, and racial contexts of multi-cultural texts? Do we ignore these and teach texts according to familiar paradigms, forms, genres, and other formal qualities of literature, or should other kinds of critical approaches be brought to these texts? Many instructors of multiethnic literature agree that new critical categories and paradigms are necessary.

Chicano writer **Rudolfo Anaya**'s *Bless Me, Ultima* will serve as one example. This text is readily taught within the traditional framework of a coming-of-age novel, the bildungsroman, in which a young protagonist (typically white, male, and middle class) develops into a more mature individual through a standard pattern of making choices, breaking away from societal institutions, overcoming obstacles, undergoing a spiritual crisis, and finally, recognizing one's self-**identity** and place in the world. In *Bless Me, Ultima* the protagonist, Antonio (who narrates the story retrospectively), adheres to many of these traditional patterns. He moves away from the security of his mother's home to experience life and discover himself, and he encounters numerous tests along the way, including the violent killings of the sheriff and Lupito as well as knowledge of sin. Antonio must choose between the confinement represented by the farms of his maternal family, the Lunas, or the freedoms represented by his paternal family, the Márezes, and their history as *vaqueroes* (cowboys). The novel follows a fairly linear pattern that readers, especially students, find accessible and familiar.

But scholars of Chicano/a literature have identified many distinctive cultural elements in the text, such as references to Mexican Catholicism, code-switching, Aztec myth and symbol, New Mexican and Southwest folklore, and the importance of modernization's threat to agricultural and ranching ways of life in the small towns of New Mexico in the early 1940s. La Llorona, the wailing woman of the river in Mexican myth and folklore, permeates Antonio's self-discovery. La Llorona is associated with the women in the novel, most pointedly Antonio's mother, Maria, who offers warmth and security that Antonio must deny if he is to become a man. By understanding the significance of La Llorona, readers understand Antonio's story, not only in universal terms of growing up, but through the lens of Mexican folklore which was very much a part of Antonio's (and Anaya's) childhood.

Feminist perspectives are also crucial to effective multiethnic pedagogy, but some ethnic feminists find mainstream feminist critical frameworks limiting. Observing that feminist criticism was initiated by and based upon white, middle-class women, critics and teachers of texts by women of color charge that mainstream feminist interpretive frameworks often omit the racialized ethnic contexts embedded in this body of work. Accordingly, they argue that women of color are multiply marginalized by gender, race, **ethnicity**, class, and other categories of difference. As a result of this perspective, scholarship in multicultural literary studies argues for providing students with relevant cultural information as they read and interpret texts within feminist frameworks.

One common mainstream approach to texts by women writers of color is to consider the text within larger categories of women's traditions, such as narrative strategies, voice, and themes. For example, feminist critics tend to view women's connections to one another as a need for reassurance that they are not alone as writers and creators, even though patriarchal culture has long viewed the woman writer as deviant or as "monsters." One only need look at Charlotte Perkins Gilman's white, middle-class protagonist (in her widely read short story, "The Yellow Wallpaper,") who is completely isolated, with the exception of the woman she imagines in the wallpaper; while her creative energy at the story's end can be read as subversive, she ends up institutionalized for her alleged madness. This traditional reading of women's relationships can be productively applied to a text like African American writer **Alice Walker**'s *The Color Purple*, illuminating the female relationships that sustain Celie and ward off descent into madness, which would seem utterly understandable given the abuse she suffered as a young girl and an adult. Celie's developing relationships with the women around her—Shug, Sofia, Squeak, and even her sister Nettie, who she is able to communicate with through letter writing—parallel her healing of mind, body, and soul.

However, because many identified women's traditions were ascertained with or by white, middle-class women writers and may not apply to women of color or poor women, mainstream feminist notions of women's connections do not account for the decidedly African American nature of women's networks of support that derive from African cultural systems and black slaves' experiences during American slavery. Thus Celie's mutually supportive relationships with Shug, Sophia, Squeak, and Nettie become crucial to her development as a fully realized human being. Through such support, Celie can resist the patriarchal rhetoric that seeks to destroy her: Alphonso's admonitions that she tell no one about the rape, his vicious words about her ugliness, and Albert's hurtful contention that she is worthless. Additionally, Celie's writing reveals the creativity passed through generations of African American women. Walker honors black women's conscious and unconscious struggles to be creative despite the oppressive conditions in which they have historically lived. Celie's sewing activities aid her acquisition of black women's agency as they directly connect Celie with a community of women, past and present.

Teaching Methods

Infusing the curricula with multicultural perspectives refers to teaching practices as well as content and critical approach. It is the recognition that teaching practices are always politically constituted. In a multicultural classroom, subjects are approached in multiple ways and through multiple perspectives rather than top-down and single (teacher) voiced. All students' voices must be heard to make the classroom a genuinely democratic setting where everyone contributes to meaning-making. Such pedagogy recognizes that all students bring valuable experiences and knowledge to their readings of texts, and that students must feel free to express their views in a mutually informing conversation of ideas. Teaching from critical multicultural perspectives means helping students, especially women and students of color, to feel safe in classrooms and to realize that their ideas are valued.

The Instructor

The instructor of U.S. ethnic literatures faces enormous challenges. The notion of identity politics in literary studies continues to provoke passionate debate about whether one's ethnic background should determine what texts one can appropriately teach. That is, must Native American literature be taught by Native Americans? Must Asian American literature be taught by Asian Americans? Although some ethnic literature specialists continue to believe that white instructors should not teach ethnic literature, most acknowledge the pragmatic implications of such limitations; discouraging white instructors from teaching U.S. ethnic literatures would severely undermine advances in curricular diversification. Many also look beyond pragmatics to assert that any instructor, regardless of race or ethnicity, can commit to teaching any literature well through sustained study of the literature and relevant culture and history.

Finally, instructors of U.S. ethnic literatures understand that bringing issues of race into the classroom is risky, unpredictable, discomforting, and potentially explosive. Instructors of multiethnic literature face numerous challenges including marginalization by the institution; negative student responses to multicultural content, including defensiveness, resistance, apathy, anger, resentment, or guilt; and lower course ratings. Yet despite (or because of) these challenges, there is an urgency and excitement about multiethnic pedagogy among teachers, scholars, and students. When instructors teach about and with race, ethnicity, class, gender, and other social categories of difference, they raise the stakes for students and themselves. They push students to think and feel beyond what they are accustomed to, and instructors must do the same for themselves. Teachers who choose to teach U.S ethnic literatures can expect the unexpected, but the unexpected often brings the most meaningful moments inside or outside the classroom.

In many ways, effective teaching of U.S. ethnic literatures requires collaboration and sharing of ideas. An enormous amount of theoretical and pedagogical scholarship exists and all instructors and students should take advantage of these resources. In addition to the books listed below, which only begin to tap available resources, the following journals are recommend: *MELUS, College English, College Literature,* and *Pedagogy: Critical Approaches to Teaching Literature, Language, and Culture.* (*See also* Multiculturalism)

Further Reading

Alberti, John, ed. *The Canon in the Classroom: The Pedagogical Implications of Canon Revision in American Literature.* New York: Garland, 1995.

Brannon, Lil, and Brenda M. Greene, eds. *Rethinking American Literature.* Urbana, IL: NCTE, 1997.

Goebel, Bruce A., and James C. Hall, eds. *Teaching a "New Canon"? Students, Teachers, and Texts in the College Literature Classroom.* Urbana, IL: NCTE, 1995.

Grobman, Laurie. *Teaching at the Crossroads: Cultures and Critical Perspectives in Literature by Women of Color.* San Francisco: Aunt Lute, 2001.

Jay, Gregory S. *American Literature and the Culture Wars.* Ithaca, NY: Cornell University Press, 1997.

Maitino, John, and David R. Peck, eds. *Teaching American Ethnic Literatures*. Albuquerque: University of New Mexico Press, 1996.

TuSmith, Bonnie. *All My Relatives: Community in Contemporary Ethnic American Literatures*. Ann Arbor: University of Michigan Press, 1993.

Laurie Grobman

PIÑERO, MIGUEL (1946–1988)

Miguel Piñero was a poet, playwright, screenwriter, and actor. He is best known for his award-winning play *Short Eyes*, which became both a Broadway show and a commercial film during the 1970s. He also wrote and acted in television crime dramas such as *Kojak, Barretta*, and *Miami Vice*. Some critics report that contemporary Hollywood images of Latinos, specifically criminals, are based on Piñero's depictions created for the previously mentioned television programs. A prolific and eloquent writer, Piñero is also credited, along with Miguel Algarín, as being one of the founders of the **Nuyorican** Poets' Café. His life was depicted in the 2000 film *Piñero*, directed by Leon Ichaso.

Considered by many scholars and critics to be a real life "outlaw," his writing, as well as his life, was a testament to his refusal to conform to the mainstream's status quo and its ideals for success. His writing can be described as a counter-discourse (connecting him to such exiled writers as the Cuban Reinaldo Arenas, and the Puerto Rican Manuel Ramos Otero) to the belief that an individual must conform to a homogenous mentality and a uniform way of life in order to achieve success as prescribed by mainstream society. Rather, his writing reflects life as he lived it and experienced it. In essence, his writing and life experiences were nonapologetic; his writing depicted life on the streets, the underworld, characters such as drug dealers and prostitutes—individuals who lived their lives in complete opposition to conventional social expectations. Unlike many contemporary media depictions of modern-day outlaws, gangsters, and drug lords, the characters and descriptions created by Piñero were based on his own experiences in the streets with the people he encountered and associated with.

His plays in particular showcase his belief in living life as an individual, avoiding conformity and presenting a reality that has often been ignored. As a matter of choice and style, his plays often attacked "the comfortable aesthetics of the middle-class theater goers" (Kanellos, 1997, 245). His work also criticized **racism**, "exploitation of the poor, colonialism (in Puerto Rico), greed, and materialism" (Kanellos 245–46).

Another aspect of his writing touches on how Puerto Ricans on the island view those individuals who call themselves "Nuyoricans" as Americanized versions of what a Puerto Rican is—and at the same time a threat to Puerto Rican island culture. This attitude is best represented in the film *Piñero* where the poet is attacked by some of his Puerto Rican audience members during a presentation of his poetry. Piñero's response was that his Nuyorican **identity** reflected his condition—a Puerto

Rican who was "transplanted" to New York and who had to adapt to his environment in order to survive.

Further Reading

Acosta-Belén, Edna. "Beyond Island Boundaries: Ethnicity, Gender, and Cultural Revitalization in Nuyorican Literature." *Callaloo* 15.4 (Autumn 1992): 979–98.

Irizarry, Roberto. "The House of Pretension: Space and Performance in Miguel Pinero's Theatre." *Latin American Theatre Review* 34 (2004): 583–601.

Kanellos, Nicolás, ed. *The Hispanic Literary Companion.* New York: Visible Ink, 1997.

Luis, William. "From New York to the World: An Interview with Tato Laviera." *Callaloo* 15.4 (Autumn 1992): 1022–33.

Enrique Morales-Diaz

PUERTO RICAN AMERICAN AUTOBIOGRAPHY

If what distinguishes memoirs from autobiography, as it has been suggested, is the emphasis on community rather than the individual, then the foundational Puerto Rican American first-person accounts fall unquestionably under the rubric of the former. Neither the *Memorias de Bernardo Vega* (1977), written in Spanish, nor Jesus Colon's *A Puerto Rican in New York and Other Sketches* (1961), both recognized by critics as fundamental texts in the history of Puerto Rican literature in the United States, aims to represent the protagonist only, but an individual life submerged in the social and political history of the Puerto Rican community on the mainland. Readers looking for details about the intimate lives of these two individuals will not find them in these texts. The period covered by both books spans roughly a hundred years, beginning with the mid-19th century. Although the personal, albeit public, eyewitness story Bernardo Vega (1885–1965) and Jesus Colon (1901–1974) have to tell begins in the second decade of the 20th century, when they both arrived in New York in search of a better life, Vega's book summarizes the state of the Puerto Rican settlement in the metropolis from about 1850 through a story told to him by a relative who had preceded him. This narrative strategy serves to trace the ongoing struggle of a colonized people in the continental United States and in crafting what is considered to be, by all accounts, a unique document for the study of the Puerto Rican community's forebears.

Written by Bernardo Vega, the manuscript of the *Memorias* was edited by César Andreu Iglesias, Vega's longtime friend, 10 years after the author's death. Born in Cayey, Puerto Rico, the self-taught Vega worked as a cigar maker since an early age. Like others in the cigar industry, then at the vanguard of the labor movement, he embarked on a long fight for social justice that led to his involvement in myriad political, cultural, and labor organizations, some of which he helped create, and his collaboration in a number of progressive and socialist newspapers of the first half of the 20th century. Vega paints a large fresco of Hispanic life in the boroughs of New York, with episodes relating to diverse topics, such as the fight of the working-class migrants for their rights and their daily interaction with other ethnic groups. Vega also records the intense activity displayed by the community in support of the independence of their native land from Spain, and later their participation in local politics. He also maps out the expansion of neighborhoods to accommodate the growth of the Hispanic community that, by 1927, may well have numbered over 100,000 inhabitants. These numbers would increase significantly in the 1940s and 1950s as a result of the push for industrialization in Puerto Rico and the concomitant displacement of peoples.

Whereas Vega offers a panoramic view of Puerto Ricans in the continental United States, Jesus Colon, another self-educated cigar maker with whom Vega would cross paths in the fight for justice, zooms in to offer thumbnail sketches of this history in *A Puerto Rican in New York and Other Sketches*. The book opens with a scene of reading in a cigar factory in Puerto Rico that lingers in the memory of the narrator. Colon recalls how the resonant voice of the *lector* (a person hired to read to the cigar makers while they worked) would reach his nearby room, filling it with the sounds of world literature and political philosophy. This opening vignette suggests a link between word and work that Colon would pursue later, when he went into journalism and labor organizing. Many of the sketches included in the book reflect his lifelong interest in reading and writing, often as a means to defend the rights of disenfranchised constituencies and to counteract the widespread misinformation on Puerto Ricans found in the mainstream media of his times. During more than 50 years, he collaborated in numerous progressive newspapers published in Spanish and English. The essays included in *A Puerto Rican in New York and Other Sketches* represent only a portion of the ones he wrote. In 1993, a selection of Colon's unpublished sketches appeared under the title *The Way It Was and Other Writings*, edited by Edna Acosta-Belén and Virginia Sánchez Korrol. Colon, a black Puerto Rican, has been credited with defining a Puerto Rican tradition in New York that served as a source of inspiration and resistance to subsequent waves of migrants from the island.

Whereas the characters that populate the above books are largely from the working class and racialized sectors of the Puerto Rican colony with a strong class consciousness, Pedro Juan Labarthe provides a window into the mindset of a different type of character in *The Son of Two Nations: The Private Life of a Columbia Student* (1931). The only child of a dressmaker and an educated and wealthy man who soon dilapidates his fortune, Labarthe becomes a pro-American Puerto Rican who advocates the annexation of the island to the United States. Following many hardships after his arrival in New York in 1924 (only a few years after Vega and Colon), Labarthe succeeds in entering Columbia University on a scholarship, where he obtains a degree that allows him to ultimately dedicate himself to teaching. If the narratives by Vega and Colon are read like memoirs, Labarthe's book is clearly an autobiography that stresses his *petite histoire* and his own ability to rise above penury in pursuit of the American dream.

The topic of **race** addressed by Colon informs **Piri Thomas**'s autobiographical novel ***Down These Mean Streets*** (1967), a classic in Puerto Rican literature and the most accomplished work within a subgenre that brings ghetto life to the fore in the tradition of Malcolm X's autobiography. The main character in *Down These*

Mean Streets, a second-generation *mestizo* Puerto Rican, agonizes over the binary racial context predominant in the United States, which precludes his mixed racial heritage. Dehumanizing social conditions in the New York urban *barrio* drive the protagonist into confrontation with the law, and into jail. Thomas's other books, *Savior, Savior, Hold My Hand* (1972) and *Seven Long Times* (1974) describe, respectively, his rehabilitation, religious conversion, commitment to social work, and experiences in jail. All three fall under the genre of autobiographical novels.

Although the above narratives stressed a male point of view that left little room for women's perspectives, the last two decades of the 20th century saw a blossoming of autobiographical accounts authored by female writers that placed women in center stage, always in relation to their surroundings. The first, Nicholasa Mohr, won acclaim with novellas and short stories of growing up in the Puerto Rican *barrio* of East Harlem, all with female characters that face up to adversity and come out strengthened by the experience. Instead of delving in the violent, drug-ridden culture found in sectors of inner cities, Mohr chooses to underscore the resilience of the average barrio family in the face of discrimination. Partly autobiographical, *Nilda* (1973) and *Felita* (1979) are two of Mohr's popular novellas that fit this description, displaying a female perspective that was lacking in the literature written by Puerto Ricans. Mohr's feminist concerns, which are evident in the collection of short stories *Rituals of Survival: A Woman's Portfolio* (1985) and other books, are also reflected in *Growing Up Inside the Sanctuary of My Imagination* (1994), an autobiography proper, where the narrator's creative skills are the tools employed to escape prescribed gender roles within Hispanic patriarchal society. Like Thomas's work, and the **Nuyorican** poetry of the 1970s, Mohr's narratives signal the coming of age of a Puerto Rican literature grounded in the streets of New York.

Survival, a recurrent theme in Puerto Rican literature, is thoughtfully approached in *Getting Home Alive* (1986), a hybrid book of prose and poetry, the outcome of a collaboration between a mother, Rosario Morales, and her daughter, Aurora Levins Morales, both creative writers. Their joint story crisscrosses not only generations, but also languages and religions. Rosario was born in New York shortly after her parents migrated from Puerto Rico in 1929, and years later, after marrying a Jewish man of Russian ancestry, made the return trip to the island, where she gave birth to Aurora. Afterward, the family moved to Chicago. Although at times the family struggled economically, both women consider themselves relatively privileged; therefore, the survival skills they hone are aimed at a larger world in which social inequality, police brutality, profit-driven multinationals, and abuse against women proliferate, making it difficult to get "home alive." Although they denounce the current state of affairs, they also celebrate their mixed racial and ethnic heritage and the multiple identities that result from that mix. One of the collection's most disseminated pieces is the "Ending Poem" in which the alternating, bilingual voices of both women reconstruct their genealogies and recognize their diasporic condition as well as their "wholeness." Ironically, only by acknowledging their multiple racial and ethnic make-up—and by remaining committed to the struggle for a better future—do they make it "home" alive.

The topic of **identity** is also crucial to **Judith Ortiz Cofer**, an award-winning poet, essayist, and fiction writer, the author of *Silent Dancing: A Partial Remembrance of a Puerto Rican Childhood* (1990). Highly skeptical of the act of remembering, the autobiographical prose and poetry of *Silent Dancing* capture discrete, defining moments in the narrator's journey toward self-discovery. Cofer was born in the town of Hormigueros, Puerto Rico, and moved to Paterson, New Jersey, in 1955. Her move was far from permanent, however, as every time her father, a U.S. Navy officer, was on duty, she, her mother, and her brother went back to the island to her grandmother's home, where several of the stories in *Silent Dancing* are set. There, while listening to the stories from the Puerto Rican oral tradition told by women relatives, the narrator begins to construct her gender and ethnic subjectivity. Accustomed to the back and forth movement of transnational migrants, neither of these identities comes across as one-dimensional. Rather, they are the outcome of a negotiation between the identity models provided by her ancestors and others learned through the English language. Cofer embraces a self-image that suits her bicultural reality; it includes a Puerto Rican **identity** that implicitly transgresses national borders and official languages. Currently Franklin Professor of English at the University of Georgia, Cofer is a prolific writer, with books such as the much-praised *The Line of the Sun* (1989) and *The Latin Deli* (1993) to her credit.

Also engaged in cultural negotiations, Esmeralda Santiago looks back down memory lane in *When I Was Puerto Rican* (1993) to offer a gendered narrative of growing up in a town near Bayamón, in the Puerto Rican countryside, and the city of Santurce. Santiago, who went on to migrate to the United States, graduating from the Performing Arts High School in New York and later Harvard University, endows her persona with an inquisitive character, one that with time leads her to question the double standard for men and women inherent in patriarchal society. The oldest daughter in a family of six children, the narrator suffers the tension and bickering between her parents due to her father's adulterous and complacent conduct. His unfaithfulness, along with his lack of ambition, prompts the mother to enter the labor market and, later, opt for migration. Only the last fifth of the book is set in Brooklyn, where the children attend public schools. The book was quickly translated into vernacular Spanish by the author herself and published in 1994. Although the use of the past tense in the title would seem to imply a conversion narrative, in the prologue to the Spanish edition Santiago portrays herself as a hybrid Puerto Rican writer who embraces both the *jíbaro* (hillbilly) tradition and American culture. In *Almost a Woman* (1998), a sequel, Santiago focuses on her sexual awakening as she grows into a young adult who establishes some distance from her indigenous culture as well as family values and traditions. The book highlights the tense relationship between mother and daughter as much as between native and adopted cultures.

Whether emphasizing the individual or the community, the autobiographical genre has served Puerto Ricans to negotiate between their two cultural worlds and expose the marginalized and "other" space from which they write due to nationality, **ethnicity**, **race**, class, or gender. Their self-referential narratives reveal commonalities across ethnic experiences as well as uniqueness, one largely derived from their neocolonial condition. (*See also* Bilingualism)

Further Reading

Aparicio, Frances R. "From Ethnicity to Multiculturalism: An Historical Overview of Puerto Rican Literature in the United States." In *Handbook of Hispanic Cultures in the United States: Literature and Art*, edited by Francisco Lomelí, 19–39. Houston: Arte Público Press, 1993.

Flores, Juan. *Divided Borders: Essays on Puerto Rican Identity*. Houston: Arte Público Press, 1993.

Hernández, Carmen Dolores. *Puerto Rican Voices in English. Interviews with Writers*. Westport, CT: Praeger, 1997.

López, Iraida H. *La Autobiografía Hispana Contemporánea en los Estados Unidos. A Través del Caleidoscopio*. Lewiston, NY: Mellen Press, 2001.

Mohr, Eugene V. *The Nuyorican Experience. Literature of the Puerto Rican Minority*. Westport, CT: Greenwood Press, 1982.

Torres-Padilla, Jose, et al. *Writing Off of the Hyphen: New Critical Perspectives on the Literature of the Puerto Rican Diaspora*. Seattle: University of Washington Press, 2008.

Iraida H. López

PUERTO RICAN AMERICAN DRAMA

When the United States annexed Puerto Rico, today officially known as the Commonwealth of Puerto Rico, in 1898 after the Spanish American War, it found its new charge to be a poverty-stricken island of coffee and sugarcane farmers. Today, Puerto Rico is primarily an urban society relying on industry and tourism as its major sources of means. Spanish, U.S., and Afro-Caribbean cultures have mixed together on the island to form a dynamic, specifically Puerto Rican culture. Spanish explorers established San Juan in the early 16th century and maintained control of the island until the end of the 19th century. Although Spanish is still the predominant language of Puerto Rico, English is spoken by many Puerto Ricans, and both languages have intermingled to form a uniquely Puerto Rican patois. Puerto Rico has several museums, libraries, and other cultural centers, including the Luis A. Ferré Fine Arts Center, a theater for drama and for musical events, in the capital city of San Juan. Puerto Rico has produced many playwrights, including the world famous and influential René Marqués, and many noted stage and film actors, including José Ferrer, Rita Moreno, Raul Julia, and Benicio Del Toro.

Since 1898, many Puerto Ricans have immigrated to the United States, though improved living conditions on the island had induced a small return to Puerto Rico by the end of the 20th century. Many have remained in the United States, however, with the number of Puerto Ricans living in the United States rising from about 70,000 in 1940 to more than 3,000,000 at the end of the 20th century, mostly in New York, though the population has recently shifted somewhat to other areas of the country.

During the great migration of Puerto Ricans to the United States, especially to New York City in the 1940s and 1950s, Puerto Rican drama began to flourish in New York's theater scene, eventually supplanting Spanish theater as the dominant form of Hispanic theater in the United States. Hispanic theater in its various forms represents several nationalities and continues to thrive in New York and in other major American cultural centers, with Puerto Rican artists continuing to make great contributions to American and world theater.

Puerto Rican American drama has often proved difficult to categorize. Puerto Ricans are American citizens whose culture is primarily Spanish in origin. However, Puerto Rican American drama is rarely anthologized in collections of American plays. Rather, Puerto Rican American plays are generally lumped with Mexican American, Caribbean American, Spanish American, and other ethnic groups of plays into a generic category called "Hispanic." Puerto Rican American drama reflects this confusion, dealing with themes of the Puerto Rican islander's longing for a "better life" in the States balanced against themes of the Puerto Rican immigrant in the States struggling to hold on to the family and Catholic values of home. At the same time, Puerto Rican American drama examines **racism**, sexism, and other forms of prejudice that Puerto Rican Americans experience in the United States.

Puerto Rican theater flourished on the island in the 1940s after the founding in 1938 of the Areyto Group by Emilio S. Belaval. The Areyto Group explored Puerto Rican history, delving into issues of slavery and encroaching modernization. The group also created plays centering around Puerto Rico's national folk hero, the jíbaro. A farmer of modest means, the jíbaro began appearing in Puerto Rican literature in the mid-19th century and remained popular well into the 20th century as a symbol of the land and the spirit of Puerto Rico, a spirit often difficult to maintain during the rapidly changing 20th century.

Puerto Rican dramatist Rene Marqués was studying playwriting in New York on a Rockefeller grant in 1940 when he began to develop a keen awareness of the Puerto Rican experience in the United States. Upon returning to San Juan, he wrote *La Carreta* (1953), a play about a rural Puerto Rican family that moves to San Juan and then to New York City in search of better living conditions. The family's journey is filled with pain and loss as it is crushed beneath an unrealizable American dream that is not meant for them. Although Marqués wrote the play in Puerto Rico, its world premiere was a Spanish-language production directed by Roberto Rodríguez Suárez in New York. It ran in an English-language production titled *The Oxcart* Off Broadway in 1966 starring Raul Julia and directed by Lloyd Richards, now known for his work with **August Wilson**. The original 1953 production is generally credited with birthing the Puerto Rican theater movement in New York. Suárez, himself a native Puerto Rican, moved to New York after matriculating at the University of Puerto Rico and established himself as an important catalyst in the growth of Puerto Rican American theater. His play *The Betrothal* (1958) captures the uncertainty of the transition of Puerto Rico from an agrarian colony to an industrial U.S. territory. Cultures and generations clash before a tapestry of religion, family, and the growing pains of modernization.

In 1954, Suárez and a group of colleagues founded the Nuevo Círculo Dramático, the first permanent Hispanic theater in New York. For five years the theater functioned as a theater school as well as a performance space. Soon other Hispanic theaters began to open and, in some cases, to flourish in New York City. Puerto Rican actress Miriam Colón, who had appeared in the 1966 production of *The Oxcart*, founded the Puerto Rican Traveling Theatre (PRTT) in 1967. Traveling the boroughs of New York City, PRTT performed in English and in Spanish. The group continues to operate, training new theater artists as it maintains its touring companies, and has had many popular successes, including Edward Gallardo's *Simpson Street* (1979), which spoke to a generation of Puerto Rican Americans who had been born in the States and thus had no memories of Puerto Rico but still felt bound together as a community because of their Puerto Rican heritage. *Simpson Street* explores the dynamics between this new generation of Puerto Rican American and their forebears as well as exploring the Puerto Rican American woman experiencing the effects of the U.S. women's liberation movement while combating the culturally instilled machismo of the Puerto Rican male.

Other Puerto Rican theaters to come along in the wake of the success of PRTT include the South Bronx's history-exploring Pregones Touring Puerto Rican Theatre Collection, the ensemble-oriented Shaman Theater Repertory Company, and Manhattan's radical **Nuyorican** Poets' Café. These theaters reach out to a traditionally disenfranchised audience that feels it has nothing in common with the mainstream face of contemporary Broadway and Off Broadway theaters. All of these theaters have been profoundly informed by the experimental New York theater of the 1960s: the theater of La Mama, the Group Theatre, and other companies radical in approach to performing techniques and subject matter.

Miguel Algarín founded the Nuyorican Poets' Café in 1973 in order to provide a home in which creative artists, particularly of the underclass, could congregate and exchange creative energy and ideas. One of the café's earliest participants was **Miguel Piñero**, whose influential prison drama *Short Eyes* (1973) was then playing at Joseph Papp's Public Theater in New York. *Short Eyes* was an enormous critical and popular success and, though not a Poets' Café production, brought attention to the café because of Piñero's involvement with the company. The Poets' Café's mission has always seemed to bolster the disenfranchised "Other" at odds with the hegemony, whether because of race or class. It has constantly endeavored to create a theater that reflects the truth of the gritty life of the streets, and Piñero and Algarín often roamed the streets of New York in the early days of the 1970s, recruiting prostitutes, junkies, and other street people as actors for the company. Originally setting out to attract a working-class audience, the Nuyorican Poets' Café did not take long to begin attracting a diverse audience made up from many social classes as word of its unique setting and mission spread. Patrons could sit and order a few beers while watching a play or poetry reading. Not restricted to works by Puerto Rican American playwrights, the café has fostered works by playwrights as diverse as Amiri Baraka and Ntozake Shange. William Burroughs dropped in frequently during the 1970s to read new work aloud. As the Nuyorican Poets Café proceeds

Miguel Pinero, circa 1977. (Michael Ochs Archives/Getty Images)

into the 21st century, it has become famous for its Poetry Slam competitions and forays into hip-hop theater.

Puerto Rican American playwrights born in the United States have dealt in recent decades with many of the same cultural **identity** conflicts that Puerto Rican–born playwrights dealt with in the 1950s and 1960s, though strategies and techniques have changed. Oscar A. Colón's *Siempre en Mi Corazón* (1986) explores issues of identity as its main character returns home to Puerto Rico after having left 20 years earlier to marry and live in the States. Carmen Rivera's *Julia* (1992) deals with issues of gender, education, and the transition from being an islander to a New Yorker. Edward Iván López, though born in Puerto Rico, was raised in New York. His *Spanish Eyes* (1982) explores issues of cultural identity through the framework of an intercultural marriage.

Perhaps the most successful Puerto Rican American playwright thus far is José Rivera, author of the popular *Marisol* (1992), *Cloud Tectonics* (1995), *References to Salvador Dalí Make Me Hot* (2000), and *Sueño* (1998), a freewheeling adaptation of Pedro Calderón de la Barca's Spanish Golden Age classic play *Life is a Dream* (1636). Rivera was born in Puerto Rico but raised on Long Island, where he saw his father work as many as three jobs at any one time to support his family. Rivera's work has been criticized by some for "not being Hispanic enough" and by others for being "too Hispanic." Full of excess and fantasy, Rivera's plays are often classified as "magic realism," and he does count Gabriel García Márquez as an influence. His plays negotiate the space between the real and the fantastic, as in *Marisol's* exploration of a postapocalyptic New York. Ruptured violently, society must begin anew as the old order falls. Populated with angels and idiots, the play explores issues of gender and religion against a backdrop of dreams and nightmares. It has proven popular among regional theater groups since it premiered at the Actors Theatre of Louisville in 1992 and won the 1993 Obie Award for Outstanding Play.

Rivera claims to come from a family of storytellers, which he cites as an intrinsic part of being Puerto Rican. His family's stories, he says, blur the lines between fantasy and reality, and this trait is evident in his own playwriting. Rivera's plays have been produced all over the country at such prestigious theaters as the Public Theater/New York Shakespeare Festival, which sponsors the annual Festival Latino; Playwrights Horizons; and the Mark Taper Forum. He has received Fulbright, National Endowment for the Arts, Rockefeller, and Whiting Foundation grants. Rivera makes his home in Los Angeles.

Further Reading

Algarín, Miguel, and Lois Griffith. *Action: The Nuyorican Poets Café Theater Festival*. New York: Touchstone, 1997.

Antush, John V., ed. *Nuestro New York: An Anthology of Puerto Rican Plays*. New York: Mentor, 1994.

Antush, John V., ed. *Recent Puerto Rican Theater: Five Plays from New York*. Houston: Arte Público Press, 1991.

Gallardo, Edward. *Simpson Street and Other Plays*. Houston: Arte Público Press, 1990.

Rivera, José. *Marisol and Other Plays*. New York: Theatre Communications Group, 1997.

Rivera, José. *References to Salvador Dalí Make Me Hot and Other Plays*. New York: Theatre Communications Group, 2003.

Torres-Padilla, Jose, et al. *Writing Off of the Hyphen: New Critical Perspectives on the Literature of the Puerto Rican Diaspora*. Seattle: University of Washington Press, 2008.

Jeffrey Godsey

PUERTO RICAN AMERICAN GAY LITERATURE

Puerto Rican literature has traditionally focused on themes that deal with various forms of **identity** (ethnic, cultural, national, or political). Contemporary literature not only continues to focus on the political status of the island, but also touches on family, tradition, culture, and gender relations. Diasporan writers also discuss topics of political importance and issues pertaining to their identity as either Puerto Ricans in the United States, as Nuyoricans or Neo-Ricans (Puerto Ricans in the United States who do not reside in New York).

However, the literature available from writers on and off the island rarely deals with sexuality as it pertains to same-sex relationships. Although there have been exceptions within the last decade, such as Angel Lozada's *La Patografía* (1998) and *Las Siete Palabras* (1999), and Mayra Santos-Febres's *Sirena Selena Vestida de Pena* (2000), not much is available in reference to gay Puerto Rican men. What literature there is on sexuality focuses on the male/female dichotomy that exist in Puerto Rican society, connected to *machismo* and *marianismo*—ideals that each man and woman must adhere to in order to be accepted by society. According to Puerto Rican anthropologist Rafael L. Ramírez, *machismo* is "invariably defined as a set of attitudes, behaviors, and practices that characterize men" (11). Puerto Ricans have often adopted a homogenous conformity, and as a result those who have left the island have brought into the diasporic communities values that continue to encourage individuals to conform to specific behavioral patterns based on their gender. Among U.S. Puerto Ricans most affected by these notions are Puerto Rican gay males, who are often perceived as anomalies to Puerto Rican masculinity and manhood.

The gender-stratified expectations of Puerto Rican society continue to inform the behavior of many, even second-generation Puerto Ricans living in the United States. As Ramírez states, "The masculine ideology, because it is a social construction that favors the masculine and belittles the feminine, places us men in a universe of categories and symbols of power that we reproduce daily. This ideology forms and guides us in our behavior as men" (15–16). However, what happens when gay Puerto Ricans do not conform to mainstream society's expectations? What happens when they refuse to accept that they must behave according to prescribed notions of proper male conduct?

Puerto Rican men find that they must reinforce the belief that the role of the "macho" or "real" man is to conquer, possess, and dominate. As a result, mainstream society on and off the island has marginalized the unique element that homosexuality adds to the diasporan experience. For the U.S. Puerto Rican gay man, the task of being able to identify himself is a challenging one as he is forced or expected to conform to both North American as well as Puerto Rican ideologies of masculinity devoid of a homosexual identity, and conform to a homogenous homosexual identity in the United States that ignores ethnic differences.

Added to these pressures is the fact that, according to David Román, both Catholicism and machismo have "combined to undervalue—if not foreclose—a 'Latino' gay identity." For this reason, some of the literature by U.S. Puerto Rican gay writers presents an internalized *machista* attitude as seen in the ways that gay men relate to each other. Some scholars such as Donald Hall would argue that this is so because there is an expectation that even homosexual relationships must reflect the ways individuals in mainstream society relate to each other: There must be a "man" and a "woman" in every relationship. This parallels Román's statement with regards to gay Latinos—machismo has played an integral role in the ways U.S. Puerto Rican gays label themselves and affects whether they identify themselves as gay or not.

However, some contemporary U.S. Puerto Rican gay writers have opted to confront the pressures imposed by the mainstream societies they are a part of in order to appropriate a sense of self that is devoid of any classification other than the one they choose. As Larry La Fountain-Stokes writes, there is a "critical mass of openly self-identified queer cultural producers" that defies any imposition pertaining to an ethno-sexual identity; the choice is up to the individual. Among these contemporary "producers" who seek to (re)present a reality often ignored by scholars who speak and write of the diasporan experience are writers, poets, and playwrights like

Larry La Fountain-Stokes, Roberto Vázquez-Pacheco, Arturo Sandoval, Emanuel Xavier, Angel Lozada, Moisés Agosto-Rosario, Rane Arroyo, Guillermo Román, Edgardo Alvarado-Vázquez, Elliot Torres, and Aldo Alvarez, whose work not only embraces their characters' and their own sexualities, but mutually acknowledges an ethnic identity that U.S. mainstream gay communities force them to deny in order to belong. Embracing their ethnic identity in the United States comes in many forms: Some writers protest mainstream society's images and biases about Puerto Ricans in general, while others explore relationships that ignore any form of categorization and focus on male/male sexual relationships as well as on the characters' relationships with their family members. They demystify stereotypes that exist with regards to the ways that U.S. Puerto Rican gays relate to their own culture and to mainstream society. Their work often focuses on "family . . . identity and its ramifications within two distinct cultures, the attempts to assimilate into U.S. gay culture . . . the efforts to cultivate a [Puerto Rican] gay culture in the United States" (Román). It presents experiences centered on an ethno-sexual identity. Their writing (re)presents an attempt at incorporating themselves within the fixed definition of what it means to be a Puerto Rican man, both in the United States and Puerto Rico, and share their own diasporic experiences. At the same time they attempt to break with the imposed masculine man/feminine woman dichotomy, rejecting conformity and defining for themselves their *puertorriqueñidad* (Puertoricanness), or what it means to be Puerto Rican.

These queer cultural producers differ in experiences and artistic style. However, an attribute that their writing shares in common is an autobiographical approach, a counterattack against heteropatriarchal norms that force U.S. Puerto Rican gay men to conform to the ideals of the society they live in, and at the same time embrace the values imposed by the ethnic culture they are a part of. Thus, the process of constructing an identity within the diasporan communities can be considered a deconstruction of fixed characteristics that marginalize them because they do not conform to accepted notions of Puerto Rican masculinity.

For instance, Robert Vázquez-Pacheco's "Brujo Time" focuses not only on his character's sexuality, but also on reconciling with his Puerto Rican heritage, which his family members denied him because they wanted him to succeed and attain the American dream. Like Vázquez-Pacheco's character, La Fountain-Stokes's autobiographical voice in "My Name, Multitudinous Mass" embraces not only his sexuality but even alludes to a more universal Latin American/Latino gay identity, specifically within the confines of a culture that believes homosexual behavior to be non-Puerto Rican/un-American.

Emanuel Xavier's "Banjee Hustler," an excerpt from his 1999 novel *Christ Like*, looks at gay Puerto Rican/Latino life in New York City, focusing on the realities that many Latino gay men face when they are not accepted by their families and must learn to survive by any means necessary. Xavier, primarily a poet, embraces his ethnic roots as seen in his poem such as "Americano" and "Burning Down the House."

Rane Arroyo in *The Singing Shark* (1996) and *Home Movies of Narcissus* (2002) also addresses ethnic and sexual identities. For example, in his poem "The Singing Shark Dream, or Toto, I Don't Think We're in Tegucigalpa Anymore," he makes references to being the son of "Tony and María," protagonists of *West Side Story*. Both a memorial and protest, this poem explores the images and biases mainstream society has about Puerto Ricans in the United States, and it also touches on the influence these images have on the way society in general view ethnic groups, and the behavioral expectations for Puerto Ricans in general.

Five Years of Solitary (2002) by Elliot Torres is a series of poems, like Xavier's *Americano* (2002), that explore the individual life of a Puerto Rican gay man and his perspective not only on his ethnicity and sexual identity, but also on his particular perspective of the world around him. *Undaunted: A Poetic Journey* (2004) picks up where his first volume leaves off in a continuing exploration of life as a gay Puerto Rican in the United States, affirming an identity that the individual is supposed to deny because it is considered "un-Puerto Rican."

The emerging Puerto Rican gay writing in the United States continues to explore the intersections of ethnicity and sexuality. Speaking from the ethnic and sexual margins of American society, the writers continue to make a radical a revolutionary attempt at interpolating themselves within the diasporan Puerto Rican community that has not embraced them because of who and what they are and the Anglo society that continues to perceive them as outsiders.

Further Reading

Acosta-Belén, Edna. "Beyond Island Boundaries: Ethnicity, Gender, and Cultural Revitalization in Nuyorican Literature." *Callaloo* 15.4 (Autumn 1992): 979–98.

Alvarez, Aldo. Blithe House Quarterly: A Site for Gay Short Fiction. www.blithe.com /bhq7.1/index.html [Winter 2003—The Puerto Rican Issue].

Cruz-Malavé, Arnaldo, and Martin F. Manalansan IV, eds. *Queer Globalizations: Citizenship and the Afterlife of Colonialism*. New York: New York University Press, 2002.

Manrique, Jaime with Jesse Dorris, eds. *Bésame Mucho: New Gay Latino Fiction*. New York: Painted Leaf Press, 1999.

Ramírez, Rafael L. *What It Means to be a Man: Reflections on Puerto Rican Masculinity*. Trans. by Rosa E. Casper. New Brunswick, NJ: Rutgers University Press, 1999.

Román, David. "Latino Literature." In *GLBTQ: An Encyclopedia of Gay, Lesbian, Bisexual, Transgender and Queer Culture*. www.glbtq.com/literature/latino_lit.html.

Enrique Morales-Diaz

PUERTO RICAN AMERICAN LESBIAN LITERATURE

Like other Latina writers, Boricua (the indigenous term for Puerto Rican) lesbian writers confront the complexities of **race**, **ethnicity**, and class within a dual cultural **identity** defined between the homeland of Puerto Rico and the mainland of the United States. The duality of two cultures, exemplified in the nation's two names (the colonial one of "Puerto Rico"—meaning "rich port"—and its indigenous Taíno one of Borinquen) is an ever-present theme in Puerto Rican literary production in general. For many lesbian writers, the notion of exile becomes a metaphor for the double and triple diaspora that they experience as both migrants between two geographic spaces and as marginalized voices within two heterosexually dominant patriarchal worlds. They must work through both a sense of urgency to address sociopolitical issues such as independence and colonization yet also are compelled to speak to the double silence surrounding women's voices generally and lesbian voices in particular. Given these personal and political exigencies, contemporary Puerto Rican lesbian texts represent the self, family, friends, and the larger world through a lens of social critique and rebellion that often defies traditional literary genres and language boundaries. Both defined and not defined by borders, Puerto Rican lesbian writing is fluid and multifaceted reflecting the many levels of self to be negotiated in the creative process.

As part of Latino/a cultural production, Boricua lesbian writing is necessarily bilingual: Texts may be exclusively in Spanish or in English, or may move between the two languages in a creative play of difference and invention. The bilingual nature of many of these texts not only structurally sets the reader up for accepting difference, but also provides an innovative avenue of resistance to cultural **assimilation**. As linguistic alienation and isolation give way to linguistic liberation, so too does lesbian existence gain a space for authentic expression through that language play. Contemporary self-identified Puerto Rican lesbian writers not only connect sexual and sociocultural identities through multiple languages, but also by blurring the lines around their literary production as essayists, short-story writers, playwrights, spoken word artists, and poets, and their work as sociopolitical activists and intellectuals. Given their immediacy and accessibility, the cultural production of contemporary Puerto Rican lesbians is most prominent in these areas of artistic and social expression.

Juanita Díaz-Cotto's 1987 anthology *Compañeras: Latina Lesbians* (published under the pseudonym Juanita Ramos) is a vital contribution to lesbian writing and is illustrative of the diversity of creative identities among the *puertorriqueñas* represented there: Rota Silverstrini is a poet, editor, and writer; Brunilda Vega, poet and social worker; Cenen, an African Boricua short-story writer and poet, to name only a few.

As with other rights movements that gained ground from the civil and social transformations of the late 20th century, the 1970s and 1980s marked the moment when self-identified Boricua lesbians began to produce and publish works that reached a wider audience. Rather than give up multiple identities of color, *raza* (race), African roots, and the diasporic condition, these writers sought to articulate and explore those differences. Nemir Matos Cintrón's *Las Mujeres no Hablan Así* and *Proemas para Despabilar Cándidos* and Luz María Umpierre's texts such as *The Margarita Poems* and *For Christine: Poems and One Letter* are late-20th-century poetic contributions that challenge the tradition of censure and prejudice that women loving women experience. Although Matos Cintrón utilizes a direct vocabulary that relies on metaphors of nature to create a highly eroticized poetry, Umpierre's work largely connects sexuality and issues of personal oppression to **racism** and colonialism. Both poets necessarily challenge and transgress phallocentric discourse by naming the unnamable. Umpierre in particular has been the subject of much critical inquiry, especially because her work's form and content was one of the first to militantly defy boundaries of language and ritual. Boricua poet and photographer Samantha Martínez, who primarily publishes in online venues, echoes this need to write for sanity and for her survival.

More recently, Aixa Ardín's sensual and political collection of poetry, *Batiborrillo* (meaning "Hotchpotch"), continues the themes expressed by her precursors in a poetry marked by rebellion and open expression of lesbian desire. Like many Puerto Rican writers, Ardín relies on references and vocabularies specific to island culture to bring her underground poetry to the surface. In the first poem of the collection, "Poesía para Mayra Montero," Ardín playfully calls herself a *plátano*—but one that cannot be used for traditional dishes. In "Pa-ul" the great island rainforest of El Yunque provides a metaphor of healing for one who dies of AIDS. As is the case with many Latina writers, Ardín plays on the gendered nature of Spanish grammar, anthropomorphizing words like "la imaginación" into a girlfriend, a best friend. Informed by lesbian sexuality and also by a rejection of colonization, these poems are out and proud, and are representative of both the rage and celebration found in writings by women-identified women.

Family is central to Latino culture and thus is an important theme in Puerto Rican lesbian writing. Radical lesbian feminist and Puerto Rican poet Teresita Bosch explains how familial estrangement is overcome by identifying and working through common spaces of oppression: in her work, coming out as a lesbian is paralleled to the repression of language that her mother experiences as the price to be paid for striving toward a middle-class lifestyle within an Anglo culture that demands assimilation of difference.

Since the publication of Ramos's anthology, online journals and websites such as *Conmoción* (which published between 1995 and 1996) have begun to provide forums for Latina lesbian writing. Yet the most visible and current cultural production has been in terms of theater and spoken work, especially within the **Nuyorican** context. Among the most notable figures here are Bronx-born Puerto Rican lesbian writer, actor, and producer Janis Astor del Valle who founded Sisters on Stage, and Brenda Cotto who, with Noelia Ortiz, wrote the wholly woman identified 1996 play *Motherlands*, which also explores the complexities of mother–lesbian daughter relationships.

In all its varied forms, Puerto Rican lesbian cultural production is intricately tied to the larger reclamation and insertion of the feminine within Boricua culture and heritage. (*See also* Bilingualism)

Further Reading
Blasius, Mark. *Sexual Identities, Queer Politics*. Princeton, NJ: Princeton University Press, 2001.

Chanady, Amaryll, ed. *Latin American Identity and the Construction of Difference*. Minneapolis: University of Minnesota Press, 1994.

Chávez-Silverman, Susana, and Librada Hernández, eds. *Reading and Writing the Ambiente: Queer Sexualities in Latino, Latin American, and Spanish Culture*. Madison: University of Wisconsin Press, 2000.

Cruz-Malavé, Arnaldo, and Martin F. Manalansan IV, eds. *Queer Globalizations: Citizenship and the Afterlife of Colonialism*. New York: New York University Press, 2002.

Dolores Costa, Marìa. *Latina Lesbian Writers and Artists*. New York: Harrington Press, 2003.

Gómez, Alma, Cherríe Moraga, and Mariana Romo-Carmona, eds. *Cuentos: Stories by Latinas*. Brooklyn, NY: Kitchen Table Press, 1983.

Martínez, Elena. *Lesbian Voices from Latin America: Breaking Ground*. New York: Garland Publishing, 1996.

Ramos, Juanita. *Compañeras: Latina Lesbians*. New Cork: Routledge, 1994.

Rivera, Carmen. *Kissing the Mango Tree: Puerto Rican Women Rewriting American Literature*. Houston: Arte Público Press, 2002.

Romo-Carmona, Mariana. *Conversaciones: Relatos por padres y madres de hijas lesbianas y hijos gay*. San Francisco: Cleros Press, 2001.

Sánchez González, Lisa. *Boricua Literature: A Literary History of the Puerto Rican Diaspora*. New York: New York University Press, 2001.

Torres, Lourdes, Inmaculada Pertusa. *Tortilleras: Hispanic and U.S. Latina Lesbian Expression*. Philadelphia: Temple University Press, 2001.

Colleen Kattau

PUERTO RICAN AMERICAN NOVEL

The first major wave of Puerto Ricans settled in New York in what would come to be known as Spanish Harlem, the Bronx (El Barrio), and the Lower East Side (Losaida) between the American Civil War and the World War I. Published novelists of this generation were few and they often wrote in Spanish. A few, however, including William Carlos Williams, published novels in English. Williams represents his generation's critique of the American dream and his advocacy of a progressive, even radical, politics of social and institutional reform. Like many of his contemporaries as well as his successors, Williams was an activist as well as a novelist, offering free care to low-income patients in his medical practice. However, another early Puerto Rican American novel, Pedro Juan Labarthe's *The Son of Two Nations* (1931), tells a largely **assimilation**ist story where Pedro, a Puerto Rican boy, embraces the American dream and through education and hard work becomes more American than Puerto Rican. *The Son of Two Nations* resembles classic immigrant novels of the early 20th century more than it does later Puerto Rican American novels. In 1917, the Jones Act granted citizenship to Puerto Ricans just as the second generation of Puerto Rican Americans, and the firstborn in the United States, came into the world. This is the generation that launched Puerto Rican American literature as we know it. In addition to the novel, throughout its history much Puerto Rican American literature takes the form of the short story, picking up perhaps on the popularity of this genre in Latin American letters. Poetry has also been important in Puerto Rican American letters with such figures as **Tato Laviera** and more recently the **Nuyorican** Poets' Café. Many Puerto Rican American novelists also write short stories and poetry. The second generation of Puerto Rican American writers saw the Puerto Rican community in New York grow to over

50,000 people. They were active in the Young Lords party and advanced their radical civil rights program; all were concerned with delineating a Puerto Rican American **identity** that belongs in America even as it resists either assimilation of second-class citizenship. They often call themselves Nuyorican, emphasizing their ties to New York but also asserting that they are not simply a hyphenated community, rather an organized part of an America whose only language is not English.

Piri Thomas's ***Down These Mean Streets*** (1967) launches the contemporary Puerto Rican American novel and still serves as the exemplary Puerto Rican American text. In *Down These Mean Streets*, we find many characteristics that continue to define the Puerto Rican American novel: a form of the coming-of-age novel, a blending of Spanish and English, a focus on the place of El Barrio, and an exploration of Puerto Rican Americans as an American ethnic group negotiating a complex set of questions about **race**, culture, language, place, gender, sexuality, and class. Piri narrates *Down These Mean Streets*, recounting his early childhood in Spanish Harlem, his encounter with racism in other parts of Harlem, and the necessary turn to violence for survival. Even as he tries to understand his relationship to black American, Puerto Rican, and poor Anglo-American communities, Piri becomes increasingly caught up in a life of drugs and crime and eventually ends up in prison. Seven years in Sing Sing prison and Comstock correctional facility force him to reconsider whether violence is the best way to assert his manhood and whether gangs and drugs are viable means of survival.

At the same time as *Down These Mean Streets*, a number of similar novels appear. They share not only the themes but also many formal elements of *Down These Mean Streets*. At the same time, each novel offers a distinct perspective on *barrio* life. Manuel Manrique's *Island in Harlem* (1966) actually precedes *Down These Mean Streets* by a year to tell the story of Antonio. Antonio's life is much like Piri's, but Manrique offers a more complex consideration of young women than does Thomas. In *Down These Mean Streets*, girls serve as the vehicles through boys to express their masculinity. *Island in Harlem* portrays Margarita, the stereotypical virgin from Puerto Rico who saves Antonio at the risk of her own perdition. But *Island in Harlem* also presents another girl, Lilliam, who is neither the typical virgin nor the typical whore: She is a smart, savvy young woman aware of the sexual power plays that go on in the barrio, and she is able to enter into them as a player, not just an object. It will take years and the appearance of women writers for more nuanced portrayals of girls to appear in a Puerto Rican American novel. Other novels in the tradition of *Down These Mean Streets* include: Lefty Barreto's *Nobody's Hero* (1976), Edwin Torres's *Carlito's Way* (1979), Abraham Rodríguez Jr's *Spidertown* (1993), and Ernesto Quiñonez's *Bodega Dreams* (2000). One notable variation on *Down These Mean Streets* are the novels of Nick Cruz Humberto Cintrón where the trajectory of poverty, violence, and drugs leads not to redemption and the return of the prodigal son, but to his final departure from the barrio and from the community.

In the 1980s, a number of Puerto Rican American women writers question the paradigms of the Puerto Rican American novel set up by Thomas. Nicholasa Mohr, **Judith Ortiz Cofer**, and more recently Esmeralda Santiago write coming-of-

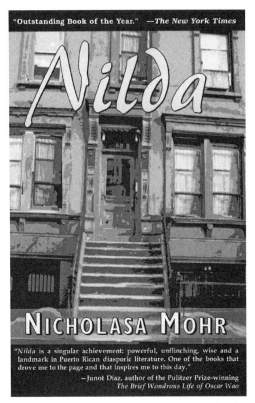

"Outstanding Book of the Year." —*The New York Times*

Nilda

NICHOLASA MOHR

"*Nilda* is a singular achievement: powerful, unflinching, wise and a landmark in Puerto Rican diasporic literature. One of the books that drove me to the page and that inspires me to this day."
—Junot Díaz, author of the Pulitzer Prize-winning *The Brief Wondrous Life of Oscar Wao*

The book cover for *Nilda*. (Reprinted with permission from the publisher, Arte Público Press—University of Houston)

age novels and employ a vernacular mix of Spanish and English, but theirs is a domestic rather than a street vernacular, and their community starts with the family rather than the gang or the block. These women describe the domestic life of Puerto Rican Americans, what happens inside the buildings that the boys are always leaving or entering only to be fed, comforted, or chastised by mothers, sisters, and girlfriends. Mohr, Cofer, and Santiago reveal the complex experience of Puerto Rican American girls who serve as linguistic and cultural translators for their families in welfare offices and schools, as well as in the arena of gender relations, negotiating the differences between the roles of girls and women in Puerto Rican and in American contexts.

Mohr's *Nilda* (1976) was the first novel written by a Puerto Rican American woman. Like Piri, Nilda grows up in Spanish Harlem in the 1940s. One of her brothers follows a path similar to Piri's, but Nilda remains closely tied to her mother, responsible for maintaining the home either by cooking and cleaning or by communicating with the Home Relief Office. Nilda negotiates her identity as a Puerto Rican American in a variety of interior spaces: homes, buildings, and institutions. Nilda struggles to make school a place where she can learn skills that will help her to survive in New York and to make New York more hospitable to Puerto Rican Americans.

Santiago's work covers many themes similar to Mohr's, although she writes of the experiences of later waves of Puerto Rican immigrants, of those of Mohr's generation and the next who were born in Puerto Rico and came to the United States as children. Santiago's novels, starting with *When I Was Puerto Rican* (1993), include much less of a mix of Spanish than do many other Puerto Rican American novels and are written in a much more "standard" English, but she also translates all of her own work into Spanish, suggesting that this literature is of interest not only to Puerto Rican Americans and to Americans, but also to Puerto Ricans on the island. Santiago's second novel, *América's Dream* (1996), makes an important move in its questioning of the ideal of Puerto Rico that stands as a sort of "Paradise Lost" in the background of so many Puerto Rican American novels.

The 21st century has already seen not only a new novel by Cofer, *The Meaning of Consuelo* (2003), but also the emergence of a new generation of Puerto Rican American authors who write about the changing faces and the enduring identity of Puerto Rican Americans. Ed Vega's *No Matter How Much You Cook or Pay the Rent You Blew It Cause Bill Bailey Aint Never Coming Home Again* (2003) is a novel of epic proportions following its female protagonist, Vidamía Farrell, as she negotiates not only her own mixed heritage (she is half Puerto Rican and half Irish) but also the increasingly mixed neighborhoods of New York.

The barrios of New York remain the place of the Puerto Rican America novel, its language remains a mixed Spanish and English vernacular, and its themes continue to turn on the understanding of hybrid identity in the context of poverty and discrimination, but now the Puerto Rican American novel has a wide and nuanced cast of characters: well-developed women and men who not only assert their identity but also explore its limits. (*See also* Bilingualism)

Further Reading

Flores, Juan. *From Bomba to Hip-Hop*. New York: Columbia University Press, 2000.
Luis, William. *Dance between Two Cultures*. Nashville: Vanderbilt University Press, 1997.
Mohr, Eugene V. *The Nuyorican Experience*. Westport, CT: Greenwood Press, 1982.
Sánchez-González, Lisa. *Boricua Literature*. New York: New York University Press, 2001.
Torres-Padilla, Jose, et al. *Writing Off of the Hyphen: New Critical Perspectives on the Literature of the Puerto Rican Diaspora*. Seattle: University of Washington Press, 2008.

Keja Lys Valens

PUERTO RICAN AMERICAN POETRY

Puerto Rican literature in all genres flourished in the United States throughout the 20th century. The political status of Puerto Rico as an Estado Libre Asociado (Associated Free State) of the United States complicates the easy classification of this corpus as ethnic "American" literature. Designations such as "mainland" and "continental" literature can be cumbersome, and "Puerto Rican American" is inappropriate. The social, historical, and cultural impact of the 1960s **Civil Rights Movement** brought the terms "Neorican" and "**Nuyorican**" into currency despite the island origin of "Nuyorican" as a derogatory term for Puerto Rican New Yorkers. "Boricua," which Lisa Sánchez-González defines as a "term of self-affirmation in the stateside community" (1), is another culturally appropriate designation (and broader than "Nuyorican"). These terms describe the Puerto Rican literature produced, primarily in English, as part of multiethnic American literature beginning in the late 1960s. Several periodicals are indispensable sources of Puerto Rican, Nuyorican, and Boricua creative writing, interviews, scholarly criticism, and literary essays over the years: the literary magazines *Revista Chicano-Riqueña* (1973–1985) and its continuation, *The Americas Review* (1986–1999); the scholarly journal *The Bilingual Review/La Revista Bilingüe* (founded in 1974); and the two-issue Chicago diaspora magazine *The Rican* (1971–1974). This body of literature also enjoys varying degrees of regional or national renown, significance, and distribution through the book publications of Bilingual Press/Editorial Bilingüe (established by the *Review* in 1976) and Arte Público Press (founded by Nicolás Kanellos in 1979), as well as the research and publishing activities of the Recovering the U.S. Hispanic Literary Heritage project (since 1992).

The Two Islands

In "La guagua aérea" (1983), a poetic essay about back-and-forth migration between Puerto Rico and New York, Luis Rafael Sánchez recounts an anecdote about a woman who identifies New York as her place of origin in Puerto Rico. This poignant and paradoxical truth underscores the role of place and **identity** in the Puerto Rican experience in the 20th century, and the rich motif of the two islands is a recurring image in the Nuyorican aesthetic. Alfredo Matilla and Iván Silén wrote in similar terms about the shared experience of Puerto Rican poets: "The poets became brothers crossing a bridge of airplanes that span language" (xviii). Several anthologies have highlighted the continuities and differences between the literatures of the two islands by bringing together writers from Puerto Rico and the mainland. The editors necessarily must consider place of residence, national identity, language choice, and aesthetic and literary affiliations, and consequently the introductions, biobibliographies, and other critical apparatus of these compilations provide invaluable secondary-source information. Matilla and Silén's *The Puerto Rican Poets/Los poetas puertorriqueños* (1972) was the first anthology of this type. The publication of this volume in a popular poetry series from Bantam Books alongside such significant (and now classic) anthologies as *The Black Poets* (1971; ed. Dudley Randall) and *The Voice That Is Great Within Us: American Poetry of the Twentieth Century* (1970; ed. Hayden Carruth) is evidence of the place of Puerto Rican poetry in the changing American literary canon of the early 1970s. María Teresa Babín and Stan Steiner's *Borinquen: An Anthology of Puerto Rican Literature* (1974), published by Knopf, also afforded the potential for mainstream attention during the crucial period of development of Puerto Rican literature in the United States. An important feature of *Borinquen* is its chronological and thematic breadth, which extends from the pre-Columbian oral tradition and early colonial historiography (Juan de Castellanos's 16th-century epic poem *Elegías de varones ilustres de Indias*) to psalms by a Lower East Side priest, David García, in the radical tradition of liberation theology. (Significantly, and an additional indication of the burgeoning Latino literary and cultural movements in the United States, Steiner also coedited, with the playwright **Luis Valdez**, a comparable early volume of Mexican and Chicano literature, *Aztlán: An Anthology of Mexican American Literature* [1972]). Julio Marzán's *Inventing a Word: An Anthology of Twentieth-Century Puerto Rican Poetry* (1980) gave much less room to Nuyorican poetry than did the previous anthologies, but nevertheless acknowledges the continuities between the two groups, particularly with respect to a shared tradition of social protest and colloquial expression, as exemplified by Pedro Pietri and Victor Hernández Cruz. Much more recently, Roberto Santiago has taken the same composite approach to

Puerto Rican literature in *Boricuas: Influential Puerto Rican Writers—An Anthology* (1995).

On the other hand, Miguel Algarín and **Miguel Piñero**'s now-**canon**ical *Nuyorican Poetry: An Anthology of Puerto Rican Words and Feelings* (1975) and Faythe Turner's comprehensive *Puerto Rican Writers at Home in the USA: An Anthology* (1991) cover only Nuyorican and Boricua literature. Algarín explains in the afterword that Nuyorican poets need to "[define] the qualities of the space in which [they] live" and so "locate their position on earth, the ground, the neighborhood, the environment" (181). Turner indicates the same notion with the geographical specification of "at home" in the expressive title of her anthology. From the 1970s forward, this space, position, or home is not the island, but New York and other places in the diaspora. Regardless of the relative merits of the chronological, geographic, thematic, or aesthetic scope or limitations of each of these anthologies published over a 20-year period (1972–1991), however, all are indispensable to a comprehensive understanding of the field of Puerto Rican poetry in the United States.

Nuyorican Poetry

The Nuyorican movement was firmly in place by the mid-1970s. In 1979, Soledad Santiago published "Notes on the Nuyoricans" in the *Village Voice*, New York's alternative weekly. These notes constitute a sweeping essay on the arts, culture, and institutions of the Nuyorican experience during a decade of vast changes in all sectors of U.S. society. The Nuyorican Poets' Café emerged as a literary and cultural arts venue on the Lower East Side in 1975, founded by poet Miguel Algarín, who with dramatist Miguel Piñero also compiled the anthology, *Nuyorican Poetry*, that introduced the poetry and poetics of this experience. Numerous New York organizations, institutions, and venues also supported the dissemination and promotion of Puerto Rican and Nuyorican literature and intellectual culture at the time, including the Association of Hispanic Arts (AHA), El Museo del Barrio, the New Rican Village Cultural and Educational Center, Repertorio Español, and Taller Boricua. The location of venues of this kind in neighborhoods such as El Barrio (also known as East Harlem or Spanish Harlem) and the Lower East Side (Loisada), bolstered in turn by the broader-reaching activities and missions of AHA and the Repertorio, granted important visibility for Nuyorican activities both within and outside of the community.

The best-known single-author book of the Nuyorican movement is *Puerto Rican Obituary* (1973) by the late Pedro Pietri (1944–2004), published by the radical Monthly Review Press. The 32 poems treat a variety of issues relating to the Puerto Rican experience in New York as seen through the eyes of a vociferous social critic: work, poverty, life in the housing projects, drug abuse, unemployment and underemployment, and the disintegration of Puerto Rican identity in the face of a hostile dominant culture. In extreme antiestablishment spirit (inherited in part from both Beat poetics of the 1950s and the social activism of the 1960s) Pietri parodies, satirizes, and blasphemes everything from mindless consumerism and authority figures to such mainstream texts as the Lord's Prayer and the Pledge of Allegiance. *Puerto Rican Obituary* includes poetry of contrasts. Puerto Rico and New York, Puerto Ricans and non-Puerto Ricans, Spanish and English, dark skin and light skin, death and life, the self and the other, rich and poor—all these oppositions come together to explore the loss of cultural identity of a group marginalized by social and political circumstances. Pietri's sharp wit and keen sense of social justice combine with a streetwise approach to poetry as oral performance to shape these differences into a multifaceted and conflicted vision of Puerto Rican reality in New York.

Irony, satire, comedy, and tragedy are the dominant modes in this self-proclaimed verse obituary, and Pietri employs both traditional and unconventional poetic and rhetorical techniques to lay bare this problem and the attendant wrath, hostility, and frustration. The hallmarks of his compositional style include intricate patterns of rhyme and repetition, the intercalation of written and oral found material, and a reliance on orality and Nuyorican speech patterns. Language—whether English or Spanish, broken or not—is also a theme in *Puerto Rican Obituary*. For instance, Juan, Miguel, Milagros, Olga, and Manuel—the generic Puerto Rican New Yorkers of the title poem, "Puerto Rican Obituary"—implausibly take lessons in broken English. Pietri revisits this ironic motif in "The Broken English Dream," which nominally underscores the linguistic ramifications of how the so-called American dream has eluded Puerto Ricans in the United States. Alfredo Matilla and Iván Silén used this same clever turn of phrase in the context of both islands: "Puerto Rican poetry of the 20th century, in Puerto Rico as well as New York . . . is a summons to awaken from this broken English dream and assume the Puerto Rican and Latin American essence that belongs to us" (xviii). The aptness of this concept to a socio-political critique notwithstanding, Miguel Algarín embraces the literary practice of code-switching in Nuyorican expression, as he explains in "Nuyorican Language," the introduction to *Nuyorican Poetry*, the anthology he edited with Piñero: "We come to the city as citizens and can retain the use of Spanish and include English. . . . The interchange between both yields new verbal possibilities, new images to deal with the stresses of living on tar and cement" (15). Two recent books that variously document, analyze, and contextualize this hybrid language—Ed Morales's *Living in Spanglish: The Search for a Latino Identity in America* (2002) and Ilan Stavans's *Spanglish: The Making of a New American Language* (2003)—underscore the growing acceptance of Spanglish as a linguistic and cultural phenomenon and exemplify an increasingly broader approach to U.S. Latino literature.

The modes of communication and topics that Pietri practiced in *Puerto Rican Obituary* and Algarín theorized in "Nuyorican Language" provide common ground for many other poets of the same period, beginning with those anthologized in *Nuyorican Poetry*. Along with Pietri, the other principal poets in Algarín and Piñero's anthology are Sandra María Esteves, Lucky CienFuegos, and Algarín and Piñero themselves. They wrote primarily in free verse and in English with sporadic Spanish or **bilingualism**. Most of the *Nuyorican Poetry* writers did not go on to distinguish themselves beyond the anthology, though: Later compilations and studies neither include nor name more than a few of the poets from the 1975 book. Nor did every important Nuyorican poet appear in the Algarín and Piñero anthology. Victor Hernández Cruz is notably absent, even though he already had published three books of poetry and an anthology by that time, most prominently *Snaps* (1969) and *Mainland* (1973), both with Random House. By the same token, Cruz and some of the *Nuyorican Poetry* poets (Algarín, Esteves, Pietri, Piñero, and José Angel Figueroa) continued publishing into the 1980s and even beyond, thus bridging the gap between the Nuyorican and post-Nuyorican periods, and defying neat periodization based on a specific cut-off date. As a corpus, this work runs the gamut from the protest and praise poetry of the Caribbean Latina of color Esteves, to Figueroa's visually conscious verse in *Noo Jork* (1981), and Piñero's allegiance to the catchy orality and musical rhythms that inspire many Nuyorican poets (and that critics and music lovers recognize as an early configuration of rap lyrics and slam poetry).

During this post–*Nuyorican Poetry* transitional period, a new generation simultaneously began to emerge and introduce aesthetic changes, as Frances Aparicio has noted (28). Louis Reyes Rivera published his poetry and edited anthologies, established the small press Shamal Books, and wrote a spirited introduction for Esteves's first book, *Yerba Buena* (1980). In *La Carreta Made a U-Turn* (1979), Tato Laviera presented a realistic alternative to René Marqués's treatment of return migration in the play *La carreta* (1951; pub. 1963). Martín Espada explored the particulars of Puerto Rican identity, his experiences in the broader Latino community, and radical causes throughout the Americas. The anthology Espada edited for the progressive Curbstone Press, *Poetry Like Bread: Poets of the Political Imagination from Curbstone Press* (1994; rev. 2000), exemplifies the extent of his commitment to a political aesthetic in contemporary U.S. and Latin American poetry. The work of **Judith Ortiz Cofer** and the mother–daughter collaboration of Rosario Morales and Aurora Levins Morales, *Getting Home Alive* (1986), added the perspectives of women and Latinas. Jack Agüeros, the former director of El Museo del Barrio (1976–1986), challenged the established precepts of two time-honored forms, the sonnet and the psalm, in his first book, *Correspondence between the Stonehaulers* (1990). Two essential books provide comprehensive access to this breadth of Nuyorican poetry as it developed from its beginnings into the 1990s, Faythe Turner's *Puerto Rican Writers at Home in the USA: An Anthology* and Carmen Dolores Hernández's *Puerto Rican Voices in English: Interviews with Writers* (1997). In addition, Turner introduces a new poet, Magdalena Gómez, and two others not usually included in this group, Luz María Umpierre and Julio Marzán. Hernández similarly assembles voices from different generations; her comparative chronology of writers and events from 1922 to 1996 is a notable contribution to the study of Nuyorican and Latino cultural and publishing history.

Into the Twenty-first Century

At the turn of the 21st century, two works of popular art—a novel and a film—have immortalized the earlier decades of Nuyorican literature. The up-and-coming New York novelist Ernesto Quiñonez, raised in El Barrio by his Puerto Rican mother and Ecuadorian father, pays homage in *Bodega Dreams* (2000) to the heyday of his

Nuyorican literary forebears. The protagonist visits the hallowed halls of El Museo and Taller Boricua, for example, and Agüeros, Algarín, CienFuegos, Espada, Esteves, Pietri, and Piñero appear at a climactic moment; the final section of the novel, "A New Language Being Born," pointedly marks the cultural relevance of Spanglish. León Ichaso's *Piñero* (2001) celebrates the work of the late Piñero (1946–1988) and, by extension, the entire Nuyorican scene of the 1970s and 1980s. The release of the biopic gave room for the *New York Times* to address the current state of Nuyorican poetry and performance. Mireya Navarro shows in "The Poetry of the Nuyorican Experience" that the scene has changed. At the Nuyorican Poets' Café, a new generation reads, performs, and slams alongside non-Puerto Ricans, as Miguel Algarín and Bob Holman's anthology *Aloud: Voices from the Nuyorican Poets' Café* (1994) clearly illustrates. Pietri later groused about slams as well as about being excluded as coeditor of this Nuyorican anthology (Hernández 118–19), but his poetry appears there nonetheless. Nor was everyone pleased with the lionization of Piñero; Espada and Esteves openly questioned the choice (Navarro B3).

Such considerations bring to the fore the ongoing relevance of comprehensive access to Boricua poetry and its place in the broader contexts of Latino and American poetry. Several anthologies of the 1990s responded to the trend of documenting the Puerto Rican presence within a pan-Latino context: *After Aztlán: Latino Poets of the Nineties* (1992; ed. Ray González), *Paper Dance: 55 Latino Poets* (1995; ed. Victor Hernández Cruz, Leroy V. Quintana, and Virgil Suárez), *El Coro: A Chorus of Latino and Latina Poetry* (1997; ed. Martín Espada), and *¡Floricanto Sí! A Collection of Latina Poetry* (1998; ed. Bryce Milligan, Mary Guerrero Milligan, and Angela de Hoyos). The encyclopedic undertakings of the Recovering the U.S. Hispanic Literary Heritage project under the editorship of Nicolás Kanellos, *Herencia: The Anthology of Hispanic Literature of the United States* (2002), and *En otra voz: antología de la literatura hispana de los Estados Unidos* (2003), offer another model for showcasing Boricua and other Latino poetry within Hispanic literature. A current anthology might follow the example of *Aloud* and feature the new voices (such as Mariposa, Ed Morales, Willie Perdomo, Mayda del Valle, and others) among not only those of earlier periods, but also as part of the corpus of American poetry, where they rightfully belong.

Further Reading

Algarín, Miguel. Introductions and Afterword. In *Nuyorican Poetry: An Anthology of Puerto Rican Words and Feelings*, edited by Algarín and Miguel Piñero, 9–20, 23–27, 81–91, 129–31, 181–82. New York: Morrow, 1975.

Aparicio, Frances R. "From Ethnicity to Multiculturalism: An Historical Overview of Puerto Rican Literature in the United States." In *Handbook of Hispanic Cultures in the United States: Literature and Art*, edited by Francisco Lomelí, 19–39. Houston: Arte Público Press; Madrid: Instituto de Cooperación Iberoamericana, 1993.

Flores, Juan. *Divided Borders: Essays on Puerto Rican Identity*. Houston: Arte Público Press, 1993.

Hernández, Carmen Dolores. *Puerto Rican Voices in English: Interviews with Writers*. Westport, CT: Praeger, 1997.

Kanellos, Nicolás, ed. *Biographical Dictionary of Hispanic Literature in the United States: The Literature of Puerto Ricans, Cuban Americans, and Other Hispanic Writers.* Westport, CT: Greenwood Press, 1989.

Kanellos, Nicolás. "An Overview of Hispanic Literature in the United States." In *Herencia: The Anthology of Hispanic Literature of the United States*, edited by Nicolás Kanellos, et al., 1–32. New York: Oxford University Press, 2002.

Lindstrom, Naomi. "Cuban American and Continental Puerto Rican Literature." In *Sourcebook of Hispanic Culture in the United States*, edited by David William Foster, 221–45. Chicago: American Library Association, 1982.

Matilla, Alfredo, and Iván Silén. Prologue. In *The Puerto Rican Poets/Los Poetas Puertorriqueños*, edited by Matilla and Silén, xiii–xviii. Bantam Poetry. New York: Bantam, 1972.

Mohr, Eugene V. *The Nuyorican Experience: Literature of the Puerto Rican Minority* [Contributions in American Studies 62]. Westport, CT: Greenwood Press, 1982.

Morales, Ed. *Living in Spanglish: The Search for a Latino Identity in America.* New York: St. Martin's Griffin, 2003.

Navarro, Mireya. "The Poetry of the Nuyorican Experience." *New York Times* (January 2, 2002): B1+.

Sánchez-González, Lisa. *Boricua Literature: A Literary History of the Puerto Rican Diaspora.* New York: New York University Press, 2001.

Santiago, Soledad. "Notes on the Nuyoricans." *Village Voice* (February 19, 1979): 1+.

Torres-Padilla, Jose, et al. *Writing Off of the Hyphen: New Critical Perspectives on the Literature of the Puerto Rican Diaspora.* Seattle: University of Washington Press, 2008.

Wall, Catharine E. "Latino Poetry." In *Critical Survey of Poetry.* 2nd rev. ed. 8 vols. Edited by Philip K. Jason, 4825–32. Pasadena, CA: Salem, 2003.

Catharine E. Wall

PUERTO RICAN STEREOTYPES

Similar to other minoritized groups in the United States, Puerto Ricans also deal with stereotyped notions of themselves held by the dominant (Anglo) culture. As Ilan Stavans discusses in his book *The Hispanic Condition* (2001), since the 1960s the U.S. government has repeatedly talked about "the Puerto Rican problem," usually referring to "criminality, the preponderance of drugs, the lack of education, poverty" and other malaises associated with working-class barrios (47). In addition, Puerto Ricans are also seen as docile: "lacking self-esteem, domesticated, harmless, submissive, gentle to the point of naiveté, out of touch with themselves" (47).

Throughout the years, Puerto Rican literature in the United States has contested these stereotypes by providing a context upon which they are addressed, explained, and subverted. For instance, **Piri Thomas's** ***Down These Mean Streets*** provides an insight into the life of a young Puerto Rican raised in the New York City's barrio who struggles to find a space in a world that seems to tell him he is insignificant (or dangerous) because he is a dark-skinned Puerto Rican. Because of the political relationship between Puerto Rico and the United States, Puerto Rican literature on the island has also dealt with and contested these notions. For instance, in his play *La Carreta* (The Oxcart) René Marquéz details the story of a family (a matriarch and her three children) looking for a way to improve their living conditions while attempting to stay together. Set in the 1940s, poverty in *La Carreta* is not the result of a cultural trait, nor is it the result of individual laziness or lack of self-esteem, but the result of an economic system in flux and disarray. In their search for a better life for themselves and their family, the main characters engage in a migratory cycle where they move from the countryside on the island to the city (San Juan), to New York, and back to the island. The topic of migration (especially migration in search of a better life) is present in much of the Puerto Rican literature and popular culture in general (e.g., music, art, press, etc.). Migration is also the central topic in Luis Rafael Sanchez's "short story turned motion picture" *La Guagua Aérea* (The Air Bus), which provides insight into the economic reasons for the constant migration of between the island and the United States, while tweaking the stereotype of submissiveness in the character of Don Faustino, the figure narrating the events. Also set in the 1940s (because of monumental changes in the economic system at the time, the 1940s marked the beginning of massive migration from the island of Puerto Rico to the U.S. mainland), Don Faustino seems like the stereotypical *jíbaro* from the countryside: the domesticated, harmless, submissive and "kind to the point of being naïve" Puerto Rican from the countryside. However, he is the one character who, in the middle of the flight, provides a heartfelt and compelling statement as to why he is flying for the first time to New York, while responding to the scolding inquiries of another Puerto Rican, one who has been portrayed throughout the story as an "Americanized" Puerto Rican. In the end, his stereotypical characteristics are the ones pushing him to fight for his land and, thus, his heritage.

The works of **Judith Ortiz Cofer**, *An Island like You* (1995) and **Silent Dancing** (1991), and Esmeralda Santiago, *When I Was Puerto Rican* (1993) and *Almost a Woman* (1998), are very important in this discussion, for they offer alternative representations of Puerto Rican **identity** via migration.

Ortiz Cofer, for instance, presents the reader with her own account of Puerto Ricanness, which she associates with her childhood, as she travels back and forth from the island to New Jersey. Santiago's account also involves detailed discussions of a Puerto Rican childhood, in this case a "one way trip" to the United States with her mother and her siblings. Santiago's family migrates to the barrio in New York, but different from the stereotypes associated with this environment, Santiago presents us with a poor but strong and caring family. It is clear through her account that their poverty is not the result of a cultural defect, but rather the result of imposing economic, political, and social structures. Thus, in the hands of Puerto Rican authors, Puerto Ricanness becomes a contesting and contested identity, in direct opposition to the traditional stereotypes associated with this **ethnicity**/nationality.

Further Reading

Stavans, Ilan. *The Hispanic Condition: The Power of a People*. New York: HarperCollins, 2001.

Carmen R. Lugo-Lugo

R

RACE

Most scholars today hold that the idea of *race* as an identification or category for classifying people is a social invention. Recent discoveries in the field of genetics have particularly discredited biological notions of race because more genetic variations exist within a socially defined racial group than between different races. To say that race is a social construct, however, is not to deny the reality of **racism**, or the effects of these social attitudes and beliefs about human difference upon various groups, both in the past and in the present. It does shift the focus of historical and literary investigations to the changing meaning of race in U.S. culture and the instrumental value that ideologies (or sets of beliefs) about race had in justifying inequalities such as in slavery or immigration restrictions, nation building, the management of class conflict, imperialism, westward expansion, cultural shifts in gender roles and norms, and political resistance movements. At the beginning of the 21st century, some people wished for or predicted the end of race as a significant marker of identity as the U.S. population becomes increasingly heterogeneous and individuals multiracial. Many peoples of color, on the other hand, continue to value race as an important source of belonging and an essential tool to rally political struggles for social justice and equality in the face of continuing institutional and cultural racism. Because art is a product of its historical context, critical race scholars have increasingly investigated the work that literature has played both in constituting U.S. society's ideas about racial **identity** and difference, but also in creating counter traditions resisting these dominant beliefs and authoring an alternative racial (or nonracial) identity.

Most scholars trace modern ideas about race to the categories of thought invented during the Enlightenment. Although 18th- and 19th-century historians located the origin of race thinking in Greek thought, the Greeks did not tie their system of classifying differences among people to a biology of race, and their practice of slavery was not reserved for people of specific skin colors or physical features. With the development in the 17th century of Enlightenment investigations into natural history and anthropology, philosophers began to turn from earlier metaphysical and theological explanations for the ordering in nature and society toward a more empirically based description and classification. Originally, to 18th-century theorists, these observable physical differences resulted from climate and social environment, which over time placed groups at various stages of civilization. In key works, however, such as the 1795 edition of Natural Variety of Mankind, Johann Friedrich Blumenbach, the father of modern anthropology, started to tie natural or physiological distinctions such as pigment or anatomy to innate and mental distinctions. Blumenbach spoke of five divisions of mankind: the Caucasian, Mongolian, Ethiopian, American, and Malay. To explain the diversity of mankind from the original Biblically based unity, he argued that, in addition to climate-based differences, each racial group had a life force or soul that determined its place in the hierarchy of civilizations. Blumenbach's ideas would influence historians who saw in theories of genius and blood explanations for differences in national character. In his reinterpretation of Greek and Roman history, Barthold G. Niebuhr (1813) would imply that each nation had a hidden and noble natural past that could be legitimated by scientific investigation and that served as a driving, if not determining, force of history. Although the word *race* had entered the European lexicon sometime in the Middle Ages to designate lineage or purity of descent in class or kinship, it slowly shifted to a genealogy of natural inheritance that was linked to national and cultural characteristics.

In the first half of the 19th century, race continued to have malleable meanings, and U.S. writers used the term *race* loosely as a convenient rhetoric to denote a number of differences, from nation, class, region, and skin color. Yet over the course of the 19th century, race would acquire a new scientific authority and would be associated—for the first time—specifically with biological differences. The intellectual movement toward biological notions of race must be connected to their value for a number of historical and socioeconomic developments. Many historians link the rise of race thinking to the need to justify slavery and colonialism. Although certainly scientific racism was appropriated to legitimate slavery and imperialism, it is important to see how it served the larger purpose of reconciling the conflict within the United States between professed beliefs in equality and the persistence of—and desire for—inequality. A language of race helped to naturalize differences and to provide an immutable ground to imagined communities of nation, class, and region.

In the 19th century, race particularly worked, according to a number of labor historians, as a divide-and-conquer strategy that separated working-class European descendants from the slave and free people of color. Although initially Africans, like many European immigrants, were brought to America as indentured servants, colony leaders introduced the differentiating language of race to create a buffer class of "whites" to identify with the planters and, in turn, to defend the established interests of the status quo. Although European stereotypes of Africans and Asians have exited for centuries, these groups were enslaved, or indentured, in the case of the Chinese and South Asians, not simply because of racism. Rather, these stereotypes developed into full-blown theories of biologically based racial inferiority because of the political utility this race thinking had in providing a cheap labor force for a trans-Atlantic plantation economy and for developing an enfranchised class of free white citizens who would identify with the ruling elite.

The assigning of racial meaning in the 19th century, however, was also a variegated system, whereby a group could have more than one racial classification. Although various European immigrants such as the Irish and later the Eastern European Jews were "white" in contrast to the African American, they were considered "black" or a racial other compared to the Anglo-Saxon.

The designation of the Anglo-Saxon as a separate race, one descended from the original English settlers in New England and the South arose as an important racial ideology in the 19th century. New Englanders continually invoked the superiority of the Anglo-Saxon race to rationalize their national prominence, their class leadership (especially in contrast to more recent immigrants), and their right to a manifest destiny in the West and overseas. The so-called Anglo-Saxon race believed they had inborn traits of self-discipline, individualism, domestic life, and intellectualism that set them apart from other races who never had—and never would—reach such a stage of evolutionary development. Thus, the Anglo-Saxons had a manifest destiny to dispossess the Native Americans and Mexicans of their land and to seize the Pacific coast before the Chinese and other "Mongolians" could settle it. Likewise, because certain racialized groups, such as the Chinese, were considered incapable of these Anglo-Saxon traits, they were deemed fundamentally unassimilable—permanent aliens who would later be barred from immigration with the Chinese Exclusion Act of 1882 (and 1888 and 1892). Not surprisingly, these exclusions also coincided with the economic depression of the 1880s, when many "nativist" workers resented cheap "foreign" labor.

The spread of race thinking in the 19th century also occurred because of its value in strengthening nationalism. Earlier ideas of citizenship were based on civic ideals or actions in the public sphere, but 19th-century theorists turned to ideas of race to provide a social cohesion and order based on nature and not politics: national membership would derive from sharing a common racial character, language, culture, and color. In his "Essay on the Inequality of the Human Races" (1853), Arthur de Gobineau, who is often called the father of modern racial thought, reimagined historical progress in terms of racial struggle. The spirit of the dominant race was key to the survival of the nation and to the future evolution of civilization, and countries had a duty to preserve their best racial traits. Likewise, the Scottish anatomist John Knox would greatly influence many prominent New England thinkers by promoting a similar determinist racial history and organic idea of national characters. Such theories would shape later debates over immigration, naturalization, and the exclusion of designated racial groups well into the 20th century.

In the last decades of the 19th century, race thinking is particularly evident in the national debates over social Darwinism and degeneration. Although Darwin himself argued against a causal link between physical (racial) features and behavior, that did not stop social theorists from appropriating his ides of evolution and the survival of the fittest to naturalize capitalist modernization, immigration restriction, and imperialism. Social positivists borrowed particularly three key principles from Darwinian influenced science: first, that history was purposive and progressed according to laws of nature, such that the triumph of the superior racial civilization was inevitable; second, that all human society was constrained by natural laws and, therefore, human beings and races were no different from animals in battling for the survival of the fittest; and, third, that mental abilities were related to physical characteristics. The pioneer criminologist Cesare Lombroso in *The Man of Genius* 1891 is particularly known for having argued that physical traits such as facial angle, ear shape, or cranial size provided a true indication of mental ability and criminal behavior. Mental deficiencies were carried as visible signs on an "abnormal" body, which was different from a Western Greco-Roman classical ideal. Such theories were adopted not only by conservatives elites who could feel reassured of their continued leadership because of the natural evolutionary progress of the superior race but also by liberals who believed that social change went hand in hand with racial improvement.

Complementary to this belief in the inevitability of racial conflict and progress, on the other hand, was an anxiety about degeneration, a fear that would lead to support for eugenics. Many theorists in the last decades of the 19th century and the first part of the 20th century feared that immigration, miscegenation, and other social changes (dance halls and public parks) that permitted racial mixing would cause racial dilution and usher in the decline and fall of the Anglo-Saxon nation. Such fears at the turn of the century lent support to many regulations on female sexuality and reproduction, as well as exhortations for increased birth rates among Anglo-Saxon women to offset the reproductive excess of immigrant races, including Southern and Eastern Europeans as well as Africans and Asians. Some initial support for white women's suffrage also stemmed from a similar desire to create a white voting block and government majority. To some theorists, such as Max Nordau in *Degeneration* (1895), experimental art forms as well were a sign of a mind atrophied by modern excess and racial pollution, and antimodernist aesthetic views arose out of overt, as well as more subtle, racial anxieties. In his *Inquiries into Human Faculty* (1883), when speculating on nations' racial future, Francis Galton first introduced the term *eugenics*, believing that a nation's average intelligence, racial behavior, and culture could be improved through racial engineering and selection. After the increase in labor movement strikes and the great wave of immigration from Eastern and Southern Europe starting in the 1890s, degeneration moved from a subcurrent of U.S. social thought to the center as differences in blood and race loomed as the causal agent of many social tensions.

In the first half of the 20th century, race theory would undergo another important alteration, as an understanding of race would shift from biology to culture. Franz Boas, a German Jew who immigrated to the United States in 1887, would be a key figure in the redefining of race. In his influential *The Mind of Primitive Man* (1911), he would vehemently oppose racial theories of identity by asserting that physiological and morphological features of race had no determination on inherited cultural traits. Race and culture had to be studied separately. Although Boas's idea would shape the thinking of key African American public intellectuals such as W.E.B. Du Bois, most theorists took up Boas's call for the primacy of culture to preserve dominant ideas of racial difference. Racial identities were now understood as discrete cultural genealogies that had created the soul or consciousness of the race, and, as a consequence, racial segregation and hierarchies would persist as cultural divides. Prior to World War II many U.S. writers saw themselves as fashioning the cultural identity of America, which was frequently spoken of as a racial one. In response, many writers of color saw themselves as forging a racial consciousness and identity figured as an opposing cultural nationalism. The 20th-century debate within many communities of color over **assimilation** versus separatism cannot be understood apart from this shift toward linking nation, race, and culture. Building a strong minority identity through resisting assimilation depended on recovering or maintaining the culture (language, beliefs, manners) of one's ancestors and the home country against a U.S. race-based nationalism.

Post–World War II U.S. culture has been greatly enriched by the art movements within various communities of color based on models of cultural nationalism, whether the Black Arts Movement, the Chicana/Chicano Movement, or the collective of Asian American writers that produced the landmark *Aiiieeeee!* anthology in 1974. Tied to political movements based on an identity politics, these art movements gave individuals a sense of belonging and a shared consciousness, and mobilized collective political struggles that transformed the United States toward greater political and social justice. Starting, however, in the 1970s there began a shift to think of these identities along models of **ethnicity** rather than race. Although Chicana and Chicano activists in the 1960s and 1970s spoke of La Raza (or "the race") to describe a pan-Latin identity, many view such collective identifications, whether of Hispanic or Latino, as a false term of unity and collectivity imposed by an Anglo-European media, entertainment industry, and government. Prior to coming to the United States, most people of Latin American and Caribbean descent would have identified themselves in national rather than racial terms and certainly would not have designated themselves within the U.S. binary racial system as simply either black or white. As a consequence, Latinas and Latinos have had two competing and shifting historical trajectories in response to race as an identity category: first, to acknowledge that U.S. Latinas and Latinos have become a racialized population and to use this portrayal as a "race" (if not a homogeneous one) to fight against discrimination and to seek the inclusion of people of Spanish-speaking descent in affirmative-action programs under the Equal Protection Clause; and, second, to resist Latinoness/Latinaness as a racial category, instead, recruiting ethnic paradigms to define *Latinidad* as a set of shared cultural practices, customs, and language. Among African Americans, the shift from the term "black" to "African American" also indicates a rethinking of racial identities in terms of ethnicity rather than biology. What unites the great diversity of black people is less a shared racial essence than a shared historical experience, collective memory, and expressive style that derives from their African diasporic cultural heritage.

The history of Asian American in the United States (a collective racial classification that can also trivialize cultural and historical differences) has been complicated by their shifting racialization within the bipolar system of U.S. race relations. In the past Asians were assigned a place in American society as both black and white. In the 19th century, for example, the Chinese's status within national censuses shifted, being considered white in 1860, Chinese in 1880, and lumped as black in 1900, if they were not born in China. After the 1952 Walter–McCarran Act reversed earlier Asian exclusion laws and allowed "non-white" citizens to be naturalized, Chinese, Korean, Japanese, and South Asian immigrants have often been seen as model minorities, who were nearer white, but they were often treated and designated as nearer black, being economically and socially discriminated against. As a result, many Asian diasporic immigrants felt pressured to adopt the racial prejudice against African Americans and to disassociate themselves from them as part of the assimilation process.

At the end of the 20th century and the first part of the 21st century, a number of theorists have turned from cultural theories of racial difference to explore questions of hybridity and creolization, and some predict that this will in turn change how people think of their membership in socially defined groups. Despite the continuing appeal of race as a positive source of identity, it can also marginalize or exclude the diversity of people who identify with this category, particularly in recent years, many sexual minorities. Many theorists believe as well that cultural theories of racial identity perpetuate false myths of the purity of a white U.S. culture, which, from the beginning, has always been shaped by the unrecognized contributions of minorities. U.S. culture is embedded with African, Asian, and Latin diasporic influences, and thus the color line between U.S. culture and African, Asian, and Hispanic American culture is always an arbitrary or tenuous one. Finally, any stagnant notion of racial identities would belie a long history of racial border-crossing, in which European-descent people and individuals of color have interacted, intermarried, and initiated productive interchanges that have created a continuum of racial identities that are never stable, always hybrid, and, most accurately, multiple.

Further Reading

Delgado, Richard, and Jean Stefanic. *The Latino/a Condition: A Critical Reader*. New York: New York University Press, 1998.

Gossett, Thomas F. *Race: The History of an Idea in America*. 2nd ed. Oxford: Oxford University Press, 1997.

Hannaford, Ivan. *Race: The History of an Idea in the West*. Washington, DC: Woodrow Wilson Center, 1996.

Jacobson, Matthew Frye. *Whiteness of a Different Color: European Immigrants and the Alchemy of Race*. Cambridge, MA: Harvard University Press, 1998.

Lowe, Lisa. *Immigrant Acts: On Asian American Cultural Politics*. Durham, NC: Duke University Press, 1996.

Niro, Brian. *Race*. New York: Palgrave Macmillan, 2003.

Oboler, Suzanne. *Ethnic Labels, Latino Lives: Identity and the Politics of (Re)Presentation in the United States*. Minneapolis: University of Minnesota Press, 1995.

Omi, Michael, and Howard Winant. *Racial Formations in the United States: From the 1960s to the 1990s*. New York: Routledge, 1994.

Said, Edward. *Orientalism*. New York: Vintage, 1979.

Takaki, Ronald. *Iron Cages: Race and Culture in 19th-Century America*. New York: Oxford University Press, 1990.

Stephen Knadler

RACISM

Racism refers to belief in a racial hierarchy based on unchangeable characteristics or assumed physiological traits as well as to practices that discriminate against a people because of their perceived or ascribed racial identities. Sometimes labeled *white supremacy* in the United States, racism still affects nearly every aspect of life and remains a central theme in a great body of American writing.

Racism cannot exist without a concept of **race**. Drawing from the biological sciences and social Darwinism, the notion of race categorizes the human species into different varieties or types on physiological grounds such as skin, hair color, physique, and facial features. Invidious distinctions based on differences in these traits among Negroes, Caucasian, Asiatic Mongols, Moors, and others have been used by Europeans to impose systems of imperialism, colonialism, and slavery. The distinctions of race are made meaningful in the contexts of culture, intellect, and morality to justify the racial superiority of the white men and women and to legitimize prejudice and hostility toward other peoples. The history of American racism dates back to Christopher Columbus's "discovery" of America in the late 15th century. For this so-called discovery, Native Americans paid a great price. As the first victims of American racism, American Indians, seen as subhumans, were virtually annihilated by acts of European violence and their spread of unfamiliar diseases. These wiped out more than 90 percent of American Indians of coastal New England. Their lands were stolen, their towns destroyed, their religious structures defiled, and their languages lost due to a long history of colonization and forced **assimilation**.

The next victims of American racism were Africans introduced to the New World as slaves. These peoples were shipped from Africa across the Atlantic Ocean—the notorious Middle Passage—primarily to Spanish and Portuguese colonies in the Caribbean, Mexico, and Central and South America in the early 16th century. From this trade, a system of American slavery developed and was fully established by about 1680. Slavery on American soil grew at such a fast rate that, by 1750, there were over 200,000 African slaves. Throughout most of the colonial period, opposition to slavery among white Americans was virtually nonexistent. Settlers in the 17th and early 18th centuries lacked a later generation's belief in natural human equality and saw little reason to question the enslavement of Africans. In molding a docile labor force, they resorted to harsh measures, including liberal use of whipping and branding, and inculcated in Africans a sense of black inferiority, helplessness, and dependence and a belief in the superior powers of their white masters. By 1860, near the start of the Civil War, the African American population had increased to 4.4 million, but the vast majority remained slaves. America condoned institutional slavery from 1619 up until the passage of the Thirteenth Amendment to the Constitution abolishing "slavery and involuntary servitude" on December 18, 1865. But constitutional abolition freed African Americans only halfway in their escape from racism. Questionable legal strategies, named for an antebellum mistral show character, called Jim Crow laws were enacted in the last third of the 19th century after Reconstruction by legislatures of the Southern states to legally impose racial segregation. Despite challenges for many decades, many of these persisted until the 1960s in many Southern states and systematically codified in law and state constitutional provisions the subordinate position of African Americans in society. Most such legal steps were aimed at separating the races in public spaces (restaurants, boardinghouses, theaters, parks, schools, hospitals, accommodations, and transportation) and denying black Americans their civil rights. Laws regulating segregation and disfranchisement were not only legitimized by the U.S. Supreme Court but also supported by brutal acts of ceremonial and ritualized mob violence such as the notorious lynching practiced by the Ku Klux Klan. Since the 1960s, the Supreme Court has struck down most such laws, but de facto segregation and disenfranchisement remain in many locales, as do other forms of racial discrimination against African Americans.

Like American Indians and African Americans, many immigrants have encountered racism to a great or certain degree, and even some European immigrants—Italians, Irish, Poles, and Jews—have not been immune to racist discrimination. But only Japanese Americans have ever been interned in the United States. In February 1942, two months after the Japanese bombing of Pearl Harbor, the federal government, under President Franklin D. Roosevelt, legalized the relocation of approximately 120,000 people of Japanese ancestry. Taken from their homes, mainly on the West Coast, they were forced into **internment** camps, also known as relocation camps, in Idaho, Arizona, Utah, California, Arkansas, Colorado, and Wyoming. Simply as *Japanese* Americans, they were seen as "enemy aliens" or, worse, "the enemy" in their own homeland. In the name of national security, this horrible act was perpetrated by the American government without regard for due process or legal remedy and most, even after repatriation, lost their most valued possessions. Like that of the Japanese, the history of Chinese immigration into the United States has been characterized by official policies of racist exclusion and violence. Chinese immigrants encountered harsh conditions, including what is called *institutionalized* racism. The Chinese Exclusion Act of 1882, the first and only immigration law in American history to target a specific nationality, banned the entry of "lunatics," "idiots," and all "Chinese laborers" into the United States. Designated as "aliens ineligible for citizenship," Chinese immigrants were unable to own land or work in California and other states. The Chinese Exclusion Act was renewed in 1892, again in 1902, and was not repealed until 1943 when China allied itself with the United States in World War II. In more recent American history, racist attitudes have been directed toward immigrants from south of the border. Rapidly becoming the largest minority in the United States, Mexican Americans and other Hispanic groups are playing a vital role in the borderlands of the American Southwest and beyond. Although Mexican Americans in the North American Southwest trace their history to pre–Anglo-American times, it was the 1848 Treaty of Guadalupe Hidalgo that brought a radical turning point for Mexican Americans. The treaty took the lands of thousands of Mexicans residents in former Mexican territories and thrust them into the United States within the region known as the American Southwest. There, as underclass American citizens, they have faced dual wage structures, job segregation, and racist treatments that force them to serve mostly as poorly paid laborers, ranch hands, farm workers, or domestic servants. In Texas during the 1930s, a sign that read "No dogs nor Mexicans allowed" was commonly written on restaurant facades.

Racism has been present blatantly or subtly throughout Anglo-American literature, and some writings have even been **canon**ized as American classics. From writers in the colonial period (particularly the Puritans) through writers of the frontier in the 18th century (such as James Fenimore Cooper) to 19th-century realist and naturalist writers (Samuel Langhorne Clemens, William Dean Howells, and Thomas Dixon, for instance)—virtually all either overtly or covertly express racist attitudes in their works. Also known as Mark Twain, Clemens is seen by many critics as a racist as well as a realist: his realist's aim to truly represent society has been called into question because his *critique* of a social problem paradoxically helps to perpetuate it. Twain's racism is evident not merely in his use of racial slurs (e.g., "nigger") but also in the racial stereotypes of Native Americans, blacks, and Chinese. In *The Adventures of Tom Sawyer* (1876), for example, the villain of the novel, Injun Joe, acts out of more than just an evil nature. He is evil *because* of his Indian blood, a claim that other characters in the novel reiterate repeatedly and also take as a cause of his sadistic nature and the vengeful fantasy Twain attributes to him. Racist expressions about Indians also appear in Twain's *Innocents Abroad* (1869) and *Roughing It* (1872). In the latter work, Twain labels "Goshoot" Indians as "gorilla," "kangaroo," and "Norway rat."

Beside Indians, Twain's racism also targets African Americans. In *The Adventures of Huckleberry Finn* (1884), Twain addresses the issue of slavery in antebellum America. His abundant use of racial slurs such as "nigger" has been excused by some readers as a necessity for its realistic historical context. Likewise, some excuse Twain because his protagonist, Huck, offers a powerful speech against racism. Even so, Twain's racism is embedded deeply in the relationship between Huck and Jim, a runaway slave who is Huck's companion. Extending beyond racism directed toward Native Americans and African Americans, Twain's play *Ah Sin* (1877), written with Bret Harte, is a reminder of the racist legacy of California's literary frontier. Ah Sin, a Chinese, is treated with contempt as a "slant eyed son of the yellow jaunders," a "jabbering idiot," and "a moral cancer," yet such a racist portrayal of Ah Sin in the eyes of Twain "reaches perfection."

Described by biographers as like a Huck Finn roaming the Michigan woods barefoot and wearing a straw hat, Ernest Hemingway once said that "all modern American literature comes from one book by Mark Twain called *Huck Finn*." Like Twain, Hemingway has been reread with racial issues in mind. A racist or an anti-Semite (along with other labels including misogynist, homophobe, cultural imperialist, and elitist), Hemingway uses the term *nigger* to refer to African Americans in his works and the word *kike* litters his personal letters. *The Sun Also Rises* (1926) well illustrates the ethnic hatreds of the upper classes in the 1920s. There, the portrayal of Robert Cohn reveals the author's anti-Semitism. In the eyes of Hemingway's narrator, Jake Barnes, Cohn is the one who possesses every negative personality trait and, most of all, a disfigured *Jewish* nose. Even as Barnes notes that Cohn's nose was flattened in a boxing match, he also avers that the blow "certainly improved" it.

Refuting presuppositions of American racism, ethnic American writers demonstrate their shared concern in their writing. The first body of ethnic writing to emerge, African American literature presents some of the most revealing investigations of racism. Early in the 19th century, slave narratives recount the dehumanizing effects of slavery. In probably the period's most famous African American text, *The Narrative of Frederick Douglass, an American Slave, Written by Himself* (1845), **Frederick Douglass**, born into slavery in Maryland, details his own experiences in slavery and articulates his dignity as a man. Refusing to submit himself to his master, he declares, "You have seen how a man was made a slave; you shall see how a slave was made a man." Although by a century later slavery is no longer present, racial discrimination still intrudes upon every aspect of the lives of African Americans and positions them as "invisible" men. **Ralph Waldo Ellison**'s *Invisible Man* (1952) depicts a quest for **identity** within the system of American racism. Ellison's unnamed black narrator's search for self-definition begins with an indictment of racial discrimination: "I am invisible, understand, simply because people refuse to see me." In her novels, Pulitzer and Nobel Prize winner **Toni Morrison** explores the history of racial hatred perpetrated upon black Americans. In her first novel, *The Bluest Eye* (1970), Morrison, also writing from a feminist perspective, describes how racism defines standards of beauty that militate against blacks, women especially, and leads to tragic consequences. That black is not beautiful has been determined by (northern) European standards of blond, blue-eyed beauty. In Morrison's novel, the child Pecola's obsession with Shirley Temple and a desire to have "the bluest eyes" cause her to descend into madness. In her tragic story, Morrison illustrates another form of the soul-killing impact of American racism on African Americans.

Exploring the unspeakable issue of the Japanese American internment, **John Okada**'s *No-No Boy* (1957) was neglected by the American dominant public and unwelcome in the Japanese American community for almost two decades after publication. The disfiguring effects of racism on the individual psyche, the family, the Japanese American community, and other ethnic Americans prevail throughout the novel. The novel also shows that blacks, Japanese, Chinese, Mexicans, Filipinos, and Jews all strive for recognition as complete beings, namely as Americans, but so far few are able to cross the "unseen walls" constructed by racism.

As old as Columbus, American racism is marked by epithets rooted in color ("The Yellow Peril," "the Red threat," "the Brown Menace") and heinous slogans ("A good Indian is a dead Indian"). Although legal statutes supporting racism have been struck down in America, racism's effects nonetheless continue to permeate American letters and society. Once dominant but now operating on the culture's fringes, white supremacy movements are still recurrent phenomena in the United States, as are racist organizations including the Ku Klux Klan, Christian Identity theology, skinheads, and neo-Nazi organizations.

Further Reading

Fredrickson, George M. *Racism: A Short History*. Princeton, NJ: Princeton University Press, 2003.

Grice, Helena, et al. *Beginning Ethnic American Literatures*. Manchester, NH: Manchester University Press, 2001.

Fu-jen Chen

RAISIN IN THE SUN, A

Lorraine Hansberry's *A Raisin in the Sun* (1959), whose title comes from a **Langston Hughes** poem, is a groundbreaking play that endowed Hansberry with the distinction of being the first African American female to have a play produced on Broadway. The play also established Hansberry as the first African American, the first woman, and the youngest American playwright to win the New York Drama Critics Circle Award for Best Play of the Year, and her play helped pave the way for African American as well as female playwrights.

A compassionate domestic drama structured as a well-made play, *A Raisin the Sun* tells the story of the Younger family living in a cramped Southside Chicago slum, yearning for a better life. Their hopes center around a $10,000 life insurance check that the family matriarch Lena (Mama) is due in the wake of her husband's death. Conflicts arise over how to use the money: Mama wants to buy a house for her family and set aside a portion to fund her daughter Beneatha's hope of becoming a doctor; however, her son, Walter Lee Younger, dreams of investing in a liquor store, envisioning himself a wealthy businessman. When Mama makes a down payment on a house in a white neighborhood, Walter Lee is furious. But she entrusts the remaining money with Walter Lee, instructing him to set up a fund for his sister's medical education and to put the rest in a bank account in Walter's name.

Meanwhile, a representative from the white community where the Youngers plan to move—Mr. Lindner—attempts to bribe the family into selling back the property at a profit, but his offer is rejected. However, after Walter Lee foolishly turns over the remaining money to a scam artist rather than following Mama's instructions, he is ready to capitulate. But when Lindner arrives to finalize the deal, Walter Lee, galvanized by the strength of his family, announces that he has changed his mind, and the end of the play depicts the Youngers leaving their slum for their new home.

A Raisin in the Sun features characters who, for better or worse, may be considered stereotypes: Mama is the stern matriarchal figure; Walter Lee is the angry young man straining to escape subservience to the white man; Beneatha is struggling to reconnect with her African roots, rejecting the affections of a wealthy but assimilated suitor in favor of a Nigerian lover who wants to take her back to his native village. But the play also reflects Hansberry's own activism in its push towards the future, its sense of racial pride, and the family's daring foray into white territory. Reflecting the contemporary struggles of African Americans to find social acceptance, the play conveys a sense of endurance, survival, and hope. (*See also* African American Drama)

Further Reading

Carter, Steven R. *Hansberry's Drama: Commitment amid Complexity*. Urbana: University of Illinois Press, 1991.

Cheney, Anne. *Lorraine Hansberry*. Boston: Twayne, 1984.

Domina, Lynn. *Understanding "A Raisin in the Sun": A Student Casebook to Issues, Sources, and Historical Documents*. Westport, CT: Greenwood Press, 1998.

Effiong, Philip U. *In Search of a Model for African-American Drama: A Study of Selected Plays by Lorraine Hansberry, Amiri Baraka, and Ntozake Shange.* Lanham, MD: University Press of America, 2000.

Kappel, Lawrence, ed. *Readings on "A Raisin in the Sun."* San Diego: Greenhaven Press, 2001.

Matthews, Kristin. "The Politics of "Home" in Lorraine Hansberry's *A Raisin in the Sun." Modern Drama* 51.4 (2008): 556–78.

Karen C. Blansfield

RECHY, JOHN (1931–)

John Rechy is a Mexican American novelist. He was born Juan Francisco Rechy in El Paso, Texas, on March 10, 1931, and first came to prominence in the 1960s as the author of sexually explicit depictions of homosexual subculture. Most early critics concentrated on the shocking and strongly autobiographical subject matter of his novels—Rechy used his extensive experiences as a male hustler as the basis for his fiction—and soon the author was labeled a gay writer. Rechy has stated that he does not like labels of any sort and hopes that eventually he will just be considered a writer who is gay. Recently, Rechy's substantial contributions to Chicano literature have been recognized, as has his role as a regional writer with the focus on Los Angeles, the "City of Lost Angels." Although Rechy has been gratified that he has finally been accepted as a Chicano writer, he has always seen himself as an outsider, an outlaw. In some of his interviews he has conceded that he has never seen himself totally fitting in the gay or the Chicano world.

Early in his career Rechy was not only labeled a gay writer but also an accidental one because the documentary style of his first novels gave critics the false impression that Rechy was lacking craftsmanship and artistry. Rechy has therefore felt the need to defend himself, and he has stressed on numerous occasions that he considers himself a literary writer and that all of his books are consciously structured and have undergone numerous revisions. Without false modesty he has stated that he is an excellent writer, a writer who is as good as any other writing today, and much better than most. The fact that he

John Rechy. (Tony Korody/Sygma/Corbis)

recently received several lifetime achievement awards is a sign that the importance of his oeuvre is finally being recognized. In 1997, he was honored by the PEN Center USA-West; in 1999, he received the Publishing Triangle's William Whitehead Lifetime Achievement Award; and in 2001, he received an award from the University of Southern California.

A close look at Rechy's novels reveals that they are indeed carefully structured and that they are a part of a long literary tradition. Essentially, all of Rechy's works are quest narratives using elements of the picaresque novel and the bildungsroman as well as Gothic literature. The author told Ramon Renteria of the *El Paso Times* that he enjoys the challenge of taking a very old form and making it seem modern. Rechy's protagonists are in a never-ending search for (sexual) **identity**, salvation, redemption, and grace. *City of Night* (1963), Rechy's groundbreaking first novel, established the pattern. The unnamed narrator traverses the United States, exploring the homosexual subculture in New York, Los Angeles, and New Orleans in search of self-affirmation and sexual identity, and meeting various colorful characters along the way, the most memorable of whom is Miss Destiny, a drag queen. The book's protagonist is a hustler who sells his body to other men and who refuses to show any affection to his clients. Being a Chicano man, he is confined to a world of machismo, which only permits a sexually active role. Patrick O'Connor has shown that this stereotype of Latin masculinity, personified by the nameless narrator, together with the stereotype of Latin femininity, the Latin drag queen, connect Rechy's book to Latino literature. The novel, which had its origin in a letter that described Rechy's experiences during carnival season in New Orleans and which he reworked into the short story "Mardi Gras" (published in the progressive *Evergreen Review*), was a commercial success but took an initial drubbing by the critics. Rechy was especially incensed by Alfred Chester's vitriolic review for the *New York Review of Books*, which was titled "Fruit Salad" and which questioned the existence of the author. Another critic who savaged Rechy's novel was Peter Buitenhuis, who wrote in the June 30, 1963, edition of the *New York Times Book Review*, "Mr. Rechy can hardly be called a novelist. He lacks the art to shape experience into developing narrative; he has little of the craftsmanship, nothing of the detached lucidity which makes the true novelist" (3).

Rechy was not deterred by such criticism and, in 1967, published *Numbers*, which can be considered a sequel to *City of Night* and which, according to Rechy's biographer Charles Casillo, is based on the author's experiences while traveling to Los Angeles with his beloved mother Guadalupe. While his mother was staying with his sister in Torrance, Rechy went on a 10-day sexual binge in order to prove to himself that he was still a sexual magnet. Like his creator, Johnny Rio, the protagonist of *Numbers*, sets himself a goal of 30 sexual conquests—hence the title of the novel—in an attempt to reaffirm his desirability and to keep the damaging effects of time at bay. Casillo has pointed out that the death Rechy describes in *Numbers* is the "death of youth" (181). *This Day's Death* (1969), which Rechy considers the worst book he ever wrote, is based on the author's close relationship with his strong-willed but ailing mother and his arrest in Griffith Park in Los Angeles for public indecency. Jim Girard, the novel's protagonist, divides his time between caring for his ill mother in El Paso and defending himself in Los Angeles against the unfounded charges. According to Casillo, Girard thus faces two kinds of prison: the metaphorical one of his suffocating relationship with his mother and the real one he might have to enter as a result of the trial (197).

Having explored the homosexual subculture in detail in his first three novels, Rechy expanded his themes in his next novels. *The Vampires* (1971), one of the author's personal favorites, shows the influence of Edgar Allan Poe, comic strips, and Hollywood films and is based on Rechy's visit to the secluded Chicago mansion of a wealthy heterosexual admirer. In the operatic novel dozens of colorful characters play dangerous, sadomasochistic mental games initiated by Richard, the mansion's eccentric owner, and Malissa, a mysterious, witchlike woman. *The Fourth Angel* (1972) refers to Jerry, a 16-year-old, who, like the novel's author, is mourning the recent death of his mother and who joins a group of hardened teenagers. These "lost angels" are led by a girl, Shell, who invents cruel mind games with strangers in order to keep boredom at bay and who takes drugs in order to cope with emotional pain. *Bodies and Souls* (1983), which David William Foster has called one of the very best contemporary novels about Los Angeles, "a sort of urban Pilgrim's Progress" (*Studies in 20th Century Literature* 25 [Winter 2001]: 196), also features several disillusioned teenagers who have traveled to the City of Angels in search for a modern paradise promising salvation only to be obliterated in a bloody shoot-out on a freeway overpass. Rechy stated in the introduction to the 2001 reprint of the novel that Los Angeles is a main character in many of his novels, and in this one a central character throughout. It was his intention "to explore beneath the clichés too often expressed about Los Angeles: its spurious obsession with artifice, not substance, its lack of defining center, its courtship of extremity, its mindless narcissism—that is, its want of profundity, of soul." As an homage to Hollywood, Rechy reproduced scenes from classic movies with the intention to "strip away romance and sentimentality from the old films in order to expose camouflaged violence." He conceived *Bodies and Souls* as an alternating series of Technicolor and black-and-white scenes.

The Sexual Outlaw (1977), subtitled *A Non-Fiction Account, with Commentary of Three Days and Nights in the Sexual Underground*, also employs cinematic elements. Rechy described the book as "the literary equivalent of a film documentary influenced by Robbe-Grillet's theories on the new novel. Plotless and black and white, it is a minute-by-minute accounting of three days and three nights of anonymous sex as Jim roams the sexual underground of Los Angeles" (Casillo 252). The book was conceived as a powerful statement of gay rage against heterosexual fascism and as a provocative defense of promiscuity. Because Rechy characterized *The Sexual Outlaw* as "a documentary," this book has sometimes been ignored in studies of the author's fiction. For Rechy, however, the line of fiction and nonfiction is blurred, and he does not see any rigid separation, as he told Richard Canning. One of his works-in-progress is tellingly titled *Autobiography: A Novel*. The title of Rechy's 1979 novel, *Rushes*, directly alludes to its connection with the cinema: Rushes is not only the name of the gay bar that serves as the book's setting, it also refers to film footage shot during a given day without editing or soundtrack. Rechy combines cinematic elements with allusions to the Catholic Mass and the Stations of the Cross in *Rushes*. It was intended as an allegory on the destructiveness of Christian rituals as well as an examination the self-hatred of gay men caused by heterosexual oppression. Considering Rechy's strong political engagement, it is surprising that he has not explicitly dealt with the devastating AIDS pandemic. He comes close to dealing with the subject in *The Coming of the Night* (1999), which describes the sexual odyssey of a large cast of characters during a single day in the summer of 1981 in Los Angeles. While alluding to the approaching crisis in the title and mentioning "a strange illness . . . Something mysterious, something new, something terrible," Rechy seems to give the reader the impression that time has stopped in the early 1980s. Consequently, O'Connor has called the book "not only a disappointment but a significant one" (416). Rechy has indicated that *Autobiography*, his work in progress, will deal directly with AIDS.

In the late 1980s and early 1990s, Rechy created a cycle of novels featuring memorable female characters. *Marilyn's Daughter* (1988) describes the quest of Normalyn Morgan, a young woman from Gibson, Texas, for her true identity. Normalyn is raised by Enid Morgan, one of Marilyn Monroe's closest friends, and when Enid commits suicide she leaves a note for Normalyn that states Marilyn Monroe is her real mother. Normalyn's quest leads her to Los Angeles, where she encounters an array of colorful characters, among them a gang of teenagers called the Dead Movie Stars, reminiscent of the groups of alienated youths in previous novels. *The Miraculous Day of Amalia Gomez* (1991), which is Rechy's most overtly Latino book, revolves around a twice-divorced Mexican American woman in Los Angeles who searches for meaning in her life after she witnesses the apparition of a cross in the sky. Rechy describes the book's origin in the introduction to the 2001 edition as follows: "On a spring day in Los Angeles, I looked up into a clear sky and saw two wisps of clouds intersect to form a very discernible cross. I watched until a breeze smeared the impression. What would one of the Mexican American women I grew up among think if she had seen that cross? What if such a woman's life was in crisis? Would she see that cross as a desperate sign of hope?" Religious elements also abound in *Our Lady of Babylon* (1996), which is based on the book of Revelation and which deals with the fate of fallen women throughout the ages. Rechy's most recent novel, *The Life and Adventures of Lyle Clemens* (2003), a picaresque bildungsroman inspired by Henry Fielding's *The History of Tom Jones* (1749), describes the hilarious trials and tribulations handsome, naive, and—for a change—heterosexual Lyle has to endure in artificial and seductive Las Vegas and Los Angeles before he can discover his real self. The novel proves yet again Rechy's ability to recast old literary conventions into something original and new. (*See also* Mexican American Gay Literature)

Further Reading

Arnold, Kevin. "'Male and Male and Male': John Rechy and the Scene of Representation." *Arizona Quarterly* 67.1 (2011):115–34.

Bredbeck, Gregory W. "John Rechy." In *Contemporary Gay American Novelists*, edited by Emmanuel S. Nelson, 340–51. Westport, CT: Greenwood Press, 1993.

Casillo, Charles. *Outlaw: The Lives and Careers of John Rechy*. Los Angeles: Advocate Books, 2002.
O'Connor, Patrick. "John Rechy." In *Latino & Latina Writers*, edited by Alan West-Duran. Vol. 1, 405–23. New York: Charles Scribner's Sons, 2004.

Karl L. Stenger

RIVERA, TOMÁS (1935–1984)

A writer, scholar, and university administrator whose 1971 novel *. . . y no se lo trago la tierra* (*. . . And the Earth Did Not Devour Him*) won the first *Premio Quinto Sol*. This novella was made into a feature film and is among the most studied works of Chicano literature. Rivera was born in Crystal City, Texas to Mexican immigrants. Because of their migrant work Tomás missed much school. Nevertheless, in 1969 he received a PhD in romance languages and literature, and in an astonishing 10 years moved up the ranks to became chancellor of the University of California, Riverside—the first minority so honored in the University of California system. Along with his award-winning novel, he published poetry, short stories, and essays. Some work was posthumously published: *The Searchers: Collected Poetry* (1990), *The Harvest: Short Stories by Tomás Rivera* (1989), and *Tomás Rivera: The Complete Works* (1995).

. . . *And the Earth Did Not Devour Him* was translated by Hermino Rios C., and later by Evangelina Vigil-Piñon. Rolando Hinojosa-Smith produced an English "rendition": *This Migrant Earth* (1987). *. . . And the Earth Did Not Devour Him* powerfully depicts the miserable conditions endured by Mexican migrants between 1945 and 1955. A young, nameless protagonist is the primary narrator, but there are other voices that sometimes act as chorus. Structurally, the novel consists of 12 chapters that roughly correspond to a year because Rivera is interested in cycles of life and harvest. Before each chapter there is a one-paragraph vignette that usually relates to the following story or to the previous one. The prologue introduces a lost year, and then the narrator falls asleep and dreams of his past—the stories that follow. The epilogue "Under the House," employs flashbacks that tie together many of the stories and add further detail. The protagonist wants to recapture all of the people from his past and embrace them. Though initially a boy is under the house, ultimately a man emerges from where he had gone to "think in peace." This tranquil setting—representative of his subconscious—allows him to make a discovery and experience an epiphany. Through memory he recaptures a lost year, and then desires to recall all the past years and all the people from them.

The first story of the collection concerns a young Mexican boy being accidentally shot by the Anglo rancher who does not want workers wasting time drinking water. This sets the tone for Rivera's narrative, but what keeps the work from being overly didactic is his style and craft, his subtlety, as well as his sense of humor, and humanity.

In "The Night the Lights Went Out" Rivera characteristically renders a complexity of voices by alternately using Ramon, Juanita, Ramiro, and neighbors as contributing narrators. Ramon, a spurned and jealous ex-boyfriend still wants to control Juanita, who insists on going to a dance without him, so he attempts to cut off the building's power supply and ends up electrocuting himself. What Rivera renders so well are the different speakers who elevate this tragic couple to a Romeo-and-Juliet-like status by concluding that Ramon must have killed himself over unrequited love.

At the center is the title story in which the protagonist finds his voice and curses God for the sunstroke of his father and brother, and for the tuberculosis of relatives. His mother, meanwhile, merely lights candles and implores God for mercy—which the boy thinks is useless. The novel's title could be loosely translated as "and lightening did not strike him," which traditionally conveys what happens to those who blaspheme. The boy curses God, but the ground does not swallow him. His cursing becomes a powerful act of self-determination and empowerment, which is significant since in the first paragraph the narrator is "at a loss for words." Cursing God also serves as a rejection of his mother's Catholicism, which is associated with superstition and passivity. Rivera's depiction of religion is clear: priests and nuns are dirty-minded; a minister's wife runs off with a carpenter; a mother bargains with God—her palpitating heart in exchange for her son's safety; a priest blesses cars for five dollars each and then vacations in Spain. Rivera also makes oblique allusions to ideas of Aztec sun worship and human sacrifice.

The double entendre of "When We Arrive," a story of migrant workers traveling like cattle in a truck, suggests the idea of interminable travel; more significantly, the repetition of the title conveys the notion that these migrants will never arrive economically or socially. Despite dehumanizing hardships, one character—suffering from diarrhea—is able to maintain humanity and transcend difficulties through his concern for others and, even more dramatically, by gazing skyward and reveling in the beauty of stars punctuating a black sky. His unwillingness to succumb to his squalid circumstances gives him courage to endure and, ultimately, to overcome such conditions.

Rivera's other collection, *The Harvest*, has not received enough critical attention although the first five stories are masterpieces of Chicano literature and rise to mythic proportion: "The Salamanders" is a gripping allegory about those socially and economically disenfranchised; "On the Road to Texas: Pete Fonseca" is about a *pachuco* who seduces a single mom and fools a migrant community; "Eva and Daniel" is a poignant story of love lost; in "The Harvest" mild magical realism depicts the migrant worker's connection to the earth's rhythms; and in "Zoo Island" José empowers a migrant camp by counting everyone and putting up a sign, "Zoo Island Pop 88 1/2." All of these uncommon stories are among Rivera's best. One story is a fragment from Rivera's lost novel *La casa grande del pueblo*; another pays homage to Jorge Luis Borges.

Despite Rivera's early death, his literary reputation is assured. His stories, novel, and poetry chronicle the life and struggles of dispossessed migrants. Although Rivera drew from his own life, his exceptional literary talent renders works rich in interpretation, nuance, and compassion.

Further Reading

Lattin, Vernon E, ed. *Contemporary Chicano Fiction: A Critical Survey*. Binghamton, NY: Bilingual Press, 1986.

Lattin, Vernon E., Rolando Hinojosa, and Gary Keller, eds. *Tomás Rivera, 1935–1984: The Man and His Work*. Tempe, AZ: Bilingual Press, 1988.

Olivares, Julian, ed. "International Studies in Honor of Tomás Rivera." *Revista Chicano-Riqueña* 13.3–4 (1985): 7–14.

Sommers, Joseph, and Tomás Ybarra-Frausto, eds. *Modern Chicano Writers*. Englewood Cliffs, NJ: Prentice Hall, 1979.

Paul Guajardo

RODRIGUEZ, RICHARD (1944–)

A Mexican American intellectual, television and radio commentator, journalist, and essayist, Richard Rodriguez writes for Pacific News Service, periodicals such as *Harper's* and the *Los Angeles Times*, and the Public Broadcasting Service show *The NewsHour with Jim Lehrer*. Richard Rodriguez exploded on the literary scene with his controversial first book, *Hunger of Memory: The Education of Richard Rodriguez, An Autobiography*, published in 1982. Ten years later *Days of Obligation: An Argument with My Mexican Father* (1992) appeared. In 2002, Rodriguez, who spells his name the English way rather than with the original Spanish accent (*Rodríguez*), published *Brown: The Last Discovery of America*, which he says "completes a trilogy on American public life and [his] private life."

Hunger of Memory begins the trilogy. Though subtitled "An Autobiography," Rodriguez notes that the book is a collection of six "fugue-like" essays, "impersonating an autobiography." The six essays and prologue reveal the history of Rodriguez's education, beginning with his uncomfortable entry into the "public" English-language classroom of the local Catholic school from the "private" intimacy of a Spanish-language household, and moving to an epiphany of sorts as a Fulbright researcher in the British museum. There he rejects the secure academic career waiting for him as he rejects the benefits of affirmative action that, he believes, unjustly make that career possible for him and not for others. And thus begins his career as a freelance writer. As language is the tool of his trade, so it is one of the main subjects of *Hunger of Memory*. An oft-excerpted section anthologized under the title "Public and Private Language" lies at the heart of his argument. At its simplest, "private" language was the Spanish of his household and family, while "public" language is the English he learned at school, the English the nuns asked his parents to use instead of their native Spanish. But more than language, it is education itself that creates an unbridgeable distance between him and his parents.

Rodriguez has been harshly criticized, and deeply praised, for his stance on affirmative action and bilingual education in *Hunger of Memory*. Other Chicanos (or Mexican Americans) in particular have rejected his views as harmful to the progress of the Chicano movement, while conservatives have seen his views as sensible. He, on the other hand, considers himself to the left of center, but has resisted the group **identity** implied by a "movement." He complains of the lack of diversity present in an all-encompassing group identity that inherently limits the identity of the individual.

Days of Obligation: An Argument with My Mexican Father (1992), selected as a finalist for the Pulitzer Prize in 1993, was received less contentiously than *Hunger*. The "days of obligation" of the title comes from the Catholicism ever-present in Rodriguez's writing. A practicing Catholic is obligated to attend Mass on Sundays and certain holy days of obligation, which at their most pared down include the Ascension (Easter), the Immaculate Conception, and the birth of Christ (Christmas). Composed of 10 chapters and an introduction, Rodriguez places himself, literally and figuratively, in Mexico and California in search of an ethnic and sexual identity. On location in Mexico with a British television camera crew, he searches for his "parents' village," just the right image for a European audience. But Rodriguez ranges through time as well as space. "India" contemplates the Indians of the Americas who later became Native Americans. He examines the story of La Malinche, who, as consort of the Spanish conquistador Hernán Cortés, gave birth to the first Mexican, a *mestizo* mix of Indian and Spanish. In his (revisionist) version she is the seductress of Spain rather than the victim of rape. She is the defiled Indian juxtaposed with Mexico's Virgin patron saint, Our Lady of Guadalupe, who appeared to a humble Indian boy in 1531. And like Mexico itself, Rodriguez cannot avoid his own heritage as a Mexican (American) with Aztec ancestors.

In "Late Victorians" Rodriguez examines sexual identity and reveals a sexual orientation only hinted at in *Hunger of Memory*. He sketches a history of gay life in San Francisco, noting that the "gay-male revolution had greater influence on San Francisco in the 1970s than did the feminist revolution. But then came the AIDS epidemic of the 1980s, and with it the phone calls reporting the diagnosis or death of one friend after another. One dying friend tells him that he, Rodriguez, will be the only one spared the AIDS plague, because he is "too circumspect."

"In Athens Once" he visits Tijuana, a bustling town across the border from San Diego, during Holy Week. In other chapters, Rodriguez visits "The Missions" founded by Father Junípero Serra, who founded 21 missions, all a day's walk apart. He tells the story of the legendary bandit Joaquín Murietta. He discusses Catholicism and visits a "Junky church" in "The Latin American Novel" and delves into the immigrant experience in "Asians." Visiting various locations in California and Mexico, Rodriguez takes the reader to physical spaces inhabited by history—the history of the past, recorded by its inhabitants, and the history of the future of America, the place and the idea that no one can resist. What is America? And who is American? are questions central to *Days of Obligation*, but no less central is Rodriguez's self-definition, his tracing of his own identity as Catholic, Mexican American, and gay, along with a kind of redefinition of the cultural contributions of those elements to America.

In *Brown: The Last Discovery of America* (2002), Rodriguez completes his trilogy. With a preface and nine chapters, *Brown* is a series of meditations not on the color brown, but brown as impurity, says Rodriguez. Even the cover of the book is brown, with its brown title word and a photo of the author designed to reveal his own brownness, his Hispanic-ness, and most especially his Aztec features.

According to Rodriguez, **race** in America has always been an issue of white and black, of what he calls "white freedom and Negro disadvantage." From Alexis de Tocqueville's "triad" of white, Indian, and Africa, America moved to a dichotomy of white and black; race, not class, as the great American divide. Thanks to the administration of President Richard Nixon ("Poor Richard"), race became five categories: black; white; Native American/Eskimo; Asian/Pacific Islander; and Hispanic, or black, white, red, yellow, and brown. The Hispanic was born, what Rodriguez calls "The Third Man." Unlike other racial categories, being Hispanic depends on culture, not blood: "there is no such thing as Hispanic blood." With the invention of the Hispanic (sometimes known as the Latino), the specificity of national identity—Peruvian, Mexican, Honduran—was erased, and affirmative action and bilingual education were born. Rodriguez remains firmly against affirmative action and the notion of "minority" as numerical rather than cultural because, once again, race, not class, is the issue. In his view, that is, the poor white kid has less chance of getting into college than the middle-class Hispanic.

Rodriguez remains equally unconvinced of the need for bilingual education, which he sees as a program that creates disadvantages for young children and prevents their **assimilation** into mainstream America. It is perhaps ironic that Rodriguez himself had to learn Spanish in college, though it was his first language.

In *Brown* Rodriguez is much more open about being Catholic and, perhaps paradoxically, about being gay. He compares himself with the church's fathers, her popes, because none of them create life. He contrasts as well the white Anglo-Saxon Protestant pronoun "I" with the brown Catholic pronoun "we" (*nosotros*). He alters the standard historical vision of America as East–West. With the trans-border agreement of NAFTA (the North America Free Trade Agreement) and the continuing influx of Hispanics, America is now North–South. Blond-haired, blue-eyed Anglos order *burritos* and say "*sí, gracias.*" In keeping with his stance on affirmative action, Rodriguez would do away with race altogether as a category. Not black versus white, but brown. Impurity, as he calls it, is the fusion of races, the fusion of cultures, and it is precisely this fusion, or confusion, that Rodriguez sees as America's best hope.

Though Rodriguez's works are often shelved in the sociology section, he might better be categorized as a cultural critic, a kind of participant–observer who makes no pretense of objectivity. He ignores the notion of political correctness, emphasizes the individual over the collective, and envisions the history of the future, rather than the past. For Rodriguez, the optimistic history of the future is brown. (*See also* Bilingualism; Mexican American Autobiography; Mexican American Gay Literature)

Further Reading

Alarcon, Norma. "Tropology of Hunger: The 'Miseducation' of Richard Rodriguez." In *The Ethnic Canon: Histories, Institutions, and Interventions*, edited by Liu D. Palumbo, 140–52. Minneapolis: University of Minnesota Press, 1995.

Fine, Laura. "Claiming Personas and Rejecting Other-Imposed Identities: Self-Writing as Self-Righting in the Autobiographies of Richard Rodriguez." *Biography* 19 (Spring 1996): 119–36.

Lim, Jeehyun. "'I Was Never at War with My Tongue': The Third Language and the Performance of Bilingualism." *Biography* 33.3 (2010): 518–42.

Schilt, Paige. "Anti-Pastoral and Guilty Vision in Richard Rodriguez's *Days of Obligation*." *Texas Studies in Literature and Language* 40.4 (Winter 1998): 424–41.

Torres, Hector A. "'I Don't Think I Exist' Interview with Richard Rodriguez." *MELUS* 28.2 (Summer 2003): 164–202.

Linda Ledford-Miller

S

SIGNIFYING

Signifying relates to a specific form of communication found in traditional African American literature that combines elements of joking and lying with the use of traditional black dialect to form a genre of its own. The joking aspect can take on the form of insult or mockery, parody, or a playful exchange used as a test of linguistic wits. The lying aspect can be merely another layer of the inherent humor, or it can be used as a sign of power in a dialectic struggle between two characters. Signifying is also popularly known as "playing the doubles." There are elements of both literary humor and struggle for social power inherent in the art of signifying.

Signifying has its roots in the oral tradition of African American folktales, examples of creativity used by those unable to read and write, often as a means of laying claim to the native language of power by utilizing the folktales of one's country of origin. One of these tales is that of the signifying monkey himself, who is the epitome of the trickster figure often seen in oral folktales. In written form, signifying can easily be seen in works such as the Uncle Remus stories penned by Chandler Harris in the late 19th century. The protagonist of Uncle Remus's tales, Brer Rabbit, is another classic trickster figure. Harris's tales remained popular into the middle of the 20th century for the same reason that signifying continues to live in both oral and written forms: The trickster, through signifying, brings a sense of justice and the hope of overcoming oppression to those seeking empowerment and equality. This was especially important, of course, as the African American community struggled through the era of Reconstruction and the turbulent years that led up to the **Civil Rights Movement**. Signifying often involves a reversal of meaning and an element of competition. Such can be seen in later examples of African American literature, as well as can the traditional model of signifying. The idea of signifying has laid the basis for a form of African American literary criticism formally formulated by Henry Louis Gates Jr. in which the traditional dialogue of signifying becomes a more sophisticated dialogue of sorts between different writers, critics, and social philosophers who build upon—or against—each other's work, most often with deep racial implications involved. Signifying also plays a part in popular culture, as it has since its inception in this country, with the oral practice of signifying continuing its usage within the African American community of our own day, for many of the same reasons that the phenomenon has always been popular.

Further Reading

Gates, Henry Louis, Jr. *The Signifying Monkey: A Theory of Afro-American Literary Criticism.* New York: Oxford University Press, 1988.

Marrouche, Mustapha. *Signifying with a Vengeance: Theories, Literatures, Storytellers*. Albany: State University of New York Press, 2002.

Watkins, Mel. *On the Real Side: Laughing, Lying and Signifying: The Underground Tradition of African-American Humor that Transformed American Culture, from Slavery to Richard Pryor*. New York: Simon and Schuster, 1994.

Terry D. Novak

SILENT DANCING

An inventive and award-winning autobiography by **Judith Ortiz Cofer** published in 1990, *Silent Dancing* is as much a meditation of the vagaries of memory as it is a chronicle of growing up biculturally. It is a nonlinear narrative that consists of a prefatory essay and 13 vignettes that are punctuated by 18 poems. By blending different generic forms, Ortiz Cofer creates a unique cross-genre autobiography.

A *Bildungsroman*, Ortiz Cofer's narrative offers a map of the narrator's evolving consciousness, her coming of age, her maturation. Born in Puerto Rico, she grows up biculturally and bilingually: her family shuttles back and forth between Puerto Rico and New Jersey. The vignettes and poems offer evocative glimpses into the joys and challenges of growing up in the cultural and linguistic borderlands. Ortiz Cofer weaves into her narratives Spanish words and phrases; sometimes she includes English translations but sometimes not. By doing so she creates in her text a trans-lingual space that poignantly reflects the personal reality of a young child who routinely navigates cultural and linguistic borders. Readers who do not understand Spanish are thus immersed into a textual space that is at times as disorienting as what young Judith must have experienced as a child growing up with Spanish at home and English at school and teased for speaking English with a Spanish accent and Spanish with a North American lilt.

Silent Dancing is also an exemplary *Kunstlerroman*, a coming-of-age

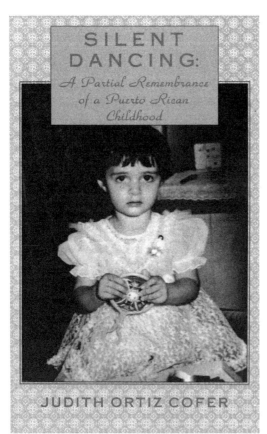

The book cover for *Silent Dancing*. (Reprinted with permission from the publisher, Arte Público Press—University of Houston)

narrative that focuses on a child who would grow up to be an artist. As a child, Judith is fascinated by the many stories of her grandmother. She becomes an avid reader; she becomes aware of the power of language to shape reality. As she grows older, she begins to imaginatively modify the stories she hears and eventually gains the confidence to invent her own stories. She becomes, like her grandmother, a teller of tales, an artist in her own right.

Many of the stories that the narrator recounts reveal and sometimes subvert the patriarchal gender codes that govern social relations in Puerto Rico. The story of Maria la Loca, for example, is a cautionary tale about a young girl who is seduced and abandoned by her lover. Traumatized by the loss and betrayal, she remains alone and emotionally unhinged. But the story of Maria Sabida is about a heroic young woman, courageous and wise, who outwits a gangster, marries him, and transforms him into an honest man. The last story in the book is the most daring one: it is the story of a boy, Marino, who is raised as a girl named Marina, who elopes with and marries a girl named Kiki, and eventually lives as a man. His transgressive transvestitism reveals the socially constructed nature of gender as well as gender roles and offers the most articulate critique of the culturally scripted machismo/mariasmo dynamic.

Further Reading

Derrickson, Teresa. "'Cold/Hot, English/Spanish': The Puerto Rican American Divide in Judith Ortiz Cofer's *Silent Dancing*." *MELUS* 28.2 (2003): 121–37.

Montilla, Patricia M. "Gathering Voices: Storytelling and Collective Identity in Judith Ortiz Cofer's *Silent Dancing: A Partial Remembrance of a Puerto Rican Childhood*." *Bilingual Review* 25.3 (2003): 205–216.

Emmanuel S. Nelson

SILKO, LESLIE MARMON (1948–)

Leslie Marmon Silko is a Native American poet, novelist, short-story writer, essayist, and photographer. Known previously for her short stories and poetry, Silko's place in Native American writing is permanently assured by her innovative first novel, *Ceremony*. Silko is one of the earliest Native American authors to celebrate the mixed-blood Indian as a source of power and a symbol of the future of the Native peoples. Her works have met with a varied critical response for their inventive and often controversial addressing of issues pertaining to Laguna culture and the dilemma of **race** in America.

Major Works

Ceremony (1977) was published in the same year that Silko won the Pushcart Prize for poetry. Written during her sojourn in Alaska where she was greatly influenced by the landscape as well as the sense of exile from Laguna that she carried with her, *Ceremony* is Silko's attempt to recreate Laguna and its surroundings. Silko's male protagonist is a scorned, alienated half-white, half-Indian war veteran who is regarded as a failure when judged by white terms of heroism. Shell shock and survivor's guilt cause Tayo to spiral into an abyss of self-condemnation and despair. It emerges that part of the strategy to combat such despair and achieve wholeness is to recover, through ceremonial rites of healing, the tribal stories and women-centered traditions that have been too readily dismissed, abused, or discarded. In a modern world where Indians still live under the ignominy and injustice of a colonizing government's policies, where violence dominates and nuclear sites desecrate the natural landscape, *Ceremony* is a cautionary tale directed not only at the whites who work against Native integration, but also at the Indians who unthinkingly embrace the values of the white world to the detriment of their own people's welfare.

Storyteller (1981) is a multigenre collection of photographs, poems, tribal tales, short stories, personal recollections, and family lore. Together, the collection exemplifies how the act of storytelling is important to the process of linking the historical and mythical past spiritually to the happenings of the present. In the title story, "Storyteller," the Alaskan landscape has as much a role as the human characters: the powerful wintry weather denying any human attempt to shape the environment permanently for their own uses.

Almanac of the Dead (1991) is Silko's magnum opus. Ten years in creation, it caricatures a country united by the soulless binding of materialism, a nation that is spiritually doomed. Dealing with sovereignty, past and present oppression of the indigenous peoples, political unrest, the drug dealing scene, mixed-blood **identity** conflicts, corruption, and bestiality as well as psychological and technological mayhem, *Almanac* is a narration of the self-destruction evident in an individualistic culture. In a dramatic restructuring of the American mythic mindscape, Silko, in an era ruled by immediate efficacy and militarism, nonetheless advocates a graduated process of change. Only thus can new ideas be introduced at a pace that is readily integrated by the community so that the transformation is constructive rather than disruptive and destructive. Hope for the future is represented by the gathering of a motley crew of characters who for personal reasons join in a community resistance to combat that force of despair. Highlighting the social and political specter of a national uprising, Silko depicts a multiracial army made up of Mexican migrants, disgruntled war veterans, the poor and the homeless, and the North American tribal peoples ready to fight for their rights to a place and land from which they had been earlier dispossessed. Here, identity is depicted as a fluid entity so much so that "enemy" whites can escape their prophesized disappearance through Silko's apparent solution of the sincere embracing of Indian values. In *Almanac*, the "Indian problem" is a universal problem, and the reader is drawn into the pattern of the plot and forced to partake in the judging of the characters' actions in the light of the author's terms for ultimate victory. Throughout, Silko is no mere propagandist for her beliefs. Rather she understands that despite her personal politics, alternatives need to be looked at objectively for a convincing evaluation of what to do next. The aesthetic underpinnings present in the complexity of the plot's design ensure that a simplistic, absolute reading of the novel's message is close to impossible.

Gardens in the Dunes (1999) is an historical novel harking back to the humanitarian and industrial contradictions of the Gilded Age at the turn of the 19th century. Here we have a white woman, Hattie, born to wealth but oppressed by her husband and the gendered values of the rigid society she lives within. Her state of physical and psychological captivity is mirrored in the Sand Lizard girl she saves and befriends, both being hemmed in by prejudices that persecute them less for what they have done but for who they are. Published 22 years after *Ceremony*, *Gardens* reflects Silko's increased engagement with the politics of religion, beliefs, and superstitions as a matter that extends across generations and countries. There is no simplistic civilized/savage dichotomy in the presentation of the Indians in *Gardens* for while highlighting the vulnerability of tribal survival in the modern world, the work challenges the privileging race as the great distinguisher of the "other." Silko walks a fine line in exposing the problematic dynamics of attempting to site difference without ultimately lapsing into oversimplification. She very deliberately introduces the issue of gender politics, with the anti-Indian elements also proving to be antifeminist. Unlike *Ceremony* and *Almanac* where the key characters whose spiritual lives we follow are often male, the onus of change and revival in *Gardens* lies with women. The Indians' struggle to survive the corruptions of the "new" world is clearly linked to a recovered spirituality grounded in the Ghost Dance, which opposes the closed reading of the Jesus story that the patriarchal, dominant-culture church propagates. In communicating her alternative reality, Silko manipulates the conventional tropes of the organized church, thus destabilizing the politically correct white religious message. Throughout, there is an irrevocable sense of the linkage between femaleness and fertility, of a sexualized women-centered society and the hope of fecundity in a truly new Eden. Providing a complex study of the relationship between tribal and European myths, the sociocultural use of gardens, imperialism, collecting fauna and the issue of interracial as well as intercultural exchanges, *Gardens* highlights the complex overlapping of identity influences.

Silko's repertoire of work also includes a book of poetry titled *Laguna Woman* (1974); the self-published *Sacred Water: Narratives and Pictures* (1993); *The Delicacy and Strength of Lace* (1986), chronicling her correspondence with poet James Wright and exploring the process of creating a work; and *Yellow Woman and a Beauty of the Spirit* (1997), a collection of essays covering largely political issues such as **racism**, immigration, and tribal disenfranchisement.

Themes

Silko writes mainly from the identity of an American Indian even though she has a mix of Laguna Pueblo, Mexican, and white ancestry. At the core of her writing is a desire to identify what it is like to grow up on the fringes of identities, neither fully fledged Laguna nor white. This lack of belonging allows her to look at Native identity both from the insider and outsider perspectives. It also pushes her to forge a path whereby her Laguna heritage may coexist with prevalent 20th-century Euro-American sensibilities. Historically, Laguna culture itself is heavily influenced by Hopi, Zuni, Jemez, and Navajo as well as miscellaneous European cultures. Thus the practice of incorporating other traditions into Laguna society has always been in evidence. Her early short story, "The Man to Send Rain Clouds," highlights the basic themes of tolerable assimilation in a humorous depiction of a burial ritual encompassing Laguna as well as Roman Catholic rites and beliefs. Similarly, the mythic role of Yellow Woman, mirrored in many of her heroines, reveals how the traditional and contemporary can coexist in that one easily misunderstood figure who transgresses boundaries for the greater purpose of spiritual service to the tribe.

Educated variously at Board of Indian Affairs schools and a Catholic school before attending the University of New Mexico, Silko locates much of her work in the Pueblo of Laguna where she grew up. Central to much of her writing is the issue of the interrelatedness of community, which she defines as comprising both the land and its people. American Indian communal and individual identities have been consistently compromised in the past 500 years by the multiple atrocities inflicted upon the land and its peoples. Hence sovereignty, community, the vitality of an evolving tradition, and the need for continuity and change are recurring themes in her works. The function of humor in her texts lends perspective to the author's view of the world and balances her rigorous addressing of issues including the role of violence in resistance. As a holder of community stories to be passed on, Silko also takes on the responsibility of an historian, combating ignorance of Native history with knowledge, a key weapon to disarm the whites who typically have the monopoly on making meaning.

Style

The role of orature and the power of storytelling to heal are very real to Silko's vision. As a child Silko learned the folklore of the Laguna and Keres people through stories told by her grandmother and aunt. As a writer, she seeks to bring the dramatic oral experience of listening to a story into the reading of a printed story. The spider's web is an important structural metaphor for her writing, with the circularity of the work and its complex weaving of different strands of the narrative suggesting connections that are difficult to untangle or assail. Incorporating verse and prose with eloquently loaded spacing, the interrelatedness of all things is demonstrated in the nonlinear narrative of *Ceremony*. Similarly, in *Almanac*, the work loops back on itself, runs into prolonged digressions, and fills its 800 or so pages with a series of narratives within narratives. Here Silko is essentially telling several stories at once, stories interlinked to touch each other at certain symbolic points. In line with Silko's borrowings from Native oral tradition is her perspective of time. Chronological time, like linear narratives, only serves to limit one's view of the history and the world. In the organic cosmology that Silko adheres to, prophecies begun five centuries ago are still in the process of being fulfilled. Constantly experimenting with and subverting Western literary forms, Silko produces a seditious style that is in itself a critique of white conventionality.

Critical Reception

Lauded with critical acclaim for her stylistic achievement and multigenre works, Silko, like many of her fellow writers, has also been criticized for exoticizing the Indian world she portrays. Despite her aim to stay true to her Laguna heritage, she has also been criticized by fellow Laguna writer, Paula Gunn Allen, for revealing tribal secrets in *Ceremony*, a situation that points to the complexity involved in forming an Indian aesthetic and critical methodology. Having left law school in favor of the activism of writing, it is unsurprising that Silko's more recent work has also been met with disapproval by mainstream critics who earlier found *Almanac* uncomfortably political. Yet new studies have begun to analyze the subversive nature of Silko's earlier works, which tie in with her political agenda, which has become more overtly evident in her later works. Storytelling as a weapon of war is a means made available both to the author as well as to her characters. As a creative artist and activist, Silko's works unceasingly undercut the supposed fixity of a situation, be the issue a geographical limitation or a gender, racial, or sexual stereotype. (*See also* Native American Novel)

Further Reading

Arnold, Ellen L., ed. *Conversations with Leslie Marmon Silko*. Jackson: University Press of Mississippi, 2000.

Graulich, Melody, ed. *"Yellow Woman": Leslie Marmon Silko*. New Brunswick, NJ: Rutgers University Press, 1993.

Lee, Robert. *The Native American Renaissance*. Norman: University of Oklahoma Press, 2013.

Salyer, Gregory. *Leslie Marmon Silko*. New York: Twayne, 1997.

Poh Cheng Khoo

SONG OF SOLOMON

Toni Morrison's third novel, *Song of Solomon* (1977), is now a **canon**ical African American novel that explores the theme of quest for **identity** and for preserving a sense of community in its rich references to African American folklore tradition and history.

Morrison chooses a male protagonist, Milkman Dead, for her National Book Critics' Circle Award–winning novel, and this choice counters her foregrounding of female characters in her previous two novels—*The Bluest Eye* (1970) and *Sula* (1973). Milkman, caught between his father's black middle-class materialism and his aunt, Pilate's, traditional values, is alienated from his community and his cultural roots. Increasingly preoccupied with his family's past and troubled with his alienation, he embarks upon a physical and spiritual journey into the South. The original reason for this journey is to recover the gold that caused the rift between Milkman's father and his sister, Pilate. Milkman's father believes that Pilate stole a bag of gold when he and Pilate escaped from the South. What he does find, however, is liberating knowledge instead of the gold: when he overhears the name *Solomon* from a song that some children sing as they play a game in a little Virginia town, Milkman realizes that the song is part of his family history and that the "Solomon" in the song is his great-grandfather, a slave who escaped his bondage by flying back to Africa.

In *Song of Solomon*, Morrison also places her narrative in a larger political context of the **Civil Rights Movement** of the 1960s by incorporating historical events, such as the murder of Emmett Till, and through the characterization of Milkman's best friend Guitar Bains, who represents a radical political position. Guitar is a member of a secret revolutionary group called the *Seven Days*. Rejecting all racial uplift strategies, the Seven Days members are dedicated to avenging racial violence: when a black person is murdered by whites, the member responsible for that day of the week avenges the death by the same manner. At the end of the novel, Milkman and Guitar find themselves locked in physical struggle, and, then, Milkman leaps off a cliff, surrendering to the wind and riding it.

In *Song of Solomon*, a text that is infused with biblical allusions, mythologies, African American folklore and the history of slavery, the Great Migration, urbanization, and the Civil Rights Movement. Morrison illustrates how ancestral and cultural roots are vital to the preservation of the African American communities through her protagonist, who ultimately embraces the richness of his ancestry and heritage.

Further Reading

Kubitschek, Missy Dehn. *Toni Morrison: A Critical Companion*. Westport, CT: Greenwood Press, 1988.

Twagilimana, Aimable. "Toni Morrison's *Song of Solomon* and the American Dream." In *The American Dream*, edited by Harold Bloom and Blake Hobby, 203–12. New York: Bloom's Literary Criticism, 2009.

Wagner-Martin, Linda. "'Close to the Edge': Toni Morrison's *Song of Solomon*." In *Teaching American Ethnic Literatures*, edited by John R. Maitino and David R. Peck, 147–57. Albuquerque: University of New Mexico Press, 1996.

Willis, Susan. "Eruption of Funk: Historicizing Toni Morrison." In *Black Literature and Literary Theory*, edited by Henry Louis Gates Jr., 263–83. New York: Routledge, Chapman, and Hall, 1990.

Seongho Yoon

SOUTH ASIAN AMERICAN LITERATURE

The first significant American writer of South Asian descent was Dhan Gopal Mukerji (1890–1936). Often referred to as "that Hindu writer" by his contemporaries, Mukerji enjoyed considerable popularity during the 1920s. He was a graduate of Stanford University and his interpretations of Hindu folklore, philosophy, and scriptures are said to have influenced such diverse American authors as Van Wyck Brooks, T. S. Eliot, Lewis Mumford, and Eugene O'Neill. Born near Calcutta (India) in 1890, he came to the States in 1910, via Tokyo University, earned a graduate degree at Stanford University, where he taught as lecturer in comparative literature until 1916; in 1918, he married Ethel Ray Dugan, an American school teacher, became a prolific writer, and died in New York in 1936 (at his own hands). In nearly 15 years, he had published seven books about Indian fables, philosophy, and civilization; three plays, two books of poems, eleven children's books, and an autobiography. His beguiling animal stories became widely popular; one of them, *Gay Neck: The Story of a Pigeon* (1928), won the year's John Newbery Medal for "distinguished contribution to children's literature." This story of an army pigeon's death-defying friendship with his trainer would be produced as a filmstrip by Miller-Brody in 1973.

If Rudyard Kipling had written jungle stories solely for children's entertainment, Dhan Gopal Mukerji used them to embody the folk wisdom and the spiritual truths of the Hindu life—mainly its principles of tolerance, nonviolence, and truth. By using animals as protagonists of his tales, the animals that worked in unison with humans, he sought to dramatize the psychological benefits of living in harmony with nature. His work, sensitive and eloquent, seems to have been written with a fullness of love for all forms of life. As a literary pathfinder, he blazed the trails that other South Asian talents would follow for a while. However, those who followed him, albeit invariably better artists, would find Mukerji's grand humanistic vision unsuitable to their purpose. His autobiography, *Caste and Outcast* (1923), recently reissued by Stanford University Press (2002), has grabbed the attention of modern, especially postcolonial, scholars by its historical accuracy about the sorry status, and the questionable reception, of immigrants from minority communities.

The following essay, sectioned according to genres, deals chronologically with the South Asian Americans' achievements in various literary categories, beginning with the memoirs, then to poetry, and ending with fiction. A word about the criteria of inclusion: an open country like the United States has welcomed writers and professionals even if they came merely to work, and not to settle here; the nature of this publication, however, permits the inclusion of only those who can be rightly called American. Also, it may be said, the essay draws upon but a selection of the American writers of Indian and Pakistani descent, especially upon those who have either already made a name for themselves or are beginning to draw public attention.

Memoirists

In his recent book, *Modern South Asian Literature in English* (2003), Paul Brians speaks of "a profound and ever-growing international appetite for fiction by South Asian authors" (3), confirming the popular belief that South Asian Americans have excelled only in fiction. However, contrary to the general notion, South Asian American writers' contributions to nonfiction genres—especially to autobiography and poetry—have surprised well-informed readers not only by the freshness, elegance, and wit of their stance and narratives but also by the unusual content of their works. It is fitting that the essay should begin with a survey of the domains the least suspected to have been cultivated by South Asian American writers.

Ved (Prakash) Mehta (1934–), arguably, towers over contemporary autobiographers writing in America. The 15-year-old boy who came from India to the Arkansas School for the Blind, in Little Rock, and went on to earn a BA from Pomona College and a BA Honors from Balliol College of Oxford University, an MA, also from Oxford, and another MA from Harvard, ended up working as a staff writer for *New Yorker*. He has had a full share of exclusions from the five cultures he had known: the Indian, British, and American; the *New Yorker*'s; and of the blind. So, to share his stories and his insights, he embarked on autobiography on an epic scale, one that would keep him returning for 32 years to different segments of his life. Unleashing the series "Continents of Exile" in 1972, a metaphor for a life of exclusions, Mehta has just completed the 11th, and perhaps the final, installment of his memoirs, the first being *Daddyji* (1972) and the last, *The Red Letters* (2004), both dealing with the long and the powerful shadow his father's life cast upon him. Each memoir, organized around a central metaphor, seeks to capture the shifting seasons of the soul at various stages of the author's life. Together, the 11 parts of the autobiography encompass the grand architecture of an eventful memory of 70 years.

Now, Mehta's memory, in the grand autobiographical tradition, is by no means made up of family relatives or personal events alone. Like Nirad C. Chaudhuri (1897–1999) and V.S. Naipaul (1932–), the two other famous political analysts of Indian diaspora, Ved Mehta has freely commented upon India's social and political conditions. *Portrait of India* (1970) inaugurates his life-long engagement with the political scene of the country he had left behind. He returns to the subject in *Mahatma Gandhi and His Apostles* (1977), if only to note the decline of Gandhian idealism among his disciples and political successors, a loss that spelled the national betrayal of a great promise. *The New India* (1978), *A Family Affair: India Under Three Prime Ministers* (1982), and *Rajiv Gandhi and Rama's Kingdom* (1994) round off his cold, detached analyses of the home conditions. Mehta has, thus, been a pilgrim of two worlds: of the rich internal world of his personal memory and psyche—its reports contained in his memoirs; and of the human world of material forces—its accounts recorded in his histories of India's contemporary politics.

Not all South Asian memoirists, however, display an equal interest in, or awareness of, the wider forces of history. Meena Alexander (1951–), poet, novelist, and critic, concentrates, in *Fault Lines* (1992), on her personal past as an allegory of an exiled woman's situation, of the dislocation of a person moving across cultures and borders, searching for herself and assessing the nature of the influences that shaped her poetic persona. Commenting upon the changes in the revised issue of *Fault Lines* (2003), Michael W. Cox, in the celebrated autobiography's review, published in *South Asian Review* 25.1 (2004), rightly observes that Alexander goes "to unearth something much closer to the truth and essence of who she is and how she came to be the present self" (351). Meena Alexander, thus, becomes the story of Meena Alexander's crafted memoir. Within that province, she searches with the alacrity—nay, the tenacity—of an Isis for the fragments of a global woman's **identity** scattered across continents, poring over them to piece together a human form. The result, one must say, is well worth the effort, for the reader is at once pulled into, and drawn along, the intriguing paths of a personal memory.

Sara Suleri (1953–), a memoirist, public intellectual, and literary critic, born in Pakistan, educated in Lahore and at Indiana University, has emerged as an intriguing and humorous autobiographer. A born stylist, wielding an exquisite language, she can nail down a sharp detail in a phrase, or light up an entire life in a sentence. Her first work, *Meatless Days: A Memoir* (1989), deals not only with the loves and tensions of a growing family but also with the conflicted existence of Pakistan torn asunder by the 1971 war with India. Nobody escapes the gloom and oppression of those times—neither a thriving family, nor an individual's psyche. Suleri's second memoir, *Boys Will Be Boys* (2003), celebrates her father's passion for politics as well as his lust for life. In "an elegy" for her Pip, the "patriotic and preposterous," an intense inner monologue is directed here at the dead father, in a manner not unlike Sylvia Plath's. In both the works, the lives of the young keep getting mangled by the history of the country. Suleri's narrative, by turns gentle, bitter, or funny, veers away from making bold historical judgments. Her voice, cool when it could be screaming, can as well be read as a measure of personal desperation as of artistic discipline.

Poetry

The body of South Asian American poetry is indeed slim but is not insignificant. Several factors can satisfactorily account for its slimness: only a few of the South Asian creative writers have devoted themselves exclusively to poetry; most of them come from a younger generation, which has not rendered its full account yet; and two very gifted poets have been lost in the very prime of their lives—Agha Shahid Ali, to cancer, and Reetika Vazirani, to suicide.

A. K. Ramanujan (1929–1993), poet, translator and folklorist, linguist, scholar, and academician, is widely acknowledged as the doyen of the American poets of Indian descent. Educated at the University of Mysore, then earning a PhD in linguistics at Indiana University (1963), he arrived at the University of Chicago in 1962 to join its departments of South Asian languages and civilizations, where he would stay, until his death, to shape the course of South Asian Studies. A transnational and transcultural genius, elected to the American Academy of Arts and Sciences (1990), Ramanujan was honored with *Padma Sri*—one of India's highest civilian awards—by the president of India and awarded the MacArthur Fellowship by the prestigious Chicago-based foundation. His poetry, laced with mischief and mysticism, written in modernist—almost laconic—English, manages alternately to carry hints of the Himalayan breeze, the metropolitan pollution, and the monsoons of the South. The narrator's voice there, sensitive yet unsentimental, cuts like a scalpel through life's daily illusions. Philosophic or ironic, playful, naughty, or just whimsical, Ramanujan's poems, much like Eliot's, or Robert Frost's, begin in surprise and end in joy. So creative was his life that the publication of four volumes of poetry, six works of translations—four of them of classical Tamil and Kannada poems—and the coauthorship of four works did not exhaust his energy. Since his death, another five volumes of poems, essays, and oral tales have joined the body of his work, and more are in the offing.

Agha Shahid Ali (1949–2001), poet, critic, and translator, has had a phenomenal success in poetry, were success measured by the boldness to modify an established tradition and to influence the very course of poetry. One of Chaucer's contributions to English poetry has been that he imported the Petrarchan sonnet from Italy; one of Ali's contributions has been that he brought Urdu ghazal from India and grafted it on to the body of American poetry. He accomplished this, first, by writing some intense and winsome ghazals in English himself; and then by translating some of the best ghazals of the legendary poet of Pakistan, Faiz Ahmed Faiz, under the title *The Rebel's Silhouette* (1995); and, finally, by persuading, as Ellen Bryant Voigt says in "In Memoriam, Agha Shahid Ali: 1949–2001," "innumerable and some unlikely American poets to commit the elaborate ghazal" (Norton Poets online). A poem of formal discipline, where the first couplet sets up the rhyme and the refrain for the entire poem, the second line of whose succeeding couplets repeats the refrain, ghazal was antithetical to the contemporary American poetry entranced by free verse. Ali, in compelling poetic attention to his work, won respect for the restricted form new to the American poetry, so that when he gave his first reading at the Academy of American Poets, James Merrill would come to listen to his work. Amitav Ghosh gives an astute assessment of Agha Shahid Ali's contribution in his article "'The Ghat of the Only World': Agha Shahid Ali in Brooklyn." He says "the formalization of the ghazal may well prove to be Shahid's most important scholarly contribution to the canon of English poetry" (*Nation* 274.5 [2002], 31). Still another influence emanates from Ali's poetry: a multicultural blend of mythologies—the Arabic, Hindu, Persian, and the Greek—one that imparts density to his own work and demonstrates to our mythless age the central importance of the poets' historic memory to their art. What is more, experimental and playful, Ali refused to be circumscribed by the traditional and the exotic alone. He mastered some elaborate and complex forms of European poetry—especially the sestina and canzone—claiming a special place in the American poetry for South Asian voices. In view of his multiple achievements, it will be some years before Ali's full significance as poet can be assessed.

Meena Alexander, poet, memoirist, novelist, and critic has, with her eight volumes of poetry, produced a remarkable body of verse. At once reflective, intense, and lyrical, a fresh voice enters contemporary American poetry with her. Especially, as one who has lived in four continents (Asia, Africa, Europe, and North America) and who speaks five languages (Arabic, English, French, Hindi, and Malayalam), Alexander brings a genuine cosmopolitan awareness to bear upon issues of feminism that are invariably the subjects of her poems. So, as with Eliot's narrator in "The Love Song of J. Alfred Prufrock," the "I" of Alexander's narrator keeps splitting into an individual and a universal person, a particular sufferer transforming into a type, in this case a universal woman—especially a postcolonial woman with harsh penalties attached to her color. The lines of her latest poems, the ones written after 9/11, especially the ones appearing in *Raw Silk* (2004), carry in their solemn march the stoic echoes of Hilda Doolittle's *The Walls Do Not Fall*, which dealt mainly with Londoners' endurance and courage during the 1940s' Battle for Britain.

Chitra Banerjee Divakaruni (1957–), poet, novelist, essayist, and social counselor, has published four volumes of poetry. In a way, her poetry reflects the spirit that she considers to be the lifeblood of good art: "Compassion and empathy." And Divakaruni's compassion is pretty wide—for a self-willed child ("Leroy at the Zoo"), the ruthless Irish nuns in India ("The Infirmary"), and the battered immigrant women in the States (*Black Candle*). Her poetry, consequently, deals with the multicultural world that Divakaruni lives and moves in. And, deriving from personal experiences, her poems blend immigrant sociology with autobiography, their lines often rolling out as declarations of a humanistic commitment. Surprisingly, they deal as easily with the Indigo past of India as with a modern Yuba City School, stitching South Asian memories onto the American landscape.

Reetika Vazirani (1962–2003), a poet and literary editor, published two volumes of poetry in her brief lifetime, and several pieces, besides, but which still remain to be collected. Intense exuberance presides over her poems, where a reckless playfulness often surprises the reader with freshly minted words or remorseless sentiments. The poems of her first collection, *White Elephants* (1996), fastening their attention upon what naturally catches a newcomer's eye—the differences between *the here* and *the there*, between *theirs* and *ours*—resolve themselves into emotional dialectics. Her second book of poems, *World Hotel* (2002), which won the 2003 Anisfield-Woolf Book Award meant "for books that explore the richness of human diversity," is the work of a knowledgeable, almost a disillusioned, person who not only understands but also accepts human infidelity and forgives opportunism, ignoring lovers' indifference or their sudden falling off. Written with gusto, but almost in haste, it is urban poetry without a trace of sentimental nostalgia. The second book is, indeed, postmodernist to the core, teasing us to speculate where Vazirani might have arrived had she lived beyond her youthful years.

Fiction

The field of fiction has, indeed, been the glorious playground where South Asian American writers have racked up an impressive record of enduring value. First, there is an abundance of talent here: every six months or so a new author, generally a woman writer, turns up with a bright and dazzling book, the title quickly noted and widely promoted. Then, together, they have created a critical mass of fresh and varied South Asian writing. Finally, the quality of their contribution to American fiction has entitled one (**Bharati Mukherjee**) to a National Book Critics Circle Award (1998), and another (**Jhumpa Lahiri**) to a Pulitzer Prize. Not only are the best of these authors distinguished by awards, they are also recognized by regular inclusion in school and college curricula and anthologies.

Roughly since the late 1950s, the South Asian English fiction had been known in the West generally, and in the States particularly, through the comic works of

Jhumpa Lahiri, 2014. (Vipin Kumar/Hindustan Times via Getty Image)

R. K. Narayan—*The Financial Expert* (1952), *The Guide* (1958), and *The Vendor of Sweets* (1967); the philosophic novels of Raja Rao—*Kanthapura* (1938), *The Serpent and the Rope* (1960), *The Cat and Shakespeare: A Tale of Modern India* (1965); and the intense tales of Kamala Markandaya—*Nectar in a Sieve* (1954), *A Handful of Rice* (1966), and *The Nowhere Man* (1972). However, as a tributary of the American fiction, the South Asian American novel truly begins with the arrival of Bharati Mukherjee on the scene. In our chronological scheme, however, Bapsi Sidhwa must take precedence, as Anita Desai's latest phase of work, the one of American orientation, must be recognized here as well.

Anita Desai (1937–), short-story writer, novelist, and critic, is identified as an Indian, rather than as a South Asian American, writer both on account of her subject and her domicile. For more than a decade, though, she has lived in and written about America, and hence the last phase of her work demands an acknowledgment here. Beginning with *Journey to Ithaca* (1995), which sends a young American couple on a tedious journey through India—virtually on their painful trials through India's ashrams—Desai's attention shifts to the American scene. Progressively, the plot of the next novel, *Fasting, Feasting* (1999), unfolds from India to the States, following a young Indian student who gets lost among the mazes of his abnormal

American host family. Her latest novel, *The Zigzag Way* (2004), the narrative of a historian's search for his family roots spreading out from States, through Mexico, to England, paints vivid scenes of contemporary Mexican life. The three novels, open-ended, tentative, and experimental, bespeak of immense resilience in the author who, after publishing 11 novels, can break an altogether fresh ground. Her virtue as artist now, as earlier, seems to lie in the sensitivity and assurance with which she handles the contemporary idiom of the global middle-class professionals. Now witty, then sardonic, her narrative becomes a source of pleasure in itself—yes, even when the story becomes a bit tedious. She remains a bright and intelligent observer of the world's social and political scene.

Bapsi Sidhwa (1938–), a Pakistani American novelist of Parsi descent, has added sociopolitical novels with a fine overlay of humor. Whether dealing with heartless wife abuse by Pakistani tribesmen, as in *The Bride* (1983), or the social manners of the Parsi community in Pakistan, as in *The Crow Eaters* (1992), she gives a comic treatment even to the issues poignant or painful, thus gathering a distance from her subjects. Because she selects her characters from minorities, servants, and vendors, her fiction proves her to be pushing the marginalized or the misrepresented to center stage. Because of this social commitment, even a fictionalized personal memoir in her hands begins to approximate to a cultural and political record, as *Cracking India* (1991), a young Parsi girl's account of the upheaval in the wake of the Partition, amply demonstrates. It is remarkable that the novel, which describes the sexual maturing of Lenny, can be read not only as her passage from innocence to knowledge but also as a feminist allegory. For, after all, the novel scours the female world governed as much by patriarchy as by a colonial regime, portraying thus the helpless condition of the young woman maimed by polio and governed by forces beyond her control. By turns humorous and raucous, Sidhwa's fiction excels at the portrayal of characters with a patina of westernization, of which the finest example is *An American Brat* (1993).

Bharati Mukherjee (1940–), novelist, short-story writer, essayist, and critic, is "the Grande Dame of the Indian diasporic fiction," as Vijay Lakshmi says in her essay "Bharati Mukherjee," in *The Routledge Encyclopedia of Postcolonial Literatures* (2005). With seven novels, two collections of short stories, and three books of non-fiction and several polemical essays to her credit, Mukherjee's claim to an eminent place in the contemporary fiction is not likely to be challenged seriously. On the contrary, her position has been strengthened by more than the volume of her work. The way she has turned the expatriate novel into a variation of American writing puts her at the head of the compatriot practitioners of the craft. By the example of her work as much as by her polemical essays, she has demonstrated how the writing of newcomers can, and ought to, move beyond the ghettoized community of expatriates, and escape the perpetual rehearsals of the nostalgia of a home left behind. She argued for, and has achieved, a veritable immigrant community's novel, whose characters fight not to preserve their identity but to transform it, affecting, while striving to be assimilated by, the larger body politic.

Above all, what gives Bharati Mukherjee's work an easy currency is her craft. It is not only her exquisite story lines, but also her tightly knit yarns and seamless narratives, all delivered in the limpid prose of modern Americana, that have won her a wide readership. Her protagonists, mostly upwardly mobile women who, constantly in the process of becoming, keep on launching out in search of a new identity, a new destiny, or an enriching fulfillment of their lives, have stuck a deep chord in the heart of contemporary generation. In keeping with the characters' ceaseless search, her plots, the hieroglyphs of internal and external motions, delineate a world in constant flux, where one who stops must stagnate. Her novels have thus opened up an avenue of new attitude for the characters in transit, one leading to hopeful and energetic assertiveness in the face of the general uncertainty and indifference they encounter in the host country. A remarkable feature of her superb stories of personal relations, whether located in Calcutta or Bombay, New York or Detroit, Montreal or San Francisco, is their circumambient universe. A family's tale is grounded in the Indian National Movement; a life is mangled by Canadian racism, or a family's future is twisted by American violence. Their various envelopes effectively displace the characters' isolating exoticism with global modernism. However, in as much as the fortuitous violence of her women's lives shapes her plots, Mukherjee's work seems to suffer from the limitations that brand the turbulent early fiction of Joyce Carol Oates.

Gita Mehta (1943–), novelist, journalist, social activist, and cultural commentator, has achieved well-deserved recognition in academic circles as well as the public media. She first attained fame with *Karma Cola: Marketing the Mystic East* (1979), a tightly knit and fast-paced account of the credulous crowd that went to India for a pop salvation of the soul. The narrative, spiked with lightning puns and crackling with wit, at once won an audience across the English-speaking world that found its postmodernist turn of mind perfectly reflected by it. For the generation of the 1970s, it seemed to do what T. S. Eliot's "Love Song of J. Alfred Prufrock" had done for the Europe of the 1920s: It cleverly and faithfully reflected the contemporary skepticism with cool detachment. Gita Mehta's fiction, meager but precious, represents two Indias: the colonial, in *Raj: A Novel* (1989), and the mystical, in *A River Sutra* (1993). In *A River Sutra*, like a thread (*sutra*), as Pradyumna Chauhan notes in his article "Gita Mehta," in *The South Asian Novelists in English* (2003), "the holy river Narmada flows through the novel, just as the great brown god Mississippi does through *The Adventures of Huckleberry Finn*, linking diverse lives and stories, myths and memories, rituals and dreams" (151). One such novel is enough to ensure an author's place in the history of South Asian American fiction.

Vijay Lakshmi (1943–), short-story writer, novelist, critic, and social commentator, has attracted global attention not only through her publications in *Paris Transcontinental, Orbis*, and *Wassafiri* (United Kingdom), *Femina* (India), *Short Story* (United States), but also through translations of her work in Chinese, French, and Spanish. Fascinated by the phenomenon of global mobility, she writes of the emotional losses and psychological consequences of deracinated communities, whether Jewish, Russian, or South Asian. Although her protagonists are often women, and although women pay the heaviest price for their emotional and physical transplantation, her characters are hardly ever victims. Well educated and cosmopolitan, her heroines take charge of their destinies by readjusting to the changed circumstances of their lives, by borrowing the humane and rational practices of the host culture, by dedicating themselves to the needs of new society, or simply by starting out as entrepreneurs in the new land of opportunities. Believing that each human being lives alone in the castle of their skin, she coasts by popular ideological pronouncements that presume all human beings to be standardized like parts of a Ford motor car. Her chief domain is, rather, the world of the interior atmosphere of the mind, forever fluid, amorphous, and evanescent. To find a match to her lyrical stories fraught with poetic images that stun the reader with their deadly accuracy and brightness, one has to go to Virginia Woolf's impressionistic passages. Anne D. Ulrich finely sums up this poetic quality in her article "Vijay Lakshmi," in *Writers of the Indian Diaspora* (1993). She says of Lakshmi's narratives: "When her characters' fears are greatest, 'horses thunder across the plains of the mind, against skies of liquid fire'. When the moments are tender, 'the fragrance of jasmine and bela', which the narrator wants so much to pack in a box to carry to America, falls off hands 'in tufts of cotton' and disappears" (179). Lakshmi's magical powers in capturing existentialist moments decidedly remain unsurpassed in contemporary American fiction.

Amitav Ghosh (1956–), anthropologist, essayist, journalist, and novelist, has carved out a reputation for prolific fiction that takes the reader's breath away. Reinforced by sound research, Ghosh's fiction cuts broad swaths through history as well as geographies—especially as represented by his last three novels: *The Calcutta Chromosome* (1996), *The Glass Palace* (2000), and *The Hungry Tide* (2004). He recreates in his *In an Antique Land: History in the Guise of a Traveler's Tale* (1993) a 12th-century Indian servant's relation to his Tunisian Jewish master, a prosperous merchant first settled in Egypt, then in Aden. In the process, the novel delivers the contrary worlds of the two parties: the mud-walled Cairo of the master and the lush Malabar coast of the servant. Filtered through the vision of a modern, Oxford-trained, anthropologist, the bondsman's story of 800 years ago, although reconstructed from medieval letters and chronicles, acquires a powerful clarity about the relationships between two old civilizations and their economic and social practices. The pervasive irony of the slave-compatriot's reading, and judging, the slave-master's documents ensures the reader's unflagging interest. However, Ghosh's work is no more a pure novel than Joyce's *Ulysses* is a classical epic. Provided with biographical information, bibliographic footnotes, and a factual prologue, in addition to blending various genres, its narrative unambiguously redefines the boundaries of the modern novel.

The Glass Palace, chronicling the fortunes of three generations, sweeps through the history of Bengal, Burma (Myanmar), and Malaysia, unfolding a panorama of Southeast Asia through war and peace, a truly Tolstoyan canvas of an imperial history done, and delivered, by a "postcolonial" subject. With his historical works, Ghosh opens up a new territory for the contemporary American novel. His fictional achievement, though, refuses to be confined to only a single category. *The Calcutta Chromosome: A Novel of Fevers, Delirium and Discovery* is a brilliant piece of science fiction that reads like a fast-paced mystery thriller. No matter in which type of fiction it is embedded, Ghosh's cross-cultural narrative, urbane and elegant, always ripples with gentle humor, verging at times on witty sarcasm. At work, behind all his fiction, is a highly intelligent and deeply moral mind, one anchored in wholesome sanity.

Chitra Banerjee Divakaruni (1956–), starting out as a poet, has arrived at a respectable place in the South Asian American fiction. Her novels no less than her stories are well known in, and outside, academia. And she has produced a robust body in genres as varied as children's fiction, such as *Neela: Victory Song* (2002); mythical writing, in *The Conch Bearer* (2003); the novel of magic realism, in *The Mistress of Spices* (1997); and realistic fiction, in *Sister of My Heart* (1999). Extremely popular—indeed, a best seller—she writes mostly about the plight and the travails of immigrant women as they seek to find their feet in the new country. Adventurous and creative as Divakaruni's characters are, one suspects that they are run through a formulaic trail to vindicate a feminist ideology. It is such commitment alone that can satisfactorily explain the repetitive patterns of stories in the hands of a richly imaginative writer. The abiding virtue of Divakaruni's fiction, at times sentimental and often melodramatic but always experimental, is that it boldly engages in the creation of alternate realities.

Vikram Chandra (1961–), filmographer, novelist, and short-story writer, has collected handsome credits for his fiction as well as for his work with films. "Passionately interested in movies," as he confessed in his interview with Kevin Mahoney (1998), Chandra has been associated either as actor, director, scriptwriter, or co-producer, with four films: *The Disenchanted* (1990), *Left Luggage* (2000), *The Quarry* (2000), and *Mission Kashmir* (2000), working with John Lynch, Jonny Phillips, Sylvia Esau, Oscar Peterson, and Jody Abrahams. For his fiction—*Red Earth and Pouring Rain* (1995), and *Love and Longing in Bombay* (1997)—he has won the Commonwealth Writers Prize for Best First Book and the Commonwealth Writers Prize for the Eurasia region. Chandra's fiction is remarkable for a ceaseless experimentation in form, and for its postmodernist resistance to genre and the inclusion of kitsch and skepticism. The action of *Red Earth and Pouring Rain*, an extensive epic stretching across three continents (Asia, Europe, and America) over three centuries, is mediated by a ghost narrator. Subverting the orderly—indeed, the organic—conventions of classicism, Chandra's fiction resorts to multiple and fractured narratives, creating a feel of multiverse. For his next work, as Chandra told Kevin Mahoney in a summer 1998 interview, he deliberately decided "to do a story of drawing-room warfare . . . a ghost story . . . a detective story, a love story, and a story about work and money" all, together, granting the writer "a many-layered apprehension of the city of Bombay" (www.geocities.com/SoHo/Nook/1082 /vikram-chandra.html). Whether caressing, or interrogating, the traditional forms of stories, Chandra links the five stories by a framing tale, all of them ending as so many meditations upon fictional form. There is something Joycean in Chandra's conscious exploitation of literary forms.

Jhumpa Lahiri (1967–), short-story writer and novelist, is a popular fiction writer whose stories have appeared in *Harvard Review, Story Quarterly*, and *The New Yorker*. The focus of her work is personal relations, yes, even when they extend across oceans. By threading her narrative through their entanglements, Lahiri seeks not to dazzle, even less to shock, but only to reveal, to take the reader into the hidden recesses of personal ties, where festering might have begun but of which the persons involved may not have any inkling. As Paul Brians says in *Modern South Asian Literature in English* (2003), "the relationships in her stories are a series of missed connections" (196). Whether working on the smaller scale of stories, or the larger canvas of a novel, Lahiri explores the physical and psychological dislocation of her immigrant characters. And in her pursuit, she employs the Jamesian method of cross-lighting the diverse characters, by juxtaposing their respective cultures together, in this case the Indian and the American. Her observation and treatment of the habits and attitudes of the second-generation characters rings true, while her portraits of *desis* (of Americanized versions of the people of Indian descent) visiting or touring India are but superficial accounts of certain stereotypes. Robin E. Field accurately observes in "Writing the Second Generation: Negotiating Cultural Borderlands in Jhumpa Lahiri's *Interpreter of Dreams* and *The Namesake*": "Lahiri's most overt project in *The Namesake* [2003], and in several of her short stories as well, is the differentiation between generations in regard to the importance and understanding of cultural roots" (*South Asian Review*, XXV: 2 [2004], 165). This disparity has earned Lahiri's work the charge of being "inauthentic," especially from South Asian critics who regard themselves as the only qualified purveyors of genuine cultural artifacts. Howsoever the future settles the charge against her, one thing is clear: as an artistic interpreter of cultural maladies, Jhumpa Lahiri hardly needs any apologies.

Anjana Appachana (1972–), story writer and novelist, deals in her fiction with the daily lives of ordinary Indian women, which, seemingly uneventful, are haunted by physical assaults, hardships, and psychological violations. *Incantations and Other Stories* (1992) recounts in various frames how the oppression of women comes not from men alone; it comes too from other women as well as the victims' collaboration with the perpetrators and their own silence. In *Listening Now* (1998), a novel made up of the life stories of six women, no one particular group or gender is blamed for women's situation and suffering, but everyone and everything about the woman's life—the folk ways, the customs, the rituals, the expectations—are alike shown to be responsible for their plight. Appachana is too much taken up, in words of Eliot's "Preludes," with "this infinitely gentle and infinitely suffering thing" to be drawn into heated debates about the politics of gender. The center of her well-told fiction is, primarily, a woman's experience of being alive with all her buried desires and pains, fantasies, and passions.

In sum, the South Asian American literature has been varied, vibrant, and abiding. New voices are breaking onto the scene, from such novelists as Kiran Desai, Amina Ali, Manil Suri, and Indu Sundaresan, a historical novelist of discernible power; they are going to provide the staying power for the coming decades. And their predecessors' impatience with social wrongs, their passion for change, their engagement with literary forms, and their freshly minted language, are all likely to have far-reaching consequences for contemporary American fiction, and not just for South Asian American fiction. After all, the work of their peers—V. S. Naipaul, Salman Rushdie, and Vikram Seth—has already altered the landscape of the modern English novel. The transformation taking place across the Atlantic holds a lesson—indeed, a promise—for the contemporary American literary scene.

Further Reading

Bahri, Deepika, and Mary Vasudeva, eds. *Between the Lines: South Asians and Postcoloniality.* Philadelphia: Temple University Press, 1996.

Brians, Paul. *Modern South Asian Literature in English.* Westport, CT: Greenwood Press, 2003.

Chauhan, Pradyumna S. "Anita Desai." In *South Asian Novelists in English: An A-to-Z Guide,* edited by Jaina C. Sanga, 47–53. Westport, CT: Greenwood Press, 2003.

Chauhan, Pradyumna S. "Gita Mehta" In *South Asian Novelists in English: An A-to-Z Guide,* edited by Jaina C. Sanga, 149–52. Westport, CT: Greenwood Press, 2003.

Mukherjee, Meenakshi. *The Perishable Empire: Essays on Indian Writing in English.* New Delhi: Oxford University Press, 2000.

Nelson, Emmanuel S., ed. *Reworlding: The Literature of the Indian Diaspora.* Westport, CT: Greenwood Press, 1992.

Nelson, Emmanuel S., ed. *Writers of the Indian Diaspora: A Bio-Bibliographical Critical Sourcebook.* Westport, CT: Greenwood Press, 1993.

Ross, Robert, ed. *International Literature in English.* New York: Garland, 1991.

Sanga, Jaina C. *South Asian Novelists in English: An A-to-Z Guide.* Westport, CT: Greenwood Press, 2003.

Wong, S. C. *Reading Asian American Literature: From Necessity to Extravagance.* Princeton, NJ: Princeton University Press, 1993.

Pradyumna S. Chauhan

SPIRITUALS

The musical counterpart to slave narratives, the spirituals have assumed a dominant presence in the canon of American folk song. They have transcended their particular context and symbolically represent a universal hope of liberation from oppression. The spirituals are principally associated with African American church congregations of the antebellum South and the earlier, more informal, and sometimes clandestine gatherings of enslaved people. Their creation, the result of a process of mutual influence and reciprocal borrowing, is credited to evangelical sermons and hymns, biblical stories, traditional African chants and praise songs, and the combined experiences of enslaved people in the South.

Most important for interpreting the meaning of the spirituals is an appreciation of the context—social and religious—in which they were performed and the insight they lend into the extraordinary power of music to shape the experience and conscious identity of a people. In the spirituals, enslaved people critically analyzed their conditions, fashioned a creative theological response, indicted their oppressors without overtly denigrating them, reasserted the influence of an African sensibility, and empowered themselves by exercising a form of resistance that would endure longer than the conditions to which they were subject.

The spirituals created by enslaved people became a unique means to "keep on keeping on" under the physical and psychological pressures of daily life, testifying to the belief that the supernatural interacted with the natural and humanity had a decisive role to play in accomplishing liberation. In creation as well as performance they exhibited the essential characteristics of spontaneity, variety, and communal interchange. The form of the spirituals was flexible and improvisational, thereby able to fit an individual slave's experience into the consciousness of group, creating at once an intensely personal and vividly communal experience.

The spirituals, as the cultural product of enslaved Africans, used rhythms and beats of various homelands. The distinguishing musical aesthetic of the spirituals derives from West African percussive forms, multiple meters, syncopation, extensive melodic ornamentation, a call-and-response structure, and an integration of song and movement, each involving improvisation. Call and response embodies the foundational principle behind the performance of the spirituals, denoting the ritual requirement of what is necessary for completion. Very much a ritual act, when spirituals were sung by enslaved people they amplified their desire for liberation and created conditions of sacred space and time wherein the biblical stories of which they sang were transformed and the history of the ancient past became the history of the present.

Designed to communicate on more than one level, the spirituals sometimes functioned as coded songs to communicate information between enslaved people. Booker T. Washington affirmed that the freedom in their songs meant freedom in this world and **Frederick Douglass** insisted that references to Caanan implied the North. But formally and thematically, spirituals were open to change and improvisation as a spiritual in one situation might mean something else in another. In nearly every instance, however, there is an intertwining of theological and social messages.

When the Civil War opened up the society in which enslaved Africans were confined and brought them in to large-scale contact with the world outside the plantation, Northerners came to appreciate their distinctive music. As with ex-slave narratives, the African American authorship of the spirituals was challenged at first. But in an 1867 article published in *The Atlantic Monthly*, Thomas Wentworth Higginson, a militant New England abolitionist who commanded the first freed slave regiment to fight against the Confederacy, was among the first to describe how he heard spirituals.

Synthesizing sacred and secular meaning, the spirituals drew images from the Bible to interpret their own experience, measuring it against a wider system of theological and historical meaning. Three themes dominate spirituals: the desire for freedom, the desire for justice, and strategies for survival. God is a liberator who is involved in history who will "trouble the waters" of oppression. Many spirituals like "Joshua Fit the Battle of Jericho" are drawn from biblical texts that stress God's involvement in the liberation of the oppressed. Although God's liberating work was not always concretely evident, enslaved people were confident that "You Got a Right" to "the tree of life."

The songs also stress a need for enslaved people's own participation in God's liberation, to be "Singing with a Sword in My Hand." They viewed their cry of "Let My People Go" as answered with the Emancipation Proclamation, when "Slavery Chain Done Broke at Last." God makes justice for the righteous and the unrighteous because "All God's Children Got Wings," but "everybody who's talking about heaven ain't going." Anyone who stands against liberation is called to account, "Were You There When They Crucified my Lord?" Jesus represents both an historical savior and whoever helps the oppressed. Jesus functions in a more personal way than God does, and is affirmed both in his divinity and humanity, especially his identification with the oppressed who believe that "A Little Talk With Jesus Makes It Right." Hence his birth is an occasion to "Go Tell It on the Mountain."

Songs like "Steal Away" may have served as a means to convene secret resistance meetings, whereas "Deep River and My Home is Over Jordan" may imply a wish to cross over to Africa or to the North. But getting to freedom is what occupies many of the lyrics that take as a theme a tired sojourner struggling through a hostile landscape while leaning and depending on God. Portraying a struggle against oppression in a variety of metaphors, many spirituals focus on the difficult movement through space and time, but with the confidence to cheer the "Weary Traveler." Spatial and temporal metaphors of movement employing a variety of methods—sailing, walking, riding, rowing, climbing—all appear for a people "Bound to Go."

The spirituals actually and symbolically moved a people toward liberation when they sang, "We Are Climbing Jacob's Ladder," even if they could only "Keep Inching Along." Noting the threat of adverse physical conditions, the creators appropriated symbols from their own situation and describe searching for God in the wilderness, rocks, darkness, storms, and valleys. Lyrics from songs such as "O Stand the Storm," gave inspiration to endure. Although an enslaved person often felt "Like a Motherless Child," faith is affirmed because "All My Troubles Will Soon Be Over." Sometimes a lonely sojourner is aided by heavenly transportation, as in "Swing Low, Sweet Chariot," or the activity of the Underground Railroad that invites "Get on Board, Little Children." But the destination is always freedom. Many writers of all ethnicities have invoked the spirituals, conscious that in doing so they were calling forth the spirit of a people struggling to be free, a people who asserted that "Before I'll be a slave/I'll be buried in my grave/And go home to my Lord and be free." (*See also* African American Slave Narrative)

Further Reading

Cone, James. *The Spirituals and the Blues.* New York: Seabury Press, 1972.
Lovell, John. *Black Song: The Forge and the Flame.* New York: Macmillan, 1972.

Kimberly Rae Connor

STREET, THE

Written with the assistance of the Houghton Mifflin Literary Fellowship Award and published in 1946, Ann Petry's novel became the first by an African American woman to sell over 1 million copies. *The Street* builds on the examples of Paul Laurence Dunbar's *The Sport of the Gods* (1902) and **Richard Wright**'s *Native Son* (1940) in the cultivation of black literary naturalism. At the same time, it marks the historical crossover of black women's writing into mainstream American reading publics.

Recently divorced from her husband and estranged from her father, the independent and self-reliant Lutie Johnson is nevertheless filled with hope that she will be able to start a profitable new life for herself in New York City.

Lutie and her son, Bub, move into a run-down apartment in a tenement on Harlem's 116th Street, and, despite her immediate surroundings, the iconic image of Benjamin Franklin as the quintessential self-made individual looms large in Lutie's thoughts. But the reality of her situation as a single black mother living in a world where economic opportunity and social advancement are foreclosed to her lot is highlighted by the characters who prey on her optimism: Superintendent Jones targets Lutie as the object of his perverse sexual fantasies and persuades Bub to steal letters from mailboxes; tenant and madam Mrs. Hedges wants to enlist her as a prostitute; bandleader Boots Smith uses her to secure his own job and advance his own career; and white slumlord Junto, Petry's narrative counterpoint to Franklin, orchestrates the entire web of exploitation through his ownership of the tenement, its first-floor brothel, and the bar in which Boots's band plays.

The one glimpse of a silver lining comes when Lutie is given the opportunity to sing for Boots's band. But her sense of relief is cut short by a series of depressing events: Jones's attempted rape of Lutie; Junto's demand that Boots find a way to make Lutie his personal concubine or risk losing his job; Boots's subsequent extortion of her; and Bub's arrest by the post office authorities. Alone, destitute, and desperate, Lutie finally appeals to Boots for funds to retain a lawyer for Bub. Before she allows him to determine her fate with Junto, however, Lutie, in a fit of pent-up rage, takes matters into her own hands and clubs Boots to death with a candlestick. She instantly recognizes the weight of her crime and flees the city, leaving her incarcerated son behind.

As with most naturalist writers, Petry has received criticism for investing in an irrevocably bleak portrait of contending human interests and desires. But her narrative, cannily situated as it is at the nexus of **race**, class, and gender exploitation, compels the genre to examine the intersecting dynamics of social inequality, particularly as they bear on black women. In that light, the novel presents a singular (anti)heroine whose capitulation to extreme conditions of socioeconomic, sexual, and psychic oppression articulates one of the most damning literary critiques of the so-called American Dream. (*See also* African American Novel)

Further Reading

Barrett, Lindon. "(Further) Figures of Violence: *The Street* in the U.S. Landscape." In *Blackness and Value: Seeing Double*, 94–128. Cambridge, UK: Cambridge University Press, 1999.

Hicks, Heather. "'This Strange Communion': Surveillance and Spectatorship in Ann Petry's *The Street*." *African American Review* 37.1 (2003): 21–37.

Lubin, Alex. *Revising the Blueprint: Ann Petry and the Literary Left.* Jackson: University Press of Mississippi, 2007.

McBride, Kecia Driver. "Fear, Consumption, and Desire: Naturalism and Ann Petry's *The Street.*" In *Twisted from the Ordinary: Essays on American Literary Naturalism*, edited by Mary E. Papke, 304–22. Knoxville: University of Tennessee Press, 2003.

Pryse, Marjorie. "'Pattern against the Sky': Deism and Motherhood in Ann Petry's *The Street.*" In *Conjuring: Black Women, Fiction, and Literary Tradition*, edited by Marjorie Pryse and Hortense J. Spillers, 116–31. Bloomington: Indiana University Press, 1985.

Kinohi Nishikawa

T

TAN, AMY (1952–)

Amy Tan is a Chinese American novelist, essayist, and writer of children's literature. She merits a place in Asian American literature as a result of her intriguing story-telling, which enriches the genre of fiction in its explorations of the connection between past and present and her characters' struggles over family relations and **identity** construction. Her novels skillfully delineate many aspects of the Chinese American individual and family, particularly in their relation to cultural memory and ethnic heritage. The popularity of and critical responses to her debut novel *The Joy Luck Club* (1989) have contributed to the recognition and validation of Asian American fiction in American literature. The bittersweet mother–daughter relationships portrayed in this fiction, inspired by Tan's own experiences with her mother in America and Europe, reveal complex familial bonds and cultural and generational differences. Tan's creative and insightful storytelling is nurtured by a combination of elements from biography and autobiography, history and folk-tale, memory, and imagination. Through the richness of her artistic innovation and crafting, Tan has explored a new possibility for fiction writing. In this sense, Tan's works enrich the literary tradition of the genre of novel writing.

Born in 1952 in Oakland, California, Amy Tan is the only daughter of Daisy and John Tan, who emigrated from China a few years before her birth. Daisy was a daughter from a wealthy Shanghai family. Having lost her father at a young age, Daisy spent part of her childhood with her mother, Jing-mei. Jing-mei was raped and forced to become a rich man's concubine before she committed suicide when Daisy was nine. Tan integrates her grandmother's story into the narrative of An-mei Hsu in *The Joy Luck Club*. In her young adulthood, Daisy lost her infant son and had to give up her three daughters when she escaped from her arranged marriage. Shortly after divorcing, Daisy came to America, where she remarried and started a new life. Tan and her husband Lou DeMattei traveled to China to accompany her mother in 1987, where she met her half-sisters. The story of Suyuan Woo in *The Joy Luck Club* and some plots in *The Kitchen God's Wife* (1991) draw inspiration from Daisy's past.

Tan's fiction usually adopts a complex structure that includes a multilayered storyline, a rupture of the linear narrative frame, and a combination of talk story, folktale, legend, personal history, dreams, and imaginations. Such a narrative con-figuration challenges the traditional definition and sheds new light on the genre of the novel. Culturally and geographically set in early 20th-century China as well as contemporary America, Tan maps out her fictional landscape in a broad range that bridges the East with the West.

Through striking storytelling, Tan's novels illuminate the identity construction of hyphenated Americans, the cultural and generational gaps within immigrant groups, and the necessity to discover or recover the past. Similar to **Maxine Hong Kingston**'s strategy in *The Woman Warrior: Memoirs of a Girlhood among Ghosts*, Tan's fiction retells stories and events in China in the past by way of the mother–daughter dichotomy. Centered on the connection between her female characters, Tan incorporates Asian Americans' cross-cultural experiences, identity construction, uncertainties and struggles between cultural heritage and adopted American life, and negotiations between gender and **ethnicity**. Individual pursuits for a distinct identity, tensions between generations, and family connections addressed in Tan's novels are of universal concern.

The Kitchen God's Wife (1991)

Addressing the relationships, at times involving conflicts and miscommunications, between a first-generation mother, Winnie, and her American-born daughter, Pearl, Tan's second novel focuses on the life story of the mother. Winnie's orphaned childhood, nightmarish arranged marriage in China, and reconstructed life in America are reminiscent of the experiences of Daisy Tan. Written amid the anxiety and pressure after the great success of her debut work, Tan's second book has proved to be another favorite among readers and reviewers alike.

The novel begins with the daughter, Pearl, and her perceptions of her agonized relationship with her mother. She narrates the first two chapters about her American life and the gaps and distance between mother and daughter. The storyline of the novel is structured by Pearl's recollections of her childhood and adolescence as well as sketches of her present life with her husband, Phil Brandt, and two daughters, Tessa and Cleo. Winnie's first-person narrative about her life in China encompasses the main body of the novel. Before departing from China at the end of World War II to start building her new life in the United States, Winnie is called Jiang Weili. Weili has suffered the early loss of her father, mysterious abandonment by her mother at six, the indifference of her uncle's family, where she grows up until her arranged marriage, continuous rape from her abusive husband Wen Fu, and the brutality and chaos of the Japanese war in the 1930s and 1940s. It is not until she meets Jimmy Louie, an American soldier of Chinese heritage, that Weili sees the hope of her salvation. She is not able to leave China, however, without being raped again. Winnie ends her story by revealing the fact that Pearl was born nine months after the last sexual attack by Wen Fu. Being shocked by her mother's tragic past and the secret of her own birth, Pearl confesses to Winnie about her multiple sclerosis, a disease she has concealed for seven years. Through revealing secrets and hidden sides of their emotion, the mother and daughter finally understand each other.

The Hundred Secret Senses (1998)

After two novels on the mother–daughter relationships, Tan turns to explore the tie between two sisters in her third. Also a multilayered narrative, *The Hundred Secret*

Senses plays with collisions between the actual and the imaginary, between this life and previous life. The major storylines happen across two centuries and two cultures. Olivia Bishop and her half-sister Li Kwan's present lives in late-20th-century San Francisco (together with their trip to Changmian, China) are paralleled with their previous lives as Nelly Banner and her loyal friend Nunumu, respectively, during the Taiping Rebellion in late-19th-century imperial China.

Having come to America at age 18, Kwan has never assimilated into American culture. While she grows up, Olivia has never taken Kwan's claim seriously that she is talented with *yin* eyes and has the ability to communicate with deceased people from "the World of *Yin.*" Telling her story episode after episode over the years, Kwan's narrative constructs the sisters' previous lives as friends in chaotic China. When Olivia is divorcing her husband Simon after their 17-year marriage, Kwan persuades them to accompany her to visit her home village in China. In Changmian, Kwan mysteriously vanishes into the caves in the village. In the end, Olivia and Simon return to America reconciled and expecting their daughter, who is suggested to be a gift from Kwan.

Similar to *The Kitchen God's Wife, The Hundred Secret Senses* has dual narrators. Olivia's narrative framework opens and closes the book in present-day California. Yet it is the central storyteller Kwan's memory, imagination, and creativity that blur the boundaries between dream and reality, and previous and present lives. Despite some criticism of the supernatural elements in the novel, responses to Tan's third novel confirm her talent in storytelling across culture, time, and space.

The Bonesetter's Daughter (2001)

In terms of the structure of fiction, *The Bonesetter's Daughter* is Tan's latest experiment. This novel both continues the theme of exploring the mother–daughter relationship, but it provides innovations in this subject matter in comparison to her earlier works. Comprising three chapters sandwiched between prologue and epilogue, Tan's fourth novel has two pairs of mothers and daughters in three generations (grandmother, mother, and daughter) across geographical and temporal boundaries.

In the prologue the mother, LuLing, laments the loss of her own mother, whose name she cannot remember. Part 1 starts with the daughter Ruth's American life as a 45-year old "book doctor" with her partner Art (a linguistics consultant), Art's two daughters from a previous marriage (Sofia and Dory), and her mother, who seems to be "permanently unhappy." Ruth's connection to her estranged mother's past begins with her recovery of a stack of paper with her mother's handwriting in Chinese.

The long second part, set during the period from late imperial China to the Japanese invasion, is told by LuLing. LuLing's life story during the years in Peking, Hong Kong, and America is paralleled with her effort to unravel the puzzle of Precious Auntie, her nursemaid in name and birth mother in reality. Years after Precious Auntie's death, LuLing understands her motherly love. Part 3 of Ruth's narrative draws the story back to the present in San Francisco, where LuLing and Ruth finally understand and forgive each other.

Dedicated to her grandmother and mother, Tan's fourth book further confirms her creative approach to storytelling. The stories about women of three generations are told in a complex structure. Ruth's narrative is the frame story, enclosed within which is LuLing's experience, told in first-person narration in her diary-like manuscripts and by pieces from Ruth's recollection. The central narrative about Precious Auntie is pieced together through LuLing's written words and Ruth's voice. Once again, the exploration in this novel of family relations, generational conflicts, and the three women's social status encompasses universal as well as ethnic concerns.

Saving Fish from Drowning (2005)

Tan's experimentation with the novelistic form continues in *Saving Fish from Drowning*. The omniscient narrator is Bibi Chen, a tour leader who plans to take 12 American tourists to a politically unstable Burma on a guided tour. She dies unexpectedly before the journey even begins, yet the tourists go on their adventure. All of them mysteriously disappear in Burma. The narrator, who is already dead, vividly describes the dangerous journeys of the travelers.

Rules for Virgins (2012)

Tan's most recent novella, *Rules for Virgins*, is an unusual text in her oeuvre. A hauntingly sensual tale set in 1912 Shanghai, the story is narrated by Magic Gourd, an aging courtesan. She forges a friendship with Violet, a young and aspiring courtesan. Magic Gourd remembers her past and her victorious seductions and advises her young protégé on the art of seduction. Despite the content, the novella does not become an explicitly erotic tale but an intensely sensual story about the complexities of the human heart.

Other Works

Collaborating with illustrator Gretchen Schields, Tan has published two picture books for children. In *The Moon Lady* (1992), Nai-nai tells her granddaughters the story of her outing as a seven-year-old girl in China, where she falls into the lake from the family boat on Moon Festival, meets the Moon Lady, and is granted a secret wish. Instead of human characters, it is a cat that tells stories in *The Chinese Siamese Cat* (1994). Ming Miao tells her kittens about the antics of one of their ancestors, Sagwa of China. Adapted from Tan's book, an animated film, *Sagwa the Chinese Siamese Cat: Cat Nights, Flights, and Delights* was released in the United States in 2002.

In her recent publication *The Opposite of Fate: A Book of Musings* (2003), Tan collects pieces that trace her life story as a second-generation Chinese American daughter and her literary journey as a writer. "A Note to the Reader," that opens the book, functions as an introduction and guide to the variety of essays, which are divided into seven sections. The "musings" on her life start from the metaphors created by eight-year-old Tan and stream along her cross-cultural girl-hood and young adulthood: the tension and love between her and her mother, life with her husband, success in the literary field, and the consequent joy and stress. Varied in length, audience, and forms, Tan's essays depict moments in her life and her writing full of pleasure and sorrow, excitement, and lament. These words arranged in various forms are filled with the author's musings about fate and hope, through which she seeks her "voice" to tell her stories in the form of fiction. In this sense, Tan's "nonfiction book" explains her process of creating fiction. Covering a long time span from her childhood until the present, her first book of essays shows Tan's skill in nonfiction writing. (*See also* Chinese American Novel)

Further Reading

Adams, Bella. "Representing History in Amy Tan's *The Kitchen God's Wife*." *MELUS* 28.2 (Summer 2003): 9–30.

Bloom, Harold. *Amy Tan's "The Joy Luck Club."* Philadelphia: Chelsea House, 2002.

Caesar, Judith. "Patriarchy, Imperialism, and Knowledge in *The Kitchen God's Wife*." *North Dakota Quarterly* 62.4 (1994–95): 164–74.

Dong, Lan. *Reading Amy Tan*. Santa Barbara, CA: ABC-CLIO, 2009.

Huntley, E. D., ed. *Amy Tan: A Critical Companion*. Westport, CT: Greenwood Press, 1998.

Kramer, Barbara. *Amy Tan, Author of "The Joy Luck Club."* Springfield, NJ: Enslow, 1996.

Smorada, Claudia Kovach. "Side-Stepping Death: Ethnic Identity, Contradiction, and the Mother(land) in Amy Tan's Novels." *Fu Jen Studies: Literature & Linguistics* 24 (1991): 31–45.

Wong, Sau-ling Cynthia. "'Sugar Sisterhood': Situating the Amy Tan Phenomenon." In *The Ethnic Canon: Histories, Institutions, and Interventions*, edited by David Palumbo-Liu, 174–210. Minneapolis: Minnesota University Press, 1995.

Xu, Ben. "Memory and the Ethnic Self: Reading Amy Tan's *The Joy Luck Club*." *MELUS* 19.1 (Spring 1994): 3–18.

Lan Dong

THEIR EYES WERE WATCHING GOD

Published in 1937, *Their Eyes Were Watching God* is **Zora Neale Hurston**'s second and most accomplished novel. Conveyed through prose that has an ear for the black vernacular of the rural, segregated South, the narrative revolves around the romances of its spirited protagonist, Janie Crawford, whose self-empowering journey from adolescence to adulthood is reflected in her marriages to three different men: Logan Killicks, Joe "Jody" Starks, and Vergible "Tea Cake" Woods.

Based on the hardships she had to endure as a slave, Nanny, Janie's grandmother, demands that Janie settle down with a mate who, above all, can offer her social stability and financial security. Nanny pushes Janie to marry the older Killicks because he is relatively well-off and owns 60 acres of farmland. But when Killicks makes it clear to Janie that he prefers to relate to her as a farmhand rather than as a wife, she wastes no time leaving him for Starks, the stylish city slicker who initially sweeps her off her feet. Starks proves that he too can neither fathom nor value Janie's desire, however: his upwardly mobile ambitions leave her confined to the general store he owns and out of public life in Eatonville. Starks's fragile self-image is so hurt by Janie's decision to talk back to him in public one day that he falls ill and eventually dies.

After these two lackluster marriages, Janie refuses to compromise her happiness for anyone or any degree of socioeconomic status and determines to follow her own desire. In the vibrant wandering blues musician, Tea Cake, Janie finds a lover who fulfills her deepest emotional, psychological, and sexual longings. Their mutually satisfying relationship is nurtured by the colorful folk who populate the "muck" of the Everglades. But at the height of the couple's shared happiness, tragedy strikes when a rabid dog bites Tea Cake as he rescues Janie from flooding caused by a hurricane. Tea Cake's subsequent descent into madness forces Janie to kill him in self-defense. She is tried for his murder but is acquitted of all charges.

Hurston's novel is widely regarded as a landmark text in black women's writing and African American letters more generally not only for its representation of a resilient female protagonist who seeks to fulfill her desire on her own terms but also for its situating Janie's quest within the rich historical and cultural contexts of black life in rural Florida. Thus, what starts off as a personal journey toward self-fulfillment and happiness turns into a romantic allegory about the fortitude and life-affirming character of African American communities conditioned but never exhausted by poverty, **racism**, and gender inequality. That Tea Cake's death is memorialized in the dialogic structure of the narrative itself, with Janie recounting her tale to her Eatonville "kissin'-friend," Pheoby Watson, implies Hurston's own desire to imagine a full and complex black love in the midst of personal injury and collective struggle. (*See also* African American Novel)

Further Reading

Awkward, Michael. "'The Inaudible Voice of It All': Silence, Voice, and Action in *Their Eyes Were Watching God*." In *Inspiriting Influences: Tradition, Revision, and Afro-American Women's Novels*, 15–56. New York: Columbia University Press, 1989.

Gates, Henry Louis, Jr. "Zora Neale Hurston and the Speakerly Text." In *The Signifying Monkey: A Theory of Afro-American Literary Criticism*, 170–216. New York: Oxford University Press, 1988.

Johnson, Barbara. "Metaphor, Metonomy and Voice in *Their Eyes Were Watching God*." In *Black Literature and Literary Theory*, edited by Henry Louis Gates Jr., 205–19. New York: Methuen, 1984.

Lowe, John. *Approaches to Teaching* Their Eyes Were Watching God. New York: Modern Language Association, 2009.

Wall, Cheryl A., ed. *Zora Neale Hurston's* Their Eyes Were Watching God: *A Casebook*. New York: Oxford University Press, 2000.

Kinohi Nishikawa

THOMAS, PIRI (1928–2011)

Piri Thomas was a Latino novelist. He was born Juan Pedro Tomás in New York's Spanish Harlem to Puerto Rican and Cuban parents. He was the oldest of seven children, four of whom lived to adulthood. Thomas's parents came to New York with the first major wave of Puerto Ricans who immigrated between the American Civil War and the World War I. In 1917, the Jones Act granted American citizenship to Puerto Ricans, and Thomas belongs to the first generation of New York–born Puerto Ricans who were raised bilingual by Puerto Rican American parents. Thomas grew up surrounded by others like him in Spanish Harlem, otherwise known as El Barrio (the neighborhood).

Thomas describes his youth in his autobiographical novel, **Down These Mean Streets** (1967). The protagonist of *Down These Means Streets* shares the name Piri Thomas and lives through the same experiences as did Thomas. The text is alternately categorized as fiction and as autobiography because a good deal of poetic license makes the story more true to the atmosphere of Thomas's childhood than it is to telling the exact real events in the exact and real order in which they occurred. Indeed, although Tomas certainly does not depict himself as perfect, he does tell the story of a young boy who rises to every challenge, who is almost superhuman in his ability to win fights and in his adherence to a code, an ethics, of the streets where he never betrays a friend and never fights an unfair fight. He remains more an exemplary hero of a novel than a real person.

The poverty, violence, and drugs that plagued El Barrio mark Piri's youth. Piri faces discrimination from multiple angles. In Spanish Harlem, close-knit families always offer a safe home and plenty of beans and rice to eat, but Piri also experiences prejudice within his own home for his dark skin. Many Puerto Ricans, including Piri's farther, have dark skin, but when Piri realizes that to Anglos he appears black rather than Puerto Rican and begins to compare himself to his African American friends, he encounters an unwillingness within the Puerto Rican community to confront the racial differences that mark them, coupled with a tacit valorization of lighter, more "Spanish" features. At the same time, after a trip to the South, Piri learns that he does not share the history or culture of African Americans. Rather, Piri eventually learns that he shares multiple alliances, tied to the Puerto Rican community in New York by history, culture, and language, tied to African Americans by **racism**, and tied to inner-city Anglos by poverty. Piri's patents eventually move to Long Island to offer their children a different environment, but Thomas soon returns to El Barrio, preferring the "mean streets" of Harlem to the racism and absence of a Puerto Rican community that he finds in Long Island. And the streets are a hard place to live, catching Piri not only in violence but also in drug use. From there he began to commit petty theft, and in 1950, Piri Thomas was wounded in an armed robbery that turned into a shootout with the police. He spent the next seven years incarcerated in Sing Sing Prison and Comstock Correctional Institution during which time he began to reevaluate his life. When he returned home, it was to work hard and to build community in nonviolent ways. *Down These Mean Streets* follows Piri's life until just after his release from prison in graphic detail and in a highly stylized street language that blends Spanish and

English with violent slang to reflect Thomas's experiences of the streets not only in the plot but also in the words of the story.

Upon its release, the *New York Times Book Review* proclaimed *Down These Mean Streets* a "linguistic event" that "claims our attention and emotional response." The novel quickly became a classic of confessional autobiography. It also became the representative text of the Puerto Rican experience in America, serving as the model for Puerto Rican American literature even today. This latter quality has earned *Down These Mean Streets* some criticism along with its great acclaim. No doubt, *Down These Mean Streets* offers a frank exploration of the painful reality of inner-city life. It describes the strength of Puerto Rican families in New York in the face of so many trials and tribulations. It provides a rare exploration of the racial identity of Puerto Ricans and describes the ways that poverty, violence, drug use, and machismo feed into one another in a cycle that is extremely difficult to escape. But *Down These Mean Streets* describes the violence of the streets so powerfully that it leaves no room for other stories. Girls and women appear in *Down These Mean Streets* only as mothers and girlfriends, either perfect martyrs or else completely lost to drugs, poverty, and prostitution. Piri's masculinity depends on his degrading women, homosexuals, and boys who do not fit his mold of violent and aggressive self-reliance. This was perhaps the reality that Thomas knew, but when the force of his novel renders it the typical Puerto Rican American reality, women and other men find it even more difficult to be granted status as full characters within the Puerto Rican American community.

Since writing *Down These Mean Streets*, Thomas has devoted his time to work with gangs and with junkies in New York, Puerto Rico, and Northern California, where he now resides with his wife and their two daughters. He provides performances and conducts workshops intended to encourage and to develop alternatives to gangs and drugs. Thomas's work emphasizes creative writing as an outlet for the disenfranchised. He not only encourages people to write, he also offers them the opportunity to perform or to have their work read alongside his own.

Thomas has also continued to write. Two other autobiographical novels, *Savior, Savior, Hold My Hand* (1972) and *Seven Long Times* (1974), detail his experiences after leaving prison. Both novels are largely marked by religious experience and by the ideas of salvation and penance, but rather than embrace any one particular religion, they follow Thomas as he learns to be a man not by proving his strength over others but by resisting the temptations of drugs and violence and instead remaining a faithful husband and father. He first learns these skills in Christian churches, but he ultimately finds Christianity in all of its forms to be tied to a universalism that is ultimately that of the "typical American" who is a middle-class white homeowner. Christianity for Thomas is not concerned with creating proud Puerto Rican Americans who can fight racism and poverty to ameliorate but not leave the barrio. Thomas's *Stories from El Barrio* (1978) covers the same themes as his earlier works for a younger audience.

Down These Mean Streets remains Thomas's most successful novel. Thomas also published several recordings of his poetry, including *Sounds of the Streets* and *No Mo Barrio Blues*, and was working on a new autobiographical novel, *A Matter of*

Dignity at the time of his death on October 17, 2011. (*See also* Puerto Rican American Novel)

Further Reading

Flores, Juan. *From Bomba to Hip-Hop*. New York: Columbia University Press, 2000.

Hernández, Carmen Dolores. *Puerto Rican Voices in English*. Westport, CT: Praeger, 1997.

Luis, William. *Dance between Two Cultures*. Nashville: Vanderbilt University Press, 1997.

Mohr, Eugene V. *The Nuyorican Experience*. Westport, CT: Greenwood Press, 1982.

Sánchez, Marta E. "La Malinche at the Intersection: Race and Gender in *Down These Mean Streets*." *PMLA* 113.1 (1998): 117–28.

Sánchez-González, Lisa. *Boricua Literature*. New York: New York University Press, 2001.

Sosa-Velasco, Alfredo. "Gerald and Thomas: The Subtext within the Text in *Down These Mean Streets*." *Romance Notes* 49.3 (2009): 287–99.

Keja Lys Valens

TRICKSTER, AFRICAN AMERICAN

Common to many cultures, especially African American, tricksters are masters of disguise and survivors in animal or human embodiment; known to be wise, cunning, and high-spirited, they oftentimes skillfully outmaneuver their foes with guile, wit, and charm. Evolving mainly from West African antecedents, where folklorists Alcee Fortier, Elizabeth Pringle, and Joseph LeConte have traced many of the tales to Senegal, Nigeria, Ghana, and Mauritius, African American trickster tales that thrived during slavery and Reconstruction remain significant to African American folklore and literature. Some of the best-known African American trickster tales to survive the oral tradition include the popular figure Brer Rabbit, in the folktales preserved by Joel Chandler Harris, John of the "John and the Old Master" tales, and the signifying monkey, each of whom thinks quickly and outsmarts those opponents of superior strength, size, and power to advance his own interests.

Sometime after the Civil War, African American trickster tales were tailored to describe the oppressive conditions of the slave and the slave community. Although the tales served as a survival mechanism, highlighting the trickster's masking and signifying skills, the image of the trickster evolved as a purely selfish, greedy imposter. Within the context of American slavery, the trickster did more than outwit his oppressor for imposing on him a value system, which constantly failed to serve as a model for action or even as the slightest reflection of his own identity. Prevented from openly revolting, the trickster emerged as a folk hero, one who used both overt resistance and subversive tactics to challenge the injustices of slavery while maintaining one's dignity and humanity.

Toward the end of the 19th century, the trickster figure took on new characteristics and became a cultural survivor. In Charles Waddell Chesnutt's *The Conjure Woman* (1899), especially in "The Goophered Grapevine," Uncle Julius McAdoo, an old, genial former slave conjurer, who entertains his Northern employer with the horrors of slavery, is a living repository of local legend and a clever manipulator who seeks to provide for his own needs and comforts such as income from a vine-yard, the use of an old schoolhouse, a secret honey tree, and so forth.

In contemporary African American novels, tricksters remain significant. Examples include Proteus Rinehart of **Ralph Waldo Ellison**'s *Invisible Man* (1952), Eli Bolton of Clarence Major's *All-Night Visitors* (1968), Ishmael Reed's PaPa LaBas of *Mumbo-Jumbo* (1972) and *The Last Days of Louisiana Red* (1974), Kristin [Hunter] Lattany's Bella Lake in *The Lakestown Rebellion* (1978), and **Toni Morrison**'s retelling of the a well-known trickster tale, *Tar Baby* (1981). The trickster also appears in other contemporary mediums such as Colleen McElroy's poem, "The Griots Who Know Brer Fox" (1979). In children's books, they appear in Gerald McDermott's *Anansi the Spider* (1972) and *Zomo the Rabbit* (1992), Ashley F. Bryan's *The Adventures of Aku* (1976) and *The Dancing Granny* (1977), Eric Kimmel's *Anansi and the Talking Melon* (1994), and Julius Lester's *The Last Tales of Uncle Remus: As Told by Julius Lester* (1994).

In more recent criticism, the trickster is linked with the development of an African American literary tradition. In the realm of literary and culture criticism, Henry Louis Gates Jr. situates the vernacular roots of this tradition in the African trickster Eshu-Elegbara and the **signifying** monkey, his African descendent. Possessing many attributes, Eshu's is a skillful storyteller and master of verbal techniques, who becomes his culture's spokesperson through which creative expression is channeled.

The trickster is a powerful force in African American literature and culture. Contesting a harsh system, he has disrupted the norm with his laughter, charm, anger, and rebellion. Yet, despite many imposed situations, he has survived and triumphed in many shapes, sizes, and forms, maintaining a strength that elevates him to the status of a folk or culture hero. (*See also* Trickster, Native American)

Further Reading

Hynes, William J., and William G. Doty. *Mythical Trickster Figures: Contours, Contexts, and Criticisms.* Tuscaloosa: Alabama University Press, 1993.

Roberts, John W. *From Trickster to Badman: The Black Folk Hero in Slavery and Freedom.* Philadelphia: University of Philadelphia Press, 1989.

Loretta G. Woodard

TRICKSTER, NATIVE AMERICAN

Trickster is a creature of constant change. Lacking a fixed **identity**, trickster is male, female, coyote, rabbit, human, cunning, foolish, and every other identity one can think of. Trickster often performs two functions in Native American oral traditions: Trickster is both a culture hero and an example of how *not* to live.

As a culture hero, trickster is typically credited with making the world ready for human habitation. In the Winnebago trickster cycle recorded by Paul Radin (1956), trickster travels the world killing off all the monsters who would make it difficult for people to survive. The trickster then convinces the animals to become food for the people. Similarly, the Anishinaabeg trickster, naanabozho, presented by **Gerald Vizenor** in *Summer in the Spring* (1993), also makes the world ready for people by risking his life to steal fire from the sun in order to warm the people. These tales also explain why the world functions as it does. In a Yakima tale, recorded by Erdoes and Ortiz (1999), the trickster Coyote goes to the land of the dead to bring his friends back to life. However, like the Greek Orpheus, Coyote does precisely what he is told not to and lets them out of their box early. As a result, the spirits return to the land of the dead.

As an example of how not to live, tricksters are not only foolish, but also exemplify traits common to tricksters in all their manifestations. Tricksters are often hungry, amoral, greedy, lustful, and driven by desires for excesses of everything. It is these very excessive desires that typically lead tricksters into trouble. Many trickster tales deal with tricksters' lustful or greedy nature and how tricksters get tricked by their own tricks. They might get their head trapped in an animal skull, burn their children alive, or burn their own anus because it failed to warn that someone was approaching to steal trickster's food.

Trickster does not just live in the oral tales of the past; trickster plays a vital role in contemporary literature as well. Just as in traditional oral tales, trickster is both a culture hero and a cunning or foolish player of tricks. Vizenor, in *The Trickster of Liberty* (1988) and *Bearheart: The Heirship Chronicles* (1990), presents characters who, like many contemporary tricksters, work to play with, revise, and deny limiting stereotypes. For example, in *The Trickster of Liberty*, Vizenor denies the dominance of the proper name. His characters have nicknames that suggest that the identity of the bearer is malleable and transitive rather than fixed and permanent. The trickster nickname exists outside of and denies white America's identification of Native Americans as either noble savages or part of a dying breed. For Vizenor, there are no rules for the trickster to follow save one: Let nothing fall under the realm of concrete definition. Similarly, Louis Owens's trickster figure in *Bone Game* (1994), Alex Yazzie, a gender-bending, lustful, and ever-hungry individual, shows that tricksters should be infinite in all their dimensions rather than definite.

In **Louise Erdrich**'s *Tracks* (1988) the trickster figure, Nanapush, not only seeks to buck the system by manipulating politics, he also plays tricks. Like Vizenor and Owens's tricksters, Nanapush despises fixed identities, and no character in the novel is as fixed as the psychotic nun, Pauline. Pauline, although native, tries to be as white as possible and limits herself to only that identity. The destruction of this rigidity would help return her to the community, so one afternoon, after Nanapush discovers that Pauline has limited her urination to twice a day as a perverse movement toward whiteness, he repeatedly doses her with tea to force her to break her "routine." Pauline summarily wets herself. However, this "trick" fails and Pauline is not convinced.

Tricksters are, and have been, more than literary constructs, and they play a vital role in Native American communities in much the same way as they always have. Tricksters are important figures in the articulation of Native rights and identities. (*See also* Trickster, African American)

Further Reading

Erdoes, Richard, and Alfonso Ortiz, eds. *American Indian Trickster Tales*. New York: Penguin, 1999.

Hyde, Lewis. *Trickster Makes This World: Mischief, Myth, and Art*. New York: Farrar, Straus, and Giroux, 1998.

Radin, Paul. *The Trickster: A Study in American Indian Mythology*. New York: Schocken, 1972 [orig. pub. 1956].

Vizenor, Gerald, ed. *Narrative Chance: Postmodern Discourse on Native American Indian Literatures*. Norman: University of Oklahoma Press, 1993 [orig. pub. 1989].

Carrie L. Sheffield

V

VALDEZ, LUIS (1940–)

Luis Valdez is a Chicano playwright, director, producer, and actor. Often called the father of Chicano theater, Valdez founded El Teatro Campesino (The Farmworkers' Theater) and directed the performances that marked the beginning of a national movement in Chicana/o political theater. He also wrote and directed *Zoot Suit*, which became a landmark play in American theater. Valdez's career in Chicana/o theater has now spanned nearly 40 years, and he remains the most widely recognized Chicana/o director and playwright in the world. Valdez has written poetry, books, and essays in addition to the plays and films for which he is so well known. His impact on Chicana/o theater is immense and continues to this day.

On June 26, 1940, Luis Valdez was born in Delano, California. Since his parents were migrant farm workers, Valdez's formal education was frequently interrupted as he and his family followed the seasonal labor of the crops. Despite this, he did well in school, and he also developed an early interest in performance. As an adolescent, he performed puppet shows for his family and friends, and when he was in high school, he appeared regularly on a local television program. While he was attending San José State College, Valdez saw his first full-length play produced. *The Shrunken Head of Pancho Villa*, a surrealistic and comedic drama about a Chicana/o family, premiered in 1964, the same year that Valdez graduated from college.

After a brief period of working with the San Francisco Mime Troupe, Valdez founded El Teatro Campesino and became its artistic director. The actors in the company, including Valdez's siblings, were all farm workers and members of Cesar Chavez's union, the United Farm Workers (UFW). Teatro Campesino was created as part of the Great Delano Grape Strike of 1965, and its first performances sought to recruit members for the UFW and discourage strike breakers. Valdez has been called the resident playwright of Teatro Campesino, but actors in the company and scholars writing about the group have contested the amount of credit given to Valdez for writing the *actos*, or short scenes, that were Teatro Campesino's first performances. The early performances of Teatro Campesino were not scripted in the traditional sense. Valdez would propose a scenario for an *acto*, and the actors would take on the roles he suggested and improvise the dialogue. Valdez later wrote down the *actos* and published them in a collection in 1971. That collection of *actos* includes *Los Vendidos* (*The Sellouts*), which is the most anthologized work of Chicana/o theater to date. The other *actos* in the collection are *Las Dos Caras del Patroncito* (*The Two Faces of the Boss*), *Quinta Temporada* (*Fifth Season*), *La Conquista de México* (*The Conquest of Mexico*), *No Saco Nada de la Escuela* (*I Don't Get*

Anything Out of School), *The Militants, Huelgistas* (*Strikers*), *Vietnam Campesino* (*Vietnam Farmworker*), and *Soldado Razo* (*Buck Private*).

After El Teatro Campesino broke away from the UFW in 1967, Valdez began writing longer texts for the actors of Teatro Campesino to perform. That year he wrote his first *mito*, or myth, titled *Dark Root of a Scream*. The *mito* condemns the Vietnam War and emphasizes the battles for social justice that Chicana/os are fighting on domestic soil. Three years later Valdez wrote another *mito* titled *Bernabé*. In this one-act play, Bernabé, the village idiot, falls in love with the allegorical figure of La Tierra (The Earth), who is portrayed as one of the women who rode with Pancho Villa during the Mexican Revolution.

After the *acto* and the *mito*, Valdez shifted into yet another theatrical mode, the *corrido*. Traditionally, *corridos* are Mexican ballads, but in Valdez's theater the audience not only hears a singer singing the *corrido* but also sees actors performing the story told in the ballad. One of Teatro Campesino's most successful plays, *La gran carpa de los rasquachis* (*The Great Tent of the Underdogs*), draws on the styles of the *acto, mito*, and *corrido*. It premiered in 1973 at the Fourth Annual Chicano Theater Festival in San Jose, California, and went on to tour both the United States and Europe to great critical acclaim.

Also in 1973 Valdez wrote an epic poem defining the neo-Mayan philosophy that continues to appear in his work to this day. The heart of this poem, *Pensamiento Serpentino*, lies in the Mayan philosophy "In Lak Ech," which translates to "*Tu eres mi otro yo*" ("You are my other self"). This poem and this philosophy fall in line with the nonviolent rhetoric of both Cesar Chavez and the Chicano Movement. It purports that any violence committed against another person is also committed against one's self. Valdez's words were written in the context of the Vietnam War and the violence committed against people of color in the United States during the **Civil Rights Movement**, and his call to nonviolence undoubtedly influenced the tone of much of the Chicana/o theater created during the Chicano Movement.

Valdez began breaking away from Teatro Campesino in 1978 when the first production of *Zoot Suit* opened at the Mark Taper Forum in Los Angeles with a cast of professional actors, most of whom were not members of Teatro Campesino. *Zoot Suit* experienced enormous commercial success in California but did not fare well in New York when it became the first Chicana/o play to run on Broadway. The play launched the careers of many successful Chicana/o actors, including Evelina Fernandez and Edward James Olmos. In 1981, Valdez adapted the script for the screen and directed the film version of *Zoot Suit*.

Valdez drew the plot and some of the characters in *Zoot Suit* from the real Sleepy Lagoon Trial of 1942, in which 18 teenage defendants were wrongly convicted of murder. The central character Hank Reyna is based on the lead defendant in the case, Henry Leyva. Reyna's alter ego, El Pachuco, serves as a Brechtian device, stopping the action of the play to provide social commentary. The play follows Reyna through his trial, incarceration, and release, and all the while Valdez's text critiques the institutions of the court, the prison, and the press.

Valdez used the money he made from the success of *Zoot Suit* to purchase an old packing shed in San Juan Bautista, California. That shed became the permanent theater and administrative offices for El Teatro Campesino, and the company remains in residence there to the present. In 1981, Teatro Campesino mounted Valdez's adaptation of David Belasco's melodrama *Rose of the Rancho*. This was Teatro Campesino's first production in the new playhouse.

Throughout the 1980s, Valdez wrote and directed *Bandido!*, *Corridos*, and *I Don't Have to Show You No Stinking Badges!* By the mid-1980s, Teatro Campesino could no longer support its actors full-time. In lieu of the collective living and creation process that had formerly characterized the company, Teatro Campesino began contracting actors just for the duration of rehearsals and performances. Valdez continued as the artistic director of Teatro Campesino, but he also began working in film in the late 1980s.

Valdez wrote and directed the film *La Bamba*, which told the story of the life and death of Chicano singer Ritchie Valens. The film was the hit of the summer of 1987 and starred Lou Diamond Phillips as the young singer. That same year Valdez adapted his play *Corridos* for television and renamed it *Corridos: Tales of Passion and Revolution*. Linda Rondstadt, Paul Rodriguez, and Valdez himself starred in this Peabody Award–winning production. Valdez continued working in television and film as a director, writer, and producer and in 1991 directed his adaptation of *La Pastorela* (*The Shepherd's Play*) for television. *La Pastorela* and *La Virgen de Tepeyac* (*The Virgin of Tepeyac*) are the two traditional Christmas plays that Teatro Campesino performs every year at Christmas, switching back and forth between the two plays annually.

Both Valdez and El Teatro Campesino continue their work in Chicana/o theater. The children of the Valdez family make up a large portion of the current troupe of actors in Teatro Campesino, and they perform both at El Teatro Campesino Playhouse in San Juan Bautista and on tour. Valdez has never stopped writing and directing, and he occasionally takes on an acting role as well. His other works include *El fin del mundo* (*The End of the World*), *El baile de los giantes* (*The Dance of the Giants*), *Tiburcio Vasquez, The Mummified Deer*, and *Earthquake Sun*, which premiered at the San Diego Repertory Theater in 2004. (*See also* Mexican American Drama)

Further Reading

Broyles-González, Yolanda. *El Teatro Campesino: Theater in the Chicano Movement*. Austin: University of Texas Press, 1994.

Elam, Harry J., Jr. *Taking It to the Streets: The Social Protest Theater of Luis Valdez and Amiri Baraka*. Ann Arbor: University of Michigan Press, 1997.

Huerta, Jorge A. *Chicano Theater: Themes and Forms*. Ypsilanti, MI: Bilingual Press, 1982.

Huerta, Jorge A. "Introduction." In *Zoot Suit and Other Plays*. By Luis Valdez. Houston: Arte Público Press, 1992. 7–20.

Ashley Lucas

VIETNAMESE AMERICAN LITERATURE

Vietnamese American literature in English has been dominated by two categories: first, the survivor memoirs of the first generation of immigrants, usually cowritten with a native English speaker and emphasizing the need to witness experience over the craft of literary writing, and second, the more varied works of writers who were born in Vietnam but immigrated to the United States in childhood, thus speaking English at least as fluently as Vietnamese. Le Ly Hayslip, one of the most well-known Vietnamese American writers, bridges and exemplifies the characteristics of both modes. Hayslip is familiar to many because her two memoirs, *When Heaven and Earth Changed Places* and *Child of War, Woman of Peace*, were made into the concluding film of Oliver Stone's Vietnam trilogy, *Heaven and Earth* (which follows *Platoon* and *Born on the Fourth of July*). Hayslip's books are being widely read in college courses, and have been among the best sellers of Vietnamese American literature.

In the context of American narratives about Vietnam, Hayslip's prominence is a major breakthrough; Hayslip's memoirs offer a perspective that had rarely been seen in films or books about the Vietnam War: a Vietnamese peasant woman's perspective. Hayslip had also seen both sides of both sides. She had been a Viet Cong heroine, and put on trial and raped by Viet Cong soldiers. She was tortured in South Vietnamese prisons and worked for the American military. She had family members allied to both North and South. In acknowledging and including all these perspectives, she created in her text a richer dialogue of what this war looked like from the Vietnamese perspective than had previously been heard.

Her work may have found such wide audience in part because its message is easy to hear. Hayslip's theme is forgiveness, and she honors the integrity and value of Vietnam War veterans and survivors, regardless of their ideological position. In doing so, she can be seen as reducing difference into a universal victimhood, applicable to all. In her second book, she also exemplifies a capitalist immigrant success story, moving from destitution to ownership of rental properties and restaurants. Experiences of exploitation, prejudice, and violence appear only within her private life. Thus, she offers a narrative that deepens understanding and sympathy for

South Vietnamese orphans heading to the United States as a result of Operation New Life. (Bettmann/Corbis)

the Vietnamese experience without fundamentally challenging the equation of Vietnam with trauma and victimization, and America with capitalist success.

Seen, however, in the context of Vietnamese American literature, Hayslip's texts mark not so much a breakthrough as a transition. Published in 1989, Hayslip's first memoir, *When Heaven and Earth Changed Places*, concludes a period in which Vietnamese American literature in English consists almost entirely of memoirs. Oscillating between memories of her life in Vietnam before 1973 and her "present-day" return to visit Vietnam in 1986, the memoir introduces a new theme that will gain prominence in this literature: the return to Vietnam. And cowritten with her son James Hayslip, her second memoir, published in 1993, subtly inaugurates a generational shift: after 1994, this literature is dominated by the "1.5 generation," those who immigrated in childhood.

Many early survivor memoirs were attempts to explain the war itself. Prominent political and military leaders of South Vietnam such as former prime minister Nguyen Cao Ky, former defense minister Tran Van Don, and former chairman of the Joint General Staff Cao Van Vien published autopsies of the Vietnam War in 1976, 1978, and 1982. Truong Nhu Tan's 1985 *Vietcong Memoir* offers an alternative perspective, chronicling the experiences of a leading member of the National Liberation Front's political organization.

In the early 1980s, a new theme enters the memoir genre: denunciation of the reeducation camps. Survivors, including Nguyen Long, Nguyen Ngoc Ngan, Doan Van Toai, and Tran Tri Vu, detail unexplained arrests and detention, forced labor, fruitless interrogations punctuated by torture and threats, filthy, pestilential prisons, and gnawing deficiencies of food and medicine. Their titles often signal the combination of despair and anger that fuel their narratives: Ngan's *The Will of Heaven: A Story of One Vietnamese and the End of His World* (1982), Toai's *The Vietnamese Gulag* (1986), Vu's *Lost Years: My 1,632 Days in Vietnamese Reeducation Camps* (1988). The reeducation camp testimonials and the military autopsies are genres dominated by men.

In the mid-1980s, memoirs by women began to appear. These narratives focus less on battles and torture, and more on civilian life and cultural changes. Most of these writers present the American war as another chapter in Vietnam's long history of invasion. Anna Kim-Lan McCauley (*Miles from Home*, 1984) and sisters Nguyen Thi Thu-Lam (*Fallen Leaves*, 1989) and Nguyen Thi Tuyet Mai (*The Rubber Tree*, 1994) all begin their narratives with childhood memories of French colonial oppression. In this context, the Americans function as a new wave of colonizers, to whom the women adjust as they have previous invaders. *Shallow Graves*, a book of poetry, captures this interaction formally. The book contains two sets of poems, one written by Wendy Larson, an American who accompanied her husband on military assignment to Vietnam, and the other arranged by Larson from her taped conversations with Tran Thi Nga, who had worked for Larson's husband in Vietnam.

Women writers also dominate the tales of immigration to America. McCauley, mentioned earlier, immigrated to America as a child in order to attend the Perkins School for the Blind. Her memoir, like several of the other women immigrants' stories, begins in a context of war, but does not focus on it. McCauley's passion is not war but delineating her experience of blindness and her desire to overcome prejudice against the blind. Other immigrant narratives, such as Linda B's *Edge of Survival* and Mai Holter's *While I Am Here* primarily emphasize conversion to Christianity, as does Nguyen Van Vu's *At Home in America*, which centers on his family's conversion to Baptist Christianity and their embrace of American capitalism.

South Wind Changing, Jade Ngoc Quang Huynh's 1994 memoir, combines the civilian and reeducation camp memoir. "Book I" tells of his rural childhood, echoing Hayslip in its portrait of a peasantry "trapped in the middle as victims." The much longer second and third books tell of his suffering in a reeducation labor camp and his escape to America. Nguyen Qui Duc's *Where the Ashes Are* (1994) similarly chronicles Duc's Vietnamese childhood, his father's arrest and detention during and after the war, the family's attempts to survive the war's aftermath, Duc's escape to the United States, and his eventual return visit to Vietnam.

Duong Van Mai Elliott's *The Sacred Willow* (1999) extends personal memoir into family genealogy, chronicling four generations of her family's life in Vietnam. Elliott incorporates the familiar themes of French oppression, ideological and geographical division within the family, and eventual escape to America. Kien Nguyen's 2003 memoir, *The Unwanted*, offers a previously unchronicled experience of the war's aftermath: his ostracization in postwar Vietnam because his father was an American.

Until the 1990s, Vietnamese American literature consisted almost entirely of memoirs, but there is one early novelist: Tran Van Dinh. Dinh's first novel is one of the first Vietnamese American authored works in English. *No Passenger on the River* was published in 1965, the year American marines first landed in Vietnam. Written at this early stage of American involvement in the war, it provides a fascinating portrait of American and Vietnamese interactions. In this portrait, the American military presence is small. Dinh describes corruption, mismanagement, and accidental tragedy in ways familiar from American veteran narratives, but differs from those narratives in presenting the war as an entirely Vietnamese endeavor. The American presence is displaced into a romance plot that parallels the military plot (which centers around the coup against and assassination of President Diem). Dinh's second novel, *Blue Dragon White Tiger* (1983), returns to the plot of a Vietnamese immigrant man in love with a native-born American woman, but the emphasis of the tale is again on the protagonist's relationship with Vietnam, chronicling his participation in and disillusionment with the Communist Vietnamese government.

Both Dinh's novels and the survivor memoirs share a concern to educate an American audience about Vietnam. This concern appears as well in Vietnamese American literature for children. Often published explicitly for school curricula, books such as *Beyond the East Wind: Legends and Folktales of Vietnam* (Duong Van Quyen and Jewell Reinhart Coburn, 1976) and *The Little Weaver of Thai-Yen Village* (Tran Khanh Tuyet, 1977) participate directly in multicultural diversification, offering bilingual texts and some including teacher's aids. *Co Thich Nhi Dong: Folk*

Tales for Children (Tran Van Dien and Winabelle Gritter, 1976), *The Land I Lost: Adventures of a Boy in Vietnam* (Huynh Quang Nhuong, 1982), *Tet, the New Year* (Kim-Lan Tran, 1992), and *Going Home, Coming Home/Ve Nha, Tham Que Huong* (Truong Tran, 2003) also seek to educate readers about the culture of Vietnam. Most of these works emphasize folkways and ancient tales, omitting direct reference to war. *The Little Weaver of Thai-Yen Village* thus stands out for its direct and unsparing engagement with war and trauma: a bomb destroys the child protagonist's house, kills her mother and grandmother, and seriously wounds her.

Equally experimental, but in a very different genre, film theorist Trinh Thi Minh-Ha's investigations of **identity**, narrative convention, language, and film have become as well known and influential among literary and film theorists as Hayslip has among more mainstream readers. In her films as well as her writing, Trinh produces complex, challenging, nonlinear, genre-crossing, and highly self-reflexive texts. Trinh exemplifies the sophistication and careful craftsmanship of the best of the 1.5 generation of writers.

As a 1994 anthology proclaimed in its title, for these writers, Vietnam is "Not a War, Not a Syndrome." It is the common history from which they write, but from which they move in varied directions, and in varied genres. Two stars of this generation, novelist Lan Cao and performance artist Maura Donohue, are discussed in further detail in separate essays in this volume.

Like Cao and Donohue, many writers of the 1.5 generation work from autobiography, but expand the genre beyond immigrant or survivor memoir. Andrew Pham, whose *Catfish and Mandala* won the 1991 Kiriyama Pacific Rim Book Prize, chronicles his physically and mentally grueling bicycle journey from San Francisco to Hanoi, and interrogates his own identity and his relationship to his ancestry. In *The Tapestries*, the novel Kien Nguyen published after the success of *The Unwanted*, Nguyen invents the romantic and intrigue-filled story of his grandfather, a weaver in the last Vietnamese imperial court. Barbara Tran's *In the Mynah Bird's Own Words* (2002) also imagines the lives of relatives in Vietnam, portraying her mother and other women in vignettes both realistic and symbolic. Novelist Monique Truong departs from both her personal ancestry and contemporary culture, to imagine lost chapters of history. *The Book of Salt* (2003), invents the story of a historical character known to us only through a casual note in the journal of Alice B. Toklas: the Vietnamese cook of Alice B. Toklas and Gertrude Stein. A stylistic tour de force, Truong's lush, sensual language mirrors the passions and flavors of her protagonist's life, even as that protagonist remains silent behind the linguistic and class barriers that divide him from his employers.

Whereas the chronological memoir was the dominant form for the first generation of writers, many of the younger generation's writers gravitate toward the vignette or fragment. Their novels and short story and poetry collections raise issues of rupture, alienation, incompleteness, and comparison both structurally and thematically. Their juxtapositions also capture the artistry, labor, and intentionality of creating connections. Poet Truong Tran explores memory, perception, and transmission both in his 2002 series of unpunctuated, poetic meditations (*dust and conscience*), and such poem cycles as "recipe 1" through "recipe 6" and "what remains one" through "what remains five" (*placing the accents*, 1999). Linh Dinh, caustic, postmodern poet and short story writer (*Drunkard Boxing*, 1998; *Blood and Soap*, 2004), offers snapshots of urban alienation in America, Vietnam, and Europe. Performance artist and novelist lê thi diem thúy's novel *The Gangster We Are All Looking For* (2003) provides vignettes of an unnamed narrator's childhood in Southern California. Like many other 1.5-generation writers, lê explores the child's role as translator for her immigrant parents, as parental companion when the family is separated during emigration, and as witness to the parent's struggles to create a new life in America. Works by these and other writers of this generation are collected in *Watermark: Vietnamese American Poetry and Prose*, edited by Barbara Tran (1998).

Further Reading

Beevi, Miriam. "The Passing of Literary Traditions: The Figure of the Woman from Vietnamese Nationalism to Vietnamese American Transnationalism." *Amerasia* 23.2 (1997): 27–53.

Christopher, Renny. *The Vietnam War/The American War*. Amherst: University of Massachusetts Press, 1995.

Fujita-Rony, Dorothy B., and Anne Frank. "Archiving Histories: The Southeast Asian Archive at University of California, Irvine." *Amerasia* 29.1 (2003): 153–64.

Janette, Michele. "Vietnamese American Literature in English, 1963–1994." *Amerasia* 29.1 (2003): 267–86.

Minh Ha, Trinh. *Woman, Native, Other*. Bloomington, Indiana University Press, 1989.

Truong, Monique. "Vietnamese American Literature." In *An Interethnic Companion to Asian American Literature*, edited by King-Kok Cheung, 219–46. Cambridge, UK: Cambridge University Press, 1997.

Michele Janette

VILLARREAL, JOSÉ ANTONIO (1924–2010)

José Antonio Villarreal was a Mexican American writer. Villarreal established himself with *Pocho* (1959), an autobiographical novel published in New York. This seminal book inspired subsequent works such as Richard Vásquez's *Chicano* (1970) and Victor Villaseñor's *Macho!* (1973), among others. Villarreal was the son of Mexican immigrants who settled in Santa Clara, California, after the Mexican Revolution. For seven years his father had fought with Pancho Villa. Although José spoke no English when he started school, he learned quickly and skipped third grade. He graduated from the University of California campus at Berkeley and later wrote *The Fifth Horseman* (1974) about the Mexican Revolution, and *Clemente Chacón* (1984), which is something of a Chicano rags-to-riches story, though success comes at the expense of cultural alienation.

Pocho begins in Mexico with Juan Manuel Rubio (the protagonist's father), who fought with Villa. This establishes historical background and serves as a striking contrast to his pedestrian life later: "Juan became a part of the great exodus that came of the Mexican Revolution." The sensational beginning presents Juan in a Mexican *cantina* shooting a "Spanish" pimp and taking a prostitute. After Rubio's arrest, it is discovered that he is a well-known colonel, and so he is allowed to flee to the United States, where he is soon brought to his knees figuratively: "this man who had lived by the gun . . . would sit on his haunches under the . . . trees, rubbing his sore knees." The traditional Mexican macho is now just another underpaid expendable migrant laborer. Eventually, Juan loses his family as the forces of assimilation insidiously invade his home. He and his wife separate, and Juan takes up residence with Pilar, a traditional Mexican immigrant.

Pocho however, is primarily the story of Richard Rubio's **assimilation**. It is the Chicano *kunstlerroman* influenced by James Joyce's *A Portrait of the Artist as a Young Man*. In Spanish *pocho* means faded, off-color, bland; the connotation, however, suggests sellout, turncoat. This may account for Richard's last name, which means blond or fair-skinned. (Ironically the tall and ruddy Juan hates Spaniards.) Richard, like Stephen Dedalus, eventually rejects his religion, his culture, and his family in order to maintain independence and creativity. As a sensitive and precocious young man, Richard rebels: "First, I know that one should never discuss matters of sex with one's parents. Second, one should not . . . discuss religion with the priests. And, last, one should not ask questions on history of the teachers." As in many Chicano novels, religion and clergy are depicted negatively. Eventually Richard tells his mother that he is through with her church; he no longer believes in God, and "at last he was really free."

Increasingly, Richard also distances himself from other Mexican Americans. When told that he should help his people, he answers "Let 'my people' take care of themselves," and then he wonders, "who the hell were his people?" He stops identifying himself as Mexican and acknowledges that he is a *pocho*: a stranger and "a traitor to his '**race**'." Although he rejects his religion, family, and culture, he is continually interested in learning, books, and writing, though he does not view education as a means toward a vocation or a more comfortable lifestyle; he merely seeks knowledge. He announces, "I'm gonna write books when I grow up," so after graduating from high school he enrolls in a creative writing class.

As Richard's family undergoes metamorphosis in America, he is saddened "to see the Mexican tradition begin to disappear." The decline of the Rubio household is explained by Villarreal: "the transition from the culture of the old world to that of the new should never have been attempted in one generation." As the Rubio family deteriorates, Richard decides that "There was nothing to be done now except run away from the insidious tragedy of such an existence." so he enlists in the military to escape. The book ends with this: "and suddenly he knew that for him there would never be a coming back." Nevertheless, Richard is still young, so perhaps this renunciation of his past is temporary; perhaps he will eventually return to his roots.

Although the novel is set in the 1930s and 1940s, and written in the 1950s, it is still a valuable and germane work. The themes Villarreal eloquently addresses resonate in subsequent Mexican American novels and autobiographies. Though by no means the first Chicano novel, it is among the most influential. (*See also* Mexican American Autobiography)

Further Reading

Jimenez, Francisco, ed. *The Identification and Analysis of Chicano Literature*. Binghamton, NY: Bilingual Press, 1979.

Lattin, Vernon E., ed. *Contemporary Chicano Fiction*. Binghamton: Bilingual Press, 1986.

Saldívar, Ramón. *Chicano Narrative: The Dialectics of Difference*. Madison: University of Wisconsin Press, 1990.

Sedore, Timothy S. "'Everything I Wrote Was True': An Interview with José Antonio Villarreal." *Northwest Review* 39.1 (2001): 77–89.

Paul Guajardo

VIZENOR, GERALD (1934–)

Gerald Vizenor is a Native American novelist, short story writer, poet, essayist, and educator. One of the most prolific writers in his field, Vizenor writes extensively about the Native American experience, culture, and literature. His writings often feature the motif of the trickster and advance his view of the métis or mixed-blood Indian as a prototypical trickster, able to move between worlds and reimagine his/her **identity**. In addition, Vizenor sees the terms "Indian" and "white" as inventions that need to be deconstructed, often by asking, "What does it mean to be Indian?" Vizenor sees the trickster as a possible answer, a mischievous, comic character whose imaginative stories shatter static certainties and create a new worldview for Native Americans.

Vizenor was born in Minneapolis, Minnesota, and spent his childhood moving between various homes after his natural father's murder. Later, Vizenor served in the U.S. Army and received his Bachelor of Arts degree from the University of Minnesota in 1960. He then took various graduate courses and has worked variously as a social worker, journalist, community advocate, and college professor.

Vizenor's first publications were collections of haiku, which he encountered while stationed in Japan: *Raising the Moon Vines* (1964) and *Seventeen Chirps* (1964), which have been praised as some of the best examples of this traditional poetry. The brief syllabic form became a fitting vehicle for Vizenor's reflections about nature and the interrelationship between the tribal and nontribal worlds. Vizenor would later give these themes more extensive treatment in his longer prose works.

An early appearance of these ideas occurs in *Wordarrows* (1978), a collection of stories blending fact and fiction in which Vizenor addresses the importance of language and the oral tradition to tribal peoples. *Earthdivers* (1981) expands on these ideas through the metaphor of the métis as earth divers, a reference to an Anishinabe creation story in which animals dive to the bottom of the ocean to retrieve grains of sand that then become land. Like the earth divers of the myth, the métis have the ability, Vizenor believes, to travel freely between white and tribal cultures and to bring the "truth" back to their people in the form of a new identity.

A métis himself, Vizenor presents mixed bloods not as victims torn between two cultures, but as mischievous tricksters whose unique worldview and celebration of contradictions allow them to mediate between the two worlds a mixed-blood inhabits. These tricksters balance contradictions between Native Americans' traditional past and the modern present. In this respect, Vizenor departs from the writings of authors such as Morning Dove, D'Arcy McKnickle, and Joseph Matthews. Like the protagonists of these writers, Vizenor's métis heroes may be victims of misguided federal Indian policy, but his characters satirize their situation, rather than view it with mournful sentimentality.

This satire and celebration of contradiction can be clearly seen in Vizenor's first major novel, *Darkness in St. Louis Bearheart* (1973), a postmodern work structured around a story within a story involving characters who are archetypes from traditional Anishinabe folktales, such as the trickster and the evil gambler. The novel centers around a mock epic journey of métis trickster Proude Cedarfair, who travels across the United States with a band of pilgrims in a postapocalyptic world plagued by a lack of natural resources. In the end, many pilgrims die violent deaths, and Cedarfair finds redemption by moving backward in time to the fourth world of the Native Americans' traditional past, thus emphasizing Vizenor's belief in the significance of traditional values.

The novel is filled with explicitly detailed violence and has been criticized as "difficult" and "shallow." However, Vizenor's postmodern work can be seen as itself a trickster tale, in which the author as trickster turns traditional narrative forms upside down; the structure and language of the novel are difficult because they are unlike the forms readers are accustomed to. In addition, Vizenor uses his trickster hero and the violent deaths of the pilgrims to point out the danger of what he calls "terminal creeds": beliefs that impose static definitions upon the world. Vizenor instead sees the need for a reimagining of terminal creeds, such as those that define who can be called an Indian.

The trickster motif takes a new turn in *Griever* (1987), where the ancient Chinese trickster, the Monkey King, blends with the traditional Native American trickster Nanabohzo. The result is a tale of a métis college professor on an exchange program in China. As the trickster hero, Griever reimagines the world around him, mocking not only the rigidity of socialist Chinese culture, but also the actions of his fellow teachers and, by association, of all humanity. Here, Griever functions as what Vizenor calls the quintessential "sociacupuntcurist." Neither white nor Indian, Chinese nor English, Griever punctures holes in the facades and stereotypes around him, and, along the way, encourages readers to reimagine their world.

In *The Heirs of Columbus* (1991), Vizenor stands the historical narrative of Columbus's discovery of the New World on its head, portraying Columbus as a Mayan Indian. This simple act of inverting the explorer's identity is a trickster move that rewrites a narrative of colonialism and exploitation into one that is liberating for the Native Americans, for if the exploiter is Native American, that throws into question the traditional view of tribes as victims. By rewriting history himself,

Vizenor gives the storytellers in the novel the power to do the same, creating a new vision of what it means to be Indian.

Tricksters and shape-shifters populate *Dead Voices: Natural Agonies in the New World* (1992). Narrated by an urban trickster who has become a bear, this novel centers around the power of storytelling as an antidote to mundane urban existence. But transformation lies at the heart of the novel, the notion that in order to survive, mixed bloods and tribal people must transform themselves to ward off the deadening effects of the stereotyping of Indian culture by whites.

The issue of repatriation of Indian remains is addressed in Vizenor's novel *Chancers* (2000), in which a group of university students attempts to retrieve native remains from a museum by sacrificing members of the faculty and administration. This group, the Solar Dancers, is opposed by a group of tricksters, the Round Dancers, and the two groups battle to a comic end. In this novel also, the tricksters have the power to rewrite history and traditional views of Indians.

In addition to novels and poetry, Vizenor has written and edited collections of short essays and literary criticism, which also center around the question of who can call themselves Indian. One good example is *Fugitive Poses: Native American Indian Scenes of Absence and Presence and Postindian Conversations* (1998), which deconstructs the contemporary image of "Indian." He has also edited collections of traditional Anishinabe prose and poetry.

Vizenor remains one of the most intriguing and prolific Native American writers, having published works in the genres of poetry, fiction, drama, and essay. However varied his genre choice, the same themes reverberate just below the surface: his celebration of the mixed blood as a hero, his belief in the importance of humor and storytelling, and his conviction that static worldviews and stereotypes must be questioned and broken down. (*See also* Native American Novel)

Further Reading

Lee, A. Robert. *Loosening the Seams: Interpretations of Gerald Vizenor*. Bowling Green, OH: Bowling Green University Press, 2000.

Madsen, Deborah, ed. *The Poetry and Poetics of Gerald Vizenor*. Albuquerque: University of New Mexico Press, 2002.

Owen, Louis. "Ecstatic Strategies: Gerald Vizenor's Trickster Narratives." In *Other Destinies: Understanding the American Indian Novel*, 225–54. Norman: University of Oklahoma Press, 1992.

Patti J. Kurtz

WALKER, ALICE (1944–)

Alice Walker is an African American novelist, essayist, poet, and activist. One of America's preeminent black intellectuals, Walker has written more than a dozen books of fiction, essays, and poetry. In her works Walker depicts the struggles of black women to uncover and nurture their individual selves and to find the strength to achieve psychological wholeness and spiritual fulfillment. Her reputation as a major American author was secured after the publication of her third novel, **The Color Purple** (1982), for which she received the National Book Award and the Pulitzer Prize. She has received numerous other awards, including several grants from the National Endowment for the Arts and a Guggenheim Memorial Foundation Award.

Alice Malsenior Walker was born in Eatonton, Georgia, the daughter of impoverished sharecroppers and the youngest of eight siblings. Although naturally precocious and vivacious from a very young age, Walker became withdrawn and introspective at the age of eight when a shot from her brother's BB gun blinded her in one eye. Ashamed of the scarred eye, she turned to reading and writing poetry for solace. Walker's mother realized her daughter's extraordinary intellectual gifts and excused her from household chores so she could spend her time reading and thinking instead. Walker won a scholarship to Spelman College in Atlanta, and eventually finished her bachelor's degree at Sarah Lawrence College in New York. During this period she traveled to Africa and became interested in social activism and the **Civil Rights Movement**, canvassing for voter registration in Georgia. In her senior year of college, Walker suffered an unwanted pregnancy and underwent an illegal abortion, a traumatizing experience that affected her as profoundly as the eye injury. Her emotions poured forth as groups of poems, which were published a few years later as *Once: Poems* (1968). The book was an immediate success, and introduced some of Walker's enduring thematic concerns, such as the search for a universal love that transcends all borders, whether spatial, cultural, or racial. After college Walker moved to Mississippi to pursue teaching and social activism. In 1967, she married a white civil rights lawyer, and the two became the only legally married interracial couple in their town. They had a daughter before divorcing in 1976. Walker now lives in San Francisco, where she continues with her writing and social activism.

Walker's early works have received less critical and popular attention than her momentous third novel, but nonetheless they are significant in their own right. Between 1970 and 1981, Walker published two novels and two collections of short stories. Her first novel, *The Third Life of Grange Copeland* (1970), pointedly criticizes African American gender relationships and underscores the debilitating social and economic oppression suffered by African Americans in the segregated South. Unable to overcome the accumulation of debt inherent in the sharecropping system and considered less than human by his white superiors, Grange Copeland vents his frustration by drinking heavily and beating his wife and son, the only people over whom he can exercise control. Copeland eventually realizes that he cannot blame the corrupt social system for his personal failings, but he is unable to pass this wisdom on to his son, who already is perpetuating his father's brutality upon his own wife and children. In this novel Walker highlights personal accountability for one's actions and stresses the inviolability of the soul despite oppression and prejudice. The short-story collection *In Love and Trouble* (1973) continues Walker's investigation of gender relationships, but focuses specifically on black women's struggles with self-definition in the face of institutionalized **racism** and abusive love relationships. Here again are men who repeatedly mistreat their wives and lovers, and yet these women largely remain loyal to them, at the expense of their psychological well-being and personal fulfillment. The women in Walker's second short-story collection, *You Can't Keep a Good Woman Down* (1981), more successfully challenge strictures upon black womanhood, deciding for themselves what will bring inner peace and psychological wholeness. Walker's second novel, *Meridian* (1976), traces the spiritual development and personal growth of a young black woman who becomes a civil rights activist. Walker experiments with form in this novel with a deliberately complicated narrative structure, which in one interview she likens to a crazy quilt.

The Color Purple (1982) achieved immediate critical and commercial success, and was adapted into a film by Steven Spielberg in 1985. Set in the rural South, the novel portrays the life of Celie, a young black girl who bears two children after her stepfather repeatedly rapes her. She is forced into a loveless marriage with the widower Mister, who needs someone to keep his house and raise his children. Celie's only comfort is her sister Nettie, who lives with them for a short while; but the sisters are separated when Mister throws Nettie out after she resists his sexual advances. Written as Celie's letters to God and then to Nettie (and later, as Nettie's letters to Celie from Africa, where she is a missionary), *The Color Purple* charts Celie's evolution from a silent, passive, unloved—even by herself—workhorse to someone who recognizes her own value and unique contributions to the world. Derided by her husband for being poor, black, ugly, and a woman, Celie nonetheless comes to realize that she is worthy of respect and love. Again questioning strictures on gendered behavior, Walker has Celie find love in the arms of another woman, Shug Avery, who is, ironically, also Mister's long-time lover. By the end of the novel, Celie has left her marriage, is reunited with Nettie and her two children (who were given away by her stepfather), runs a successful business, and is the matriarch of her extended family. Walker continues to experiment with form in this novel, for although *The Color Purple* is ostensibly an epistolary novel, it also contains elements of the epic, romance, realist, and bildungsroman traditions. Critics have praised Walker's use of the African American vernacular for Celie's voice, noting that Walker legitimizes the black oral tradition in her text. Of some concern to other critics, however, is Walker's negative portrayal of African American men, which some believe is overly harsh.

However, Walker does allow some of the oppressive men to reform by the end of the novel. *The Color Purple* remains one of the most provocative and oft-studied novels in the **canon** of African American literature.

Walker revisits some of the characters from *The Color Purple* in her subsequent two novels, *The Temple of My Familiar* (1989) and *Possessing the Secret of Joy* (1992). The former was strongly criticized for its blatant sociopolitical agenda and sprawling storyline covering 500,000 years. More warmly received, *Possessing the Secret of Joy* investigates the practice of female genital mutilation, a topic that Walker also explores in her nonfiction book and film *Warrior Marks: Female Genital Mutilation and the Sexual Blinding of Women* (1993). Narrated by angels, the novel *By the Light of My Father's Smile* (1998) portrays, in a creative reversal, how the dead are required to honor the living by undoing the wrongs they enacted while alive. The short-story collection *The Way Forward Is with a Broken Heart* (2000) contains an autobiographical account of Walker's puzzlement over the dissolution of her previously fulfilling marriage.

Though known best for her fiction, Walker is also respected as a poet and essayist. Her first five volumes of poetry were collected in *Her Blue Body Everything We Know: Earthling Poems, 1965–1990 Complete* (1991). Walker has been praised for her strong, persuasive poetic voice. She explores the themes of female identity and self-exploration in her early poems, while also promoting a vibrant female sexuality unfettered by societal mores. Her yearning for a universal love that transcends **race** and, indeed, encompasses all living creatures, including plants and trees, becomes increasingly prominent in her later poetry. As an essayist, Walker has made significant contributions to the African American literary and cultural traditions. In her first collection of essays, *In Search of Our Mothers' Gardens* (1983), Walker considers her lack of literary role models and her joy in discovering the African American author **Zora Neale Hurston**, whose genius had not been recognized in her lifetime. Walker subsequently edited *I Love Myself When I Am Laughing* (1979), a collection of Hurston's work. Walker also reflects upon the effects of the Civil Rights Movement upon her life and the black community. Her second collection of essays, *Living by the Word* (1988), expands her notion of wholeness beyond the reconciliation of the individual self to encompass unity among all living beings and within the entire world. Walker's most recent essay collection, *Anything We Love Can Be Saved: A Writer's Activism* (1997), reflects her embrace of the activist stance once again after a period of rejection, although she modifies her definition to include not only political, but also cultural and spiritual work. Ultimately, Alice Walker secured her place as an essential African American writer early in her career, and her recent books only add to the richness and complexity of her already impressive oeuvre. (*See also* African American Novel)

Further Reading

Lauret, Maria. *Alice Walker*. New York: Palgrave Macmillan, 2011.
Winchell, Donna Haisty. *Alice Walker*. New York: Twayne, 1992.

Robin E. Field

WAY TO RAINY MOUNTAIN, THE

Navarre Scott Momaday's *The Way to Rainy Mountain* (1969) recounts the Kiowa myths of his grandmother, who lived in the shadow of Rainy Mountain in Oklahoma. It also tells the story of Momaday's encounter with the sacred Tai-me medicine bundle of the Kiowas, details his journey to the graves of his father's family, and reflects upon what unites him with—and separates him from—the traditions of his Kiowa heritage. The oral storytelling tradition plays an important role; Momaday's research for the book included collecting oral stories from elders, although he was often at a disadvantage because he did not know the Kiowa language. However, he had heard many of the stories from his grandmother as a child, and his father, Al Momaday, was able to translate the Kiowa stories Momaday himself could not understand.

The novel is divided into two-page chapters, with each chapter in turn divided into three voices, those of myth, history, and memory. The chapters contain a great deal of white space between these different voices, and that space is also a part of the narrative, part of Momaday's effort to convey the oral tradition in written form. Further, the book is subdivided into three parts: "The Setting Out," which focuses on the origin stories of the Kiowa tribe and its traditions; "The Going On," which largely provides stories about Kiowa culture and history after their migration and before European colonization; and "The Closing In," which relates stories of the Kiowa after colonization.

One of the stories in this collection, which Momaday also discusses in his book *The Man Made of Words*, is the story of the arrowmaker (chapter XIII); this story illustrates many of the themes in *The Way to Rainy Mountain*. A Kiowa arrowmaker, alone in his tipi with his wife, sees an intruder outside. He tells his wife in Kiowa that they should speak as if nothing is wrong, and then proceeds to ask the man outside, in Kiowa, to identify himself by speaking his name. When the intruder does not answer, the arrowmaker knows that he does not speak Kiowa and is an enemy, and shoots him through the heart. This legend demonstrates the importance of language and the power of words in creating identity, much as Momaday is recovering his Kiowa **identity** in writing this book. At the end of the chapter, in the voice of memory, the narrator speaks of an old arrowmaker he knew when he was a boy, whom he can still imagine in his mind's eye, praying. The passage ends with an evocation not of language, but of silence, the silence at dawn; like the white space in the book's passages, silence too is an essential part of language and of story. (*See also* Native American Novel)

Further Reading

Momaday, N. Scott. *The Man Made of Words: Essays, Stories, Passages.* New York: St. Martin's, 1997.

Schubnell, Matthias. "The Indian Heritage: *The Way to Rainy Mountain.*" In *N. Scott Momaday: The Cultural and Literary Background*, 140–65. Norman: University of Oklahoma Press, 1985.

Miriam H. Schacht

WHITENESS

Whiteness is often the unspoken **race** in American literature. Early American historical documents reveal attempts early on in the slaveholding society to define and maintain the privileges of whiteness. To be American was to be white. Since the late 1980s, literary critics and historians have brought to the forefront the idea of whiteness as an explicit social and political construction and an implicit norm in literature and society. Whiteness Studies is now an area of literary, cultural, and historical studies, and its goal is not to continue the privileging of whiteness, but to deconstruct the ways whiteness has been equated with American **identity** in literature and culture, despite the overturning of the legal privileging of whiteness with civil rights legislation over the last century. Without recognition of the power of this social and political construct, reinforced by literature and culture, its power will continue.

Whiteness in American History

David Roediger's important books *The Wages of Whiteness: Race and the Making of the American Working Class* (1991) and *Towards the Abolition of Whiteness* (1994) encouraged historians to examine the construction of whiteness as an integral part of American history. As Roediger notes, most Americans hear the word "race" and think black, Hispanic, Asian, or Native American—they do not consider white a race, but the norm from which all other races deviate. In his examination of American labor history, Roediger reveals how whiteness was both a political and social construct developed to maintain the power of white Anglo-Saxon Protestants. Other historians have noted that Italians, Jews, and the Irish were considered "not white" at some point in American history, only becoming white as they assimilated into American "white" culture.

Valerie Babb in *Whiteness Visible* (1998) also examines the printed historical record of early American political documents that explicitly construct and define whiteness. She reminds us that race, as a socially constructed concept, includes class, culture, and beliefs as well as biological attributes, rather than biological fact. For example, as Theodore Allen notes in his book *The Invention of the White Race* (1994), the British defined the Irish as a distinct race despite the fact that they shared the same "whiteness." By making the Irish another race, the British could justify oppressing them.

Even more ironically, according to Babb, in written historical records, whiteness is not always seen as a sign of privilege: Chinese and Arab historians described the white people they encountered as barbarians, and Aristotle's *Politics* suggested that the cold climate of northern Europe led to racial inferiority. It wasn't until European colonization that racial identification became as powerful as geographic identification. English settlers in North America originally differentiated themselves from the Native Americans with the Christian/heathen distinction, but that quickly changed to civilized/savage and finally white/nonwhite as the colonists desired more land and as colonial political leaders realized that one way to unify the ethnically diverse population of the soon-to-be-new nation was to unify through whiteness. However, figures such as John Jay and Benjamin Franklin, although both saw the new nation as a white nation, differed on the definition of white. Jay spoke generally about whites, whereas Franklin distinguished between different ethnic groups, with the British being the most white, and the Swedes and Germans as nonwhite, or "swarthy." Thus the debate about who was white began. In 1790, Congress enacted "that all free white persons" shall have the right of citizenship—whiteness was tied with Americanness early in the country's history.

In order to include more ethnic groups (such as Scots, Germans, French) into the definition, however, by the 19th century the idea of a white racial antecedent, separate from national origin, was needed in order to confirm the creation of a white race; thus we get the idealized past of the Teutonic or Anglo-Saxon (and later, Nordic) origins of whiteness fulfilling the need for a racial history that confirmed the idea of America as a white nation biologically rather than socially constructed (Babb 37–40). The "one-drop rule" was a pseudoscientific social and legal practice of the 19th century to justify slavery and, later, Jim Crow (segregation) laws of the late 19th through mid-20th centuries: a single drop of "black" blood made one black. Whiteness was thus clearly the absence of a racial sign, perpetuating the idea of white purity. Although some states made it law (such as Virginia's Racial Integrity Law of 1924), for the most part it was simply ascribed to common knowledge that insidiously entered the legal, cultural, and social fabric of the United States. Two novels of the 1890s, Mark Twain's *Puddn'head Wilson and the Comedy of Those Extraordinary Twins* (1893) and Frances Harper's *Iola Leroy, or Shadows Uplifted* (1894), refer to the one-drop rule. In the Twain novel, Roxy is described as only one-sixteenth black, and thus although she looked white, she was raised a slave, as was her child, Chambers, who was one part black and thirty-one parts white. And in *Iola Leroy*, both Iola and her mother appear to be white, but their drop of black blood ultimately makes them slaves. Iola escapes slavery when she works as a nurse for the Union soldiers during the Civil War, but when a white doctor asks her to marry him, she declines, very much aware that their marriage would not be acceptable because of her heritage.

This ideology of whiteness led to the idea of white privilege: that those with white skin (a physical distinction not always agreed upon, and with the "passing" of many African Americans in American history, not always theoretically accurate) had better access to social and economic success and privileges. This privilege has become so ingrained that Peggy McIntosh's article "White Privilege" (1988) identifying 46 privileges continues to surprise white readers who do not recognize that they have such privileges, including "I can swear, or dress in secondhand clothes, or not answer letters, without having people attribute these choices to the bad morals, the poverty, or the illiteracy of my race" (167). White privilege is institutionalized in museums, film, toys, and literature, where the depiction of whites as the norm, as the privileged, reinforces this ideology.

Whiteness Studies in American Literature

Before 1990, it was rare that "whiteness" as a category of study was part of any literary analysis class, although discussions of and entire courses on **ethnicity** and race (usually black, Asian, or Hispanic) were already common. Except for the epithet given to the traditional American or British literature course, "Dead White Male Writers," the idea that whiteness was as much a social construction as blackness was not yet recognized as relevant to literary analysis. **Toni Morrison**'s book, *Playing in the Dark: Whiteness and the Literary Imagination* (1992) ignited the discussion of whiteness across academia. Morrison argues that the slave Jim in *Adventures of Huckleberry Finn* is so painfully not free in the last chapters because white freedom depends on the actual or perceived enslavement of blacks. She recognizes that Twain deliberately has Tom and Huck imprison Jim after the reader has seen Jim as a caring and compassionate father figure and friend to Huck, and it is within this drastic dichotomy that Twain allows the unspoken to speak: white privilege needs the antithesis of black enslavement. Morrison ends her work with emphasis that blackness in American literature is both "evil and protective . . . fearful and desirable" but that at least it is recognized: Whiteness is not acknowledged at all (59).

W.E.B. Du Bois's argument in *The Souls of Black Folk* (1903) originally brought up the idea that white American culture only exists because of black American culture and that the two are intertwined. Twain scholar Shelley Fisher Fishkin, author of *Was Huck Black? Mark Twain and African-American Voices* (1993), picks up on such an analysis of the influence of black culture on American identity with her argument that the dialect and stories in *Adventures of Huckleberry Finn* come from black speakers and oral traditions. As she describes in one of her essays on the subject, "Interrogating Whiteness" (1996), her discovery proves that **canon**ical American literature—and Ernest Hemingway praised Twain's novel as the origin of all modern American literature—could not exist without black cultural influences.

Whiteness is often the ignored center of most American literature of the 19th century, according to Morrison, referring specifically to the works of Edgar Allan Poe, Herman Melville, Nathaniel Hawthorne, Mark Twain, Ernest Hemingway, F. Scott Fitzgerald, and Willa Cather. As an example, she notes that in *Moby-Dick* (1951) the whiteness of the whale signifies the invention of whiteness as the norm in reaction to **racism** against blacks. Melville's antipathy toward slavery is well known, and his struggle with how to depict the complexity of such racism is the unspoken theme of the novel. Morrison suggests that literary representations of "white American identity" were responses to nonwhiteness (14).

Valerie Babb also uses Melville's *Moby-Dick* to illustrate at least one 19th-century writer's exploration of the ideology of whiteness in the story of a hunt for a white whale. The passages in the novel that focus on philosophy, history, and art specifically examine how white dominance has been justified, particularly in the chapter titled "The Whiteness of the Whale." Babb summarizes the chapter's references to several connotations of whiteness throughout history, including the negative associations that Ishmael has of the noncolor.

More books and articles followed by critics who began to examine the interrelationships between black and white writers, especially in the 19th century, and the influence of black culture (dialect, stories, and music) on white writers ranging from Harriet Beecher Stowe to Gertrude Stein. Even popular culture did not escape the scrutiny: Fishkin quotes from David Roediger's essay "A Long Journey to the

Hip Hop Nation" (1994) where he analyzes Bugs Bunny's black cultural roots, from his language to his origins as a trickster figure in West African folklore.

A more contemporary and explicit examination of the effect of the concept of whiteness on blacks is illustrated in Morrison's first novel *The Bluest Eye* (1970): the narrator, 11-year-old Claudia, destroys the white doll she gets for Christmas, much to the horror of her parents. However, Pecola, the 12-year-old in the novel, is destroyed by her obsession with Shirley Temple and her desire for her blue eyes. Morrison begins each chapter with quotations that echo the Dick and Jane children's stories popular in the first half of the 20th century, quotations that become increasingly distorted as their image of the white middle-class family increasingly distorts Pecola's mental state. *The Bluest Eye* is one of the few novels that explicitly depicts the effects of the privileging of whiteness on blacks. For the most part, depictions of whiteness are unmentioned or symbolized rather than directly confronted.

Another area that whiteness literary studies has examined is "white trash" or the Southern poor white character as a popular literary figure since the 18th century. Early on, two conflicting views of poverty were established: environment and biology, though biology won out in most fiction and newspaper articles in the 19th and 20th centuries, which do not consider the social, economic, or historical conditions that create poverty, but rather blame the victim. Poor whites also became comic figures. By the 1930s the Southern poor were given lots of press, and more people became aware of them, but the popular culture still won out. Dorothy Allison's novel *Bastard Out of Carolina* (1993) broke new ground in its attempt to show the hunger, despair, limited choices, and shame of white poverty. What Allison found absent or caricatured in romantic literary depictions of poverty and the heroic poor was self-hatred among poor whites. Her novel does not shy away from a depiction of poverty as dreary, deadening, and shameful. The characters internalize this shame; they see themselves as basically lazy, shiftless, and unlovable, and give in to the stereotypes. In the novel, Anney passes on this shame to Bone, with her desperate need to change the birth certificate and have her children act "middle class" all indicate internalization of white trash self-shame.

Literature of "Passing"

There is one category of fiction that has always explicitly dealt with whiteness as a social construct and that is the literature of "passing": when the protagonist chooses, or chooses not to, pass as white. Such choices often lead to tragic consequences as depicted in the literature, and thus the archetypal figure of the "tragic mulatto" emerges. In James Weldon Johnson's *Autobiography of an Ex-Colored Man* (1912) the narrator chooses to be white as an adult. The unnamed protagonist is born in Georgia to a former slave mother and a white father who once owned slaves. With his mother, he moves to Connecticut as a young boy and with his mother's tacit approval, he assumes he is white until a teacher at school reveals that he is black. Throughout the novel, he fights society's need to categorize him: as an adult, he allows the world to accept him as white, an act of passive resistance. At the same time, although he feels great responsibility to the black race, he never reveals his racial **identity** to his children.

Another **Harlem Renaissance** writer, Jessie Redmon Fauset, also writes about the "tragic mulatto" who takes the chance to pass for white. In her novel *Plum Bun* (1928), Angela Murray is a light-skinned painter who leaves her darker-skinned sister, changes her name, and moves to New York to live as a white woman and attend art school. The climax of the novel has her denying knowing her sister when she comes to visit unexpectedly, yet soon after, Angela announces that she is black to a roomful of reporters in order to support another black art student.

A more explicitly "tragic mulatto" theme is found in **Nella Larsen**'s novel ***Passing*** (1929), which details the tense relationship between Irene Redfield, a privileged, light-skinned black woman, and her childhood friend, Clare Kendry, who has spent her adult life passing for white. The two women meet again as adults, and Clare pushes to resume their friendship, mostly to feed her hunger for the black society she hasn't known since childhood. Through Irene, Clare is able to reenter black society, but soon Irene is jealous of the beautiful Clare. At the end, Clare's white, racist husband bursts into a party at Irene's house to confront her with what he's discovered about her true racial identity, but when he enters, Irene runs to Clare, who is sitting at an open window of the 17th-floor apartment building and Clare falls (or is pushed by Irene) to her death.

The theme of passing continues in more contemporary literary works. In Philip Roth's novel *The Human Stain* (2000), English professor Coleman Silk, raised in a black working-class family, lives his adult life as a Jewish man, never revealing to his wife, children, and colleagues that he is black. Silk recognizes that his choice to live as a white man is, in part, as critic Kathleen Pfeiffer points out, a rejection of what he perceives to be the oppressiveness of racial solidarity. The irony of the novel is that he is charged by several black students with racism, a charge he cannot fight and that effectively ends his academic career in dishonor.

On the other hand, the desire to return to a positive sense of racial solidarity also appears in the literature of passing. Danzy Senna's heroine in her novel *Caucasia* (1998), Birdie Lee, wants to return to her black family. Her parents divorced, and her white mother took light-skinned Birdie, and her black father took her dark-skinned sister. Unlike in most other novels of passing, Birdie wants to reintegrate with the black community.

Conclusion

The awareness of the powerful construction and privileging of whiteness has led to changes in literary studies today. The publication of the second edition of *The Heath Anthology of American Literature*, general editor Paul Lauter, led to its adoption throughout the country in American literature survey courses. In this edition, Lauter and others make a point of redefining American literature and its canon: The text, now in its fifth edition, continues to be popular. The canon is thus no longer as segregated into American literature and "other" literature (black, ethnic, women's) as it used to be. Such texts allow for the analysis of whiteness in literary works as well as analysis of the interrelationship between socially constructed definitions of whiteness and blackness, the influence of black culture on white American culture, and the connection between whiteness and being an American. (*See also* Race; Racism)

Further Reading

Allen, Theodore. *The Invention of the White Race*. London: Verso, 1994.

Babb, Valerie. *Whiteness Visible: The Meaning of Whiteness in American Literature and Culture*. New York: New York University Press, 1998.

Fishkin, Shelley Fisher. "Interrogating 'Whiteness,' Complicating 'Blackness': Remapping American Culture." In *Criticism and the Color Line: Desegregating American Literary Studies*, edited by Henry B. Wonham, 251–90. New Brunswick, NJ: Rutgers University Press, 1996.

Hill, Mike, ed. *Whiteness: A Critical Reader*. New York: New York University Press, 1997.

Ignatiev, Noel. *How the Irish Became White*. London: Routledge, 1996.

Jacobson, Matthew Frye. *Whiteness of a Different Color: European Immigrants and the Alchemy of Race*. Cambridge, MA: Harvard University Press, 1999.

Keating, Ann Louise. "Interrogating 'Whiteness,' (De) Constructing 'Race'." *College English* 57.8 (December 1995): 901–17.

McIntosh, Peggy. "White Privilege: Unpacking the Invisible Knapsack." In *Race, Class, and Gender in the United States: An Integrated Study*. 4th ed. Edited by Paula S. Rothenberg, 165–69. New York: St. Martin's, 1998.

Morrison, Toni. *Playing in the Dark: Whiteness and the Literary Imagination*. New York: Vintage Books, 1993.

Morrison, Toni. "Unspeakable Things Unspoken: The Afro-American Presence in American Literature." In *Criticism and the Color Line: Desegregating American Literary Studies*, edited by Henry B. Wonham, 16–29. New Brunswick, NJ: Rutgers University Press, 1996.

Pfeiffer, Kathleen. *Race Passing and American Individualism*. Amherst: University of Massachusetts Press, 2003.

Roediger, David. *Towards the Abolition of Whiteness: Essays on Race, Politics and Working Class History*. New York: Verso, 1994.

Roediger, David. *The Wages of Whiteness: Race and the Making of the American Working Class*. Rev. ed. New York: Verso, 1999.

Sollars, Werner. *Beyond Ethnicity: Consent and Descent in American Culture*. New York: Oxford University Press, 1986.

Stacey Lee Donohue

WILSON, AUGUST (1945–2005)

August Wilson was an African American playwright, as well as one of the country's most important and prolific contemporary dramatists. His reputation rests primarily on a cycle of 10 plays (which he completed in 2005 with *Radio Golf*) that chart the cultural experience of African Americans in the United States through the course of the 20th century. Each play is set in a specific decade and a particular year, with his characters defined and influenced by the time periods in which they live. Historical markers as well as social, cultural, and political forces shape his characters' attitudes, opportunities, and actions. For example, in *Fences* (1986)—perhaps Wilson's most well-known play—the main character is very much affected by Jackie Robinson having broken the sports color barrier in 1947.

Born Frederick August Kittel, Wilson is a child of mixed heritage, son of an African American mother, Daisy Wilson, whom he adored, and a white father, Frederick Kittel, a German immigrant baker whose presence was sporadic and who abandoned the family when Wilson was quite young. Daisy subsequently married David Bedford, an African American who was much more influential than Wilson's biological father (and who in many ways provided the model for Troy Maxson in *Fences*). Eventually, Wilson dropped his birth surname to adopt that of his beloved mother.

Growing up in a slum area of Pittsburgh known as the Hill District—the setting for most of his plays—Wilson dropped out of school as a teenager because of racial prejudice and taunting. To avoid letting his mother know, he spent his days in the public library, where he read voraciously, from classics to science to philosophy, attaining a remarkably broad and diverse self-education. He also rambled the streets of Pittsburgh, listening to the stories, language, and rhythms of the people that would later infuse his plays. Wilson's dramatic characters are inveterate storytellers, and his dialogue carefully reproduces authentic verbal styles and nuances. His plays are also informed by what Wilson has often cited as the "four B's" that most influenced him: artist Romare Bearden, writer Amiri Baraka (formerly LeRoi Jones), Argentinian author Jorge Luis Borges, and most importantly, the **blues**.

In fact, Wilson first came to prominence with his play *Ma Rainey's Black Bottom* (1985), based on the real-life recording star who was considered the "mother of the blues" and who served as mentor to legendary singer Bessie Smith. Set in 1927, an era when blues and **jazz** were blossoming, the play explores the exploitation of African American musicians in a white-dominated recording industry, while also contrasting Ma Rainey's brand of the blues with the changing styles of swing that were coming into vogue. Such conflict and resistance to change mark much of Wilson's work, with characters struggling to reconcile the past with the present, and the present with the future.

Wilson's status as a preeminent dramatist was indisputably confirmed the following year with *Fences*, one of his most popular and renowned works. Starring the indomitable James Earl Jones in its Broadway production, *Fences* earned Wilson his first Pulitzer Prize as well as four Tony awards. Set in 1957, a time when the complacency and indolence of the Eisenhower era had begun to erode, and with the insurrection and explosiveness of the 1960s already in stir, *Fences* centers around Troy Maxson, a man embittered by the racial oppression that has literally and symbolically fenced him out of his ambitions and dreams and into a life limited by his race. An aspiring baseball player who attained high stature in the Negro Leagues, Troy resents the fact that he was too old for the Major Leagues when Jackie Robinson broke the color barrier in 1947. Despite the rise of such African American athletes as Hank Aaron—who led the Milwaukee Braves to victory in the 1957 World Series and won the award for Most Valuable Player—Troy refuses to recognize that times are changing and that new opportunities and freedoms for African Americans are on the horizon. Because of the prejudice he has suffered all his life, Troy refuses to allow his son Cory to accept a college football scholarship, fearing that he will encounter similar indignities and rejection. The father–son conflict results in an unbreachable gap, symbolic of the enormous changes wrought by the onset of the fiery 1960s as well as of the generational differences between African Americans trapped in the mentality of a prewar era and those who came of age in times of increasing freedom. A similar rift erupts between Troy and his loyal, long-suffering wife Rose, when she learns that Troy has been having an affair, resulting in a pregnancy. When Troy's mistress dies in childbirth, the loving Rose agrees to raise the baby, but she physically and emotionally shuts Troy out of her life.

In 1990, Wilson garnered his second Pulitzer Prize with *The Piano Lesson*, which also earned him the Tony Award for Best Play, among other honors. Furthermore, Wilson enjoyed the unusual honor of having two plays running on Broadway simultaneously, the other being *Joe Turner's Come and Gone* (1988).

Set in the Depression era of 1936, and inspired by Romare Bearden's painting *Piano Lesson*, Wilson's play directly confronts the importance of acknowledging and preserving cultural heritage while pitting the importance of ancestry against the lure of **assimilation** through capitalism. A piano whose legs are carved with family images is the central character in the play and the source of dissent among its owners, the Charles family, descendants of slaves whose owner had originally bought the piano for the price of two Charles family members. The character of Boy Willie wants to sell the piano in order to purchase the Mississippi land where his ancestors had toiled, but his sister Berniece is determined to keep it because it depicts the family's heritage. Both characters have noble if irreconcilable intents. The conflict fuels Wilson's theme of whether—and how—to retain or release one's cultural past, with the piano serving as a literal victim in this visionary clash. At a time when African Americans were still disenfranchised, and when America itself was in economic and moral decline, the struggle to reclaim or retain a cultural heritage and dignity is symbolized through the "lesson" of the piano itself.

Wilson's other plays continue to invoke racial memory and heritage through characters who fight to maintain cultural pride in a world that keeps changing. Although his 10 plays trace the African American experience through the 20th century, Wilson did not write them chronologically. In fact, his ninth play, *Gem of the Ocean*—first produced in 2003—initiates the cycle. Set in 1904, *Gem of the Ocean* incorporates characters from other plays of the cycle and also places onstage the powerful character of Aunt Ester, an ancient woman who represents black America's links to its cultural roots. In subsequent works, however, she will figure only as a mystical offstage presence. Wilson notes that Aunt Ester has gradually emerged for him as the most significant character in his cycle of plays.

Joe Turner's Come and Gone (1988), inspired by another Bearden painting, *Mill Hand's Lunch Bucket*, is set in 1911, a time when the descendants of the freed slaves are strangers in a strange land, wandering American cities in search of new identities and better lives, yet struggling to reconnect with severed memories. The title character is an actual historical figure, the brother of Tennessee's governor, who—long after the Emancipation—captured and enslaved black men for a period of seven years each.

Seven Guitars (1997) takes place in 1948, when African Americans, despite serving their country in World War II, are still overlooked, and the play addresses this injustice by viewing history through the spiritual center of African Americans. The 1960s are explored in *Two Trains Running* (1992), which won a Tony nomination for Best Play. This play too is set late in the decade, 1969, in the wake of assassinations—John F. Kennedy, **Martin Luther King Jr.**, Malcolm X—and with civil rights activism in decline. A sense of death and violence thus pervades the play, reflected further in the fact that the main character's restaurant—the setting of the action—is slated for demolition to make way for gentrification. Wilson has noted that the play's title reflects its two central ideas of cultural assimilation and cultural separatism—recurring themes in Wilson's work.

The action of *Jitney* (2001), which is actually the first play Wilson wrote, takes place in a cab station in 1977 and recounts the daily routines of the cab drivers. As in *Two Trains Running*, the dilapidated building that houses the company is to be razed to make way for new housing, though the implication is that it will simply end up boarded and abandoned, like other buildings in the neighborhood. Allusions to the Vietnam War, the growth of inner-city slums, and increasing opportunities for African Americans in education and home ownership also help demarcate the play's historical framework. Despite the bleak outlook, however, *Jitney* ends on a positive note, with the cab company's owner determined to save the building and, after his sudden death, his estranged son's decision to carry on that legacy.

The 1980s are explored in *King Hedley II* (1999), set in the Reagan era of 1985 and reflecting the failure of supply-side economics to "trickle down" to the African American community. The play reflects a growing anger toward the injustice and violence inflicted upon the African American community, an attitude embodied by Hedley's bitter wife Tonya, who is determined to have an abortion so as not to bring into the world yet another black youth who will be shot down.

Wilson addresses the 1990s in *Radio Golf*. The setting is Pittsburgh, and the action takes place in 1997; the focus in on the ambitious and upwardly mobile black middle class. Harmond Wilks, the protagonist, is a self-made millionaire whose ruthless pursuit of political goals reveals a deep disconnection from the very community that he wants to be a part of. *Radio Golf* is a contemporary cautionary tale that rearticulates many of Wilson's themes. He has completed a remarkable and unique body of work. His 10 plays depict the African American experience in this vast saga of the 20th century. One auspice of a new career came in 2003, when Wilson performed a one-man show at the Seattle Repertory Theatre as part of its Festival of New Works, a performance he plans to develop further.

Wilson's numerous honors attest to his distinguished stature in American and African American theater. Besides his two Pulitzers and the many Tony and other theater rewards, Wilson has earned a Guggenheim, Rockefeller Playwriting Fellowships, a Whiting Foundation Writers Award, a McKnight Fellowship, and a

Bush Fellowship, as well as memberships in the American Academy of Arts and Sciences and the American Academy of Arts and Letters, and some two dozen honorary degrees. In 1996, the William Inge Festival in Kansas devoted its season to Wilson's work; Minnesota's Penumbra Theatre—which nurtured much of Wilson's early work—did the same for its 2002–2003 season, and New York's Signature Theater will devote its 2005–2006 season to Wilson's oeuvre. (*See also* African American Drama)

Further Reading

Bigsby, C.W.E. *Modern American Drama 1945–2000.* Cambridge, UK: Cambridge University Press, 2000. 291–308.

Bloom, Harold, ed. *August Wilson.* Bloom's Major Dramatists. Broomall: Chelsea House Publishers, 2002.

Bogumil, Mary L. *Understanding August Wilson.* Columbia: University of South Carolina Press, 1999.

DiGaetani, John L., ed. "August Wilson." In *A Search for Postmodern Theater: Interviews with Contemporary Playwrights,* 275–84. Westport, CT: Greenwood Press, 1991.

Elam, Harry J. *The Past as Present in the Drama of August Wilson.* Ann Arbor: University of Michigan Press, 2004.

Elkins, Marilyn, ed. *August Wilson: A Casebook.* New York: Garland, 1994.

Johann, Susan. "On Listening: An Interview with August Wilson." *American Theatre* 13.22 (April 1996): 22.

Little, Jonathan. "August Wilson." In *Dictionary of Literary Biography,* Vol. 228. Twentieth Century American Dramatists, 2nd Series, edited by Christopher J. Wheatley, 289–305. Detroit: Gale, 2000.

Moyers, Bill. "August Wilson." In *A World of Ideas,* edited by Betty Sue Flowers, 167–80. New York: Doubleday, 1989.

Nadel, Alan, ed. *May All Your Fences Have Gates: Essays on the Drama of August Wilson.* Iowa City: University of Iowa Press, 1994.

Roudané, Matthew. *American Drama since 1960: A Critical History.* New York: Twayne, 1996.

Shafer, Yvonne, ed. *August Wilson: A Research and Production Sourcebook.* Westport, CT: Greenwood Press, 1998.

Wang, Qun. *An In-Depth Study of the Major Plays of African American Playwright August Wilson: Vernacularizing the Blues on Stage.* Lewiston, NY: Edwin Mellen Press, 1999.

Wolfe, Peter. *August Wilson.* New York: Twayne, 1999.

Karen C. Blansfield

WILSON, HARRIET E. (1827?–1863?)

Harriet E. Wilson was an African American novelist. Little is known about the person of Wilson, whose sole claim to literary fame is the autobiographical novel *Our Nig* (1859), the proper title of which includes the lengthy but significant subtitle, *Or, Sketches from the Life of a Free Black in a Two-Story White House, North. Showing that Slavery's Shadows Fall Even There.* What we know about Wilson's life is due almost exclusively to the literary detective work of Henry Louis Gates Jr., who followed up his rediscovery of the obscure *Our Nig* in the early 1980s with an intense investigation into the life of the author. Gates's work was followed by that of fellow literary scholar Barbara A. White. What has come from the work of these two scholars is the well-accepted presumption that Wilson was born Harriet Adams around the year 1827 in New Hampshire and that she was married in that same state to Thomas Wilson in 1851. Harriet gave birth to the couple's only child, George, in 1852. Sometime before 1859 Harriet Wilson and her son moved, with or without Thomas, to the Boston area, where young George died of a lingering illness in 1860. By this time Thomas had either died or abandoned the family. Harriet returned to New Hampshire on her own after the death of her child. This is where the trail of her life ends.

Before Harriet Wilson married, she worked for a number of years in the home of the Hayward family, a well-to-do family in Milford, New Hampshire. It is largely this work experience that forms the basis of Wilson's autobiographical novel and only written work. *Our Nig* tells the story of the young mulatto Frado, who is abandoned by her white mother and left to become the servant of the Bellmont family. Frado spends her formative years with this family. Despite her living in the North, Frado is treated for all practical purposes as a slave, especially by Mrs. Bellmont. Wilson paints Mr. Bellmont as a weak man who succumbs to his wife's wishes, despite the nagging of his conscience. Wilson further portrays the various ways that Northern whites typically treated blacks of their acquaintance through the other characters in the book. Especially telling is her portrayal of Jack, the Bellmont son who is indeed kind to Frado and who even protects her from the wrath of his mother on several occasions. Despite his sympathy, however, Jack believes that there is a fundamental difference between black and white people, with white people being far superior. This would have been a popular albeit undiscussed stance for a white American to take in the 19th-century Northern United States.

Though Frado is legally able to break her bonds with the Bellmont family when she becomes an adult, her health is so precarious after so many years of physical abuse that she cannot work at any one job for long and finds herself largely at the mercy of the charity of the Bellmont family and others for some time. Eventually Frado learns the trade of hat-making, which helps her financial situation, and she marries. In *Our Nig*, Frado's husband abandons Frado while she is pregnant.

There are many poignant aspects to Wilson's *Our Nig*. The most poignant, perhaps, is the fact that she wrote the book in a desperate attempt to raise funds so that she could procure proper medical treatment for her ailing son. Wilson was well aware of the fact that some **African American slave narrative**s were being published to the financial advantage of their writers. As her story has many similarities to the classic slave narrative, she undoubtedly thought that her narrative also could sell well. In addition, she recognized that she had an important story to tell about the North, a story of which she felt too few people were aware. Unfortunately, Wilson was unable to procure the type of solid sponsorship from the white community that others had been able to get. Without such sponsorship, even publication itself, let alone readership, would have been tremendously difficult to procure. Even her personal written plea for assistance, used as the preface to her book, failed to help sales. Tragically, Wilson's son died within months of the 1859 publication of the unsuccessful book.

Harriet E. Wilson is arguably the first African American to publish a novel. This is an extremely significant part of Wilson's legacy, as, prior to the scholarship of Gates, that accolade had been given to another. We also know her as writer who was concerned about both gender and **race** issues, especially as she lived the problems of both issues. Wilson portrays the concerns of the single, young working woman in her book, an issue that was becoming increasingly important to her society. She also tackles the topic of Christianity and what believing in such is supposed to mean in her society. She even uses motherhood as a theme, in that both Frado's own mother and Mrs. Bellmont are portrayed in ways that oppose the social idea of true womanhood that was so popular in Wilson's day. Wilson is indeed a woman who broke through many social stereotypes in her one piece of published writing. For that, she takes a significant place in the **canon** of American literature at large and in the canon of African American literature specifically. (*See also* African American Novel)

Further Reading

Gates, Henry Louis, Jr. "Introduction." In *Our Nig*. Harriet E. Wilson, edited by Henry Louis Gates Jr., xi–lv. New York: Random House, 1983.

Landry, H. Jordan. "Bringing Down the House: The Trickster's Signifying on Victimization in Harriet E. Wilson's *Our Nig*." *Callaloo* 36.2 (2013): 440–60.

White, Barbara A. "Our Nig and the She-Devil: New Information about Harriet Wilson and the 'Bellmont' Family." *American Literature* 65 (1993): 19–52.

Terry D. Novak

WOMAN WARRIOR: MEMOIRS OF A GIRLHOOD AMONG GHOSTS, THE

Maxine Hong Kingston's *The Woman Warrior: Memoirs of a Girlhood among Ghosts* (1976) remains a **canon**ical work in Asian American literature and one of the most widely read literary college texts written by a living American author. Well received by readers and critics alike, Kingston's memoir has been integrated into the curricula across academic disciplines. It is one of the pioneer works that have contributed to building up the foundation of Asian American literature, paving the way for other writers to follow. Moreover, discussions and explorations generated by *The Woman Warrior* continue to guide the development of Asian American studies as a recognized field. The book is not only the signpost that Asian American literature has entered the mainstream, but it also embodies a crucial point in the experimentation of genre and writing techniques in American literature.

The Woman Warrior starts with the story of "No Name Woman," Kingston's paternal aunt, who dishonors her family by having an affair and kills herself and her illegitimate infant. The punishment for the aunt's disloyalty extends from outcast and abandonment during her lifetime to sturdy silence about her existence, transforming her into a family secret. "White Tigers," the chapter that follows, recreates a Chinese folk story about the cross-dressing woman warrior Fa Mu Lan, as compensation for the tragic destiny of the "no name" aunt and for young Kingston's disappointment with her American life. Kingston employs certain elements from the Chinese legend but reinvents her woman warrior to represent the intersection of gender and **ethnicity** in her upbringing as a second-generation Chinese American daughter. The debates on *The Woman Warrior* usually focus on Kingston's (mis)representation of cultural authenticity and her transformation of tradition in the ethnicized and gendered context. The release of Disney's animated feature film *Mulan* (1998) further confirms the far-reaching influence of Kingston's book through visualizing Fa Mu Lan as an American cultural idol. The third chapter, "Shaman," focuses on Kingston's mother's life in China and America. Depicted as a strong-minded pioneer woman, Brave Orchid has a strong influence on young Kingston's rearing. Compared to Kingston's other aunt Moon Orchid in the fourth chapter, "At the Western Palace," who since coming to America has become disoriented and eventually insane, Brave Orchid seems to be a modern woman warrior. "A Song for a Barbarian Reed Pipe" completes the book with the adapted story of ancient Chinese woman poet Ts'ai Yen, utilizing an intricate structure of conversations between the narrator and her mother, emanating from both reality and the imagination.

Through recollecting her memories and retelling her mother's stories, the narrator conveys the stories of the female members of her family who have traveled to America. The daughter's remembrance of her childhood, intertwined with her imagination and her mother's talk stories, enables the reader to experience the multiple perspectives of Kingston's book. The mother–daughter relationship in *The Woman Warrior* thus has become a narrative structure for other writers such as **Amy Tan** and Mei Ng to follow.

Through the young narrator's experiences of growing up not only as an ethnic minority but also as a woman, *The Woman Warrior* highlights some significant themes in ethnic American literature: silence, struggle over **identity** construction, negotiation between gender and ethnicity, and generational (mis)communication. First published as nonfiction, *The Woman Warrior* resists any single categorization. It breaks down the boundaries between fiction and nonfiction, novel and biography, and thus has illuminated the possibility for a new literary genre. (*See also* Chinese American Autobiography; Chinese American Novel)

Further Reading

Bolaki, Stella. "'It Translated Well': The Promise and the Perils of Translation in Maxine Hong Kingston's *The Woman Warrior*." *MELUS* 34.4 (2009): 39–60.

Cheung, King-kok. "'Don't Tell': Imposed Silences in *The Color Purple* and *The Woman Warrior*." In *Reading the Literatures of Asian America*, edited by Shirley Geok-lin Lim and Amy Ling, 163–89. Philadelphia: Temple University Press, 1992.

Frye, Joanne S. "*The Woman Warrior*: Claiming Narrative Power, Recreating Female Self-hood." In *Faith of a (Woman) Writer*, edited by Alice Kessler-Harris and William McBrien, 293–301. Westport, CT: Greenwood Press, 1988.

Goldman, Marlene. "Naming the Unspeakable: The Mapping of Female Identity in Maxine Hong Kingston's *The Woman Warrior*." In *International Women's Writing: New Landscapes of Identity*, edited by Anne E. Brown and Marjanne E. Gooze, 223–32. Westport, CT: Greenwood Press, 1995.

Li, David Leiwei. "The Naming of a Chinese American 'I': Cross-Cultural Signification in *The Woman Warrior*." *Criticism* 30.4 (1988): 497–515.

Outka, Paul. "Publish or Perish: Food, Hunger, and Self-Construction in Maxine Hong Kingston's *The Woman Warrior*." *Contemporary Literature* 38.3 (1997): 447–82.

Wong, Sau-Ling Cynthia. *Maxine Hong Kingston's The Woman Warrior: A Casebook*. New York and Oxford, UK: Oxford University Press, 1999.

Lan Dong

WRIGHT, RICHARD (1908–1960)

Richard Wright was an African American poet, short-story writer, novelist, auto-biographer, essayist, and travel writer. Wright is one of the preeminent writers in United States literature in the 20th century, and a key figure, however controversial, in black American literature. His major works include *Uncle Tom's Children* (1938, 1940), *Native Son* (1940, 1991), **Black Boy** (1945, 1991), *The Outsider* (1953, 1991), *Eight Men* (1961), and *Lawd Today* (1963, 1991). *Uncle Tom's Children* is a collection of short stories of varying quality, with "Big Boy Leaves Home" being for many readers the most successful. The story begins with a scene that appears often in Wright's work, a group of young black males in a hostile white environment. All they are interested in is going to a swimming hole to have a good time, but they see, and are seen naked by, a young white woman at the hole. What in a rational world would be a nonevent leads to fatal violence: all three of Big Boy's companions are killed (two are shot, one burned alive); Big Boy himself flees to Chicago to escape from his terrifying "home," as Wright himself did in 1927. Of the other four stories in the collection, "Down by the Riverside" is concerned with the unstoppable determination of the black community to endure, no matter what; "Long Black Song" with a black husband's response to his wife's sexual violation by a white man; "Fire and Cloud" with a black minister's realization that organization is the key to black resistance to white oppression; and "Bright and Morning Star" with a brave black woman's revenge on the white men who murdered her son.

Native Son, Wright's second book, is his most powerful and frequently discussed novel. It is focused on, and told largely from the point of view of, its protagonist, Bigger Thomas. Debate has centered on whether or not he is a homicidal lunatic or a figure who grows in self-understanding. After killing two women—Mary Dalton, his employer's daughter, because he fears being detected in her bedroom by her blind mother, and Bessie Mears, his girlfriend, because he fears she will betray him to the police—Bigger is sentenced to execution. Wright had been concerned that *Uncle Tom's Children* had been judged sentimental, but there was no danger of that response on the part of readers of his first novel, as both the murders in it are extremely brutal: The first one includes Bigger's decapitating Mary so that her corpse will fit into a furnace, and the second one is committed by Bigger's smashing Bessie's head in with a brick. Wright is particularly concerned with the cause of these two killings. In the eyes of the law, Bigger is judged responsible for Mary's murder (Bessie's murder is not an issue at the trial), but in the author's view Bigger is a native son, in some sense a product of American society, which had told him repeatedly and in many different ways that he was subhuman. Wright may be suggesting that although Bigger committed two gruesome murders, the responsibility for the crimes lies partly in the environment.

A movie poster for *Native Son* from 1951. (John D. Kisch/Separate Cinema Archive/Getty Images)

Wright's most famous novel is also notable for the world it creates—a world of sensational journalism; escapist movies; tough detectives; wealthy whites who go slumming in the black community; black families who have to live in one-room tenement apartments where they fight rats; and a city, Chicago, which fascinates and destroys its citizens. The central character is Bigger Thomas, a 19-year old. Wright sets the novel in February, so the ubiquitous snow reinforces the sense of Bigger's being like the rat he killed in that he lives in an extremely hostile environment that affects him at every turn. Driving this powerful fictional world is the author's effective use of naturalism (environmentalism) combined with modernism (the heavy use of patterns of figurative language and symbols). As Wright said in his autobiography, realism and naturalism are what he hungered for as a reader (he also loved pulp fiction, which is echoed in his use of elements of the detective novel in *Native Son*). All in all, this novel, although tendentious and repetitive sometimes, is an unforgettable literary experience. It makes a compelling case that the sociological novel can be a work of art.

Wright followed his first novel with his autobiography, *Black Boy*, which helped explain why he himself did not become a Bigger Thomas. The story of a very sensitive and imaginative youth, it relates his experiences growing up in the white South in the first third of the 20th century. Although we know that he made many changes in the factual record, that is, wrote a novel rather than factual history, the emotional truths he conveys are very compelling. Using words as weapons, he told the white and black South that they had never known him, because in the case of the former, he was treated as less than human, and in the case of the latter, he was treated as someone who did not fit in even in his own community. To survive, Wright conformed outwardly often enough, but his mind retained its autonomy. After Wright left the United States with his young family and moved to France in 1947, he did not publish another book until 1953, when *The Outsider* appeared. Debate continues about whether or not expatriation harmed his writing, but in any case the existentialism often noted in this novel comes out of his experiences in the Deep South as much as from French philosophy. Centered on the life of Cross Damon, the novel explores the consequences of the rejection of social conventions. However artificial, they are needed, Wright suggests, to enable some form of restraint. Cross causes the deaths of many, including himself, because he cares more about making a philosophical point than he does about other people.

Two of Wright's books, *Eight Men* (1961) and *Lawd Today* (1963, 1991), were published after his death. The former collects previously published short stories and two plays for radio; the most notable story, "The Man Who Lived Underground," seems to lie in the background of **Ralph Waldo Ellison**'s *Invisible Man*. Wright's fascination with the repressed side of American society is vividly depicted in the nightmarish life of Fred Daniels, after he hides from the police in a sewer. There he sees an aborted fetus, a butcher shop where a butcher reminiscent of Hitler works, and a black church. Daniels comes to realize the arbitrariness and conventionality of aboveground values, but when he tries to convey his insight to the surface world, he is killed by a policeman named Lawson, who realizes what a threat Daniels would be aboveground. The tale is unique in Wright's work for its persistent use of allegory. Also of interest is "The Man Who Was Almost a Man," a brief narrative concerned with the protagonist's assumption that if he can buy a gun, he will be respected, but the result of his acquiring one is that he kills a mule with it, and ends up having to pay for the dead animal; he eventually flees north, where he thinks he can be a man. "Big Black Good Man," another story in *Eight Men*, can be approached as a conversation with Twain's *Huckleberry Finn*, but Wright's Jim is perceived as a physical and sexual threat by the diminutive white hotel clerk, although Jim means him no harm. Worth mentioning briefly also are the two plays, which were badly misconstrued at first because critics did not realize they were meant to be read over the radio. "Man of All Work" depicts the case of a black man who pretends to be a woman to get a job so he can support his family. It has particular resonance now because of the intense interest in cross-dressing and gender boundaries. The other radio play, "Man, God Ain't Like That," is also of interest now in that it concerns postcolonialism and the third world: the black African protagonist's misreading of Christianity results in the death of his white American mentor and also dramatizes the shortcomings in the West's imperialistic attitudes toward Africa.

Lawd Today was written in the 1930s but published in 1961. In a nod to James Joyce's *Ulysses*, it is set in Chicago during one day in the life of Jake Jackson, a postal clerk, as Wright himself was for a time. Jake's life revolves around pointless diversions, from gambling to alcohol to women. Wright has little sympathy for him, as he makes no effort to counter his environment but instead just reacts to it. He is a pitiful and hopeless creature, who takes his frustrations out on his wife, instead of trying to understand them. (*See also* African American Autobiography; African American Novel)

Further Reading

Fabre, Michel. *The Unfinished Quest of Richard Wright*. 2nd ed. Urbana: University of Illinois Press, 1993.

Felgar, Robert. *Student Companion to Richard Wright*. Westport, CT: Greenwood Press, 2000.

Joyce, Joyce Ann. *Richard Wright's Art of Tragedy*. Iowa City: University of Iowa Press, 1986.

Kinnamon, Keneth. *The Emergence of Richard Wright*. Urbana: University of Illinois Press, 1972.

McCall, Dan. *The Example of Richard Wright*. New York: Harcourt Brace, 1969.

Tuhkanen, Mikko. *The American Optic: Psychoanalysis, Critical Race Theory, and Richard Wright*. Albany: State University of New York Press, 2009.

Robert Felgar

Selected Bibliography

Aldema, Frederick Luis. *A User's Guide to Postcolonial and Latino Borderland Fiction*. Austin: University of Texas Press, 2009.

Allatson, Paul. *Latino Dreams: Transcultural Traffic and the U.S. National Imaginary*. Amsterdam: Rodopi, 2002.

Alvarez-Borland, Isabel. *Cuban-American Literature of Exile: From Person to Persona*. Charlottesville: University Press of Virginia, 1998.

Anderson, Eric Gary. *American Indian Literature and the Southwest: Contexts and Dispositions*. Austin: University of Texas Press, 1999.

Andrews, William L., ed. *African American Autobiography: A Collection of Critical Essays*. Englewood Cliffs, NJ: Prentice-Hall, 1993.

Andrews, William L. *To Tell a Free Story: A First Century of Afro-American Autobiography, 1760– 1865*. Urbana: University of Illinois Press, 1986.

Andrews, William L., et al., eds. *The Oxford Companion to African American Literature*. New York: Oxford University Press, 1997.

Anzaldúa, Gloria. *Borderlands/La Frontera: The New Mestiza*. San Francisco: Spinster/Aunt Luve, 1987.

Awkward, Michael. *Inspiriting Influences: Tradition, Revision, and Afro-American Women's Novels*. New York: Columbia University Press, 1989.

Baker, Houston, Jr. *Modernism and the Harlem Renaissance*. Chicago: University of Chicago Press, 1987.

Balshaw, Maria. *Looking for Harlem: Urban Aesthetics in African American Literature*. London: Pluto, 2000.

Bell, Bernard. *Bearing Witness to African American Literature*. Detroit: Wayne State University Press, 2012.

Bennet, Michael, and Vanessa D. Dickerson, eds. *Recovering the Black Female Body: Self-Representation by African American Women*. New Brunswick, NJ: Rutgers University Press, 2000.

Benston, Kimberly W. *Performing Blackness: Enactments of African American Modernism*. New York: Routledge, 2000.

Bloom, Harold, ed. *Asian American Women Writers*. Philadelphia: Chelsea House, 1997.

Bloom, Harold, ed. *Black American Women Poets and Dramatists*. New York: Chelsea House, 1996.

Bloom, Harold, ed. *Major Modern Black American Writers*. New York: Chelsea House, 1995.

Boelhower, William. *Through a Glass Darkly: Ethnic Semiosis in American Literature*. Oxford, UK: Oxford University Press, 1987.

Bow, Leslie. *Betrayal and Other Acts of Subversion: Feminism, Sexual Politics, Asian American Women's Literature*. Princeton, NJ: Princeton University Press, 2001.

Braxton, Joanne M., and Andrée Nicola McLaughlin, eds. *Wild Women in the Whirlwind: Afra-American Culture and the Contemporary Literary Renaissance*. New Brunswick, NJ: Rutgers University Press, 1990.

Brennan, Jonathan, ed. *When Brer Rabbit Meets Coyote: African–Native American Literature.* Chicago: University of Illinois Press, 2003.

Brill de Ramírez, Susan Berry. *Contemporary American Indian Literatures and the Oral Tradition.* Tucson: University of Arizona Press, 1999.

Brooks, Joanna. *American Lazarus: Religion and the Rise of African-American and Native American Literatures.* New York: Oxford University Press, 2003.

Bruce, Dickson D., Jr. *The Origins of African American Literature.* Charlottesville: University of Virginia Press, 2001.

Chang, Joan Chiung-Luei. *Transforming Chinese American Literature: A Study of History, Sexuality, and Ethnicity.* New York: P. Lang, 2000.

Cheung, King-kok. *An Interethnic Companion to Asian American Literature.* New York: Cambridge University Press, 1988.

Christian, Barbara. *Black Women Novelists.* Westport, CT: Greenwood Press, 1980.

Chu, Patricia P. *Assimilating Asians: Gendered Strategies of Authorship in Asian America.* Durham, NC: Duke University Press, 2000.

Connor, Kimberley Rae. *Conversions and Visions in the Writings of African-American Women.* Knoxville: University of Tennessee Press, 1994.

Cullum, Linda, ed. *Contemporary Ethnic American Poets.* Westport, CT: Greenwood Press, 2004.

Dalleo, Raphael. *The Latino/a Canon and the Emergence of Post-Sixties literature.* New York: Palgrave Macmillan, 2007.

Darraj, Susan Muaddi. *Scheherazade's Legacy: Arab and Arab American Women on Writing.* Westport, CT: Praeger, 2004.

Davies, Carole Boyce. *Black Women, Writing, and Identity: Migrations of the Subject.* New York: Routledge, 1994.

Dubey, Madhu. *Signs and Cities: Black Literary Postmodernism.* Chicago: University of Chicago Press, 2003.

Duncan, Patti. *Tell This Silence: Asian American Women Writers and the Politics of Speech.* Iowa City: University of Iowa Press, 2004.

Dureski, Carole. *Writing America Black: Race Rhetoric in the Public Sphere.* New York: Cambridge University Press, 1998.

Eng, David L. *Racial Castration: Managing Masculinity in Asian America.* Durham, NC: Duke University Press, 2001.

Eng, David L., and Alice Y. Horn, eds. *Q&A: Queer in Asian America.* Philadelphia: Temple University Press, 1998.

Ervin, Hazel Arnett. *African American Literary Criticism, 1773 to 2000.* New York: Twayne, 1999.

Eversley, Shelly. *The Real Negro: The Question of Authenticity in Twentieth-Century African American Literature.* New York: Routledge, 2004.

Fabre, Geneviève, and Michael Feith, eds. *Temples for Tomorrow: Looking Back at the Harlem Renaissance.* Bloomington: Indiana University Press, 2001.

Fabre, Michel. *From Harlem to Paris: Black American Writers in France, 1840–1980.* Urbana: University of Illinois Press, 1991.

Foster, David William. *Chicano/Latino Homoerotic Identities.* New York: Garland, 1999.

Foster, Frances Smith. *Witnessing Slavery: The Development of Ante-bellum Slave Narratives.* Madison: University of Wisconsin Press, 1994.

Frederickson, George M. *Racism: A Short History.* Princeton, NJ: Princeton University Press, 2003.

Gallagher, Charles A. *Rethinking the Color Line: Readings in Race and Ethnicity*. New York: McGraw-Hill, 1999.

Gates, Henry Louis, Jr. *Figures in Black: Words, Signs, and the "Racial" Self*. New York: Oxford University Press, 1987.

Gates, Henry Louis, Jr., ed. *Reading Black, Reading Feminist: A Critical Anthology*. New York: Meridian, 1990.

Gates, Henry Louis, Jr. *The Signifying Monkey: A Theory of Afro-American Literary Criticism*. New York: Oxford University Press, 1988.

Gish, Robert Franklin. *Beyond Bounds: Cross-Cultural Essays on Anglo, American Indian & Chicano Literature*. Albuquerque: University of New Mexico Press, 1996.

Gruesz, Kirsten Silva. *Ambassadors of Culture: The Transamerican Origins of Latino Writing*. Princeton, NJ: Princeton University Press, 2001.

Gutiérrez, Ramón A., and Genaro N. Padilla. *Recovering the U.S. Hispanic Literary Heritage*. Houston: Arte Público Press, 1993.

Harris, Trudier. *Saints, Sinners, Saviors: Strong Black Women in African American Literature*. New York: Palgrave, 2001.

Harris, Trudier, and Thadius M. Davis, eds. *Afro-American Writers, 1940–1955*. Detroit: Gale, 1988.

Harris, Trudier, and Thadius M. Davis, eds. *Afro-American Writers after 1955: Dramatists and Prose Writers*. Detroit: Gale, 1985.

Harris, Trudier, and Thadius M. Davis, eds. *Afro-American Writers before the Harlem Renaissance*. Detroit: Gale, 1986.

Harris, Trudier, and Thadius M. Davis, eds. *Afro-American Writers from the Harlem Renaissance to 1940*. Detroit: Gale, 1987.

Harris-Lopez, Trudier. *South of Tradition: Essays on African American Literature*. Athens: University of Georgia Press, 2002.

Hathaway, Heather, et al., eds. *Race and the Modern Artist*. New York: Oxford University Press, 2003.

Heflin, Ruth J. *I Remain Alive: The Sioux Literary Renaissance*. Syracuse, NY: Syracuse University Press, 2000.

Holmes, David Glen. *Revisiting Racialized Voice: African American Ethos in Language and Literature*. Carbondale: Southern Illinois University Press, 2004.

Huang, Yunte. *Transpacific Displacement: Ethnography, Translation, and Intertextual Travel in Twentieth-Century American Literature*. Berkeley: University of California Press, 2002.

Hull, Gloria T. *Color, Sex and Poetry*. Bloomington: Indian University Press, 1987.

Hutchinson, George. *The Harlem Renaissance in Black and White*. Cambridge, MA: Belknap Press of Harvard U, 1997.

Jarrett, Gene Andrew. *Representing the Race: A New Political History of African American Literature*. New York: New York University Press, 2011.

Jinqi, Ling. *Narrating Nationalism: Ideology and Form in Asian American Literature*. New York: Oxford University Press, 1998.

Kanellos, Nicolás, ed. *The Greenwood Encyclopedia of Latino Literature*. Westport: Greenwood Press, 2008.

Kanellos, Nicolás. *Hispanic Literature of the United States: A Comprehensive Reference*. Westport, CT: Greenwood Press, 2003.

Kavane, Bridget A. *Latino Literature in America*. Westport, CT: Greenwood Press, 2003.

Knippling, Alpana Sharma, ed. *New Immigrant Literatures of the United States*. Westport, CT: Greenwood Press, 1996.

Kramer, Victor A., and Robert A. Russ. *The Harlem Renaissance Re-Examined.* Troy, NY: Whitson, 1997.

Krupat, Arnold. *Ethnocriticism: Ethnography, History, Literature.* Berkeley: University of California Press, 1992.

Krupat, Arnold. *Red Matters.* Philadelphia: University of Pennsylvania Press, 2002.

Krupat, Arnold. *The Turn to the Native: Studies in Criticism and Culture.* Lincoln: University of Nebraska Press, 1996.

Laliotou, Ioanna. *Transatlantic Subjects: Acts of Immigration and Cultures of Transnationalism between Greece and America.* Chicago: University of Chicago Press, 2004.

Lee, Yoon Sun. *Modern Minority: Asian American Literature and Everyday Life.* New York: Oxford University Press, 2013.

Li, David Leiwei. *Imagining the Nation: Asian American Literature and Cultural Consent.* Stanford, CA: Stanford University Press, 1998.

Lim, Shirley Geok-lin, and Amy Ling, eds. *Reading the Literature of Asian America.* Philadelphia: Temple University Press, 1992.

Lowe, Lisa. *Immigrant Acts: Asian American Cultural Politics.* Durham, NC: Duke University Press, 1996.

Lundquist, Suzanne Evertsen. *Native American Literatures: An Introduction.* New York: Continuum, 2004.

Ma, Sheng-mei. *The Deathly Embrace: Orientalism and Asian American Identity.* Minneapolis: University of Minnesota Press, 2000.

Maitano, John R., and David R. Peck, eds. *Teaching American Ethnic Literatures.* Albuquerque: University of New Mexico Press, 1996.

Morrison, Toni. *Playing in the Dark: Whiteness and the Literary Imagination.* New York: Vintage, 1993.

Myrsiades, Kostas, and Linda Myrsiades, eds. *Race-ing Representation: Voice, History, and Sexuality.* Lanham, MD: Rowman & Littlefield, 1998.

Nelson, Emmanuel S., ed. *African American Authors, 1745–1945.* Westport, CT: Greenwood Press, 2000.

Nelson, Emmanuel S., ed. *African American Autobiographers.* Westport, CT: Greenwood Press, 2002.

Nelson, Emmanuel S., ed. *African American Dramatists.* Westport, CT: Greenwood Press, 2004.

Nelson, Emmanuel S., ed. *Asian American Novelists.* Westport, CT: Greenwood Press, 2000.

Nelson, Emmanuel S., ed. *Contemporary African American Novelists.* Westport, CT: Greenwood Press, 1999.

Nelson, Emmanuel S., ed. *Gay and Lesbian Writers of Color.* Binghamton, NY: Haworth, 1993.

Ostrom, Hans, and J. David Macey Jr., eds. *The Greenwood Encyclopedia of African American Literature.* 5 vols. Westport, CT: Greenwood Press, 2005.

Pelaud, Isabelle Thuy. *This Is All I Choose to Tell: History and Hybridity in Vietnamese American literature.* Philadelphia: Temple University Press, 2011.

Piatote, Beth H. *Domestic Subjects: Gender, Citizenship, and Law in Native* American *Literature.* New Haven: Yale University Press, 2013.

Porter, Joy, and Kenneth M. Roemer, eds. *The Cambridge Companion to Native American Literature.* New York: Cambridge University Press, 2005.

Pryse, Marjorie, and Hortense J. Spillers, eds. *Conjuring: Black Women, Fiction, and Literary Tradition.* Bloomington: Indiana University Press, 1985.

Rader, Dean, ed. *Speak to Me Words: Essays on Contemporary American Indian Poetry.* Tucson: University of Arizona Press, 2003.

Rivera, Carmen S. *Kissing the Mango Tree: Puerto Rican Women Rewriting American Literature*. Houston: Arte Público Press, 2002.

Roemer, Kenneth M., ed. *Native American Writers of the United States*. Detroit: Gale, 1997.

San Juan, E., Jr. *From Exile to Diaspora: Versions of the Filipino Experience in the United States*. Boulder, CO: Westview, 1998.

Sánchez-González, Lisa. *Boricua Literature: A Literary History of the Puerto Rican Diaspora*. New York: New York University Press, 2001.

Schaefer, Richard T. *Race and Ethnicity in the United States*. 3rd ed. Upper Saddle River, NJ: Prentice Hall, 2004.

Schwarz, Christa A. B. *Gay Voices of the Harlem Renaissance*. Bloomington: Indiana University Press, 2003.

Singh, Amritjit, et al., eds. *Postcolonial Theory and the United States: Race, Ethnicity, and Literature*. Oxford: University Press of Mississippi, 2000.

Sollors, Werner, and Maria Diedrich. *Black Columbiad: Defining Moments in African American Literature and Culture*. Cambridge, MA: Harvard University Press, 1994.

Spiners, Hortense J. *Black, White, and in Color: Essays in American Literature and Culture*. Chicago: University of Chicago Press, 2003.

Srikanth, Rajni. *The World Next Door: South Asian American Literature and the Idea of America*. Philadelphia: Temple University Press, 2004.

Sumida, Stephen H. *Literary Tradition of Hawai'i*. Seattle: University of Washington Press, 1991.

Sundquist, Eric. *The Hammers of Creation: Folk Culture in Modern African-American Fiction*. Athens: University of Georgia Press, 1992.

Tate, Claudia, ed. *Black Women Writers at Work*. New York: Continuum, 1983.

Trotman, James C. *Multiculturalism: Roots and Realities*. Bloomington: Indiana University Press, 2002.

Ty, Eleanor, and Donald C. Goellnicht, eds. *Asian North American Identities: Beyond the Hyphen*. Bloomington: Indiana University Press, 2004.

Walker, Cheryl. *Indian Nation: Native American Literature and Nineteenth-Century Nationalisms*. Durham, NC: Duke University Press, 1997.

Wall, Cherly A. *Women Writers of the Harlem Renaissance*. Bloomington: Indiana University Press, 1995.

Wiget, Andrew. *Handbook of Native American Literature*. New York: Garland, 1996.

William, Luis. *Dance between Two Cultures: Latino Caribbean Literature Written in the United States*. Nashville: Vanderbilt University Press, 1997.

Witalee, Janet, and Trudier Harris-Lopez, eds. *Harlem Renaissance: A Gale Critical Companion*. Detroit: Gale, 2002.

Wonham, Henry B. *Criticism and the Color Line: Desegregating American Literary Studies*. New Brunswick, NJ: Rutgers University Press, 1996.

Xu, Wenying. *Eating Identities: Reading Food in Asian American Literature*. Honolulu: University of Hawaii Press, 2008.

Yamamoto, Traise. *Making Selves, Making Subjects: Japanese American Women, Identity and the Body*. Berkeley: University of California Press, 1999.

Yin, Xiao-huang. *Chinese American Literature since the 1850s*. Urbana: University of Illinois Press, 2000.

About the Editor and Contributors

THE EDITOR

EMMANUEL S. NELSON is professor of English at the State University of New York at Cortland. The recipient of two Fulbright teaching grants—one to Germany, the other to Trinidad and Tobago—he was a postdoctoral research fellow at the University of Queensland, Australia, in 1984–1986. Author of more than 70 articles on various international literatures, he has edited 20 reference volumes, including *The Greenwood Encyclopedia of American Multiethnic Literature* (2005), *African American Autobiographies* (Greenwood, 2002), *Asian American Novelists* (Greenwood, 2002), and *Contemporary African American Novelists* (Greenwood, 1999).

THE CONTRIBUTORS

CORA AGATUCCI is professor of English at Central Oregon Community College. She has published widely on African, Afro-Caribbean, and African American literatures.

FREDERICK LUIS ALDAMA is distinguished professor of English at the Ohio State University. He teaches Latino/a and postcolonial literatures and is the author of several books, including *Dancing with Ghosts: A Critical Biography of Arturo Islas* (2004) and *Postethnic Narrative Criticism* (2003).

PAUL ALLATSON is senior lecturer in Spanish and U.S. Latino Studies at the Institute for International Studies, University of Technology, Sydney, Australia. Author of *Latino Dreams: Transcultural Traffic and the U.S. National Imaginary* (2002), he has published widely on Hispanophone, postcolonial, and queer literary and cultural studies.

EBERHARD ALSEN is professor emeritus of the State University of New York College at Cortland. His most recent book is *A Reader's Guide to J. D. Salinger* (Greenwood, 2002).

T. J. ARANT was until recently the President of Friends University in Wichita, Kansas.

SARA SCOTT ARMENGOT, who received her PhD candidate in comparative literature at Pennsylvania State University, is now assistant professor in the Department of Languages and Cultures at Rochester Institute of Technology.

KARINA A. BAUTISTA is lecturer in the Department of Romance Languages at Wake Forest University, North Carolina.

MELANIE R. BENSON received her doctorate in English from Boston University in 2004. She is currently associate professor of Native American Studies at Dartmouth University.

KAREN C. BLANSFIELD is dramaturge at Deep Fish Theater Company in Chapel Hill, North Carolina. She has published numerous articles on American and European playwrights in a variety of journals. She has also contributed chapters to a number of collections and reference works.

NICHOLAS BRADLEY is assistant professor of English at Victoria University in Canada.

LINDA M. CARTER is associate professor of English at Morgan State University. She has coedited four books and authored more than forty articles on African American literature and culture.

HARISH CHANDER is professor of English at Shaw University, North Carolina. He has contributed chapters to various reference volumes on African American and post-colonial literatures.

VIJAY LAKSHMI CHAUHAN, author of *Pomegranate Dreams and Other Stories* (2002), teaches at the Community College of Philadelphia. Educated at the University of Rajasthan (India) and at Yale University, she has published a book on Virginia Woolf and more than two dozen scholarly articles.

PRADYUMNA S. CHAUHAN is professor of English at Arcadia University. Editor of *Salman Rushdie Interviews: A Sourcebook of His Ideas* (Greenwood, 2002), he has published more than 30 articles and chapters on American, British, Caribbean, and South Asian authors.

FU-JEN CHEN is assistant professor of English at the National Sun Yat-sen University, Taiwan. He has published numerous articles on Asian American literature.

KIMBERLY RAE CONNOR is the author of *Conversations and Visions in the Writings of African American Women* (1994), *Imagining Grace: Liberating Theologies in the Slave Narrative Tradition* (2000), and dozens of articles on African American literature and multicultural pedagogy. She teaches at the University of San Francisco.

SUSAN MUADDI DARRAJ is an Arab American writer and critic. Her most recent publication is a collection of short stories titled *Inheritance of Exile* (2011).

ROCÍO G. DAVIS is professor of American and postcolonial literatures at the City University of Hong Kong. She is the author of *Transcultural Inventions: Asian American and Asian Canadian Short Story Cycles* (2001).

EDUARDO R. DEL RIO teaches at the University of Texas at Brownsville. He is the editor of *The Prentice Hall Anthology of Latino Literature*.

LAN DONG received her PhD candidate in comparative literature at the University of Massachusetts at Amherst. Currently she is associate professor of English at the University of Illinois, Springfield.

STACEY LEE DONOHUE is associate professor of English and Chair of the Humanities Department at Central Oregon Community College in Bend, Oregon.

JULIET A. EMANUEL is associate professor of English at the Borough of Manhattan Community College.

CAROL FADDA-CONREY is assistant professor of English at Syracuse University.

SUSAN FARRELL teaches courses in American literature and women writers at the College of Charleston. She has published a book on Jane Smiley and articles on Toni Morrison, Louise Erdrich, Tim O'Brien, and other contemporary American authors.

KEITH FELDMAN is assistant professor of ethnic studies at the University of California, Berkeley.

ROBERT FELGAR is professor of English at Jacksonville State University in Alabama. He is the author of *Richard Wright* (1980), *Understanding Richard Wright's "Black Boy"* (1998), and *Student Companion to Richard Wright* (2000).

ROBIN E. FIELD is associate professor of English at King's college in Wilkes-Barre, Pennsylvania.

JEFFREY GODSEY received an MA in liberal studies with emphasis on dramatic theory and criticism from the University of Memphis. He is an actor, a dramaturge, and a doctoral candidate at the University of Wisconsin, Madison.

JOSE B. GONZALEZ is professor of English at the United States Coast Guard Academy. He is the coeditor of *Latino Boom: An Anthology of Modern Latino Literature* (2005).

CAROL GOODMAN teaches in the English department at Memorial University of Newfoundland, Canada.

GURLEEN GREWAL is associate professor in the Department of Women's Studies at the University of South Florida. Author of *Circles of Sorrow/Lines of Struggle: The Novels of Toni Morrison* (1998), she is interested in the intersections of ethnic American and postcolonial literatures and theories.

LAURIE GROBMAN is associate professor of English at Pennsylvania State University, Berks—Lehigh Valley College. She is the author of *Teaching at the Crossroads: Cultures and Critical Perspectives in Literature by Women of Color* (2001).

PAUL GUAJARDO, author of *Chicano Controversy* (2002), is associate professor of English at the University of Houston.

JANE HALADAY holds a PhD in Native American Studies from the University of California at Davis. Her scholarly work has appeared in *Studies in American Indian Literatures* and *Paradoxa: Studies in World Literary Genres*. Currently she is associate professor of American Indian Studies at the University of North Carolina, Pembroke.

ROXANNE HARDE is associate professor of English at the University of Alberta. She has published articles on American literature in *Critique, Legacy*, and *Mosaic*.

KEVIN M. HICKEY is assistant professor of English at Albany College of Pharmacy.

KUʻUALOHA HOʻOMANAWANUI is a Native Hawaiian scholar born and raised in Hawaiʻi. She teaches at the University of Hawaiʻi at Manoa, where she received her PhD in English. She is the chief editor of *Oiwi: A Native Hawaiian Journal*, the first contemporary publication dedicated to the art and literature of Native Hawaiians.

GUIYOU HUANG is vice president for academic affairs at Norwich University in Vermont. He has authored and edited several reference books including *Asian American Autobiographers* (2001), *Asian American Poets* (2002), and *Asian American Short Story Writers* (2003).

SHUCHEN SUSAN HUANG received her doctorate in comparative literature at the University of Massachusetts at Amherst. She is currently assistant professor at Temple University.

ANUPAMA JAIN, author of *How to Be South Asian in America* (2012), is an educator and diversity consultant in Philadelphia.

MICHELE JANETTE is associate professor of English and director of cultural studies at Kansas State University. Her primary areas of research and teaching interest are Asian American literature and film.

KIMBERLEY M. JEW is assistant professor of theatre at Washington and Lee University.

LEELA KAPAI is professor of English at Prince George's Community College in Largo, Pennsylvania. She has contributed chapters to several reference works on ethnic American literature.

PERSIS KARIM is associate professor of English and comparative literature at San Jose State University. She is the coeditor of *A World Between: Poems, Short Stories, and Essays by Iranian Americans* (1999).

COLLEEN KATTAU is associate professor of Spanish at the State University of New York at Cortland. She has published articles on the works of Isabel Allende, Julia de Burgos, and the Latin American New Song Movement.

POH CHENG KHOO is an independent scholar. She is a graduate of the University London and the National University of Singapore.

MARTIN KICH is professor of English at Wright State University's Lake Campus and a recipient of the university's Trustees' Award, which recognizes sustained excellence in teaching, scholarship, and service. He is the author of *Western American Novelists* (1995) and *An Encyclopedia of Emerging Writers* (2005).

STEPHEN KNADLER is associate professor of English at Spelman College. Author of *Fugitive Race: Minority Writers Resisting Whiteness* (2002), his scholarly work has appeared in journals such as *Cultural Critique* and *Modern Fiction Studies*.

PATTI J. KURTZ is associate professor of English at Minot State University, where she also directs the Writing Center.

PAUL LAUTER is Allen K. and Gwendolyn Miles Smith Professor of Literature at Trinity College, Connecticut. He is general editor of the groundbreaking *Heath Anthology of American Literature*, which was instrumental in helping introduce many ethnic writers into the American literature curriculum. His most recent books include *From Walden Pond to Jurassic Park* (2001) and, with Ann Fitzgerald, *Literature, Class, and Culture* (1999).

AMANDA M. LAWRENCE is associate professor of English at Young Harris College, Georgia. She is the coauthor of two textbooks on writing.

LINDA LEDFORD-MILLER teaches Spanish and Portuguese in the Department of Foreign Languages and Literatures at the University of Scranton, Pennsylvania.

KRISHNA LEWIS teaches at the Pennsylvania College of Art and Design. She has published on American and other literatures and is currently writing a book on South Asian women's voices in American literature.

STEPHANIE LI, who received her PhD in English at Cornell University, holds the Susan D. Guber Chair in Literature at Indiana University, Bloomington..

IRAIDA H. LÓPEZ is professor of Spanish and literature at the School of American and International Studies at Ramapo College of New Jersey. She is the author of *La autobiografía hispana contemporánea en los Estados Unidos: A través caleidoscopio* (2001) and coauthor of *Cofre literario: iniciación a la literatura hispánica* (2003).

SERI LUANGPHINITH is associate professor of English at the University of Hawai'i at Hilo. Her articles have appeared in a variety of journals including *Transformations, Texas Studies in Literature and Language*, and *The Contemporary Pacific*.

ASHLEY LUCAS is associate professor of theatre and drama at the University of Michigan.

CARMEN R. LUGO-LUGO is associate professor in the Department of Comparative Ethnic Studies at Washington State University.

SUZANNE HOTTE MASSA teaches multicultural literature at a high school for at-risk students in Ithaca, New York. She has contributed to various reference volumes published by Greenwood Press.

CRYSTAL MCCAGE is associate professor of English at Central Oregon Community College.

PARVINDER MEHTA teaches at Sienna Heights University in Michigan.

KIM MIDDLETON is associate professor of English at the College of Saint Rose in Albany, New York.

NINA MIKKELSEN has taught at universities in Florida, Pennsylvania, and North Carolina. She has published widely in the field of children's literature.

ENRIQUE MORALES-DIAZ is professor of Spanish at Westfield State University. He has published on the works of Esmeralda Santiago and various contemporary U.S. Puerto Rican gay writers.

JULIE CARY NERAD is associate professor of English at Morgan State University. Her scholarly work has appeared in *American Literature* and *African American Review*.

KINOHI NISHIKAWA is assistant professor of English at the University of Notre Dame.

TERRY D. NOVAK is associate professor of English at Johnson and Wales University in Rhode Island. She has contributed several chapters on African American authors to various reference volumes.

RICARDO L. ORTIZ teaches in the English department and the American Studies program at George Washington University. He is the author of *Diaspora and Disappearance: Political and Cultural Erotics in Cuban America* (2005).

YOLANDA W. PAGE is vice president for academic affairs at Dillard University in New Orleans.

W. DOUGLAS POWERS is associate professor of theatre at Susquehanna University; his scholarly work focuses on Cherokee ritual, dance, and drama. A professional actor and director, he is of Chickasaw and Cherokee descent.

ELIZA RODRIGUEZ Y GIBSON is associate professor of English at Loyola Marymount College in Los Angeles. Her scholarly work appears in journals such as *Legacies* and *Studies in American Indian Literatures*.

JOYCE RUSSELL-ROBINSON holds a PhD in English from Emory University and currently teaches at Fayetteville State University in North Carolina.

BILL R. SCALIA earned his PhD in English from Louisiana State University in 2002. He is lecturer in English at St. Mary's Seminary and University in Baltimore.

MIRIAM H. SCHACHT is assistant professor of Native American literature at the University of Wisconsin, Oshkosh.

LYNN ORILLA SCOTT is the author of *James Baldwin's Later Fiction: Witness to the Journey* (2002). She has taught writing and literature at Michigan State University.

PHILLIP SERRATO is associate professor of English at San Diego State University. His research interests include children's literature, gender studies, and Latino/a cultural studies.

CARRIE L. SHEFFIELD is senior lecturer at the University of Tennessee, Knoxville.

MELISSA S. SHIELDS, who received her PhD candidate in English from Harvard University, is assistant professor of English at Wake Forest University.

ANDREW SHIN is associate professor of Asian American literature at California State University, Los Angeles.

ELLEN MCGRATH SMITH is a poet and critic who teaches at the University of Pittsburgh.

MICHAEL SOTO is associate professor of English at Trinity University. He is the author of *The Modernist Nation: Generation, Renaissance, and Twentieth-Century American Literature.*

KARL L. STENGER is associate professor of German at the University of South Carolina at Aiken. He has published several articles on African American authors and gay literature.

LAURA TANENBAUM received her PhD in comparative literature from New York University; she is currently assistant professor of English at LaGuardia Community College.

MATTHEW TEOREY is assistant professor of English at Peninsula College in Washington.

BARBARA Z. THADEN, formerly associate professor of English at St. Augustine's College, North Carolina, is now a freelance writer, editor, and researcher.

STELLA THOMPSON is associate professor of English at Prairie View A & M University.

JIE TIAN is a reference librarian at California State University, Fullerton. She holds graduate degrees in English and American Studies as well as library and information science.

CYNTHIA TOLENTINO is director of Special Programs in Paris, France, for the University of Oregon.

ZOE TRODD received her PhD in the History of American Civilization Program at Harvard University. She is now professor of American literature at the University of Nottingham, England.

AIMABLE TWAGILIMANA is professor of English at Buffalo State College. Among his publications are *The Debris of Ham: Ethnicity, Regionalism, and the 1994 Rwandan Genocide* (2003) and *Race and Gender in the Making of an African American Literary Tradition* (1997).

KEJA LYS VALENS received her PhD in comparative literature from Harvard University; she is now associate professor of English at Salem State University.

ALEXANDER WAID teaches at the United States Coast Guard Academy. His research work focuses on Latino identity theory, border studies, and technology enhanced language learning.

CATHARINE E. WALL teaches at Osher Lifelong Learning Institute at University of California, Riverside Extension. Her articles on Latin American and U.S. Latino literature have appeared in a variety of scholarly journals.

MICHELLE S. WARE is associate professor of English at North Carolina Central University.

DEBORAH WEAGEL teaches at the University of New Mexico. She has published articles in a variety of journals, including *Word and Music Studies* and the *Journal of Modern Literature.*

KATHRYN WEST is professor of English and director of honors program at Bellarmine University. She is the coauthor of *Women Writers in the United States: A Timeline of Literary, Cultural, and Social History* (1996).

LORETTA G. WOODARD is associate professor of English at Marygrove College, Detroit. Her scholarly articles appear in various journals such as *African American Review, The Journal of African American History*, and *Obsidian*. She has contributed chapters to various reference works on African American literature.

DONALD R. WRIGHT is distinguished teaching professor of history at the State University of New York at Cortland. Author of *African Americans in the Colonial Era* (2000) and *The World and a Very Small Place* (2004), he was a scholar-in-residence at the Rockefeller Foundation Study Center in Bellagio, Italy, in 2003.

ZHOU XIAOJING is associate professor of English at the University of the Pacific, California. She is the author of *Elizabeth Bishop: Rebel in Shades and Shadows* and coeditor of *Asian American Literature: Form, Confrontation, and Transformation* (2005).

SEONGHO YOON earned his doctorate in English at the University of Massachusetts, Amherst. He is currently assistant professor of English at Hanyang University in Korea.

DARCY A. ZABEL is now interim president at Friends University. She is the author of *The (Underground) Railroad in African American Literature* (2004).

Index

Bold page numbers indicate main entries; those in *italics* followed by *p* indicate photos.